# THE LEGAL LIABILITY
## OF HOSPITALS

## SEVEN DAY LOAN

This book is to be returned on
or before the date stamped below

**UNIVERSITY OF PLYMOUTH**

# PLYMOUTH LIBRARY

Tel: (01752) 232323
This book is subject to recall if required by another reader
Books may be renewed by phone
CHARGES WILL BE MADE FOR OVERDUE BOOKS

# THE LEGAL LIABILITY
# OF HOSPITALS

*by*

Marésa Cronjé-Retief

## KLUWER LAW INTERNATIONAL
THE HAGUE / LONDON / BOSTON

A C.I.P. Catalogue record for this book is available from the Library of Congress

ISBN 90-411-1450-5

Published by Kluwer Law International,
P.O. Box 85889, 2508 CN The Hague, The Netherlands.

Sold and distributed in North, Central and South America
by Kluwer Law International,
675 Massachusetts Avenue, Cambridge, MA 02139, U.S.A.

In all other countries, sold and distributed
by Kluwer Law International, Distribution Centre,
P.O. Box 322, 3300 AH Dordrecht, The Netherlands.

*Printed on acid-free paper*

Printed in the Netherlands.

*This book is based on an unpublished
thesis approved for the LL.D. degree
in the Faculty of Law, Criminal Law
and Medical Law Department at the
University of the Orange Free State.
Promotor: Prof. Dr. T. Verschoor*

Maresa Cronjé-Retief
2000

*Every man has an absolute right*
*to the absolute security of his own person*
*by the hand of every other man*
*except the Higher Hand*

'… the right of absolute security of the person.'
*Stoffberg* v. *Elliott* 1923 CPD 148, Watermeyer J.

# Table of Contents

# Preface

This book was compiled in order to enable professionals to establish an international perspective on the **legal liability of hospitals**. It is a comprehensive international work of reference on the topic and is aimed at the market of medico-legal practitioners, healthcare management officials and academic lawyers.

The book presents, from an international legal perspective, research on the legal liability of hospitals in the USA, CANADA, the UNITED KINGDOM, AUSTRALIA, and SOUTH AFRICA.

Chapter 1 presents a general introduction. In Chapter 2, the health care systems of various countries are discussed. In Chapter 3 the *hospital* is then researched in various contexts. The origin and history of medicine and hospitals and the history of the law pertaining to the malpractice liability are also discussed in this chapter. Chapter 4 deals with a general discussion of the legal grounds of hospital liability, and presents an invaluable *Comparative Diagram*. In Chapters 5–9, every individual consecutive chapter on hospital liability of the above-mentioned countries is introduced by a short discussion of their unique health care systems and hospitals. Thereafter, from every legal system's unique perspective, legal principles, doctrines and legal grounds for the liability of hospitals are identified with full reference to their case law. Chapter 10 and the *Summary* conclude the book.

The book covers a wide range of topics: health care; health care systems; hospitals (state and private); hospital companies; the hospital industry; the history of hospitals; medicine and medical law. This wide range of subjects will be of benefit to a large range of legal and medical professionals.

*In toto*, it will be useful to all lawyers and all those involved in the medico-legal profession to be able to consult an international reference on the legal liability of hospitals. It could facilitate court proceedings and proposed legislative interventions and could also assist the establishment of a concise hospital liability law worldwide.

It should be noted that the legal principles set out in this book, were also successfully applied to the liability of AIRLINES and SHIPPING COMPANIES and other groups. The exposition of and the clear distinction between legal grounds which can establish GROUP LIABILITY were also expounded.

Whilst perfection is not readily achieved in human matters such as the writing of a book, I sincerely believe that this book will facilitate the professional's search for clarity on this vast subject.

M Cronjé-Retief

mcronjeretief@hotmail.com

# Acknowledgements

Special gratitude is due to my husband André, who has enabled me to do extensive international research on this subject. I would also like to thank both my husband and my dear daughter Michelle for their patience and support.

A word of thankfulness is extended to Prof. Dr. T. Verschoor for his professional expert advice concerning the writing of this book.

# Chapter 1

# Introduction

Most countries in the world have their own political system, legal system, culture(s), language(s), and other particular characteristics. Similarly, most countries have their own health-care industry comprising, amongst other main components, of a health-care system, health-care services, a health-care provider industry and a health-care insurance industry.

An international perspective will reveal that health-care systems are completely diversified in structure, administration, function, policies and the laws applying to them. Countries can be categorized according to their similarities or dissimilarities regarding their health-care industries. A national perspective illustrates that the health-care system of a country is uniquely established by interacting dynamic forces.[1] Consequently every country in effect has its own health-care industry, health-care provider industry (e.g. hospital industry), resulting in its own health-care provider liability (e.g. hospital liability) system and structure.

The purpose of the investigation into and comparison of the health-care systems of various countries lies in the exposition of the different bureaucratic or administrative health-care structures and bureaucratic or other administrative health-care provider structures. Every health-care system and institutional health-care provider system has its own structure. An examination of these structures clearly reveals the nature of the health-care system and the type of health-care facility (hospital) and the important authoritative role players in each system. This examination becomes necessary and most relevant when trying to identify and select the appropriate institutional or representative defendant(s) for the liability of a hospital in medical malpractice cases. For example, where the health-care system is run predominantly by the state, and hospitals are state controlled, the defendant would be a state entity or state representative. Following an investigation of the health-care structures, and hospital governance structure, it will appear clearly which state entity or state representative to sue. When a hospital is, for example,

---

[1] Field *Health* 15–28.

established by a corporation, investigation of relevant statutes or regulations, hospital by-laws, hospital standards and its governance structure will likewise establish an appropriate institutional or other appropriate defendant.

The description of the appropriate institutional or representative defendant will also differ from country to country. In Great Britain the hospital or 'hospital authority', in the United States of America the 'corporation' or hospital or medical centre or university or health authority, in South Africa a state representative such as the 'Minister of Health' or a corporation or hospital and in France a 'regional council' or hospital may be considered and named as the responsible entity.

It must also be taken into consideration that hospitals are legal entities or legal persons who derive their powers, duties and responsibilities from a legal basis.[2] On the ground of a distinct legal basis and composition, hospitals can be categorized into different types of organizations.[3] A selection of health-care providers or hospitals which are akin to most countries are the following: private facilities, governmental institutions, non-profit institutions or corporations, for-profit institutions or corporations, partnerships or sole proprietorships.[4] These distinctive forms of organizations also have a dramatic influence on the potential liability of a hospital and the determination of an appropriate defendant.

Furthermore, it must be taken into account that the hospital itself may not be the only obvious institutional choice for liability.[5] Departments or sections within the hospital (e.g. the anaesthesiology or cardiovascular department, the emergency section, etc.) and co-ordinated groups of hospital doctors who find themselves in a group akin to a partnership, are other institutional defendant possibilities.[6]

**Hospital liability** has experienced dramatic development and expansion. Charitable institutions were the first facilities that were established and kept by means of donations and legacies. They were places of refuge for the poor and disabled and a place where the sick died. The rich stayed at home and were treated by family members and later by private physicians. Hospital liability was then unheard of. The doctrine of charitable immunity became firmly rooted and hospitals were protected as charitable institutions by

---

[2]  Miller *Hospital Law* 14–20. Southwick and Slee *Law of Hospital* 103–113. See Chapters 3 & 8.

[3]  Miller *Hospital Law* 14.

[4]  See also Miller *Hospital Law* 14, 15–20.

[5]  Chapman *Medicine* 65–66, 71–75.

[6]  *Op. cit.* 65–67, 71–75.

courts. The reason for this was to protect the financial viability of the charitable institutions which provided invaluable community services.[7]

Hospital immunity from liability was, however, phased out within forty years. The legal systems of England, Australia, Canada, the United States, South Africa and many others each partook in this dramatic development. The expansion of hospital liability is thoroughly discussed with regard to most relevant legal systems with special reference to their case law, relevant legal grounds and legal principles.[8]

The main field of investigation of this thesis will thus be the various legal grounds and doctrines regarding hospital liability, which have been employed by courts over decades. They have not only been instrumental in imposing liability on hospitals, but have succeeded in expanding this liability to medical malpractice. This development has taken place due to major social and especially radical economic changes[9] that have caused a crisis in the economic sphere of the health-care field.

The following six forms of liability pertaining to hospitals will be discussed:[10]

**Indirect or vicarious liability** has by far been the most common ground on which hospitals have been held liable. After having enjoyed an effective immunity from liability for the negligence of professional staff, hospitals are now being treated similarly to other employers with respect to vicarious liability.[11] Traditionally, vicarious liability basically entails that the employer is held liable for the delictual wrongs committed by the employee during the course or in the scope of employment. The doctrine of *respondeat superior* is mostly employed by courts to establish the liability for the acts of employees. Traditional requirements for the application of this theory have, however, been adapted considerably in the hospital setting.

**The direct or primary or corporate liability** of a hospital is established for the negligent acts of medical staff including independent contractor/doctors under the doctrine of **(corporate) negligence**. Direct or corporate hospital liability is imposed as a result of a personal duty which is owed

---

[7] See Chapter 3.

[8] See Chapters 4–9.

[9] Louisell and Williams *Medical Malpractice* § 15.02 15–2 and 15–8.

[10] When gaining an international comparative perspective on hospital liability, it becomes clear that most writers either acknowledge or discuss most of the legal grounds which are scrutinized here. Every individual writer(s) has his own distinctive approach and unique exposition of the relevant legal grounds and principles which found hospital liability. Yet, the following grounds embrace most of those perspectives. See Chapter 4.

[11] Jones *Negligence* 392.

directly to the patient by the hospital. Direct duties which the hospital owe the patient consist of all organizational obligations which include the provision of proper administration, competent staff, safe systems and reasonable health care.

**Hospital liability** is established for the acts of independent contractor/doctors where **non-delegable duties** of care are constructed and construed as being owed to the patient by the hospital. Many non-delegable duties are founded in common law. Responsibility for the duties cannot be delegated by the hospital, only performance thereof. The hospital is liable to the patient where the conduct of an employee, an independent contractor or other medical staff is at stake. The purpose of this legal ground, which founds a faultless employer liability, is to especially establish such responsibility for the employer, for the negligence of an independent contractor. This liability ensures the quality and high performance standards of a health-care system *in toto*.

The **liability of hospitals** is established for the acts of independent contractor/doctors under doctrines such as **apparent agency** or **agency by estoppel**. The hospital is held liable for injury resulting from any services which it purports to, or does in fact provide to patients. The liability of the hospital is based on the fact that the doctor is supposedly an agent of the hospital, and that the patient relies on the hospital for treatment. The hospital is thus held liable for the negligent act(s) of even an independent contractor.

**Breach of contract** is also a possible legal ground which can establish hospital liability in the appropriate circumstances.

**Strict hospital liability** has been introduced in many legal systems. The expansion of hospital liability seems to be evolving towards a general approach of strict liability.

The modern trend, therefore, is towards an expansion of hospital liability. The institution is by far more economically sound and financially capable of accommodating astronomic settlement fees or damage awards.

Every sovereign independent legal ground has been subject to some kind of adaptation towards this extended hospital liability. The expansion of the liability of hospitals has rid the legal system of rigid barriers such as the unnecessary or questionable distinction between employees and independent contractors in order to determine liability. Likewise, the sole application of the control test and all its variants has been labelled by some modern writers as ineffective and outdated. A variety of tests should be taken into consideration and applied in accordance with their relevance to a specific case. Hospital liability has therefore been expanded significantly for the performances of independent contractors.

The expansion of hospital liability and the consequential cost-controlling crisis of the medical malpractice arena, can be approached in more than one way: Policies concerning the regulation/control or possible expansion of hospital liability with inclusion of relevant solutions, requirements and/or legal grounds should be provided for in legislation. Legal experts who specialize only in the medical malpractice field should be appointed to medical malpractice cases. Legal procedures should be streamlined and legal costs reduced. Independent medical malpractice boards and/or courts could be established. Professional medical staff should be thoroughly legally enlightened, effectively regulated and reasonably controlled. Alternative social insurance plans should be investigated. All possible precautionary measures should be taken in order to avoid and reduce the incidence of medical misadventures, and ultimately limit legal claims. If the number of legal claims could be reduced and consequential economic burdens lifted, this would in turn prevent increased costs of liability insurance and relieve the taxpayer's burden.[12] Preventive medicine and/or measures rather than defensive medicine is therefore advocated.

A system of strict hospital liability could be the answer. A regime of strict or no-fault liability could be a likely cure for the medical malpractice crisis many countries face.[13] However, at this stage, a responsible expanded hospital liability system, which is based on the acknowledgement of the presence or non-presence of fault of hospitals and/or medical professionals, is still advocated.

---

[12] Chapman *Medicine* 55–56. See also Kennedy and Grubb *Medical Law* 528 and 538 for their proposed measures

[13] See also Chapman *Medicine* 55–58, 100–102 and Kennedy and Grubb *Medical Law* 509–512, 529.

# Chapter 2

# Health-Care Systems

## 2.1 INTRODUCTION

The purpose of the discussion on health-care systems is not to indulge in a detailed exposition of various internationally recognized health-care systems. This discussion is only a useful briefing on the identification of various countries into different categories. Countries that fall into the same category have certain basic similarities and their health-care structures bear some resemblance. It is meant only to indicate whether public or private enterprise are the dominant or more important authoritative role players in a country's health-care system influencing the identification of defendants in medical malpractice cases. It will thus serve to give a rough indication of the expected type of health-care system and consequential health-care liability system.

Health-care systems are constant only in their tendency to change.[1] Technological discoveries, scientific breakthroughs and changing political and health policies ensure highly flexible and modern health-care regimes and systems.

An **international perspective** reveals that health-care systems are diversified in structure, administration, function, policy, and the laws applying to them. The diversification is unique to every country. A study of various countries' health-care systems reveals differing health laws, statutes or regulations and different bureaucratic or administrative structures. This in turn reveals that every country in effect creates its own health-care provider liability system or structures. Certain similarities or common denominators and dissimilarities can be identified when comparing various countries' health-care structures. Countries can therefore be categorized according to similarities in the characteristics of their health-care structures.

---

[1]  Roemer *World Perspective* ix.

A **national perspective** emphasizes every country's unique bureaucratic or administrative structures in their health-care and institutional health-care provider (hospital) system, The investigation of different health-care systems reveals the variation in bureaucratic or administrative health-care and health-care provider (hospital) structures. The purpose of the investigation and comparison of these structures lie in the identification of important authoritative role players in each system or structure. This identification becomes necessary and most relevant when trying to establish and select the appropriate institutional or representative defendant(s) for the liability of a hospital in medical malpractice cases.

**Hospitals** are the most important institutional health-care providers, and form an integral part of any health-care system.[2] When considering a health-care structure, relevant health policy and institutional health-care provider structures, one may establish which (state) entity or organization controls the health-care facility and which institution or representative to hold ultimately responsible for the hospital's liability.

## 2.2  NATIONAL PERSPECTIVE ON HEALTH-CARE SYSTEMS

### 2.2.1  Universal and Particular Determinative Factors

Universally speaking the political system, legal system, culture, language and other particular characteristics of every country differ. Likewise, every country has its own health-care industry or system which is inclusive of a unique health-care provider industry.

The health-care system of every country is mainly determined and formed by two dynamic-sovereign, though inter-active and developing forces. The 'universalistic'[3] aspects on the one hand, are aspects such as modern science, medical knowledge, medical research and modern technology. The 'particularistic'[4] characteristics of a country on the other hand, are its political system, legal system, economic policy and associated dynamics. The universalistic elements are implemented and introduced in a unique and specific manner in each country, depending on the country's particularistic

---

[2]   See also Carmi *Hospital Law* 6.

[3]   Field *Health* 21 23 27 28. 'Universalistic' is the phrase used by Field.

[4]   Field *Health* 21 23 27 28. 'Particularistic' is the phrase used by Field.

elements. The unique interaction of these forces establishes and determines each country's health-care system.[5]

Every country's health-care system as well as the institutional health-care provider systems, in terms of which they are established, exist, function and incur liability, are individually founded on that country's particular elements. The particular elements comprise of political ideologies, socio-economic principles, legal concepts and the implementation of policies. In short, a country's type of civilization determines the success of its health policy and health-care.

The dominating political philosophy of a country is the primary casting mould for the ensuing administrative and executive structures of a health-care system and institutional health-care providers. Thus, politics and civilization mastermind national health-care initiatives.

The political ideologies of a country establish its own unique constitution, statutory laws and health policies. The constitution, statutes and policies in turn produce its own, distinctive administrative and other organizational systems and structures and thus naturally implicate specific liability frameworks. Liability adheres to and is dependent on an authoritative framework or structure for the determination of appropriate defendants in medical malpractice cases. All large organizations — be they private or public — maintain impersonal hierarchical structures in which diversified ranks of superiors and subordinates feature, and are known as bureaucratic organizations.[6] These organizational structures implicate health-care liability systems or structures. Constitutions, statutory laws and policies thus initiate and determine bureaucratic structures. There are, however, sometimes radical differences between the theoretical exposition of authoritative structures — in a constitution, statute or health policy, and the practical implementation or execution of authoritative concepts.

The legal system or judicial machinery of a country can independently of the constitution, statutory law and health policies, regulate and determine, for example, health-care systems, health-care provider issues and eventual medical malpractice cases. As Max Weber demonstrated, 'law is the dominant technique whereby the hierarchical, impersonal and rationalized structure of modern bureaucracies is organized.'[7] The law thus creates and controls — at all levels of government — complicated networks of institu-

---

[5]   Field *Health* 21 23 27 28. Bridgman and Roemer *Hospital* 74–75.

[6]   Baxter *Administrative Law* 72.

[7]   *Ibid.*

tions, powers, rights and duties.[8] The law also controls legal relationships that are relevant to hospital liability in medical malpractice cases. When the structures of modern bureaucracies such as the health-care system and hospital governance structure are scrutinized, authoritative role players are identified. The establishment of the appropriate defendant(s) and all relevant parties to a hospital liability suit then follows easily. Appropriate defendants to these legal relationships consist of the state, the hospital authorities and other health-care providers and corporations. Delictual, contractual and administrative-law principles apply in determining the liability of these parties.

Furthermore the executive structures of countries, i.e. the executive departments, administrative agencies and other executive bodies enforce health acts and health policies dependent on the economic structures and allocated funds.

### 2.3  COMPARATIVE INTERNATIONAL PERSPECTIVE ON HEALTH-CARE SYSTEMS

#### 2.3.1  Relevance of the Discussion

A comparative international perspective of different countries' health-care systems and their administrative structures will demonstrate 'a range of differing patterns of health service organization'.[9] The world perspective will further define the place of every country in a theoretical framework, upon investigation of the level of government involvement in every country or of the 'relationships of the health department to medical care'.[10] Health-care is one of the world's most highly regulated industries.[11]

This perspective also illustrates the way in which countries world-wide are at present running their health-care systems. Determinative similarities and differences are described. It has, however, been announced in the media and published world-wide, that from October 1993 revolutionary changes are to be expected in the evolution of the health-care systems of *inter alia* the United States of America, the United Kingdom and South Africa.

---

[8]   *Op. cit.* 73, 74.
[9]   Roemer *World Perspective* 252.
[10]  *Ibid.*
[11]  Scully *Health Care Facilities* 9.

The relevance of the discussion lies in the determination of the nature of every health-care system and the identification of the type of the relevant institutional health-care provider or hospital. The identification of these structures and authoritative role players, will aid the legal representative in establishing the appropriate defendant for hospital liability in medical malpractice cases. It will also provide a clear indication of which kind of legal liability to expect. In other words: The pursuant liability of these parties — whether private or public, delictual, contractual or administrative — becomes obvious from classifying and perusing the various health-care systems and hospital governance structures.

Where the health-care system is run predominantly by the state, and hospitals are controlled similarly, the appropriate defendant would be a state entity or state representative. Following an investigation of the health-care structures and hospital governance structure, it will appear clearly which state entity or state representative to sue. When a hospital is established by a corporation, investigation of relevant statutes or regulations, hospital by-laws, hospital standards and its governance structure will likewise establish an appropriate institutional or representative defendant.

The terminological description of the appropriate institutional or representative defendant, will also differ from country to country. In Great Britain the 'hospital authority', in the United States of America the 'corporation' or hospital, medical centre, university or health authority, in South Africa a state representative like the 'Minister of Health' or a 'provincial or regional division' or a corporation or hospital, and in France a 'regional council' or hospital may be considered and named as the responsible entity.

### 2.3.2 Models on the Classification of Health-Care Systems

Two models will be illustrated briefly. The model of Roemer comprises of four components.[12] The model of Field comprises of five elements.[13] Each component or element of both the two models comprises of certain countries of the world. The countries are grouped together or classified on the basis of the level of government involvement.[14]

---

[12]  Roemer *World Perspective* 252.

[13]  Field *Health* 23 24.

[14]  Davis and George *States* 102; Roemer *World Perspective* 252.

### 2.3.2.1  Roemer's model [15]

Roemer classifies countries' health-care systems into a model consisting of four components which are:

(i)     free enterprise,

(ii)    social insurance,

(iii)   public assistance, and

(iv)    universal service.

(i)  Free enterprise systems

Free enterprise predominates in the United States of America. The private sector provides many health-care facilities and much funding. Consumers contract with private health insurance companies and private hospitals where doctors are paid on a fee-for-service basis.[16] Consumers are responsible for their own health-care costs.[17] The government is involved in funding and subsidizing health-care and has many public health insurance schemes. Government therefore plays a residual role, providing for those who cannot afford private treatment.[18]

(ii)  Social Insurance

The social insurance system of health service organization predominates in western continental Europe. Social insurance systems provide medical and hospital services in countries such as France, Germany, Italy and Scandinavia. The health system of Japan also shows resemblance. The insurance funds which sponsor health-care are organized by a mixture of government, employer and religious groups.

Hospitals are mainly governmental and under local and provincial authority. Doctors are salaried in hospitals or receive fee-for-service payments from the insurance in private practice.[19]

---

[15]  Roemer's classification of health-care systems into four different components will be discussed in paragraph 3.2.1. All information related here, concerning these systems, was obtained from Roemer *World Perspective* 252–255.

[16]  This follows from the discussion by Davis and George of Roemer's model: Davis and George *States* 103.

[17]  *Ibid.*

[18]  *Ibid.*

[19]  *Ibid.*

(iii) Public assistance

The public assistance system of health service is found in developing countries. The provision of health-care under this system involves free medical care to the majority of the population by the government. Hospital and medical services are provided in public hospitals by salaried medical professionals. Eligibility is secured by a means test and the minimum number of non-poor,[20] arrange private care by doctors who are paid fee-for-service.

(iv) Universal service

This system is found in Great Britain. The National Health Service (NHS) of Britain greatly resembles this type of health service. Roemer also categorizes the Soviet Union (now defunct) and New Zealand here. The government provides almost complete and unrestricted health-care to the whole nation by means of general revenues. This service exceeds that of or are equal to services of the free-enterprise and social insurance countries. Many hospitals are owned and controlled by government. Patients may be treated by salaried doctors in public clinics or hospitals.[21] Only ten per cent of health costs accrues to the private sector.[22]

*Roemer's comment*

Roemer's most profound conclusion on the general hospital which is regarded by many as the 'health center of the community'[23] involves the following: The hospital as public facility — as in most countries of the world — is promoted as being the 'key physical instrumentality'[24] in establishing a unified health administration in general for each country. He also advocates health department participation in medical care programmes. Roemer furthermore observes — but does not advocate — a trend in all countries from free enterprise towards universal service systems which involves socially organized and financed health services. He predicts that health departments at local levels are the true community health administration of the future.[25]

---

[20]   *Ibid.*

[21]   *Ibid.*

[22]   *Ibid.*

[23]   Roemer *World Perspective* 255.

[24]   *Ibid.*

[25]   *Ibid.*

## 2.3.2.2  *Field's classification* [26]

Field distinguishes between five different categories or types of health-care systems. They are:

(i)     the emergent type

(ii)    the pluralistic system

(iii)   the insurance — social security system

(iv)    the national health service system and

(v)     socialized medicine

Major issues such as the nature of the health-care system, government involvement, the role of authoritative institutions and the private sector, financial arrangements, the role of the doctor and specialization are outlined.

(i)  The emergent system

The so-called emergent systems might also be referred to as 'primitive systems'. These systems existed mainly in the nineteenth century, for example in Russia, certain countries of Western Europe and the USA. At present countries which fit into this category are, for example, Mauritius, India, and various Third World countries.

These systems are characteristically unorganized and underdeveloped. They consist basically of a few health-care facilities or units which are privately owned and controlled, private practitioners working independently with few hospitals and almost no involvement by the polity. The systems outlined below evolved from the emergent systems.

(ii)  The pluralistic system

Typical examples of the pluralistic system are found in the United States, Switzerland and South Africa. Characteristic of the system is a combination of different types of organizations and schemes that jointly provide health-care services. Health-care facilities and health-care providers, for example hospitals and other institutions, are owned and controlled by either the state or private entrepreneurs. The state is indirectly, though increasingly, involved in health-care. Physicians are either state-employed and salaried or work privately. Professional associations play a powerful role. Health-care is

---

[26]   Field's classification of health-care systems into five different categories will be discussed in paragraph 3.2.2. All information related here, concerning these systems was obtained from Field *Health* 15, 21–28.

predominantly a consumer good or service, the consumer being the patient or person in need of medical care.

### (iii) The insurance-social security system

The system is essentially a twentieth century Western European phenomenon. It is to be found in countries such as Germany, France, Sweden and Italy. But it is also to be found in Canada and Japan.

Health-care is basically regarded as an insured or guaranteed consumer good or service. Hospitals and other institutional health-care providers are controlled by either public or private enterprise. Health-care services or medical services are guaranteed and provided as a basic right of citizenship. Financial arrangements are dependent on funding, the degree of insurance and state subsidies. A reimbursement system, i.e. a retrospective payment arrangement, is mostly created in which the organized medical profession as autonomous body contracts with insurance companies and/or the state's social-security system. Remuneration for medical services rendered is paid by the state on a subsidized basis, and by insurance companies in terms of the relevant policies. These bodies reimburse retrospectively. The role of the polity is thus significant (though indirect). In this reimbursement system, constant tension is created between the state and the medical profession regarding finances.

### (iv) The national health service system (NHS)

The British system is the prototype of the NHS. Another such system is found in Australia. This system is not widely imitated.

The system revolves around a central government that initiates a structure for all such services and finances it largely with public monies with prospective payment arrangements.

The government contracts with doctors who are regarded as independent professionals. The doctor has to tend to a certain number of patients and provide all non-hospital services for them. He or she is paid a *per capita* fee, irrespective of the extent of services provided. Specialists are regarded as consultants, work in hospitals or clinics and are paid salaries.

Ownership and control of hospitals and other providers of health-care are for the most part public. The liability of the state and its relevant authorities will thus be first and foremost, their control being central or direct. Health-care is provided as a state-supported consumer good or service.

### (v) Socialized medicine

The prototype was formerly found in the Soviet health-care system (early twentieth century), and is adopted now in Eastern Europe, Cuba and Chile.

The state has an absolute monopoly on all health and health-care services, providing most of it. In this system the state, however, spends the least on health-care in comparison with all the systems discussed. The state owns and controls all medical facilities, i.e. hospitals and other health-care institutions. Most doctors are trained, employed and salaried by the state and are not seen as professionals. Health-care is considered as a state-provided public service.

### 2.3.2.3  Conclusion

The models of both Roemer and Field basically group the same countries' health-care systems together. Although making use of different concepts and terminology, they basically concur.

## 2.4  CONCLUSION

The profound progress that has been made in the evolution of health-care industries and health-care provider industries of the world, can be attributed to the diffusion of modern knowledge and unprecedented multi-faceted developments in most societies. Together with major technological developments, changes in political systems and economic policies have always anticipated radical changes in health-care, health-care policies and institutional health-care provider conditions. The law has been equally flexible, adapting freely to new manifestations of mankind. When relevant policies have changed, so have bureaucratic or administrative health-care structures and health-care provider structures. These structures give clear indications of potential defendants for hospital liability in medical malpractice cases. Social and economic changes thus create different and changing health-care liability systems.

Grouping countries with similar health-care systems gives a clear vision of the manner in which health-care systems could be operated. It creates a potential educational environment for countries in which to learn from each other and distinguish viable systems from those not so successful. It should however be taken into consideration that what works for one country, might not necessarily be successful in another.[27]

The ultimate question, whether it really matters how health systems are organized, has to be posed. No existing health system perfectly fits any model, but only serves to indicate some combination of public and private

---

[27]    Roemer *World Perspective* ix.

health-care. Davis and George[28] have offered three reasons for answering this question positively:

First, **access** to medical services are discriminately affected and determined by the values and principles of each health-care system. The organization and structure of every health-care system thus determine the accessibility of every country's medical services. Second, **costs of services** are borne differently, because health-care resources rank differently on every country's list of national priorities. In South Africa health expenditure in 1994 amounted to ten per cent (10%) of the Gross National Product (GNP), whilst in most Western industrialized societies it amounted to seven per cent (7%) of GNP. In every society with its distinctive health-care system, primary health-care costs are borne by different sectors of the population. In the light of the fact that health costs have risen dramatically and health status has not, Davis and George advocate public regulation in order to control and fairly distribute health-care costs. Third, the **effect or cost** on the **health status** or quality of health care of a population is evaluated. There is no direct correlation between 'the arrangements of health-care, expenditures and health status'. Distribution of services have been influenced by doctors' resistance to governmental intrusion into professional practice. This remains notwithstanding large governmental funding. This and other important factors influence rising health-care costs. Legal procurement of accountability of the medical profession, also works against stabilizing health costs. Davis and George eventually advocate that only a radical change of health policy will bring about a reduction in health costs with a simultaneous improvement in health status.

I am of the opinion that any relevant or radical change of health-care policies will most probably lead to a change in health-care systems and their administrative structures. This in turn will most probably lead to a change in health-care liability systems and structures. The liability of health-care professionals and institutional health-care providers is and will always be dependent on the health-care system and administrative health-care structures of every community or country. Change in health-care systems and structures therefore has far-reaching effects for the legal system and liability sphere of all institutional or authoritative health-care role-players. Careful consideration must therefore be given to the evolution of health-care systems, hospitals and other providers of health-care services. No pains should be spared at achieving success in establishing reasonable access to,

---

[28] All information on the three reasons for analysing health-care systems was obtained from Davis and George *States* 103–105.

superb quality and balanced control of health-care. The quality of health-care will ultimately affect the health and happiness of all people.

# Chapter 3

# Hospitals
# The Hospital in Perspective

## 3.1 THE HOSPITAL

Today, the term **hospital** means an 'institution providing medical and surgical treatment and nursing care, for ill or injured people',[1] or as Speller aptly states it 'means any institution maintained for the reception, care and treatment of those in need of medical or surgical attention'.[2] Hospitals have undergone revolutionary development. At first, hospitals were no more than places of refuge for the destitute, poor and sick. Today, they are indispensable health facilities, furnished with modern medicine and technological equipment, that serve the whole population.

In considering the meaning of the word **hospital**, a brief survey of the historical development of this most important health facility may be useful. The word hospital comes from the Latin *hospes*, which means *host* or *guest*.[3] It has also been suggested that *hospital* comes from the Greek *hospitium*, which means a place for the reception of strangers and pilgrims.[4] The medieval Latin term *hospitale* for *hospital*, means place of reception for guests.[5] *Hospitale* is the neutral singular of *hospitalis*, from which the words *hostel* and *hotel* are derived.[6] The medieval hospital (*hospitale*), embraced mainly six types of institutions:[7]

---

[1]  *Oxford Advanced Learner's Dictionary* Tenth impression 1994.

[2]  Speller *Hospitals* 1.

[3]  *Cassell's Latin Dictionary* by DP Simpson 5 ed. 1979 Seventh Impression New York; see also McConnell *Health Care* 15.

[4]  McConnell *Health Care* 15.

[5]  *Oxford English Dictionary* Volume VII 2 ed.1989 414.

[6]  *Ibid.*

[7]  *Ibid*; see also Carlin *Hospital* 21.

1.  They were hospices or houses of reception, entertainment and rest for pilgrims, travellers and strangers.
2.  Charitable institutions, housing and maintaining the destitute, infirm, aged and needy (almshouses).
3.  An institution that cared for the sick, poor or wounded.
4.  A house of entertainment ('open house').
5.  A place of lodging.
6.  Leper houses.

The first hospitals were established during the Middle Ages.[8] Religious orders mainly cared for the sick poor. The rich stayed at home and were attended by family members and later by doctors. Quality care and survival were ensured not by being admitted to, but rather evading hospitals.[9] Today, hospitals are the most important institutional health-care providers, or health facilities. The discussion on the legal liability of hospitals will also be relevant to the liability of other institutional health-care providers of health facilities. Health facilities include the following:[10]

1   Hospitals
2   Clinics
3   Free-standing surgical outpatient facilities
4   Homes for the aged
5   Nursing homes
6   Outpatient physical therapy and speech pathology facilities
7   Kidney disease treatment centres
8   Ambulatory health-care service facilities
9   Drug treatment facilities
10  Laboratories
11  Birthing centres or maternity homes
12  Sperm banks
13  Blood banks
14  Eye banks
15  Psychiatric hospitals

---

[8]  Peters *et al. Medical Practice* 3.

[9]  *Ibid.* McConnell *Health Care* 15–16. Picard 1981 *MGLJ* 1000.

[10]  See Peters *et al. Medical Practice* 74–79 for more examples. Speller *Hospitals* 1–3.

## 16    Hospices

The hospital has also become the largest employer of health-care personnel inclusive of health-care professionals. Health-care professionals who are also non-institutional health-care providers are for example doctors, nurses and others. Other health professions which have emerged are that of pharmacist, dentist, optometrist and many more. According to McConnell 'health-care as an industry is a stronghold of professionalism'. Few other industries rely so heavily on so many highly trained and specialized workers.[11]

Most importantly, a hospital is an independent legal entity. The legal basis[12] of the hospital establishes the institution and determines the type and nature of the hospital. Hospitals can be categorized into various types of business organizations. We can distinguish, on their differing legal basis, between governmental institutions, private facilities, for-profit institutions or corporations and non-profit institutions or corporations, proprietorships and partnerships.[13] These health-care facilities derive their specific powers, restricted duties, governance structure and therefore their discerning characteristics from their legal basis.[14]

A corporation is a fictitious person created by law, existing separately from those who create it, own it or serve it.[15] Natural persons are however designated to form a governing body and are generally known as the board of directors or board of trustees.[16] These individuals exercise corporate powers and may be held liable for their corporate decision-making.[17] Institutions that are not incorporated, are not fictitious persons and powers and responsibilities are held by one or more natural persons,[18] or authorities.

Every country has different types of hospitals. We will therefore find various types of hospitals or legal organizations in every country. However, we can basically differentiate between public and private health services or health-care providers in every country. Both the public and private enterprises are common phenomena to all countries. The only difference between countries is the degree of involvement by each public and private sector. The scope of public-sector involvement as opposed to private-sector involvement

---

[11]    McConnell *Health Care* 15 16.

[12]    Miller *Hospital Law* 14–15.

[13]    *Ibid*; Southwick and Slee *Law of Hospital* 106; Pozgar *Health* 199.

[14]    Miller *Hospital Law* 14–16; Pozgar *Health* 199.

[15]    Southwick and Slee *Law of Hospital* 106; Pozgar *Health* 199.

[16]    Pozgar *Health* 199.

[17]    *Ibid*.

[18]    *Ibid*.

will naturally vary from country to country. Furthermore every country with its own hospitals, have different governance structures for these hospitals. The organization of every hospital relies on the governance structure, and the form of legal organization has its own implications for the governance of the hospital.[19] The hospital governance structure or organization of the hospital basically includes a governing body (consisting of directors or trustees) or hospital council, an administrator or superintendent and organized medical staff.[20] This is an over-simplified but basic structure akin to every hospital only differing terminologically from hospital to hospital and from country to country.

## 3.2  THE HOSPITAL WITHIN THE HEALTH-CARE SYSTEM

Hospitals have become the largest most dynamic institutions in the health-care industry and form an integral part of any health-care system. Hospitals have also evolved into the most important[21] institutional health-care providers. They are funded by means of a substantial part of the state or national health-care budget.[22]

## 3.3  THE HOSPITAL INDUSTRY

In the United States of America the hospital industry is the third largest national industry while in Canada it is the largest industry.[23] The health-care system of the United States *in toto* is the seventh largest business industry in the world. The hospital industry has evolved universally into a comprehensive high-risk business enterprise. That is especially true of the private health-care sector of certain countries, especially that of the United States of America. The primary contemporary propensity of the industry is oriented towards financial gain, which seems to enjoy preference over all other priorities. It would appear that financial gains and profiteering come first, and health-care follows. There are of course always exceptions to the rule. Here we think of the hospital industry of Great Britain. Their population enjoys the benefit of the National Health Service (NHS). At the moment the

---

[19]  Miller *Hospital Law* 16.

[20]  *Op. cit.* 15, 16.

[21]  See also Carmi *Hospital Law* 6.

[22]  *Ibid.*

[23]  Picard 1981 *MGLJ* 998: The largest service industry.

system is experiencing financial and other difficulties, because of the government's heavy financial subsidies or funding of the health-care system. South Africa's and other countries' state hospitals also come into mind as big funders of their health-care. When the liability of hospital authorities and other health-care providers is calculated monetarily, the financial factors represent serious — if not catastrophic — consequences.

## 3.4 HISTORICAL BACKGROUND

The perspective gained from analysing thousands of years of medical practice and legal concepts, will probably lead us to the identification of problem areas, and the subsequent negotiation of some solutions to the ever-increasing crisis concerning hospital liability.[24] Religion gave birth to the practical and noble sciences of law and medicine.[25] Although idealistically speaking, they compliment each other — both exhibiting a distinct love for intellectualism and elite acknowledgement — it might appear they could have severed the ties of friendship from the beginning of times. The highlights in the evolution of these sciences will now be outlined and it will be demonstrated how they irrevocably became entwined.

### 3.4.1 An Outline of the History of Medicine and Hospitals

**The origin of medicine:** The history of medicine is introduced and made known to modern man, through the science of palaeopathology.[26] **Palaeo-pathology**, that is the 'scrutiny of the history of disease and its morbid manifestations in prehistoric periods',[27] has demonstrated that with the first manifestations of life on earth, there was an almost synchronous existence of disease.[28] Investigations revealed forms of life and disease even antecedent

---

[24] See Peters *et al. Medical Practice* 1.

[25] Deutsch 1979 1 *IJML* 81; King 1984 *JAMA* 2204 describes the conflict between law and medicine since 1856.

[26] 'Palaeo-' *Oxford Advanced Learner's Dictionary* 10th impression 1994. 'Palaeo-pathology' as spelt by Castiglioni *Medicine* 13. palaeo-, palae-, US paleo-, pale- *comb. form.*: Indicates ancient or prehistoric; [Greek *palaio-*, from *palaois*, ancient, from *palai*, long ago.] *Reader's Digest Universal Dictionary* 1988 1113. Pathology n. 1. The scientific study of the nature of disease, its causes, processes, development, and consequences. 2. The anatomical or functional manifestations of disease, or of a particular disease, for example changes in organs and tissues. *Reader's Digest Universal Dictionary* 1988 1134.

[27] Castiglioni *Medicine* 13.

[28] *Ibid.*

to the existence of human life on earth. Prehistoric palaeozoic times evidenced diseases in fossilized animals that we recognize and treat today.[29] Palaeopathology[30] later, as a result of the 'study of diseases in ancient human populations as revealed by their skeletal and mummified remains',[31] provided modern man with the first obscure evidence of primitive man's medicine.

The first known forms of medicine which emerged during these centuries and were akin to the primitive peoples, were 'instinctive medicine, empirical medicine, magic medicine and priestly medicine'.[32]

The most fundamental characteristic of the era of **prehistoric medicine** was the belief in the supernatural:[33] supernatural forces were thought to cause diseases;[34] supernatural means were accordingly used as diagnostic methods;[35] and treatment was supernatural in character.[36] It is the super-natural element that distinguishes primitive medicine from modern medicine.[37]

**Mesopotamian medicine** arose and developed in the eastern Mediterranean civilizations in the period 5000 to 4000 BC.[38] The medicine was predominantly of a magical or religious nature. Priests practised religious medicine.[39] Later, Assyrian and Babylonian doctors became famous and popular to the extent that they consulted as far as Egypt at high fees. Doctors drew up medical texts containing descriptions of various diseases and corresponding prescriptions.[40] The Code of King Hammurabi of Mesopotamia, dating from about 1792 BC, confirmed the doctor's important role in the society. This code was the most significant, though not the first

---

[29]  Castiglioni *Medicine* 13 14 51; According to Peters *et al. Medical Practice* 1 scientists have established that disease forms have essentially remained the same throughout millions of years.

[30]  As spelt by Peters *et al. Medical Practice* 1.

[31]  Peters *et al. Medical Practice* 1.

[32]  Castiglioni *Medicine* 16–30.

[33]  Peters *et al. Medical Practice* 2.

[34]  *Ibid*; Castiglioni *Medicine* 19.

[35]  Peters *et al. Medical Practice* 2.

[36]  *Ibid*; Castiglioni *Medicine* 19.

[37]  Peters *et al. Medical Practice* 2.

[38]  Castiglioni *Medicine* 31.

[39]  *Op. cit.* 33–44; Peters *et al. Medical Practice* 2.

[40]  Castiglioni *Medicine* 39.

recorded system that expounded medical ethics. The doctor's penal and civil responsibility was established, and medical fees were specified.[41]

In comparison, the medicine of this era was developed in observation of and in relation to the universe (i.e. the stars, waters and plants). It was less objective in scientific approach than the Egyptian civilization and less advanced in legal regulation than the Jewish.[42] The concepts of social medicine and hygiene also emerged.[43]

The development of ancient **Egyptian medicine** took place parallel and independently to that of Mesopotamia. It extended over a period of five or six millenia.[44] In **Ancient Egypt** treatment of illness was still haunted by supernaturalism, but rationalization of patients' diagnoses and diseases steadily emerged. Patients were carefully examined, case histories were made and tests of urine, faeces and blood were invented.[45] However awesome the mummification processes, the tombs and other Egyptian monuments were, the Egyptian physicians were known for their excellence and skill, and Egyptian medicine was known for its shrewd perspicuity.[46] All this declined after Persia conquered Egypt.[47]

**Jewish medicine**: In the eighth century BC,[48] a thousand years after Hammurabi,[49] the pre-exile prophets, especially Amos,[50] Jeremiah[51] and Isaiah[52] brought a powerful ethical message to the leaders of Israel and Judah.[53] On the basis of the Lord's spoken word, they[54] independently and fearlessly delivered a message of justice and righteousness to kings and nations to return to the straight and narrow path.[55]

---

[41]   *Op. cit.* 40; *Chapman Physicians* 4–5; Peters *et al. Medical Practice* 2.

[42]   Castiglioni *Medicine* 44.

[43]   *Ibid*; Peters *et al. Medical Practice* 2.

[44]   Castiglioni *Medicine* 45–63.

[45]   Peters *et al. Medical Practice* 2; Castiglioni *Medicine* 46 51 62 63 (45–63).

[46]   Castiglioni *Medicine* 59 62–63.

[47]   *Op. cit.* 61–62.

[48]   *Op. cit.* 8–9.

[49]   *Op. cit.* 8.

[50]   The book of Amos 7:14; 5; 23–24.

[51]   The book of Jeremiah 23:28; 33:15.

[52]   The book of Isaiah 32:1; 5:15; 33:16.

[53]   Chapman *Physicians* 8–11.

[54]   The pre-exile prophets were also called classical prophets: Chapman *Physicians* 9.

[55]   Chapman *Physicians* 9.

Centuries later, this ethical message was redirected to include the medical profession which enjoyed the same status as priests and judges at that time.[56] By the beginning of the Talmudic period (200 BC to AD 600) the medical calling had — according to the apocryphal book of Ecclesiasticus 38:1–3 — gained favour both in the sight of God and man.[57] From AD 400 doctors were granted privileges and their liabilities were carefully expounded and restricted.[58]

According to Castiglioni, the crux of Jewish medicine lies in the superior ethical concept of monotheism.[59] Biblical medicine's main and valuable contribution to medicine was its laying of a foundation for social ethics and even social hygiene until the relevant legislation was eventually passed.[60]

Medicine of **ancient Persia and India** also emerged and was migrated into the Mediterranean basin between 3000 and 1000 BC. It spread to distant places but was later almost completely destroyed and is today maintained only by oral tradition. It consisted mainly of the belief of a demonistic origin of all ills and healing was perceived as a magical experience which changed into a religious ideation.[61]

**Chinese medicine** originated during the Chinese civilization which dates back to centuries before the reign of Emperior Fi, who reigned about 2800 BC.[62] Chinese medicine made great strides but stagnated completely about AD 1000, due to the overemphasizing of detail and the deletion of principle facts. At — about 2700 BC — however, the technique of acupuncture had been invented. Surgery flourished and fifty-two volumes consisting of two thousand prescriptions were compiled. Chinese medicine spread to **Japan** through Korea about AD 400.[63] Chinese doctors were called to court. The Empress Komyo built the first Japanese hospital AD 758, and by AD 982 smallpox hospitals already existed in Japan.[64]

---

[56] *Op. cit.* 12.

[57] Chapman *Physicians* 12–13. Hoffman *et al. Legal Medicine* 35: In ancient Mosaic Law, the Israelites perpetuated the concept of 1 'Lex Talionis' or 'Law of Talion' by demanding 'an eye for an eye, a tooth for a tooth'. See Castiglioni *Medicine* 76–77 in connection with the Talmudic period.

[58] Chapman *Physicians* 13–14.

[59] *Op. cit.* 79.

[60] Such as sanitary legislation: Castiglioni *Medicine* 67, 79.

[61] Castiglioni *Medicine* 80–97.

[62] *Op. cit.* 98.

[63] *Op. cit.* 98–112.

[64] *Op. cit.* 108.

**Ancient Greek medicine** started about 500 BC.[65] Greek physicians initially still maintained the belief that the gods punished people through illness.[66] They thus engaged in ritual sacrifices and purification ceremonies to cure their patients.[67] Apollo was first honoured as the god of healing.[68] Apollo was replaced by his son, Asclepius in 500 BC.[69] Asclepius' staff and holy snake are still the symbols of the medical profession.[70] **Hippocratic medicine**: Hippocrates (about 460 – 360 BC),[71] known as the father of medicine and the wisest physician of antiquity, fortunately came to the rescue of ancient Greek medicine. The supernatural stigma and speculations were exchanged for rational considerations of scientific value, such as the clinical observation[72] of patients which created a consistent doctrine of theory and practice.[73]

The Hippocratic Corpus consists of seventy titles and was published between 430 and 350 BC.[74] The Hippocratic Oath[75] — one of the tributes of the *Corpus* — has bound physicians for centuries.

---

[65] Peters *et al. Medical Practice* 2; see Castiglioni *Medicine* 113–188 on ancient Greek medicine.

[66] Peters *et al. Medical Practice* 2.

[67] *Ibid.*

[68] *Ibid.* Chapman *Physicians* 18–19.

[69] Chapman *Physicians* 18–19.

[70] Peters *et al. Medical Practice* 2; Castiglioni *Medicine* 122–123.

[71] Hippocrates counted himself a lineal descendant of Asclepius; so did Aristotle: Chapman *Physicians* 18. Peters *et al. Medical Practice* 2; Chapman *Physicians* 19–26; see Castiglioni *Medicine* 148–178 on Hippocratic medicine.

[72] Peters *et al. Medical Practice* 2.

[73] Chapman *Physicians* 20.

[74] *Ibid*; Peters *et al. Medical Practice* 2; Castiglioni *Medicine* 146 151. It was supposedly written by different authors at different times.

[75] Peters *et al. Medical Practice* 3; Chapman *Physicians* 20–26; Chapman 25 declares that the oath '… cannot be looked on as a great source of medical ethics, its chief purpose having been, as Edelstein has shown, much more mundane and pragmatic.' Edelstein *Legacies* 61 66–75: The oath was not composed before 400 BC. Edelstein states that the Hippocratic Oath became the nucleus of all medical ethics. All men of all religions embraced the Oath and its ideals as being the embodiment of truth. Castiglioni *Medicine* 144 153–156.

# OATH[76]

I swear by Apollo Physician and Asclepius and Hygicia and Panaccia and all the gods and goddesses, making them my witnesses, that I will fulfil according to my ability and judgment this oath and this covenant:

To hold him who has taught me this art as equal to my parents and to live my life in partnership with him, and if he is in need of money to give him a share of mine, and to regard his offspring as equal to my brothers in male lineage and to teach them this art — if they desire to learn it — without fee and covenant; to give a share of precepts and oral instructions and all the other learning to my sons and to the sons of him who has instructed me and to pupils who have signed the covenant and have taken an oath according to the medical law, but to no one else.

I will apply dietetic measures for the benefit of the sick according to my ability and judgment; I will keep them from harm and injustice.

I will neither give a deadly drug to anybody if asked for it, nor will I make a suggestion to this effect. Similarly I will not give to a woman an abortive remedy. In purity and holiness I will guard my life and my art.

I will not use the knife, not even on sufferers from stone, but will withdraw in favour of such men as are engaged in this work.

Whatever houses I may visit, I will come for the benefit of the sick, remaining free of all intentional injustice, of all mischief and in particular of sexual relations with both female and male persons, be they free or slaves.

What I may see or hear in the course of the treatment or even outside of the treatment in regard to the life of men, which on no account one must spread abroad, I will keep to myself holding such things shameful to be spoken about.

If I fulfil this oath and do not violate it, may it be granted to me to enjoy life and art, being honoured with fame among all men for all time to come; if I transgress it and swear falsely, may the opposite of all this be my lot.

---

[76] The Oath attributed to Hippocrates, pagan version, as translated by Ludwig Edelstein. Ludwig Edelstein 'The Hippocratic Oath — Text, Translation, and Interpretation' Supplement No I, Bull Hist Med (1943) p. 3. Chapman *Physicians* 22.

Greek schools of medicine were established and organizations of physicians were formed during the same period.[77] Physicians were classified as belonging to the class of 'demiurgoi' (the workers useful for the people) or as a 'technites' or 'artificers'. Medicine was prepared by the physician himself or by the rhizotomist (cutter of roots). The latter later became pharmacists.[78] Midwives appeared and a textbook of midwifery also saw the light of day.[79]

Greek medicine stands out in the history of medicine. This period was characterized by rational investigations of life itself and an unequalled search for new knowledge. From these facts scientific medicine could arise.

**Greek medicine** officially came to Rome in 292 BC, during a major epidemic.[80] The Romans initially bestowed little or no honour on their own physicians, considering them of low status and thus contracting Greek doctors.[81] The first Greek physician by the name of Archagathus arrived in Rome in 219 BC.[82] The Romans took over Greece in 146 BC, and maintained Athens as university city and intellectual capital until AD 529.[83]

**Roman medicine** did not nearly achieve or equal the scientific developments of the Greeks. Medical history, however, credits the Romans for having introduced an outstanding Roman system of law in which medical law or legal medicine featured. The Romans also eventually raised the doctors from an initially humble position to an invincible, dignified class, protected by law.[84]

At first, Rome did not have professional medical practitioners. The *paterfamilias* fulfilled that function.[85] Doctors from Greece were later introduced to Rome and were initially treated with disrespect.[86] Their superior knowledge eventually earned them great wealth and high positions. Asclepiades of

---

[77] Castiglioni *Medicine* 144.

[78] *Op. cit.* 146. The rhizotomist was regarded as the assistant of the physician. He collected roots, dried and pulverized them and then prepared the product as medicine.

[79] Castiglioni *Medicine* 146.

[80] Chapman *Physicians* 36: It was '... possibly bubonic plague ...'. See also Castiglioni *Medicine* 244.

[81] Chapman *Physicians* 36–38; Peters *et al. Medical Practice* 3; Castiglioni *Medicine* 196 (232) describes Cato's hate and fear for physicians, forbidding his son to see one.

[82] Chapman *Physicians* 35–36.

[83] *Op. cit.* 35.

[84] Castiglioni *Medicine* 240–241; Peters *et al. Medical Practice* 3.

[85] Castiglioni *Medicine* 196.

[86] *Op. cit.* 196, 232.

Prusa who came to Rome in 100 BC, was most sought after by the rich and famous. Once, upon investigation of a 'corpse' on its way to be buried, he detected signs of life, manipulated the body and brought it back to life. He became well known.[87]

Rome — most importantly — initiated an historical transformation of the Greek healing craft (*ars*) into the medical profession (*professio*)[88] as known and respected universally today. Scribonius Largus was a Roman physician of the first century AD, who clearly stated the physician's obligation to place the patient's interests first, and his guild and medical colleagues second.[89] He was also the first to refer in writing to medicine as a profession.[90] Yet, 'Rome's physicians never reached the top of the social ladder', but were always one step behind the patrician class.[91]

Julius Caesar granted all doctors Roman citizenship in 46 BC, with the result that dignity of the practice of medicine was enhanced. Medical schools were established which furnished the entire Roman empire with doctors.[92] Toward the end of the Empire, the status and dignity of doctors in Rome were clearly established. Their opinions carried great weight in medical matters, matters of hygiene and even concerning political problems.[93] Since 27 BC the Romans established sickness insurance associations and medical societies.[94] The state employed physicians and specialization began to emerge.[95]

In the early centuries of Christianity (*circa* 100–300 AD) plagues occurred frequently and were extremely contagious, causing enormous loss of human life.[96] It has been cited as a major factor in the decline of the Roman Empire. It was, however, during the time of these epidemics that Christians first established institutions to care for the aged and the sick.[97]

---

[87]    *Op. cit.* 197–200.

[88]    Chapman *Physicians* 38–43, 161: It was Scribonius who first made use of the word *professio*.

[89]    Chapman *Physicians* 40–42.

[90]    *Ibid.*

[91]    *Ibid.*

[92]    Castiglioni *Medicine* 233.

[93]    *Op. cit.* 234–235.

[94]    Peters *et al. Medical Practice* 3; *Chapman Physicians* 42.

[95]    Peters *et al. Medical Practice* 3.

[96]    Up to 800,000 people died of one plague in Numidia alone: Castiglioni *Medicine* 244.

[97]    Castiglioni *Medicine* 246: 'The influence of Christianity on the history of medicine of this period is also manifest in the fact that it attracted and held the most active minds and the

Institutions described as 'Roman military hospitals' were discovered near Vienna, at Bonn in Germany and at Baden in Switzerland. The institutions referred to as hospitals, and pharmacies were revealed in 1904. 'Real hospitals, in the modern sense of establishments designed to receive and treat all sorts of patients, were only instituted, as we shall see, much later.'[98] The hospitals for soldiers and slaves were called *valetudinaria*. There were also *valetudinaria* for athletes, for wounded gladiators and for the legions. Well-known doctors like Galen, attended the athletes and gladiators. There were many doctors, specialists, dentists, gynaecologists, otologists, midwives and nurses.[99]

**The medieval era (AD 500–1500):**[100] **The Early Middle Ages,**[101] especially after AD 600, were pervaded with the Christian belief that disease stemmed from sin, the devil or witchcraft and could be countered only by prayer, and recovery was perceived as a miracle.[102] The rendering of medical services was therefore confined to monasteries.[103] The care of the sick was until then mainly the responsibility of family members.[104]

The second period or **Late Middle Ages**[105] (starting about 950 AD)[106] was famous for the founding of universities.[107] Medicine taught at these universities was known as scholastic medicine, and relied on Greek philosophies.[108]

The establishment of **hospitals** during the Middle Ages is considered the greatest medical accomplishment of that period.[109] The establishment and development of hospitals stretched over centuries and occurred throughout the Middle Ages. In the early centuries of the Middle Ages, monastic infirmaries were first reported to have been founded and designed exclus-

---

most elevated intellects to such an extent that one can say that intellectual activity converged almost exclusively upon great religious problems and the ethical problems that derived from them. The practice of medicine was regarded as a work of charity.'

[98]  Castiglioni *Medicine* 238–239.

[99]  *Ibid.*

[100]  Peters *et al. Medical Practice* 3.

[101]  Giesen *International* 3 footnote 8.

[102]  Peters *et al. Medical Practice* 3.

[103]  *Ibid*: After the sixth century.

[104]  Carmi *Hospital Law* 6.

[105]  Giesen *International* 3 footnote 8.

[106]  Peters *et al. Medical Practice* 3.

[107]  *Ibid*; Giesen *International* 4.

[108]  Peters *et al. Medical Practice* 3; Castiglioni *Medicine* 375.

[109]  Peters *et al. Medical Practice* 3.

ively for monks, and hospitals for the laity arose near the infirmaries only much later.[110]

Christians founded the first hospitals[111] as a result of the duty they perceived they had to their fellow man.[112] The Jewish hospice, which existed in the pre-Christian Talmudic period, has been mentioned as a possible model for the Christian institutions. Most hospitals were owned by churches or monastic orders.[113] Small hospitals near monasteries (about 700–900 AD) were places of collection, where ancient medical knowledge was compiled and where monastic medicine was also practised until restricted at first, and eventually forbidden, by the Church.[114]

These medieval hospitals were philanthropic and spiritual institutions[115] which offered hospitality to the socially unfit, that is the mentally ill, the disabled, the old, the poor and homeless,[116] rather than being acclaimed for their medical treatment. Peters states that the first hospitals were small, overcrowded, under-equipped, and mainly the place where sick people died.[117]

The first hospitals in England were also established during the Middle Ages, under the influence of the Christian church.[118] St Bartholomew's Hospital was founded by a cleric named Rahere in London in 1123, with assistance from both the king and the bishop. This hospital is still in operation. These institutions later became known as voluntary general hospitals and involved both the state and the church in their organization. The English Medieval hospitals have been described as having been

---

[110] Castiglioni *Medicine* 320 (about AD 700–900) according to Castiglioni *Medicine* 298.

[111] Peters *et al. Medical Practice* 3. Prior to the mediaeval period and its hospitals, we find that temples were probably the first institutions concerned with the sick. Religious traditions of ancient Judaism, Christianity and Islam have been mentioned to have had a distinct influence in this regard: see Carmi *Hospital Law* 7. Castiglioni *Medicine* 304 refers to hospitals in 1100 AD.

[112] Carmi *Hospital Law* 7; compare Castiglioni *Medicine* 246.

[113] Carmi *Hospital Law* 7.

[114] Castiglioni *Medicine* 298–299: (1131–1212 AD): At the beginning of the thirteenth century medicine became almost entirely a lay activity: see Castiglioni *Medicine* 320. The Benedictines founded a hospital in Italy toward the end of the seventh century BC.

[115] Carmi *Hospital Law* 7.

[116] Peters *et al. Medical Practice* 4; Carmi *Hospital Law* 7.

[117] Peters *et al. Medical Practice* 125.

[118] Bridgman and Roemer *Hospital* 143; see also Carlin *Hospital* 21–61 on Medieval English hospitals.

'predominantly ecclesiastical in character, charitable and pious in tone and stable and effective in activity ...'.[119]

In France, most hospitals were established and owned by the Christian Church during the Middle Ages.[120]

Charitable hospitals evolved or were revolutionized only into medical institutions during the thirteenth century.[121] This was due to the administration of hospitals being taken over by cities.[122] The first public pharmacies were established in Italy at the end of the thirteenth century.[123]

At about the beginning of the fourteenth century, as a result of major social factors, such as public health and heavy soldier and other traffic, the need for hospitals where pilgrims, soldiers, strangers, artisans and others could be treated was recognized.[124] This resulted in a slow but definite development of medical institutions (hospitals) throughout Europe. In some cities they reached an exemplary standard.[125]

It was the larger Italian cities, in particular, which invested in hospitals with magnificent architectural features, bestowing 'objets d'art' on the buildings and laying out substantial funds for the charitable care of the sick. Noteworthy amongst these hospitals are the hospital of Sienna (with valuable frescoes by Dominico di Bartolo), the Hospital of Milan, (magnificent for its Lombard art), the Hospital of Santa Maria Nuova in Florence (1288), and the Hospital of the Ceppo at Pistoia (ornamented with marvellous bas-reliefs of Giovanni della Robbia (1469–1529)).[126]

The fifteenth century saw the establishment of the first hospital on the American continent in old Mexico.[127] This took place during the reign of Montezuma, the last Aztec ruler.[128]

At the end of the fifteenth century hospitals in Europe were well organized, especially in Italy, and cities maintained and supported these institutions with unprecedented generosity.[129]

---

[119] Carlin *Hospital* 21.

[120] Bridgman and Roemer *Hospital* 111.

[121] Peters *et al. Medical Practice* 4 *supra* 123; Castiglioni *Medicine* 320.

[122] Peters *et al. Medical Practice* 4.

[123] Castiglioni *Medicine* 404.

[124] *Op. cit.* 391, 393, 404.

[125] *Op. cit.* 393.

[126] *Op. cit.* 393–394.

[127] Peters *et al. Medical Practice* 125.

[128] *Op. cit.* 126.

[129] Castiglioni *Medicine* 393 394.

**The Renaissance (beginning *circa* 1500)**: This was a time of great learning and 'self-discovery of man'.[130] Major advances were made in the field of anatomy. Knowledge of anatomy was gained due to artists' profound interest therein and to an increasing number of dissections being performed on human cadavers,[131] which in turn gave rise to astounding progress in surgery.[132] The sixteenth century gave birth to scientific psychopathology, a new epidemiology, and the application of chemistry to medicine. The clinic and surgery also experienced a rebirth.[133] A scientific exposition of a contagious disease was published in book form in 1526, though it was only confirmed in the nineteenth century. This period was also known for its publications of cheap medical works in Greek and Latin.[134]

King Henry VIII (1511–12) awarded the medical profession in England a professional status of exclusive standing, laying down strict conditions for the examination of and admittance to the fellowship.[135] This was achieved by means of '*An Act concerning Physicians & Surgeons*' of 1512.[136] The earliest occasion of doctors acquiring professional acclaim can be traced to Northern Italy.[137]

In 1518 further legislation was enacted in England in the form of the *Royal Charter of Incorporation*, establishing a governing body regulating the profession.[138] It was later to become the Royal College of Physicians.[139] '*An Act concerning Phisicions*' was introduced in 1523, expanding the scope of the above-mentioned rulings, organizing the profession, enlarging granted privileges and controlling required ethical conduct.[140]

---

[130] Peters *et al. Medical Practice* 4.

[131] *Ibid*: Dissections became more widely practised in the fifteenth century. Castilioni *Medicine* 410–417: Leonardo Da Vinci known for his ingenious mind initiated a new era of anatomical and physiological studies known as the 'Renaissance of Anatomy'. He was being acclaimed a great scientist, architect, geologist, physicist, mechanical engineer, apart from being the greatest artist, painter and sculptor of his day. He also performed dissections.

[132] Peters *et al. Medical Practice* 4: This progress was made in the sixteenth century.

[133] *Op. cit.* 4.

[134] *Ibid*.

[135] Chapman *Physicians* 63; Giesen *International* 4.

[136] *Ibid*.

[137] *Ibid*.

[138] Chapman *Physicians* 63–64; Giesen *International* 5.

[139] *Ibid*.

[140] Giesen *International* 5.

In England and other countries the influence of the above-mentioned legislation and subsequent statutes had a lasting effect on the medical profession[141] both in the nineteenth[142] and twentieth centuries.[143]

The exclusivity and status of the medical profession were thus procured at a very early stage by an elite sector of society. People involved in politics, economics and law were firmly convinced of the value of the services rendered. They sponsored the medical profession and thus ensured its continuing prosperity. The medical profession experienced a steady progress since the founding of the universities to our day. The legal profession developed in a similar way.[144]

Hospitals in France were subjected to some government supervision from the sixteenth century. Municipal authorities established their own new hospitals and were represented on the governing boards of church hospitals.[145]

**The seventeenth century**: The first hospitals appeared in the major cities of the United States and Canada in the seventeenth and eighteenth centuries.[146] These hospitals were understaffed, overcrowded and too small. They were still charitable institutions providing medical care for the impoverished sick.[147]

The seventeenth century saw the birth of physiology and microscopic anatomy; the circulation of blood was finally discovered and advances in respect of knowledge about digestion, respiration, pathology, surgery and clinical medicine were made.[148]

Seventeenth-century medicine experienced a co-operation of medicine and the natural sciences, introducing experimental medical science.[149]

---

[141] *Ibid.*

[142] 'The General Council of Medical Education and Registration of the United Kingdom' took over from the Royal college some of its most important functions in terms of *An Act to regulate the Qualifications of Practitioners in Medicine and Surgery* (The Medical Act, 1858): Giesen *International* 5 footnote 25.

[143] Henry VIII's Act of 1511–12 remained in the statute book until 1948: Giesen *International* 5 footnote 26; Chapman *Physicians* 63.

[144] Giesen *International* 6.

[145] Bridgman and Roemer *Hospital* 111.

[146] Also compare Castiglioni *Medicine* 659–660, Peters *et al. Medical Practice* 126.

[147] Peters *et al. Medical Practice* 126.

[148] *Op. cit.* 4: William Harvey, an Englishman, made the final discovery on the circulation of blood following research which had already started in the sixteenth century. Castiglioni *Medicine* 431–442, 516, 550.

[149] Castiglioni *Medicine* 577.

Specialties developed and surgery was accorded the dignity of being comparable to medicine.[150] Other disciplines developed on scientific foundations. Extensive integration of knowledge and structuring of systems prepared the way for modern medicine.[151]

Physicians of the seventeenth century experienced a dramatic improvement in social status and enjoyed more respect and admiration in society.[152]

Medical journalism was initiated which expedited the exchange of international medical discoveries and other important medical information.[153]

The **eighteenth century**: Leading countries started to organize national health services, although this development progressed very slowly.[154] The central office of such an organization was situated in the capital, being headed by men of first rank. The health service in smaller towns and cities was established by planned legislation.[155]

The eighteenth century also saw a world-wide growth in hospitals. Major political and social currents created a fertile environment for developments in this area.[156]

In England the eighteenth century was a very prosperous time, due to the rise of industry and the expansion of trade. 'It has been called the 'Age of Hospitals',' because voluntary groups established many general hospitals.[157] Hospitals were founded in Great Britain from the middle of the eighteenth century in particular.[158] These health institutions housed medical schools, became clinical research centres and models for hospital administration policies. Cities or large towns established their own general hospitals or voluntary infirmaries.[159] The great Rotunda Hospital at Dublin was founded by Mosse in 1751–7. The British Lying-in Hospital in London followed in 1749 and Queen Charlotte's in 1752.[160]

---

[150]  *Ibid.*

[151]  *Ibid.*

[152]  *Op. cit.* 569.

[153]  *Op. cit.* 574.

[154]  *Op. cit.* 659; Carmi Hospital Law 7; Peters Medical Practice 7.

[155]  Castiglioni *Medicine* 659.

[156]  Carmi Hospital Law 7.

[157]  Bridgman and Roemer *Hospital* 143.

[158]  Castiglioni *Medicine* 659.

[159]  Bridgman and Roemer *Hospital* 143.

[160]  Castiglioni *Medicine* 658–659.

In North America public "almshouses" were the first infirmaries or public institutions which forerun the American hospital.[161] Later, state and local institutions were established which primarily housed the poor and the homeless and were called "hospitals".[162]

In North America, the first hospitals, medical schools and societies were established in the second half of the eighteenth century:[163] Local governments of cities such as Philadelphia and New York started the first hospitals in North America.[164] After the American Revolution (1776) this trend continued.[165] The Pennsylvania Hospital founded in 1751 by Benjamin Franklin, Thomas Bond and others is said to be the oldest independent hospital of the American colonies.[166] The present Philadelphia General Hospital started as the Infirmary of the Almshouse in 1731, and still exists. The Bellevue Hospital in New York started in 1735 and has a similar history. A combined hospital and almshouse was opened in New Orleans in 1737. The New York hospital which later combined with the Cornell Medical School in the exquisite Medical Centre in New York City, started in 1771. Dispensaries were established in Philadelphia in 1786 and in New York in 1791.[167]

In the late eighteenth and early nineteenth centuries these public institutions were supplemented by private voluntary non-profit hospitals financed by donations and bequests.[168] Religious groups also established hospitals.[169] Units of local and state (provincial) government, established institutions for the mentally disordered and sufferers of tuberculosis. Hospitals were founded for merchant mariners by the federal government in 1798.[170]

---

[161] Annas *et al. American Health Law* 10; the public almshouses received the incurable, those with infectious diseases, the destitute and the homeless elderly.

[162] *Op. cit.* 10.

[163] Castiglioni *Medicine* 659.

[164] Bridgman and Roemer *Hospital* 87.

[165] *Ibid.*

[166] Castiglioni *Medicine* 659.

[167] *Op. cit.* 659–660.

[168] Annas *et al. American Health Law* 10. The voluntary hospitals offered convalescent (not curative) care to patients with a prospect of recovery; Bridgman and Roemer *Hospital* 87.

[169] Bridgman and Roemer *Hospital* 87. The Roman Catholic Church especially.

[170] *Ibid.*

In France, the government took over all hospitals at the time of the French Revolution (1798) and handed supervision over to the municipalities.[171]

Conditions in the hospitals and prisons of Europe were disgraceful toward the end of the eighteenth century. A campaign was eventually launched, thanks to the work of Howard, to bring about true reforms in these institutions. Rational treatment of the sick followed; asylums for the insane were erected and these patients were treated with patience and kindness. Barbarous methods such as chaining, forced bathing, 'bastonade' and isolation in cells were abandoned after centuries of abuse.[172]

Marine hospitals were found to be most helpful in combating childhood diseases and tuberculosis. Fresh sea air and sunlight were valued in the founding of the following institutions: A hospital with sixteen beds at Margate, England, in 1796; a hospital at Viareggio founded by G Barellai in 1862, (present-day Italy has more than forty marine hospitals with a total of seven thousand beds) and the Berck-sur-Mer in France, which now is a government hospital.[173]

Physicians of the eighteenth century experienced exceptional social honour, wealth and professional independence. The profession acquired fame, especially in England where the practice of medicine was very well organized.[174]

During the eighteenth century great developments took place in the field of chemistry.[175] But from 1780 until 1850 so-called 'heroic' medicine prevailed, known for its extensive bloodletting and the prescribing of dangerous mineral drugs.[176] Homeopathy,[177] eclectic medicine[178] and

---

[171] Bridgman and Roemer 111.

[172] Castiglioni *Medicine* 659. 'Bastinado' should be the correct spelling. (Spanish *'bastonada'*. *Oxford Advanced Learner's Dictionary* 86.

[173] Castiglioni *Medicine* 659, 858: Marine hospitals.

[174] Castiglioni *Medicine* 654.

[175] Peters *et al. Medical Practice* 5. Castiglioni *Medicine* 580: Oxygen and other gases were discovered.

[176] Peters *et al. Medical Practice* 5.

[177] Reader's Digest *Universal Dictionary* 1988 737: 'A system of medical treatment based on the use of minute quantities of remedies that in large doses produce effects similar to those of the disease being treated.'

    Homeopathy was developed by Samuel Hahnemann, a German physician: Peters *et al. Medical Practice* 5.

[178] 'Eclectic medicine was yet another medical movement of the era, developed by Worster Beach, a medical school graduate who also studied with botanical practitioners. Beach

Thompsonism arose in response to heroic medicine.[179] Vaccination was invented by Jenner,[180] an English physician.

Medicine of the eighteenth century provided the foundations on which mankind could discover and develop the structures of modern medicine. Mysticism was finally exchanged for true scientific knowledge concerning anatomy, physiology and pathology, which was cultivated by universities and dispersed internationally by the rapid exchange of knowledge acquired and discoveries made.[181]

**The nineteenth century**: The rapid progress of different sciences and technological expansion provided medicine with unprecedented information concerning the human body.[182]

Laboratory medicine through clinical observation introduced a new science of bacteriology by means of which infectious diseases could be traced.[183] Louis Pasteur's studies in this regard — being the father of this science — led to the invention of various preventive vaccines against anthrax, chicken cholera and, in 1885, rabies.[184] Joseph Lister discovered antiseptics and thus furthered germ-free operations and even brain surgery.[185] Osteopathy and preventive medicine were developed.[186] Doctors' diagnoses were based on rational scientific grounds rather than moral inclinations. René Laënnec (1781–1826) discovered the stethoscope[187] and Morton and Long, anaesthesia.[188]

The history of medicine was recorded by various historians, the first of whom was Daniel le Clerc (1652–1728).[189] This subject became part of the university curriculum.[190]

---

used vegetable remedies and rejected mineral drugs and bloodletting.' Peters *et al. Medical Practice* 5.

[179] Peters *et al. Medical Practice* 5.

[180] Castiglioni *Medicine* 620, 621, 641–644.

[181] *Op. cit.* 666: Medicine of the eighteenth century.

[182] Peters *et al. Medical Practice* 6.

[183] *Ibid.*

[184] *Ibid.*

[185] *Ibid*; Annas *et al. American Health Law* 3.

[186] Peters *et al. Medical Practice* 5.

[187] Castiglioni *Medicine* 698, 700.

[188] *Op. cit.* 713; Annas *et al. American Health Law* 3.

[189] Castiglioni *Medicine* 751.

[190] *Op. cit.* 756.

Physicians of the nineteenth century[191] won respect and admiration that surpassed that of previous centuries. They were considered leaders of great intellectual currents, excelled as scientists and were honoured by both governments and patients.[192] Corporations and associations of physicians were formed.[193]

Women were accepted into some medical schools as early as 1847,[194] but only in the 1970s did this become a common phenomenon when women also entered several other predominantly 'male professions'.[195]

Most important of all, the number of hospitals increased dramatically in the nineteenth century, and indeed flourished.[196] Great hospitals were founded.[197] This was due to increasing urbanization as a result of the Industrial Revolution.[198] Clinical observations and autopsies were performed because of newly sponsored technology and newly invented facilities in hospitals.[199] Hospitals were staffed with a greater number of physicians and a large sanitary personnel, and equipped with an abundance of clinical material and other resources.[200] Laboratories reinforced and supported hospitals, and the construction of railways facilitated patient transport to

---

[191] Castiglioni *Medicine* 760 described the 19th century physician as follows: 'He is no longer the sorcerer of remote ages, the priest of ancient times, the clerk of the Middle Ages, the astrologer or alchemist of the fifteenth century, the blood-letter of the seven-teenth, or the philosophising academician of the eighteenth. His costume is no longer that of white linen, or of red robe with silken bonnet. His office is no longer in the temple, or in the pharmacist shop, or in the Academy. He no longer depends on the Church, or on the State, or on the conservative conventicles of bewigged academicians. The physician of the nineteenth century ... is simply the scientist detached from the temple and the academy to take his proper place at the bedside of the patient.'

[192] Castiglioni *Medicine* 760.

[193] Castiglioni *Medicine* 760. Since the late 1700s, a few American states initiated medical licensing legislation controlling the practice of medicine and reserving it for those properly trained and credentialed. It was, however, only at the end of the nineteenth century that all American states finally required all medical practitioners to hold medical licenses. Only in the year 1912 did patients start benefiting medically from consulting these elected doctors. Annas *et al. American Health Law* 3–5. Chapman *Physicians* 103–104 describes this evolution in detail.

[194] Peters *et al. Medical Practice* 6; Castiglioni *Medicine* 932–933.

[195] Peters *et al. Medical Practice* 7.

[196] *Op. cit.* 6.

[197] Castiglioni *Medicine* 757.

[198] Peters *et al. Medical Practice* 6; Picard *et al. Liability* 2.

[199] Peters *et al. Medical Practice* 6.

[200] Castiglioni *Medicine* 757–759.

hospitals and clinics.[201] All facilities promoted medical instruction, research and progress.

Military medicine was introduced during the wars of the nineteenth century and reorganized thereafter.[202] Mobile hospitals, base hospitals, ambulance trains, hospital ships and aeroplane transport established efficient hospitalization which dramatically reduced figures of morbidity and mortality.[203]

England, in the early nineteenth century revised their Poor Laws and established the public hospital for the poor, under the sponsorship of local (government) authorities.[204]

France passed a law in 1851 which confirmed the conception of the hospital at that time, as a facility mainly for the needy.[205] Hospitals were to be supported by local tax funds and from income derived from its own endowment.[206]

All American hospitals of the nineteenth century were institutions for the poor.[207] Medical care was mostly administered to the not so poor at home or at the physician's office. Because of the appalling circumstances in the hospitals where unhygienic conditions prevailed, where wards were overcrowded and where there was a general lack of medical skills and knowledge, only the desperate sought refuge there. Upon admission they also had to apply for sponsorship from the hospital's patrons. The doctors therefore had little contact with private or public hospitals and surgery was performed elsewhere than in hospitals.[208]

The late 1800s saw scientific breakthroughs introducing antisepsis, anaesthesia, X-ray diagnosis, modern medicine and sophisticated surgical techniques. These revelations procured the American hospital as a more acceptable haven for all. It enhanced the hospital's role in the training of physicians under tutelage of leader physicians, and the hospitals claimed the free services of physicians to patients in wards. Physicians, considering it

---

[201] *Op. cit.* 759.

[202] *Op. cit.* 913.

[203] *Op. cit.* 917.

[204] Bridgman and Roemer *Hospital* 143.

[205] *Op. cit.* 112.

[206] *Ibid*: 'Many hospitals owned valuable properties'.

[207] Annas *et al. American Health Law* 10.

[208] *Ibid.*

unethical to charge patients in wards, only charged private patients who sought physicians with good reputations from hospitals.[209]

The evolution of hospitals also influenced the nursing profession.[210] Florence Nightingale, described as the first true health-care administrator, brought about revolutionary changes in 1854 during the Crimean war.[211] The training of nurses, organizational skills and order, hygienic principles and morality emerged.[212] In 1860 she started the Nightingale School of Nursing in England from which fifteen nurses graduated in 1863.[213] Nursing schools were established by American hospitals in the 1870s. Educational reform and the upgrading of nurses' conditions and status were at first met with resistance.[214] However, Baccalaureate education, expanding responsibilities and status have been the major developments in the nursing profession ever since.[215]

**Twentieth century medicine** has become extremely sophisticated and reached a superb standard. Every known field of medicine has undergone qualitative evolution and unknown fields of medicine have been deployed. Modern medicine and the modern physician have become dynamic agents in a life-administering call manifesting profound effects on millions of lives.

The contemporary modern hospital is found mostly in large urban areas and is often a building of enormous size.[216] Hospitals of different countries have diverse and complex organizational and administrative systems.[217] Their financial support comes from states, municipalities, private charities or enterprises and religious groups. The hospitals accommodate anything from wards and private rooms for hundreds of patients to medical research centres, laboratories, lecture rooms and other sophisticated facilities.[218]

Hospitals of the twentieth century have experienced an unprecedented increase in numbers of patients and there has been a marked development[219]

---

[209]  *Ibid.*

[210]  *Ibid.*

[211]  Pozgar *Health* 298.

[212]  *Ibid*; Annas *et al. American Health Law* 11.

[213]  Pozgar *Health* 299.

[214]  Annas *et al. American Health Law* 11; Pozgar *Health* 299.

[215]  Pozgar *Health* 299. See Fiesta *Nurses* 13–14 on this development.

[216]  Castiglioni *Medicine* 951.

[217]  *Ibid.*

[218]  *Ibid.*

[219]  The twentieth century saw increasing and large-scale vaccination as prevention against serious diseases. Antibiotics and other scientific discoveries also increased the life expect-

in every sphere of the institution. They have been transformed from pathetic places of charity for the consolation of the dying, into modern high-technological institutions rescuing ill-fated patients from possible death.

Hospitals once existed as sovereign autonomous[220] bodies, where hospital management could be described as 'isolationist'.[221] Through revolutionary change, these self-regulating entities have become national responsibility. The health-care industry has become the subject of national economic and political debate and has been expounded and regulated on both national level and in the vast legal domain.

The astounding progress in the development of hospitals can be attributed to a variety of reasons.

Politics, governmental powers, social and economic structures, advancing technologies and legal expansion have played more than a major role not only in shaping health-care services but also other crucial aspects of national health policy.

The dynamic development of hospitals has been marked by a shift in emphasis from the community's helping hand towards the dying, to a highly responsible and structured governmental organization and intervention creating medical liability and health insurance, providing revolutionary medical technology, facilities and professional medical care.

### 3.4.2 The History of the Law Pertaining to Medical Liability

**Mesopotamia:** The oldest legal regulation and ethical admonition of the healing calling in writing that was recovered originated from Mesopotamia and dates back to approximately 3000 BC.[222] Several codes — often more of an ethical than a legal nature — followed in later centuries.[223]

---

ancy of people: Peters *et al. Medical Practice* 7. See Castiglioni *Medicine* 924 on hospitals in the world for those suffering from tuberculosis alone.

[220] Greek *autonomous*, meaning self-ruling; *nomos* means law.

[221] Carmi *Hospital Law* 7; Castiglioni *Medicine* 951–952.

[222] Chapman *Physicians* 1; Mesopotamian medicine started about 4000–5000 BC: Castiglioni *Medicine* 31.

[223] Chapman *Physicians* 2–4. The various codes were: Code of Urukagina (about 2350 BC); Code of Urnammu (2112–2095 BC); Code of Lipit-Ishtar (1934–1924 BC); Code of Eshnunna (Bilalama) (about 2000–1800 BC); Code of Hammurabi (1792–1750 BC); Castiglioni *Medicine* 38–40.

The Code of King Hammurabi of Mesopotamia[224] was the most re-
nowned, although not the first recorded, authoritative system that expounded
medical ethics.[225] It also specified medical fees[226] and punished medical
malpractice[227] such as medical negligence. The Code had 282 statutes.
Statutes 215–223 read as follows:

> 215. If a surgeon has made a deep incision in the body of a free man with a
> lancet of bronze and saves the man's life or has opened the caruncle in the eye
> of a man with a lancet of bronze and saves his eye, he shall take 10 shekels of
> silver.
>
> 216. If the patient is a villein, he shall take five shekels of silver.
>
> 217. If the patient is the slave of a free man, the master of the slave shall give
> two shekels of silver to the surgeon.
>
> 218. If the surgeon has made a deep incision in the body of a free man with a
> lancet of bronze and causes the man's death or has opened the caruncle in the
> eye of a man and so destroys the man's eye, they shall cut off his fore-hand.
>
> 219. If the surgeon has made a deep incision in the body of a villein's slave
> with a lancet of bronze and causes his death, he shall replace slave for slave.
>
> 220. If he has opened his caruncle with a lancet of bronze and destroys his
> eye, he shall pay half his price in silver.
>
> 221. If a surgeon mends the broken bone of a free man or heals a diseased
> muscle, the injured person shall give the physician five shekels of silver.
>
> 222. If he is a villein, he shall give three shekels of silver.
>
> 223. If he is the slave of a free man, he shall give the surgeon two shekels of
> silver.

One of the most important achievements of past Mesopotamian dynasties
and millennia, was the socio-legal transition from blood revenge to the

---

[224] It was promulgated by Hammurabi (1792–1750 BC) of the first Babylonian Dynasty. Of
the 282 statutes, nine related to services of healers (translated surgeons) of some sort; they
are statutes 215–223. Statutes 218–220 regulate unsatisfactory therapeutic result or death
by a healer, in which case a penalty was inflicted on the healer. Statutes 215–217, 221–
223 prescribed medical fees for certain services rendered. Chapman *Physicians* 2–4;
Castiglioni *Medicine* 40 41; Strauss *Doctor* (1984) 292; Carstens 1988 *De Rebus* 345;
Peters *et al. Medical Practice* 2; Kramer *Medical Malpractice* 5; Moore and Kramer
*Medical Malpractice* 1; Hoffman *et al. Legal Medicine* 35.

[225] Chapman *Physicians* 5; Peters describes the Code as 'the earliest known system of
medical ethics', which is not in accordance with the view of Chapman *Physicians* 5.
Peters *et al. Medical Practice* 2.

[226] Statutes 215–217, 221–223 of the Code of Hammurabi: Chapman *Physicians* 4–5; Peters
*et al. Medical Practice* 2.

[227] Statutes 218–220 of the Code of Hammurabi. Chapman *Physicians* 4–5; Peters *et al.*
*Medical Practice* 2.

principle of monetary compensation.[228] This transpired in an age when the acknowledgement of the concept and theory of the medical profession and required accompanying ethical codes were still to be introduced.[229]

**Jewish regulation:** In 800 BC, a thousand years after Hammurabi,[230] the pre-exile prophets, especially Amos,[231] Jeremiah,[232] and Isaiah[233] brought a powerful ethical message to the leaders of Israel and Judah. They delivered a message of justice and righteousness.[234] Centuries later, the ethical message was redirected to include the medical profession which enjoyed the same status as priests and judges at that time.[235] According to the book of Ecclesiasticus 38:1–3, by the beginning of the Talmudic period (200 BC — AD 600) the medical calling had gained favour both in the sight of God and man.[236] From AD 400 doctors were granted privileges and their liabilities were carefully expounded and restricted.[237]

The Hebraic and Greek cultures developed independently but parallel for several centuries.[238] The Golden Age of Greece occurred mainly in the fifth century BC.[239] The splendour of this period has been acclaimed for the invention of democracy, a free market economy and valued philosophies.[240]

**Greek law** not only evolved a unique description of the legal relationship between physicians and patients,[241] but from 450 BC onwards physicians acquired a respectful position by legal custom.[242]

Plato described the plight and duties of physicians.[243] Aristotle revered their honour and impartiality and found it to be in stark contrast with those

---

[228] Chapman *Physicians* 8.

[229] *Ibid.*

[230] Chapman *Physicians* 8–9.

[231] The book of Amos 7:14; 5; 23–24.

[232] The book of Jeremiah 23:28; 33:15.

[233] The book of Isaiah 32:1; 5:15; 33:16.

[234] Chapman *Physicians* 9.

[235] *Op. cit.* 12.

[236] *Op. cit.* 12–13; Hoffman *et al. Legal Medicine* 35; Castiglioni *Medicine* 76–77.

[237] Chapman *Physicians* 13–14.

[238] *Op. cit.* 14–15.

[239] *Op. cit.* 15.

[240] *Op. cit.* 16.

[241] *Op. cit.* 25–26. The legal relationship between physicians and patients has been described since Hippocrates: Giesen 3.

[242] Chapman *Physicians* 30–31; Giesen *International* 3.

[243] *Ibid.*

of politicians.[244] He also indicated that the word 'doctor' was used in three senses: for ordinary physicians, specialists and for laymen with a general knowledge of medicine.[245] Chapman suggests that 'the Greek patient in Aristotle's time must therefore have had available a variety of providers of health services'.[246] Greek law, however, neglected the subject of medical negligence or incompetence on the part of the physician — unlike Roman law.[247] Greek law was nonetheless studied prior to the drawing up of the Twelve Tables in 450 BC, during the early Roman Republic.[248]

**Roman law** has had an invaluable and remarkable influence on most Western legal systems from the establishment of its comprehensive and codified laws until the present day. Roman law was under constant revision from its inception and underwent continuous evolution by means of juristic interpretations and praetorian extensions.[249] Roman law as explicitly dealt with in the *lex Aquilia*, a plebiscite or Act from 286/287 BC,[250] (contained in Book 9, Title 2 of Justinianus' *Digest*)[251] superseded table VIII (*iniuriae*) of the Twelve Tables.[252] The *lex Aquilia* was one of the most important sections of Roman law. This Act still applies in South Africa although it has undergone many changes and extensions.[253]

The *lex Aquilia* deals mainly with the casuistic Roman law of delicts,[254] resulting from liability on the ground of *damnum iniuria datum*.[255] The *actio legis Aquiliae* was primarily a penal action which governed compensation

---

[244] *Ibid.*

[245] Chapman *Physicians* 31–32.

[246] *Ibid.*

[247] Chapman *Physicians* 32; Giesen *International* 3. Chapman *Physicians* 89 points out that ancient Greek law and probably early English common law as well, held the physician liable only if he injured his patient by specific intent; he was not legally liable for damages if injury to the patient resulted from ignorance or neglect.

[248] Chapman *Physicians* 35–36: 'Tradition has it that the Roman Republic sent a delegation to Athens to study Solon's Laws prior to drawing up its Twelve Tables in 451–450 BC.'

[249] Van der Walt *Delict* 12. Van der Walt and Midgley *Delict* 9.

[250] Van der Walt *Delict* 11. Van der Walt and Midgley *Delict* 9. Neethling *et al. Delict* 9 determines the date as 287 BC. Chapman *Physicians* 36 refers to this date as 286 BC; Lawson *Negligence* 4 refers to the date as 287 BC.

[251] Chapman *Physician* 37, 160.

[252] *Op. cit.* 36; See also Kaser Roman Private Law 3.

[253] Neethling *et al. Delict* 8–13.

[254] *Op. cit.* 8–10; Van der Walt *Delict* 15; Chapman *Physicians* 37.

[255] Neethling *et al. Delict* 8–9. Van der Walt *Delict* 11. Van der Walt and Midgley *Delict* 9.

for persons who had suffered patrimonial damage.[256] The *Lex Aquilia* consisted of three chapters, the first and third of which are still recognized today, while the second fell into desuetude during Roman times.[257]

The Aquilian action was initially only available to the owner of damaged property (corporeal assets). Where damage to things occurred by burning, breaking or destroying or the wounding or killing of a slave or four-footed animal, Aquilian liability could ensue. The field of application of this action was, however, extensively expanded.[258] It eventually provided a legal remedy not only for the owner, but also for the injured freeman (*liber homo*) or father of an injured child, where the wrongdoer was, for example, a layman or even a doctor, and patrimonial damage resulted from the injuries.[259] The *actio legis Aquiliae* was therefore also made applicable to other instances of patrimonial loss resulting from bodily injuries.[260] Liability ensued where there was any kind of physical infringement of a thing or in the cases of bodily injuries mentioned. Another consequence was that compensation was due for all patrimonial damage that resulted from the wrongful act. Furthermore other holders of real rights could claim, and not only the owner.[261]

Roman law was clearly hampered by the restriction that where 'a person suffered harm which was not caused by a physical infringement, the Roman jurist had no criterion by which the act could be evaluated.'[262] Progress was, however, already made in Roman law times from a liability based on damage to property, to a more general liability for patrimonial loss. The Aquilian action could therefore, in future, be expanded into a general remedy to claim damages for all patrimonial loss caused wrongfully.[263]

---

[256] Van der Walt *Delict* 11. Van der Walt and Midgley *Delict* 9.

[257] Neethling *et al. Delict* 9; see also footnote 35 on 9; Van der Walt *Delict* 11. Van der Walt and Midgley *Delict* 9.

[258] Neethling *et al. Delict* 9.

[259] Chapman *Physicians* 160: '*Delictum* in Latin meant (literally) fault or crime'. *Culpa* in Latin means fault or blame and is equated with 'negligence' as is frequently found in Book IX of the Digest of Justinianus. 'Digest IX.2.31, p. 91: ... there is fault when what could have been foreseen by a diligent man was not foreseen. The phrase diligent man is the ancestor of the common law's reasonable or prudent man'. Neethling *et al. Delict* 9–10. Van der Walt *Delict* 11–14. Van der Walt and Midgley *Delict* 9–11. Kaser and Wubbe *Romeins Privaatrecht* 247–248.

[260] Neethling *et al. Delict* 9.

[261] *Op. cit.* 9–10.

[262] *Op. cit.* 10.

[263] *Ibid.*

It is the *lex Aquilia*, in particular, that has a bearing on the issue of medical liability. The *lex Aquilia*, which contained the Roman law of delicts included 'several references to physicians and medical care'.[264] The following provisions were included and are interpreted as follows:

(i)  According to Hunter:[265]

'If a man undertook a task requiring special skill, then want of skill was considered equivalent to negligence as, for instance, when a doctor kills a slave by bad surgery or by giving him wrong drugs.' ... Then ... 'he is chargeable with negligence if the damage resulted from want of skill, or even from want of the strength of an ordinary man.'

According to Lawson:[266]

'Proculus says, if a doctor operates unskilfully on a slave, an action lies either *ex locato* or under the *lex Aquilia*. The law is the same if he makes a wrong use of a drug. Moreover, one who operates properly and then omits further treatment will not get off free but is considered guilty of negligence.'

According to Chapman:[267]

'If a surgeon operated negligently on a slave or abandoned his patient, he is deemed to be guilty of negligence.'

(ii)  When a son lost his eye as a result of an accident, the perpetrator was responsible for medical costs involved as well as compensation to the victim's father to the value of lost services.[268]

(iii)  If a slave died as a result of blows received, legal action would ensue where death was not attributed to the attending physician's ignorance.[269]

(iv)  Midwives were considered guilty of murder where they administered fatal potions with their own hands.[270]

---

[264]  Chapman *Physicians* 36 37; Giesen *International* 3; Castiglioni *Medicine* 196.

[265]  Hunter *Roman Law* 147. This work was edited by FH Lawson.

[266]  Lawson *Negligence* 87.

[267]  Chapman *Physicians* 37 159; Chapman concludes that in Roman law, negligence had no precisely defined meaning comparable to the definition that has evolved in Anglo-American common law. See also Van der Walt *Delict* 12. Van der Walt and Midgley *Delict* 10.

[268]  Chapman *Physicians* 37, 159; Van der Walt *Delict* 14. See also Van der Walt and Midgley *Delict* 11. Neethling *et al. Delict* 8–10.

[269]  Chapman *Physicians* 37, 159; See also Van der Walt *Delict* 11 and Van der Walt and Midgley *Delict* 9.

[270]  Chapman *Physicians* 37; Lawson *Negligence* 87 89.

(v)   The injured free man (*liber homo*) was entitled to damages for his injuries.[271]

The *Lex Aquilia* did not, however, set forth a law of medical malpractice as such. The obligatory payment of compensation in cases of fault or negligence was only introduced at a later date.[272] Also Roman law never developed rules which provided a penalty (compensation) for the death of a free man, caused by the negligence of a physician or a layman, much less for non-fatal injury.[273]

According to Chapman, Roman law — at first glance — regarded slaves merely as property, and not as beings with legal rights of their own. Lawson, however, pointed out that slaves were eventually regarded as both persons and things by Roman law. Under the *lex Aquilia*, harm inflicted upon slaves due to negligence was also personal injury, and had, ultimately, to be regarded as such.[274]

In AD 533–4 Emperor Justinianus ordered that a further codification of Roman law be carried out.[275] The *Corpus Iuris Civilis* was compiled. An experienced commentator and codifier of law and medicine, named Tribonius, together with his sixteen assistants, started this formidable work late in AD 530.[276] The *Corpus Iuris* describes both the contractual[277] and delictual[278] (civil) liability of physicians when dealing incompetently (*imperite*) with patients: '*si medicus servum imperite secuerit, vel ex locato vel ex lege Aquilia competere actionem*'.[279] If a physician administered the wrong medicine, or operated carefully but later abandoned the patient, the consequence was the same.[280]

---

[271] Neethling *et al. Delict* 9; Van der Walt *Delict* 14. Van der Walt and Midgley *Delict* 11.

[272] Chapman *Physicians* 37; Van der Walt *Delict* 17. Van der Walt and Midgley *Delict* 13.

[273] Chapman *Physicians* 37.

[274] *Op. cit.* 37, 159; Lawson *Negligence* 21–27.

[275] Chapman *Physicians* 43 162; Giesen *International* 3; Van Zyl *Justice* 10–11; Kaser *Roman Private Law* 7.

[276] Chapman *Physicians* 162.

[277] *I.e.* the law of contract for services: Giesen *International* 3.

[278] *I.e.* delict (torts): Giesen *International* 3.

[279] D.9.2.7.8 (Ulpianus): 'if a physician treats a slave incompetently, an action (for damages) lies both according to the law of contract for services and according to the lex Aquilia, i.e. delict (torts)'. See also Giesen *International* 3; Deutsch 1979 *IJML* 81 89.

[280] D.9.2.8 (Gaius): idem iuris est, si medicamento perperam usus fuerit. sed et qui bene secuerit et dereliquit curationem, securus non erit, sed culpae reus intelligitur. See also Giesen *International* 3; Deutsch 1979 *IJML* 81; Strauss Doctor (1984) 292.

The *Corpus Iuris Civilis* survived not only the fall of the Western Roman Empire in AD 476, but also the Middle Ages. It experienced a dramatic revival at the end of the eleventh century, 'the impact of which on the Civil Law countries (and beyond) can hardly be over-estimated'.[281] It still forms the basis of South African common law.

It was under the influence of the church that the dormant Roman law experienced its revival at the end of the eleventh century.[282] Both Roman and Canon Law were taught at the newly-founded universities.[283]

**Medieval law** was formulated by jurists adhering strictly to the principles and concepts of the *Corpus Iuris Civilis*. They emphasized the penal element of Roman delictual actions and postulated fault as the foundation of delictual liability. The medieval courts executed a policy process of generalization of liability, applying a general principle that all damage to person or property that was caused *dolo* or *culpa* was recoverable.[284]

At English common law the medical profession was regarded as a humble calling. The apothecary, barber, common carrier and innkeeper were treated in a similar way.[285]

According to Chapman, 'fourteenth-century England judges began to require physicians to treat their patients with diligence.'[286] It was required by law that when the doctor attended patients, he do so with proper care and skill.[287] The doctor thus had to adhere to a duty imposed by law.[288] Failure to comply with the legal requirement of a certain degree of skill made the physician liable to an action of trespass on the case for negligence, and he could thus be sued in tort.[289] Liability for negligent conduct was applied only in the field of professional malpractice, and expanded only in the nineteenth century.[290]

---

[281] Giesen *International* 3. 'It was the growing influence of the church which greatly contributed to the survival and revival of the Roman heritage. It was hand in hand that Roman and Canon Law also entered the young universities of Oxford and Cambridge': Giesen *International* 3–4 footnote 8.

[282] Giesen *International* 3 footnote 8.

[283] *Op. cit.* 4 footnote 8.

[284] Van der Walt *Delict* 16. Van der Walt and Midgley *Delict* 17.

[285] Giesen *International* 4; Picard *et al. Liability* 1.

[286] Chapman *Physicians* 89.

[287] Picard *et al. Liability* 1; Holdsworth 3 *History* 385.

[288] Holdsworth 3 *History* 385.

[289] *Op. cit.* 386; Giesen *International* 4; Picard *et al. Liability* 2.

[290] Chapman *Physicians* 90; Chapman *Physicians* 90 172 states the negligence theory: 'defendant owes to those whom he may injure (accidentally) a duty to exercise due care

The first medical malpractice case in England was reported in 1374.[291] Action was brought against a surgeon and the claim was upheld in principle, but failed on a technicality. Other medical malpractice cases followed in the fourteenth century.[292]

During the reign of Edward I, decisions in both the criminal and civil courts were collected.[293] The first 'year-book' was published during this period, consisting of a compilation of informal notes on cases and comments made by lawyers and students.[294] The body of decisions and the application of these earlier decisions of the cases of the royal court became known as the 'common law' which was taken by early colonists from England to the United States of America.[295]

**The Renaissance** (beginning *circa* 1500), was a time of great learning and 'self-discovery of man'.[296] It laid the foundation for major advances in later ages.

The first authentic works on the **medico-legal** field were Italian and the first of these was published as early as 1598. The first work was written by Fotunatas Fidelis and 'emphasized the **interrelationship** of the subject to both medicine and the law.'[297] The interdisciplinary medico-legal field was thus established.

The second earliest publication of Paulo Zacchias dealt with a vast range of legal and medical subjects and was truly a legal as well as a medical textbook. This work, published in the period 1621 to 1661, was the first to demonstrate the phrase 'medico-legal', to describe this interdisciplinary

---

— the care of an ordinarily prudent and careful man. The breach of that duty is actionable negligence.'

[291] Moore and Kramer *Medical Malpractice* 1: A surgeon's negligent treatment of a wound was involved. Kramer *Medical Malpractice* 5; 'Morton's case (1374) 48 Edw 11: Picard *et al.* *Liability* 1 footnote 1; Morton's case (1374) YB 46 Edw III pl 11: Giesen *International* 4 footnote 10. However, see Pozgar *Health* 6. Pozgar reports that English common law records its first case of medical malpractice in AD 1329. When the College of Physicians of London was incorporated in 1518, malpractice litigation was common enough for the charter to set out disciplinary provisions for malpractice.

[292] Giesen *International* 4 footnote 10.

[293] In England during the fourteenth century: Hoffman *et al.* *Legal Medicine* 35.

[294] Hoffman *et al.* *Legal Medicine* 35.

[295] *Ibid.* The state of Louisiana's legal system is however based on the Napoleonic Code from France resulting from initial French control, and does not follow the English common law.

[296] Peters *et al.* *Medical Practice* 4.

[297] Curran *Health* 2. The medico-legal field is today termed Medical Law.

field. Curran suggests that the term is now so common, that it would be appropriate to drop the hyphen, and use it as a single word.[298]

Together with the upliftment of the medical profession, profound developments occurred in the law of contract.[299] In regard to the issue of liability of physicians, contractual liability gained preference.[300] The physician's liability was held to flow from contract rather than being founded on tort,[301] as was the case previously. This led to implied or express contractual agreements[302] being formed between doctors and their patients respectively. The consequence for physicians was that the law introduced many implied terms into contracts[303] for example, that physicians possess and use due care and skill.[304]

The term '**forensic medicine**' was created in the Germanic states by about the middle of the seventeenth century.[305] Johann Michaelis, professor of pathology in the University of Leipzig, was the first to present lectures under this title in 1650. The subject was essentially medical in content, not legal, and not a combination of both. The Germanic medico-legal educators however, dropped the term 'forensic medicine' and adopted the term 'gerichtliche medizin' which means 'courtroom medicine' or 'judicial medicine'.[306]

**Legal medicine** made its first appearance in Italy as a new medical discipline following the anatomical and surgical progress of that period.[307] Autopsies were performed for legal purposes and a whole new subject evolved.[308] Many medico-legal experts who produced authoritative writings emerged.[309] The term 'legal medicine' was received from the French in the

---

[298] *Ibid.*

[299] Giesen *International* 6; Picard *et al. Liability* 1–2.

[300] Giesen *International* 6; Holdsworth 3 *History* 448. Picard *et al. Liability* 1; *Everard* v. *Hopkins* 1615.

[301] *Ibid.*

[302] Picard *et al. Liability* 2; Holdsworth 3 *History* 448.

[303] Giesen *International* 7; Picard *et al. Liability* 2.

[304] *Ibid.*

[305] 'Forensic medicine' has come to mean that part of the medical field concerned with the presentation of medical data in courts of law: Curran *Health* 2.

[306] Curran *Health* 2–3.

[307] Castiglioni *Medicine* 557.

[308] *Ibid.*

[309] *Op. cit.* 558.

late eighteenth and early nineteenth centuries.[310] This subject covered amongst other things medical areas of legal significance such as diagnosis, treatment, and rehabilitation of criminals and the criminally insane.

Continental medico-legal texts written in academic Latin were the origin of the term and subject of '**medical jurisprudence**'.[311] It was, however, Andrew Duncan, professor of the institutes of medicine of the University of Edinburgh (1791), who established the latter title and subject firmly in the British Medical education of the British Isles.[312] The subject was introduced in American lectures as early as 1804. An American lecturer by the name of Rush, who presented lectures in this field, as early as 1810 included subject areas like forensic psychiatry, traumatic medicine, toxicology, forensic pathology, forensic obstetrics, occupational medicine, military medicine and public health regulation. These subjects were most exhaustive even by modern standards.[313] Curran, however, objects to Duncan's use of the term 'medical jurisprudence' since he almost exclusively covered a medical field which was only of significance to practising doctors. In those centuries 'jurisprudence' was mainly an academic synonym for 'law', but Duncan did not discuss 'medical law'. In contemporary American and English legal education, the term has been used in the sense of the 'philosophy of law'.[314]

Natural-law jurists of the seventeenth and eighteenth centuries finally accepted fault, not only as general basis of delictual liability, but as universal foundation of liability. The courts followed this principle of generalization. The main contribution of these jurists was to propagate codification which eventually occurred in the nineteenth century.[315]

**The eighteenth century:** The legal inclination that medical malpractice was tortious in nature was never fully relinquished.[316] In 1768 Sir William Blackstone, a most distinguished graduate and professor of Oxford, stated that the proper common law remedy for damages against physicians was an

---

[310] Curran *Health* 3. 'The French medicolegal subject covered primarily the same medical evidentiary matters with which the Germanic states were concerned, but it was broad enough in meaning to cover other medical areas of legal significance such as diagnosis, treatment, and rehabilitation of criminals and the criminally insane, an area of particular interest among French medicolegal practitioners': Castiglioni *Medicine* 636.

[311] Curran *Health* 3.

[312] *Ibid*: The cycle of medicolegal terminology of the western world was completed in Great Britain when Duncan used the term "medical jurisprudence".

[313] Curran *Health* 4.

[314] *Op. cit.* 4–5.

[315] Van der Walt *Delict* 16. Van der Walt and Midgley *Delict* 17–18.

[316] Giesen *International* 7.

action for trespass on the case.[317] This action entailed that physicians and surgeons were held responsible for all personal wrongs and injuries, unaccompanied by force caused by neglect or want of skill, for which damages were then awarded.[318] Blackstone was also one of the first authors to use the word 'malpractice' in this context.[319]

The first reported American malpractice case was said to have been brought in 1794.[320] This Connecticut case involved a successful action by a man against a physician stemming from the latter's negligent performance of an operation.[321]

Late in the eighteenth century, another terminological area in the medico-legal field, namely 'public health regulation', received little attention in the Germanic states of Continental Europe. In 1764, public health policy and governmental health regulation were introduced by Wolfgang Thomas Ban under the title 'medical police'.[322]

Johann Peter Frank (1745–1821) compiled a six-volume treatise entitled (in translated form) 'A Complete System of Medical Police', which was published 1779 to 1817. In the United States, Great Britain and on the Continent this broad field later became known as 'state medicine'. Three areas were encompassed by this field:[323] (i) public health regulation; (ii) public welfare medicine for the poor and chronically ill; and (iii) traditional forensic or courtroom medicine. The term 'state medicine' disappeared in the early decades of the twentieth century as the above-mentioned three fields developed separately.[324]

**The nineteenth century:** In the field of legal medicine[325] illustrious representatives appeared. Scientific methods for use by the police were

---

[317] *Op. cit.* 7 footnote 38; his conclusion was based on both the Roman law and Dr Groenvelt's case (1694); Chapman *Physicians* 92.

[318] Giesen *International* 7.

[319] *Ibid.*

[320] The case was registered in 1790 according to Giesen *International* 4 footnote 10; Pozgar *Health* 9: Pozgar reports that the first American malpractice case occurred in 1794. Kramer *Medical Malpractice* 5 states that this case occurred in 1794. Moore and Kramer *Medical Malpractice* 1 confirm the date as being 1794.

[321] Moore and Kramer *Medical Malpractice* 1.

[322] Curran *Health* 5.

[323] *Ibid.*

[324] *Op. cit.* 5–6.

[325] Castiglioni *Medicine* 742–743.

developed to combat crime and promote crime-prevention. Notorious writings were compiled.[326]

During this period Britain evolved a fine law of medical malpractice which was adopted almost intact in the United States about the mid-nineteenth century.[327] American judges at the time effected only slight modifications to this branch of law to accommodate the American ideals they thought appropriate.[328]

The Industrial Revolution also initiated new legal developments. The negligence action sprang from the English Common Law concept of a duty in the doctor-patient relationship.[329] This English principle of negligence was also established in American law about 1853.[330]

Both Britain and the United States, however, met with crises due to industrialization, when courts were overloaded with personal-injury cases flowing from industrial accidents.[331] In 1873 Britain introduced a radical reform of its legal system and America reacted by a major restructuring of tort law focusing on a more objective and refined definition of fault and negligence.[332]

The **twentieth century**: The issue of medical malpractice liability during the past century-and-a-half has been dominated by the tort of negligence,[333] and for nearly a century most actions against doctors have been based on negligence.[334] In the 1960s the United States faced a 'malpractice crisis'.[335]

Currently, claims brought for medical malpractice are based primarily on allegations of negligence, which is usually contended by strict liability,[336] a situation which has expanded liability quite dramatically. No-fault com-

---

[326] *Op. cit.* 743.

[327] Chapman *Physicians* 88 100: This occurred about 1847 when the AMA adopted an English code of Percival.

[328] Chapman *Physicians* 88 100.

[329] Fleming *Torts* 113, 137, 138; Picard *et al. Liability* 2; Giesen *International* 4.

[330] Chapman *Physicians* 94: The American principle entails 'that physicians are required to possess an ordinary degree of skill but not the highest degree possible'.

[331] Chapman *Physicians* 94.

[332] *Ibid.*

[333] Giesen *International* 7; Picard *et al. Liability* 2; Fleming *Torts* 114–116.

[334] Picard *et al. Liability* 2; Giesen *International* 7.

[335] Giesen *International* 101.

[336] Giesen *International* 8.

pensation schemes brought into being in Sweden, New Zealand and Finland — and recently proposed in Australia — have also won acclaim.[337]

The modern usage of certain terms has also been under investigation: In the middle 1960s, British and German medico-legal societies recommended independently, that the French term 'legal medicine' be adopted by medical schools and medico-legal institutes. According to Curran some progress was made to this effect in Germany, but multiple terminology persists in Britain.[338] The United States of America has also used them interchangeably during the twentieth century.[339] Confusion has however reigned concerning the correct use of the titles, especially in medico-legal departments of American medical schools.[340] Curran, therefore set out with a proposal of reform, by defining terms with regard to correct utilization in the medico-legal field. Thirteen definitions were set out which should, if applied correctly, rule out any further confusion or misconceptions.[341]

### 3.5 HOSPITAL LAW

'A distinction should be made between hospital liability and hospital law.'[342] Hospital law deals with the activities and various functionaries of hospitals, the system of relations and the interaction of hospitals with any external factors.[343] The modern hospital has become a very complex professional system. Hospital law therefore necessitates a comprehensive codification, although many laws already exist concerning the activities of hospitals.[344]

Hospital law must be enforced by means of a completely new system. Control mechanisms should ensure the fulfilment of new standards and conditions. These requirements should be formulated by the consensus and co-operation of health-care providers and lawyers, relying on both ethics and reality.[345]

---

[337] *Ibid.*

[338] Curran *Health* 6.

[339] *Ibid.*

[340] *Op. cit.* 7.

[341] *Op. cit.* 8–10.

[342] Carmi *Hospital Law* 14.

[343] *Ibid.*

[344] *Ibid.* Existing laws and regulations deal with liability for the provision of care, administration, ancillary and support services, facility standards, informational practices, financial practices and educational services.

[345] Carmi *Hospital Law* 14–15.

# Chapter 4

# Hospital Liability

## 4.1 Charitable Immunity to Hospital Liability

As already set out above, the first hospitals were established in the Middle Ages.[1] Religious orders mostly owned and controlled these institutions.[2] Hospitals were charitable institutions from the start, which offered hospitality to the sick, poor, the disabled, the old and the homeless.[3] These institutions were small, under-equipped, overcrowded and a place where people died rather than being cured. The wealthy did not attend these facilities, but were treated at home by family members and later by private doctors.[4]

The hospital as charitable facility developed through the centuries. It was eventually sustained amongst other by legacies, endowments and voluntary contributions from various groups, persons and churches.[5]Governments also made contributions, in particular where special populations were cared for like the military, pilgrims and other public health groups.[6] This led to the charitable trust being created in England, in which all funds were kept to safeguard the livelihood and continual existence of each hospital.[7]

The doctrine of charitable immunity was invented by the courts, and protected hospitals from liability from the mid-nineteenth century until the mid-twentieth century.[8] This doctrine protected voluntary non-profit

---

[1]   Peters *et al. Medical Practice* 3.

[2]   Carmi *Hospital Law* 7.

[3]   *Ibid.* Peters *et al. Medical Practice* 4; Strauss *Doctor* (1991) 300.

[4]   Peters *et al. Medical Practice* 125. Picard 1981 *MGLJ* 1000.

[5]   Picard 1981 *MGLJ* 997; Speller *Hospitals* 3; Castiglioni *Medicine* 393–394.

[6]   Carmi *Hospital Law* 7; Castiglioni *Medicine* 393.

[7]   Speller *Hospitals* 3–5; Picard 1981 *MGLJ* 997.

[8]   Morris and Moritz *Law* 387 confirm this statement. See also *Avellone* v. *St John's Hospital* 165 Ohio St 467 135 NE 2d 410 (Ohio) 1956). Werthmann *Malpractice* 1, however describes the doctrine of charitable immunity as having existed only from the late nineteenth century. Mason and McCall Smith 1987 *Encyclopaedia* 582.

charitable hospitals from liability for negligence of hospital employees in the care and treatment of patients where employees had been duly selected. The doctrine — which was regarded as an exception to ordinary principles of liability — had three bases:[9]

(i) Charitable hospitals provided invaluable community services, and therefore their financial viability had to be protected at all cost. (ii) Charitable trusts had to be protected and could not be spent for purposes other than that intended by the trustor. (iii) It was held that the negligence of the doctors could not be ascribed to the hospital, since the former exercised control over the facilities. The hospitals were not capable of committing any medical negligence, representing a mere collection of facilities and manpower.

Hospital immunity from liability did, however, change completely to hospital liability within less then forty years.[10] In *Yepremian* v. *Scarborough General Hospital* Blair J A stated:

> ...the oft-told tale of how the Courts in a period of less then 50 years eliminated the anomaly which exempted hospitals from the ordinary rules of liability for negligence of doctors, nurses and other professionals acting within the scope of their employment need not be repeated.[11]

This development started with Australia in 1923,[12] Canada in 1938,[13] England in 1942[14] and the USA[15] and other Common Law countries like South Africa followed in 1957.[16]

Charitable hospitals eventually evolved into medical institutions where medical care could be provided to all population groups and people could be cured in stead of waiting on death. Hospitals were managed effectively. Facilities were organized, staff were hired and food and equipment were purchased. Consequently, both the impoverished as well as the paying

---

[9]    Werthmann *Malpractice* 1: The writer provides three reasons for the existence of this doctrine.

[10]   This is the most common perception. See also Giesen *International* 53 footnote 151.

[11]   (1980) 13 *CCLT* 105 (Ont CA) at 164.

[12]   *Cummins* v. *Hobart Public Hospitals Board* (1923) 19 TAS LR 18. See also *Henson* v. *Board of Management of Perth Hospital* (1939) 41 WALR 15.

[13]   *Sisters of Joseph* v. *Fleming* [1938] SCR 172. Giesen *International* 52.

[14]   *Gold* v. *Essex Country Council* [1942] 2 KB; 293 [1942] 1 ALL ER 326.

[15]   *Bing* v. *Thunig* 163 NYS 2d 3 (1957). See also Giesen *International* 52.

[16]   *Esterhuizen* v. *Administrator Tvl* 1957 (3) SA 710(T). See also Giesen *International* 52.

patients could be accommodated.[17] Hospitals thus forming legal relationships with patients necessarily became accountable under contracts.[18]

In both Common Law and Civil Law jurisdictions, there is still a general progression towards greater hospital accountability.[19] Policy considerations[20] which are in favour of an extended hospital liability become obvious

(i)     in England when perusing the sequence of common law cases, and the National Health Service Act 1946, repealed, and now the National Health Service Act 1977;[21]

(ii)    in Scotland under the National Health Service Act 27 of 1947, repealed, and now the National Health Service (Scotland) Act 29 of 1978;[22]

(iii)   in Australia with special reference to the *Henson*,[23] *Samios*,[24] *Albrighton*,[25] *Ellis*[26] and other cases and relevant publications;[27]

(iv)    in Canada with special reference to the *Yepremian* [28] case and Picard's [29] works;

(v)     in the United States where hospital liability cases are rife and the doctrine of apparent authority[30] is applied increasingly, expanding hospital liability likewise.

Courts have in general extended hospital liability and placed responsibility on hospitals and hospital authorities by accommodating almost all plaintiff-

---

[17]   Speller *Hospitals* 3–4; Picard 1981 *MGLJ* 997; Werthmann *Malpractice* 1.

[18]   Picard 1981 *MGLJ* 997.

[19]   Giesen *International* 55.

[20]   *Ibid.*

[21]   *Op. cit.* 55; see footnote 167.

[22]   *Op. cit.* 55; see footnote 169.

[23]   (1939) 41 WALR 15.

[24]   [1960] WAR 219.

[25]   [1979] 2 NSWLR 165; [1980] 2 NSWLR 542.

[26]   [1989] 17 NSWLR 553 (CA).

[27]   Compare the publications of Fleming *Torts*, Trindade and Cane *Torts* and Whippy 1989 *ALJ* 182–204. Giesen *International* 56 footnote 170.

[28]   (1980) 13 *CCLT* 105 (Ont CA).

[29]   Picard *et al. Liability* and Picard 1981 *MGLJ*. Giesen *International* 56 footnote 171.

[30]   Louisell and Williams *Medical Malpractice* §15.02 15–8, §16.08 16–3. Giesen *International* 56.

patients in finding a vast variety of medical staff negligent,[31] which include nurses,[32] house pharmacists,[33] laboratory technicians,[34] audiologists,[35] physiotherapists,[36] psychiatrists,[37] radiographers and radiologists,[38] anaesthetists,[39] general surgeons,[40] orthopaedic surgeons and neurosurgeons,[41] pathologists,[42] gynaecologists and other specialists,[43] whole-time (or resident) assistant medical officers,[44] part-time medical officers,[45] senior registrars[46] and consultants.[47]

---

[31] Giesen *International* 52–53, 55 for a discussion of all relevant medical staff.

[32] Louisell and Williams *Medical Malpractice* § 3–26 [7]. *Morris* v. *Winsbury-White* [1937] 4 ALL ER 494. *Henson* v. *Board of Management of Perth Hospital* (1939) 41 WALR 15. Picard *et al. Liability* 392–394.

[33] Giesen *International* 52. *Collins* v. *Hertfordshire County Council* [1947] 1 KB 598 (per Hilbery J).

[34] Giesen *International* 52. *Neufville* v. *Sobers* (1983) 18 ACWS 2d 407 (Ont HC).

[35] Giesen *International* 52. *Bartlett* v. *Children's Hospital* (1983) 40 Nfld & PEIR 88 (Nfld TD).

[36] Giesen *International* 52. *Mc Kay* v. *Royal Inland Hospital* (1964) 48 DLR 2d 665 (BCSC).

[37] Giesen *International* 52. *Landau* v. *Werner* (1961) 105 SJ 1008 (CA).

[38] Louisell and Williams *Medical Malpractice* §3.23 3–82 to 3–88. *Gold* v. *Essex County Council* [1942] 2 KB 293, CA. *Samios* v. *Repatriation Commission* [1960] WAR 219.

[39] Louisell and Williams *Medical Malpractice* § 3.03 3–6 to 3–15. *Jones* v. *Manchester Corporation* [1952] 2 QB 852. *Roe* v. *Minister of Health* [1954] 2 QB 66.

[40] Louisell and Williams *Medical Malpractice* § 3.08 3–18 to 3–19. *Cassidy* v. *Ministry of Health* (1951) 2 KB 343. *Collins* v. *Hertfordshire County Council* (1947) 1 KB 598.

[41] Louisell and Williams *Medical Malpractice* § 3.10 § 3.11 and § 3.15. *Albrighton* v. *Royal Prince Alfred Hospital* [1980] 2 NSWLR 542 (CA).

[42] Louisell and Williams *Medical Malpractice* § 3.17. Giesen *International* 53.

[43] Louisell and Williams *Medical Malpractice* § 3.13. Giesen *International* 53. *Clark* v. *MacLennan* [1983] 1 ALL ER 416.

[44] Giesen *International* 53. *Barnett* v. *Chelsea HMC* [1968] 1 ALL ER 1068.

[45] Giesen *International* 53. *Collins* v. *Hertfordshire County Council* [1947] 1 KB 598. *Razzel* v. *Snowball* [1954] 3 ALL ER 439 CA. *Roe* v. *Minister of Health* [1954] 2 ALL ER 131 CA. *Yepremian* v. *Scarborough General Hospital* [1980] 13 *CCLT* 105 (Ont CA, Arnup J A at 133–142).

[46] Giesen *International* 53. *Wilsher* v. *Essex AHA* [1987] 1 QB 730.

[47] Giesen *International* 53. *Razzell* v. *Snowball* [1954] 3 ALL ER 429 CA. *Albrighton* v. *Royal Prince Alfred Hospital* [1980] 2 NSWLR 542 CA. *Samios* v. *Repatriation Commission* [1960] WAR 219. *Yepremian* v. *Scarborough General Hospital* [1978] 6 *CCLT* 81 (Ont HC). (1980) 13 *CCLT* 105 (Ont CA). *Darling* v. *Charleston Community Hospital* 211 NE 2d 253 (Ill 1965).

It becomes evident that a comprehensive vicarious hospital liability has developed as well as an extensive direct hospital liability for its organizational failures. Liability is concentrated on hospitals and other institutionalized health-care providers and undertakings,[48] which are financially viable and economically sound participants in the health-care industry. These institutions are economically most able to absorb great costs and to procure compensation for injured plaintiffs by means of the principle of loss-distribution.[49] Where modern compensation legislation is lacking, it avoids ruining negligent individuals financially and benefits the patient-physician relationship.[50]

A chronological description of the systematic decay of the doctrine of charitable immunity and resultant expansion of hospital liability will be given. The development of hospital liability in every legal system will be discussed separately. This will be demonstrated by expounding the relevant principles, legal grounds and case law peculiar to every system.

## 4.2 LEGAL GROUNDS OR THEORIES OF HOSPITAL LIABILITY (IN GENERAL)

### Introduction

The phenomenon of the evolution of hospital immunity into expanded hospital liability, has been attended by the formulation of various constructions or theories, and its inherent doctrinal devices, in order to rationalize and facilitate its application. Theories of liability and doctrinal devices[51] have been employed by courts in order to impose liability on hospitals. The expansion of hospital liability has been stimulated by social and economic developments in the health care industry.[52] These legal grounds are common to most legal systems. They will at first be discussed as legal grounds in general under 4.2 and 4.3 — and later with particular reference to the relevant legal systems.

---

[48] Giesen *International* 58–59; this has been described by both Common Law authorities and Civil Law courts.

[49] Atiyah *Vicarious* 22–28. Giesen *International* 58–59.

[50] Giesen *International* 59.

[51] Louisell and Williams *Medical Malpractice* § 15.02 15–8.

[52] *Op. cit.* § 15.02 15–2 to 15–8.

Summary

The following legal grounds or theories can be distinguished and employed in order to establish hospital liability:[53]

### 4.2.1  Indirect or Vicarious Liability

**Indirect or vicarious liability** most often establishes hospital liability. The doctrine of *respondeat superior* is usually employed here. Vicarious liability basically entails that the employer is held liable for the delictual wrongs committed by the employee during the course of employment. Traditional requirements for the application of this theory have, however, been changed and expanded substantially. This legal ground and doctrine is of English origin.

### 4.2.2  Direct or Primary or Corporate Hospital Liability

**The direct or primary or corporate liability** of a hospital is established for the negligent acts of medical staff including independent contractor/doctors under the doctrine of (corporate) negligence. Direct or corporate hospital liability is imposed as a result of a personal duty which is owed directly to the patient by the hospital. For example, the hospital owes a patient an independent or sovereign duty to provide competent medical personnel, breach of which may lead to its being held liable. It also includes all incidents of organizational failure which would occur as a result of the malfunctioning of the systems of a hospital.

---

[53] Most of the theories or legal grounds in this summary are acknowledged or discussed by most writers who know and research hospital liability law. See also Louisell and Williams *Medical Malpractice* § 15.02 15–8, Picard *et al. Liability*, Carmi *Hospital Law*, Christoffel *Health*, Claassen and Verschoor *Negligence*, Curran *Health*, Dix *et al. Australia*, Dornette *Hospital Liability*, Dugdale and Stanton *Negligence*, Fleming *Torts*, Giesen *International*, Gordon, Turner and Price *Medical Jurisprudence*, Fiscina *Legal Medicine*, Jackson and Powell *Negligence*, Jones *Negligence*, Kennedy *Medical Responsibility*, Kennedy and Grubb *Medical Law*, Kelly and Jones *Healthcare*, Kramer and Kramer *Medical Malpractice*, Miller *Hospital Law*, Moore and Kramer *Medical Malpractice*, Oerlikoff and Vanagunas *Hospitals*, Pozgar *Health*, Rozovsky *Law*, Sharpe *Canada*, Southwick *Hospital Liability*, Southwick and Slee *Law of Hospital*, Trindade and Cane *Torts*, Wallace *Law*, Werthmann *Malpractice*, McWilliams and Russell 1996 *SCLR* 432, Osode 1993 *AALR* 289, Whippy 1989 *ALJ* 182, for their valuable contributions.

### 4.2.3  Hospital Liability in Terms of the Non-Delegable Duty

Thirdly hospital liability is established for the acts of independent contractors/doctors or employees where **non-delegable duties** of care are constructed and construed as being owed to the patient by the hospital. Many non-delegable duties are founded in common law. Responsibility for the duties cannot be delegated by the hospital, only performance thereof. The hospital may be liable to the patient where the conduct of an employee, an independent contractor or other medical staff is negligent. The actual purpose of the doctrine is especially to establish the responsibility of the employer, for the negligence of an independent contractor. This liability ensures the quality and high performance standards of a health-care system *in toto*.

### 4.2.4  Doctrines Invoking Hospital Liability

Liability of hospitals can also be established under doctrines such as the doctrines of **apparent agency** or **agency by estoppel**. This liability follows for the acts of independent contractor/doctors. The hospital is held liable for injury resulting from any services which it purports to, or does in fact provide to patients. The liability of the hospital is based on the fact that the doctor is supposedly an agent of the hospital, and that the patient relies on the hospital for treatment. These doctrines are applied in the law of the USA. The hospital is thus held liable for the negligent act(s) of even an independent contractor. The relevant doctrines will be discussed as they are encountered in the various legal systems.

### 4.2.5  Breach of Contract

**Breach of contract** is also a possible legal ground which can establish hospital liability in the appropriate circumstances.

### 4.2.6  Strict Hospital Liability

**Strict hospital liability** has been introduced in many legal systems. The whole expansion of hospital liability seems to be evolving towards a general approach of strict liability.

## 4.3  GENERAL DISCUSSION

### 4.3.1  Indirect or Vicarious Hospital Liability

The law invokes the principle of vicarious liability when one person is held responsible for the misconduct of another, while the former has no personal blameworthiness or fault.[54] The employer becomes responsible/liable for the perpetrator, where the latter's blame is imputed to the former.[55]

The word *vicarious* is derived from Latin and means substitute.[56] In all professional and business spheres the principal delegates various assignments, performances, tasks and duties to substitutes for which he could ultimately be held liable.[57]

#### *4.3.1.1  Indirect and direct liability*

The law of vicarious liability is an older and more settled area of law that also founds hospital liability. It is only one basis to be considered in establishing the liability of a hospital. It serves as an alternative to direct liability which is introduced by the 'direct, or personal or corporate duty'.[58]

Indirect or vicarious liability and direct liability most often form alternative bases for the foundation of a hospital's liability, although they are not the only doctrinal devices which found hospital liability. In theory one can distinguish between these not always easily identifiable or separable fields of liability in order to establish the liability of the responsible entity. Issues concerning the classification of the non-delegable duty either as a form of vicarious or direct liability, will be discussed later.[59]

#### *4.3.1.2  Medical malpractice*

Medical law has adopted principles of vicarious liability with ease and has liberally flexed and extended its applicability, especially in the area of liability of hospitals. Medical malpractice cases are often resolved through

---

[54]   Fleming *Torts* 409; Mason and McCall Smith 1987 *Encyclopaedia* 582.

[55]   Fleming *Torts* 409,412. Markesinis and Deakin *Tort Law* 532.

[56]   Scott *Negligence* 109.

[57]   *Ibid.*

[58]   Picard 1981 *MGLJ* 1016–7. Jones *Negligence* 392.

[59]   *Ibid.*; Whippy 1989 *ALJ* 182.

the application of the principles of indirect or vicarious liability.[60] The law of vicarious liability becomes most relevant when trying to establish the potential liability of a hospital or hospital authority for the negligence of its medical staff.[61] It is also taken into consideration when assessing other medical negligence issues, such as the potential liability of the general practitioner or doctors for the negligence of nurses or professional assistants which they employ.[62] These principles apply aptly in medical context.

### 4.3.1.3 Vicarious hospital liability

Hospital liability can also be established by applying the principle of vicarious liability.[63] A hospital, a corporation, a board of trustees or governors, or a health authority might incur such liability where it undertakes responsibility for the treatment and care of patients, and a patient consequently suffers injury due to its employees' negligence.[64] Hospitals traditionally incur vicarious liability for the employees' acts and omissions under the doctrine of *respondeat superior*.[65]

The successful application of this legal ground will depend on the identification of the relevant health-care provider as a government controlled or state funded institution or as a private institution. Traditionally, employee perpetrators of the state hospitals will easily implicate such a vicarious liability, whereas the independent contractor staff of private institutions will consequently necessitate another legal ground to redress.[66]

### 4.3.1.4 Application in legal systems

*Respondeat superior* is also the doctrine of vicarious liability. This theory imposes liability on the employer for the torts committed by the employee in the course of his employment.[67] The principle of vicarious liability is

---

[60] See also Giesen *International* 38.

[61] Giesen *International* 50–51: 'when the hospital, a corporation, a board of trustees or governors, or a health authority undertakes responsibility for a patient's treatment and the latter is injured due to the employees' negligence, liability may incur for the hospital … The hospital can be vicariously liable on the doctrine of *respondeat superior*.'

[62] Giesen *International* 38.

[63] *Op. cit.* 47, 50–59. Scott *Negligence* 115.

[64] Giesen *International* 50. That is traditionally speaking.

[65] *Op. cit.* 51.

[66] See also Scott *Negligence* 115.

[67] Cowdrey *Law* 44. Dugdale and Stanton *Negligence* § 22.06 539.

originally an English law principle.[68] According to English common law, hospitals were regarded to be vicariously liable for the negligence of their medical staff.[69] Common law provisions have been adopted and applied in many foreign legal systems.[70] Principles of vicarious liability have become well established in modern law, and form an undeniable part of the South African positive law.[71]

### 4.3.1.5  Origin

The doctrine of *respondeat superior* originated in old England at a time when landlords or masters maintained large family estates. The maxim literally means 'let the master answer'. The English doctrine generally implied that the master is liable in certain cases for the wrongful acts committed by the servant.[72]

The historic background involved the wealthy master or landlord who provided room, board and pitiful remuneration to very poor peasant servants. The king or queen of England at that time, set down proclamations of law or writs concerning the payment of pecuniary damages to a person intentionally injured by another. Where the law was violated, the sheriff would issue a writ of enforcement.[73] This doctrine was initiated for example, due to the following circumstances: where wealthy landowners would injure one another intentionally over disputes, damages would be sought and eventually forced to be paid. But clever people seeking revenge would send their penniless peasant to settle the score. No harmful consequences would then ensue for the vindictive master nor for the penniless servant. The doctrine of *respondeat superior* was then introduced, in cases where it became impossible to recover damages. Where any injury or damages followed as a result of the master's instructions or directions, the latter was held liable for the servant's wrongful acts. The doctrine was later evolved to include negligent

---

[68]  Claassen and Verschoor *Negligence* 95. Van der Merwe and Olivier *Onregmatige Daad* 508. Neethling *et al. Delict* 373. According to Fleming *Torts* 409 it became part of most systems of primitive law.

[69]  Picard 1981 *MGLJ* 1016–7. Whippy 1989 *ALJ* 182. Lee 1979 *ALR* 313.

[70]  Such as South African Law, Anglo-Australian and Anglo-Canadian case-law.

[71]  Claassen and Verschoor *Negligence* 95. Van der Merwe and Olivier *Onregmatige Daad* 508. See also Strauss 1991 *Doctor* 299.

[72]  Cowdrey *Law* 44. See Fleming *Torts* 409.

[73]  *Ibid.*

acts of the servant performed in the course of his doing something for the master and being authorized by the master.[74]

Early in the 19th century the policy was tempered to involve only those acts of the employee committed in the course of his employment.[75] This represented a compromise between the innocent victim and the financially responsible defendant and the unnecessary burdening of business enterprise.[76]

Today, the doctrine of *respondeat superior* includes, 'liability assessed against a principal for the acts of his or her agents'.[77] Case law in the 1940s and 1950s further developed the principle of agency law to include the 'borrowed servant' rule. The implementation of this rule rendered the doctor vicariously liable for the acts of non-employee medical assistants. The 'captain of the ship' rule was also introduced with similar effect.[78] These rules are, however, no longer greatly in use.

### 4.3.1.6 Joint liability

Vicarious liability is thus based on the doctrine of *respondeat superior*.[79] It basically entails that the defendant employer becomes liable for the wrongful act(s) or omission(s) of another.[80] The liability is now founded on the servant's wrongdoing and the relationship between the employer and employee.[81] It implies for example that where an employee (amongst others) commits a wrongful act against a third person whilst executing his duties, action for damages or redress can be instituted by the third party against the

---

[74] Cowdrey *Law* 44–45 on the origin of vicarious liability.

[75] Fleming *Torts* 409.

[76] *Op. cit.* 409–410.

[77] Cowdrey *Law* 44.

[78] *Ibid.*

[79] Picard 1981 *MGLJ* 1016. Giesen *International* 51. Speller *Hospitals* 256. Louisell and Williams *Medical Malpractice* by Nelson LJ III, Chapter XV §15.02 15–8, 15–15 to 15–19. The latter stipulates the two traditional requirements to establish vicarious liability under the doctrine of *respondeat superior* as: (i) the physician must be a servant or agent of the hospital; (ii) the physician must commit the tort within the scope of his employment. Picard *supra* states that this doctrine rather is a 'vehicle to achieve a goal that seems fair and necessary'.

[80] Giesen *International* 38. Neethling *et al. Delict* 372. Strauss (1991) *Doctor* 299.

[81] Lipschitz 1981 *Responsa Meridiana* 117.

employer.[82] Vicarious liability is therefore a form of joint liability.[83] It implies that both the person who commits the wrongful act as well as the person vicariously liable for him may be liable.[84]

### 4.3.1.7  Strict Liability

Vicarious liability is also a form of strict liability.[85] Where the law holds a person responsible for the misconduct of another, although he is himself free from personal fault or blame, vicarious liability is invoked. It is thus a form of strict (no-fault) liability.[86] Common Law countries as well as France and Scandinavia, and Germany (in respect of the law of contract), adheres to this form of strict liability.[87]

No fault or personal blame (even negligence) is required from the person who is vicariously liable, even where the wrongful act complained of requires that the perpetrator's negligence actually be proved.[88] The fundamental principle of delictual liability implies that the person liable, must comply with the element or requirement of fault.[89] Because the employer himself is free from personal blame or fault his vicarious liability could therefore either not be delictual by nature, or it could be strict delictual liability. Vicarious liability therefore deviates from delictual liability because the element of fault is lacking in the person whom the law holds responsible for the misconduct of another.[90] Vicarious liability thus imposes an (objective) legal liability on a person or organization for the wrongful act committed by another, with no fault or personal blame attaching to the person or organization which is being held responsible.[91]

---

[82]  Claassen and Verschoor *Negligence* 95. Van der Merwe and Olivier *Onregmatige Daad* 508.

[83]  Neethling *et al. Delict* 376. Kennedy *Medical Responsibility* 154, 156: the medical staff or a member thereof is also liable. Dugdale and Stanton *Negligence* § 22.06 539.

[84]  Kennedy *Medical Responsibility* 154.

[85]  Kennedy *Medical Responsibility* 154. Fleming *Torts* 409. Giesen *International* 38.

[86]  *Ibid.*

[87]  Giesen *International* 38.

[88]  Kennedy *Medical Responsibility* 154.

[89]  This is also a valid principle in South African law. Authors who describe this liability as not being delictual: Claassen and Verschoor *Negligence* 95. Van der Merwe and Olivier *Onregmatige Daad* 508.

[90]  *Ibid.* Van der Walt 1964 *THRHR* 42 professes it to be strict or faultless delictual liability. *Supra* 9.3.1.

[91]  *Ibid.* MacFarlane *Health Law* 26.

### *4.3.1.8 Traditional requirements:*

The **traditional** perspective on the application of vicarious liability as a general principle,[92] which is founded on three traditional requirements, applied or still applies in most legal systems.[93] The traditional perspective and formulation of the vicarious principle or *respondeat superior* doctrine reads as follows: The employer (master) is fully liable for the damage where the employee (servant) negligently commits a wrong whilst acting within the scope or during the course of his employment.[94] The traditional or most common situation in which the vicarious principle is applied, is that of employer and employee, or master and servant.[95] The traditional test applied in order to establish vicarious liability consisted of the following three requirements:[96]

4.3.1.8.1    **There must be an employer-employee relationship at the time when the wrongful act is committed.**

4.3.1.8.2    **The employee must act within the scope or during the course of his employment or in the execution of his duties when committing the wrongful act.**

4.3.1.8.3    **The employee must commit a wrongful act or an actionable wrong.**

4.3.1.8.1    There must be an **employer-employee relationship** at the time when the wrongful act is committed. In other words the doctor or physician

---

[92]    Atiyah *Vicarious* 3, 6–8.

[93]    *Ibid.* Giesen *International* 38, 50–51. Kennedy and Grubb *Medical Law* 431–440. Louisell and Williams *Medical Malpractice* § 16.01, § 16.02, § 16.03. Kennedy *Medical Responsibility* 154–155. Jackson and Powell *Negligence* 490. Jones *Negligence* 392. Picard 1981 *MGLJ* 1016. Picard *et al. Liability* 381. Mac Farlane *Law* 26, 31–32. Fleming *Torts* 409, 413–426. Claassen and Verschoor *Negligence* 95–98.

[94]    *Ibid.* See *infra.*

[95]    MacFarlane *Health Law* 26, 31–32. Kennedy *Medical Responsibility* 154–155. Atiyah *Vicarious* 3,6.

[96]    Atiyah *Vicarious* 3,6. Giesen *International* 38, 50–51. Kennedy and Grubb *Medical Law* 431–440. Louisell and Williams *Medical Malpractice* § 16.01, § 16.02, § 16.03. Kennedy *Medical Responsibility* 154–155. Jackson and Powell *Negligence* 490. Jones *Negligence* 392. Picard *MG LJ* 1016. Picard *et al. Liability* 381. Mac Farlane *Law* 26, 31–32. Fleming *Torts* 413–426. Claassen and Verschoor *Negligence* 95–98. Van der Merwe and Olivier *Onregmatige Daad* 508–519. Neethling *et al. Delict* 373–378. Or as Strauss (1991) *Doctor* 299 defines: 'Vicarious liability ordinarily arises in those cases where a person employs another to perform a lawful activity, and the servant then does not proceed with the required or expected measure of skill and care, and causes harm to others'.

must be a servant of the (employer) hospital. 'Such a relationship exists where someone, by agreement, places his manpower or his capacity for work at the disposal of another for remuneration, in such manner that the latter can exercise control over the former'.[97] A contract of employment (*locatio conductio operarum*)[98] is thus required. This is also known as the 'contract of services'.[99] On the other hand, where the contract of mandate (*locatio conductio operis*)[100] or 'contract for services' was identified, it was tradition-ally held to exclude vicarious liability.[101] The mandator could in such a case not be held responsible for the wrongful acts of the independent agent. Such a contract contained that the agent undertook to render services for the mandator for remuneration, without being subject to the control of the mandator during the rendering of such services.[102] The distinction between the two agreements (*locatio conductio operarum et locatio conductio operis*) is founded upon the control or absence thereof, of the superior over the services of the other person.[103]

The **traditional test** or factor applied by the courts in England and our own courts, in order to ascertain whether a person was an employee, was whether the employer had employed the person (employee), and whether the latter's work and the manner in which it was undertaken, was under the control of the employer. This is the so-called **control test**. Therefore, the servant and the independent contractor were also distinguished from one another by means of the 'control' factor.[104] At first, it was regarded as the 'final test' and considered to be of 'vital importance' to establish vicarious liability ultimately.[105] Yet in borderline cases where it was difficult to differentiate

---

[97] Claassen and Verschoor *Negligence* 96. Van der Merwe and Olivier *Onregmatige Daad* 508.

[98] 'A hiring of services' according to Claassen and Verschoor *Negligence* 96 footnote 14. Neethling *et al. Delict* 373–374.

[99] Finch *Law* 82.

[100] 'A letting and hiring of work' according to Claassen and Verschoor *Negligence* 96. Neethling *et al. Delict* 374.

[101] *Ibid.* Finch *Law* 81–82. Fleming *Torts* 413.

[102] Claassen and Verschoor *Negligence* 96. Neethling *et al. Delict* 374.

[103] *Ibid.*

[104] Lipshitz 1981 *Responsa Meridiana* 118.

[105] *Performing Rights Society* v. *Mitchell and Booker Ltd* [1924] 1 KB 762 at 767. See also Lipshitz 1981 *Responsa Meridiana* 118.

between employers and agents or their relevant contracts, **other indicia**[106] were acknowledged as indicative of contracts of service. They were:

(a)     the master's power of selection of the servant;

(b)     the payment of wages;

(c)     the master's right to control the method of doing the work;

(d)     the master's right of dismissal or suspension.

It was commended that control was only one of several indicia from which it could be concluded that an employer-employee relationship existed. Control was to be considered together with other indicia before reaching a conclusion. Control was no longer regarded as the only essential criterion or sole determining factor which could establish vicarious liability. Every case had to be evaluated on its own merit.[107]

Denning LJ, however, discarded the traditional control test in *Cassidy*.[108] The control test was demonstrated there as being ineffective in the hospital setting. Authors have described it as being bankrupt in hospital cases.[109] Kahn-Freund discredited the control test in the same year, and postulated an alternative — the organization test.[110]

Thereafter, some courts[111] and authors have tried to 're-interpret' or resuscitate the control test. Control was re-defined as not meaning real factual control but only as the capacity (power) or right to control. It was considered to be the 'most important and therefore decisive factor ... in determining whether the wrongdoer is an employee or an independent contractor'.[112] The significance of the control test has only been reduced by stating that it should not be considered as the only factor, but should be

---

[106]   *R* v. *AMCA Services* 1959(4) SA 207 (AD) 211 per Schreiner JA. Lipshitz 1981 *Responsa Meridiana* 119.

[107]   *R* v. *AMCA Services* 1959 (4) SA 207 (AD) 211 per Schreiner JA. Lipshitz 1981 *Responsa Meridiana* 118, 119, 121, 124–125.

[108]   *Cassidy* v. *Ministry of Health* [1951] 2 KB 343. Picard 1981 *MGLJ* 1017.

[109]   Picard 1981 *MGLJ* 1017.

[110]   Kahn-Freund 1951 *MLR* 504–509. Lipshitz 1981 *Responsa Meridiana* 123. Picard 1981 *MGLJ* 1017 footnote 116.

[111]   *Rodrigues* v. *Alves* 1978 (4) SA 834 (AD) per Viljoen AJA stated at 842 A: 'the requirement is not that there should be actual control. The requirement relates to the power or right to control.' *Mhlongo* v. *Minister of Police* 1978 (2) SA 551 (AD) at 568 B. *Smit* v. *Workmen's Compensation Commissioner* 1979 (1) SA 51 (A) 62.

[112]   Neethling *et al. Delict* 374–375, *Deliktereg* 364.

considered together with all the circumstances of the specific case, in order to determine the relationship of the parties.[113]

In the light of the fact that the control test is no longer deemed the sovereign or absolute parameter to establish vicarious liability, **alternative tests** have been introduced:

- **the organization test;**[114]
- **the dominant impression test;**[115]
- **the composite test.**[116]

4.3.1.8.2 The employee must act **within the scope or during the course of his employment, or in the execution of his duties** (when committing the wrongful act).[117] This transpires when actions are performed as direct obligations or incidental to or in the general course of his duties.[118] The terms and the nature of the service contract, the nature of the assignments and the particular circumstances of the case should be considered in order to

---

[113] *Ibid.* See the discussion of Markesinis and Deakin *Tort Law* 532,535–538 on the control test.

[114] The organization test: the question asked here was whether the employee was 'part of the employer's organisation in the sense that his work was an integral part of the master's business?' Lipshitz 1981 *Responsa Meridiana* 123. Fleming *Torts* 416–418. Claassen and Verschoor *Negligence* 97 footnote 23. *Cassidy* v. *Ministry of Health* [1951] 2 KB 343 per Denning LJ. Picard 1981 *MGLJ* 1016–1017. Kahn-Freund 1951 *MLR* 504–509. *Stevenson, Jordan and Harrison Ltd* v. *MacDonald and Evans* 1952 1 TLR 101 (CA). *Bank Voor Handel en Scheepvaart N.V.* v. *Slatford* [1953] 1 QB 248 (CA).

[115] The dominant impression test: the court had to classify the contract on the basis of the dominant impression it made upon it. Many indicia were considered here but the test was found wanting. Lipschitz 1981 *Responsa Meridiana* 124. Claassen and Verschoor *Negligence* 97 footnote 23.

[116] The composite test: this test was introduced in *Market Investigations Ltd* v. *Minister of Social Security* 1969 (2) WLR 1 by Cooke J. This test was formulated by Cooke J as follows: 'The fundamental test to be applied is this. Is the person who was engaged himself to perform these services performing them as a person in business on his own account? If the answer to that is 'yes', then the contract is a contract for services. If the answer is 'no', then the contract is a contract of service'. See also Beyleveld on *Smit* v. *Workmen's Compensation Commissioner* 1979 (1) SA 57 (AD) in 1979 *THRHR* 446 at 448. Lipshitz 1981 *Responsa Meridiana* 124. See also Markesinis and Deakin *Tort Law* 537, who calls this test the 'economic reality test'.

[117] Finch *Law* 83–86. Lipshitz 1981 *Responsa Meridiana* 118. Claassen and Verschoor *Negligence* 97. Fleming *Torts* 420–422. Neethling *et al. Delict* 376–378. Van der Merwe and Olivier *Onregmatige Daad* 514–518. According to Jones *Negligence* 399 this is treated as a question of fact in each case. MacFarlane *Health Law* 31 states the test is whether the employee was doing the employer's work.

[118] Claassen and Verschoor *Negligence* 97.

determine whether the employee acted according to this prerequisite.[119] The traditional perspective entailed that where a wrongful act (or delict) was committed by the employee outside the limits of his service contract, vicarious liability would no longer follow for the employer.[120]

This requirement has been applied well in medical negligence cases.[121] If a surgeon were to operate outside the sphere of his experience, it could constitute his acting outside the scope of his employment. Only extreme circumstances and the degree of deviation would, however, determine such a situation. The circumstances that can lead to responsibility are not only limited to the provision of treatment, but can extend to cases such as the patient falling out of a hospital bed.[122]

**4.3.1.8.3 The employee must commit a wrongful act or an actionable wrong.**[123] The vicarious liability of the employer is only established, when the act of the employee meets all the requirements of the wrongful act in order to render himself liable. The employer is then entitled to raise any defence at the employer's disposal. The employer and employee are co-perpetrators, because the employee is also delictually responsible. Where the employer is sued and ordered to pay damages as a result of the wrongful act of the employee, the employer has a right of recourse against the employee.[124]

### *4.3.1.9 Comment*

**4.3.1.9.1 The employer-employee requirement:**[125] The traditional rigid scrutiny of legal (contractual) relationships,[126] to determine the existence of the traditional requirements ((i) to (iii)) in order to establish vicarious liability, has proved unsatisfactory in practice. The rigid conformation to traditional requirements ((i) to (iii)) has led to unreasonable and undesired consequences. The imposition of hospital liability for medical staff in the

---

[119] *Ibid.*

[120] *Ibid.*

[121] Jones *Negligence* 399.

[122] *Ibid.*

[123] Claassen and Verschoor *Negligence* 98. Fleming *Torts* 422–424.

[124] *Ibid.* See also Lipshitz 1981 *Responsa Meridiana* 118.

[125] A thorough conclusive discussion on this requirement will follow in the final chapter of this thesis.

[126] *I.e.* the relationships between the hospitals and their employed or engaged staff, in relation to the injuries of third parties. See also Finch *Law* 94.

area of medical law is thus no longer dependent on legal niceties[127] such as the required employer-employee ratio nor excluded by the independent contractor agent. The control test which founded this distinction has also been discarded.[128]

Modern but more reasonable and flexible approaches and constructions have been developed and have expanded the law of vicarious liability. Vicarious liability is now seen, in essence, as a mechanism of modern law which enables an injured third party to proceed against a party who can through insurance or other funds, meet his claim.[129] This would most likely be the employer, rather than the employee.[130] The law also does not always clearly define the absolute criteria necessary for vicarious liability.[131] The success of the injured party in recovering compensation, should therefore not be dependent upon the detail or minutiae of the contractual relationship between two other parties of which the plaintiff has no knowledge in any case.[132] According to Kennedy it should (for example) rather depend on 'the undertaking of responsibility by one and the subsequent delegation to the other'.[133] Other constructions or ratio which enhance the plaintiff's chances for success, have also been formulated and will be discussed later. Therefore, it should make no difference to the eventual outcome of the hospital's liability, whether the person committing the wrongful act was an employee, an independent contractor or any other member of the medical staff. In other words the minutiae of the contractual relationship[134] between the person committing the wrongful act and the person or body sued vicariously, should not prescribe the outcome of the case. The legal relationship between hospitals and their medical staff — in relation to injury to third parties — should not be regarded as a sovereign or absolute factor in establishing the liability of a hospital. Liability of hospitals and hospital authorities should be imposed irrespective of and independent to legal niceties distinguishing between employees and independent contractors for the purposes of the incidence of third party liability.[135] One cannot formulate liability and try to

---

[127] Finch *Law* 94. Markesinis and Deakin *Tort Law* 535 on the term 'employee'.

[128] A discussion concerning this statement will follow *infra*.

[129] Kennedy *Medical Responsibility* 154–155.

[130] *Op. cit.* 155.

[131] *Ibid.*

[132] *Ibid.* Whippy 1989 *ALJ* 202. Jones *Negligence* 408.

[133] Kennedy *Medical Responsibility* 154–155.

[134] See also Finch *Law* 94–95.

[135] *Ibid.*

achieve justice, but the moment the member of staff does not comply with a technicality, the vicarious liability vanishes.[136] Vicarious liability should be imposed independent to trivial contractual detail in the face of sometimes severe injuries to third parties. It is not thereby meant that every misadventure should be punished or labelled as liability, but that reasonable justice should be enforced. Vicarious liability, being a form of strict liability and implicating the liability of the person responsible for that of the perpetrator, should not apply only to employees but also to independent contractors and other members of the medical staff.

Judicial decisions dealing with vicarious liability should, however, be constrained by the following: Hospitals and hospital authorities should not only be fixed with legal (vicarious) liability because they can better pay the bill and in order to provide the injured third parties with compensation. The fault of the staff member should still be exhaustively proved in stead of being assumed.[137]

4.3.1.9.2 The control test: The general inadequacy of the control test has been discussed by many foreign and modern authors. Its application in the founding of vicarious hospital liability in medical malpractice cases, has also been discounted.

Kahn-Freund[138] discredited the control test in 1951, when he condemned the application of the test in modern technological societies with advanced social conditions. He advocated the implementation of the organization test. Atiyah[139] discussed the obvious deficiencies of the control test as 'a sufficient condition of the existence of a contract of service', with particular reference to company directors and skilled and professional men. He concluded that control could no longer be treated as a decisive test in all circumstances, but rejecting it in its traditional form would be an 'over-simplification'.

---

[136] *Ibid.*: 'Problems arising from the incidence of vicarious liability and its general absence in the case of injuries caused to third parties by independent contractors become most acute in the context of hospital activities'.

[137] Finch *Health* 95 also accentuates that when hospitals are fixed with vicarious liability in order to pay the bill, the valued personal reputations of medical staff may be at stake. Direct liability implying the breach of the hospital's own duty, rather than vicarious liability should then attach. Thereby avoiding the problems concerning the status or reputations of employed or engaged staff.

[138] Kahn-Freund 1951 *MLR* 504–509. See also Markesinis and Deakin *Tort Law* 535.

[139] Atiyah *Vicarious* 45–49.

Picard has rejected the application of the control test in the hospital setting, most decisively. Attention should be drawn to the almost famous and often quoted passage by Picard:

> All of the principles of the law of vicarious liability are applied to hospitals, but therein lies the problem. Those principles, set up for masters and servants, shop keepers and clerks, do not fit the hospital and its professional staff. But most courts doggedly try to stretch the old garments to fit the new flesh. The concept that was the material measurement of vicarious liability, the control test, no longer covers modern hospital-doctor relationships. The new, more viable organization test, has yet to be worked into Canadian Law. The reluctance of courts to move towards the more modern approach has resulted in a restriction in the liability of hospitals.

She proceeds to find that the control test's deficiencies were obvious from the moment it went into service. The employer of the professional doctor, for example, may have no knowledge concerning medicine and is not only not in a position to control the doctor, but if he should attempt to do so, would find that the doctor-employee had already exercised his own form of control over the situation and would quit.[140] She also recommended the organization test.

Jones considers the control test as an inadequate determinant of the employer-employee relationship in modern economic conditions.[141] Employers can often not supervise and control the manner in which skilled employees perform their work, because they (the employers) do not have the required technical expertise. He admits that the current approach in English law concerning the identification of the employer-employee relationship, is that no single test is applied. A number of possibly conflicting factors have to be weighed in order to ascertain whether the work performed is under a 'contract of service' or a 'contract for services'.[142]

Lee found that the control test had no logical foundation and that it would falter in almost every industrial situation today.[143] Finch also stated that it was once thought that the 'acid test of distinction between employees and independent contractors lay in the degree of control which an employer could expect, and be expected to exercise over the activities and conduct of the employee, and the relative absence of such control in the case of

---

[140]   Picard 1981 *MGLJ* 1016–1017. See Picard *et al. Liability* 382.

[141]   Jones *Negligence* 393.

[142]   *Ibid.*

[143]   Lee 1979 *ALR* 321.

independent contractors.'[144] This does not apply any more in the light of English case law.[145]

Fleming[146] remarked that the control test had been adjusted. It no longer involved a question of factual supervision, but rather 'whether ultimate authority over the person in the performance of his work resided in the employer so that he was subject to the latter's orders and directions.' He added that a more flexible approach also included the consideration of other factors, such as the power of dismissal or the power to delegate the work by the employee. He recommended the more useful test or organization test which was more appropriate in 'hospital cases'. Kennedy[147] described the control test as 'outdated' concerning the vicarious liability of hospitals.

In the light of the fact that the modern approach discounts the control test, the slight transformation of the control test into the 'right or power to control test', or however modified, does not provide it with the necessary resur-rectional power.[148] Control is still absent, with respect, in the hospital context, no matter how the control is purported to be exercised. The only 'control' in the hospital context would be correctly summarized in the dictum of Denning LJ in the *Cassidy* and *Roe* cases[149] — discussed *infra* — as being the right of the employer to choose and dismiss their staff. This was indeed the criterion which was created by Denning LJ in order to determine vicarious liability in the light of the fact that the employer could not control its staff.

Even if the 'control test' was to remain relevant in the context that it could be considered together with other factors in establishing vicarious liability, its main purpose namely identifying the employer-employee relationship becomes irrelevant seen from the angle of modern legal research and case law and this comment. The distinction between an employee and an agent becomes irrelevant — according to modern writers — in order to establish hospital liability.

The correct approach to the control test is with respect, that it should be discounted as an absolute test or 'most important test' which determines the traditional employer-employee relationship in order to establish the vicarious

---

[144] Finch *Health* 94–95.

[145] See also Kennedy *Medical Responsibility* 155; Speller *Hospitals* 258. *Roe* v. *Minister of Health* [1954] 2 QB 66.

[146] Fleming *Torts* 414–416, 415.

[147] Kennedy *Medical Responsibility* 155.

[148] *Supra et infra.* Markesinis and Deakin *Tort Law* 535.

[149] *Cassidy* v. *Ministry of Health* [1951] 2 KB 343. *Roe* v. *Minister of Health* [1954] 2 QB 66. See the discussion *infra*.

liability of hospitals. If it were in any way still to be considered as being relevant to this matter, it could only come into consideration as one of many factors or tests weighed in order to establish vicarious liability, or should not be considered at all.

### 4.3.1.10 Justification

The formulation of the principles of the law of vicarious liability and the criteria that are necessary to establish this form of liability in the context of modern hospital activities, have not occurred without creating consequential problems. The law has up to date not been successful in defining or providing exact or absolute required criteria. Criteria applied in the establishment of hospital liability are still 'appropriately unclear'[150] and comparatively inconsistent or differing in respective legal systems. Therefore, the rationale, sole theoretical basis of or justification for vicarious liability has until now, not absolutely been defined or identified.

Both the Common Law countries and the Civil Law jurisdictions present various explanations concerning the basis of vicarious liability.[151] In Common Law countries alone we can distinguish between nine different theories to found this liability.[152] Giesen does, however, categorize certain jurisdictions into two main groups of thinking, concerning the theoretical basis of vicarious liability.[153]

1.      According to certain Common Law countries, France, Scandinavia, and (regarding the law of contract) Germany as well, the basis of vicarious liability is a form of strict or no-fault liability.[154] It implies that the liability arises from the servant's acts or omissions and fault and not from the master's conduct who is also free from fault or blame.[155]

In German Law, strict vicarious liability has been introduced in almost all cases by imposing non-delegable duties of organizational care and control not only on employers but on others as well. Medical malpractice cases are also included where desirable.[156]

---

[150]   Kennedy *Medical Responsibility* 155.

[151]   Giesen *International* 38.

[152]   Ibid.; Atiyah *Vicarious* 12–28.

[153]   Giesen *International* 38.

[154]   *Ibid.* Kennedy *Medical Responsibility* 154. Fleming *Torts* 409.

[155]   *Ibid.*

[156]   Giesen *International* 39.

2.    According to Austria, Switzerland, and (as far as the law of delict is concerned) Germany as well, the basis of liability is the fault or conduct of the master himself. In German law liability arises from the fault of the employer through poor choice of a servant, for example his *culpa in eligendo*. In Swiss law the employer's negligent conduct in failing to avoid the occurrence of damage, will establish liability. The fault or capacity to negligent conduct of the servant, is irrelevant. Technically, this liability is not vicarious, but direct.[157]

3.    Other theories or justifications for vicarious liability: Although vicarious liability can rest with a party or employer who does not necessarily have any fault or is not to blame, it is commendable because it grants the plaintiff a remedy and does give him recourse to the master.[158] Justifications for this rather unusual but outstanding doctrine have been all but few. Various other theories[159] have been designed, to justify its existence:

a)    The risk or danger theory: It implies that the master creates risks of prejudice or harm to others for his own benefit. When employing others to do his work, he should be held responsible when harming others on the grounds of fairness and justice.[160]

b)    The solvency theory: It implies that the master be held liable since he is usually financially stronger to pay the bill. It is also said: "Let the deeper pocket pay".[161]

c)    The interest or profit theory: The master should bear the burdens for which in correlation, he enjoys the benefits of the servant's services.[162]

d)    The identification theory: The master is identified as acting when the servant acts; the latter only being the arm of the master.[163]

---

[157] *Op. cit.* 38–39 on this comparative perspective.

[158] Lipshitz 1981 *Responsa Meridiana* 117. Fleming *Torts* 409–429.

[159] *Ibid.*

[160] *Ibid.* Scott *Middellike Aanspreeklikheid* 30–40. Neethling *et al. Delict* 373. Scott *Negligence* 110. Dugdale and Stanton *Negligence* § 22.06 539.

[161] *Ibid.*

[162] Neethling *et al. Delict* 373.

[163] *Ibid.*

e)   The principle of loss — distribution: This implies that the mas-
     ter can distribute his losses easier by means of insurance and
     price increases and should therefore take the loss. This theory
     seems the most realistic and commendable in certain circum-
     stances, and in accordance with the modern law of delict.[164]

To take it one step further, a particular form of loss — distribution can be recommended namely a form of national medical
malpractice insurance or scheme. This can compensate for any
form of medical malpractice especially including cases of hospital malpractice and consequently hospital liability. Thus a national responsibility or national subsidization for medical malpractice can be established which could be formulated
according to principles of reasonableness, fairness and equity.[165]

### 4.3.2  Direct Hospital Liability

### Direct or Primary or Corporate Hospital Liability

The development of the policy of direct or corporate liability of hospitals, is
based on the perception that the hospital is the primary institution and
provider of quality health-care.[166] The hospital is no more the place of refuge
for the destitute, but the modern institutional health facility equipped with
highly skilled health professionals and high tech equipment, providing the
best health-care. This has resulted in strong, well-defined legal relationships
between modern patients and modern hospitals.[167]

Direct or corporate hospital liability entails that hospital authorities
should be responsible for all hospital organizational distributions, task
distributions and control of responsibilities.[168] This is comprehensive of co-

---

[164] Lipshitz 1981 *Responsa Meridiana* 117. Giesen *International* 39. Scott *Negligence* 110.
Dugdale and Stanton *Negligence* § 22.06 539. Atiyah *Vicarious* 22–28.

[165] See also Atiyah *Vicarious* 25–28, where he discusses the same principles in relation to
motor car accidents, business enterprises and industries.

[166] Mason and McCall Smith 1987 *Encyclopaedia* 582. Giesen *International* 47. Kennedy
and Grubb *Medical Law* 402. Picard 1981 *MGLJ* 997.

[167] Kennedy and Grubb *Medical Law* 403. Picard 1981 *MGLJ* 997–998.

[168] This was implied and stated most aptly by the German Federal Supreme Court in *BGJ*, 8
May 1979 *NJW* 1979, 1935 (1036) and *BGJ*, 16 October 1979 *NJW* 1980, 650 (651) and
elsewhere. Giesen *International* 64.

operation in hospital teams, co-ordination and control of personnel, facilities and equipment in order to provide proper patient care.[169] Hospital organizational regulations[170] should be drafted to enforce the above-mentioned guidelines, in order to maintain high standards of quality health-care and prevent injury to life caused by careless ignorance.

The legal implication is that the hospital, as organization, owes a direct or personal or corporate,[171] and independent,[172] duty of care to its patients. This duty of care includes the provision of reasonable care in the organization, administration and staffing of the hospital.[173] Where negligence occurs as a result of an unsafe or unreliable system, organizational errors or bad administration, a claim for damages could be brought as a result of breach of this duty,[174] and primary or direct liability could ensue for the hospital authority.[175] An effective organization or reliable system could thus be ensured by — amongst other things — providing sufficient, properly qualified and competent medical staff and non-medical staff, providing efficient supervision and training for them, maintaining the general safety and standard of adequate equipment and the premises, adhering to general requirements of hygiene and in providing proper systems and supplies.[176] Non-compliance to these requirements could lead to direct or corporate liability.[177]

A comprehensive **list of direct duties** which may establish hospital liability, can be compiled:

The scope of the direct duty was according to precedents expanded to include the following direct duties:[178]

(a)     to select competent and qualified employees;

---

[169]  *Ibid.*

[170]  *Ibid.*

[171]  Kennedy and Grubb *Medical Law* 403. Picard 1981 *MGLJ* 997–998.

[172]  Mason and McCall Smith 1987 *Encyclopaedia* 582.

[173]  Kennedy *Medical Responsibility* 156.

[174]  *Ibid.*

[175]  Jackson and Powell *Negligence* 492.

[176]  Giesen *International* 47, 59. Dugdale and Stanton *Negligence* § 22.04 538.

[177]  *Ibid.*

[178]  Picard 1981 *MGLJ* 997–1019. Picard stated that the courts have called the other duties into existence, but that it was not always clear whether the hospital's accountability was then founded on direct or vicarious liability. Further duties could always be created, but most cautiously by courts, with regard to their attitude concerning the law of negligence in general. See Kennedy and Grubb *Medical Law* 403.

(b)    to instruct and supervise them;

(c)    to provide proper facilities and equipment;

(d)    to establish systems necessary to the safe operation of the hospital.

Other direct duties[179] are:

(e)    to establish appropriate procedures such as aseptic procedures and
       infection control and procedures concerning administration of drugs
       and control of contagious or dangerous diseases;

(f)    to provide adequate resources.

The list of direct duties now also includes the following:[180]
     A hospital should:

    (i)    employ an adequate number of personnel eg. one fully qualified
              anaesthetist cannot attend three operations in two different
              theatres simultaneously;[181]

    (ii)   not allow one nurse to monitor five patients in intensive care
              simultaneously;[182]

    (iii)  be held liable for maintaining a negligent system of providing
              dangerous drugs such as anaesthetics;[183]

    (iv)   be liable for employing an inexperienced doctor and allowing
              the latter to administer anaesthetics without proper supervi-
              sion;[184]

    (v)    be liable for an inadequate communication system,[185] or an in-
              adequate interdepartmental communication system;[186]

---

[179]  Picard 1981 *MGLJ* 997–1019. Kennedy and Grubb *Medical Law* 403.

[180]  Giesen *International* 64–69.

[181]  *Op. cit.* 64–65. German case law.

[182]  Giesen *International* 65. This happened in Canada: *Laidlow* v. *Lions Gate Hospital* (1969)
       70 WWR 727 (BCSC). Also *Jinks* v. *Cardwell* (1987) 39 *CCLT* 168 (Ont HC McRae J at
       174): Two nurses handled thirty-three mentally ill patients in the latter case.

[183]  Giesen *International* 65. *Collins* v. *Hertfordshire County Council* [1947] 1 KB 598.

[184]  Giesen *International* 65. *Jones* v. *Manchester Corporation* [1952] 2 QB 852.

[185]  *Bull* v. *Devon Area Health Authority* 1989 (unreported). Jones *Negligence* 401. Kennedy
       and Grubb *Medical Law* 413–415.

[186]  Giesen *International* 65 and footnote 250.

(vi)   be liable for negligently allowing unqualified staff to administer an intravenous injection;[187]

(vii)  be liable for failure to adequately protect a disturbed person from injuring himself or others (patients or visitors), or persons outside the hospital premises, with effective systems;[188]

(viii) be liable for failing to rotate sufficient personnel without danger to patients;[189]

(ix)   be liable for failure to provide training programmes for hospital staff;[190]

(x)    be liable for failing to provide a proper and safe system for: handling drugs; injections or infusions; transfusions; patient surveillance for patients with suicidal tendencies, with risks, of self-injury, or suffering from epilepsy, for dangerous or psychiatric patients, or newly-born babies, or other children;[191]

(xi)   protect their patients from falls;[192]

(xii)  protect patients from infections and illnesses, and not discharge such persons untimeously;[193]

(xiii) comply with basic organizational rules such as the following of only aseptic procedures, providing and maintaining proper facilities, and operational equipment which are constantly repaired, replaced and/or refilled. Non-compliance will lead to hospital liability;[194] and

(xiv)  provide the best and most modern equipment used only by staff who are trained in its functioning and control it during its op-

---

[187] *Murphy* v. *St Catherine's General Hospital* (1963) 41 DLR 2d 697 (Ont HC). Giesen *International* 65 and footnote 251.

[188] *Jinks* v. *Cardwell* (1987) 39 *CCLT* 168 (Ont HC). *Pallister* v. *Waikato Hospital Bd* [1975] 2 NZLR 725. *Jones* v. *United States* 272F Supp 679, 399 F 2d 936 (2 Cir 1968). Giesen *International* 65–66, and footnotes 252–254.

[189] *Laidlow* v. *Lions Gate Hospital* (1969) 70 WWR 727 (BCSC). *Krujelis* v. *Esdale* [1972] 2 WWR 495 (BCSC). Giesen *International* 66 and footnote 256.

[190] *Bartlett* v. *Children's Hospital Corp.* (1983) 40 NFld & PEIR 88 (Nfld TD). Giesen *International* 66 and footnote 256.

[191] Giesen *International* 66–67.

[192] *Op. cit.* 67.

[193] *Evans* v. *Liverpool Corporation* [1906] 1 KB 160. *Lindsey C C* v. *Marshall* [1936] 2 ALL ER 1076 HL. Giesen *International* 67–68.

[194] Giesen *International* 68.

eration.[195] A hospital has to keep trend with new techniques and developments and may not adhere to old or out-dated procedures. They need not have the 'latest or most modern facilities', but should comply with 'standards which properly prevailed at the time of the injury complained of'.[196]

Failure to comply with organizational standards required by law, resulting in ineffective management or control systems, will thus render a hospital liable.[197] Where a court is, however, satisfied that all arrangements were beyond reproach, no liability would follow for the hospital.[198]

Organizational failure therefore entails that the authority itself is personally at fault for the manner in which it has performed its functions, without having or being able to identify any particular negligent employee.[199] In case of the vicarious liability of the hospital, the hospital has no personal fault at stake. It only takes responsibility for the fault or blameworthiness of someone else. By following the avenue of the direct liability of a hospital, the reputations and status of the employed or engaged staff are protected. In case of vicarious liability their fault could be assumed in stead of exhaustively proved. However, in the case of direct liability this is completely discarded, because the primary liability of the hospital is assumed on account of breach of its own duty.[200]

Justification for imposing direct or corporate hospital liability is to ensure quality health-care and to prevent a substandard in the health-care system as a whole.[201] A proper organizational structure consisting of effective systems in providing competent medical staff, adequate equipment and other necessary means, is the only way to establish such a proficient health-care industry. Consequently, **'unsafe systems of health-care are legally unacceptable'**.[202] Economic considerations always play an important part in the justification of any form of institutional health-care provider or hospital liability. The institutional health facility is far more able, in terms of

---

[195] *Jones* v. *Manchester Corporation* [1952] 2 QB 852. Giesen *International* 68.

[196] *Roe* v. *Minister of Health* [1954] 2 QB 66; [1954] 2 ALL ER 131. Giesen *International* 69.

[197] Giesen *International* 69.

[198] *Ibid.*

[199] Jones *Negligence* 399.

[200] Finch *Law* 95.

[201] Giesen *International* 61.

[202] *Op. cit.* 62.

financial structures and resources, to accommodate any damages than any individual.[203] This applies to direct hospital liability as well.

### 4.3.3 Hospital Liability in Terms of the Non-Delegable Duty

Hospital liability has been expanded by introducing the non-delegable duty to hospital law. This doctrine or legal ground constitutes an independent form of liability. It deserves a sovereign status in the area of the law of torts.[204]

The non-delegable duty can be imposed as a legal ground to establish the employer's (or hospital's or hospital's authority's) liability, for the negligence of an independent contractor. The employer is held liable through no fault of his own, on account of the breach of his own personal non-delegable duty towards patients only. The negligence consists of the malperformance of a delegated duty by an independent contractor, employee or other medical staff from which the employer could not escape or for which he could not delegate his legal responsibility.[205] In both Common Law and Civil Law jurisdictions the non-delegable duty of the hospitals extends not only to the provision of staff, but includes the provision of competent treatment.[206]

At this stage there are no absolute or defined principles which govern the application of this doctrine. However, circumstances in which it is applied, are somewhat fixed.[207]

By analysing distinct features of the non-delegable duty, its independent nature will become clearer when comparing it with other legal grounds or doctrines such as vicarious liability. Although it boasts some similarities to both the indirect and direct liability, its independent status stands.

#### 4.3.3.1 Vicarious liability or not

*Employer liability without personal blame:* The argument has been raised that the non-delegable duty may be some kind of (disguised) form of vicarious liability. According to some authorities 'the doctrine of the non-delegable duty differs both conceptually and practically from vicarious

---

[203] Atiyah *Vicarious* 20, 25–28. Chapman *Medicine* 535.

[204] Whippy 1989 *ALJ* 182, 203.

[205] See also: Jones *Negligence* 399–400. Fleming *Torts* 412–413, 434–435. Kennedy and Grubb *Medical Law* 414–415. Nelson-Jones and Burton *Law* 24. Whippy 1989 *ALJ* 182, 203. Dugdale and Stanton *Negligence* § 22.01 537. Giesen *International* 60.

[206] Giesen *International* 61.

[207] Jones *Negligence* 400.

liability'.[208] The similarities displayed between vicarious (indirect) liability and the non-delegable duty are that in both instances, (i) the employer (hospital/hospital authority) has no personal blame or fault.[209] In both instances, (ii) person(s) in the hospital[210] acted negligently. In case of vicarious liability the employee was negligent and the employee-negligence is then *imputed*[211] to the employer. Whereas in the case of the non-delegable duty, the independent contractor (employee or other medical staff) was negligent. The employer is then held responsible/liable for the contractor's negligence which consists of non-performance of a duty, which occurrence in turn *constitutes* breach of the employer's non-delegable duty of responsibility.[212]

Although both the vicarious liability and the non-delegable duty are occasioned by the employer's liability or responsibility, without any personal fault of the employer, the two doctrines cannot be equated and remain separate grounds for hospital liability. In case of vicarious liability the negligence of the employee is imputed to the employer, and in case of the non-delegable duty the contractor's negligence indicates the occurrence[213] by which the employer's duty is breached.

*Servant-employees and/or independent contractors:* The non-delegable duty is a comprehensive legal ground which eliminates needless judicial minutiae, such as the differentiation between employees and independent contractors as a prerequisite to establish vicarious hospital liability.[214] Under this duty, hospital liability could be established for medical staff including employees and/or independent contractors.[215] Having regard to the English case law and

---

[208]  Whippy 1989 *ALJ* 198. *Kondis* v. *State Transport Authority* (1984) 154 CLR 672 at 688 per Mason J. *Staveley Iron and Chemical Co Ltd* v. *Jones* [1956] AC 627 at 639 per Lord Morton and at 646 per Lord Tucker.

[209]  Fleming *Torts* 409,412. Jones *Negligence* 400: 'In this situation there is no 'personal' fault by the employer'.

[210]  Whippy 1989 *ALJ* 198.

[211]  *Ibid.* Fleming *Torts* 412.

[212]  *Ibid. Cassidy* v. *Ministry of Health* 343 at 362 per Lord Denning. Jones *Negligence* 400: '... it is the employer's primary duty to the plaintiff that is broken.'...'Sometimes referred to as a duty to see that care is taken, as opposed to a duty to exercise reasonable care: ...'.

[213]  Whippy 1989 *ALJ* 198.

[214]  The first and foremost requirement to establish traditional vicarious hospital liability, has been that the negligent performing person had to be an employee before his blame could be imputed to the hospital.

[215]  *Cassidy* v. *Ministry of Health* [1951] 2 KB 343 at 362–363 per Lord Denning. *Roe* v. *Minister of Health* [1954] 2 QB 66 at 82 per Lord Denning. Whippy 1989 *ALJ* 199.

developments there and elsewhere, liability could also be extended to include negligent actions of other medical staff. 'Professional men and women who are to give treatment', house surgeons, resident medical officers, nurses, doctors, surgeons and radiographers have been included in the list of those for whom hospital authorities should take responsibility.[216] Medical student interns, house surgeons, visiting consultants[217] and anaesthetists[218] — irrespective of the basis or terms of performance — have also been added to the list of the non-delegable duty.

In this respect the non-delegable duty differs from the traditional vicarious liability where the latter doctrine only comes into operation where the culprit could be proven to have employee status. In other words, traditional vicarious hospital liability is established only where the negligent act(s) were performed by an employee. Breach of the non-delegable duty could, however, establish hospital liability by the negligent act(s) of a variety of individuals as employees, independent contractors and other medical staff. Where the non-delegable duty is invoked, the control test and organization test will consequently have no relevancy.[219]

*Scope of employment:* This requirement was one of three which was applied to establish traditional vicarious liability. The unlawful act performed by the employee, was required to be within the scope of his employment to render the hospital vicariously liable.

The scope of employment is, according to professor Atiyah, immaterial where the personal duty is invoked, and only an essential element of vicarious liability.[220] Whippy[221] states that this requirement is apparently abandoned in English hospital law, when establishing hospital liability by relying on the breach of the hospital's non-delegable duty. Following this argument, it would appear that the omission of this requirement could

---

Fleming *Torts* 412,413,417. Jones *Negligence* 399–400. Mason J stated the following in *The Commonwealth* v. *Introvigne* (1982) 150 CLR 258 at 270: 'If, as I have indicated, liability on the part of the hospital is for breach of a 'personal' duty to which the hospital authority is subject then the distinction between servant and independent contractor is immaterial'.

[216] *Cassidy* 343 at 362 per Lord Denning.

[217] Whippy 1989 *ALJ* 199. Jones *Negligence* 408.

[218] *Roe* v. *Minister of Health* [1954] 2 QB 66 at 82 per Lord Denning: 'It does not matter whether they are permanent or temporary, resident or visiting, whole-time or part-time. The hospital authorities are responsible for all of them'.

[219] Whippy 1989 *ALJ* 199.

[220] Atiyah *Vicarious* 339. Whippy 1989 *ALJ* 199.

[221] Whippy 1989 *ALJ* 199.

broaden the application of the doctrine and extend the liability of hospitals. The unlawful negligent acts, however, only relate to the medical treatment or care of the patient. Negligence itself, becomes a limiting factor because it occasions a breach of duty only in relation to the medical treatment of the patient. Whippy concludes that consequently there is no basis for the contention that the breach of the non-delegable duty will be upheld by negligent acts which do not directly relate to the medical treatment of the patient,[222] (or would be outside the scope of the perpetrator's employment[223]).

Jones, however, categorically states that the employer is not liable for *acts of collateral negligence* by an independent contractor, in the event of a non-delegable duty being established.[224] He distinguishes between collateral acts as acts which are not performed as delegated work, and acts which are merely a manner of performing the delegated work.[225] Denning LJ also accepted the distinction in *Cassidy* v. *Ministry of Health*. He stated that it was of no importance in that case 'because we are not concerned with any collateral or casual acts of negligence by the staff, but negligence in the treatment itself which it was the employer's duty to provide'.[226] Jones then comes to the conclusion that the employer has no comparable restriction in vicarious liability, 'provided the employee's negligence occurred in the course of employment'.[227]

Having regard to the case law and contemplating the contents of the phrases *collateral or casual acts of negligence* and *acts outside the scope of employment*, one can arrive at no other conclusion than to equate them. Although collateral acts are freely in use and description with the non-delegable duty, and the scope of employment requirement adheres tradition-ally to the vicarious liability, they serve the same purpose i.e. limiting the sphere of hospital liability for only certain relevant negligent acts. In effect, they could be one and the same thing.

### 4.3.3.2 Primary liability or not

*Own primary personal duty:* The non-delegable duty manifests a phenome-non of primary liability in the respect that breach of the primary personal

---

[222] *Ibid.*

[223] My interpretation.

[224] Jones *Negligence* 408.

[225] *Op. cit.* 408 and footnote 85. This distinction was upheld in *Padbury* v. *Holliday & Greenwood Ltd* 1912 28 TLR 494. *Holliday* v. *National Telephone Co* [1899] 2 QB 392.

[226] [1951] 2 KB 343, 365.

[227] Jones *Negligence* 408.

duty which a hospital owes a patient, is breach of its own duty.[228] Negligence incurred by the behaviour of hospital staff is therefore not imputed to the hospital. The hospital derives its liability from breach of its own duty without fault of its own. The duty is not owed by a member of staff to a patient. In this respect, the non-delegable duty is not a vicarious liability.[229]

Vicarious liability centres more on the relationship between the hospital and the employed medical staff. The non-delegable duty concentrates on the relationship between the hospital and the patient.[230]

Two characteristics of the non-delegable duty can be highlighted here: Firstly, the hospital owes a primary personal duty of its own and secondly, it is owed to patients only. Consequently an action for breach of duty will fail, where the plaintiff was not a patient of a hospital at the relevant time.[231]

### 4.3.3.3 Other relevant aspects

4.3.3.3.1 The duty to ensure that care is taken — a strict duty: The non-delegable duty entails that the employer has a primary duty to the plaintiff:

(i)    to ensure that the duty is performed[232] and

(ii)    to be responsible for the manner in which it is performed.[233]

The performance of the duty is delegated to the independent contractor, but the responsibility for the performance and manner of performance remains with the employer.[234]

The hospital complies with this strict duty by ensuring that all medical staff engaged, provide patients with reasonably competent treatment and

---

[228]    According to Lord Denning in *Cassidy* [1951] 2 KB 343 at 360 the hospital has no ears to listen through the stethoscope and could not hold the surgeon's knife; therefore it has to delegate performance of duties to staff. Responsibility could however not be delegated where performance was inadequate. Whippy 1989 *ALJ* 199. Jones *Negligence* 400.

[229]    Whippy 1989 *ALJ* 199. *The Commonwealth* v. *Introvigne* (1982) 150 CLR 258 at 271 per Mason J and at 280 per Brennan J. *Kondis* v. *State Transport Authority* (1984) 154 CLR 672 at 688 per Mason J.

[230]    Whippy 1989 *ALJ* 199. Jones *Negligence* 400,405,406.

[231]    Whippy 1989 *ALJ* 199.

[232]    Fleming *Torts* 413,434. Jones *Negligence* 400. Dugdale and Stanton *Negligence* § 22.02 537. Giesen *International* 60. Kennedy and Grubb *Medical Law* 414–415, however, disagree.

[233]    Jones *Negligence* 400. Fleming *Torts* 434. Dugdale and Stanton *Negligence* § 22.01 537.

[234]    Jones *Negligence* 400.

care.[235] The defence that the hospital had done everything it could reasonably be expected to do by delegating medical duties to experienced, qualified and selected personnel, would then not succeed in case of breach of the non-delegable duty.[236] This stresses the more stringent nature of this duty. If it was only an ordinary duty to exercise reasonable care, such a defence would have been in order.[237] The non-delegable duty thus becomes a stricter duty. This personal duty places the hospital under the responsibility to assure that reasonable care is taken for the patients' safety.[238] There is a universal growing tendency that liability is taken for independent contractors based on 'a more exacting standard of responsibility in view either of exceptional risks or special claims to exceptional protection'.[239]

Mason J typified the non-delegable duty as follows in Kondis's[240] case:

> The principal objection to the concept of personal duty is that it departs from the basic principles of liability in negligence by substituting for the duty to take reasonable care a more stringent duty, a duty to ensure that reasonable care is taken.

It must be kept in mind, however, that every legal system differs concerning the acknowledgement of this duty as well as this specific interpretation thereof. Not every legal system seems eager to accommodate the non-delegable duty and its interpretation of being a strict duty. The differing legal approaches will be discussed separately under every legal system.

---

[235]  Whippy 1989 *ALJ* 200. Fleming *Torts* 413.

[236]  Jones *Negligence* 400. *McDermid* v. *Nash Dredging and Reclamation Co Ltd* [1987] 2 ALL ER 878, 887, per Lord Brandon.

[237]  Whippy 1989 *ALJ* 200.

[238]  Fleming *Torts* 413.

[239]  *Ibid.*

[240]  *Kondis* v. *State Transport Authority* (1984) 154 CLR 672 at 681, 686. See Whippy 1989 *ALJ* 200.

4.3.3.3.2 Doctors employed by patients: If a patient had selected, employed and paid a doctor himself, he would have recourse under the doctrine of vicarious liability if he could prove that the doctor was an employee of the hospital. Under the same circumstances he would, however, have no redress under the non-delegable duty.[241] It applies especially where a patient in a clinic or hospital calls in his own private medical specialist or private doctor.[242]

Denning LJ stated the following in *Roe*:

> It does not matter whether they are permanent or temporary, resident or visiting, whole-time or part-time. The hospital authorities are responsible for all of them. The reason is because even if they are not servants, they are agents of the hospital to give the treatment. The only exception is the case of consultants or anaesthetists selected and employed by the patient himself. 'I went into the matter ... in *Cassidy* ... and I adhere to all I there said.'[243]

4.3.3.3.3 *Res ipsa loquitur*: *Res ipsa loquitur* means 'the thing speaks for itself'. In other words, the fact of the occurrence of the damage itself, is highly suggestive[244] of and raises an inference[245] of negligence. This maxim can be applied in medical negligence cases.[246] Plaintiff-patients can rely on the maxim of *res ipsa loquitor* especially in cases concerning hospitals.[247]

The burden of proof seems impossible when confronted by professional people displaying unknown skills, expertise and techniques and patients who are anaesthetized and cannot testify except to the fact of their own eventual injuries.[248] The plaintiff-patient then relies on *res ipsa loquitur*. Depending on the merit of the circumstances, evidence and explanations, the defendant then begets the onus of disproving[249] such a presumption of negligence. If the

---

[241] *Roe* at 82. This view has been upheld by most courts.

[242] Whippy 1989 *ALJ* 200. According to Whippy at 200, situations where the doctor is under an arrangement with the hospital, or exercises a right of private practice with full use of the hospital's facilities to treat patients, are less clear. See also *Gaynor* v. *Milton and Ulladulla Hospital and Others* (No 245 of 1980) an unreported decision of the New South Wales Court of Appeal.

[243] *Roe* 82; *Cassidy* 362.

[244] Scott *Negligence* 101, 102–107.

[245] Fleming *Torts* 353.

[246] Brazier *Law* 156.

[247] Scott *Negligence* 101.

[248] *Ibid.* Fleming *Torts* 355, 359.

[249] Scott *Negligence* 101, 103.

defendant then does not advance an explanation which displays his exercise of proper care, he could be held liable.[250]

*Res ipsa loquitur* is described by some as a general rule of the law of negligence[251] and by others as a mere aid in the evaluation of evidence.[252] It entails that where the defendant is in complete control of events and an accident occurs which would not occur if proper care had been taken, such an event would be reasonable evidence of negligence.[253] It is basically a question of common sense, projecting that according to life's experience a certain thing sometimes tells its own story.[254]

Actions against hospitals founded on the legal ground of the non-delegable duty, creates a situation under which *res ipsa loquitur* can be applied successfully and evidentiary problems be eliminated.

In the *Hillyer* [255] case, *res ipsa loquitur* was invoked under the vicarious liability. As a result of the fact that the negligent staff comprised of both a servant and an independent contractor, the plaintiff could not recover from either of them individually. Negligence could neither be proven against the hospital authority.[256] The non-delegable duty eludes this problem. Lord Denning gave effect to this reasoning in the *Cassidy* [257] case. He suggested there that it would be an impossible task to prove which particular individual was negligent.[258] He stated on the question of evidence:

> If the plaintiff had to prove that some particular doctor or nurse was negligent, he would not be able to do it. But he was not put to that impossible task.[259]

He further stated that if you went into a hospital with two stiff fingers, but came out with a useless hand, it should not have happened if due care had been used. A *prima facie* case would then have been established against the

---

[250]  Brazier *Law* 156.

[251]  *Ibid.*

[252]  Fleming *Torts* 353.

[253]  Brazier *Law* 156.

[254]  Fleming *Torts* 353.

[255]  [1909] 2 KB 820.

[256]  *Hillyer* 827, 828. See also Whippy 1989 *ALJ* 200. Fleming *Torts* 417. Jones *Negligence* 393.

[257]  [1951] 2 KB 343 at 365–366. See also Whippy 1989 *ALJ* 201. Fleming *Torts* 350–351, 353–356. See also *Lindsay* v. *Mid-Western Health Board* (1991) Irish Times LR 102, 106–107 and *Voller* v. *Portsmouth Corporation* (1947) 203 LTJ 264.

[258]  *Cassidy* 365.

[259]  *Cassidy* 365.

hospital.[260] The authority then had the onus to prove or explain how the tragedy could have occurred without any of its employees being negligent.[261] Somervell LJ relied outright on *res ipsa loquitur* in *Cassidy* and stated:

> ... the result seems to me to raise a case of *res ipsa loquitur*: ...[262]

He also relied on *respondeat superior*,[263] thus invoking vicarious liability.

In *Roe* v. *Minister of Health and Another*,[264] *res ipsa loquitur* was discussed thoroughly, although not even applied. Somervell LJ cited Lord Radcliffe[265] on the following:

> I find nothing more in that maxim than the rule of evidence, of which the essence is that an event which in the ordinary course of things is more likely than not to have been caused by negligence is by itself evidence of negligence.[266]

Denning LJ confirmed:

> I pause to say that once the accident is explained, no question of *res ipsa loquitur* arises ... I do not think that their failure to foresee this was negligence. It is so easy to be wise after the event and to condemn as negligence that which was only misadventure. We ought always to be on our guard against it, especially in cases against hospitals and doctors.[267]

Morris LJ added:

> ... they then said '*res ipsa loquitur*'. But this convenient and succint formula possesses no magic qualities: ... expressed in Latin: ... 'I submit that the facts and circumstances which I have proved establish a *prima facie* case of negligence against the defendant.' It must depend upon all the individual facts and the circumstances of the particular case whether this is so. There are certain

---

[260] *Cassidy* 366. Denning L J stated: 'I am quite clearly of opinion that raises a prima facie case against the hospital authorities.' He did, however, not once explicitly use or refer to the maxim of *res ipsa loquitur*. All that was, however, said and implied by Denning L J refers to nothing else but the application of this maxim.

[261] Brazier *Law* 157.

[262] *Cassidy* 348.

[263] *Cassidy* 351.

[264] [1954] 2 QB 66, at 80.

[265] From *Barkway* v. *South Wales Transport* [1950] AC 185; [1950] 1 ALL ER 392, 403. *Roe* 80.

[266] *Roe* 80. Somervell L J proceeded: 'In medical cases the fact that something has gone wrong is very often not in itself any evidence of negligence. In surgical operations there are inevitably risks. On the other hand, of course, in a case like this, there are points where the onus may shift, where a judge or jury might infer negligence, particularly if available witnesses who could throw light on what happened were not called.'

[267] *Roe* 83.

happenings that do not normally occur in the absence of negligence, and upon proof of these a court will probably hold that there is a case to answer.[268]

It is the private patient that might have a problem. If contracting an independent surgeon and/or anaesthetist who do not operate as staff of a hospital, *res ipsa loquitur* cannot be raised against the hospital. *Res ipsa loquitur* would only be raised against the surgeon and/or anaesthetist if negligence could be pinned on either. And the strategy of 'conspiracy of silence'[269] amongst the brotherhood of medical professionals might then present itself as an immovable obstacle to the plaintiff-patient.

Consequently, relying on *res ipsa loquitur* and alleging breach of the hospital's personal non-delegable duty, can become a facilitating mechanism to ensure success for the plaintiff-patient. This would be the case especially where teams of ordinary and specialized medical staff are involved in the performance of complicated surgery, and it is impossible to single out an individual member as being negligent.[270] The *res ipsa loquitur* doctrine has been applied thus, in many cases.[271]

There is, however, another more contemporary trend concerning the application of *res ipsa loquitur*. If not disallowed, it is applied only sparingly and then only by facilitating the defendants' rebuttal with all kinds of technical strategies.[272] Were the procedural disadvantages of the defendant to be increased, *res ipsa loquitur* could become 'a more effective device for imposing strict liability under the pretence of administering rules of negligence'.[273]

---

[268]  *Roe* 87–88.

[269]  Brazier *Law* 157–158. According to Brazier the plaintiff should then once again resort to the judgment of Denning L J in *Roe* v. *Minister of Health* [1954] 2 QB 66 at 82: '... I do not think that the hospital authorities and (the doctor) can both avoid giving an explanation by the single expedient of throwing responsibility on to the other.

If an injured person shows that one or other or both of two persons injured him, but cannot say which of them it was, then he is not defeated altogether. He can call on each of them for an explanation.' See also Fleming *Torts* 359.

[270]  Whippy 1989 *ALJ* 201.

[271]  *Ibid.* Fleming *Torts* stated at 359 that the doctrine of *res ipsa loquitur* has 'occasionally been invoked even at the cost of distorting its evidentiary basis, in order to advance a distinct policy objective' ... and has been 'used as a straddle between fault and strict liability'.

[272]  Such as those mentioned by Scott *Negligence* 107 by allowing the defendant to prove that they had taken all reasonable care. Fleming *Torts* 359 adds to this the alternative that the defendant should prove that the accident was due to a cause which does not connote negligence on his part.

[273]  Fleming *Torts* 363.

### 4.3.3.4 Justification for imposing the non-delegable duty

There is to date no absolute or standing phrase or principle to denote the possible universal acceptance of or justification for the somewhat irregular application of this duty. In other words, no sound policy has been designed to explain the how, when and why of the non-delegable duty.[274]

Although this duty has been handled critically in Canadian Law,[275] the Australian law[276] has more than accepted this doctrine evolving from English law. American law has equally found ways to accommodate this doctrine.[277]

The most commonly accepted and discussed policy considerations for the implementation of this 'logical fraud' would be the expectations of the plaintiff-patient and consequently that of the community.[278] If a person frequents a place which holds itself out as being a place of safety and which specializes in the provision of health care, it would not suffice to say — in cases of injury — that the perpetrator was contractually insufficiently employed or engaged. Arguments concerning legal niceties such as the differing official appointments would be of no concern to patients and would not negate their injuries. Fact remains, finding a simple justification for the non-delegable duty is far from simple.[279]

---

[274] See also Whippy 1989 *ALJ* 201–203.

[275] *Yepremian* v. *Scarborough General Hospital* (1980) 110 DLR (3d) 513, 532 (Ont. CA) per Arrup J A. He stated: 'In all the circumstances, the hospital *ought* to be liable' — (as a result). He critically considered this to be the case concerning all non-delegable duties, and was therefore not eager to apply it.

[276] *Ellis* v. *Wallsend District Hospital* (1989) 17 NSWLR 553. *The Commonwealth* v. *Introvigne* (1982) 150 CLR 258, 271. *Kondis* v. *State Transport Authority* (1984) 154 CLR 672, 687.

[277] *Infra.* See the discussion on American Law. See also Kennedy and Grubb *Medical Law* 540.

[278] Whippy 1989 *ALJ* 202–203. Atiyah *Vicarious* 335. Jones *Negligence* 408 and footnote 88.

[279] See also Atiyah *Vicarious* 335.

## 4.4  A COMPARATIVE DIAGRAM
## HOSPITAL LIABILITY

| | DIRECT LIABILITY | VICARIOUS LIABILITY | NON-DELEGABLE DUTY |
|---|---|---|---|
| EMPLOYER | Personal fault<br>Employer has fault | No (personal) fault<br>Employer has no fault/blame | No (personal) fault<br>Employer has no fault/blame |
| NEGLIGENCE | By employer<br>Corporate negligence | By employee | By independent contractor (mostly)<br>or employee<br>or other medical staff. |
| INCIDENT | i) Employer/authority liability for independent contractor or another's negligence but breach of own personal duty. Not always possible to identify perpetrator.<br><br>Employer takes blame for own negligence. | i) Employee negligence imputed to employer. | i) Employer / authority responsibility for independent contractor or another's negligence but breach of own personal duty. Not always possible to identify perpetrator. |
| | ii) Employer liability for organizational failure(s) or improper system(s). | ii) Employer responsibility / liability: *respondeat superior* | ii) Employer responsibility / liability: *stricter duty* to ensure. |
| | iii) Employer's direct own personal or corporate duty which necessitates personal performance. | iii) Employee's duty: performance is delegated but not responsibility. | iii) Employer's own personal duty: Performance is delegated but not legal responsibility for it. |
| DUTY | Duty to provide or exercise (reasonable health-care). | Duty to take reasonable care. | Duty to ensure that care is taken. |
| JUSTIFICATION | Mostly monetary / economic considerations. | Economic considerations. | Economic considerations and common sense. |
| LIABILITY | Fault-based liability<br>Corporate/institutional/ direct hospital liability | Strict or faultless liability<br>Vicarious hospital liability | Strict or faultless liability<br>Hospital liability in terms of the non-delegable duty |

SUMMARY

The profound distinction between legal grounds which found hospital liability, merits a simplistic comparison:

- **Direct hospital liability** constitutes a **fault-based** employer liability for organizational failures or improper systems, due to breach of the employer's own direct personal duty which necessitates personal performance, as a result of which the employer is negligent, and consequently directly liable.

- **Indirect or vicarious hospital liability** constitutes a strict or **faultless** employer liability due to breach of the employee's duty to take reasonable care of patients, whose negligence is imputed to the employer, where the employee commits a wrongful act in the course of his employment, for which performance the employer is held vicariously liable.

- **Hospital liability in terms of the non-delegable duty** constitutes a strict or **faultless** employer liability, due to breach of the hospital's own non-delegable duty to ensure that reasonable care is taken by his employees or independent contractors, of which duty performance is delegated but not the responsibility, as a result of which the hospital is rendered liable in terms of a non-delegable duty.

# Chapter 5

# The English Law

## 5.1 HEALTH CARE IN THE UNITED KINGDOM LAND AREA: 130,000 SQ. KM.[1]

### 5.1.2 Health Care System[2]

The NHS (National Health Service) provide the following services:

(i)     Primary Health Care Services, which is inclusive of:

-       General Medical Services
-       Primary Health Care Teams
-       General Dental Services
-       Pharmaceutical Services
-       Ophthalmic Services
-       Chiropody Services

(ii)    Hospital Services, which include:

-       Specialist Care, provided through referral from primary health care
-       Inpatient, outpatient and day patient services

(iii)   Private Health Care which provides:

-       Private Medical practice which is small
-       Outpatient and inpatient care
-       Inpatient care which is provided in private beds in NHS hospitals and private hospitals

---

[1]     Affordable Health Care Singapore 1993: Appendix B Subject 1.

[2]     *Op cit*: Appendix B Subject 10.

### 5.1.3  Health Financing[3]

The NHS provides 97–98% of all health care. The NHS is nationally financed. Income is derived from government taxation (89%), the NHS Insurance Contributions (9%) and charges (2–3%).

## 5.2  INTRODUCTION

The English law will be discussed with regard to the origin of hospital immunity and its development into an expanded field of hospital liability. The discussion on charitable immunity in Chapter 3, not only serves as a highly relevant introductory passage to the liability of hospitals in this legal system, but to every other legal system that will be discussed in this thesis. Relevant legal grounds such as indirect or vicarious liability, direct liability, the non-delegable duty and other relevant doctrines will be considered, concerning the establishment of hospital liability in the English hospital law. Since the English common law founds many legal systems on this topic, the exposition is of prime importance.

When discussing the liability of health institutions in English law, we are concerned firstly with the hospitals or institutions within the National Health Service (NHS). These hospitals and/or providers of medical services fall under a health authority. The authority could be a Health Authority (HA) (a 'directly managed unit').[4] The hospital could also be a NHS Trust hospital. Other authorities include the NHS Trust,[5] Primary Care Trusts,[6] local health

---

[3]   *Op cit:* Appendix B Subject 9. Concerning the hospital and its development in the United Kingdom, you are referred to 3.1 and 3.4.1.

[4]   Health Authorities have replaced District Health Authorities and Family Health Service Authorities in terms of the Health Authorities Act, 1995. Jones *Negligence* 397. Kennedy and Grubb *et al. Principles* 446–448. See also Kennedy and Grubb *Medical Law* 401–402.

[5]   The NHS Trust are increasingly dominating the provision of hospital services. Kennedy and Grubb *Medical Law* 401–402. Kennedy and Grubb *et al. Principles* 446. Markesinis and Deakin *Tort Law* 260–262. Jones *Negligence* 397.

[6]   Created in terms of the Health Act, 1999. Kennedy and Grubb *et al. Principles* 1999 Second Cumulative Supplement § 1.116 7.

authorities,[7] the Secretary of State[8] and private health care institutions.[9] Institutional liability has both legally and practically imposed a financial responsibility on the organisation that provides health care and/or medical services.[10]

### 5.3 INDIRECT OR VICARIOUS LIABILITY

#### Introduction

Indirect or vicarious hospital liability, direct/primary or (corporate) hospital liability and hospital liability in terms of the non-delegable duty, should be acknowledged as three separate, sovereign and independent legal grounds which establish hospital liability, each displaying unique characteristics and requirements for such liability to be successful.

Traditionally, vicarious liability implies the faultless or strict liability of the employer for the negligence of the employee in committing a wrongful act within the course of his employment.[11]

Vicarious liability is both acknowledged and frequently applied in English law.[12] Firstly, vicarious hospital liability will be discussed. English case law which is relevant to hospital liability *in toto* is set out and analysed in detail, with special reference to vicarious hospital liability.

---

[7]  Markesinis and Deakin *Tort Law* 260–262. Kennedy and Grubb *Medical Law* 401–402. Kennedy and Grubb *et al. Principles* 446. Jones *Negligence* 397.

[8]  Kennedy and Grubb *Medical Law* 402: '… in the context of the provisions of services which he has not delegated to any other NHS body.' Kennedy and Grubb *et al. Principles* 467–468.

[9]  Kennedy and Grubb *et al. Principles* 447, 466 on private institutions.

[10]  Kennedy and Grubb *et al. Principles* 447.

[11]  Kennedy and Grubb *et al. Principles* 451–452.

[12]  See the discussion on *Vicarious Liability* § 4.3.1 in Chapter 4 as introductory passage to this discussion. The following authors discuss indirect or vicarious liability in the English Law: Jones *Negligence* 392–399; Kennedy and Grubb *Medical Law* 431–440; Kennedy and Grubb *et al. Principles* 448–456; Finch *Law* 94–96, 81–84; Kennedy *Medical Responsibility* 154–156; Jackson and Powell *Negligence* 490–492; Brazier *Law* 87–89, 142–143; Speller *Hospitals* 253–265; Dugdale and Stanton *Negligence* 537–546. Nelson-Jones and Burton *Law* 20–23; Markesinis and Deakin *Tort Law* 532–557; Brazier and Murphy *Street on Torts* 503–524.

## 5.3.1  English Case Law

1.   1906: *Evans* v. *Liverpool Corporation* [1906] 1 KB 160
2.   1909: *Hillyer* v. *Governors of St. Bartholomew's Hospital* [1909] 2 KB 820
3.   1912: *Foote* v. *Directors of Greenock Hospital* (1912) SC 69
4.   1914: *Davis* v. *London County Council* (1914) 30 TLR 275
5.   1935: *Marshall* v. *Lindsey County Council* [1935] 1 KB 516
        *Lindsey County Council* v. *Marshall* [1936] 2 ALL ER 1076 HL
6.   1938: *Wardell* v. *Kent County Council* [1938] 3 ALL ER 473
7.   1942: *Gold* v. *Essex County Council* [1942] 2 KB 293; [1942] 1 ALL ER 326
8.   1947: *Collins* v. *Hertfordshire County Council* [1947] 1 KB 598; [1947] 1 ALL ER 633
9.   1951: *Cassidy* v. *Ministry of Health* [1951] 2 KB 343; [1951] 1 ALL ER 574 CA
10.  1954: *Roe* v. *Minister of Health* [1954] 2 QB 66; [1954] 2 ALL ER 131
11.  1954: *Razzel* v. *Snowball* (1954) 1 WLR 1382; [1954] 3 ALL ER 439 CA

### 5.3.1.1  English case law discussion

1. The modern history of the liability of English hospitals or English hospital authorities starts with the **Evans v. Liverpool Corporation** [13] case of 1906. One of the Evans' sons contracted a mild attack of scarlet fever upon which he was taken to hospital by ambulance. The Evans boy stayed in hospital for a month and was then taken home. Three other Evans boys developed the same symptoms following their brother's premature discharge from hospital. Mr Evans (the father) sued the Liverpool Corporation for 55 shillings as a result of his expenses due to the early discharge. Walton J decided that the defendant's duty extended only to the provision of reasonably skilled and competent medical staff, and that the plaintiff should therefore not succeed. Since the doctor and matron involved, fell into such required category, plaintiff had no recourse. The judge's ratio for declining the hospital authority's liability, was based on the control test. He found that the corporation could not control the doctor's opinion in any way, and would be wrong if they attempted to do so. The judge's argument — in this case — was not an attempt to protect the hospital authority from any threatening claim, for 55 shillings would not have ruined them. It was based on the application of the control test in finding that

---

[13]   [1906] 1 KB 160. In *Hancke* v. *Hooper* (1835) 7 C & P 81, a surgeon was held liable for the negligence of his apprentice. A surgeon is not liable for the negligence of nurses or other medical staff in carrying out his orders, unless he is personally supervising the treatment: *Perionowsky* v. *Freeman* (1866) 4 F & F 977 (nurses administered excessively hot bath); *Morris* v. *Winsbury-White* [1937] 4 ALL ER 494 (resident medical staff replacing tubes which were originally inserted by the defendant surgeon) Jackson & Powell *Negligence* 490 footnote 49. The modern history is only discussed from 1900.

the hospital authority would not have detected scarlet fever had they examined the infant Evans personally.[14] The court therefore basically found that the hospital was not vicariously liable for the negligence of the doctor-employee in the execution of his professional duties, because the hospital could not control his professional activities. He could therefore not be considered an employee of the hospital.

2. The case of *Hillyer v. Governors of St. Bartholomew's Hospital*[15] followed in 1909. Most writers introduce the modern English history of hospital liability with the discussion of the *Hillyer v. Governors of St. Bartholomew's Hospital*[16] case. Few take cognizance of the *Evans* case,[17] nor realise that the verdict in the latter case was actually followed in the *Hillyer* case. Kennedy LJ actually stated in the *Hillyer* case that 'I am deciding in accordance with the judgement … in … *Evans* v. *Liverpool Corporation* and I entirely concur in the reasoning upon which that judgement is based.'[18]

The facts of the *Hillyer* case are the following: Hillyer was a medical doctor, in need of a detailed medical examination under anaesthetic. He entered the charitable hospital as a non-paying patient. The examination was carried out by medical staff including a consulting surgeon at the defendant's hospital. During the procedure both his arms were allowed to hang over the sides of the operating table. Consequently one arm was burnt and the other badly bruised, as a result of which he suffered traumatic neuritis and paralysis of both arms. His profession as a doctor came to an end. Although he cited three surgeons, an anaesthetist, three certified nurses and two 'box carriers' (theatre orderlies) as persons responsible for the injuries, he was not success-ful. There was no direct evidence of negligence of the hospital staff, and the *Evans* case was followed. The Court of Appeal (Cozens-Hardy MR, Farwell and Kennedy LJJ), dismissed the patient-plaintiff appeal in an action for negligence against the hospital.

Farwell LJ first of all formulated a duty undertaken by the defendants:

> The only duty undertaken by the defendants is to use due care and skill in se-lecting their medical staff.[19]

---

[14] Lee 1979 *ALR* 314–315.

[15] [1909] 2 KB 820 CA.

[16] *Ibid.*

[17] *Supra*; Lee 1979 *ALR* 313–314. Jackson & Powell *Negligence* 490. See also Picard *et al. Liability* 381.

[18] *Hillyer* 830.

[19] *Hillyer* 826: '… a duty arising *ex contractu* — …'

This was also formulated and confirmed by Kennedy LJ. But most impor-
tantly Farwell LJ formulated a passage concerning the employee nurses.
Because this passage has been discussed in almost every case to follow the
*Hillyer* case and by almost every writer, it[20] is quoted:

> But although they are such servants for general purposes, they are not so for the
> purposes of operations and examinations by the medical officers. If and so long
> as they are bound to obey the orders of the defendants, it may well be that they
> are their servants, but as soon as the door of the theatre or operating room has
> closed on them for the purposes of an operation (in which term I include ex-
> amination by the surgeon) they cease to be under the orders of the defendants,
> and are at the disposal and under the sole orders of the operating surgeon until
> the whole operation has been completely finished; the surgeon is for the time
> being supreme, and the defendants cannot interfere with or gainsay his orders.

This dictum was critically examined in *Gold* v. *Essex* and was found to have
no English authority nor any relevance to that case.[21] Lee suggested that after
*Gold*, 'Farwell's judgement that inside the operating theatre the surgeon was
'supreme' was no longer acceptable.'[22]

Kennedy LJ[23] found that a *prima facie* case had been established on the
issue of negligence, while the defendants had admitted that all the persons
cited were in fact their employees. Nevertheless, Kennedy LJ proceeded to
formulate a **legal duty** which the hospital authority undertakes towards
patients which would drastically limit its corresponding liability.[24] Kennedy
LJ, described this legal duty which the hospital authority undertakes towards a
patient who receives the privilege of skilled surgical, medical and nursing aid
within its walls, as 'an inference of law from the facts.'[25] Kennedy LJ in fact
found that the only duty the hospital authority undertakes towards a patient is
the provision of reasonable competent medical staff and proper apparatus and
appliances.[26] He formulated his finding as follows:

> The governors of a public hospital, by their admission of the patient to enjoy in
> the hospital the gratuitous benefit of its care, do, I think, undertake that the pa-
> tient whilst there shall be treated only by experts, whether surgeons, physicians

---

[20]   *Ibid*. This dictum will be discussed in detail in the discussion of *Gold* v. *Essex* [1942] 2 KB
      293, *infra*.

[21]   [1942] 2 KB 293: discussion follows *infra*.

[22]   Lee 1979 *ALR* 321. See also Whippy 1989 *ALJ* 183.

[23]   For a discussion of Kennedy L J's judgment, see my discussion of *Gold* v. *Essex infra*.

[24]   *Hillyer* 829: 'In my view, the duty which the law implies in the relation of the hospital
      authority to a patient and the corresponding liability be limited.'

[25]   *Hillyer* 828.

[26]   *Hillyer* 826. Farwell L J confirmed this duty at 826.

or nurses, of whose professional competence the governors have taken reasonable care to assure themselves; and, further, that those experts shall have at their disposal, for the care and treatment of the patient, fit and proper apparatus and appliances.[27]

Kennedy LJ held further that he could hold the hospital authority liable only for the purely ministerial or administrative duties which the hospital owed its patients. He could not include professional staff and matters of professional care and skill. The reason that the distinction was held to exist between the potential liability for negligently performed administrative acts, but none for negligently performed professional acts, lay in the 'perceived absence of control of the employer over those professional activities.'[28] No liability could be found for professional acts. This incorrect ruling was based on the view that when professional activities were executed by staff, professional judgment was at stake which necessitated the exercise of a discretion, which the hospital authority could not control. Due to this perceived absence of control, the hospital staff ceased to be 'employees' of the hospital.[29] This made the professional staff look more like independent contractors.[30] Kennedy LJ's application of the control test brought about the unsuccessful implementation of vicarious liability in order to found hospital liability.

The application of the 'control' test had once again resulted in artificial reasoning. In modern economic conditions, the control test is no longer considered an adequate determinant of the employer/employee relationship. Employers often do not have the necessary technical expertise, skills or knowledge to supervise and control the judgment of or manner in which skilled employees perform their work. The modern approach to identify the employer/employee relationship or to establish liability ultimately, is to consider various tests and weigh many conflicting factors in order to reach the correct conclusion.[31]

Atiyah[32] and Lee[33] point out that the courts in these cases asked the wrong question, namely:

---

[27]   *Hillyer* 829.

[28]   Picard *et al. Liability* 381. See also Whippy 1989 *ALJ* 182–183.

[29]   Jones *Negligence* 393.

[30]   Osode 1993 *ALR* 295. Chapman 1990 *Osgoode Hall L J* 531. Dickens *Medicine* 531.

[31]   Jones *Negligence* 393. See also Lee 1979 *ALR* 321. The 'control test' is discussed *supra*.

[32]   Atiyah *Vicarious Liability* 88.

[33]   Lee 1979 *ALR* 315–316.

What is the duty of the hospital authority? rather than: Is the hospital authority
vicariously liable for the negligence of its professional staff?[34]

These two grounds can both establish the liability of hospitals when applied
correctly. They have already and should be accepted and developed in order to
determine the hospital authority's liability. By applying these grounds
separately and correctly, they can both ensure the same result. Liability can be
procured by means of applying the law of vicarious liability *or* by applying
the 'concept of duty' required from the hospital,[35] which can constitute direct
liability.

Approximately eighty-five years ago, — as Picard summarizes — a patient
had some recourse against a hospital:

> ...in contract, depending on the terms thereof, or in tort, if the hospital had
> breached its duty to select competent staff and to supply proper equipment, or
> by vicarious liability, subject to the restriction in the *Hillyer* case.[36]

In the light of the fact that charitable hospitals — at this time — were only
frequented by the indigent, and received their service gratuitously, successful
legal action claiming compensation was extremely difficult. The action in
contract could easily fail for lack of intention, uncertainty of terms or lack of
consideration.[37] The action in tort could also fail because consent could be
implied rather easily.[38] Only in the mid-nineteenth century the liability of a
hospital could be established on two main bases, namely a direct duty of care
and vicarious liability. But as Kennedy and Grubb point out these grounds
were carefully controlled in order to afford hospitals maximum immunity to
the suits of patients.[39]

*Hillyer's* case was followed in *Strangeways — Lesmere* v. *Clayton*[40] and in
*Marshall* v. *Lindsey County Council.*[41]

3. The Scottish case of **Foote v. Directors of Greenock Hospital**[42] followed in
1912. Mrs Foote upon leaving a local hotel, broke her thigh bone. She had a

---

[34]  *Ibid.*

[35]  *Infra.*

[36]  Picard 1981 *MGLJ* 997.

[37]  Kennedy and Grubb *Medical Law* 402. Picard *et al. Liability* 1–4, 17–25, 365–366.

[38]  *Ibid.*

[39]  Kennedy and Grubb *Medical Law* 402–404.

[40]  [1936] 2 KB 11. See also Jackson & Powell *Negligence* 491. Whippy 1989 *ALJ* 183,
footnote 3.

[41]  [1935] 1 KB 516. The House of Lords confirmed this decision in 1937 (1937) AC 97.

[42]  1912 SC 69. See also Lee 1979 *AALR* 316.

contract for 'board and medical treatment' for which she paid £2.2s per week. She was however treated only for a sprained knee joint for which she sued the hospital. Two English authorities were once again followed. 'Medical treatment' was considered to mean no more than the supply of competent medical staff.

4. In the **Davis v. London County Council** [43] case of 1914 the London Education Authority was not held liable for the injury suffered by a child under anaesthetic when having had her tonsils removed upon recommendation of the body. Thirty years transpired after this case, before a hospital authority was challenged again.

5. In **Marshall v. Lindsey County Council**,[44] a case of 1935, Mrs Marshall had attended the Cleethorpes Maternity Home. Upon arrival she was admitted unhesitatingly and without warning that there had been an outbreak of puerperal fever. She eventually caught the fever after being admitted to the open ward where it had started. The ward had been disinfected inadequately with the result that a second lady developed fever and later five more patients (including the plaintiff) suffered similar attacks. Mrs Marshall sued and alleged negligence and breach of duty on the part of both the council and the two doctors and matron, for whom the council was responsible.

In *Marshall* v. *Lindsey County Council*, Greer LJ commented on the *Evans* and *Hillyer* cases stating that according to his judgment 'the decision of Walton J in *Evans* v. *Liverpool Corporation* applies to the present case. It was approved in *Hillyer* v. *St. Bartholomew's Hospital* and we are bound to follow it.'[45] The Court of Appeal did however find that the matron had been negligent in not informing the patient of the risk, and found for the plaintiff. In *Lindsey County Council* v. *Marshall* the House of Lords confirmed the matron's negligence.

In the Court of Appeal, Greer LJ found that the doctor had not acted in a purely administrative capacity as defendants tried to argue in order to avoid liability, whereas Lord Wright of the House of Lords, found that it was not necessary to discuss the distinction between administrative and professional duties. The House of Lords did however find by word of Lord Wright, that the appellants had a duty towards Mrs Marshall, breach of which had rendered them negligent and responsible for the patient's subsequent illness.

---

[43]   1914 30 TLR 275. See also Lee 1979 *AALR* 316.

[44]   [1935] 1 KB 516, a Court of Appeal decision subsequently approved by the House of Lords (1937) A C 97.

[45]   [1935] 1 KB 516.

The significance of the House of Lord's ruling in *Lindsey County Council* v. *Mary Marshall* [46] is the following: Their Lordships did not extend the principles enunciated in the *Hillyer* case to the present case since those principles were not applicable to the facts of this case.[47] Differing from the *Hillyer* case, the appellants in the Lindsey case did not provide medical attendance for the respondent nor did the nurses display any lack of skill and care in her attendance. Furthermore, the suitability of the law defined in the Hillyer case was for the first time questioned at the highest judicial level.[48] Viscount Hailsham reminded that the correctness of earlier decisions such as *Hillyer*, concerning the limits of a hospital's liability — could still be reviewed by the House of Lords.[49] To this was added that 'it may be necessary to delimit the frontiers of liability'.[50] In the Marshall case, the plaintiff had ultimately succeeded against the hospital authority with no reference to the vicarious liability rule.

6. It was only in 1938, in the case of ***Wardell* v. *Kent County Council*** [51] that the winds of change began to set in. A fully trained nurse heated a tin of antiphologistine. It exploded and injured her severely. Compensation was claimed under the Workmen's Compensation Act 1925. The County Court Judge however found that she was not a servant of the hospital authority. Fortunately the Court of Appeal — on appeal — ruled that 'she was subject to the rules and regulations of the hospital as to the times of sleeping, meals, recreation and was generally under the control of the matron.[52] The initial decision was therefore reversed and the nurse compensated. As Lee[53] suggests, it was indeed a small step from here for Mr A T Denning K C counsel for the appellants in *Gold* v. *Essex County Council*,[54] to advocate that the relationship of master and servant existed there, as a result of the legal consequences of the *Wardell* decision.

The general principle or English doctrine that was applied in 'hospital liability' cases until 1942, thus maintained that the hospital (authority) could

---

[46]  *Supra.*

[47]  *Lindsey* at 108 per Viscount Hailsham LC, at 114 per Viscount Sankey, and at 125 per Lord Wright M R.

[48]  Whippy 1989 *ALJ* 183.

[49]  *Lindsey County Council* v. *Mary Marshall* at 107.

[50]  *Lindsey* at 114 by Viscount Sankey. Whippy 1989 *ALJ* 183.

[51]  [1938] 3 *ALL* ER 473.

[52]  Slesser LJ is quoted.

[53]  Lee 1979 *ALR* 320.

[54]  [1942] 2 KB 293.

not be held liable for the negligence of its professional staff in the performance of their professional duties. This was based on the charitable conception
that the hospital was a charitable institution for the sick and needy,[55] of which
the financial viability was to be secured at all costs.

Only from 1942, all misleading concepts and unnatural limitations on the
formulation of hospital liability were gradually phased out. In 1942 the first of
the famous English trilogy[56] of cases, was decided.

7. *Gold* v. *Essex County Council* [57] (1942) was a milestone case. The five-
year-old plaintiff had warts on her face for which she consulted a visiting
dermatologist at the public hospital. Oldchurch county hospital was maintained by the defendant county council. The dermatologist prescribed
treatment by Grenz rays. She received the treatment by the hand of a qualified
and competent radiographer who was employed full-time by the defendants,
under a contract of service. The plaintiff was a paying patient. The radiographer was negligent on one occasion, in that he did not cover the child's face
with the required lead-lined rubber cloth but only with a piece of lint. This
resulted in permanent disfigurement which Tucker J described as 'very
unpleasant'. The county council was consequently sued for damages.
Argument for the plaintiff was presented most remarkably by Denning KC.[58]
The council was held vicariously liable for the negligence of the radiographer.

The Court of Appeal — Lord Greene MR, Mac Kinnon LJ and Goddard
LJ — first of all, critically examined the *Hillyer* case. Lord Greene MR
looked at the judgment of Farwell LJ for the real *ratio decidendi*.[59] Two
branches of Farwell LJ's judgment had to be treated as equally authoritative.[60]

---

[55] Carmi *Hospital Law* 7–8. Werthmann *Malpractice* 1. Strauss 1991 *Doctor* 300–301.

[56] The famous English trilogy of cases are *Gold* v. *Essex County Council* [1942] 2 KB 293,
*Cassidy* v. *Ministry of Health* [1951] 2 KB 343 and *Roe* v. *Minister of Health* [1954] 2 QB
66. See Speller *Hospitals* 253–261 on these cases.

[57] (1942) 2 KB 293.

[58] In this case Denning K C most successfully represented the plaintiff. Lord Denning
recollects: 'My clients were so pleased that they presented me with a table lamp for my
room in chambers.' (The Discipline of Law [London 1979] 238): Giesen *International* 52
footnote 125.

[59] *Gold* 298.

[60] *Ibid*: According to Lord Greene M R. According to Whippy 1989 183, 'Their Lordships
were unanimous in the view that the ratio of Hillyer was contained in the judgment of
Farwell L J, which was, as he had explained in a subsequent case, that the plaintiff in
Hillyer had failed to prove negligence against the nurses and other staff.' The writer had
obviously — with respect — no cognisance or had attached little weight to Farwell L J's
first argument as mentioned by both Lord Greene at 298–299 and discussed by MacKinnon
L J at 306–307 and Goddard L J at 310–311. MacKinnon L J in any case by his dictum at

In the first argument he held that the hospital authorities could not as a matter of law be liable for the negligence of anyone present.[61] Secondly he held that in any case it was not shown that the hospital authority or any staff, were responsible for the act of negligence complained of. Farwell LJ in his first argument, found that nurses were only servants of hospital authorities for 'general purposes' but ceased to be so in the operating theatre where they were under the sole orders, control and direction of the surgeon who was supreme there.[62] Lord Greene not only rejected this reasoning, but found it not to extend to the present case.[63] MacKinnon LJ also found that the nurses remained the servants of the hospital in the operating theatre, but that the 'hospital would not be liable for their acts if they were doing, without personal negligence, what the surgeon directed them to do.'[64] This argument had no relevance — according to MacKinnon LJ — to the present case.[65] Goddard LJ also discounted this argument.[66] The Court of Appeal thus found that the dictum of Farwell LJ in *Hillyer* did not in any way oblige them to follow any other path of liability than that which they had decided on. It could not restrict their finding the hospital authority liable *in casu*.

Kennedy LJ's judgment in *Hillyer* was also rejected unanimously by the Court of Appeal.[67] Kennedy LJ had limited the liability of the hospital drastically by describing the only duty it had assumed or responsibility undertaken towards patients, was providing competent medical staff and fit and proper apparatus and appliances. Lord Greene MR found that there

---

306, discounts Whippy's finding of this ratio of Farwell L J, as being the ratio of the *Hillyer* case.

[61]   Gold 298.

[62]   Farwell L J confirmed in *Smith* v. *Martin* [1911] 2 KB 775, 784 (a judgment given two years after *Hillyer*) that the *ratio decidendi* of Hillyer was indeed the second argument referred to by Lord Greene at 298. Of this MacKinnon at 306 in *Gold* v. *Essex* remarked: 'But Farwell L J's summary in *Smith* v. *Martin* is clearly not a correct summary of his own reasoned judgment in *Hillyer's* case;'

[63]   *Gold* v. *Essex*: Lord Greene MR at 299: 'The idea that the same nurse is at one moment a servant of the hospital and at another not in one which, with all respect, I find difficult to understand.'

[64]   MacKinnon LJ at 307.

[65]   Gold 307–308.

[66]   Gold 310–311: He found that Farwell L J's judgment was 'no authority for the proposition that the governing body of a hospital are not liable for the negligence of a servant acting within the scope of his authority, although the negligent act arose during the exercise of the professional skill for which the servant was employed.'

[67]   [1942] 2 KB 293: Lord Greene MR at 300–301, MacKinnon LJ at 307–308, Goddard LJ at 311–312.

existed no English authority for such an argument. He indeed expanded the reasoning considering the obligation undertaken by the hospital and the extent thereof, considerably.[68] Furthermore the unfounded dichotomy created by Kennedy LJ which resulted in a distinction between professional and administrative activities, was also discarded as being 'not merely unworkable in practice but contrary to the plain sense of the position.'[69] The finding that a hospital authority could not be liable for the negligence of staff acting in professional capacity, was thus repudiated. The *Gold* case illustrated that the liability of the employer is not dependent upon the classification of the duties of his servant. In other words legal niceties like distinguishing between professional and administrative duties do not automatically oust principles of liability.[70] By not following the *Hillyer* case, the Court of Appeal in the *Gold* v. *Essex* case, created a wonderful opportunity for the formulation of legal principles founded on logical and rational considerations, on which to establish the ratio of hospital liability.

Examining the appropriate grounds on which a hospital should be found liable, Lord Greene (in *Gold*) made some comments that had far-reaching results for both the English law and other legal systems.[71] His Lordship stated that the basis upon which a hospital's liability is founded, could be determined by the extent of an **obligation** which one person assumes towards another.[72] The obligation assumed could be inferred from the circumstances of each case

---

[68]  *Gold* per Lord Greene MR at 301–304. See also MacKinnon LJ at 307; *Infra.*

[69]  *Gold* 302. Picard *Liability* 313 labels it as 'unworkable and contrary to common sense.' See Gold at 300–303, 307–308, 311–313. See also Whippy 1989 *ALJ* 184–185: He claims that the arbitrary and practically unworkable distinction basically had two objectives in mind namely avoiding a decision that would render the hospital liable and exempting public hospitals from liability on the ground that they were charitable institutions.

[70]  Such as the principle of *respondeat superior.*

[71]  Lord Greene's comments were followed in later English decisions and were influential in the development of Australian Law, Canadian Law, South African Law and American Law. He was quoted at great length by Hilbery J in *Collins* at 616–618 and referred to at 614–616.

[72]  [1942] 2 KB 293 at 301–302. It was described as follows that: 'the first task is to discover the extent of the obligation assumed by the person whom it is sought to make liable. Once this is discovered, it follows of necessity that the person accused of a breach of the obligation cannot escape liability because he has employed another person, whether a servant or agent, to discharge it on his behalf, and this is equally true whether or not the obligation involves the use of skill. It is also true that, if the obligation is undertaken by a corporation, or a body of trustees or governors, they cannot escape liability for its breach, any more that can an individual, and it is no answer to say that the obligation is one which on the face of it they could never perform themselves. Nor can it make any difference that the obligation is assumed gratuitously by a person, body or corporation which does not act for profit ... .'

such as the hospital's organization, medical staff, equipment and the nature of the statutory powers under which the defendant hospital was maintained.[73] His Lordship came to the conclusion that he could draw no other inference than that the obligation assumed by the hospital, was to treat the patient by the hand of the alleged negligent radiographer with the apparatus provided. This was according to him a natural and reasonable inference to draw from the defendant's method of conducting their affairs and the nature of the radiographer's engagement.[74]

According to both MacKinnon LJ and Goddard LJ the hospital authority was vicariously liable for the negligence of the radiographer.[75] MacKinnon LJ discussed the principles of *respondeat superior* and applied them to the case, finding for the plaintiff.[76] Goddard also stated that the superior will be liable for the acts of the servant or agent on the doctrine of *respondeat superior*.[77] Goddard LJ found that the radiographer had been employed under a contract of service and was therefore an employee of the hospital.[78] A distinction had been drawn between those employed under a 'contract for services' and a 'contract of service' in which case the hospital authority would only be held liable for the negligent acts of the latter group.[79] Goddard LJ further considered that the doctors employed under a contract of service, could render the hospital liable in the case of negligence. Visiting surgeons and physicians were, however, considered to be employed under a contract for services.[80]

Another remarkable finding of the court involved their questioning and discounting of the 'control test' which is used to determine the legal relationship between employer and staff in order to impose liability on a health or

---

[73]  *Gold* at 302–304: 'Once the extent of the obligation is determined the ordinary principles of liability for the acts of servants or agents must be applied.'

[74]  *Gold* 303.

[75]  *Gold* 305, 312.

[76]  *Gold* 304–305.

[77]  *Gold* 312: 'If he does that which he promises or professes by a servant or agent, he is liable for their acts on the doctrine of *respondeat superior*. Otherwise it is difficult to see how any corporate body could ever be liable for the acts of their servants.'

[78]  *Gold* Goddard L J at 310–311.

[79]  *Ibid.*

[80]  *Gold* 310 and 313: '... I am not considering the case of doctors on the permanent staff of the hospital. Whether the authority would be liable for their negligence depends, in my opinion, on whether there is a contract of service, and that must depend on the facts of any particular case.'

hospital authority.[81] This was done by way of their findings and the examples by means of which they illustrated their findings.

It was accentuated by Morris LJ in *Roe* at 89 that Greene MR had initiated the 'organization test' in *Gold* at 302. Morris LJ consequently applied the test in *Roe*. This test is favoured to the control test and can also found the (vicarious) liability of a hospital.

To summarize, the Court of Appeal in the case of *Gold*, found the hospital authority liable for the negligently performed professional act of a radiographer: MacKinnon LJ and Goddard LJ discussed the doctrine of *respondeat superior* and consequently found the authority vicariously liable for the radiographer, who was employed under a contract of service and consequently an employee of the hospital. Although the control test was in effect discounted — which in effect delimits the hospital's liability — another test which required the distinction between a 'contract of service' and a 'contract for service', was now employed in order to limit the employer's liability. Greene MR invented the obligation on which he founded the hospital's liability.

## Conclusion on Gold

The most important development was the invention of the obligation as legal ground to found hospital liability by Greene MR. Denning LJ[82] stated the following concerning the dictum of Lord Greene MR in *Gold's* case:

> He made the liability depend on what was the obligation which rested on the hospital authorities. He showed that hospital authorities were under an obligation to use reasonable care in treatment; ... that they cannot get rid of that obligation by delegating it to someone else, not even to a doctor or surgeon under contract for services.

The obligation was formulated as legal basis to establish hospital liability. The extent of this obligation was to be inferred from the circumstances (facts). The only question that remained was on which ground this principle was indeed founded.

When considering the following passages one can easily reach more than one conclusion:

(i)  'Once this is discovered, it follows of necessity that the person accused of a breach of the obligation cannot escape liability because he has employed another person **whether a servant or agent**, to discharge it on his behalf, and this is equally true whether or not the obligation in-

---

[81]  *Gold* 299, 305–307, 310–313. Osode 1993 *ALR* 296. Dickens *Medicine* 531.
[82]  *Cassidy* 364.

volves the use of skill.' '... They cannot escape liability ...' (My accentuation) (*Gold* at 301.)

(ii)    'Once the extent of the obligation is determined the **ordinary principles of liability** for the acts of **servants or agents** must be applied.' (My accentuation) (*Gold* at 302.)

(iii)   'If they exercise that power, the obligation which they undertake is an obligation to treat, and they are **liable** if the **persons employed** by them to perform the obligation on their behalf act without due care. I am unable to see how a body invested with such a power and to all appearance exercising it, can be said to be assuming no greater obligation than to provide a skilled person and proper appliances.' (My accentuation) (*Gold* at 304.)

The dictum by Greene MR in *Gold* can either constitute or be based on:

-    Vicarious liability which transcends the traditional limited liability which requires an employer-employee relationship but now includes the possibility of vicarious hospital liability for agents or independent contractors. This seems even more probable in the light of his possible introduction of the organization test at *Gold* 302.[83] See the exposition of Morris LJ in *Roe* 89 on the organization test where he quotes Greene MR in *Gold* 302. Morris applies this test in his exposition of vicarious liability.

-    Direct corporate liability which is founded by the obligation (duty) which is separately and directly owed to the patient by the hospital.

-    The obligation which evolved into the non-delegable duty which dogmatically can establish hospital liability and should preferably be seen as an independent legal ground which founds hospital liability. The obligation (non-delegable duty) can found a liability for both servants and agents.

Finally, the *dicta* in *Gold* established a hospital liability which is founded on indirect/vicarious liability and/or direct liability or the non-delegable duty. Hospital liability is thus achieved by introducing the relevant criteria or legal principles, which apply to either indirect or direct hospital liability, or the non-delegable duty as an independent legal ground.

---

[83]   See the exposition of Morris LJ in *Roe* 89 on the organization test where he quotes Greene MR in *Gold* 302.

8. In ***Collins* v. *Hertfordshire County Council and Another***[84] (1947) a patient died in the Wellhouse Hospital after being injected by the visiting surgeon with a mixture containing a lethal dose of cocaine. He believed he injected a harmless local anaesthetic containing procaine which he had ordered by telephone from the junior house surgeon. The latter was not yet a qualified medical practitioner, although she had already passed a final pharmacology examination. She was in temporary but full-time employment of the hospital and the visiting surgeon accepted an appointment as employee of the staff. Both were on the hospital's pay list.

Concerning the vicarious liability of the hospital for the negligent acts of the junior surgeon, visiting surgeon and pharmacist, Hilbery J pondered on the distinction between 'contracts for services' and 'contracts of services' — as formulated in *Gold* v. *Essex*. It was again applied and discussed *in casu*.[85] The court, however, came to the conclusion that the hospital authorities could not in any way control how the visiting surgeon was to perform his duties. The hospital could, however, direct the junior house surgeon what to do and how to do it.[86] Consequently the hospital authority was held vicariously liable for the negligently performed professional acts of the resident junior house surgeon. The hospital authority was not held vicariously responsible for the conduct of the visiting surgeon who was engaged on similar written terms (temporary but part-time) to the resident junior houseman.[87] The court also stated that the pharmacist was 'certainly and most clearly' negligent.[88]

The only conclusion one can come to when reading the judgment of Hilbery J, is that he tried to but could not apply the test of 'contract of service' and 'contract for service' correctly. The conclusion Hilbery J had reached is indeed strange in the light of his willingness to adhere to the ratio of *Gold* v. *Essex*,[89] but can be ascribed to his incorrect application of the 'control test' in order to enforce the 'contract for/of services' test. The liability of the hospital authority for the houseman but not the visiting surgeon, also seems artificial and without any logical foundation. The further application of the now outdated 'control test' was totally inappropriate. As Lee mentions, it is easy to

---

[84]  [1947] 1 KB 598, 614–620; per Hilbery J. See also: Lee 1979 *ALR* 321; Jones *Negligence* 394; Jackson & Powell *Negligence* 491.

[85]  *Collins* 609, 615, 618–619.

[86]  *Collins* 619.

[87]  *Collins* 620: 'In the circumstances, while I think that the hospital was vicariously responsible for Miss Knight's acts of negligence or negligent omissions in the course of the performance of her duties, the same does not apply to Mr Hunt.'

[88]  *Collins* 620.

[89]  See Hilbery J's quotations of and references to *Gold* v. *Essex* at 614–618.

criticize the 1947 decision in later years, but the control test would certainly 'falter in almost every industrial situation in the light of the vast technological changes which have taken place since 1947.'[90] The unacceptability of the 'control test' is discussed in detail *supra*.

Hilbery J also dealt with the direct liability of the hospital, in addition to the hospital's vicarious responsibility. He found the hospital directly liable as a result of its own improper, negligent system to provide dangerous drugs. This is discussed in the following section on the direct liability of hospitals in English case law.[91]

9. *Cassidy* v. *Ministry of Health*[92] (1951): This case was one of the most important English authorities on hospital liability, which affected all modern developments of law in this field. The facts were as follows: The plaintiff, a general labourer suffered from a contraction of the third and fourth fingers on his left hand, which his doctor diagnosed as Dupuytren's contraction. Dr Fahrni, a full-time (employee) medical officer at the hospital, confirmed the diagnosis and recommended and performed an operation. After the operation, the patient's arm and hand was in a splint for 14 days. When the splint was removed, his left hand was useless. After two unsuccessful manipulative operations, all attempts to remedy the condition were abandoned. The plaintiff alleged negligence during his post-operative treatment. During this time he was under the care of Dr Fahrni, Dr Ronaldson, a house surgeon and hospital nursing staff. The trial judge dismissed the action for damages against the hospital, on the ground that he had failed to prove any negligence in treatment. The Court of Appeal unanimously allowed the appeal (Somervell, Singleton and Denning LJJ). This became the first English case in which the hospital became liable for the negligence of an employee doctor and house surgeon.[93]

The judgments of Somervell and Singleton LJJ were quite similar. Somervell LJ[94] found that both the doctors had contracts of service with the hospital authority. They were employed like the nurses as part of the permanent medical staff. He found that the execution of their professional skills did not oust the principle of *respondeat superior*. After carefully examining the distinction between 'a contract for services' and 'a contract of services' as set

---

[90]　Lee 1979 *ALR* 321. See also Jones *Negligence* 393–394.

[91]　*Infra* at 5.3.1.

[92]　[1951] 2 KB 343. See also Taylor *Malpractice* 47.

[93]　See also Whippy 1989 *ALJ* 185.

[94]　*Cassidy* 351.

out in *Simmens* v. *Heath Laundry Co*,[95] *Yewens* v. *Noakes* [96] and *Gold* v. *Essex*,[97] he concluded that the medical staff *in casu* had contracts of service. This was to be decided as a question of fact by all the circumstances of the case.[98] He also found that the result seemed to raise a case of *res ipsa loquitur*.[99] He concluded by finding the defendants vicariously liable and allowing the appeal.[100]

Singleton LJ found that those responsible for the post-operational treatment were all full-time employees of the Liverpool Corporation — which was the hospital authority at the time of Mr Cassidy's treatment.[101] He did not find it necessary to establish precisely which individual employee was negligent.[102] He quite unhesitatingly ruled that the hospital had been negligent in that it had not met an **obligation** 'to provide the plaintiff with competent, or proper, post-operational treatment.[103] He arrived at the following conclusions:[104]

(i) The plaintiff's *prima facie* case had not been displaced.

(ii) Negligence existed in regard to the post-operational treatment.

(iii) It was impossible to say that the 'negligence was the negligence of any particular individual: it may be that a number of people were at fault, or that lack of system was the cause.' He furthermore found that everything was under the control of the hospital authorities, and those concerned (*in casu*) were in the employ of the corporation.

(iv) Responsibility lay with the defendants or the Ministry, whether the negligence was that of Dr Fahrni, Dr Ronaldson or of the nursing staff. Accordingly Singleton LJ found the hospital liable and allowed the appeal.

Singleton LJ's conclusion in (iii) played with both the direct liability and vicarious liability of the hospital. Emphasizing the 'control' of the hospital,

---

[95] [1910] 1 KB 543.

[96] (1880) 6 QBD 530, 532.

[97] [1942] 2 KB 293.

[98] *Cassidy* 353.

[99] *Cassidy* 348.

[100] Whippy 1989 *ALJ* 187; Lee 1979 *ALR* 322.

[101] *Cassidy* 354–355.

[102] *Cassidy* 355, 359: He added that 'Everything was under the control of the hospital authorities, and those immediately concerned were in the employ of the corporation.'

[103] *Cassidy* 357, 359.

[104] *Cassidy* 359.

implicates the control test which directs whether professionals are employees or independent contractors of the hospital, once again implicating vicarious liability. Finding that the negligence would have been that of one or more people or *lack of system*, implicates the direct liability of the hospital. We shall deal with this in section 5.3.1 on English case law and direct liability. Making use of all relevant concepts, he indeed arrived at the hospital's liability without pinpointing it on either vicarious or direct liability.

Denning LJ's judgment was by far the most important dictum ever delivered on hospital liability and had far-reaching results. Firstly the hospital authorities' duty of care in the treatment of their patients was described unambiguously. This duty was purported to involve the use of reasonable care and skill to cure patients of their ailments. Once the task was undertaken, they came under a duty to use care in so doing, whether they did it for reward or not. Lord Denning stated that this duty remained unconditional and irrespective of whether the patient paid directly, indirectly, through insurance companies or paid nothing at all, and was treated out of charity.[105] This could be interpreted as extending the liability of the hospital.[106]

His Lordship then proceeded with a rational consideration of grounds on which the hospital's liability could be founded.[107] He stated that the hospital authorities would remain liable for the negligent acts of professional men and women. The skill of persons who protest to 'tolerate no interference by their lay masters in the way they do their work' and who 'take no orders from anybody' would in no way aide the authorities from escaping liability. The reason for their liability was not due to the fact that they could control the way in which the work is done. He stated that the employer more often did not even have sufficient knowledge to do so. He thereby not only discarded the control test but refrained from being drawn into an employee or independent contractor debate, which resulted from the control test.[108] According to

---

[105]  *Cassidy* 359–360. Denning L J delivered a most remarkable passage at 360: 'In my opinion authorities who run a hospital, be they local authorities, government boards, or any other corporation, are in law under the selfsame duty as the humblest doctor; whenever they accept a patient for treatment, they must use reasonable care and skill to cure him of his ailment. The hospital authorities cannot, of course, do it by themselves: they have no ears to listen through the stethoscope, and no hands to hold the surgeon's knife. They must do it by the staff which they employ, and if their staff are negligent in giving the treatment, they are just as liable for that negligence as is anyone else who employs others to do his duties for him … Once they undertake the task, they come under a duty to use care in the doing of it, and that is so whether they do it for reward of not.'

[106]  See the discussion in 5.3.1 on the possible implications of this part of his judgment.

[107]  *Cassidy* 360.

[108]  *Ibid.* See also Whippy 1989 *ALJ* 185.

Whippy[109] Lord Denning was the only member of the Court who rejected the control test outright, because he found the distinction between employees and independent contractors to be irrelevant. Denning LJ did find that the hospital authority would be liable for their professional medical staff by undertaking a task and assuming a duty because 'they employ the staff and have chosen them for the task and have in their hands the ultimate sanction for good conduct, the power of dismissal'.[110] This discussion of Denning LJ in *Cassidy* at 360 implies that he:

(i) either excluded vicarious liability (as ground for his judgment) and introduced another ground such as direct liability;

(ii) or wished to introduce other more reasonable requirements for the application of vicarious liability, such as the power to employ and dismiss;

(iii) or introduced new grounds together with the non-delegable duty which could found hospital liability.[111]

The case of *Hillyer* was then critically examined. The judgment of Kennedy LJ in *Hillyer* had brought about the following: For over thirty years '— from 1909 to 1942 — it was the general opinion of the profession that hospital authorities were not liable for the negligence of their staff in the course of their professional duties.'[112] His Lordship considered this judgment as 'undoubtedly an error' which was due to the desire to relieve charitable hospitals — relying on voluntary contributions — from liabilities which they could not afford.[113] Farwell LJ's judgment was also discounted by his remarking that because hospital authorities employ nurses, pay them and nurses are liable to be dismissed by them there was 'no doubt now that nurses remain the servants of the hospital authorities, even when they are under the directions of the surgeon in the operating theatre.'[114]

---

[109] Whippy 1989 *ALJ* 187. See also his footnote 36. See also Osode 1993 *ALR* 297.

[110] Lord Denning in *Cassidy* at 360. According to Whippy 1989 *ALJ* 187 this finding could result in the introduction of the so-called 'organisation test' which poses the question whether the prospective servant was part of the employer's business or organization. Vicarious liability could thus follow even where the traditional 'control test' was not applied. (See also footnote 36.)

[111] The purpose of (the extent of) the non-delegable duty, is to make the hospital liable for independent contractors.

[112] *Cassidy* 360.

[113] *Cassidy* 361.

[114] *Cassidy* 361.

Denning LJ then dealt with the distinction that Goddard LJ had created in *Gold* in order to establish the hospital's liability. The latter had distinguished between 'contracts for services' and 'contracts of services'. This distinction was discounted by Denning LJ with the following statement:

> It does not depend on whether the contract under which he was employed was a contract of service or a contract for services. That is a fine distinction which is sometimes of importance; but not in cases such as the present, where the hospital authorities are themselves under a duty to use care in treating the patient. … But the liability of the hospital authorities should not, and does not, depend on nice considerations of that sort.[115]

He again emphasized on 364:

> Hence the courts have drifted almost unconsciously into the error of making the liability of hospital authorities depend on whether the negligent person was employed under a contract of service or a contract for services.[116]

According to Denning LJ, 'the only time the distinction between a contract of service and a contract for service becomes of importance, is 'when it is sought to make the employer liable, not for a breach of his own duty of care, but for some collateral act of negligence of those whom he employs.'[117] Speller states that concerning this dicta of Denning LJ it may be relevant — in a case concerning vicarious liability — to discern whether the actual wrongdoer was an employee or an agent, if the wrongdoing was in some collateral matter.[118] When perusing *Cassidy* 365 where Denning LJ explicitly illustrates such cases as meant or described in the last quote, it becomes obvious that Lord Denning was only trying to eliminate cases, which would traditionally not qualify as accommodating acts falling within the scope of employment. In other words where acts transpire by independent contractors or agents which are not within the scope of employment, liability will not follow.

Logical and reasonable criteria were recommended in order to establish the principles of the law of hospital liability: Denning found that the liability of the hospital for doctors should depend on the question: Who employed the

---

[115] *Cassidy* 362–363, 365.

[116] Kennedy *Medical Responsibility* 155 however stated that he courts still draw this distinction whereby the 'contract of service' 'which is regarded as the classic employment contract' can establish vicarious liability, and the 'contract for services' 'whereby a person is regarded as an independent contractor' cancels any possibility of vicarious liability.

[117] *Cassidy* 364. He follows: 'He cannot escape the consequences of a breach of his own duty, but he can escape responsibility for collateral or casual acts of negligence if he can show that the negligent person was employed, not under a contract of service, but only under a contract for services.'

[118] Speller *Hospitals* 253.

doctor or surgeon — is it the patient or the hospital authorities?[119] Consequently if the patient had selected and employed the doctor, the hospital authorities would not be liable for his negligence. Had the doctor — being a consultant or not — been employed and paid by the hospital authorities and not the patient, the former would be liable for the negligence of the doctor in treating the patient. In other words where the patient **selects, employs and pays** the doctor, the hospital will not be liable. Where the hospital selects and pays the doctor, the hospital will be liable.

Denning LJ also stated that the hospital will be liable for their medical staff because they not only employ (choose) them, but may dismiss them.[120] As Dickens remarks, we see that 'Denning LJ's 'power of dismissal' serves to imply hospital liability as much for the misconduct of physicians who are independent contractors as for the acts of employees in some kind of master-servant relation.'[121] He pleads for a systematic account of the grounds for vicarious liability and indeed expansion of vicarious hospital liability, but without depending on the problematic distinction between independent contractors and employees.[122] This test of Denning could be seen to introduce the so-called organization test in stead of the control test in order to establish hospital liability. His Lordship then clearly formulated the non-delegable duty as a new basis for founding the liability of a hospital or hospital authority. This concept is discussed in 5.4.

Having found that the *prima facie* case against the hospital authorities had not been displaced, the appeal was allowed, by their Lordships.[123]

**Conclusion on Cassidy**
Somervell LJ found the Ministry responsible and consequently vicariously liable. He considered the principle of *respondeat superior* and concluded that

---

[119] Denning L J in *Cassidy* at 362: 'I think it depends on this: who **employs** the doctor or surgeon — is it the patient or the hospital authorities? If the patient himself selects and employs the doctor or surgeon, as in Hillyer's case (66), the hospital authorities are of course not liable for his negligence, because he is not employed by them. But where the doctor or surgeon, be he a consultant or not, is employed and paid, not by the patient but by the hospital authorities, I am of the opinion that the hospital authorities are liable for his negligence in treating the patient.' This was confirmed in *Roe* at 82.

[120] Denning LJ in *Cassidy* at 360: 'The reason why the employers are liable in such cases is not because they can control the way in which the work is done — they often have not sufficient knowledge to do so — but because they **employ** the staff and have chosen them for the task and have in their hands the ultimate sanction for good conduct, the power of dismissal.'

[121] Dickens *Medicine* 65.

[122] *Ibid.*

[123] *Cassidy* 366, 359, 353.

the medical staff had contracts of service. The judgment of Singleton LJ centred on the dictum of Green MR in *Gold* and thus emphasized the 'obligation' of the hospital authorities. Singleton LJ referred to the obligation as the 'responsibility' of the corporation. He stressed that all those concerned were employees and that the corporation was in control of everything. It is, however, not perfectly clear or declared whether he founded his judgment exclusively on either indirect or direct liability. It is also not clear whether the whole concept of the obligation or non-delegable duty was meant to be founded on either indirect or direct liability or was introduced as a sovereign legal ground. Denning LJ discarded the control test and the distinction between contracts for service and contracts of service. He employed the test concerning 'the power to select, employ, pay and dismiss' instead.[124] He paid exceptional attention to the non-delegable duty which the hospital authority owed the patient, which founded the hospital liability.

It could, however, be concluded that Denning LJ founded his judgment on the non-delegable duty as an independent legal ground in order to establish hospital liability, supported by logical and rational considerations of legal consequence.

10. *Roe v. Minister of Health* [125] (1954) was the last in the trilogy of English decisions. Two patients underwent minor operations on the same day. Both received a spinal anaesthetic, nupercaine, which was injected by the specialist anaesthetist, Dr Graham, assisted by theatre staff of the hospital. Both patients developed severe symptoms of spastic paraplegia after the operations. This resulted in permanent paralysis from the waist down. The nupercaine had been contained in sealed glass ampoules, which were stored in a solution of phenol. The primary judge had found that the paralysis was caused by phenol that had percolated into the ampoules through invisible cracks or molecular flaws. The two anaesthetists worked part-time, had private anaesthetic practices, but were under obligation to provide regular services to the hospital. The plaintiffs brought actions for personal injuries against the Minister, as successor in title to the trustees of the hospital, and against Dr Graham.

The Court of Appeal (Somervell LJ, Denning LJ and Morris LJ), unanimously found that Dr Graham was not negligent and exonerated him from any liability.[126] This was due to the fact that at that time a competent anaesthetist could not have foreseen the risk that phenol could permeate the nupercaine

---

[124] His formulation of this test could be regarded as introducing the so-called organization test, which could theoretically implicate vicarious liability.

[125] [1954] 2 QB 66.

[126] *Roe* 77–79, 87, 91–93.

ampoules through invisible cracks, nor was he personally aware of a precautionary tinting technique which would have disclosed any dangerous percolation.[127]

Somervell LJ held that if negligence had been proved, he would have found the hospital vicariously liable.[128] After making specific reference to the principle of *respondeat superior*[129] he concluded that the hospital would be responsible for Dr Graham and the nursing staff.[130] He regarded both the anaesthetists as 'part of the permanent staff, and, therefore, in the same position as the orthopaedic surgeon in *Cassidy's* case.'[131]

Denning LJ also held that the hospital authority would have been liable if negligence had been proved. They would have been considered responsible for the whole of the staff, not only for the nurses and doctors, but also for the anaesthetists and the surgeons. He further stated that:

> It does not matter whether they are permanent or temporary, resident or visiting, whole-time or part-time. The hospital authorities are responsible for all of them. The reason is because, even if they are not servants, they are the agents of the hospital to give the treatment.

The only exception would be the case of consultants or anaesthetists selected and employed by the patient himself.[132] His Lordship stated that he furthermore adhered to all he had said in *Cassidy*. He could not find the hospital authority liable, since every misadventure could not be condemned as negligence.[133] Liability could not be imposed for everything that goes wrong,[134] and *res ipsa loquitur* could not be invoked.[135]

Denning LJ gave a summary of crucial questions to be answered in every case:

(i) 'The first question in every case is whether there was a **duty** of care owed to the plaintiff; and the test of duty depends, without doubt on what you should foresee.'[136] (My accentuation)

---

127 *Roe* 83–86. See also Whippy 1989 *ALJ* 187.

128 *Roe* 80.

129 *Roe* 76.

130 *Roe* 80–81.

131 *Roe* 79–80.

132 *Roe* 82.

133 *Roe* 87.

134 *Roe* 86.

135 *Roe* 83, 87–88.

136 *Roe* 84.

(ii)     'The second question is whether the neglect of duty was a 'cause' of the injury in the proper sense of that term; and **causation**, as well as duty, often depends on what you should foresee.'[137] (My accentuation)

(iii)    The third question, **remoteness** of damage, comes into play only when the first two questions — duty and causation — are answered in favour of the plaintiff. The extent of the liability is found by asking: 'Is the consequence fairly to be regarded as within the risk created by the negligence?'[138] (My accentuation)

'Instead of asking three questions ... in many cases it would be ... better to ask the one question: is the consequence within the risk?'[139]

Morris LJ first concluded that Dr Graham was a servant or agent of the hospital.[140] Lord Morris greatly relied on Lord Greene's formulation of the hospital's obligation (non-delegable duty) in the *Gold* case.[141] He confirmed it and found that the hospital had *in casu* undertaken the obligation of anaesthetizing the patients. The hospital's obligations were to be decided on the circumstances of each particular case.[142] He invoked the 'organization test', finding that Dr Graham was a member of the 'organization' of the hospital and engaged to do what the hospital had undertaken to do.[143] The professional skill of Dr Graham did not avoid the application of the rule of *respondeat superior*. Ultimately he held that if negligence could be established, it would not matter if the exact person or persons could not be pointed out in that regard. The hospital authority would have been liable.[144] The appeal was accordingly dismissed by their Lordships.

The following could be inferred from this case: According to Somervell LJ and Morris LJ vicarious liability could follow irrespective of the fact that hospital staff were servants (employees) or independent contractors. The liability of hospitals was not dependent on peculiarities in the nature of the contractual relationship between the hospital and the staff[145] of which the patients in any case were totally ignorant. Since the anaesthetist was not an

---

[137]  *Roe* 84–85.

[138]  *Roe* 85.

[139]  *Roe* 85.

[140]  *Roe* 88.

[141]  *Roe* 88–90.

[142]  *Roe* 88.

[143]  *Roe* 89, 91.

[144]  *Roe* 91.

[145]  Osode 1994 *ALR* 297.

employee contracted under a contract of service, the hospital's potential vicarious liability represented the court's abandonment of the 'control test'. Vicarious liability once depended on the employer being able to control the job to be done and how it should be done. Liability could follow here with the absolute lack of control in that respect. This signalled the negation of the outdated 'control test'.[146] Most importantly Morris LJ incorporated the obligation or non-delegable duty into his exposition of and in defining the extent of vicarious liability.[147]

Conclusively, three different approaches could one again lead to the same result, i.e. hospital liability. But, because negligence had not been proven or found, breach of the hospital's duty could not be constituted.[148]

11. *Razzel* v. *Snowball* [149] (1954) finally dispelled all doubts concerning the liability of hospital authorities for visiting consultants and part-time surgeons. Mr Snowball, a part-time surgeon was found to be an acting servant or agent of the Minister of Health. He needed to prove this in order to gain protection under section 21(1) of the Limitation Act 1939 (now repealed).[150] Three judges held that he fell within this category. Denning LJ denoted his place in the hierarchy of hospital staff as follows:

> He is a senior member of the staff but nevertheless just as much a member of the staff as the house surgeon.[151]

The hospital authority was consequently held responsible to provide treatment under the National Health Service Act 1946 and was responsible for the acts and omissions of those by whom treatment was given.[152]

The National Health Service had introduced 'NHS indemnity', which in terms of HC (89) 34 render NHS hospital authorities vicariously liable also for consultants and agency staff.[153] Health authorities within the NHS then do not argue that certain persons are employees when engaged in NHS work.[154]

---

[146]  Kennedy *Medical Responsibility* 155.

[147]  See also Whippy 1989 *ALJ* 188.

[148]  *Op. cit.* 188–189.

[149]  (1954) 1 WLR 1382.

[150]  Jackson & Powell *Negligence* 491–492.

[151]  *Op. cit.* 1386.

[152]  See also Kennedy and Grubb *Medical Law* 432–433.

[153]  See also Jones *Negligence* 396–397.

[154]  *Ibid.*

The courts will, however, still be faced with issues of *respondeat superior* when dealing with the dynamic private sector, outside the NHS.[155]

### 5.3.2 Conclusion

The *dicta* in the English case law, have manifested various reasonable and logical criteria which can be employed in order to establish the liability of hospitals or hospital authorities. Selected instances will be highlighted.

In the *Hillyer* case, Kennedy LJ worked with the 'perceived absence of control' test, as a result of which vicarious liability was unsuccessfully implemented to establish hospital liability. He also accommodated and most importantly initiated a legal duty which was no more than an inference of law from the facts, to establish hospital liability. It concerned the provision of skilled staff and proper appliances.

The initiation of the 'legal duty' by Kennedy LJ in the *Hillyer* case, led to the formulation or construction of the 'obligation' by Greene MR in the *Gold* case and the eventual '(non-delegable) duty' by Denning LJ in the *Cassidy* case. These constructions can dogmatically be classified as the doctrine of either indirect or direct hospital liability or it can be classified as an independent legal ground implemented to found hospital liability. The latter perspective is preferred.

In the *Gold* case, Greene MR developed the legal duty of Kennedy LJ into a more sophisticated 'obligation' (which could not be delegated in order to escape liability), to found hospital liability. Denning KC at that time represented the plaintiff.

In the *Cassidy* case, Denning LJ formulated the non-delegable duty required of hospitals or hospital authorities. This was a spontaneous evolution of the legal duty of Greene MR which Denning LJ acknowledged and gave full credit to.

In the *Roe* case, Morris LJ accommodated the non-delegable duty in his effort to find the hospital vicariously liable.

Most of the *dicta* delivered, were clearly founded on vicarious liability, making use of or criticizing criteria akin to this legal ground of hospital liability. Other *dicta* such as those mentioned above did not clearly state their foundations as being direct or indirect liability. They could also have established new independent or sovereign grounds of liability.

Conclusively, whatever the constructions or principles applied, it was done in order to found hospital liability. In other words, hospital liability can be

---

[155] Kennedy and Grubb *Medical Law* 433.

established on various grounds or in many ways. The ultimate goal remains: The establishment of responsibility for and the legal liability of hospitals or hospital authorities in a legally responsible way.

### 5.3.3 Private Medical Care

The proprietors of a private hospital or private nursing home, or where incorporated, the appropriate incorporated body, are vicariously liable for the negligence of the medical staff they employ.[156]

Where a patient is treated privately, the hospital can still be sued where the doctor or other staff acted negligently as employees of the health care provider. Where the patient has, however, contracted directly and individually with the doctor, who is not an employee of the hospital, the patient must sue the doctor individually.[157] The hospital will then not be liable for the doctor's negligence. If, however, the hospital holds the doctor out to the patient as an employee, the hospital could be liable.[158] Where the patient contracts directly with the hospital a non-delegable duty can sometimes be construed based on the hospital's undertaking to provide treatment, with ensuing liability.[159] If the hospital only provides facilities for use by independent contractor doctors who have 'admissions privileges', the hospital will not be vicariously liable nor become liable as a result of an (undelegable) duty, when the patient selects and employs the doctor.[160]

Some private hospitals and clinics do contract to provide 'a whole package of care and treatment.' If the hospital undertakes to provide total care, (the operation, anaesthetic, post-operative care, etc.) then failure to adhere to a required standard of care can constitute a breach of contract. The hospital can

---

[156] Kennedy *Medical Responsibility* 157. Lewis *Negligence* 179. Kennedy and Grubb *et al. Principles* 455–456, 466.

[157] Jones *Negligence* 398–399. Lewis *Negligence* 179. Brazier *Law* 88.

[158] Jones *Negligence* 398. See also his footnote 32 on 398; E.g. *Rogers* v. *Night Riders* [1983] RTR 324, CA: Where the minicab hire firm was held accountable under a non-delegable duty regarding the safety of vehicles. The drivers were independent contractors. This is also in accordance with the modern trends of medical law in the USA. Kennedy and Grubb *et al. Principles* 455, 466.

[159] Jones *Negligence* 398. Kennedy and Grubb *et al. Principles* 455–456, 488.

[160] *Ibid.* In *Roe* v. *Minister of Health* [1954] 2 QB 66, 89, Morris LJ made the following remark: 'While the requisite standard of care does not vary according to whether treatment is gratuitous or on payment, the existence of arrangements entitling the plaintiffs to expect certain treatment might be a relevant factor when considering the extent of the obligation assumed by the hospital.' Kennedy and Grubb *et al. Principles* 455, 466 and footnote 161.

also incur a direct or primary liability in tort according to Kennedy and Grubb.[161] The status of the surgeon, anaesthetist, or anyone else then becomes irrelevant.[162]

The hospital may even — in this instance — owe the patient a non-delegable duty of care, and thus become liable for the negligence of the non-employee doctor.[163] This can be illustrated as follows: In *Powell* v. *Streatham Manor Nursing Home* [164] two nurses had inserted a catheter which punctured the patient's bladder. The nursing home was held vicariously liable for the negligence of the two employed nurses. However, in the case of *Urry* v. *Bierer and Another* [165] the following transpired: The patient suffered injury when a swab was left in his body after an operation. He then sued his surgeon and the proprietors of the private nursing home. Because the patient had a separate contractual arrangement with the doctor who had medical privileges at the nursing home or hospital, vicarious liability could not ensue for the surgeon. Both the surgeon and the theatre nurse, (the latter was employed by the nursing home), were found to have been negligent. Consequently the surgeon was made personally liable for half of the damages and the proprietor was made vicariously liable for the other half.[166]

### 5.3.4 The General Practitioner

Health Authorities make provision for 'personal medical services' to those for whom they are responsible, in terms of a statutory duty. General practitioners provide patients with primary care on behalf of the Health Authorities.[167] General practitioners are therefore not the employees of the Health Authorities and (formerly the Family Health Service Authorities).[168] They are still

---

[161] Brazier *Law* 88–89: 'It is directly responsible for its own breach of contract.' This constitutes a confusion of legal grounds, with respect. 'Breach of contract' and 'direct liability' of hospitals should be distinguished as do Kennedy and Grubb *et al. Principles* at 456, 466.

[162] Brazier *Law* 88–89. It will not matter whether they are employees or independent contractors.

[163] Kennedy and Grubb *et al. Principles* 456.

[164] (1935) AC 243.

[165] *The Times*, July 15, 1955. Kennedy *Medical Responsibility* 157.

[166] Kennedy *Medical Responsibility* 157.

[167] Kennedy and Grubb *et al. Principles* 453–454 and footnote 63 and the 1999 Second Cumulative Supplement § 8.10 42.

[168] Health Authorities Act 1995, s 1. Jones *Negligence* 397–398 and footnote 29. According to Kennedy and Grubb *et al. Principles* 454, 488 and the 1999 Second Cumulative Supple-

independent contractors.[169] Consequently, a Health Authority can not be held vicariously liable for the negligence of such a general practitioner.[170] The individual general practitioner will therefore have to be pursued in case of a claim for negligence against the doctor.[171]

Liability, other than personal liability, can be established in terms of the Partnership Act, 1890 where a general practitioner works in a group with other general practitioners.[172] Where the group is a partnership in law, then the partnership, as a legal entity, can be held (vicariously[173]) liable[174] for any negligence in the performance of any of the individual partners' duties.[175] Each of the partners may also be jointly and severally liable for the negligence of the other partners.[176] If the general practitioner or his partnership employs staff (e.g. receptionists, nurses, physiotherapists), then the partnership can be vicariously liable as employers, for the negligent performance of duties by the employees.[177]

It is likely that a *locum tenens* or deputising doctor will be classified as an independent contractor.[178] The general practitioner will therefore not be

---

ment § 8.10 42: GPs may, however, be the employees of (i) other GPs (together with other health professionals) under a 'pilot scheme' or (ii) an NHS Trust, creating a potential vicarious liability for the employer. Where NHS employees or junior medical staff have a NHS contract of employment — even attending private patients in NHS hospitals — the hospital will be vicariously liable for their negligence, with consequential responsibility for the Health Authority or NHS. Where a GP has contract of employment with a health authority or NHS Trust, NHS indemnity applies, when treatment is given under that contract.

[169] Kennedy and Grubb *et al. Principles* 454. Kennedy *Medical Responsibility* 156; Lewis *Negligence* 179. Brazier *Law* 89. Jones *Negligence* 397–398 and footnote 29; The relationship is contractual: *Roe* v. *Kensington and Chelsea and Westminster Family Practitioner Committee* (1990) 1 Med. LR 328. Compare *Kapfunde* v. *Abbey National* (1998) 45 BMLR 176 (CA): The GP working for a company was considered an independent contractor.

[170] *Supra* footnote 168. Kennedy *Medical Responsibility* 156–157. Nelson-Jones and Burton *Law* 20. Kennedy and Grubb *et al. Principles* 454.

[171] Jones *Negligence* 397–398.

[172] Kennedy *Medical Responsibility* 157. Kennedy and Grubb *et al. Principles* 454.

[173] Kennedy *Medical Responsibility* 157.

[174] Brazier *Law* 89. Kennedy and Grubb *et al. Principles* 454.

[175] Kennedy and Grubb *et al. Principles* 454. Kennedy *Medical Responsibility* 157.

[176] Kennedy and Grubb *et al. Principles* 454. Brazier *Law* 89.

[177] Kennedy *Medical Responsibility* 157. Jones *Negligence* 398. Brazier *Law* 89. Mason and McCall Smith 1987 *Encyclopaedia* 582. Kennedy and Grubb *et al. Principles* 454.

[178] This would depend on the agreement between the locum and the doctor. The contract could be one of employment or one of an independent contractor. In *Rothwell* v. *Raes* (1988) 54 DLR (4th) 193 262 (Ont HC), the independence of the locum's professional judgment was

vicariously liable for the negligent acts of locums and deputies.[179] It is also unlikely that the general practitioner will be burdened with an undelegable duty regarding the negligence of a locum.[180] The general practitioner may, however, incur liability by failing to select a competent locum or deputising service, failing to check the latter's qualifications, standard of service, professional background and his professional indemnity insurance.[181]

### 5.3.5  The Health Authorities: Appropriate Defendants

Under the National Health Service (Primary Care) Act 1977, s 1, the Secretary of State — under a duty — provides England and Wales (to such an extent as he considers necessary to meet all reasonable requirements) with a comprehensive health service: hospital and similar accommodation; medical, dental, nursing and ambulance services; other related facilities for the prevention and treatment of illness.[182] Health authorities have been entrusted and delegated the local administration of these services.[183] These authorities (rather than the Secretary of State) should be sued for acts negligently performed by hospital staff.[184]

Under the National Health Service and Community Care Act 1990, section 5, the Secretary of State may set up NHS trusts, in order to own and manage hospitals or other facilities formerly managed or provided by health authorities. Under section 4 of the 1990 Act, a health service body can (e.g. a health authority or NHS trust) contract with another health service body to provide the latter with goods or services. The provider health service body will then be directly liable to the patient, in case of negligence. Furthermore the acquiring

---

in fact confirmed, to that effect. See also Jones *Negligence* 398 and footnote 31. Kennedy and Grubb *et al. Principles* 455.

[179]  Brazier *Law* 89. Kennedy and Grubb *et al. Principles* 455.

[180]  Jones *Negligence* 398. Lewis *Negligence* 174, 179, however, refers to *Hancke* v. *Hooper* (1835) 7 C & P 81, where a physician was held liable for the apprentice's negligence, and consequently states that the G P would be the appropriate defendant where he engages a locum who performs negligently. Kennedy and Grubb *et al. Principles* 455.

[181]  Brazier *Law* 89–90. Kennedy and Grubb *et al. Principles* 455.

[182]  See also Jackson and Powell *Negligence* 493. Kennedy and Grubb *et al. Principles* 467. Section 3(1) of the same Act imposes the duty to provide certain services.

[183]  Jackson and Powell *Negligence* 493. Kennedy and Grubb *et al. Principles* 467.

[184]  Jackson and Powell *Negligence* 493. National Health Service Act 1977, Sched. 5, par 15(1). Kennedy and Grubb *et al. Principles* 468.

authority can be liable when placing a contract which does not provide for an adequate standard of treatment.[185]

It is the general rule — that in case of negligent NHS treatment in a hospital or — when a NHS hospital is sued, that the appropriate defendant will be the Health Authority.[186] If the hospital is not within the Health Authority's remit, the hospital itself will be the correct defendant. For example, when dealing with NHS Trust hospitals, the hospital itself should be sued.[187] Many institutions and health care services are now NHS Trusts, in which case the NHS Trust is the correct defendant.[188] If a claim rises out of the conduct of a service, such as the ambulance service, the authority that operates the service, will be the appropriate defendant.[189]

The liability of the NHS hospital authorities could be vicarious for the negligently performed acts of the employees.[190] Where it is difficult to precisely ascertain which member of the medical team is responsible for the negligent conduct, it facilitates to sue the employer who is responsible for the acts of the whole team.[191] It could also be a direct primary liability for failing to provide an adequate system of care and competent staff.[192] Where the health authority undertakes to provide reasonable, careful, competent and skilled care and treatment, the authority or hospital will not only be vicariously liable but directly responsible to the patient.[193]

Hospital doctors are by contract required to be insured. They are insured with one of the medical defence organisations: for example the Medical Defence Union or the Medical Protection Society.[194] Hospitals do not,

---

[185] Jackson and Powell *Negligence* 494: 'The NHS contract itself does not give rise to any contractual rights or liabilities'. See the discussion on this aspect under 5.3 direct liability: *NHS and its contracts*. This incurs primary or direct liability. Kennedy and Grubb *Medical Law* 429–430.

[186] This applies to NHS hospitals under the financial control of an HA (a 'directly managed unit'): Jones *Negligence* 397. Kennedy and Grubb *et al. Principles* 446. Brazier *Law* 87. Lewis *Negligence* 177.

[187] Jones *Negligence* 397. Kennedy and Grubb *et al. Principles* 446.

[188] *Ibid.*

[189] Jones *Negligence* 397.

[190] Jones *Negligence* 396–397, such as consultants. Kennedy and Grubb *et al. Principles* 452–453.Brazier *Law* 87.

[191] Nelson-Jones and Burton *Law* 20. Markesinis and Deakin *Tort Law* 262.

[192] Brazier *Law* 87.

[193] *Ibid*; See Lord Denning's judgment in *Cassidy*.

[194] Kennedy and Grubb *et al. Principles* 448. Markesinis and Deakin *Tort Law* 262. Nelson-Jones and Burton *Law* 20. Finch *Law* 97.

however, require many paramedical practitioners and most nurses to be insured. The plaintiff can sue both the health authority and any named doctor.[195] The benefit — in some circumstances — for adding the doctor as defendant, is that suing two parties who are both good for damages can increase the prospects of a settlement. On the other hand the doctor can be offended at putting his reputation at risk and decide to defend.[196] Lewis feels strongly on the point that the doctor should not be added as defendant where it is clear that the health authority is liable for the negligence of the doctor. It not only facilitates proceedings but can also for example prevent the destruction of a young doctor's career.[197] If, however, the danger does exist that the defence may profit unduly — in any way — from not listing the doctor as defendant, he may be listed as defendant only after discovery and interrogatories are concluded. Then a deal can be struck with the defence to drop the doctor without paying his costs.[198]

One employee can not be held vicariously liable for the acts of another employee. A consultant will not be vicariously liable for the acts of his registrars.[199] Nursing staff, nowadays, remain the employees of the hospital. Surgeons do not usually employ nurses in the ward or in the operating theatre. Where nurses negligently carry out instructions — that they have been given with regard to patient treatment — surgeons will not be liable.[200] Where nurses act under instructions of a surgeon or doctor, the hospital will only escape liability not because '*pro hac vice* she ceases to be the servant of the hospital, but that she is not guilty of negligence if she carries out the orders of the surgeon or doctor, however negligent those orders may be.'[201]

---

[195] Nelson-Jones and Burton *Law* 20. Finch *Law* 97. Mason and McCall Smith 1987 *Encyclopaedia* 582.

[196] Nelson-Jones and Burton *Law* 20. See Finch *Law* 95, 97 concerning valued reputations. Problems concerning status or reputations of doctors can be avoided by treating this liability rather as the direct or primary liability of hospitals. Mason and McCall Smith 1987 *Encyclopaedia* 582.

[197] Lewis *Negligence* 177–178.

[198] *Idem* 178.

[199] *Rosen* v. *Edgar* 1986 302. See also Nelson-Jones and Burton *Law* at 20.

[200] Jones *Negligence* 397.

[201] *Gold* v. *Essex Country Council* [1942] 2 KB 293, 299 per Lord Greene MR. *Johnston* v. *Wellesley Hospital* (1970) 17 DLR (3d) 139, 152 (Ont. HC). Goddard LJ at [1942] 2 KB 293, 313 did, however, stipulate that the nurse does not necessarily act with reasonable care by mechanically following a doctor's orders. If a nurse receives an instruction that was obviously incorrect, the nurse would have a duty to seek confirmation from the doctor. See also Jones *Negligence* 397 and footnote 28.

## 5.4 Direct or Primary or Corporate Hospital Liability[202]

### Introduction

English case law, relevant to direct or corporate hospital liability, will be discussed. A hospital or hospital authority can be directly liable where **organizational failures** occur which result in negligence.[203] Actions were formulated thus, to achieve the liability of hospitals where professional staff were involved. This overcame the historic argument that the hospital could not be vicariously liable for the negligence of professional staff,[204] performing professional duties. In this case the hospital is itself at fault for failing to perform its functions or duties properly[205] by means of professional people or staff. It might even be impossible to identify any (one) individual who was negligent.[206] The primary liability of a hospital can be construed by analysing the extent of the duty of a hospital to provide the patient with a reasonable regime of care through good administration, adequate and competent staff, effective systems, adequate materials and proper supervision.

Direct hospital liability is part of English law.[207] It constitutes a fault-based employer liability, due to the breach of the employer's own personal direct duty to provide reasonable health care, rendering the employer negligent and therefore directly liable.

---

[202] See the discussion on Direct Liability in § 4.3.2 Chapter 4 as introductory passage to this exposition. The following authors discuss direct (hospital) liability in English law: Kennedy and Grubb *Medical Law* 402–431; Kennedy and Grubb *et al. Principles* 456–472 and 1999 Second Cumulative Supplement § 8.14 42–43; Jones *Negligence* 392, 399–405; Jackson and Powell *Negligence* 492–493; Dugdale and Stanton *Negligence* § 22.04 538 (very briefly) explicitly recognize direct or primary hospital liability, in the English law.

[203] Jones *Negligence* 399, 400–405. Kennedy and Grubb *et al. Principles* 456–460.

[204] Jones *Negligence* 392–393, 400.

[205] *Op. cit.* 399. Kennedy and Grubb *et al. Principles* 458.

[206] *Ibid.*

[207] Kennedy and Grubb *Medical Law* 413 and 414.

## 5.4.1  English Case Law

### *Miscellaneous*

1.  1842: *McLoughlin* v. *Pryor* (1842) 4 M & G 48
2.  1853: *Ellis* v. *Sheffield Gas Consumers Co* (1853) 2 E & B 767
3.  1916: *Pinn* v. *Rew* (1916) 32 TLR 451
4.  1948: *Bernier* v. *Sisters of Service* [1948] 2 DLR 468 (Alta SC)
5.  1937: *Lindsey County Council* v. *Marshall* [1937] AC 97
6.  1969: *Laidlow* v. *Lions Gate Hospital* (1969) 8 DLR (3d) 730 (BCSC)
7.  1971: *Krujelis* v. *Esdale* (1971) 25 DLR (3d) 557 (BCSC)
8.  1980: *Denton* v. *South West Thames Regional Health Authority* (1980) unreported QBD
9.  1984: *Bergen* v. *Sturgeon General Hospital* (1984) 28 CCLT 155 (Alta QB)
10. 1985: *Blyth* v. *Bloomsbury Health Authority* (1985) (unreported) QBD 1987 (CA)
11. 1988: *D & F Estates Ltd* v. *Church Commissioners for England* [1988] 2 ALL ER 992
12. 1991: *Johnstone* v. *Bloomsbury Health Authority* [1991] 2 All ER 293
13. 1997: *Robertson* v. *Nottingham HA* [1997] 8 Med LR 1
14. 1999: *Kent* v. *London Ambulance Service* [1999] Lloyd's Rep Med 58 (CA)

### *Cases discussed*

### *Direct hospital liability*

1.  1947: *Collins* v. *Hertfordshire County Council and Another* [1947] 1 KB 589
2.  1951: *Cassidy* v. *Ministry of Health* [1951] 2 KB 343
3.  1952: *Jones* v. *Manchester Corporation and Others* [1952] 2 QB 852 [1952] 2 ALL ER 125 (CA)
4.  1986: *Wilsher* v. *Essex Area Heath Authority* [1987] 1 QB 730 [1986] 3 ALL ER 801 (CA)
5.  1993: *Bull* v. *Devon Area Health Authority* 1989 (unreported) (CA) [1993] 4 Med LR 117 (CA)

### *Allocation of resources*

1.  1980: *R* v. *Secretary of State for Social Services, Ex parte Hincks* (1980) 1 BMLR 93 (CA)
2.  1987: *R* v. *Central Birmingham Health Authority, Ex parte Walker* (1987) 3 BMLR 32
3.  1988: *R* v. *Central Birmingham Health Authority, Ex parte Collier* 6 January 1988 unreported (CA)
4.  1997: *R* v. *North Derbyshire HA, Ex parte Fisher* [1997] 8 Med LR 327

5.  1990: *Re HIV Haemophiliac Litigation* [1990] 140 NLJR 1349 (CA)
6.  1995: *Danns* v. *Department of Health* (1995) 25 BMLR 121

### 5.4.1.1 English case law discussion

The direct liability of a hospital may exist in various circumstances: The hospital will be primarily liable:

(i) Where it does not establish adequate procedures to safeguard patients from cross-infection.[208]

(ii) For having failed to provide an adequate number of staff to care for patients.[209]

(iii) Where it has no system to check the safety of equipment.[210]

(iv) For having failed to enforce its own rules and regulations, for example to keep accurate records and notes.[211]

(v) Where the duty to inform and warn patients about the side-effects of drugs is not accommodated in an effective system.[212]

(vi) Where no effective communications systems exist or are in place.[213]

(vii) Having an ambulance service, accepting a call for such service, but failing a prompt or effective response service to such call.[214]

Direct personal liability will prevail for the negligent acts of an independent contractor:[215]

---

[208] *Lindsey County Council* v. *Marshall* [1937] AC 97. Jones *Negligence* 401 and footnote 48.

[209] *Laidlaw* v. *Lions Gate Hospital* (1969) 8 DLR (3d) 730 (BCSC). *Krujelis* v. *Esdale* (1971) 25 DLR (3d) 557 (BCSC). *Johnstone* v. *Bloomsbury Health Authority* [1991] 2 ALL ER 293. *Pinn* v. *Rew* (1916) 32 TLR 451. Jones *Negligence* 401–402 and footnote 53. Kennedy and Grubb *et al. Principles* 457–459.

[210] *Denton* v. *South West Thames Regional Health Authority* (1980) unreported QBD. Jones *Negligence* 401 and footnote 46.

[211] *Bergen* v. *Sturgeon General Hospital* (1984) 28 CCLT 155 (Alta QB). *Bernier* v. *Sisters of Service* [1948] 2 DLR 468 (Alta SC). Jones *Negligence* 401 and footnote 52.

[212] *Blyth* v. *Bloomsbury Health Authority* [1993] 4 Med LR 151 CA. Jones *Negligence* 401 and footnote 49.

[213] *Robertson* v. *Nottingham HA* [1997] 8 Med LR 1, 13. In this case Brooke LJ effectively distinguished between the vicarious liability and the direct liability of the health authority. Kennedy and Grubb *et al. Principles* 458–459.

[214] *Kent* v. *London Ambulance Service* [1999] Lloyd's Rep Med 58 (CA). Kennedy and Grubb *et al. Principles* 1999 Second Cumulative Supplement § 8.14 42–43.

[215] Jones *Negligence* 399–400.

(i)     Where the person or institution ratifies or authorizes the tort.[216]

(ii)    Where the person or institution is negligent in selecting an incompetent contractor.[217]

(iii)   Where there is interference with the manner in which the work is done, which results in damage.[218]

(iv)   Where work which is done in a foreseeable dangerous fashion with (possible) resulting negligence, is condoned.[219]

1. *In* **Collins v. Hertfordshire County Council and Another** [220] (1947) the direct liability of the hospital was expounded. The negligence in the management and control of the hospital was found to be the cause of action.[221] The negligence of the hospital was contained in their system of administrating drugs, which was described as being 'utterly defective and dangerous'.[222] No adequate procedures had been established to safeguard patients from the risk of errors in providing dangerous drugs.[223] The hospital had regulations, which had never been implemented or had never come to the knowledge of the junior medical officer. This consisted of certain requirements in the 'Routine Procedures', which expressly required written prescriptions initialled by a qualified person.[224] The hospital was therefore held directly or primarily liable for having a negligent system in the provision of dangerous drugs.[225] Proper and effective systems will consequently exclude the possibility of hospital liability.

---

[216]  *Ellis* v. *Sheffield Gas Consumer Co* (1853) 2 E & B 767. Jones *Negligence* 399.

[217]  *Pinn* v. *Rew* (1916) 32 TLR 451. Jones *Negligence* 399.

[218]  *McLoughlin* v. *Pryor* (1842) 4 M & G 48. Jones *Negligence* 399–400.

[219]  *D & F Estates Ltd* v. *Church Commissioners for England* [1988] 2 ALL ER 992, 1008. Jones *Negligence* 400.

[220]  [1947] 1 KB 598. See the discussion in 5.2.1 on this case. It contains an exposition of the facts and vicarious liability of the hospital.

[221]  *Collins* 622, 624: '… there was negligence on the part of the hospital, …'. Hilbery J gave judgment for the plaintiff against each of the defendants at 622: 'Each of the defendants is responsible, because each was guilty of what the law calls negligence, that is to say, a failure to exercise reasonable skill and care in the treatment of the patient, Collins, with the result that Collins died.'

[222]  *Collins* 608.

[223]  Jones *Negligence* 401 and footnote 49.

[224]  *Collins* 608–609. See also Jones *Negligence* 401 footnote 49.

[225]  Jackson and Powell *Negligence* 492. Kennedy *Medical Responsibility* 156. Mason & McCall Smith 1987 *Encyclopaedia* 582. Jones *Negligence* 401.

2. In ***Cassidy* v. *Ministry of Health***[226] (1951) Singleton LJ first touched on direct liability — knowingly or unknowingly — when referring to the obligation of the hospital in providing competent, proper, post-operational treatment to the patient, and later in coming to the conclusion that *lack of system* could have been the cause of negligence (involving any number of people). The lack of system implied the primary or direct liability of the hospital, for failing to have safe and effective procedures concerning the post-operational care of a patient *in casu*.

However, where it becomes impossible to establish whether:

(i)   the system was inadequate or ineffective and/or

(ii)   whether any number of individuals had been negligent in implementing (an adequate) system, it has 'the effect of blurring the distinction between the hospital's primary liability for organizational errors and vicarious liability'.[227]

The whole of Singleton LJ's summary of conclusions on 359, exactly displayed the latter global finding.[228] His whole judgment centred on concepts that include findings of direct and vicarious liability and even included the non-delegable duty when referring to the obligation of the hospital. It illustrates the flexibility in establishing the liability of a hospital, making use of all relevant concepts, although it might become a bit confusing to some.

Denning LJ's judgment in this case, had also extended the direct or primary liability of the hospital or Health Authority, substantially. He stated:

> In my opinion authorities who run a hospital, be they local authorities, government boards, or any other corporation, are in law under the selfsame duty as the humblest doctor; whenever they accept a patient for treatment, they must use reasonable care and skill to cure him of his ailment. The hospital authorities cannot, of course, do it by themselves: they have no ears to listen through the stethoscope, and no hands to hold the surgeon's knife. They must do it by the staff which they employ; and if their staff are negligent in giving the treatment, they are just as liable for that negligence as is anyone else who employs others to do his duties for him. What possible difference in law, I ask, can there be between hospital authorities who accept a patient for treatment, and railway or shipping authorities who accept a passenger for carriage? None whatever. Once they undertake the task they come under a duty to use care in the doing of it, and that is so whether they do it for reward or not.[229]

---

[226] [1951] 2 KB 343. For the exposition of facts and its principles of vicarious liability see 5.2.1.

[227] Jones *Negligence* 401 footnote 51.

[228] Refer to the discussion in 5.2.1 on the *Cassidy* case.

[229] *Cassidy* 360.

His statement has the following implications:[230]

Direct liability can result from

(i)     bad administration, unsafe systems of work, dangerous and ineffective procedures, and organizational errors in the hospital

(ii)    negligent behaviour or performance by hospital staff

(iii)   lack of resources where proper treatment was not provided

(iv)    provision of staff or doctors without sufficient skill and experience[231]

(v)     bad management and control by the hospital, hospital board, or health authority.[232]

3. In *Jones v. Manchester Corporation and Others* [233] (1952) the patient was accepted at Ancoats Hospital with first degree burns on his face and neck. After having first anaesthetized the patient with gas by means of a mask over his face, the impracticality dawned on the house surgeon in charge, Dr Sejrup. He had been qualified for two years. It was then decided to remove the mask and give the patient a further anaesthetic by injecting pentothal. This was done by Dr Wilkes, who had five months' experience. Ten cubic centimetres pentothal was then administered — in addition to the gas first administered. This was a normal dose of pentothal for a patient not under another anaesthetic. The patient died. The plaintiff, the widow, claimed damages against the hospital board and Dr Wilkes.[234] She based her action on negligence in the administration of the anaesthetic.[235]

Singleton J found that Dr Wilkes was negligent in administering the pentothal, in regard to the volume and speed of the injection and for not having observed the patient with care.[236] He found that she was not only inexperienced, but had not followed recognized practice. He found the hospital board primarily or directly liable. They had contributed to the damage and bore some responsibility for the damage,[237] for failing to instruct or advise Dr

---

[230] See Jackson and Powell *Negligence* 492–493; Kennedy *Medical Responsibility* 156; Jones *Negligence* 400–401; Kennedy and Grubb *Medical Law* 402–404.

[231] *Wilsher v. Essex Area Health Authority* 1987 QB 730.

[232] *Collins* 618 per Hilbery J.

[233] [1952] 2 QB 852.

[234] Jones 854, 867, 871. It is a pity that the plaintiff did not include Dr Sejrup in her action. According to Denning LJ, Dr Sejrup was more to blame than Dr Wilkes.

[235] Jones 854, 865.

[236] *Jones* 866.

[237] *Jones* 865.

Wilkes as to the use of drugs.[238] The hospital board was therefore negligent, and not merely vicariously.[239]

Denning LJ once again referred to the fact that the hospital board had, by accepting the patient, come under a duty to use reasonable care and skill in their treatment of him.[240] The learned judge explicitly stated the far reaching effect of such a duty. He stated that the duty serves both the vicarious and the direct liability.[241]

Concerning the hospital board, Denning LJ continued:

> The law does not regard them as innocent. It says that they are themselves under a duty of care and skill; and if that duty is not fulfilled, it regards them as tortfeasors and makes them **liable** as such, **no matter whether the negligence be their personal negligence or the negligence of their staff**.[242] (my accentuation)

In other words the duty of the hospital creates a liability irrespective of the fact that the perpetrator concerned was a servant or an independent contractor. Denning LJ had already discarded such a distinction in *Cassidy*. Furthermore, he created a hospital liability, as a result of a (non-delegable) duty, which superseded the question as to precisely where the negligence fell. As long as the hospital or staff was negligent, hospital liability would ensue. In the light of this finding, it could be inferred that the non-delegable duty could have been formulated to embrace both forms of direct and indirect liability, or stand independently. However, it seems that Denning LJ — more likely — could have identified the non-delegable duty as a form of direct liability and/or as an independent legal ground. Denning LJ did however find that the hospital board was *in casu*, itself a tortfeasor. He found that the responsibility of the hospital board was more than that of either Dr Wilkes or Dr Sejrup. The hospital should not have been run to incur such mistakes.[243] He found that the

---

[238] *Jones* 866.

[239] The trial judge Oliver J, referred to the liability of the hospital, as resulting from the system or lack of system: *Jones* 864.

[240] *Jones* 867.

[241] *Jones* 869: 'It is true that in those cases the principal himself is under a duty of care which he cannot get rid of by delegating it to an independent contractor: but that is also the position in most cases of master and servant. it is certainly the position in these hospital cases. The hospital board are under a duty of care and skill to the patient which they cannot escape by delegating it to a doctor on the staff: *Cassidy* v. *Ministry of Health*.

[242] *Jones* 870.

[243] *Jones* 871.

hospital board should not have left patients in such inexperienced hands without proper supervision.[244]

Both Singleton J and Denning LJ therefore found that the hospital board were negligent. Primary liability ensued as a result of its own negligence which was not merely vicarious. They found Dr Wilkes also to be negligent. In the absence of an express contractual stipulation, the hospital board had no right of indemnity against the doctor, neither any claim to contribution or indemnity under the common law.[245] The responsibility was apportioned (under statute) under section 6 of the Law Reform (Married Women and Tortfeasors) Act, 1935 as to 20 per cent on the doctor and 80 per cent on the hospital board. (Hodson LJ dissented)

The court thus found the hospital board to be negligent, and consequently primarily liable in allowing a doctor with little experience to administer anaesthetics (like pentothal by injection) without proper supervision.[246] The hospital board was itself at fault.

4. In *Wilsher* v. *Essex Area Health Authority*[247] (1987) the plaintiff was born prematurely and placed in a special care baby unit at the hospital. The unit was managed by a medical team consisting of two consultants, a senior registrar, several junior doctors and trained nurses. The plaintiff suffered from various illnesses and also had an oxygen deficiency. The oxygen should have been administered by inserting a catheter into an umbilical artery. This would have ensured that his blood oxygen levels could be accurately read on an electronic monitor. An inexperienced junior doctor however, mistakenly inserted the catheter into the umbilical vein. The monitor gave a lower reading and the doctor asked the senior registrar to check what he had done. Both saw that the readings on the monitor were wrong and both failed to see that the catheter had been wrongly inserted into the vein, as showed on the X-rays. The registrar replaced the catheter in exactly the same way. Once again the monitor failed to register correctly the amount of oxygen in the plaintiff's blood. Only the next day, it become clear that the plaintiff had been supersaturated with oxygen for between 8 to 12 hours. After about 30 hours, a catheter was inserted into the artery. Thereafter, there were again periods when monitoring the arterial blood oxygen levels, they were considered too high.

---

[244] *Jones* 871–872.

[245] *Jones* 869.

[246] See also: Jones *Negligence* 401–402; Jackson and Powell *Negligence* 492; Kennedy *Medical Responsibility* 156.

[247] [1987] 1 QB 730; ([1986] 3 ALL ER 801 (CA)). See also Kennedy and Grubb *et al. Principles* 458.

The plaintiff developed retrolental fibroplasia, which resulted in near blindness to the eyes, as a result of the excess oxygen in his bloodstream. The plaintiff brought action against the health authority and claimed damages. The trial judge had awarded the plaintiff £116,199. The Court of Appeal dismissed the appeal. The Court of Appeal stated the following concerning the health authority's primary duty of care:

Mustill LJ decided that the case was conducted exclusively on the basis of vicarious liability. He pointed out that counsel for the plaintiff had explicitly disclaimed that they had put forward a case of direct liability. He therefore found that it was unnecessary to decide on direct liability as alternative basis or on its validity in English law.[248] He did however state that the defendants could have been directly liable. This 'would focus attention on the performance of the unit as a whole'. He concluded that this line of argument would have shown that the defendants owed the patient a duty, to ensure that staff knew how to operate the device and how to detect when it was wrongly inserted. 'Finally it might have been said that, if the junior doctors did not have sufficient skill or experience to provide the special care demanded by such a premature baby, the defendants were at fault in appointing them to the posts which they hold.'[249] In the end the judge found that the plaintiff had established both a breach of duty[250] by the defendants and a sufficient causal connection with the loss suffered. This established liability.[251]

Sir Nicholas Browne-Wilkinson V-C categorically excluded the possibility of a finding of vicarious liability *in casu*. He stated that:

In English law, liability for personal injury requires a finding of personal fault (e.g. negligence) against someone. In cases of vicarious liability such as this, there must have been personal fault by the employee or agent of the defendant for whom, the defendant is held vicariously liable.[252]

---

[248] *Wilsher* 748. Kennedy and Grubb *Medical Law* 412–413.

[249] *Wilsher* 747: He also mentioned at 748 B-C that: 'Unfortunately this does not deprive the point of all practical significance in the present context. Possibly because the statement of claim could be read as raising a direct claim and possibly also because the circumstances of the trial precluded a systematic analysis of the plaintiff's real complaints ... .'

[250] The duty to which the learned judge referred, related not to the individual, but to the post which he occupied. At *Wilsher* 751 he stated: 'In a case such as the present, the standard is not just that of the averagely competent and well-informed junior houseman (or whatever the position of the doctor) but of such a person who fills a post in a unit offering a highly specialised service. ... different posts make different demands.'

[251] *Wilsher* 772 D-E.

[252] *Wilsher* 777.

In other words, in order to establish the vicarious liability of the defendant health authority, the personal fault of one or more individual doctors had to be established, even though no claim had been made against the individual doctor.[253] The general standard of care required by the doctor was found to exist in that 'he should exercise the skill of a skilled doctor in the treatment which he has taken upon himself to offer.'[254] The judge found that by taking up a specialist field, the doctor had set out to acquire a professional qualification and specialist skills which he did not possess at that time. He could not make the necessary analysis or display the necessary skills at that time. Therefore, 'such doctors cannot in fairness be said to be at fault if, ... , they lack the very skills which they are seeking to acquire.'[255] In view of the fact that the English law rests liability on personal fault, and the doctor had no fault, the health authority could not be held vicariously liable.[256]

Browne-Wilkinson V-C based his judgment and the liability of the hospital authority, on direct liability. The hospital authority was found to be negligent and therefore directly liable for having failed to provide doctors of sufficient skill and experience to give treatment offered at the hospital.[257] Its organization was at fault in appointing doctors without the necessary skills and

---

[253]  *Ibid.*

[254]  *Ibid.*

[255]  *Wilsher* 777.

[256]  *Wilsher* 777; It was stated: 'In my judgment, so long as the English law rests liability on personal fault, a doctor who has properly accepted a post in a hospital in order to gain necessary experience should only be held liable for acts or omissions which a careful doctor with his qualifications and experience would not have done or omitted. It follows that, in my view, the health authority could not be held vicariously liable (and I stress the word vicariously) for the acts of such a learner who has come up to those standards, notwithstanding that the post he held required greater experience than he in fact possessed.'

[257]  *Wilsher* 777–778: Browne-Wilkinson V-C: ... 'I agree with the comments of Mustill LJ as to the confusion which has been caused in this case both by the pleading and the argument below which blurred the distinction between the vicarious liability of the health authority for the negligence of its doctors and the direct liability of the health authority for negligently failing to provide skilled treatment of the kind that it was offering to the public. In my judgment, a health authority which so conducts its hospital that it fails to provide doctors of sufficient skill and experience to give the treatment offered at the hospital may be directly liable in negligence to the patient. Although we were told in argument that no case has ever been decided on this ground and that it is not the practice to formulate claims in this way, I can see no reason why, in principle, the health authority should not be so liable if its organisation is at fault: see *McDermid* v. *Nash Dredging & Reclamation Co Ltd* [1986] QB 965 especially at pp. 978–979.' See also Kennedy and Grubb *Medical Law* 412–413.

experience in specialist posts and for further failing to train them in the management of advanced equipment such as monitors.[258]

Glidewell LJ agreed with the Vice Chancellor concerning the direct liability of the hospital authority:

> I agree with Sir Nicholas Browne-Wilkinson V-C that there seems to be no reason in principle why, in a suitable case different on its facts from this, a hospital management committee [sic] should not be held directly liable in negligence for failing to provide sufficient qualified and competent medical staff.[259]

He found that the defendants should be liable for any proven damage to the plaintiff caused by the negligence.[260]

The Court of Appeal in *Wilsher* seemed tentative to accept the legal ground of primary or direct liability. It seems even more strange in the light of the foregoing judgments or background of hospital liability.[261] It is, however, clear that this form of direct liability (i.e. to provide a safe system) is part of English law. It was accepted as such by the Court of Appeal in *Bull* v. *Devon Area Health Authority.*[262]

5. In ***Bull* v. *Devon Area Health Authority***[263] (1989), the defendant Health Authority was sued on behalf of Mrs Bull and her disabled son. The baby had been born at the Exeter City Hospital for which the defendant and its predecessors were responsible. Due to the negligence of the Health Authority and its staff, the baby was disabled due to asphyxia at birth. The direct claim against the Health Authority, was founded on the fact that a doctor was not able to attend to her at birth, which delayed the delivery which in turn caused the asphyxia.

Slade LJ held that the duty the Authority owed Mrs Bull's son was indisputable. The duty in this case purported 'to provide a woman admitted in labour with a reasonable standard of skilled obstetric and paediatric care, in order to ensure as far as reasonably practicable the safe delivery of the baby

---

[258] Nelson-Jones and Burton *Law* 24. Jackson and Powell *Negligence* 493. Jones *Negligence* 402.

[259] *Wilsher* 775.

[260] *Wilsher* 774.

[261] Kennedy and Grubb *Medical Law* 413: 'Perhaps it is surprising that the court was so tentative in accepting the notion of primary or direct liability ... given the background we have already seen.'

[262] 1989 (unreported), CA. See [1993] 4 Med LR 117 CA. Kennedy and Grubb *Medical Law* 413.

[263] 1989 (unreported) CA [1993] 4 Med LR 117 (CA). See Kennedy and Grubb *Medical Law* 413–415 and Jones *Negligence* 402–403. Kennedy and Grubb *et al. Principles* 459.

... and the health of the mother and offspring thereafter.'[264] According to the judge the liability was most likely due to (i) the inefficient system of the hospital in 1970 to summon doctors to assistance and (ii) negligence by some individual(s) in the working of that system.[265]

Dillon LJ found the Health Authority directly liable for breach of its primary duty.[266] Mustill LJ held that the Authority was in breach of duty.[267]

The Court of Appeal thus held that the Health Authority owed Mrs Bull and her son a duty of care directly. It consequently held the Health Authority directly liable in negligence.[268] The direct liability ensued as a result of the ineffective or faulty system of the hospital, which operated on two sites and could not summon their doctors. Direct hospital liability was once again established as a result of an improper system or organizational failure(s).

### 5.4.2  Secretary of State

Primary liability can also be extended to include not only institutions (such as hospitals) or bodies (such as health authorities), but possibly the Secretary of State. The Secretary of State can be liable for negligence, and possibly liable for breach of statutory duty.[269]

Kennedy and Grubb point out that any civil claim for damages may be established as: (a) civil liability for breach of a statutory duty; and (b) negligence.[270] Liability for breach of statutory duties would usually be founded in public law, whereas a private cause of action would arise only in exceptional circumstances.[271]

---

[264]  *Ibid.*

[265]  *Ibid.*

[266]  Kennedy and Grubb *Medical Law* 414.

[267]  *Ibid.*

[268]  *Ibid.*

[269]  Kennedy and Grubb *Medical Law* 415, 418. Jones *Negligence* 403–405. Kennedy and Grubb *et al. Principles* 468.

[270]  Kennedy and Grubb *et al. Principles* 468.

[271]  *Ibid.*

## A. Statutory duty and breach thereof:

Direct liability may follow for the Secretary of State or its delegate, for breach of statutory duty.[272] The National Health Service Act 1977,[273] s 3 (1) provides:

It is the Secretary of State's duty to provide throughout England and Wales, to such extent as he considers necessary to meet all reasonable requirements–

(a)    hospital accommodation;

(b)    other accommodation for the purpose of any service provided under this Act;

(c)    medical, dental, nursing and ambulance services;

(d)    such other facilities for the care of expectant and nursing mothers and young children as he considers are appropriate as part of the health service;

(e)    such facilities for the prevention of illness, the care of persons suffering from illness and the after-care of persons who have suffered from illness as he considers are appropriate as part of the health service;

(f)    such other services as are required for the diagnosis and treatment of illness.

The vast majority of the Secretary of State's functions derived from the above-mentioned duty, are delegated to health authorities by statutory instrument. Failure to perform the duty under s 3, determines the health authorities — and not the Secretary of State — the party to be sued under par 15(1) of schedule 5 of the Act.[274] Consequently, proceedings concerning the 'enforcement of such rights and liabilities shall be brought, and brought only, by or, as the case may be, against the authority in question in its own name.'[275] Claims against the Secretary of State directly, are limited to (i) the (non)-

---

[272] Kennedy and Grubb *Medical Law* 418. Jones *Negligence* 403–405. Kennedy and Grubb *et al. Principles* 468–469.

[273] *Ibid.* See also ss 4 and 5 of this Act concerning mental hospitals and school medical services, contraceptive services, a microbiological service and research.

[274] Kennedy and Grubb *Medical Law* 418 on health authorities. Par 15.(1) An authority shall, notwithstanding that it is exercising any function on behalf of the Secretary of State or another authority, be entitled to enforce any rights acquired in the exercise of that function, and be liable in respect of any liabilities incurred (including liabilities in tort) in the exercise of that function, in all respects as if it were acting as a principal. Kennedy and Grubb *et al. Principles* 467–468.

[275] Kennedy and Grubb *Medical Law* 418.

exercise of a retained function and (ii) an ancillary function of the Secretary of State.[276]

Where the Secretary of State or health authorities have been challenged on public law grounds concerning decisions on resource allocation, such challenges have been unsuccessful.[277] If the plaintiff had sustained injury through inadequate provision of resources such as funds, equipment, staff or drugs, it would best be to prove that the lack of resources was due to negligence in the *organization* of the hospital itself.[278] Thus, establishing direct hospital liability as a result of an improper system or organizational error. Where it is merely indicated that the lack of resources existed as a result of resource allocation decisions over which the hospital has no control, it will not suffice to establish hospital responsibility.[279]

The Secretary of State and health authorities are granted discretion under statutory powers, to allocate resources and make relevant decisions. When trying to prove the decision had been made negligently, it must by applying public law principles, first be established that the discretion was exercised *ultra vires* the statutory power. In cases of health resources, courts have seemed reluctant to make such a finding.[280]

1. In ***R* v. *Secretary of State for Social Services, ex parte Hincks***[281] (1979), a local hospital decided to postpone its expansion, due to cost. Four patients who had been waiting for orthopaedic operations, challenged the decision, relying on section 3. Application for judicial review failed. Lord Denning MR suggested that section 3(1) should be implied to read as follows:

> ... to such extent as he considers necessary to meeting all reasonable require-
> ments **such as can be provided within the resources available**.[282]

Bridge LJ commented that resources available to the health service should be limited by current **'government economic policy'**.[283]

---

[276]  Kennedy and Grubb *et al. Principles* 468.

[277]  Jones *Negligence* 403.

[278]  *Ibid.*

[279]  *Ibid.*

[280]  Jones *Negligence* 404–405. Compare Jackson and Powell *Negligence* 493.

[281]  (1979) 123 SJ 436; (1980) 1 BMLR 93 (CA); Jones *Negligence* 403–404. Kennedy and Grubb *et al. Principles* 477–478.

[282]  The accentuated words were added to section 3(1) by Lord Denning MR, by his interpretation thereof.

[283]  According to Bridge LJ the accentuated words were to be implied and read into section 3(1).

Two cases followed in which parents sought intervention to procure staff and facilities from a hospital, in order to perform heart surgery on two young children. They were unsuccessful in both applications for judicial review.

2. In *R* v. *Central Birmingham Health Authority, ex parte Walker*[284] (1987), Sir John Donaldson MR said that the court could not substitute the discretion or judgment of those who allocated resources with their own judgment. The court could only intervene where a *prima facie* case had been established and the failure to allocate resources had been *Wednesbury*[285] unreasonable. He explained that the jurisdiction indeed existed but had to be used 'extremely sparingly'.[286]

3. Then in *R* v. *Central Birmingham Health Authority, ex parte Collier*[287] (1988), Brown LJ confirmed this view even in circumstances where the child's health was in danger according to medical evidence. Gibson LJ held that the court had no role as investigator of social policy and of allocation of resources. It's jurisdiction was limited to breaches of duty under law and unreasonable decisions made by public authorities.

4. In *R* v. *North Derbyshire HA, ex parte Fisher*[288] (1997), the applicant sought a judicial review of the Health Authority's decision not to allocate resources for the prescription of a new and expensive drug, beta-interferon. The applicant had been diagnosed as suffering from the relapsing / remitting form of multiple sclerosis, and was in need of the drug. A national policy had already been introduced in a Circular,[289] that beta-interferon be provided. The Health Authority, however, refused to authorize the applicant's treatment. They decided not to take the Circular into account and disregarded it.[290] It was held that their policy was therefore unlawful, 'because it was not a proper application of the guidance, contained in the Circular', by failing to properly take into account the national policy.[291] Dyson J in no way made a decision

---

[284] (1987) 3 BMLR 32, 35–36. Jones *Negligence* 404.

[285] *Associated Provincial Picture Houses Ltd.* v. *Wednesbury Corporation* [1948] 1 KB 223. The *Wednesbury* case in Administrative law determined the reasonable standard.

[286] *Ibid.*

[287] (1988) unreported CA. Jones *Negligence* 404. See also *R* v. *Cambridge Health Authority ex parte B* [1995] 2 ALL ER 129 (CA). Kennedy and Grubb *et al. Principles* 482.

[288] [1997] 8 Med LR 327. See also Kennedy and Grubb *et al. Principles* 480–481.

[289] An executive letter EL (95) 97 ('the Circular').

[290] *R* v. *North Derbyshire HA* 336, 337: They did so because they were opposed to it. 'That is something which in my judgment they were not entitled to do.'

[291] *R* v. *North Derbyshire HA* 337.

concerning allocation of resources, which did not entail any new law-making. He only ordered the implementation of an already existing national policy.[292]

These cases illustrate that where actions are instituted because of failures to provide adequate resources due to negligence, they will not likely succeed.[293] However, the possibility of a successful action for breach of statutory duty has been suggested by judges in *Yepremian* v. *Scarborough General Hospital*.[294] The issue also arose directly in *Re HIV Haemophiliac Litigation*.[295] Gibson LJ declared that the duties imposed by the 1977 Act, did 'not clearly demonstrate the intention of Parliament to impose a duty which is to be enforced by individual civil action.'[296] To this, Bingham LJ and Sir John Megan agreed. Kennedy and Grubb (*Medical Law* 1995) suggested that the better view might be that the 1977 Act 'only imposes a duty amenable to control in *public law* through the judicial review procedure.'[297]

## B Negligence:

An action in negligence can be brought against the Secretary of State, (or his delegate), based on the (non)-exercise of statutory powers under the 1977 Act. It will have to be proved that the Secretary of State (or his delegate) owes the individual a duty of care.[298] In the light of the fact that most decisions are taken at the highest level of the NHS, are not delegated but based on policy considerations, the plaintiff-patient will not easily succeed in bringing a claim.[299]

---

[292] Kennedy and Grubb *et al. Principles* 481: 'Thus *Fisher* does not break new ground. It affirms the existing view of the role of the courts in public law in matters of non-provision of resources: that such matters are non-justiciable and, thus, that it has no role.'

[293] Jones *Negligence* 404.

[294] (1980) 110 DLR (3d) 513 at 564 per Blair JA. Kennedy and Grubb *Medical Law* 418.

[295] [1990] NLJR 1349 CA.

[296] *Ibid*. Kennedy and Grubb *Medical Law* 419. The Court of Appeal held that sections 1 and 3(1) of the 1977 Act did not initiate an action for breach of statutory duty: *Re HIV Litigation* [1996] PNLR 290 (CA). Kennedy and Grubb *et al. Principles* 469.

[297] Kennedy and Grubb *Medical Law* 419. The judicial review procedure under RSC Order 53. Kennedy and Grubb *et al. Principles* 469 concluded (in 1998) that it is most unlikely that breach of any duty relating to the health service would be construed as giving rise to a claim of damages. However, see their discussion and the author's conclusion *infra* at 5.5.

[298] Kennedy and Grubb *Medical Law* 415. Kennedy and Grubb *et al. Principles* 469–472.

[299] Kennedy and Grubb *Medical Law* 415. Kennedy and Grubb *et al. Principles* 471: 'A patient's remedy will lie, if at all, in public law.' See *supra* footnote 271.

5. In ***Re HIV Haemophiliac Litigation*** [300] (1990), 962 haemophiliacs, their wives and children had developed AIDS or would do so after being treated under the NHS and receiving blood made out of Factor VIII concentrate, infected with the HIV virus and imported from the USA. The 962 plaintiffs brought action against, *inter alia*, the Department of Health, the licensing authority under Medicines Act 1968, the committee on the safety of medicines, all regional and district health authorities in England and Wales, and the central blood laboratories authority. The plaintiffs alleged that the Department of Health was in breach of its statutory duty under sections 1 and 3(1) of the National Health Service Act 1977,

'to promote a comprehensive health service in England and Wales designed to secure improvement

(a)    in the physical and mental health of the people and

(b)    in the prevention, diagnosis and treatment of illness, and to provide throughout England and Wales facilities for the prevention of illness and the care of persons suffering from illness, and was negligent in failing to ensure that the country was self-sufficient in blood supplies thereby causing haemophiliacs to be treated with infected blood from the USA.'[301]

They also applied for discovery of documents to which the department claimed public interest immunity on the grounds that ministers discreetly formulated public policy concerning blood products, allocation of resources and other aspects.[302]

Gibson LJ confirmed that it would be difficult to prove a case of negligence with regard to the nature of the duties under the 1977 Act and with regard to the law of negligence. It would have to be proved that the party charged, did in fact by exercising discretion and forming judgments on the allocation of public resources, negligently breach a duty. He did however state that it was possible that there could in law be such a claim in negligence.[303]

Gibson LJ held that the department could have eliminated or reduced the risk by taking practicable steps, and if those steps had been taken, the injury would not have been caused.[304] The error of judgment did not have to be

---

[300]    [1990] 140 NLJR 1349 (CA). Compare Kennedy and Grubb *Medical Law* 415–418 and Kennedy and Grubb *et al. Principles* 469, 471–472.

[301]    *Re HIV* 1349.

[302]    *Ibid.*

[303]    *Re HIV* 1350.

[304]    *Ibid.*

grave, but consisted of an error of failing to act appropriately upon available information which was in turn caused by a failure of some level to pass such information to those who were required to make the decisions. A *prima facie* case had therefore been established that the 'decisions were such that no reasonable or responsible person could properly make them'.[305] A case of negligence had been made up and consequently the necessary documents were ordered to be produced.[306] Bingham LJ and Sir J Megan concurred.[307]

6. In ***Danns* v. *Department of Health*,**[308] Wright J dismissed the plaintiff's actions. It was alleged that the Secretary of State had been negligent and therefore in breach of a duty under section 2 of the Ministry of Health Act 1999, in failing to disseminate information concerning the risks of diseases and defects (in this case of the particular vasectomy), to the public. The court refused to impose a duty of care on the Department of Health in terms of section 2 of the Ministry of Health Act 1999, since the defendant had exercised a statutory discretion entailing a policy decision. Imposing such a duty, was considered to be contrary to public policy.

Conclusively, the authority's discretion and policy-making functions which are derived from statutory powers which infer statutory duties, can attract primary or direct liability when assumed negligently or unreasonably.

The question of resource allocation coupled with the discretionary policy-making powers of an authority or its delegates, provides the courts with an undesired or troubling responsibility.[309] When addressing issues on the availability of resources or the allocation of sufficient resources, two conflicting interests are weighed: Courts have to bear in mind that when setting legal standards for defendants, resources are finite, and there might not be enough for all. On the other hand, when courts deny compensation to patients, they might elude their duty to hold the government accountable.[310]

---

[305] *Ibid.*

[306] *Re HIV* 1351.

[307] See also Kennedy and Grubb *Medical Law* 417–418.

[308] (1995) 25 BMLR 121. Kennedy and Grubb *et al. Principles* 472, applaud this verdict and suggest that it is likely to be followed in analogous cases.

[309] *Re J* (A Minor) Wardship Medical Treatment [1992] 4 ALL ER 614 Lord Donaldson MR at 623–4. Kennedy and Grubb *Medical Law* 420.

[310] *Ibid.* See also the proposed analysis and solution to this problem by Kennedy and Grubb *Medical Law* 420–421. See Kennedy and Grubb *et al. Principles* 476–477.

### 5.4.3  The National Health Service and its Contracts

Concerning the 'internal market' of the NHS, NHS contracts may exist between a health authority, (purchaser) and a NHS Trust (provider).[311] A Primary Care Trust can also enter into NHS contracts both as a 'commissioner' of services and as a provider for another Primary Care Trust or Health Authority.[312] Where the purchaser enters into a NHS contract, and inadequate provision of services results in harm to a patient, primary liability could ensue. Likewise direct liability could follow where the purchaser failed to properly monitor the performance of the contract or the services provided under it.[313] In other words where minimum reasonable necessary standards — according to expert evidence — are not met, primary liability will be established. To this effect, the guidelines to health authorities issued by the NHS Management Executive concerning minimum standards of quality and regular monitoring of performances, should be consulted,[314] and adhered to.

### 5.4.4  Conclusion

Various structures can be construed which fundamentally are offshoots from the concept of organizational failures or management defaults, which in turn could lead to a finding of primary or direct hospital liability. The global hospital industry is interspersed with unique examples of such errors or breach of duties which lead to a finding of negligence and ultimate accountability of the appropriate defendants. We find a selection of failures to provide the proper staff, equipment, facility controls, administration, procedures or resources. In short, unsafe systems and bad administration are ideal circumstances set for injuries, resulting in negligence and finally, direct or primary hospital liability. Every hospital must have proper and effective systems and appropriate management to safeguard patients against catastrophes or

---

[311] See discussion under 5.2 Vicarious Liability: The Health Authorities: Appropriate Defendants. Kennedy and Grubb *Medical Law* 429–430.

[312] A Primary Care Trust is established under the Health Act 1999. See *supra*. It qualifies as 'health service body' under the National Health Service and Community Care Act 1990, s 4 (2), (Sch 4, para 54). National Health Service Act 1977, s 18 A, inserted by Health Act 1999, s 5. See Kennedy and Grubb *et al. Principles* 1999 Second Cumulative Supplement § 1.40 4.

[313] Reasonable requirements derived from statutory duty under section 3 of the National Health Service Act 1977, must be met: Kennedy and Grubb *Medical Law* 429.

[314] *Working for Patients, Contracts for Health Service*: Operating Contracts (HMSO, 1990). Kennedy and Grubb *Medical Law* 430.

tragedies. The duty to provide safe and proper systems which forms an independent legal ground of primary hospital liability, is not only recognized in English law, but is indeed part of English law. The English primary hospital law provides us with excellent examples and principles to govern intricate situations and cases.

## 5.5 Hospital Liability in Terms of the Non-Delegable Duty

### Introduction

The non-delegable duty is the hospital's own non-delegable duty to ensure that reasonable care (or skill) is taken of patients, by its employees or independent contractors, of which (non-delegable) duty, performance is delegated but not responsibility. Breach of the worker's (employee/ independent contractor) duty in attending patients negligently, without reasonable care or skill, constitutes breach of the hospital's own non-delegable duty, rendering the hospital strictly liable in terms of a non-delegable duty.[315]

The non-delegable duty is neither a form of indirect (vicarious) liability nor a form of direct (primary) liability. These legal grounds should be distinguished from one another and expositions, formulations and terminology should be technically sound.

Legal grounds differ in a fundamental area, since vicarious hospital liability is a strict or **faultless** employer liability, direct hospital liability is a **fault-based** employer liability and hospital liability in terms of the non-delegable duty is a **strict faultless** employer liability due to a strict(er) duty. Much less can the non-delegable duty be a form of direct liability, since direct liability is **fault-based** (employer) liability and liability in terms of the non-delegable duty is a **faultless** (employer) liability.[316]

---

[315] The section on the Non-Delegable Duty in § 4.3.3 in Chapter 4 serves as introductory passage to this discussion. The following authors discuss the non-delegable duty in English law: Jones *Negligence* 405–409; Kennedy and Grubb *et al. Principles* 460, 461–466; Kennedy and Grubb *Medical Law* 402–415; Dugdale and Stanton *Negligence* 537–538, 543–545; Brazier and Murphy *Street on Torts* 251–256, 510–513; Markesinis and Deakin *Tort Law* 523–531, 556–557.

[316] See § 4.4: A Comparative Diagram at 96. Jones *Negligence* 405–409 and Kennedy and Grubb *et al. Principles* 460, 461–466, (highly respected authors), recognise the non-delegable duty. They do, however, classify the non-delegable duty as a form of direct (hospital) liability, which, with utmost respect, cannot be condoned. Hospital liability in terms of the non-delegable duty and direct hospital liability should be regarded as separate, independent and sovereign legal grounds. See also Kennedy and Grubb *Medical Law* 404,

## 5.5.1 English Case Law

1.  1951: *Cassidy* v. *Ministry of Health* [1951] 2 KB 343
2.  1952: *Jones* v. *Manchester Corporation and Others* [1952] 2 QB 852
3.  1954: *Roe* v. *Minister of Health* [1954] 2 QB 66
4.  1954: *Razzle* v. *Snowball* (1954) 1 WLR 1382
5.  1998: *M* v. *Calderdale and Kirklees HA* [1998] Lloyd's Rep Med 157

### *5.5.1.1 English case law discussion*

The relevant English case law and relevant statutory obligation(s) will be addressed firstly:

The non-delegable duty which a hospital authority owes to patients in a hospital, was formulated first of all in case law: Denning LJ created the non-delegable duty in *Cassidy* v. *Ministry of Health*[317] as a result of Lord Greene's obligation in *Gold* v. *Essex County Council*.[318]

In ***Cassidy* v. *Ministry of Health***[319] (1951), Singleton LJ referred to the obligation of the hospital to provide the patient with competent, proper, post-operational treatment.[320] He quoted from the *Gold* case quite extensively, which introduced the obligation which could not be delegated and for which breach, the body of trustees or governors could not escape liability. This also — on his part — introduced the non-delegable duty, for which he ultimately found the corporation or employers responsible at 358. He once again resorted to the concept of 'employees of the corporation' finding that all those concerned, were in fact employees.[321] He then condemned the 'scheme or system of examination' of the surgeon's patients, when the surgeon would go away for a weekend. This would theoretically display a ground for a finding

---

414–415. Dugdale and Stanton *Negligence* 537, 543–546: Apparently, they consider the non-delegable duty as an independent legal ground to establish hospital liability, and they state nothing to the contrary that could merit any other conclusion. The exposition of Brazier and Murphy *Street on Torts* at 250–253, and 510–513, is concise and clear but unfortunately they refer to the '*direct* non-delegable duty' (my italics) at 512. Jackson and Powell *Negligence* 492, however, discuss the Cassidy-case under the heading of 'Primary liability'.

[317] [1951] 2 KB 343.

[318] [1942] 2 KB 293.

[319] [1951] 2 KB 343.

[320] *Cassidy* 357.

[321] *Cassidy* 359: Thus resounding to or implicating vicarious liability.

of direct hospital liability as a result of an ineffective or dangerous system.[322] Nonetheless, the Ministry was held responsible.[323]

Denning LJ formulated a new basis for the founding of a hospital's liability.[324] He did in effect create the concept of the **undelegable duty** which was similar to the duty formulated and initiated by Lord Greene in *Gold's* case. Lord Greene's duty was the same in content but was just termed 'obligation'[325] and not undelegable or non-delegable duty. Lord Greene's duty or *obligation* was mainly a question of fact relying on the circumstances of each case, signifying a more flexible approach. It could even accommodate the vicarious liability.[326] Lord Denning's undelegable duty was a matter of law. Although a stricter formulation, it brought about certainty and consistency to the law.[327] Despite these subtle nuances, in content, they both created the non-delegable duty for the hospital.[328]

Denning LJ stated:

> I take it to be clear law, as well as good sense, that, where a person is himself under a duty to use care, he cannot get rid of his responsibility by delegating the performance of it to someone else, no matter whether the delegation be to a servant under a contract of service or to an independent contractor under a contract for services.[329]

If this basis is correct, then the fact that the consultant is engaged as employee or independent contractor becomes irrelevant. The duty cannot be discharged by delegating its performance to an independent contractor, under a contract for services.[330] The hospital will be liable for its negligence.[331]

Denning LJ confirmed his judgment in *Cassidy* in both ***Jones* v. *Manchester Corporation*** [332] and again in ***Roe* v. *Minister of Health*.**[333] Although the non-delegable duty is absolutely condemned by some as extending hospital liability too far and equating it with strict liability, Denning LJ did not

---

[322] *Cassidy* 359.

[323] *Ibid.*

[324] Whippy 1989 *ALJ* 186. Jones *Negligence* 399–400, 405, 408–409.

[325] I.e. the obligation that rested on the hospital authorities.

[326] Whippy 1989 *ALJ* 189.

[327] *Ibid.*

[328] *Ibid.*

[329] *Cassidy* 363.

[330] *Cassidy* 363–364.

[331] Jones *Negligence* 395. Whippy 1989 *ALJ* 182–204.

[332] [1952] 2 QB 852 at 867, 869, 870–872.

[333] [1954] 2 QB 66, 82.

— even by making use of the non-delegable duty — find the hospital authority liable in *Roe*. He also refused to apply the *res ipsa loquitur* doctrine in that case.[334] The majority of the Court of Appeal in *Cassidy* and *Roe* relied on *respondeat superior* and found the hospital/health authorities to be vicariously liable for the doctor-employees.[335]

According to various authors,[336] authority for Denning LJ's proposition remained uncertain, and in England the question had yet to be decided directly.

---

[334] *Roe* 83.

[335] In *Jones* v. *Manchester Corporation and Others* [1952] 2 QB 852 the majority of the court also founded its findings on vicarious liability.

[336] See *infra* 5.5.2 and 5.5.3. Kennedy and Grubb *et al. Principles* 461, 462, 464–466, 465 and footnote 158. Kennedy and Grubb *et al. Principles* 462: 'This issue remains open in the modern case law.' (Before their discussion of *M* v. *Calderdale & Kirklees HA* (1998) in the 1999 Second Cumulative Supplement). See *infra*. Kennedy and Grubb *Medical Law* 414. Jackson and Powell *Negligence* 493 § 6.65: 'the question had not been directly addressed by the courts.' Jones *Negligence* 405–406 and footnote 73. At 405: '... the question has not arisen directly for decision in this country.' Dugdale and Stanton *Negligence* § 22.20 544–545: '... this approach has not gone unchallenged as representing common law principles.' Most of the above-mentioned discussions were given before 1998.

Uncertainty tainted the decision in *Barnett* v. *Chelsea and Kensington HMC* [1969] 1 QB 428; [1968] 1 ALL ER 1068 where Nield J acknowledged a duty to ensure that care was taken by the defendant, which had been breached by the doctor's negligence in failing to examine a patient in the Accident and Emergency department (A&E). The decision restricted the legal finding to the A&E department. Legal certainty was yet to follow. See Kennedy and Grubb *et al. Principles* 465.

In *X (minors)* v. *Bedfordshire CC*, [1995] 2 AC 633; [1995] 3 ALL ER 353 (HL), Lord Browne-Wilkinson referred to the judgments of Lord Greene MR in *Gold* and of Denning LJ in *Cassidy* and *Roe*, and other judgments. However, at 372, he formulated a 'breach of the duty of care (if any) owed directly by the authority to the plaintiff' and other formulations from which it is not clear whether he was indeed accommodating the non-delegable duty or implementing direct (hospital) liability. Compare criticisms of this case: Jones *Negligence* 405–406 and footnote 73: Jones remains undecided on the implications of this case. Kennedy and Grubb *et al. Principles* 461–462: 'What is to be made of this statement is unclear.' However, see Dugdale and Stanton *Negligence* § 22.20 545 who find that this court had regarded Denning LJ's approach, concerning the non-delegable duty, as representing the law: Although the approach of Denning LJ — in this country — had 'not gone unchallenged as representing common law principles, it was regarded as representing the law in *X* v. *Bedfordshire County Council*'.

In *Wilsons and Clyde Coal Co Ltd* v. *English* [1938] AC 57, the House of Lords, by word of Lord Wright formulated an employer non-delegable duty which is personal, to take reasonable care for the safety of workmen by providing: competent staff, adequate material and a proper system which includes effective supervision. The extension of the application of these general criteria, to the field of medical law, should be considered. See also: Jones *Negligence* 406 and footnote 73a. Brazier and Murphy *Street on Torts* 251. Markesinis and Deakin *Tort Law* 523, 528–531.

## 5.5.2  The Statutory Duty

Secondly, it is suggested that the National Health Service Act 1977 places a duty on the Secretary of State, which in turn places a statutory duty or obligation on a health authority which puts the NHS hospital authority under a non-delegable duty to provide medical services to the patient.[337]

In *Razzel* v. *Snowball* [338] (1954), the Court of Appeal held that section 3(1)(c) of the National Health Service Act 1946 placed a duty on the Minister of Health. The latter duty was not limited only to provide competent specialists, but extended to provide treatment by means of their services. This ruling implied that the defendant doctor was carrying out the minister's duty. He could therefore claim the benefit of a one-year period of limitation which applied to acts executed under any act of parliament or any public duty under section 21 of the Limitation Act 1939. Basing this duty on statute, thus ensures that it is non-delegable in nature.[339]

A further implication of the *Razzle* ruling could be that section 3(1)[340] or the whole of section 3[341] of the National Health Service Act 1977, could likewise create a non-delegable statutory duty to provide treatment services. The duty would not be discharged by appointing competent staff, whether it

---

In *McDermid* v. *Nash Dredging and Reclamation Co Ltd* [1986] 2 ALL ER 676; [1987] 2 ALL ER 878; [1986] QB 965, (978–979) the House of Lords established employer liability in terms of a (personal) non-delegable duty to devise and operate a safe system of work, regarding the safety of employees. It is submitted that such a principle could also be applied in cases of hospital liability. See *supra* the discussion of this case in *Wilsher* v. *Essex Area Health Authority* [1986] 3 ALL ER 801 CA; [1987] 1 QB 730 under Direct liability 5.4.1.i. Jones *Negligence* 400 footnote 42, 402 footnote 55, 406 footnote 73a. Brazier and Murphy *Street on Torts* 251–253. Markesinis and Deakin *Tort Law* 556–557.

[337]  Jones *Negligence* 407. See *infra* Dugdale and Stanton *Negligence* § 22.20 544–545.

[338]  (1954) 1 WLR 1382. [1954] 3 ALL ER 439 CA.

[339]  Dugdale and Stanton *Negligence* § 22.20 545.

[340]  Jones *Negligence* 408.

[341]  Dugdale and Stanton *Negligence* § 22.20 545. They state: It seems likely that an identical result is achieved as a result of the interpretation that has been placed on the National Health Services Act 1977, s 3.'

be an employee or an independent contractor such as a consultant.[342] This issue, thus remained 'open in the modern case law'.[343] A Canadian court[344] did, however, relying on the *Razzle* decision, declare that the liability of hospitals in the UK 'now rests on a clear statutory foundation'.[345]

In *Smith* v. *Cammell Laird & Co Ltd* [346] and *The Pass of Ballater* [347] the principle was already laid down that where a statute imposed an 'absolute' duty, the responsibility for the performance thereof could not be delegated.[348] Determining whether a duty is 'absolute', the construction of the statute is to be examined. A duty to use 'due diligence' could be such a duty.[349]

## The non-delegable duty: enforced

In *M* v. *Calderdale & Kirklees HA* [350] (1998), the plaintiff was seventeen years old, and pregnant. Due to unfavourable circumstances she wanted to terminate the pregnancy. A doctor employed by the first defendant — who agreed to the abortion — referred the plaintiff to and contracted with the second defendant, a private clinic. The third defendant effected the procedure incompetently at the second defendant's clinic. Consequently the plaintiff give birth to a normal boy. Action was brought against the defendants, claiming damages for negligence. Plaintiff obtained judgments against both the third and second defendants. However, neither of them was apparently insured and the second defendants were subject to a winding-up order.

The liability of the first defendant was expounded by Judge Garner. The court held:

---

[342] Jones *Negligence* 408 emphasized in footnote 85 that *in casu* it was the defendant who claimed that he was performing the Minister's non-delegable duty, and the plaintiff argued that the Minister's Duty was merely to provide specialists and not the treatment. See Dugdale and Stanton *Negligence* § 22.20 544–545.

[343] Kennedy and Grubb *et al. Principles* 462. See *supra* 5.5.1 footnote 335 and the discussion of *X* v. *Bedfordshire County Council* [1995] 2 AC 633, [1995] 3 ALL ER 353, HL.

[344] *Yepremian* v. *Scarborough General Hospital* (1980) 110 DLR (3d) 513.

[345] *Yepremian* v. *Scarborough General Hospital* (1980) 110 DLR (3d) 513 at 565 per Blair JA. See Jones *Negligence* 408 footnote 85.

[346] [1940] AC 242.

[347] [1942] P 112.

[348] See also Jones *Negligence* 408 footnote 85.

[349] *Riverstone Meat Co Pty Ltd* v. *Lancashire Shipping Co Ltd* [1961] AC 807. Jones *Negligence* 408 footnote 85.

[350] [1998] Lloyd's Rep Med 157. For the facts see 157–159.

(i)     The first defendant had accepted plaintiff into their care, from which
        care the plaintiff could not deviate, thus fully relying on such care.
        Consequently, the first defendant had a duty to 'bring about for her the
        effective provision of services either by providing that themselves or
        causing others to effect this on their behalf.'[351] In other words, once
        having accepted plaintiff into their care, the first defendant had a duty
        to provide an effective procedure or services for the plaintiff them-
        selves, or to secure such effective services from another source.

Relying on the cases of **Gold** and **Cassidy**[352] and referring to *Street on Torts*,[353]
Judge Garner found that 'the National Health Service may well owe a non-
delegable duty generally. In the particular circumstances of this case I find
that they do.'[354] The statutory obligation contained in s 1 of the National
Health Service Act of 1977, had thus, in these circumstances, been interpreted
to imply a non-delegable duty, for breach of which the Health Authority could
be held liable.

(ii)    The first defendant had not taken reasonable care dealing with second
        defendant and had therefore been negligent in failing to (a) establish
        whether second defendant carried indemnity insurance or not; (b) have
        an available copy of the contract between the parties; (c) have up to
        date information about the competence of the second defendant or its
        staff; (d) (enquire themselves), but seemed to have relied upon enquir-
        ies assumed to be ongoing by others and an apparent absence of com-
        plaints.[355]

First, Judge Garner had constructed a non-delegable duty for the NHS, of
which they were in breach, in terms of s 1 of the National Health Service Act
1977. (Thus, breach of a statutory non-delegable duty could give rise to a
claim in damages). Second, they were found to be in breach of their common
law duty of care to a plaintiff.[356] This had been the first time that an English

---

[351]  *M* v. *Calderdale & Kirklees HA* 160.

[352]  See *supra*.

[353]  The learned judge referred to *Street on Torts* 9th ed. (1993) at pages 492–494. See also
       *Street on Torts*, 10th ed. (1999) pages 510–513 and especially at 511: 'The categories of
       non-delegable duties are not closed. NHS authorities may well owe such a duty.'

[354]  *M* v. *Calderdale & Kirklees HA* 160.

[355]  *M* v. *Calderdale & Kirklees HA* 160–161.

[356]  *M* v. *Calderdale & Kirklees HA* 160–161.

court held an NHS institution to be under a non-delegable duty, which entailed a duty to ensure that reasonable care was provided by another.[357]

What can be commended, with respect, is the fact that the verdict was both in principle and terminologically sound. Not once, did Garner J himself, explicitly refer to or qualify the non-delegable duty as being a direct duty or 'directly owed' to the plaintiff.[358] Thus the independent status of the non-delegable duty as a sovereign legal ground on which to establish hospital liability (or the liability of a health care provider — in this case the HA), had been established.

On account of this judgment, it can be concluded that the non-delegable duty is acknowledged as an independent legal ground upon which hospital liability or the liability of a Health Authority can be founded in English law.

### 5.5.3  Part of the English Law or Not

It will now be endeavoured to establish whether the non-delegable duty or the '*duty to ensure* that care is taken in the provision of health services or health care treatment' is indeed part of the English law.

Initially, Kennedy and Grubb applied a most cautious stance on the status of the non-delegable duty in English Law.[359] However, in June 1998, Grubb made the following concession in recognition of the non-delegable duty:

> Consequently, it is suggested that Denning LJ may have been correct and that, within the NHS, a hospital does owe a non-delegable duty to its patients to ensure that reasonable care is taken of them during their time in hospital.[360]

---

[357] Kennedy and Grubb *et al. Principles* 1999 Second Cumulative Supplement § 8.23, 8.30 & 8.38 43.

[358] Only at 159, stating the plaintiff's case as presented to the court by the plaintiff's counsel, was there any reference to the non-delegable duty '... each of these duties being **directly** owed to the plaintiff.' (My accentuation) See also 158 of the case for an exposition of the plaintiff's case, referring to the 'primary duty'. However, not once did the learned judge explicitly condone this particular exposition, although he stated at 160, that he had preferred the submissions of Mr Hone (in general, I might presume with respect).

[359] Kennedy and Grubb *Medical Law* 404, 414–415. At 414 it was previously stated that 'an English court is most unlikely to accept it.' But see *supra* 5.5.2 and the discussion relating to the development in the English law. In *Ellis* v. *Wallsend District Hospital* (1989) 17 NSWLR 553 (NSW CA) Kirby P held that by analogy, NHS hospitals undertake a duty to ensure that a patient receives reasonable care in the hospital. (An Australian case: see *infra*.)

[360] Kennedy and Grubb *et al. Principles* 465 and 462, on this issue (at that time) still remaining 'open in the modern case law.'

The complicated issue regarding the implementation of the non-delegable duty in English law, has presented various authors with a quest for legal certainty.[361] However, since the introduction of *M* v. *Calderdale & Kirklees HA*[362] legal certainty can be said to have been founded in English law.[363] What will be even more interesting, is the reasonable expectation of new developments and future implementation of the non-delegable duty in this area of law.

### *In the past:*

The policy has been adopted that where the patient receives negligent NHS treatment in NHS hospitals with resulting injury to the plaintiff, the distinction between employees and independent contractors is discarded.[364] Much of the argument about non-delegable duties thus becomes superfluous. Health authorities accept vicarious liability for medical staff irrespective of the fact whether they are engaged under a contract for services or a contract of service.[365]

As regards the NHS Trusts, one trust may lend a doctor to another. The trust hospital lending the doctor might be vicariously liable for the doctor if remaining its employer, where the doctor does not enter into a separate agreement with the borrowing hospital.[366] The trust hospital that borrows the doctor could only be liable under the non-delegable duty where no separate agreement has been made with the doctor.[367]

Regarding private medical treatment, the following arguments are presented: If an independent contractor engages a private clinic or private hospital for use of its staff and facilities, liability for the private institution under this duty, will be possible.[368] It will become the only form of liability, with exclusion of any direct liability of the institution concerning the provision of a proper system.[369] Under the law of contract, only a duty to exercise reasonable care will be implied and imposed upon a clinic. The latter

---

[361] *Supra* 5.5.1 footnote 320 and 5.5.2 footnote 327. Dugdale and Stanton *Negligence* § 22.20 544–545. Jones *Negligence* 405–406 and footnote 73. Jackson and Powell *Negligence* 493.

[362] [1998] Lloyd's Rep Med 157.

[363] See the comment of Kennedy and Grubb *et al. Principles* 1999 Second Cumulative Supplement § 8.23, 8.30 & 8.38 43–44.

[364] Jones *Negligence* 409.

[365] *Ibid.*

[366] Kennedy and Grubb *Medical Law* 414.

[367] *Ibid.*

[368] Kennedy and Grubb *Medical Law* 414–415.

[369] *Ibid.* I.e the direct liability of an institution as discussed under 5.3.

will however give rise to direct liability as discussed under 5.3. The only way in which a non-delegable duty can be raised contractually, is when the (private) clinic has accepted responsibility for the acts of its medical staff by express term. This will hardly (if ever) occur.[370] Where the private clinic however has a reputation in the 'market place' on which grounds the patient chooses the clinic, it is then judged accordingly. If the hospital holds itself out as such, it is considered to have undertaken to provide a level of service which amounts to a guarantee of reasonable care. This in turn advocates the application of the non-delegable duty.[371]

Practically speaking, in cases of private medical treatment, if a doctor's negligence is proved, a patient will have a claim against the doctor. If the doctor is an independent contractor he will probably have insured against liability through a medical defence organization. In such a case the private hospital's non-delegable duty becomes irrelevant.[372] If the doctor was not negligent, no action for breach of the hospital's non-delegable duty will be necessary. The non-delegable duty becomes of practical importance where either the plaintiff sues only the hospital and not the doctor[373] or where the doctor has limited or no insurance cover.[374]

### 5.5.4 Conclusion

The decision in **M v. *Calderdale and Kirklees HA*** [375] has, with respect, initiated a new development regarding the implementation of the non-delegable duty as an independent legal ground on which to establish hospital liability in English law.

The imposition of the non-delegable duty on hospitals, is based on economic considerations. The hospital becomes the guarantor of the independent contractor's solvency. The hospital rather than the plaintiff carries the risk of the independent contractor's insolvency or lack of insurance cover.[376]

---

[370] Kennedy and Grubb *Medical Law* 414–415.

[371] *Ibid.*

[372] Jones *Negligence* 409.

[373] This transpired in *Yepremian* v. *Scarborough General Hospital* (1980) 110 DLR (3d) 513 (Ont CA).

[374] This was the case in *Ellis* v. *Wallsend District Hospital* (1989) 17 NSWLR 553, 569. Jones *Negligence* 409.

[375] [1998] Lloyd's Rep Med 157.

[376] Jones *Negligence* 409.

Consequently, the hospital will have either a 'contractual claim for indemnity or a right to contribution under the Civil Liability (Contribution) Act 1978.'[377]

There seems to be a vast difference between advocating (in the past) that the non-delegable duty may not or should not be a part of the English law, and the reality of it already being implemented in and a necessary guideline to the English law.

## 5.6  APPORTIONMENT OF LIABILITY

The liability of hospital authorities developed dramatically with the introduction and exposition of every case.[378] When hospital authorities were sued for negligence prior to 1954, it was common for them to bring third party proceedings against the member of staff who was alleged to be at fault.[379] The Ministry of Health directed that hospital authorities should do all possible to defend staff involved in negligence claims.[380] However, under section 6 of the Law of Reform (Married Women and Tortfeasors) Act 1935, doctors or the appropriate union could be joined as defendants, and it could be asked that they be ordered to contribute to the damages and costs.[381] This indeed was done in *Jones* v. *Manchester Corporation*, in 1952. An inexperienced doctor and anaesthetist administered a full dose of pentothal to Mr Jones, after he had already been anaesthetized, thereby causing his death. The Manchester corporation was sued, and the doctor and the hospital board were added as defendants. The court found that the doctor had herself been negligent, not by reason of her inexperience, but because she had not done what she had been trained to do. The hospital board's negligence (not merely vicariously), existed of the fact that they had failed to provide appropriate supervision. The Court of Appeal allocated 20 per cent of the contribution to the doctor, and 80 per cent to the hospital board. In *Payne* v. *St Helier Group Hospital Management Committee* [382] a patient who had been kicked by a horse, sustained abdominal injuries which were not correctly diagnosed by the

---

[377]  *Ibid.*

[378]  Lee 1979 *ALR* 324.

[379]  Jackson & Powell *Negligence* 494.

[380]  Lee 1979 *ALR* 324–325.

[381]  *Ibid.* Kennedy and Grubb *et al. Principles* 447: Now: 'While, in the case of vicarious liability, the employee will in theory remain legally liable to the patient and the employer will have an indemnity claim against the employee, in practice it is the institution who is sued and who pays the damages award.'

[382]  (1952) CIYB 2442.

casualty officer. Donovan J held that the hospital was not negligent in its system of examination of abdominal injuries, but the casualty officer was negligent. The hospital authority was granted a full indemnity against the casualty officer.

In ***Romford Ice and Cold Storage*** v. ***Lister*** [383] the Court of Appeal held that the master should have a right to indemnity against the vicarious liability for the servant. This would arise out of an implied contractual term that the servant should act with all reasonable skill and care. The House of Lords held on appeal, that the employer could recover damages for breach of a contractual obligation from the employee. The employee, however, was not entitled to be indemnified by the employer, because there was no implied term — to such an effect — in the contract of service. The effect of these decisions made it possible for the employer to obtain a full indemnity against a negligent servant, either under 1935 Act or for breach of an implied term of a contract of employment.[384] Where the employee had not been negligent alone, the claim for full indemnity could not succeed.[385]

In 1949 the Ministry offered guidelines to hospital authorities concerning the Law Reform Act 1935 by a Circular RHB (49) 128. This policy was reversed in 1954 by a further Department of Health Circular, HM (54) 32.[386] Contribution legislation which had been introduced by the Law Reform Act 1935, had been used in medical litigation, for example the *Jones* case. Its significance was however greatly reduced in the case of actions against NHS hospital doctors, since the introduction of the 1954 Circular.[387] The Department implicitly acknowledged — by the Circular — that the Health Authorities were vicariously liable for the negligence of members of the medical staff, of whatever rank and whatever their contractual relationship. The Circular introduced a private arrangement of agreement between doctors' Defence Societies and the Department of Health whereby the compensation paid to the plaintiff was apportioned between the defendants (the doctor and the Health Authority) as privately agreed upon, or in the absence of such an

---

[383] (1955) 3 WLR 631. A complete indemnity was granted.

[384] Lee 1979 *ALR* 326.

[385] *Ibid.*

[386] Lee 1979 *ALR* 327–328; Kennedy *Responsibility* 156; Jones *Negligence* 411; Jackson & Powell *Negligence* 494. Kennedy and Grubb *et al. Principles* 486.

[387] Jones *Negligence* 411; The Law Reform (Married Women and Tortfeasors) Act 1935, (and particularly section 6, has now been repealed and replaced by The Civil Liability (Contribution)n Act 1978, (s 2 (2)). The latter section is a more extensive provision which 'allows the court to exempt any person from liability to make contribution or to direct that the contribution to be recovered from any person shall amount to a complete immunity.'

agreement, in equal shares.[388] Consequently, the Circular provided a formal, though not legally binding, mechanism which reduced the costs of the defendants and presented them as a united front in litigation.[389] As a result third party or contribution proceedings were no longer brought.[390]

From January 1, 1990 the 1954 arrangement was replaced by the 'NHS indemnity', introducing a new arrangement concerning hospital doctors.[391] In terms of this arrangement health authorities assumed responsibility for new and existing claims of medical negligence. They no longer require their medical and dental staff to subscribe to a defence organization. The health authority's indemnity covers only health authority responsibilities, namely their 'vicarious liability for the negligence of staff acting in the course of their employment, and there is no attempt to seek contribution from the employee.'[392] It also includes consultants and staff provided by external agencies. The NHS indemnity applies also only to those general practitioners who provide treatment under a NHS contract of employment. Where a claim is instituted against both a health authority or NHS Trust and a doctor, the possibility of a contribution claim exists. But in such a case the Circular requests both these parties to co-operate fully in the formulation of a defence, and to reach a private agreement as to the apportionment of their respective liabilities.[393] The NHS indemnity scheme does not apply to private hospitals or private work which is undertaken by consultants in a NHS hospital. Questions of apportionment can thus still arise in that context.[394]

The NHS hospitals further cover work done by junior medical staff which is within the scope of their employment or under their contract, for example the care of private patients. 'Good Samaritan' acts assisting at an accident are not covered whilst negligence by a locum doctor provided by an internal or external agency, falls within the scheme.[395]

---

[388] *Ibid*; Kennedy *Responsibility* 156. Finch *Law* 97. See also Taylor *Malpractice* 54–57. Kennedy and Grubb *et al. Principles* 486.

[389] Kennedy and Grubb *et al. Principles* 486.

[390] Jackson & Powell *Negligence* 494.

[391] Jones *Negligence* 411; Jackson & Powell *Negligence* 494–495. Kennedy and Grubb *et al. Principles* 486–488.

[392] Jones *Negligence* 411–412. Kennedy and Grubb *et al. Principles* 487.

[393] Jones *Negligence* 412. Kennedy and Grubb *et al. Principles* 488.

[394] Jones *Negligence* 412; Jackson & Powell *Negligence* 494–495. Kennedy and Grubb *et al. Principles* 488.

[395] Jones *Negligence* 412. Kennedy and Grubb *et al. Principles* 488.

NHS Trust hospitals do not fall within NHS indemnity.[396] NHS Trusts bear their own losses arising from claims for clinical negligence from April 1, 1991. They are, however, unlike health authorities, free to enter into private insurance agreements to cover their risks. They will thus bear the cost of claims against doctors and not seek any contribution from them, in order to avoid problems in recruiting or retaining staff.[397]

Contribution claims under the Civil Liability (Contribution) Act 1978, will thus be limited to actions arising from private medicine, and disputes between general practitioners and pharmacists, and general practitioners and hospitals.[398] Defendants can, of course, always find a gentleman's agreement in respect of their responsibilities, instead of a recourse to the legislation or courts.[399]

---

[396] Jones *Negligence* 412.

[397] *Ibid*. Kennedy and Grubb *et al. Principles* 488 and footnote 223.

[398] Jones *Negligence* 410, 414.

[399] *Ibid*; Lee 1979 *ALR* 329–330. Compare Kennedy and Grubb *et al. Principles* 486.

# Chapter 6

# The Australian Law

## 6.1 HEALTH CARE IN AUSTRALIA
### LAND AREA: 7,680,000 SQ. KM.[1]

### 6.1.1 Health Care

Health is defined as 'a state of complete physical, mental and social well-being and not merely absence of disease and infirmity'.[2] The health of people is thus considered to encompass both their illness and wellness.[3] The health and well-being of Australian people is regulated by a comprehensive health care industry which is supported by a dynamic health care system.[4]

### 6.1.2 Health Care System

In the Australian health care system many sectors of society participate to ensure the well-being of the nation: The Federal government and local governments; State and regional health bureaucracies such as the government departments of Social Security and Veteran's Affairs and Repatriation; State and Territory instrumentalities; religious and charitable organizations.[5] The Australian health care system also illustrates features of the federal system in the provision of their health services.[6] The health care system is

---

[1]  Affordable Health Care Singapore 1993: Appendix B Subject 1.

[2]  This definition is found in the preamble to the constitution of the World Health Organization (WHO) of 1946.

[3]  Clinton *et al. Health Care* 3.

[4]  See also Clinton *et al. Health Care* 2–11.

[5]  *Ibid.*

[6]  Ryden and Mackay *Health* 204.

characterized by the development of inter-state co-operation, inter-governmental authorities and uniform legislation.[7]

Australian health care is delivered through a mixed system of providers. The providers are from the government, quasi- or non-government non-profit-seeking and private profit-seeking agencies as well as private professional practitioners.[8]

(i)    Primary health care is provided by:[9]

-    Community health centres
-    General practitioners
-    Private specialists and
-    Pharmacists.

(ii)   Institutional care is provided by:[10]

-    Public hospitals ranging from rural hospitals providing basic medical or surgical care to large urban district hospitals;
-    Teaching hospitals with full range of services.
-    Private hospitals and mental institutions.
-    Nursing homes.

(iii)  Domiciliary care services and

(iv)   Aerial medical services[11] are also provided.

### 6.1.3  Health Financing

The Australian health care system has various funding sources which consist of the Commonwealth, States and Territories, Health insurance funds and individuals.[12] The Commonwealth bears direct responsibility for 'the national Medicare, Pharmaceutical Benefits, Nursing Home Benefits, the war veterans 'health care programs' and 'the quarantine service'. It also provides financial assistance to a variety of health and health-related activities including medical research. The Commonwealth controls ± 40 per

---

[7]    *Ibid.*

[8]    Dewdney *Health Policy* 61.

[9]    Affordable Health Care Singapore 1993: Appendix B Subject 10.

[10]   *Ibid.*

[11]   *Ibid.*

[12]   Clinton *et al. Health Care* 5 figure 1.2: Components of the Australian health care system.

cent of Australia's health expenditure.[13] Government channels also provide the health care system with funds.[14] The state governments, together with local government authorities, currently control approximately one-third of total health service expenditure.[15] The state governments (or public sector) subsidize financially 'a range of personal and institutional health services at federal, state and local levels'.[16] State governments also have major legislative responsibilities concerning health matters, while local government authorities have some involvement in health matters.[17]

Health care is also financed by:[18]

(i)     A national health insurance scheme called Medicare. Medicare is financed from taxes. It covers the full costs in public hospitals and partial costs in private hospitals.

(ii)    Private health insurance is available for private patients in public hospitals or in case of private hospital charges.

(iii)   The Federal Pharmaceutical Benefits Scheme assists in meeting costs of drugs.

Australia's health expenditure in 1991, was A$30.9 billion and averaged 8 per cent of GDP (gross domestic product).[19] It has remained fairly constant over the last ten years. Australia proportionally spends less than the United States but more than the United Kingdom or Japan, and is on a par with other OECD countries like Canada and France.[20] The A$30.9 billion health care expenditure represents the total amount spent by both the private and public sectors. The federal government spent A$14761 million on health in 1992/3 with a projected spending of A$17688 million for 1995/6.[21]

---

[13]   Dewdney *Health Policy* 61.

[14]   *Ibid.*

[15]   *Ibid.*

[16]   Gardner and McCoppin *Health* 1.

[17]   Dewdney *Health Policy* 61.

[18]   Affordable Health Care Singapore 1993: Appendix B Subject 9.

[19]   Clinton *et al. Health Care* 3.

[20]   *Ibid.* The 'six Organization for Economic Cooperation and Development (OECD) countries' discussed here are Australia, the UK, Canada, Japan, NZ and the US.

[21]   *Op. cit.* 4.

## 6.2 THE HOSPITAL IN AUSTRALIA

The first hospital in Australia was constructed in Sydney Cove in 1788 by the colonial government. Since then state public authorities have built, owned and operated hospital institutions, thus creating a hospital system. Voluntary bodies like churches started building hospitals in the nineteenth century. They did, however, become dependent on state government grants to provide for the poor, and were designated as 'public hospitals', though still controlled by private entities. Private hospitals which operated as profit and nonprofit hospitals for paying patients, evolved later.[22]

Currently, the Australian health care system can be divided into institutional and non-institutional health care services.[23] Institutional services are provided by means of public hospitals, private hospitals, repatriation hospitals, public mental hospitals, nursing homes, other residential services and ambulance services.[24] Non-institutional services include medical services, dental services, pharmaceutical benefits, aids and appliances, administration, research and other non-institutional support or other services.[25] The health care system and its services are supported by public and health legislation and initiatives.[26] The institutional health care provider sector, which also provides hospital care, is the largest and most costly component of the Australian health care system.[27] The hospital system of Australia forms a major part of the social and economic activity of the nation.[28] Hospital expenditure in 1989–90 amounted to over A$10 billion.[29]

Every Australian state manifests a unique administrative system and organizational structure or plan for the delivery of health care services which is often changed, due to technological and other variants.[30] The provision of institutionalized health care or hospital care is as diversified in the various states as it is diversified in different institutions in those states. It is one of

---

[22]  Roemer and Roemer *Health* 104.

[23]  Clinton *et al. Health Care* 5.

[24]  *Op. cit.* 5.

[25]  *Ibid.*

[26]  *Ibid.*

[27]  *Op. cit.* 6.

[28]  *Ibid.* See the National Health Strategy 1991 b p10.

[29]  Clinton *et al. Health Care* 5.

[30]  See also chapter 2 *supra*. See also Roemer and Roemer *Health* 96 and Sax *Health* 234, 250.

the most diversified health services.[31] There are both public hospitals and private hospitals — which are each classified into non-profit and for-profit institutions[32] — in every state.

In 1986, there were 1,067 hospitals, exclusive of psychiatric institutions,[33] consisting of 734 public hospitals and 333 private institutions.[34] However, in 1992 A\$31 billion was spent, which paid for 1,000 acute care hospitals, 60 public psychiatric hospitals, 1,500 nursing homes and 1,000 hostels.[35] This hospital count was not even inclusive of all the hospitals in Australia.

### 6.3 LEGAL GROUNDS OF HOSPITAL LIABILITY IN AUSTRALIA

#### 6.3.1 Indirect or Vicarious Hospital Liability

In Australian law, the principle of vicarious liability based on the doctrine of *respondeat superior*, is also applied.[36] It basically entails that the master is held responsible (liable) whenever the employee commits a wrong during the course of his employment.[37] A legal liability is imposed on an organization or person for the wrong of another, with no personal fault attaching to the institution or person.[38] This doctrine stems from the common law principle that the master takes responsibility for his servant. Vicarious liability is therefore 'an incident which the law impresses upon certain relationships, of which that of employer-employee is the most notable'.[39]

Consequently the institutional health care provider or hospital in question can be held vicariously liable for the negligence of employees acting in the

---

[31] Roemer and Roemer *Health* 104.

[32] *Ibid.*

[33] Sax *Health* 235.

[34] *Ibid.*

[35] Clinton *et al. Health Care* 6–7.

[36] Wallace *Law* 157–161. MacFarlane *Health Law* 26–33, 36. Bates *et al. Hospital Liability* 4. Cahill *et al. Hospital Liability* 2–3. Trindade and Cane *Torts* 717–745. Fleming *Torts* 409–429. Whippy *ALJ* 182. The discussion in 4.2.1 serves as an introductory passage to this discussion.

[37] *Ibid.*

[38] Trindade and Cane *Torts* 717: Vicarious liability is a form of strict liability 'in the sense that the person held vicariously liable may not have been personally at fault'. Dix *et al. Australia* 311 § 1151.

[39] Dix *et al. Australia* 311 § 1151. Wallace *Law* 157.

course of their employment.[40] The hospital is also under a common law duty to provide reasonable care and treatment to patients.[41] Even if the employer endeavours to provide the best treatment, lack of knowledge of the negligent activity will not indemnify him/her against liability, where the employee resumes activities which are a part of the employer's enterprise.[42] The institutional health-care provider or hospital and/or responsible staff can be sued, and the court will order the respective parties to pay damages. The hospital or facility is usually regarded as the appropriate defendant to sue and to recover compensation for the plaintiff-patients, because of its financial resources and insurance.[43] Samuels JA did, however, state that institutions and individuals are insurance-wise, equally protected nowadays.[44]

### 6.3.1.1  Traditional requirements of vicarious liability

The traditional requirements[45] that apply in the most common situation of vicarious liability, have also been accepted and adhered to in Australian law. They are:

6.3.1.1.1  Master and servant (employer-employee) relationship

6.3.1.1.2  In the course/scope of employment or in the execution of duties

6.3.1.1.3  Actionable wrong(s)

---

[40]  Dix *et al. Australia* 311 § 1151.

[41]  Wallace *Law* 157: It can also be contractually obliged to provide reasonable treatment in terms of the contract between the hospital and the patient.

[42]  Wallace *Law* 157. Trindade and Cane *Torts* 728, 735–736. Fleming *Torts* 420–422, 426. MacFarlane *Health Law* 26.

[43]  *Ellis* v. *Wallsend District Hospital* (1989) 17 NSWLR 553 (CA) 569 per Kirby P: 'Where, as here, the honorary surgeon was not fully indemnified, the question is where the law should assign the loss. It is preferable, in my view, that is should be fixed upon the hospital which has far better facilities (and can be expected) to insure itself fully. That insurance can readily cover all staff — honorary and otherwise. Only in this way can the patient be protected from the predicament which now faces Mrs Ellis because of the under-insurance of the late Dr Chambers: cf *Ybarra* v. *Spangard* 154 P 2d 687 (1944) at 690; *Bing* v. *Thunig*.' Wallace *law* 157. Whippy 1989 *ALJ* 202. Fleming *Torts* 411. Dix *et al. Australia* 311 § 1151.

[44]  *Ellis infra* 606 B per Samuels and Meagher JJA.

[45]  Fleming *Torts* 412–426. Trindade and Cane *Torts* 717–725, 735–736, 742–744. Cahill *et al. Hospital Liability* 2. MacFarlane *Health Law* 26. Wallace *Law* 157–160. *Ellis* v. *Wallsend District Hospital* (1989) 17 NSWLR 553 Samuels and Meagher JJA 590.

### 6.3.1.1.1 Master and servant (employer-employee) relationship

A basic traditional rule exists that the employer will be vicariously liable only for the wrongful acts of servants (employees), and not for the wrongs committed by independent contractors (agents).[46] The distinction is determined on all the facts and circumstances of a particular case.[47] A uniform set of principles have emerged — with possible underlying policy issues — which govern the finding of whether a worker is a servant or not, in whatever context it might arise.[48] A parallelled application of this classification is found in other areas of law: taxation, social security, workers' compensation, industrial safety and long-service leave.[49] The existence of the employee-status has been considered by scrutinizing various tests in order to establish whether a person was indeed an employee or an independent contractor. The control test,[50] the organization test[51] and other tests[52] such as the independent business test,[53] have been considered.

### *6.3.1.1.1.1 Relevant tests*

(a)    The control test

(b)    The organization test

(c)    The independent business test

(d)    Other tests

(a)    The control test[54]

It seems that the control test has been taken cognizance of in Australian law, in many different forms and in different situations. According to Australian law the conventional mode of distinguishing between a servant and an independent contractor — or a contract of service and a contract for services[55] — is that the employee is a servant if he/she is 'subject to the

---

[46]    *Ibid.*

[47]    Trindade and Cane *Torts* 718.

[48]    *Ibid.*

[49]    *Ibid.* Fleming *Torts* 416.

[50]    Wallace *Law* 158, 245.

[51]    *Ibid.*

[52]    *Op. cit.* 158–159, 245.

[53]    Trindade and Cane *Torts* 724–725.

[54]    *Op. cit.* 718–723. Fleming *Torts* 414–416. Wallace *Law* 158, 245: Wallace recommends the control test as the 'foremost test'.

[55]    The terminology stems from the (Australian) Workers' Compensation Acts. Fleming *Torts* 414.

command of the master as to the manner in which he shall do his work',[56] while 'an independent contractor undertakes to produce a given result but is not in the actual execution of the work, under the order or control of the person for whom he does it.'[57] According to Fleming the employee was considered a servant if the superior could tell him/her **what** and **how** to do the work. This test was successful in primitive industrial and social conditions where the master's knowledge and experience equated that of the servant.[58]

It has, however, become 'increasingly difficult to apply the control test as a meaningful working rule to many modern situations'.[59] Technological developments, individualized professionalism and modern conditions negate control. The control test was adjusted accordingly. The question then became 'whether ultimate authority over the person in the performance of his work resided in the employer so that he was subject to the latter's orders and directions'.[60] It became a more flexible approach which incorporated circumstantial factors such as the power of dismissal, provision of own equipment, selection of own subordinates, delegation of work and subordination to detailed orders.[61] Fleming remarks that in the light of this development, the word 'servant' perhaps becomes unfortunate because it carries a connotation narrower than its legal meaning. He suggests the usage of the term 'contract of service' instead.[62]

Trindade and Cane mention that the one indicium to distinguish between a servant and an independent contractor could be whether they were employed under a contract **of** service or a contract **for** services.[63] It could also be asked whether the employer was entitled to tell the employee what and how to do and, ultimately has the 'power of dismissing the worker for

---

[56]  *Yewens* v. *Noakes* (1880) 6 QBD 530, 532 per Bramwell LJ.

[57]  *Queensland Stations* v. *FCT* (1945) 70 CLR 539, 545 per Latham CJ.

[58]  Fleming *Torts* 414.

[59]  *Ibid.*

[60]  *Humberstone* v. *Northern Timber Mills* (1949) 79 CLR 389, 404 per Dixon J. Cf. *Zuijs* v. *Wirth Bros* (1955) 93 CLR 561, 571: 'The duties to be performed may depend so much on professional skill or knowledge ... or the necessity of the employee acting on his own responsibility may be so evident, that little room for direction or command in detail may exist. But that is not the point. What matters is lawful authority to command so far as there is scope for it.'

[61]  Fleming *Torts* 415. Trindade and Cane *Torts* 720.

[62]  Fleming *Torts* 415–416.

[63]  Trindade and Cane *Torts* 718–719.

failure to observe instructions'.[64] In certain cases which involve more than one employer, the ultimate question would be, how much control was transferred to a particular employer.[65] They also suggest that the test should not be for factual control, but for the right to control.[66] They did not only dilute the inherent significance of control, but also reduced its authoritative nature in determining master-servant relationships. It was stated 'that control (in the sense of the right to control) is one, but only one, factor relevant to classifying particular employment relationships'.[67]

This broad approach has been supported by the High Court.[68] Concerning the justification of vicarious liability in this regard, it has been concluded that:

> At all events, if we adopt a functional approach to vicarious liability and view it as a technique for allocating losses so as to maximize the chance that injured plaintiffs will be compensated in the most economically efficient way, there seems very little justification for the rule.[69]

The fundamental approach of Wallace[70] still maintains an absolute loyalty to the control test — in any desired form. The control or right to control test is recommended as the 'foremost test' that should be applied, which is regarded as the most important indicium by which the employer-employee relationship is identified.[71] The control test considers the amount of control the employer exerts over the conditions, workplace, tools, the manner in which it is carried out, hours of performance and many more.[72] The more positive answers to these questions, the more likely it becomes that the person is an employee.[73] However, when the skill, expertise or judgment of the professional exceeds that of the employer, the employer does not have much scope to control the employee's actions.[74] Then the question posed is whether the employer has 'authority to command in as much as there is

---

[64]   *Op. cit.* 719. Also '... it is clear that control is only one relevant factor'.

[65]   *Op. cit.* 720.

[66]   *Op. cit.* 721.

[67]   *Op. cit.* 722.

[68]   *Ibid. Stevens* v. *Brodribb Sawmilling* (1986) 160 CLR 16.

[69]   Trindade and Cane *Torts* 721–722.

[70]   Wallace *Law* 158, 245 footnote 1, 248–249.

[71]   *Ibid.*

[72]   *Op. cit.* 158, 245 footnote 1.

[73]   *Op. cit.* 158.

[74]   *Ibid.*

scope for it'.[75] In *Zuijs* v. *Wirth Bros Pty Ltd*,[76] a trapeze artist was held to be an employee of the circus. The circus management could direct the places and times of performances, pay and leave conditions, rehearsal times and other supplementary duties.

(b)    The organization test

After the control test had been discounted in some common law cases,[77] other courts[78] experienced increasing strain on the traditional formulation. Alternative tests were proposed.[79] The 'organization' (and 'entrepreneur'[80]) tests, were introduced. The organization test considers whether the person participates in or is part of the employer's organization, or the extent to which a person's work contributes to the general organization of the employer.[81] Fleming formulates as follows:

> Was his work subject to co-ordinational control as to the 'where' and 'when' rather than the 'how'?[82]

In respect of hospital cases, the untenability of the control test had especially been ousted by the reasonableness of the organization test. Fleming[83] states that the uncontrollability of professionals in hospital settings no longer precludes recovery, as long as they form part of the organization of the hospital, thus initiating support for the organization test. He even goes so far as to say that the differentiation between employees and independent contractors — for which purpose the control test and organization test have ultimately been implemented — becomes irrelevant when affording liability

---

[75]    *Ibid.*

[76]    (1955) 93 CLR 561. Wallace *Law* 158.

[77]    *Gold* v. *Essex* [1942] 2 KB 293, 299, 305–307, 310–313; *Cassidy* v. *MOH* [1951] 2 KB 343 per Denning LJ at 360, 363–364; *Roe* v. *Minister of Health* [1954] 2 QB 66 per Morris LJ (and Somervell LJ) at 88–89, *infra*.

[78]    *Cassidy* v. *MOH* [1951] 2 KB 343 per Somervell J. *Humberstone* v. *Northern Timber Mills* (1949) 79 CLR 389 at 404 per Dixon J. Fleming *Torts* 416: 'Was he part of his employer's organization?'

[79]    A test like: 'Was he in business on his own account?', was invented in *Market Investigations* v. *Minister of Social Security* [1969] 2 QB 173. Other tests also include conditions 'such as the right to dismiss, to set the conditions and hours of work, the right to the exclusive services of the person', which according to Wallace *Law* 158 indicate that the person is an employee rather than an independent contractor. See *infra*.

[80]    Fleming *Torts* 416, 417–418. The entrepreneur test considers if the person was 'in business on his own account, …'.

[81]    *Ibid.* Wallace *Law* 158.

[82]    Fleming *Torts* 416.

[83]    *Op. cit.* 417.

to the hospital by means of the non-delegable duty. Such an exercise to expand the liability of the 'deep pockets', has been equally applied to other institutions, like in schools for example where injury occur to pupils, and in other circumstances.

Wallace states that when the health care professional provides health care in the hospital, his health care contribution to the general organization of the hospital facility as employer — under a contract of employment — will be integral to the employer's activities rather than peripheral (which could entail a hospital building's development).[84] This would constitute compliance with the organization test and grant the health professional employee-status.

Trindade and Cane[85] suggest that the organization test implies that the employer has a high degree of control over a core organization, but sometimes supplements the core with workers over which he exercises considerably less control. However, if the business had not been organized in such a two-tier way, or where there was no evidence concerning the organization of the defendant's business, the test would not be of much use.

Most Australian authors refer to the organization test with regard to its implementation in common law and its applicability or suitability in Australian law. At **common law**, the 'organization test' was first briefly referred to in *Gold* v. *Essex County Council* by Lord Greene.[86] The organization test was introduced in *Roe* v. *Minister of Health* by Morris LJ where he stated:

> I consider that the anaesthetists were members of the 'organization' of the hospital: they were members of the staff engaged by the hospital to do what the hospital itself was undertaking to do.[87]

Denning LJ formulated the organizational employer-employee test as follows in *Bank Voor Handel en Scheepvaart NV* v. *Slatford*:

> ...the test of being a servant does not rest nowadays on submission to orders. It depends on whether the person is part and parcel of the organization.[88]

---

[84] Wallace *Law* 158.

[85] Trindade and Cane *Torts* 723–724.

[86] [1942] 2 KB 293 at 302: 'He will find an organization which comprises consulting physicians and surgeons, presumably also house physicians and surgeons, a staff of nurses, equipment for administering ... treatment and a radiographer, ... employed to give that treatment.' At 304: 'I am unable to see how a body invested with such a power and to all appearance exercising it, can be said to be assuming no greater obligation than to provide a skilled person and proper appliances.'

[87] [1954] 2 QB 66 at 89, 91.

[88] [1953] 1 QB 248, 295. Cf *FCT* v. *Barrett* (1973) 129 CLR 395, 402 per Stephen J.

In *Stevenson, Jordan and Harrison Ltd* v. *MacDonald and Evans,* Lord Denning reaffirmed the organization test:

> It is often easy to recognise a contract of service when you see it, but difficult to say wherein the difference lies. A ship's master, a chauffeur, and a reporter on the staff of a newspaper are all employed under a contract of service; but a ship's pilot, a taxi-man, and a newspaper contributor are employed under a contract for services. One feature which seems to run through the instances is that, under a contract of service, a man is employed as part of the business, and his work is done as an integral part of the business; whereas, under a contract for services, his work, although done for the business, is not integrated into it but is only accessory to it.[89]

In Australian law there seemed to be a shift from vicarious liability to a personal liability in terms of the non-delegable duty for an authoritative **organizer** in the *Introvigne* and *Kondis* cases.[90] Yet according to Trindade and Cane there could be no sufficient implementation of the organization test in the case of *Massey* v. *Crown Life Insurance Co.*[91]

The Australian High Court did, in any case, reject the organization test in **Stevens** v. **Brodribb Sawmilling Co Pty Ltd.**[92] (1986). In the *Stevens* case, the Australian High Court considered an appropriate test in order to determine whether a person was an employee or an independent contractor.

(1) The court firstly decided that a 'prominent factor in determining the nature of the relationship ... is the degree of control'[93] which the party who engages the other exercises over the latter. The control test was thus once again accommodated, if only in disguised form, namely 'the right of the employer to exercise'[94] control. Mason J continued to find that control was not the sole indicia or criterion to be considered in determining the nature of the relationship. Relevant matters that could be inferred from the engagement such as 'the mode of remuneration, the provision and maintenance of equipment, the obligation to work, the hours of work and provision for holidays, the deduction of income

---

[89]  [1952] 1 TLR 101 at 111. See also *Whittaker* v. *Minister of Pensions* [1967] 1 QB 156, 167. See also Osode 1993 *AALR* 302 footnote 33. See also Fleming *Torts* 416–417.

[90]  *Commonwealth* v. *Introvigne* (1982) 150 CLR 258. *Kondis* v. *State Transport* (1984) 154 CLR 672 at 690. These cases involved a school as organizer of the supervision of pupils and the organization of a construction project. Fleming *Torts* 418.

[91]  [1978] 2 ALL ER 576. Trindade and Cane *Torts* 724.

[92]  (1986) 60 ALJR 194; (1986) 160 CLR 16. Wallace *Law* 158. MacFarlane *Health Law* 27–29. Trindade and Cane *Torts* 724.

[93]  *Stevens* 24.

[94]  *Stevens* 24.

tax and the delegation of work by the putative employee',[95] were to be considered as well.

(2) Mason J proceeded to disclaim the organization test since he argued that the organization test could not result in a finding that a contract of service existed, when the control test independently or together with other indicia indicated that there was a contract for services. Choosing between the organization test and control test he concluded that '[o]f the two concepts, legal authority to control is the more relevant and the more cogent in determining the nature of the relationship.'[96]

(3) The organization test was further discarded by rejecting the effect of imposing this test. Mason J stated:

> ... the organization test has the effect of imposing liability on the proprietor of the organization, whether he had the capacity to control the contractor or not. Whether the court should impose vicarious liability on a proprietor in these circumstances is a very large question on which we have not had the benefit of argument.[97]

Commenting on the above, with respect:[98]

(1) Any reliance on the control test or any of its replicas, cannot be approved in the medical malpractice context. The general discussion in Chapter 4 on Indirect Liability, dealt with the inappropriateness of the control test in determining hospital liability.

(2) The organization test had been recommended implicitly in a few cases. Even disregarding this fact, it remains difficult to reject a test on hypothetical grounds without having concretely subjected all the circumstances to an organization test scenario. A test should also not be dismissed merely because the result of such a test is not favoured. However, the matter had not been properly argued before the court nor was it fully considered by the court, thus forfeiting an ideal opportunity to contemplate its proper application.

(3) The element of control was in effect regarded as the main element. It could seem that the rejection of the organization test, was therefore not founded on contemplated merit, but on the idea suggesting that if liability was not concluded by acknowledging the element of control,

---

[95] *Stevens* 24.

[96] *Stevens* 27.

[97] *Stevens* 28.

[98] The comments and conclusion are presented with all respect.

no liability should be established. Liability which could be established without accrediting control, could not be contemplated since the judge commented that the saga involving the organization test had not been argued before the court.

With all due respect, this decision and its deliberations on the organization test and other related matters will not facilitate similar pending critical issues in hospital cases. In conclusion this decision should not be relied upon to determine the employer-employee requirement for vicarious liability, due to the following reasons:

(a)     Firstly the decision presents no thorough investigation of the potential of the organization test. It was not properly argued before the court nor reviewed in an in-depth discussion.

(b)     Most importantly, it is submitted that the employee requirement should eventually not be regarded as an independent determinative factor or absolute prerequisite to establish vicarious hospital liability. This will be discussed *infra*.

(c)     The independent business test

The Privy Council formulated a test in *Lee Ting Sang* v. *Chung Chi-Keung*,[99] in order to establish the status of a worker. The test did not cover the degree of control exercised by the employer over his workers, nor the nature of the employer's business but rather the economic status of the worker. If he was a 'skilled artisan earning his living by working for more than one employer as an employee', he would be a servant. If he was 'a small businessman venturing into business on his own account as an independent contractor with all its … risks', he would not be a servant. If he was 'performing services as a person in business on his own account', he would also not be a servant, but an independent contractor.

Trindade and Cane suggest that under certain circumstances, where work is scarce, and bad conditions are rife, workers should be protected:

> Under such circumstances it may seem only fair that the common law should, by extending the notion of 'servant' to cover such workers, offer them such protection as it can and shift responsibility for the torts of such workers on to those who benefit most from their work.[100]

---

[99]   [1990] 2 AC 374.

[100]   Trindade and Cane *Torts* 725.

## (d)    Other tests

Australian courts have indicated that all facts must be considered in order to determine that a person is an employee rather than an independent contractor.[101] Other factors[102] which are recognized are: mode of remuneration, provision and maintenance of equipment, the obligation to work, provision of holidays, deduction of income tax, delegation of work by the putative employee, the right to dismiss and to set the conditions, working hours and the right to the exclusive services of the person.

The Australian courts have also clearly distinguished between non-institutional health care providers who have been selected by the institutional treating body and those who are selected by patient-clients to treat them in a hospital, clinic or other institutional facility.[103] In *Albrighton* v. *Royal Prince Alfred Hospital*[104] (and other cases)[105] it was held that in instances where the health care professional who treats the patient is selected by the patient (and not the institutional facility or hospital), the hospital will not be responsible for the negligence of that professional. This principle is however subject to certain conditions according to Wallace.[106] 'If they are required to abide by hospital rules, standards and procedures, for example, thereby submitting to some extent to the hospital's control, they may become part of the organization and the hospital may well be found liable for their negligence. In the *Albrighton* case the court considered that because the doctors accepted and complied with the hospital's forms and routines, and had abided by its by-laws they were employees'.[107] [*sic*] It is, however, submitted that the conclusion that the doctors were employees should be followed, but that the basis on which it was found, namely that of 'control' which qualifies them as being 'part of the organization', is not necessary and with respect, quite excessive. The control test is really out-dated and the use of control to establish compliance with the organization test, is extraordinary. The same result could have been achieved by just considering the relevant factors, at the expense of using the control test.

---

[101]    Wallace *Law* 158, 245 footnote 1. *Stevens* v. *Brodribb Sawmilling Co Pty Ltd* (1986) 160 CLR 16.

[102]    Wallace *Law* 158, 245 footnote 1.

[103]    See *infra* the discussion on *A condition which limits hospital liability.* See also Wallace *Law* 159.

[104]    [1980] 2 NSWLR 542.

[105]    See *infra.*

[106]    Wallace *Law* 159.

[107]    *Ibid*

## Conclusion on tests

In conclusion, according to Australian sources, some[108] tests or all[109] tests are ultimately unsatisfactory. The elements that are assessed in every case are incommensurable factors or variable indicia which produce variant value judgments, which are influenced by the relevance of the relationship.[110] It is claimed that the system lacks a stable prototype external test, undergirded by certain parameters which could establish an objective criterion to ensure a balanced answer to the ultimate question.[111]

## A condition which limits hospital liability

In effect, from the vestiges of the English doctrine of charitable immunity which had a surprising universal effect little else remained than strained formulations of the control test. The control test had been implemented to protect hospitals from liability. That protection became unnecessary with the development of publicly financed hospitals which replaced privately supported charities.[112] Hospital liability progressed even in Australian law[113] except for certain honoraries.[114] 'The uncontrollability for such professionals in the performance of their tasks no longer precludes recovery, so long as they are subordinated to the hospital organization.'[115] This becomes most evident from English legislation which renders the distinction between employees and independent contractors irrelevant for hospital liability in terms of the non-delegable duty.[116] The distinction also became irrelevant in the sense that it was no longer necessary to precisely identify where the fault

---

[108]   *Ellis* v. *Wallsend District Hospital* (1989) 17 NSWLR 553 per Samuels JA at 596 G, 597 A-C, * D-G, 598 A-C.

[109]   Trindade and Cane *Torts* 725.

[110]   *Ibid. Ellis supra.*

[111]   *Ibid.* Trindade and Cane *Torts* 725 state: 'For this reason it is very strange that the courts, as we have noted, insist that the term 'servant' has a uniform meaning throughout the law'.

[112]   Fleming *Torts* 417.

[113]   See the discussion on Australian Case Law in this chapter; cf *Henson* v. *Perth Hospital* (1939) 41 WALR 15.

[114]   *Ellis* v. *Wallsend District Hospital* (1989) 17 NSWLR 553 (CA). But not so in *Albrighton* v. *RPA Hospital* [1980] 2 NSWLR 542 (CA). Fleming *Torts* 417.

[115]   Fleming *Torts* 417. This suggests implementation of the organization test. See *infra.*

[116]   See Chapter 5 on the discussion of the Non-Delegable Duty. The National Health Service Act 1946 s 3 of the English law. Fleming *Torts* 417. Jones *Negligence* 409.

had originated in the organization.[117] In other words the status of the perpetrator did not matter any more. It was irrelevant whether the person acting negligently was an independent contractor or an employee or had any other status at the relevant hospital. Liability could still rest with the hospital, irrespective of the perpetrator's status.

The general trend in the expansion of hospital liability holds the perspective that the hospital is no longer just a venue for the performance of medical procedures or the offering of facilities, but the provider of medical treatment.[118] For that reason it is held liable vicariously or under a non-delegable duty. The integrated institution has to take responsibility for all officers who are part of it.[119] The hospital thus becomes liable in terms of various doctrines for various officers or perpetrators.

But there is, however, a condition to this expanding approach to hospital liability. The condition has been implemented to limit the extent of hospital liability both in terms of vicarious (hospital) liability as well as in terms of the non-delegable duty. The condition seems to be in Anglo-Australian law — where not negated by legislation or modern legal judgments — that where the patient selects, employs and pays the doctor, no liability is in question for the hospital.[120] Usually, the institutional health care provider or hospital will be liable vicariously if the medical officer who committed the wrong had been selected by the institution or its personnel, irrespective of the status of the officer or practitioner.[121] But where the alleged wrongdoer was selected by the patient, no vicarious liability will follow for the institutional health care provider or hospital.[122] This also applies in case of the non-delegable duty. Usually, hospital liability could ensue in terms of the non-delegable duty for the wrongs committed by an independent contractor, if the patient selects the hospital for treatment. But the application of this condition — the patient selecting and employing the practitioner — cancels

---

[117] As in *Albrighton* v. *RPA Hospital supra. Yepremian* v. *Scarborough Hospital* (1980) 110 DLR (3d) 513 (Ont CA). This was, however, not the case in *Ellis* v. *Wallsend District Hospital* (*supra* footnote114). Fleming *Torts* 417.

[118] *Ellis* v. *Wallsend District Hospital* at 566. 568 per Kirby P. Jones *Negligence* 406–407.

[119] *Ibid.*

[120] *Cassidy* v. *Ministry of Health supra* at 362 per Denning LJ. *Ellis* v. *Wallsend District Hospital* per Samuels and Meagher JJA at 598–599, 600B, 601B & C, on vicarious liability; 604–606 on the non-delegable duty. Trindade and Cane *Torts* 728–729. Jones *Negligence* 406–407.

[121] *Ibid.* Especially Bates *et al. Hospital Liability* 4–5, who limits his discussion on this subject to the vicarious liability.

[122] *Ibid.* With Kirby P dissenting at 562–573.

the liability opportunity of a hospital for an independent contractor in terms of the non-delegable duty,[123] as well as the vicarious hospital liability for medical officers.[124]

### 6.3.1.1.2 In the course of employment[125]

This requirement constitutes that the servant should have been acting in the course of his/her employment at the time the wrong was committed. The specification confines the responsibility of the employer for wrongs committed by the employee-servant.[126] It suggests a judicial compromise between the employer's responsibility for wrongs and his not being responsible for all wrongs, committed by the servant.[127] Whether the servant had been acting within the course of his/her employment, is a question of fact.[128] No fixed criteria or high degree of precision has been attained to pinpoint this concept, despite a vast volume of case law.[129]

Australian authors have defined the test as follows: The test 'course of employment' is considered to entail: whether the employee was pursuing the employer's interest, i.e. doing the employer's work.[130] Wallace states that 'activities which are directed or authorised by an employer, or those which are reasonably incidental to directed or authorised activities are considered to be within the course of employment'.[131] Trindade and Cane contend that the employer will be vicariously liable if the employee commits 'authorised acts or acts that were an unauthorised mode or method of doing an authorised act'.[132] Fleming affirms this view: The course of employment test is said to 'encompass such unauthorised acts by the servant as can be regarded

---

[123] *Cassidy supra* 362 per Denning LJ. *Ellis supra* 604–606 per Samuels and Meagher JJA. Jones *Negligence* 406–407. Trindade and Cane *Torts* 728.

[124] See *supra*.

[125] Fleming *Torts* 420–426. Trindade and Cane *Torts* 735–739. Wallace *Law* 160. MacFarlane *Health Law* 31–32. Cahill *et al. Hospital Liability* 2. Whippy 1989 *ALJ* 199.

[126] Fleming *Torts* 421. Cahill *et al. Hospital Liability* 2.

[127] See also Fleming *Torts* 421.

[128] Trindade and Cane *Torts* 735.

[129] Fleming *Torts* 421.

[130] MacFarlane *Health Law* 31.

[131] Wallace *Law* 160. At 128 the requirement is also defined as 'carrying out activities which are part of the employer's enterprise'.

[132] Trindade and Cane *Torts* 735. They follow: '… negligence is always just an unauthorized mode of acting rather than an unauthorized act'.

wrongful and unauthorised *modes* of performing an authorised task'.[133] Applying this to hospital liability, the following conclusions can be drawn: The hospital could be liable for what the employee had done or had failed to do despite precautions taken by the employer.[134] The restrictions on the health provider's liability would once again feature, in that the employee's conduct must be in close association[135] to the work he/she was employed to do. This portrays a varied formulation of the 'in the course of employment' test. The employee's conduct should, of course also be tortious.

The hospital or health care institution will thus be vicariously liable if the employee is employed for an activity, but undertakes this activity in an unauthorized way.[136] The hospital would, however, not be vicariously liable for an activity which the employee undertakes for which he was not employed.[137] A hospital or health care agency will therefore be liable vicariously for damage resulting from negligence, if a health care professional or nurse acts contrary to express instructions[138] or contrary to certain policy guidelines developed by a hospital.[139] Consequently, where health care professionals act negligently, and authorized duties are performed by means of unauthorized modes or methods, they become unauthorized acts in the course of their employment.

### 6.3.1.1.3 Actionable wrong

This requirement speaks for itself and needs no independent discussion in this chapter.

---

[133] Fleming *Torts* 421: 'But the limit is exceeded when, instead of acting in furtherance of the assigned task, the servant indulges in an unrelated and independent venture of his own, that is 'when he so acts as to be in effect a stranger in relation to his employer with respect to the act which he has committed'.

[134] See also Cahill *et al. Hospital Liability* 2.

[135] *Ibid.*

[136] MacFarlane *Health Law* 31–32.

[137] *Op. cit.* 32.

[138] *Ibid.* MacFarlane suggests at 32 and 44 that there should be distinguished whether the prohibited act was an unauthorized mode of doing the employer's work or an independent wrongful act. Ignoring a prohibition such as to leave the pharmacy door closed at all times, could qualify as acting contrary to an express instruction. In *Rose v. Plenty* (1976) 1 WLR 141, the employer was held to be vicariously liable for breach of a prohibition to use children, to assist with milk deliveries. In *Kooragong Investments v. Richardson and Wrench* (1981) 36 ALR 142, the employer was held to be vicariously liable where valuations were prepared contrary to the employer's instructions.

[139] *Ibid.*

### 6.3.1.2 Vicarious liability on the basis of agency

Where professional staff like nurses are employed through an agency or by a patient directly, the nurse is considered an independent contractor. The agency is then not considered as being an employer, but simply as a source of finding work.[140] If nurses are therefore engaged directly through an agency or nursing agency to treat patients in a hospital, legal grounds and distinctive liability tests are applied in order to establish whether the hospital will be vicariously liable or if the nurse(s) will be personally liable to the patient.[141] Vicarious hospital liability becomes more probable if the hospital engages the nurses through an agency. An important indicium 'will be who pays the nurse'.[142] Furthermore, if no contract of employment exists where the nurse is engaged privately or otherwise, it is best that the engaged person acquires indemnity insurance.[143] Indemnity insurance provides automatic insurance cover,[144] which some unions do provide.[145]

### 6.3.1.3 Private practice

The medical practitioner in private practice is, as in other legal systems, vicariously liable for acts committed by his employees in the course of their employment.[146] Employees are inclusive of assistant medical practitioners, nurses and others who act in the course of their employment.[147] Liability is also imposed upon a firm for the negligence of a partner, by the Partnership Acts[148] of every State (and the ACT). All members of such a partnership will

---

[140] MacFarlane *Health Law* 32.

[141] *Ibid.* Wallace *Law* 159.

[142] MacFarlane *Health Law* 32. Wallace *Law* 159 recommends the organization test in these circumstances.

[143] *Samios* v. *Repatriation Commission* (1960) WAR 219, where the radiologist acted as agent for the hospital. *Gold* v. *Essex County Council* [1942] 2 KB 293. MacFarlane *Health Law* 32 and footnote 2. Wallace *Law* 131.

[144] MacFarlane *Health Law* 32. Wallace *Law* 131.

[145] Wallace *Law* 159–160.

[146] MacFarlane *Health Law* 32, 44. Dix *et al. Australia* 313 § 1154.

[147] Dix *et al. Australia* 313 § 1154.

[148] Partnership Acts 1891 Qld s 13 reads as follows: Liability of the firm for wrongs. Where, by any wrongful act or omission of any partner acting in the ordinary course of the business of the firm, or with the authority of his co-partners, loss or injury is caused to any person not being a partner in the firm, or any penalty is incurred, the firm is liable therefore to the same extent as the partner so acting or omitting to act.

be vicariously liable for the negligence of every partner 'committed during the course of the firm's business or with the authority of the co-partners'.[149]

### 6.3.2 Direct Hospital Liability

In Australian law, the direct corporate liability of a hospital or health care agency, is founded on the common law direct duty, which purports that the hospital owes the patient who presents himself there for treatment, a direct duty of care.[150] The extent of the hospital's direct duty depends first of all on whether the health care institution was a public or private provider.[151] The duty to exercise reasonable care is also defined by the circumstances of the case, the degree of risks, and alternative safe systems.[152] Traditional facets of the direct duty have been extended to include the following **categories of direct duties**: (i) the provision and proper selection of adequate skilled and competent staff; (ii) the provision of proper and safe systems of work; (iii) the provision and maintenance of proper machinery, equipment and adequate facilities; (iv) relevant training to provide reasonable and safe care to patients;(v) the provision of adequate measures to prevent the spreading of infections, contagious diseases or contamination; (vi) the provision of emergency services or systems to deal with certain emergency circumstances or disasters.[153]

Direct hospital liability mostly ensues as a result of bad administration, improper instruction or training and inadequate systems or supervision.[154] The hospital is then directly in breach of a duty of care owed to the patient.[155] When addressing direct hospital liability,[156] Australian authorities rely on the English cases of *Wilsher, Marshall, Jones* and *Collins* — amongst others.

There has, however, not been a thorough investigation into the direct hospital liability in Australian law and there is no clearly formulated case

---

Relevant Partnership Acts in the jurisdictions are: Partnership Acts 1891 Qld s 13; Victoria s 14; New South Wales s 10; South Australia s 10; Tasmania s 15; Western Australia s 17; Australian Capital Territory s 14. MacFarlane *Health Law* 44 footnote 3.

[149] Dix *et al. Australia* 313 § 1154.

[150] MacFarlane *Health Law* 33, 36.

[151] *Op. cit.* 33.

[152] *Op. cit.* 36.

[153] *Ibid.* Wallace *Law* 155, 254–255.

[154] Dix *et al. Australia* 312 § 1153.

[155] *Ibid.*

[156] *Ibid.* See *supra* the discussion on English law and Direct Hospital Liability under 5.3.

law which is correct in terms of its description, outlay or terminological formulation. In other words, direct hospital liability has been initiated and even relied on superficially, but no in-depth discussions on this subject have come to light. It must be added that this criticism is based on the submission that the non-delegable duty should not be deemed to be a form of direct liability. It is common knowledge that the non-delegable duty has been discussed continuously in the Australian hospital liability law. When acknowledging that the non-delegable is a *sui generis* legal ground and does not conform to all traits of the direct hospital liability, there will be consent as to the under-usage of the direct liability as a legal ground to found hospital liability in the Australian hospital liability law.

### 6.3.3  Hospital Liability in Terms of the Non-Delegable Duty[157]

In law there are some tort duties that qualify as 'duties of absolute obligation'.[158] They are formulated to the extent that responsibility is encompassed not only for the conduct of the person self, but also for a variety of other people. For example: A common carrier is liable for loss of goods, even if it is caused by strangers;[159] A shipowner could be liable for 'unseaworthiness even if the defect was due to faulty workmanship by an independent supplier or repairer.'[160]

Australian courts have also imposed the non-delegable duty (or obligation) as a legal ground to found the liability of hospitals and other authoritative or governing bodies or institutions. The implementation of the non-delegable duty can be inferred in most of the cases discussed in 6.5 Australian Case Law.[161] The liability of hospitals for patients, the responsibility of schools for pupils and the liability of companies for independent contractors have been expanded by the introduction of the non-delegable personal duty of the governing body. It also entails that the health care providers, hospitals or other institutions have a non-delegable duty to ensure

---

[157]  The discussion in 4.3.3 should be regarded as an introduction to this discussion. See Whippy 1989 *ALJ* 182–204 for a formidable discussion on the application of the non-delegable duty in the Australian law.

[158]  Fleming *Torts* 412–413, 434–435.

[159]  *Ibid.* There are certain exceptions to this rule.

[160]  Fleming *Torts* 412.

[161]  It is submitted that it can be inferred in all the discussed cases except in *Cummins* v. *Hobart Public Hospitals Board* (1923) 19 TAS LR 18. But compare Cahill *et al. Hospital Liability* 2. Cahill states that the non-delegable duty was only first applied in *Albrighton.* Dix *et al. Australia* 313 § 1153.

that reasonable care and skill is taken in the provision of treatment, care and safety to patients who select and engage the hospital for such treatment.[162] The liability of a body in terms of the non-delegable duty involves a liability for independent contractors, employees and in fact any staff of such a governing body or hospital — identifiable and non-identifiable persons.

There is a tendency to increase instances of liability for independent contractors.[163] The application of the non-delegable duty in the law of torts is one such an instance. A higher standard of responsibility is established, in the light of modern and exceptional risks,[164] which induce exceptional relationships in need of special protection.[165] The standard of responsibility involved not only requires that reasonable care be taken, but it becomes imperative to ensure that reasonable care is taken in the interest of the patient. It 'imposes on the employer a more stringent obligation than that imposed by the general duty to exercise reasonable care and skill, ... .'[166] This standard of care was assessed in *Burnie Port Authority* v. *General Jones Pty Ltd*:

> Indeed, depending on the magnitude of the danger, the standard of 'reasonable care' may be so stringent as to amount practically to a guarantee of safety.[167]

Hospitals in Australia 'owe an independent and non-delegable duty to ensure that the treatment it undertakes to provide is performed with reasonable care'.[168] This was confirmed by all the members of the NSW Court of Appeal in *Ellis*.[169] However, on the facts of that case, hospital liability was denied on the ground that the surgeon was directly engaged by the patient and not by the hospital.[170] The most important factors to consider here are

---

[162] *Supra*. Fleming *Torts* 412–413, 434–435. Bates *et al. Hospital Liability* 5. Cahill *et al. Hospital Liability* 3. Whippy 1989 *ALJ* 182–204. MacFarlane *Health Law* 38–42 indicates that the statutory duties of employers relating to the health and safety of employees are manifold in the Australian law. It has, however, not been indicated whether these statutory duties — or at least some of them — would be considered to be non-delegable, in Australian law.

[163] Fleming *Torts* 413.

[164] *Op. cit.* 413, 435.

[165] *Kondis* v. *State Transport Authority* (1984) 154 CLR 672 at 687.

[166] Kondis *supra* 681. At 686 it was stated: '... by substituting for the duty to take reasonable care a more stringent duty, a duty to ensure that reasonable care is taken.'

[167] (1994) 120 ALR 42. Fleming *Torts* 413 describes the non-delegable duty as a personal duty to assure that reasonable care is taken. See also Fleming *Torts* 434–435.

[168] Dix *et al. Australia* 313 § 1153.

[169] *Ellis*. See *infra*.

[170] *Ibid*.

firstly, the relationships amongst the hospital, the doctor and the patient and secondly, which obligations the hospital assumed.[171] When, however, taking cognizance of the development of the Australian law in this field over recent years, it could be postulated that courts would construct a duty for hospitals to provide for all medical needs of patients.[172] This would suffice unless it be proven that the hospital merely undertook to exist as a custodial institution or place of abode where medical professionals could treat patients.[173]

### 6.3.3.1 Policy justifications for the duty

Judicial expositions on policy reasons for and against the imposition of the non-delegable duty, have been deliberated: Two arguments have been advanced against the implementation of the non-delegable duty. Both are based on the ground that this duty presents another ground of liability for independent contractors in the law of torts. It is firstly contended that when the hospital is sued first in terms of the non-delegable duty and the latter then recovers indemnity from the negligent surgeon, such a rule of law causes waste of time and money, for the hospital then should not have been a party to the action in the first place. In such a case both the hospital and surgeon need insurance cover which increases costs and limits medical services to the public.[174] Secondly, where professionals with professional skills are involved, the stricter standard or (higher duty) of the non-delegable duty compels the hospital to insure against materialization of risks. But it is said that where such professionals provide specialized treatment or complex surgery, they who have high skills and are in control, are best equipped to avert risks and should therefore be held liable.[175] The oldest persuasive argument for the acceptance of the non-delegable duty, was presented by Denning LJ in *Cassidy,* where he stated that the patient knows nothing of the terms of employment of staff, and therefore the patient must be protected by the hospital.[176]

---

[171] Dix *et al. Australia* 313 § 1153.

[172] *Ibid.*

[173] *Ibid.*

[174] Whippy 1989 *ALJ* 202.

[175] *Ibid.*

[176] [1951] 2 KB 343 at 365: 'I decline to enter into the question whether any of the surgeons were employed only under a contract for services, as distinct from a contract of service... The plaintiff knew nothing of the terms on which [the hospital authorities] employed their staff: all he knew was that he was treated in the hospital by people whom the hospital

Australian courts have applied the non-delegable duty to found the liability of not only hospitals, with ease. No single absolute judicial policy justification had, however, been formulated. In Anglo-Australian judgments, several legal explanations have been formulated on the suitability of the non-delegable duty in the law of torts:

In *Albrighton* the description of the non-delegable duty came closest to any suggestion of a justification: The non-delegable duty was described as an 'overriding and continuing duty' which rested on the hospital as an organization, irrespective of the fact that others treated, diagnosed and cared for the patients in terms of other legal duties. The overriding duty existed because the hospital was no longer regarded only as a mere custodial institution where medical personnel met and treated persons who lodged there.[177] Yet, in *Introvigne* the legal justification was defined as follows:

> ... the law has, for various reasons, imposed a special duty on persons in certain situations to take particular precautions for the safety of others ...[178]

This dictum was confirmed in *Kondis* at 687.[179] Mason J evolved this ratio. He further stated that in certain relationships, an exclusive special responsibility was generated by the hospital or institution's (authoritative) undertaking to provide care, supervision and control to patients (people) who are dependent upon the hospital and in special need of care. The institution or body accepts people into its care, for which in return people reasonably expect that due care will be exercised. Under such circumstances, proper and safe appliances, premises and systems must be provided.[180]

Considerations on the justification of the non-delegable duty were most appropriately expounded in *Ellis* v. *Wallsend District Hospital*.[181] Kirby P — as discussed *infra* — concluded that the law should assign the loss to the hospital. The hospital has the best facilities (insurance or otherwise) to compensate the plaintiff-patient in full, for any wrong(s) committed in or arising out of the activities at the hospital. This principle would protect patients from financial predicaments such as the appellant faced *in casu*.

---

authorities appointed; and the hospital authorities must be answerable for the way in which he was treated.' Whippy 1989 *ALJ* 202.

[177] *Albrighton* v. *Royal Prince Alfred Hospital* [1980] 2 NSWLR 542, at 562 A–B.

[178] *The Commonwealth* v. *Introvigne* (1989) 150 CLR 258, 271.

[179] *Kondis* v. *State Transport Authority* (1984) 154 CLR 672, 687.

[180] *Kondis* 687.

[181] (1989) 17 NSWLR 553 (CA) 569 B–F. At 569 E: 'It is preferable, in my view, that it should be fixed upon the hospital which has far better facilities (and can be expected) to insure itself fully'.

This ratio is basically founded upon the principle of loss-distribution or on the principle of 'let the deeper pocket pay'. This is an economically sound perspective.

Samuels JA also explored the policy reasons for the non-delegable duty in *Ellis*.[182] His judicial exposition enhanced the perspective of Mason J in *Introvigne* and *Kondis*, on this subject. He stated:

> It arises from a relationship which combines the dependence of A upon the reasonable care, skill and judgment of B with the legitimate expectation that B will ensure that those qualities will be exercised in protection of the person or property of A. A further policy decision will be required to determine when that peculiar combination of dependence and expectation — the generative element identified by Mason J in *Kondis* (at 687) — exists. But it can scarcely be doubted that it does so in the case of the relationship between hospital and patient.[183]

Samuels JA furthermore considered that the principle of loss distribution was potentially relevant at a time when parties were likely to be under-insured, or uninsured against public risk. But in contemporary times no reason existed to believe that surgeons (independent contractors) would be 'significantly less protected' by underwriters than hospitals are. He concluded that:

> The basis of the duty is, more persuasively, the satisfaction of expectations about where liability ought to be sheeted home.[184]

## 6.4 CONTRIBUTION AND INDEMNITY

Some relevant aspects concerning the joint liability of wrongdoers and their obligations to contribute to damage awards, which apply to medical practitioners and/or hospitals, can be highlighted. If two or more persons are held liable for the same damage, each of them is liable in full to the plaintiff.[185] Consequently the plaintiff has an unfettered right to recover the full amount of the damages awarded, from such a person.[186] All Australian jurisdictions do, however, have legislation which allow for contribution to be

---

[182]  *Ellis* 605 G–606 C.

[183]  *Ellis* 605 G–606 B.

[184]  *Ellis* 606 B.

[185]  Dix *et al. Australia* 313 § 1155. Wallace *Law* 166.

[186]  *Ibid.*

sought between joint tortfeasors.[187] This entails that a person liable in tort reserves 'a right to recover a contribution from any other person who is or would, if sued, have been liable in tort in respect of the same damage'.[188] Although the principle of vicarious liability relieves the employee (medical officer) of paying for damages due to his/her negligence in the course of his employment, the employer (hospital) may in theory, resort to contribution (and rely on a defence of contributory negligence) depending on the status and the indemnity insurance of the health care professional or practitioner.[189] The court determines the amount of the contribution in accordance with its discretion.[190] The court can either order one party to totally indemnify all others or totally exempt one or more such persons.[191] The legislator intended that the plaintiff should never risk not recovering a part or all of the award, but that the perpetrators should also have the benefit of apportioning the liability between themselves.[192] The result is that when a wrongdoer might be or becomes insolvent, the risk is borne not by the plaintiff, but by others.[193] When a defendant is thus sued, the latter is entitled to and usually will join any other persons thought to be liable, as defendants in the action.[194] The court will then firstly, make a damage award for the full amount to the

---

[187] Law Reform (Miscellaneous Provisions) Act 1965 (NSW), s 10 (1). Wrongs Act 1958 (Vic), s 26 (1). Wrongs Act 1936 (SA), s 27 a (3). Law Reform (Tortfeasors' Contribution, Contributory Negligence, and Division of Chattels) Act 1952 (Qld), Pt III: Tortfeasors and Contributory Negligence Act 1954 (Tas), s 4(1). Law Reform (Miscellaneous Provisions) Act 1955 (ACT), s 15. Law Reform (Miscellaneous Provisions) Act 1956 (NT), s 16 (1). The Law Reform (Contributory Negligence and Tortfeasor's Contribution) Act 1947 (WA), s 4 (1) gives rise to a liability in tort and to the defence of contributory negligence. MacFarlane *Health Law* 33 and footnote 4. Wallace *Law* 160–161. *Ellis* v. *Wallsend District Hospital* (1989) 17 NSWLR (CA) 553 per Kirby P at 569 B–F. Dix *et al. Australia* 313 § 1155. Fleming *Torts* 288–301.

[188] Dix *et al. Australia* 313 § 1155.

[189] Except in NSW, South Australia (SA) and the Northern Territory. Dix *et al.* Australia 314 § 1155. Fleming *Torts* 302–324. MacFarlane *Health Law* 33, Trindade and Cane *Torts* 690–691, 744–745, 752–756.

[190] *Ibid.* Dix *et al. Australia* 313 § 1155: It is 'such amount as may be found by the court to be just and equitable, having regard to the extent of that person's responsibility for the damage'.

[191] Dix *et al. Australia* 313 § 1155.

[192] *Ibid.*

[193] *Ibid.*

[194] *Op. cit.* 314 § 1155.

plaintiff against each of the defendants separately and secondly, the court will make contribution orders in respect of every defendant.[195]

Concerning the employer-employee relationship: When both the employer and employee are liable in terms of vicarious or direct liability, the same right of contribution prevails between the two defendants.[196] The right of contribution between employer and employee has, however, been condemned in practice for being 'contrary to good industrial relations'.[197] New South Wales, South Australia and the Northern Territory formally abolished the right of contribution by an employer against its negligent employee.[198] Employees have also been afforded the entitlement to complete indemnification by the employer, except where the employee is entitled to an indemnity from another source and except in cases of his 'serious and wilful misconduct'.[199] In other Australian jurisdictions, the employer is usually expected to completely protect and indemnify the employee, where the employer is vicariously liable for the employee.[200] Dix *et al.* have postulated relevant and probable scenarios. Applying the above-mentioned ratios to the medical and hospital context, the following could be concluded: A plaintiff may decide to sue and recover damages from the employed practitioner alone and to ignore the employer's potential liability. The practitioner will then be able to join the employer as defendant and seek a contribution.[201] If the plaintiff does decide to recover only from the employer (hospital), the employer will (except in New South Wales, South Australia and the Northern Territory) seek a full indemnity or at least a contribution from the practitioner.[202]

The following conclusions can be drawn concerning the practices of New South Wales, South Australia and the Northern Territory: 'Honoraries' or members of the 'consultant or visiting medical staff' of a hospital may be considered employees of a hospital for the purpose of finding the hospital vicariously liable, but would for the purpose of contribution not be consid-

---

[195] *Ibid.*

[196] Dix *et al. Australia* 314 § 1155.

[197] MacFarlane *Health Law* 33. Dix *et al. Australia* 314 § 1155.

[198] *Ibid.* Trindade and Cane *Torts* 744–745. Fleming *Torts* 411, 298–300. Wallace *Law* 132.

[199] *Ibid.* See also Employees Liability Act 1991 (NSW) s 3. Wrongs Act 1936 (SA). Law Reform (Miscellaneous Provisions) Act 1984 s 22 A. MacFarlane *Health Law* 33 and footnote 5.

[200] Dix *et al. Australia* 314 § 1155.

[201] *Ibid.*

[202] *Ibid.*

ered employees of the hospital. On this hypothetical basis, 'they still will be liable to an action for contribution by their employer'.[203] Medical professionals who have contracts of service, such as resident medical officers, staff specialists and contracted employees of private practitioners, are deemed to be in the most secure position in this respect in these three jurisdictions. They should be immune from an action for contribution by their employer and should be entitled to an indemnity by their employer, where not entitled to an indemnity by their employer or another source.[204] Dix *et al.* further submit that practitioners who are members of the recognized medical defence organizations may not be entitled to an indemnity from such a body and in such a case would not lose the right to be indemnified by their employer.[205] In New South Wales, however, where practitioners had taken out professional indemnity insurance instead of medical defence, they might lose the 'statutory right to an indemnity from their employer, in the unlikely event that they, and not the employer, are sued'.[206]

Dix *et al.* conclude that applying the relevant principles in the medical context, might become complex if not confusing. They advocate that all medical practitioners practising in Australia — whether employed or not — should be covered by adequate professional indemnity insurance or should be members of a recognized medical defence organization.[207] Nurses are, however, not completely immune form liability. The hospital — it is said — will certainly not stand behind the nurse and merely take all responsibility. Compensation cannot be extracted from employees with no money, but some contribution will be sought from a negligent nurse and disciplinary measures might follow.[208] Kirby P mentioned in *Ellis* [209] that:

> The defendants, if they are deferentially insured, will reach their own agreement concerning the conduct of the litigation and insurance contribution or such contribution may be settled by reference to established principles.

---

[203] *Ibid.*

[204] *Ibid.*

[205] *Ibid.*

[206] *Ibid.*

[207] *Ibid.*

[208] Wallace *Law* 161.

[209] *Ellis* v. *Wallsend District Hospital* 569 D–E.

## 6.4.1 Relevant Legislation

In terms of the Insurance Contracts Act 1984 (Cth), s 66,[210] the employer is precluded from seeking contribution from the employee where the employer had recovered the amount paid as damages from an insurance company.[211] However, it does not apply under policies of State insurance or where the employee's conduct amounts to serious and wilful misconduct.[212]

Statutory provisions can also require an employer to indemnify the employee against any damages that the latter could cause in the course of employment, and become liable for.[213] Certain policy guidelines are also provided by the State Government in terms of which legal representation and indemnification is provided for public servants where the Crown employee had diligently and conscientiously (although negligently) performed assigned duties.[214] Certain Statutes exclude liability altogether.[215]

## 6.5 AUSTRALIAN CASE LAW

1.  1923: *Cummins* v. *Hobart Public Hospitals Board* (1923) 19 Tas LR 18.
2.  1939: *Henson* v. *Board of Management of Perth Hospital* (1939) 41 WALR 15.
3.  1960: *Samios* v. *Repatriation Commission* [1960] WAR 219.
4.  1979: *Albrighton* v. *Royal Prince Alfred Hospital* [1979] 2 NSWLR 165;
    1980: [1980] 2 NSWLR 542.

---

[210] Insurance Contracts Act 1984 (CTH) section 66:

Where:

(a) the rights of an insured under a contract of general insurance in respect of a loss are exercisable against a person who is his employee; and

(b) the conduct of the employee that gave rise to the loss occurred in the course of or arose out of the employment and was not serious or wilful misconduct,

the insurer does not have the right to be subrogated to the rights of the insured against the employee.

[211] See MacFarlane *Health Law* 33.

[212] *Ibid.* Fleming *Torts* 411.

[213] In terms of Qld Health Services Act 1991 s 2.14 (3): it concerns the work of Quality Assurance Committees; s 3.35 concerns acts done as part of employment with a Regional Health Authority. MacFarlane *Heath Law* 33 and footnote 6.

[214] MacFarlane *Health Law* 33, 44 footnote 7; for example Queensland Government guidelines.

[215] Queensland Health Act 1937 s 50 excludes liability for acts or omissions done in good faith and without negligence pursuant to that part of the Act concerning notifiable diseases. MacFarlane *Health Law* 33 and footnote 8.

5.   1982: *The Commonwealth* v. *Introvigne* (1982) 150 CLR 258.
6.   1984: *Kondis* v. *State Transport Authority* (1984) 154 CLR 672.
7.   1989: *Ellis* v. *Wallsend District Hospital* (1989) 17 NSWLR 553 (CA).
8.   1994: *Burnie Port Authority* v. *General Jones Pty Ltd* (1994) 120 ALR 42.
9.   1995: *Woods* v. *Lowns* (1995) 36 NSWLR 344.

     1996: *Lowns & Anor* v. *Woods & Ors* (1996) Australian Torts Reports 81–376 (*Lowns* v. *Woods*).

1.  *Cummins* v. *Hobart Public Hospitals Board*,[216] (1923): Cummins had brought action in the Supreme Court, for having suffered damages as a result of (i) negligent treatment in the hospital which necessitated an expensive operation later, and (ii) as a result of absence of employment. The alleged negligent and improper treatment had been provided by the Surgeon Superintendent of the Hobart General Hospital. A question of law was raised, since the Crown Solicitor contended that the Board was not liable in damages for the Surgeon Superintendent's negligence in his professional capacity.[217] The point was reserved and the trial proceeded, during which the Chief Justice found for the plaintiff.[218]

The Full Court of the Tasmanian Supreme Court gave judgment on the question of law. The *Evans* and *Hillyer* cases had been considered in argument,[219] but were not even mentioned in judgment. Nicholls CJ did find that the Surgeon Superintendent had full control of the professional work of the hospital. Thus implying that where there was control, liability could follow even for professional acts (as opposed to liability for administrative acts only in *Hillyer*). He did however state that it would be absurd to suggest that the Board should have any right to interfere with the treatment of patients, thus denying the Board any form of control over patients or any consequential liability as a result of control.[220] He held that the case was 'founded upon the supposition that the Board is liable for all negligent acts of any of its medical officers'.[221] If this was indeed considered a valid ground on which to establish hospital liability, it would have far-reaching effects, such as implying that hospital liability (i) could follow for both administra-

---

[216]   (1923) 19 TAS LR 18.

[217]   *Cummins* 18. This was held to be the case in *Hillyer.*

[218]   *Cummins* 18.

[219]   *Cummins* 18.

[220]   *Cummins* 19.

[221]   *Cummins* 19.

tive and professional acts[222] in the provision of health-care treatment and (ii) could follow for employees and non-employees (any) medical staff.[223]

The whole judgment and consequently the founding of the hospital board's liability, was held to be determined by the provisions of 'The Hospitals Act, 1918' (Tas).[224] The board was created under this legislation and it stipulated the board's legal duties. Nicholls CJ, with whom Crips J concurred, held that in terms of this Act, the hospital board's sole duty comprised of using the necessary care in ensuring that the medical officers were so 'qualified by their skill and trustworthy by their character as to fit them for the office'.[225] Considering there was no allegation of a failure concerning this duty at the Board, it was held that no breach of a statutory duty had been proved against the Board. The hospital board was thus not held liable on account of the negligence of the Surgeon Superintendent of the Hobart General Hospital.[226]

This judgment introduced a new judicial approach which demonstrated that the determination of hospital liability could depend on the interpretation of its enabling legislation. A statutory non-delegable duty (the duty to provide skilled and trustworthy medical officers) which had been created in effect by legislation, was identified and formulated by the court. This reminds of the non-delegable statutory duty which was recognized only later in English law and was discussed in Chapter 5. Regulating public hospitals by statute and establishing its liability by legislation, could become 'a more logical proposition for the courts'[227] in future.

2. In *Henson* v. *The Board of Management of the Perth Hospital and Another* [228] (1939), the plaintiff had been surfing as a result of which he suffered from a noise in the left ear. He went to the casualty department of the Perth Hospital for treatment. A resident doctor from the defendant hospital had, during his performance in the casualty department, given oral

---

[222] Thus discarding the illogical distinction between administrative and professional acts in establishing hospital liability, as was held in *Hillyer*.

[223] This would discard the employer-employee requirement which is traditionally applied to found vicarious hospital liability. It would also be in accordance with the dictum of Denning LJ in *Cassidy*. This would indeed constitute a very modern and logical indicium in the handling of hospital liability.

[224] *Cummins* 18–19.

[225] *Cummins* 19,

[226] *Cummins* 19.

[227] Whippy 1989 *ALJ* 190.

[228] (1939) 41 WALR 15.

instructions to a pupil nurse with merely eighteen months' experience. Glycerine and acid carbol drops were to be administered to the plaintiff's infected left ear. The initial instructions were misunderstood. The doctor did not record his prescribed treatment on a hospital card. The pupil nurse then tried to confirm with a senior staff nurse who was also uncertain, and further instructions were also unclear. The nurses eventually and mistakenly poured acid carbol into a bottle and handed it to the plaintiff. The latter had some drops administered to his ear, as a result of which he suffered permanent injury.[229]

The hospital board or board of management of the Perth Hospital — a body incorporated under the Hospitals Act 1927, as the controlling authority of that institution — was sued for breach of contract in treating the plaintiff medically. In the alternative a claim in tort was added against the board and the doctor for the negligence of the doctor and nurses employed by the board. The plea was subsequently amended to include a claim that the board had failed to exercise proper care in the selection of the nurse who treated him.[230]

Wolff J found both the pupil and the staff nurse to be negligent, which resulted in the injury to the plaintiff's ear. The doctor was also found to be negligent both in giving instructions to a pupil nurse and in the manner the instructions were given.[231] The hospital board and consequently the hospital was held liable for the negligence of the nurses.[232]

In consideration of the legal liability of the board, many issues were assessed. The English authorities were reviewed.[233] The *Hillyer* case was explicitly discussed. The latter case was portrayed as being inadequate regarding its artificial differentiation and uncertain legal lines of demarcation, concerning the administrative and professional categories of duties of

---

[229] *Henson* 15, 20–25.

[230] *Henson* 20.

[231] *Henson* 23.

[232] *Henson* 15, 31.

[233] The following cases were discussed: *Hillyer* v. *The Governors of St Bartholemews Hospital* [1909] 2 KB 820. *Evans* v. *Mayor of Liverpool* [1906] 1 KB 160. *Ingram* v. *Fitzgerald* 1936 NZLR 905. *Nyberg* v. *Provost Municipal Hospital Board* 1927 Can SCR 226. *Laverre* v. *Smith's Falls Public Hospital* 1915 24 DLR 866. *Logan* v. *Waitaki Hospital Board* 1935 NZLR 85. *Strangeways-Lesmere* v. *Clayton* [1936] 2 KB 11. *Powell* v. *Streatham Manor Nursing Home* 1935 AC 243. *Lindsey County Council* v. *Marshall* 1937 AC 97.

medical staff, which could qualify or not for hospital liability.[234] Wolff J
stated that the *Hillyer* case had neither been expressly dissented from, nor
had it been accepted as authority in the Dominions.[235] Wolff J then proceeded
to discuss numerous other cases.[236] He concluded that the professional or
administrative test was unsatisfactory. Wolff J made the following findings:
He insisted that irrespective of the law of England concerning the liability of
hospital authorities with regard to the professional acts of nurse employees,
he imported no implied condition of immunity or limitation to the contract
between the board and plaintiff concerning the actions of nurses.[237] He
founded the contractual liability of the board or hospital on statutory
grounds. He quoted from the Hospitals Act 1927 (No 23 of 1927) in terms of
which the board could make staff appointments and recover costs from
patients.[238]

Thereafter he announced that the doctor and two nurses were employees
of the board and under the control of the Chief Resident Medical Officer
concerning professional and administrative functions. By referring to the
employees and the element of control, he could be implicating a vicarious
hospital liability.[239] Whippy has suggested that vicarious liability should
attach to hospitals in the same way that it attaches to all other employers, and
that this case was an early Australian confirmation of such a view.[240] The
judge then expounded an obligation which the board owed the plaintiff by
contract. The contract included the obligation to 'supply whatever actual
treatment was necessary by the nurses'. He stressed that it would be quite a
fiction to limit the obligation of the board to only supply a hospital, its
equipment and competent nurses.[241] This dictum was a very strong reminder
of the invention of the obligation by Lord Greene in the *Gold* case and the
undelegable duty by Denning LJ in *Cassidy* in years to follow. In effect the
obligation of Wolff J could be nothing other than the non-delegable duty

---

[234] *Henson* 29 per Wolff J: 'I find it impossible to point to this decision as an authority for the
proposition that a hospital is not liable for negligence in the course of the professional acts
of nurses employed by a hospital'.

[235] *Henson* 29.

[236] See *supra. Henson* 25–30.

[237] *Henson* 30–31.

[238] *Henson* 31.

[239] *Henson* 31.

[240] Whippy 1989 *ALJ* 191. This case should not however be considered an ideal example of
vicarious hospital liability, because this legal ground was considered too briefly or
touched upon unknowingly.

[241] *Henson* 31.

bestowed upon the hospital and/or hospital board, which infers hospital liability for not ensuring that proper treatment was provided by qualified nurses.

The hospital's liability was depicted as existing on two independent grounds: In the first place, the court stated that the hospital was liable for having permitted a pupil nurse, who was not generally competent, to take instructions from the doctor. Had a qualified nurse taken the instructions, the mistake would probably not have occurred. Due to this, the rule in the *Hillyer's* case was not applied. Secondly, the hospital was held to be contractually liable, and the board was considered responsible for the negligence of the nurses. The plaintiff was entitled to recover damages from the board and the doctor.

3. Australian hospital law was only considered again twenty years later in **Samios v. Repatriation Commission** [242] (1960), by the Supreme Court of Western Australia. The plaintiff was an epileptic. On 15 October 1955 he had suffered a posterior dislocation of the right shoulder, for which he was treated quite successfully at the Hollywood Hospital by Dr Pannell, a visiting surgeon. On 18 October 1955 the plaintiff fell once again due to an epileptic fit, and again dislocated the right shoulder. He returned to the defendant Commission's hospital, requesting treatment. Dr Waters who was on duty in the casualty section failed to make the correct diagnosis upon a clinical and X-ray examination.[243] He was sent home. On 19 October he was admitted again to the hospital as a result of his own personal doctor's intervention. Dr Du Coudray from the hospital had a second set of X-rays taken. Dr Fraser from the clinic, with which the hospital had an arrangement, examined the X-rays and reported that there was no evidence of a dislocation or bone injury to the right shoulder. A third set of X-rays were taken on 20 December and referred to Dr Fraser, the defendant radiologist. The medical evidence suggests that the dislocation was evident at that stage.[244] Dr Fraser did however find no fracture and referred the patient back for stereoscopic views, to determine if there was any clinical suspicion of redislocation. Dr Fraser was at this stage aware of the previous dislocation, and had a complete file on the plaintiff's medical history. The hospital received the latest report, whereupon Dr Traub decided that the plaintiff suffered from a muscular strain to the right shoulder and subsequently discharged him.[245] In

---

[242]  [1960] WAR 219.

[243]  *Samios* 222.

[244]  *Samios* 219, 223, 227.

[245]  *Samios* 223.

February 1956 the plaintiff, still being in pain, had X-rays taken by the clinic. The dislocation was indicated. He was referred to the hospital. It was endeavoured to reduce the dislocation, but redislocation occurred at once. The possibility of an operation was discussed. Circumstances surrounding the discussion were unclear.[246] He was referred to an orthopaedic surgeon eight weeks later, by which time it was too late to perform an operation successfully.[247] The shoulder and arm became partially disabled.

The plaintiff sued the Repatriation Commission of the Commonwealth for damages for the negligence of its servants or agents at the hospital, in failing to diagnose and treat the dislocated shoulder with resulting disability. The clinic was sued for the negligence of Dr Fraser for failing to detect the dislocation on the X-rays and to report accordingly.[248]

Jackson SPJ held as follows: In law, a duty of care can be construed to exist between a doctor and a patient even where no contract exists, and where the patient was not known or seen.[249] The liability arises *ex delicto* for having failed to take reasonable or proper care.[250] *In casu* Dr Fraser had failed to exercise proper care in failing to detect the dislocation from the second set of X-ray films on 21 December, and for not making a strongly worded report calling for better films.[251] He was thus in breach of such a duty of care. The Commission was explicitly found to be **vicariously** liable for the negligence of Dr Fraser, as a member of the clinic, which was at that time an agent of the hospital in interpreting X-ray films.[252] He then quoted from *Gold* v. *Essex* where Greene MR stated that the extent of the obligation is first to be established, and that liability is not escaped where a servant or

---

[246] *Samios* 224.

[247] *Samios* 225.

[248] *Samios* 220, 222.

[249] *Samios* 225.

[250] *Samios* 226–227.

[251] *Ibid.*

[252] *Samios* 227–228. The judge stated: 'I should say ... that, in my view, the Commission is, in law, vicariously responsible for the negligence of Dr Fraser as a member of the clinic which was, at the material time, the agent of the hospital for the purpose of interpreting the X-ray films of the plaintiff. The evidence shows that the Commission undertook to provide for the plaintiff full hospital and medical treatment including examination by X-rays. For that purpose the hospital supplied a medical and nursing staff and in the normal course of events the hospital's own employee, Dr Grant, would have pronounced upon the X-rays. In his absence the hospital employed the clinic and its partners to do so, and it seems to me as a matter of law that that makes no difference at all so far as the plaintiff is concerned. ... I would adopt, with respect, what was said by Lord Greene, MR, in *Gold* v. *Essex Country Council* [1942] 2 KB 293 at p301. ... .'

agent has been employed to discharge the duty on its behalf. Whether the duty is undertaken by a corporation, body, trustees or assumed by a person, body or corporation, makes no difference. The principles of liability apply for the acts of servants or agents alike.[253] Proclaiming the view that the negligence of an independent contractor or agent engaged by agreement or emergency, can constitute breach of the hospital's obligation, duty or non-delegable duty towards the patient, is with respect correct. Responsibility is not always marred by lack of formalities, such as personal contracts, personal knowledge of patients, geographical precincts of the hospital, or employee-status of the perpetrator.[254]

Conclusively: First of all, the finding of vicarious hospital liability for the negligence of an agent, departs from the traditional perspective of vicarious liability for the negligence of an employee only. It is however, an acceptable modern trend in the hospital setting and one to be recommended contemporarily.

Vicarious liability for an agent was furthermore complimented by another (sovereign) legal ground which founds hospital liability, namely the 'obligation' or non-delegable duty. The judge had already found the hospital vicariously liable for the negligence of the agent, when he did refer to the **obligation** in the same paragraph. Thus, to make sure that liability would ensue for the hospital in those circumstances, the obligation was introduced. Hospital liability was in fact confirmed by or separately founded by the non-delegable duty.

The legal grounds of vicarious liability and the non-delegable duty (the obligation) can be combined successfully in certain circumstances. Where vicarious liability is introduced for an agent and it becomes risky to establish hospital liability by not adhering to traditional requirements, the non-delegable duty or obligation concept can become extremely useful.[255] Morris LJ also combined vicarious liability based on the rule of *respondeat superior* for members of staff — identified or not identified — with the obligation in *Roe* v. *Minister of Health*.[256] Theoretically, two sovereign legal grounds are implemented to secure hospital liability.

---

[253] See *supra. Samios* 228.

[254] See also Whippy 1989 *ALJ* 193.

[255] Whippy 1989 *ALJ* 192.

[256] [1954] 2 QB 66 at 88–91.

Jackson SPJ also found the Commission vicariously liable for the negligence of its servants[257]: The hospital had failed to diagnose the plaintiff's condition correctly and had discharged him from hospital.[258]

With regard to the hospital's failure to diagnose and to discharge the plaintiff, the judge also briefly referred to the 'hospital system' which should 'not escape some criticism'.[259] The hospital was also held to be negligent for not adequately advising him of the necessity of having an immediate operation.[260] Jackson SPJ confirmed the hospital's 'responsibility in law' as a result of 'some breakdown in the system' for failing to advocate an operation.[261] The mere usage of such terminology, could infer the introduction of direct hospital liability. Moreover, such train of thought coupled with such formulation, usually implicates direct hospital liability. On the other hand, the judge could have merely intended these grounds to be part of the hospital's vicarious liability for its servants. The terminological reference to the hospital's system could have been purely coincidental. Alternatively, the reference to the hospital's system could be an extension of the hospital's non-delegable duty to ensure that a safe hospital system existed which would thoroughly advocate necessary operations.

**Conclusion**: Altogether three separate legal grounds for founding hospital liability could have been introduced. Vicarious and direct hospital liability as well as the non-delegable duty was relied upon — knowingly or unknowingly — to establish hospital liability.

In *Ramsay* v. *Larsen*,[262] Kitto J of the High Court however stalled the progressive effect of the verdict in the *Samios* case. The judge reiterated that the hospital will not be vicariously liable under the principle of *respondeat superior*, for a surgeon or specialist who acts on his own account as an independent contractor or agent of the hospital. The hospital would only be liable where the surgeon is a servant of the hospital, performing a duty in service of the hospital for which breach the hospital is held accountable.

### 4. *Albrighton* v. *Royal Prince Alfred Hospital and Others* [263] (1979, 1980):
Nigar Albrighton suffered from spina bifida and gross kypho-scoliosis. She was treated by means of a halo-pelvic traction in the defendant hospital. Her

---

[257] *Samios* 228.

[258] *Samios* 228.

[259] *Samios* 228.

[260] *Samios* 228–229.

[261] *Samios* 229.

[262] (1964) 111 CLR 16.

[263] [1979] 2 NSWLR 165; [1980] NSWLR 542.

spinal cord was severed in the process, as a result of which she became a paraplegic. An action for damages for negligence was brought against the hospital, Dr Tyer the orthopaedic surgeon and Professor Gye the consulting neurosurgeon. The two surgeons were also honorary medical officers.

The defendants applied for a verdict by direction, which Yeldham J granted at first instance.[264] The judge held that there was no evidence upon which the jury could find that the hospital was vicariously responsible in law for any negligence, if either of the doctors were found to be negligent, in terms of the relationship between them or either of them and the hospital.[265] Most important, was his dismissal of the English cases. Relevant English law cases which were 'principally concerned with the functioning of hospitals under the National Health Scheme and with full-time or part-time paid consultants and specialists',[266] indicated that hospitals could be liable for the negligence of such persons in certain circumstances. He referred to Lord Denning who had in several cases, stated that as a general rule, a hospital is so liable. 'But I consider that, in New South Wales, by the application of the general principles concerning vicarious liability, the position, in general, is different.'[267] He thereby discounted the English authorities as well as the possibility of founding hospital liability on the legal ground of the non-delegable duty as expounded by Denning LJ. Yeldham furthermore relied on the control test,[268] with which the facts of the present case did not comply. He finally concluded from various statements in the English cases of *Gold, Cassidy* and *Roe* — except for Lord Denning's statements — that the main view in England was that for honorary doctors who were not full or part-time employees of a hospital, hospitals were not held vicariously liable for their negligently performed acts.[269] This he applied to the present case. The defendants were thus not held responsible.

The plaintiff appealed to the New South Wales Court of Appeal. Reynolds JA delivered the leading judgment. Hope and Hutley JJA agreed. Reynolds JA ordered a new trial against each defendant.[270] He found the

---

[264] *Albrighton* [1979] 2 NSWLR 165, 168C–D, 170G.

[265] *Albrighton* 165, 168D–E.

[266] *Albrighton* 168E–F.

[267] *Albrighton* 168E–F.

[268] *Albrighton* 168G: 'The critical test, in my opinion, is still whether it has been shown that the hospital, in addition to having the power of directing the doctor as to what he is to do, is also invested with the power, whether or not it exercises it, of directing him as to the manner in which he should carry out his work.' Whippy 1989 *ALJ* 194.

[269] *Albrighton* 169A–B.

[270] *Albrighton* (1980) 551, 562C–D, 564.

three respondents to be in breach of the duty of care, concerning the use of due care in the medical management of the appellant.[271] There was therefore enough evidence to submit to the jury in each case against the respondents.[272] The liability of the hospital was discussed, after examining the evidence against the doctors.

Reynolds JA first of all, discussed the hospital's vicarious liability.[273] The finding of Yeldham J that the hospital could not be (vicariously) liable for the tortious conduct of the two medical practitioners in the course of their duties, because no appropriate relationship existed between them and the hospital and because there was no control over them, was rejected.[274] Reynolds JA stated that 'this is a concept which has long since been eroded, and which goes hand in hand with the concept that a hospital fulfills its duty of care to persons treated in it'[275] by merely selecting and appointing competent medical staff. The concept had its origin in England when hospitals were charitable institutions, and were protected by legal doctrines from financial responsibilities they could not bear.[276] According to the judge traditional concepts such as charitable immunity or limiting the duty of the hospital in unrealistic fashion, was unacceptable in confining the scope of the hospital's liability.

> So far as the control test is concerned, it is no longer acceptable in its full rig-our; and, as the law stands today, the uncontrollability of a person forming part of an organization as to the manner in which he performs his task does not preclude recovery from the organization, and does not preclude the finding of a relationship of master and servant.[277]

In other words control was no longer deemed a prerequisite to establish a master-servant relationship or to ultimately establish vicarious liability. Liability was said to follow where there was no control and should therefore — as a matter of inference — also follow in cases of agents or independent contractors.

The judge quoted extensively from other cases equating the hospital authority's liability for radiologists, with cases where shipowners should be liable for faulty navigation of ships, or the public undertakers which should

---

[271]  *Albrighton* (1989) 553E–F, 557C.

[272]  *Albrighton* (1980) 555B–C, 557E.

[273]  *Albrighton* (1980) 557E–F. He did, however, not use the word 'vicarious'.

[274]  *Albrighton* (1980) 557E–G, 558A–C.

[275]  *Albrighton* (1980) 557F–G.

[276]  *Albrighton* (1980) 557F–G.

[277]  *Albrighton* (1980) 557G–558A.

be liable for the failure of constructional works for the lack of care and skill by their engineers.[278] He suggested that professionality, importing the exercise of professional skills, should be observed in terms of a relationship between two parties which could lead to liability.[279] He quoted from *Yewens* v. *Noakes*[280]:

> The duties to be performed may depend so much on special skill or knowledge or they may be so clearly identified or the necessity of the employee acting on his own responsibility may be so evident, that little room for direction or command in detail may exist. But that is not the point. What matters is **lawful authority to command** so far as there is scope for it. And there must always be some room for it, if only in incidental or collateral matters. Even if Mr Phillip Wirth could not interfere in the actual technique of the acrobatics and in the character of the act, no reason appears why the appellant should not be subject to his directions in all other respects.[281]

By introducing this quote the judge did implicate or allow for some (slight) form of control, or if only as an authoritative challenging presence, being the most powerful party to the relationship. But effectively, control was possibly acknowledged, although not in 'full rigour' whereas at 557G–558A he discarded control or at least acknowledged it as not being fully acceptable.

Referring to Fleming, the court found that hospitals had become liable for their 'nurses, resident medical officers, radiographers and even part-time anaesthetists and special consultants.'[282] The judge remarked that there was progression in this field.[283] Surely trying to keep pace with the development he had just discussed, he decided that the present case would not be determined by judicial dicta or the view of text writers. The position of 'honoraries, consultants or visiting doctors' in other countries, in other hospitals, at other times was irrelevant.[284] 'The submissions based on English dicta made to us that honorary medical officers are not servants of a hospital afford no assistance whatever. The problem is to be solved by looking at the evidence in this case to ascertain what it is capable of showing as to the relationship between the hospital and the doctors, however they may be described. That evidence consists in the account of their activities within the hospital, their use of, and compliance with, hospital forms and routines, and

---

[278] *Albrighton* (1980) 558A–B, B–F.

[279] *Albrighton* (1980) 558A–B, B–F, F–G*, 559A.

[280] (1980) 6 QBD 530, 532, 533.

[281] *Albrighton* (1980) 558G–559A. My accentuation.

[282] *Albrighton* (1980) 559B.

[283] *Albrighton* (1980) 559B (50).

[284] *Albrighton* (1980) 559C–D.

the operation of the by-laws which were admitted in evidence.'[285] Considering this, he concluded that a relationship of master and servant existed
between the hospital and the doctors.[286] He considered this to be a question
of fact.[287]

In this respect the judgment was of remarkable importance for it created a
norm in terms of which the hospital's liability could be formulated, without
clinging to out-dated or traditional formulae which could prejudice the
patient as well as the development of the liability of hospitals. As Whippy
suggests, the judge made 'an observation, which, it is submitted, not only
represents a realistic and preferable judicial attitude towards a hospital's
liability, but also highlights a recognition by him of the main deficiency in
the general approach taken by certain of the English judges.'[288]

Reynolds JA did however present another or alternative basis upon which
the hospital's liability could be founded — according to the appellant. The
hospital owed the patient-plaintiff a duty (directly) which it could not divest
itself by delegation.[289] It was nothing other than the famous non-delegable
duty, however, (unfortunately) termed in direct terminology.

The determination of the duty was formulated to differ from case to case
and was to be dependent on the facts of every individual case. The duty
would therefore differ in extent in every given situation, relying on the
proven facts. The judge stated:

> It seems to me that, in any case where it is sought to establish the existence of
> a duty, the relationship between the parties must be determined as a question
> of fact; and where a hospital, or a nursing home, or an infirmary, or any other
> type of medical institution is involved, it is not enough merely to speak of the
> duty owed by any hospital to a patient.[290]

Concerning the duty he quoted from *Roe* v. *Minister of Health*[291] where
Morris LJ stated:

> A hospital might assume the obligation of nursing: it might on the other hand
> merely assume the obligation of providing a skilful nurse. But the question as
> to what obligation a hospital has assumed becomes, as it seems to me, ulti-

---

[285]  *Albrighton* (1980) 559C–D.

[286]  *Albrighton* (1980) 560G.

[287]  *Albrighton* (1980) 560F–G.

[288]  Whippy 1989 *ALJ* 195.

[289]  *Albrighton* (1980) 561A–B.

[290]  *Albrighton* (1980) 561B.

[291]  [1954] 2 QB 66, (a) 89. In this case on which Reynolds JA relied frequently, Morris LJ
combined the vicarious liability with the non-delegable duty to secure a finding of
hospital liability.

mately a question of fact to be decided having regard to the particular circumstances of each particular case: the ascertainment of the fact may require in
some cases inference or deduction from proved or known facts.[292]

According to Reynolds JA the evidence in the present case supported the
view that the institution undertook to provide the appellant with

> ...complete medical services through its staff, including surgeons, consultants,
> an anaesthetist, a radiologist, a physiotherapist, pathologists and various other
> persons necessary to provide that complete medical care and all chosen, not
> by her, but by the institution.[293]

*In casu* it was found that the evidence made a case which provided a basis
for the finding that the hospital did owe a duty of care to the appellant
'which it could not fulfil merely by delegation to a person who **could not
properly be described as its servant.**'[294] (my accentuation). On the previous
page (560G) the judge had found that there was evidence upon which the
jury could find that a relationship of master and servant existed.[295] Perhaps in
the light of the fact that this proposed relationship would not make a sure,
definite or proper finding — since the traditional element of control could be
lacking — Reynolds JA resorted to the alternative legal ground of the non-
delegable duty to ensure hospital liability.

Reynolds JA concluded that the hospital, 'by admitting the appellant,
could be regarded as undertaking that it would take reasonable care to
provide for all her medical needs; and, whatever legal duties were imposed
upon those who treated, diagnosed or cared for her needs from time to time,
there was an overriding and continuing duty upon the hospital as an
organization. It was not a mere custodial institution designed to provide a
place where medical personnel could meet and treat persons lodged there, as
it might have been regarded in years long since gone by.'[296] Reynolds JA first
had established the extent of the obligation or duty on the proven facts of the
case and then proceeded to formulate the non-delegable legal duty of the
hospital within those boundaries. According to this approach in judgment,
fact-finding the obligation will be unique for every case since the evidence
of every case will differ. Consequently, the non-delegable legal duty which is
formulated and determined by the factual obligation, will also vary from
case to case.

---

[292] *Albrighton* (1980) 561 (56) B–C.

[293] *Albrighton* (1980) 561 (57) C–D.

[294] *Albrighton* (1980) 561G.

[295] *Albrighton* (1980) 560G.

[296] *Albrighton* (1980) 562 A.

This approach is a flexible one and differs in this respect from the general comprehensive non-delegable duty which had no restrictions, formulated by Denning LJ in *Cassidy* — not that the latter would not have approved of a less strict duty in the appropriate circumstances.[297]

## Conclusion on Albrighton

Concerning the hospital's vicarious liability,[298] the control test was at first explicitly denounced in its full rigour. The uncontrollability of the person's manner of acting whilst forming part of the organization, in no way deterred from recovering from the organization nor from finding a master-servant relationship between the actor and the organization. It was indeed stated that such a relationship is determined as a question of fact by analyzing the evidence of every case. Proving the medical officer to be an employee would depend, not on judicial dicta or text writers' opinions on medical officers in other countries in other hospitals at other times. Employee-status was *in casu* established by considering the medical officer's activities in the hospital, their use of, and compliance with, hospital forms and routines, and the operation of the by-laws concerning the administration of the hospital and its employment of medical officers.

Establishing the master-servant relationship without relying on the out-dated concept of control, was indeed a big step in the right direction — with respect. But it is suggested that by implementing the organization test the same result of hospital liability could have been accomplished, without resorting to either the control or the forced master-servant relationship requirements. Easier still, hospital liability in terms of the non-delegable duty can *per se* establish hospital liability for even an independent contractor or an agent. This judgment did indeed on an alternative basis, establish a flexible mode of introducing the non-delegable duty as an adaptive legal ground for the founding of hospital liability.

Another consequence of this judgment for Australian law, is where a medical practitioner falls within the hierarchy of a particular hospital and is

---

[297] See Whippy 1989 *ALJ* 197 for his interpretations of this judgment; see especially his first alternative interpretation of the concept of the duty at 196. I would with respect differ on that interpretation. Reynolds JA did not once refer to the judgment of Denning LJ, whereas Yeldham J did so in the initial hearing. Reynolds JA based his judgment almost entirely on the verdict of Morris LJ in the *Roe* case. It would therefore with respect be fruitless to speculate on Reynolds JA's interpretation of Denning LJ's judgment if Reynolds JA did not even once refer to him, or if Reynolds' judgment did not convey such an intention or contain such contents.

[298] *Albrighton* (1980) 557–560. Dix *et al. Australia* 311–312. See also Wallace *Law* 130. Wallace did however again rely on the control element, to some extent.

as such appointed to a case, a master and servant relationship is established between the medical practitioner and the hospital. The hospital will consequently be vicariously liable for such an officer's negligent behaviour.[299]

The High Court of Australia

5. *The Commonwealth of Australia* v. *Introvigne*[300] (1982): In this case the non-delegable duty that was formulated and implemented by Denning LJ in *Cassidy* v. *Ministry of Health* concerning the hospital authority, was imposed on a school authority. The duty was formulated as follows:

> The liability of a school authority in negligence for injury suffered by a pupil attending the school is not a purely vicarious liability. A school authority owes to its pupils a duty to ensure that reasonable care is taken of them whilst they are on the school premises during hours when the school is open for attendance.[301]

Mason J, with whom Gibbs CJ agreed, remarked that the duty imposed on a school authority 'is akin to that owed by a hospital to its patient'.[302] In this case it was also not discharged by the mere appointment of competent teaching staff, and leaving it to the staff to take care of the children by taking appropriate steps.[303]

Mason J then quoted from Denning LJ in the *Cassidy* case:

> ... where a person is himself under a duty to use care, he cannot get rid of his responsibility by delegating the performance of it to someone else, no matter whether the delegation be to a servant under a contract of service or to an independent contractor under a contract for services.[304]

From this passage the unfortunate interpretation followed that the duty to ensure that reasonable steps would be taken for the safety of the children, was 'a duty the performance of which cannot be delegated'.[305] In an otherwise remarkable application of the theories of hospital liability, the only demarcation to its creativity was this latter interpretation. It should, with respect, be considered that the performance is indeed delegated; it is only the legal responsibility for that performance which is non-delegable. That would

---

[299]  See also Dix *et al. Australia* 312 § 1152.

[300]  (1982) 150 CLR 258.

[301]  *Introvigne* 269.

[302]  *Introvigne* 270.

[303]  *Introvigne* 270.

[304]  *Introvigne* 270.

[305]  *Introvigne* 270.

also, with respect, correspond with Denning LJ's formulation where he states that one cannot get rid of the **responsibility** (my accentuation) by delegating... .

Other remarkable features of the judgment are contained in the following statements: Firstly, Mason J expressed the view that in certain circumstances such as the school setting, a special responsibility is created for a school authority to care for pupils' safety, 'one that goes beyond a mere vicarious liability for the acts and omissions of its servants'.[306] In other words where the application of a traditional legal theory such as vicarious liability is not deemed fit for a unique set of circumstances, legal responsibility requires that other legal grounds be resorted to. Secondly, he remarked that when applying the legal ground of a non-delegable (personal) duty to found hospital liability, to which the hospital authority is subject, the distinction between servants and independent contractors become immaterial.[307] In other words, this is one of the advantages of the application of this legal ground. The authorities' liability is founded irrespective of the fact that the perpetrator was a servant, an agent or not identifiable at all. Thirdly, Mason J negated the criticism against the non-delegable duty as a strict duty:

> It has been said that the concept of a personal duty departs from the basic principles of liability and negligence by substituting for the duty to take reasonable care a more stringent duty, a duty to ensure that reasonable care is taken. This criticism fails to acknowledge that the law has, for various reasons, imposed a special duty on persons in certain situations to take particular precautions for the safety of others, e.g. the occupier of premises.[308]

This conclusion is with respect brilliant in creating a criterion by which legal grounds could be applied in future, where no express norms exist.

By this judgment the applicability of the non-delegable duty as legal ground to found the liability of authorities, was justified and confirmed.

The High Court of Australia

6. *Kondis* v. *State Transport Authority* [309] (1984): Mason J once again held his stance on the non-delegable duty. Deane and Dawson JJ agreed. Mason J confirmed that the employer was under a personal non-delegable duty to provide a safe system of work which he failed to accomplish through his independent contractor. The independent contractor had negligently failed to

---

[306] *Introvigne* 271.

[307] *Introvigne* 270.

[308] *Introvigne* 270–271.

[309] (1984) 154 CLR 672. See also Munkman *Liability* 84.

adapt a safe system of work for which the employer was held liable. Hospital liability founded on the non-delegable duty was once again discussed shortly, and the relevant English common law cases were referred to. The special responsibility which creates the duty to ensure that care is taken, was highlighted as being appropriate in cases where authority was an element in a relationship. An alternative ground for the founding of liability in an authoritative relationship was suggested as being the failure to prescribe and provide a safe system for people in the workplace which could constitute the direct liability of the employer, which involved the negligence of an independent contractor.

Conclusively, the High Court of Australia has on two occasions ( in the cases of *Introvigne* and *Kondis*) approved, obiter, that the liability of a hospital to a patient can be based on the personal non-delegable duty.[310]

7. *Ellis* v. *Wallsend District Hospital* [311] (1989): The New South Wales Court of Appeal presented a divided opinion on the circumstances which found vicarious liability and the non-delegable duty in hospital liability, in *Ellis* v. *Wallsend District Hospital*. Mrs Ellis had been consulting Dr Chambers, a neurosurgeon, at his consulting rooms since 1971. After Dr Newman had removed a lump under her right ear, she had experienced intractable and very severe neck pain, and was referred to Dr Chambers. Since that time she had a medical history of drug dependence, drug overdoses and a failure of another surgical intervention in 1972. During 1974 to 1975 a five-nerve separation microsurgery was suggested by Dr Chambers. He warned her only of the possible risk of some slight numbness in her right hand, as a result of the operation. He had never warned her of the slight or remote risk of developing paraplegia and the more substantial risk of failing to relieve the pain. She agreed to have the operation. Dr Chambers arranged the admission of Mrs Ellis to the Wallsend District Hospital. The neurosurgeon performed a laminectomy and a cervical posterior rhizotomy of the nerve roots at the cervical vertebrae 2 to 6, on 18 June 1975, at the respondent hospital. During surgery, 'troublesome haemorrhage was encountered and controlled' and 'numerous adhesions were found surrounding the [spinal] cord' — according to the surgeon's notes. The doctor did not use the microscope, but wore thick glasses. An exploratory operation followed on the unconscious woman on 25 June. On 25 June 1975 the paralysis or quadriplegia was established.

---

[310] Jones *Negligence* 406–407. See also Whippy 1989 *ALJ* 197–198.

[311] (1989) 17 NSWLR 553 (NSW CA). For the facts of the case see 557, 574–576, 592–595. See also Kennedy and Grubb *Medical Law* 404–405.

Dr Chambers was an 'honorary medical officer' appointed to the 'honorary medical staff' under the by-laws and rules of the hospital. These officers could make use of the operating theatres for their own patients on a roster basis. The hospital did not remunerate honorary medical officers for services performed there. The hospital would book a patient for surgery according to the date and time the doctor was appointed to use the theatres. The patient would be admitted by means of a signed admission request form. The doctor's fee was settled privately between the doctor and the patient.

Mrs Ellis sued Dr Chambers and the hospital. Dr Chambers died in 1986. Her claim was settled against the executors of his estate on 6 June 1988, just before the trial was to begin. The amount of the settlement was A$500,000, which was limited by the insurance policy for professional negligence applicable to Dr Chamber's acts and omissions in 1975. She then claimed against the hospital, in the light of the fact that the settlement fee was less appropriate in the year it was awarded, given the effects of inflation and the erosion of money values. She claimed on the grounds that (i) the hospital was vicariously liable for Dr Chamber's negligence; (ii) that the hospital owed the patient a non-delegable and independent duty to ensure that she received proper medical treatment and was warned of all material risks concerning the surgery, of which it was in breach.

The President of the Court of Appeal stated that the case centred on the liability of a public hospital to a patient injured during the course of an operation by the negligence of an honorary consulting surgeon. Kirby P introduced his judgment as follows:

> The appeal is the latest step in a journey which has taken the common law from the virtual exemption of hospitals from liability for the negligence of medical staff (expressed in the English Court of Appeal in *Hillyer* v. *Governors of St Bartholomew's Hospital* [1909] 2 KB 820) to the quite different position reached by the law today. Now, in most jurisdictions of the common law, hospitals are liable, both vicariously and directly, for the proved negligence of employees and independent professional staff who work in their highly integrated activities. No authority binding on this Court determines the important question before it. It is therefore necessary to answer it by reference to the principles of the common law emerging from decisions dealing with analogous fact situations, a reflection on the direction in which the common law has moved in this regard and a consideration of applicable policy questions which help to suggest the response which should be given in this case.[312]

Kirby P discussed the doctrine of charitable immunity which endorsed 'the gratuitous benefit of its care'[313] to patients and was enforced in England and

---

[312]  *Ellis* 556–557.

[313]  *Ellis* 562D–E.

elsewhere for decades. Hospitals were not held liable for the negligent acts of professional staff. But the turnaround came in Canada in *Sisters of Joseph of the Diocese of London in Ontario* v. *Fleming* [1938] SCR 172; [1938] 2 DLR 417. A new doctrine was emerging. It reached Australia in *Henson* v. *Board of Management of the Perth Hospital* (1939) 41 WALR 15, England in *Gold* v. *Essex County Council* [1942] 2 KB 293, and South Africa in *Esterhuizen* v. *Administrator, Transvaal* 1957 (3) SA 710 (T). Almost all common law countries had by then rejected the *Hillyer* principle. Ireland did so belatedly in *O'Donovan* v. *Cork County Council* [1967] IR 173, and the United States followed with *Bing* v. *Thunig* 163 NYS 2d 3 (1957) (NYCA).[314] The judge thus examined the initial development of hospital liability in Canada, Australia, England, South Africa, Ireland and the United States.

The relation between the hospital and its professional staff also evolved rapidly. Requirements to establish the employer-employee relationship and the duty of the employer, changed. The judge stressed that the 'control' test was eventually considered inadequate to establish the employer-employee relation given the progress in 'education, tehnology, the role of the modern corporation and social changes which necessarily enhance individual autonomy'.[315] Courts sought a new criterion by which to determine such a relation in order to establish vicarious liability where highly qualified individuals were performing tasks relevant to the interests of a body. 'In place of this test the High Court of Australia suggested the need to look to a number of indicia from which the nature of the relationship and the responsibilities deriving from it would be defined.'[316] The organization test suggested by Denning LJ in *Cassidy* was, however, in Australia 'although not rejected as irrelevant ... not accepted as sufficient or as an independent method for determining that vicarious liability arises.'[317] In other words the 'control' test became inapplicable and the organization test was not accepted in Australia. After quoting from *Cassidy*[318] and *Yepremian*[319] Kirby discussed the statements of Giesen and Atiyah who both conceded to the expansion of hospital liability with exclusion of hospital immunity. Both also covered

---

[314] *Ellis* 562E–G.

[315] *Ellis* 563A–B.

[316] *Ellis* 563B–C: See *Stevens* v. *Bodribb Sawmilling Co Pty Ltd* (1986) 160 CLR 16 at 24.

[317] *Ellis* 563 C; The organization test implicates that the subordinate works in the superior's organization.

[318] *Ellis* 563D.

[319] *Ellis* 564C.

ground — implicitly or explicitly — to suggest that hospitals should not escape responsibility for injury caused by honorary surgeons.[320]

Kirby P listed the following relevant facts to reach his finding: He perceived that Dr Chambers was appointed to the 'honorary medical staff' of the hospital. The doctor was 'available for duty' according to a roster prepared by the board. He was appointed for three years. He had to resign by giving 28 days' notice. The board retained the 'power of dismissal'.[321] Dr Chambers was 'under the control of'[322] the hospital's chief executive officer for duties other than professional duties. The judge concluded that Dr Chambers was inextricably tied to the organization of the hospital, and integrated into the discipline and direction of the hospital.[323] He therefore found that the hospital was vicariously liable for the negligent acts of the honorary medical officer, or neurosurgeon, Dr Chambers.[324] The second legal ground on which Kirby P founded the liability of the hospital, he termed the direct liability.[325] He referred to the *Gold, Cassidy*[326] and *Albrighton*[327] cases which with respect was — according to this writer — founded on the non-delegable duty. He also referred tot the *Yepremian* and *Wilsher*[328] cases which are with respect — typical examples of direct corporate hospital liability. Kirby P consequently found that the non-delegable duty was a form of direct liability.[329] He proceeded to find that the two High Court decisions of Australia — *Kondis* based on the 'non-delegable duty' and *Introvigne* based on the 'direct liability of a school authority' — were binding on this Court.[330] He was not bound by English, Canadian or other differing opinions. The High Court's principle in *Kondis* was in line with other common law and civil law jurisdictions (as demonstrated by Giesen's text). This principle was 'supported by reasons of policy and practicality in the modern circumstances of Australian hospitals.'[331] Kirby P therefore found that the hospital was an

---

[320]  *Ellis* 565B–D.

[321]  *Ellis* 565E–G.

[322]  *Ellis* 565–566.

[323]  *Ellis* 566A–B, 567E: Dr Chambers was integrated into the activities of the hospital.

[324]  *Ellis* 572–573A–C.

[325]  *Elllis* 566E–F.

[326]  *Ellis* 566F.

[327]  *Ellis* 567F.

[328]  *Ellis* 567.

[329]  *Ellis* 568A–D.

[330]  *Ellis* 568E.

[331]  *Ellis* 568F–G.

integrated institution[332] of which the honorary medical officer was also part, and that the hospital was not a mere venue where private surgical procedures were performed.[333] Kirby P finally concluded that the hospital was either vicariously liable, or directly liable by means of a non-delegable duty, for the negligence of an honorary member of staff.[334] He found that the hospital was vicariously liable for Dr Chambers' failure to give the patient an adequate warning. The hospital was under an independent or non-delegable duty to ensure that such a warning was given.[335]

He motivated his finding on further monetary grounds. He said that the patient 'should be able to look to the hospital to ensure (by insurance or otherwise) that proved wrongs by health care staff occurring at the hospital or arising out of its activities are compensated in full degree.[336] ... It is preferable, in my view, that it should be fixed upon the hospital which has far better facilities (and can be expected) to insure itself fully. That insurance can readily cover all staff — honorary and otherwise.'[337]

Samuels JA, with whom Meagher JA agreed, expounded hospital liability as follows: Samuels JA first and foremost investigated the possibility that the hospital could be vicariously liable for Dr Chambers' failure to warn Mrs Ellis of the possible dangers and limited benefits of the proposed surgical procedure.[338] He based his judgment in this matter on the traditional perspective that vicarious liability of the principal could only follow for the wrongful acts of the employee committed in the course of his employment. Vicarious liability for the principal would not follow for the wrongs of an independent contractor during the course of his engagement.[339]

In order to establish the employer-employee relationship which could introduce vicarious liability, he first discussed the control test — as a prerequisite — in its original form.[340] He then proceeded to deal with it in its

---

[332] *Ellis* 569B.

[333] *Ellis* 568G.

[334] *Ellis* 569A. At 573A Kirby P stated that the hospital was vicariously liable for his negligence and also bore a direct and un-delegable duty to Mrs Ellis for negligence on the part of Dr Chambers.

[335] *Ellis* 562A–B.

[336] *Ellis* 569D.

[337] *Ellis* 569E.

[338] *Ellis* 590G.

[339] *Ellis* 590G–591A.

[340] *Ellis* 591A–C.

diluted form as formulated in *Zuijs* v. *Wirth Brothers Pty Ltd.*[341] He then dealt with the 'modern approach'[342] in order to establish the master and servant relationship. This according to *Stevens* v. *Brodribb Sawmilling* [343] existed not only of control as indicium but of factors additional to control:

> Other relevant matters include, but are not limited to, the mode of remuneration, the provision and maintenance of equipment, the obligation to work, the hours of work and provisions for holidays, the deduction of income tax and the delegation of work by the putative employee.[344]

Samuels JA stated that the Australian courts look at the 'totality of the relationship between the parties'[345] 'although control remains a significant and therefore relevant indicium of an employer and employee relationship.'[346] In determining this relationship, the organization test[347] was once again underestimated. The judge stated that:

> As a matter of Australian law, the application of the organization test is, at best, one relevant element in discerning the nature of the relationship between the parties. It is not a conclusive factor.[348]

The judge suggested that the question whether the person is an employee, was to be determined by facts.[349] All the incidents of the relationship as

---

[341] *Ellis* 591C; (1955) 93 CLR 561 at 571: 'what matters is lawful authority to command so far as there is scope for it. ... *Stevens* v. *Brodribb Sawmilling Co Pty Ltd* (1986) 160 CLR 16 at 24, 29 per Mason J 'It is sufficient if this lawful authority to control be 'only in incidental or collateral matters'.'

[342] *Ellis* 591D–E, 597C–D.

[343] *Supra* footnote 341.

[344] *Supra* footnote 342 — *Stevens* per Mason J, also at 24, 29: 'But the existence of control whilst significant, is not the sole criterion by which to gauge whether a relationship is one of employment. The approach of this Court has been to regard it merely as one of a number of indicia which must be considered in the determination of that question.'

[345] *Stevens* v. *Brodribb Sawmilling* per Mason J with whom Brennan and Deane JJ agreed at 29. *Ellis* 591F.

[346] *Ellis* 591F.

[347] *Ellis* 591–592: In *Stevenson Jordan and Harrison Ltd* v. *MacDonald and Evans* [1952] 1 TLR 101 at 111, Denning LJ, a proponent of the test, put it thus: '...One feature which seems to run through the instances is that, under a contract of service, a man is employed as part of the business, and his work is done as an integral part of the business; whereas, under a contract for services, his work, although done for the business, is not integrated into it but is only accessory to it.'

[348] *Ellis* 592A, 596E–F.

[349] *Ellis* 592D: 'The question whether a person is the employee of another is a question of fact: ... .'

disclosed by the evidence of the case[350] was to be considered in this regard. Samuels JA discarded both the potency of the control test[351] and the Australian totalitarian test which considers 'the totality of the relationship between the parties'[352] According to him the latter test seemed likely to generate a problem[353] for not providing 'any external test of requirement by which the materiality of the elements'[354] could be assessed. The modern approach thus posed the same problem, by having regard to a variety of criteria.[355]

The judge considered the ultimate question formulated by Wilson and Dawson JJ in the *Stevens* case which was:

> The ultimate question will always be whether a person is acting as the servant of another or on his own behalf.

Samuels JA eventually re-formulated his own ultimate test:

> In treating the appellant was Dr Chambers engaged in his own business or the hospital's?: ... .[356]

Samuels JA proceeded to examine all relevant indicia:

> that is to say all facts capable of elucidating the question: In treating the appellant was Dr Chambers acting as the employee of the hospital (... on the hospital's behalf) or on his own behalf?[357]

He highlighted that Dr Chambers received no remuneration from the hospital and that the hospital board had only a slight degree of control over his

---

[350] *Ellis* 592E.

[351] *Ellis* 596A–E.

[352] *Ellis* 596F–G: 'Hence *Stevens* v. *Brodribb Sawmilling* authorises and entails consideration of 'the totality of the relationship between the parties' (at 29), a methodology presumably synonymous with 'the traditional approach of balancing all the incidents of the relationship between the parties' (at 28).

[353] *Ellis* 596G.

[354] *Ellis* 597A–B.

[355] *Ellis* 597C–D: '... This approach is not without its difficulties because not all of the accepted criteria provide a relevant test in all circumstances and none is conclusive. Moreover, the relationship itself remains largely undefined as a legal concept except in terms of the various criteria, the relevance of which may vary according to the circumstances.' This quote was taken from the *Stevens* case at 35. See also Kennedy and Grubb *Medical Law* 435.

[356] *Ellis* 598 B–C. Samuels JA quoted from *Federal Commissioner of Taxation* v. *Barrett* (1973) 129 CLR 395 at 402 per Stephen J.

[357] *Ellis* 598A–C.

activities.[358] In considering the totality of the relationship between the parties, he concluded that Dr Chambers was engaged in his own business and not the hospital's. He conducted his own independent practice as neurosurgeon.[359] He was never at any time an employee of the hospital, but under all circumstances retained his independency as independent specialist.[360]

The judge came to the following conclusion: Consequently, because vicarious liability is founded on the relationship between employer and employee, and upon the analysis of the relationship the conclusion was made that (i) he was never an employee and (ii) that the relationship did not accommodate the necessary viables to establish vicarious liability, the hospital could not be vicariously liable for the negligence of Dr Chambers or any other member of the honorary medical staff in the treatment of patients at the hospital.[361] Samuels JA posed an alternative basis for the possible finding of hospital liability. The foundation of the non-delegable duty was based on the relationship between the hospital and the patient,[362] and not the relationship between the hospital and the doctor — as is the case in vicarious liability. The independent and non-delegable duty was once again presented as a form of direct liability which could found hospital liability. It had to be established whether the hospital owed the plaintiff-patient such a duty directly, 'of which it could not divest itself by delegation', and of which it was in breach.[363]

Samuels JA found the perfect solution to the problem in the finding of Houlden JA in *Yepremian*:[364] 'First, a general hospital may function as a place where medical care facilities are provided for the use of a physician and his patient. The patient comes to the hospital because his physician has decided that the hospital's facilities are needed for the proper care and treatment of the patient. This use of the hospital is made possible by an arrangement between the hospital and the physician by which the physician is granted hospital privileges. Where a hospital functions as merely the provider of medical care facilities, then, as the trial Judge pointed out, a hospital is not responsible for the negligence of the physician. The present

---

[358]  *Ellis* 598G.

[359]  *Ellis* 599A.

[360]  *Ellis* 599E.

[361]  *Ellis* 601B–D.

[362]  *Ellis* 601C & D. Jones *Negligence* 406.

[363]  *Ellis* 601C & D.

[364]  *Yepremian v. Scarborough General Hospital* (1980) 110 DLR (3d) 513, 581A–D (Ont CA). *Ellis* 603B–E.

case does not, of course, come within this classification. Second, a general hospital may function as a place where a person in need of treatment goes to obtain treatment. Here the role of the hospital is that of an institution where medical treatment is made available to those who require it. The present case falls in this second classification. Tony Yepremian was brought to the Scarborough General Hospital because he was in need of treatment. Does a hospital in these circumstances have the duty to provide proper medical care to a patient? In my judgment, it does.'

The judge observed that the first situation applied in the instant case and the second was exactly that which obtained in *Albrighton*.[365] The majority judges distinguished between the hospital which functions as a mere provider of facilities as a result of an arrangement between the hospital and the doctor, and a hospital which functions as a place where a person in need of treatment goes to obtain treatment.[366] The non-delegable duty could arise in the latter case, but would not extend to a case where the patient engaged the doctor directly, and the latter did not act on behalf of the hospital.[367]

The judge's final conclusion, included a thorough investigation of the Australian law[368] regarding the non-delegable duty: The case of *Kondis*[369] authoritatively determined for this court, the nature and scope of non-delegable duties in tort.[370] It firstly implied that as a result of a special relationship, a special responsibility is generated in terms of which a duty to ensure that care is taken emerges in various circumstances.[371] The non-delegable duty of the hospital — to ensure that reasonable care is issued in the provision of treatment — was, however, subject to the limitations expressed in common law cases[372] i.e. that 'that duty does not extend to treatment which is performed by a doctor pursuant to a direct engagement with the patient, and not on behalf of the hospital'.[373] The scope of the duty was to be determined by what medical services the hospital had undertaken to supply, which was to be established on the facts. In other words, where proof of the relationship between the hospital and the patient could project

---

[365] *Ellis* 603E.

[366] *Ellis* 603E. See also Jones *Negligence* 406–407.

[367] *Infra.*

[368] *Ellis* 603A & E.

[369] *Kondis v. State Transport Authority* (1984) 154 CLR 672.

[370] *Ellis* 603E.

[371] *Ellis* 603F & G, 604A–E.

[372] *Gold, Cassidy* and *Roe. Ellis* 604E.

[373] *Ellis* 604F.

some kind of a special duty, its legal binding enforcement would only be established by its scope on the facts. Conclusively, where the patient goes directly to the hospital for treatment and advice, the hospital will upon acceptance and admittance of the patient to medical and surgical benefits, remain responsible to ensure that proper treatment is provided with reasonable care and come under a duty that 'cannot be divested by delegation'.[374] The duty of the hospital could be limited by fact.[375] In the present case it was held that the appellant did not look to the hospital for medical care, but to Dr Chambers.[376] No relevant non-delegable duty could therefore be ascribed to the hospital which could render it liable for the negligence of Dr Chambers for the injury of the appellant. The judge concluded that

> ... in the circumstances of this case the relationship between the appellant and the hospital was not such as to generate a special independent or non-delegable obligation on the part of the hospital to ensure that the operation was performed with proper care.[377]

The hospital was not liable and the appellant's claim failed.[378]

Samuels JA thus found that where a patient approached a doctor for medical intervention, he was considered an independent contractor although being an honorary medical officer of the hospital. In terms of his privileges he had himself arranged the operation. The hospital was no more than a mere provider of facilities for care and treatment and could therefore come under no non-delegable duty towards the patient.[379]

## Comment

Comment on Kirby P's judgment in *Ellis*:

(i)     It is, with all respect, the opinion of the present writer, that his Lordship's outlay of relevant factors upon which the vicarious liability of the hospital was founded, presents the implementation of nothing other than the organization test (in disguised form).

Comment on Samuel JA's judgment in *Ellis*:

(i)     Samuel JA, with all respect adhered to the out-dated or traditional approach to vicarious liability of requiring the employer-employee

---

[374]   *Ellis* 604G–605B, F. *Ellis* 601C&D.
[375]   *Ellis* 605B.
[376]   *Ellis* 605D.
[377]   *Ellis* 606C.
[378]   *Ellis* 606D.
[379]   See also Jones *Negligence* 406 and MacFarlane *Health Law* 35–36 on this case.

relationship in order to establish such a liability. In other words in terms of his perspective, vicarious liability can never follow for independent contractors.

(ii) The profits of dealing with the non-delegable duty, is that it caters for the wrongful acts of independent contractors. Liability could follow for the wrongs committed by independent agents in terms of the non-delegable duty. But in view of the limiting factors expounded by Samuels JA, liability will not follow in such cases where the patient approaches the independent contractor who acts on his own behalf or is an honorary member of a hospital.

(iii) If a patient — of his own accord — goes to an independent contractor who is not sufficiently linked to a hospital, it could be difficult for the patient to establish

(a) the precise nature of the contract between the hospital and the doctor, and

(b) whose negligence (the hospital's or the doctor's) caused the patient's injury and/or damage. In terms of this perspective, the plaintiff seals or determines his fate to compensation by the hospital, by such an unknowing act. By this judgment the patient limits or prevents possible hospital liability by his own choices and acts by which he obtains medical intervention, as a result of lack of legal knowledge. He could, however, sue and recover compensation from the doctor.

The perspective of the judgment *in toto* shows that hospital liability is established by relationships i.e. — the relationship between the hospital and the patient (resulting in a possible non-delegable duty) and the relationship between the hospital and the doctor (resulting in possible vicarious liability).

The High Court of Australia

8. In **Burnie Port Authority v. General Jones Pty Ltd** [380] (1994) the High Court of Australia once again considered the non-delegable duty. The appellant had occupied premises which it owned. An independent contractor carried out unguarded welding operations which were close to stacked cardboard cartons of Isolite, an insulating material which burns ferociously if in contact with a flame. Due to negligence of the contractor, a fire erupted and destroyed frozen vegetables of the respondent non-owing occupier in adjoining cold-rooms. The appellant was found liable for damages at first

---

[380] (1994) 120 *ALR* 42, 43, 61–69, 70–97.

instance, and on appeal in the Supreme Court of Tasmania. The High Court of Australia also dismissed the appeal.

Mason CJ, Deane, Dawson, Toohey and Gaudron JJ (Brennan and McHugh JJ contra) found that in certain categories of cases, in identification of special relationships which generates a particular responsibility for people in special dependence or vulnerability, such proximity is marked by 'the central element of control'.[381] Principal categories were identified as proposed by Mason J in *Kondis*.[382] These categories of cases which give rise to the special non-delegable duty to ensure that reasonable care is taken, were:

> ...adjoining owners of land in relation to work threatening support or common walls; master and servant in relation to a safe system of work; **hospital and patient**; school authority and principal; and (arguably), occupier and invitee.[383]

It was concluded that under the principles of negligence, when a person in control of premises introduces dangerous substances, allows dangerous activities or allows another to do them, the former owes a non-delegable duty of reasonable care to ensure that reasonably foreseeable risks of injury or damage to persons or property, are avoided.[384] *In casu* the appellant owed the respondent a non-delegable duty of care, which extended to ensure that the independent contractor took reasonable care in preventing the Isolite to be set alight as a result of (dangerous) welding activities. They did not take such reasonable care and their liability was confirmed.[385]

9. In ***Woods* v. *Lowns***[386] (1995) the plaintiff child, Patrick Woods who was 11 years old, once again suffered a very serious epileptic fit with consequential hypoxia and resultant extensive brain damage and quadriplegia. The plaintiff's mother had sent the daughter to call a doctor. She ran to Dr Lowns' surgery, about 300 metres from their home, and asked him to assist,

---

[381] *Burnie* 62–63. It is with respect, a pity that the High Court had to rely on 'control' in any form, to come to an otherwise credible solution. The common element was unfortunately typified as 'control'. It could have been 'authority' or 'special responsibility' or 'organizational duties or requirements', or 'higher care'.

[382] *Kondis* v. *State Transport supra* at 679–687.

[383] *Burnie* 62. My accentuation.

[384] *Burnie* 67.

[385] *Burnie* 69.

[386] *Woods* v. *Lowns* (1995) 36 NSWLR 344 (Badgery-Parker J at first instance). Dix *et al. Australia* 271–272 § 1106. *Lowns & Anor* v. *Woods & Ors* (1996) Australia Torts Reports 81–376 ('*Lowns* v. *Woods*'). Day 1996 *SLR* 386–400.

upon which he refused. The trial court accepted her testimony. Other doctors were also involved in treating the plaintiff who were also sued. It was alleged that the plaintiff had received inadequate and improper medical treatment. The plaintiff succeeded at first instance in a claim for damages for negligent breach of the doctor's duty in failing to attend and treat the patient in an emergency.

The court took account of several factors, one of which was the circumstances that indicated, that refusal to attend without reasonable cause would have implied professional misconduct in contravention of '(the then in force [1150] ) section 27(1) of the Medical Practitioners Act 1938–1987 (NSW)'.[387] This section did not impose a statutory obligation in favour of the plaintiff, but the judge took it into consideration in founding a common law duty.[388]

On Appeal: In **Lowns & Anor v. Woods & Ors** [389] the New South Wales Court of Appeal gave judgment on two controversial issues in medical malpractice: a common law duty which requires medical practitioners to attend non-patients in an emergency and the relevance of usual medical practice to the standard of care.

It had been held and confirmed that the Australian law acknowledges a common law duty for all medical practitioners to attend and treat a person in an emergency who had never been nor at that time was, his patient. The Australian common law had not known such a duty or a duty to rescue a person when injury or death was/is foreseeable when failing to assist.[390]

The majority of the Court of Appeal (Kirby P and Cole JA) upheld the decision that Dr Lowns had owed a duty of care to the plaintiff, of which there was breach by failing to attend to the boy.[391] They had recognized that the common law was reluctant to impose positive duties, even to prevent foreseeable injury.[392] A duty was not founded sufficiently on foreseeability of harm alone, but in addition sufficient proximity between the doctor and plaintiff could establish the existence of a duty to attend.[393]

Other common law jurisdictions have held that a doctor has no duty to attend a sick person despite an emergency, if that person was not nor had

---

[387] Dix *et al. Australia* 272 § 1106.

[388] *Ibid.*

[389] (1996) Australian Torts Reports 81–376 ('Lowns v. Woods').

[390] Day 1996 *SLR* 386.

[391] *Lowns* 63, 156 per Kirby P; *Lowns* 63, 176 per Cole JA.

[392] *Lowns* 63, 155 per Kirby P; *Lowns* 63, 175 per Cole JA. See also Day 1996 *SLR* 388.

[393] Day 1996 *SLR* 388.

ever been a patient of that doctor.[394] The distinct Australian law of torts has thus been expanded significantly by *Lowns* v. *Woods*.[395] This decision of the Court of Appeal has far-reaching consequences for medical malpractice liability and especially for hospital liability. The creation of such a duty implies the enforcement of the duty with special reference to hospitals, where medical professionals might be working for an institution. The hospital can be held liable on account of such a duty by means of vicarious liability. In an emergency setting, this duty which relates to emergencies can activate a finding of hospital liability on the grounds of a non-delegable duty. The hospital could have delegated the provision of emergency services which the doctor neglected, for which the hospital cannot delegate responsibility. The doctrine of ostensible agency can also be considered in this regard, with possible consequential hospital liability.

Remarkable was the Court's discretion to create new law and formulate a new common law duty. This is something Blair JA had suggested and implemented in *Yepremian*,[396] a Canadian case. In that case the majority of the Court of Appeal had refused to create a policy, formulate a duty or create new law and had preferred to leave it to the legislature.


## 6.6 CONCLUSION

1.  Vicarious hospital liability cases are not few in number and are easily identifiable in Australian judicial reports. The control test has not yet been abandoned completely. It was actually reinstated by the High Court in *Burnie Port Authority* v. *General Jones Pty Ltd* (1994) 120 ALR 42. The organization test was, however, snubbed by the Australian High Court in *Stevens* v. *Brodribb Sawmilling Co Pty Ltd* (1986) 160 CLR 16.

2.  Concerning the direct liability of hospitals, Australian judgments have not, with respect, presented scientifically clear or terminologically correct cases, which can beyond a doubt be classified as thorough examples of direct or corporate hospital liability which are not founded on the non-delegable duty.

3.  The non-delegable duty has, by frequent application in Australian courts, become a permanent part of the Australian law. Its full poten-

---

[394] *Op. cit.* 386.

[395] *Supra* footnote 388.

[396] See Chapter 7 on the Canadian Law: The Non-Delegable Duty.

tial has not yet been realized and no single judicial exposition of an absolute justification has yet been mastered. Its development is, however, significant and should be taken cognizance of by other legal systems which are always endeavouring to improve their own perspectives and reasoning.

Unfortunately the Australian courts have, with all respect, categorized the non-delegable duty as a form of direct liability. It is with respect, an unnatural and unnecessary process by which squares are fitted into round holes. The main difference lies in the fact that in the case of direct liability, the employer has personal fault or blame, whilst in the case of the non-delegable duty, the employer has no personal fault or blame. They are not completely identical in terms of prerequisites, content or formulation. It is suggested, with all respect, that they should be considered as distinct and independent legal grounds, which separately found hospital liability. (See the Comparative Diagram at 4.4)

# Chapter 7

# The Canadian Law

## 7.1 HEALTH CARE IN CANADA
## LAND AREA: 10,400,000 SQ. KM.[1]

### 7.1.1 Health Care

Health Canada[2] aims at providing service excellence in the provision of health care, to the people of Canada. Their vision centres on:

-   A renewed national health system
-   National leadership and partnerships on health; and
-   The provision of timely, responsive and evidence-based advice and action on health issues.

Health Canada is organized by means of five branches and a departmental secretariat. It is represented in five regions throughout Canada: Atlantic, Québec, Ontario, Manitoba/Saskatchewan and Pacific West. Some branch activities only operate at national level and are not always represented in the regions.[3]

The **Departmental Secretariat** 'coordinates the interface between the executive and political levels of the Department in activities such as parliamentary relations and ministerial correspondence, and serves as a focal point for corporate planning, priorities and initiatives'.[4]

---

[1]   Affordable Health Care Singapore 1993: Appendix B Subject 1.

[2]   Most of the information on 'Health Care in Canada' is obtained from Internet: ABOUT HEALTH CANADA http://hbp1.hwc.ca/links/healthcan/abthc_e.htm 5/8/96 11:44 AM. See also Brown *Malpractice* 274–293.

[3]   *Ibid.*

[4]   *Ibid.*

**Branch operations**[5]

-       **Health Promotion and Programs Branch (HPPB)** institutes
        programs for the health and well-being of Canadians. Issues relating
        to family health, nutrition, tobacco, alcohol and drug use, AIDS and
        other diseases are addressed.

-       **Health Protection Branch (HPB)** conducts programs by which the
        safety of food supply, pharmaceuticals and cosmetics, medical or ra-
        diation-emitting devices and the environment are ensured. They also
        protect Canadians from hazardous consumer products or materials in
        the work place. Inspections, surveillance and research are carried out
        to prevent amongst other things disease outbreaks and product haz-
        ards.

-       **Medical Service Branch (MSB)** provides community health services,
        which include the provision of goods and services, to specified groups
        of people.

-       **Policy and Consultation Branch (PCB)** provides vital information
        and data to senior management and program branches through strate-
        gic planning, policy development and public information activities.
        This branch is responsible for a number of program areas, including
        'Communications, Health Insurance, International Affairs and the
        Women's Health Bureau'.

-       **Corporate Services Branch (CSB)** supports departmental programs
        through 'financial planning and administration, human resources man-
        agement, information systems, office accommodation, internal audit,
        facilities management and general administrative direction in line with
        departmental and government-wide policies'.

### 7.1.2  Health Financing[6]

Health care in Canada is provided through

(i)     A National Health Plan which is financed through taxation.

(ii)    The provincial governments pay for the medical care of all citizens
        with provincial and federal funds. There is no privately financed
        medical system.

---

[5]   *Ibid.*

[6]   Affordable Health Care Singapore 1993 Appendix B Subject 9: Health Financing (i) to
      (iv).

(iii)   All medical care is free, including long-term home care and nursing home care.

(iv)   Patients under 65 pay for outpatient medications.

The Canadian health-care system provides universal access to comprehensive home, office and hospital care based on the insurance principle. The federal government subsidizes each province to almost half the cost, and the rest of the cost is met by complying with national mandates.[7]

### 7.1.3  Health Care System[8]

(i)   Primary health care is provided by specialists and general practitioners. Public health nurses provide care in sparsely populated areas.

(ii)   Institutional care is provided as follows:

-   Secondary care is provided in area hospitals and tertiary care in regional hospitals.

-   Hospitals provide outpatient and ambulatory care services as well as public health programmes through their Community Health Centres.

-   About 75% of the doctors are office based and most have hospital admitting privileges.

The Canadian health care model, is considered with respect and interest by US reformers and legislators. The national health-care costs of Canada average a considerably lower percentage of their gross national product (GDP), than does the US health-care costs. The health-care system seems quite satisfactory to the Canadians. American critics, however, argue that the waiting period for Canadian elective procedures and distances travelled for special treatments or studies, are unacceptable.[9]

---

[7]   Silver *Health-Care Systems* 1993 Grolier Electronic Publishing Inc.

[8]   Affordable Health Care Singapore 1993 Appendix B Subject 10: Health care system (i)–(ii).

[9]   Silver *Health-Care Systems in European Countries* 1993 Grolier Electronic Publishing Inc.

## 7.2 THE HOSPITAL IN CANADA

The first hospitals were exclusively primitive places of refuge for the destitute and the poor.[10] Much later, both the wealthy and the poor were treated at the hospital.[11] The hospital was initially also a place which only provided facilities and abode for the patient. Thereafter, treatment and care was made available by the professionals they selected and employed. Responsibility of health institutions was, however, restricted by courts because funding was limited.[12] As a result of the doctrine of charitable immunity which was instituted in English law, 'the protectionist attitude of courts had taken seed, germinating in the form of immunities which have affected legal analysis and shaped the modern law relating to hospitals'.[13]

Today, the modern hospital in Canada is part of an extensive health care system. The health care system is one of the largest service industries in Canada.[14] The legal status and physical presentation of the hospital has therefore changed dramatically.[15] The hospital has become a centre of advanced professional skill and knowledge equipped with modern high tech apparatus, thus becoming the primary institution[16] for health care. The legal relationships between the modern hospital, the medical officers and the patients, have become strongly defined with far-reaching ramifications. The terms of the relationships are regulated by legislation, hospital by-laws, conduct of the parties and even public expectations. This perpetuates high risks of possible hospital liability, resulting in high legal fees and astronomical settlement fees or damage awards.[17]

**Definition**

In terms of the Public Hospitals Act, c 410, RSO (1980), section 1(e), 'hospital' means any institution, building or other premises or place established for the treatment of persons afflicted with or suffering from

---

[10]   Rozovsky *Law* 15. See also Picard 1981 *MGLJ* 997 and Osode 1993 *AALR* 290.

[11]   Rozovsky *Law* 15.

[12]   *Ibid.* Picard 1981 *MGLJ* 997. Osode 1993 *AALR* 290.

[13]   Picard 1981 *MGLJ* 998.

[14]   *Ibid.* The health care system was the largest service industry in Canada in 1980.

[15]   Osode 1993 *AALR* 291.

[16]   *Ibid.* Rozovsky *Law* 15.

[17]   Osode 1993 *AALR* 292. Picard 1981 *MGLJ* 1001. Chapman *Medicine* 56–102. Rozovsky *Law* 15–16.

sickness, disease or injury or for the treatment of convalescent or chronically ill persons.[18]

When encountering the Canadian public hospitals, there are essentially two kinds of public hospitals to be identified. Firstly, there are public hospitals owned by a religious order or other benevolent organization(s). They are operated as an arm of the religious order in terms of its constitution. The religious order often appoints an advisory group which it controls, to the hospital. Secondly, there are public hospital corporations. These hospitals are established by provincial corporation legislation or private act of the legislature. Trustees or a board of directors control such hospitals.[19] There are also private hospitals.

## 7.3 LEGAL GROUNDS OF HOSPITAL LIABILITY IN CANADA

The general categorization and application of most legal grounds of hospital liability have been discussed in 4.2 and 4.3. It is clear that there are various legal grounds of hospital liability of which the most important are: indirect or vicarious hospital liability; direct, primary or corporate liability; the non-delegable duties; various doctrines which invoke hospital liability and strict liability.

In Canadian law, as regards the legal grounds (heads) of hospital liability, Osode distinguishes between vicarious liability based on *respondeat superior*, corporate negligence and breach of contract.[20] Picard selected: the action in negligence, the duties owed by hospitals to patients and the vicarious liability of hospitals.[21] Five legal grounds relevant to the Canadian hospital liability will be discussed.

### 7.3.1  Indirect or Vicarious Hospital Liability

The indirect or vicarious liability of hospitals, as based on the doctrine of *respondeat superior*, is acknowledged in Canadian law.[22] It is presented as

---

[18]  In Canadian law. See also Osode 1993 *AALR* 289.

[19]  Sharpe *Canada* 123. Corporate hospital liability can be established for these hospitals.

[20]  Osode 1993 *AALR* 292.

[21]  Picard 1981 *MGLJ* 1003–1019.

[22]  Picard 1981 *MGLJ* 1016–1019. Chapman *Medicine* 531–533. Picard *et al. Liability* 381–397. Osode 1993 *AALR* 292–307. Sneiderman *et al.* Canadian 110–112. Sharpe *Canada* 109–126. Sharpe and Sawyer *Doctors* 73–86. Rozovsky *Law* 17.

the oldest and most common basis upon which hospital liability is founded.[23] The most general application of this principle purports that the employer will be liable for the negligent wrongs committed by the employee within the scope of his employment, but not for the wrongs committed by an independent contractor.[24]

It is, however, common knowledge in the common law provinces of Canada, that the principles of vicarious liability display a deficient application in founding hospital liability, with special reference to the inappropriateness of the control test in modern circumstances.[25] Picard concluded:

> Thus today, with a longstanding recognition that vicarious liability should be determined from analysis far broader in scope than that of the control test, the liability of hospitals is being decided by reference to a narrow, outdated test that by its very nature protects the hospital from liability for a large number of professionals who facilitate the achievement of hospital objectives.[26]

### 7.3.1.1  Traditional requirements of vicarious liability

The traditional requirements that apply in the most common situation of vicarious liability are acknowledged and taken cognisance of in the Canadian law.[27] Constructive criticisms have been formulated on these requirements, and these arguments should be considered.[28] The traditional requirements are:

7.3.1.1.1    Employer-employee relationship

7.3.1.1.2    Wrong(s) committed in the course of employment

7.3.1.1.2    Actionable wrong(s)

---

[23]  Picard 1981 *MGLJ* 1016–1019. Chapman *Medicine* 531–533.

[24]  See *supra* footnote 21.

[25]  Picard 1981 *MGLJ* 1016. See *supra* p. 85–86, where Picard is quoted.

[26]  Picard 1981 *MGLJ* 1019. Osode 1993 *AALR* at 293 stated: '… the Canadian law on hospitals' vicarious liability for the negligence of their professional staff significantly lags behind the present position in English law even though the same cannot be said with respect to Canadian law governing 'professional' full time employees of the hospital'.

[27]  Osode 1993 *AALR* 292–307. Picard *et al. Liability* 381.Picard 1981 *MGLJ* 1016. Sneiderman *et al. Canadian* 110.

[28]  *Ibid.*

## 7.3.1.1.1 Employer-employee (master and servant) relationship

Osode considers this requirement as 'central to a court's finding of vicarious liability'.[29] Two indicia exist which initiate the conclusion that such a relationship exists. The first is that the employee's services should be rendered under a 'contract of service', and not a contract for services. Secondly, the employer must have control as to the 'what and how' of the work to be done. Consequently, as the argument runs, employers are not vicariously liable for wrongs committed by independent contractors, because they render services in terms of contracts for services.[30]

### (1) Professional medical staff

Problems do however arise when trying to apply the principles and indicia of vicarious liability to hospital liability, and Canadian authors recognize this problem.[31] Professional medical staff whose conduct could result in injury to patients, act independently and are not subject to any kind of control from the hospital in the performance of their duties.[32]

The principle formulated in the *Hillyer*[33] decision — in the English common law — which created a ministerial-professional distinction of duties for professionals for the sake of eliminating or creating hospital liability, has experienced progressive handling by Canadian courts. At first the Canadian courts applied the principle,[34] although not consistently. It was, however, restricted in 1916 by an Ontario court.[35] In 1938, the Supreme Court of Canada[36] pronounced that it was not bound to follow the ministerial-professional distinction, but granted it their respect. Other cases[37] followed in which courts were not prepared to accommodate the principle, but nevertheless found the negligent conduct to be ministerial. In *Fraser* v. *Vancouver*

---

[29]  Osode 1993 *AALR* 294.

[30]  *Ibid.*

[31]  *Ibid.* Picard 1981 *MGLJ* 1016. See *supra.*

[32]  *Ibid.*

[33]  [1909] 2 KB 820 (CA). Sharpe *Canada* 110–111.

[34]  *Abel* v. *Cooke* [1938] 1 WWR 49 (Alta CA). *Vuchar* v. *Toronto General Hospital Trustees* [1937] OR 71 (CA). Picard *et al. Liability* 383.

[35]  *Lavere* v. *Smith's Falls Public Hospital* (1915) 26 DLR 346 (Ont CA). Picard *et al. Liability* 383: This court found that the principle should not be regarded as an exposition of the whole law.

[36]  *Sisters of St Joseph of the Diocese of London* v. *Fleming* [1938] SCR 172. The nurse's negligent action was classified as being ministerial. Picard *et al. Liability* 383.

[37]  *Nyberg* v. *Provost* [1927] SCR 226. Picard *et al. Liability* 383 footnote 145.

*General Hospital* [38] and *Petite* v. *MacLeod* [39] (albeit *obiter* in the latter case), the *Hillyer* principle was rejected by Canadian courts.

Developments in Canadian law, as elsewhere, have indicated that hospital liability has been expanded extensively. Hospital liability for medical professionals inclusive of doctors and nurses, has been established in Canadian law.[40] Canadian and other sources have provided some indicia to establish such liability.

### (2)    Doctors

The vicarious liability of hospitals for doctors, will be determined by the relationship among the hospital, doctor and patient.[41] Doctors who treat patients in Canadian hospitals, fall into two categories. The first category comprises of professionals who are private medical practitioners[42] and have been granted hospital privileges by the hospital board. This entitles them to make use of hospital facilities, equipment and personnel, when having their private patients admitted and for the treatment of them there. They do consult with patients who are not theirs, but only when attending in the emergency department of the hospital or when consulting on request of the hospital or a fellow doctor when treating the latter's patient.[43] In such cases the doctors are paid by the patient through the Provincial Health insurance plans or directly by the patient, but not by the hospital.[44] The patient employs, pays and dismisses the doctor. This category comprises of the majority of doctors who practise in North America.[45] The other category of doctors are employed and paid directly by the hospital or the medical school of a university, for example doctors employed as house staff (residents or interns).[46] There is, however, a third category of doctors who do not fit into

---

[38]    [1952] 2 SCR 36: The hospital was held liable for the negligence of an intern. Picard *et al. Liability* 383.

[39]    [1955] 1 DLR 147 (NSSC). The hospital was not held liable since the doctor was not on the house staff and the evidence (regarding a swab) was insufficient. But, the court decided upon all the law and found, *obiter*, that no difference existed between professional and non-professional acts. Picard *et al. Liability* 383.

[40]    Picard 1981 *MGLJ* 1016–1019. Picard *et al. Liability* 381–397. Osode 1993 *AALR* 292–307. Sneiderman *et al. Canadian* 110–112. Sharpe *Canada* 109–126. Sharpe and Sawyer *Doctors* 73–86.

[41]    Picard *et al. Liability* 383.

[42]    Like surgeons, specialists and consultants.

[43]    Osode 1993 *AALR* 294. Picard *et al. Liability* 383–384.

[44]    Osode 1993 *AALR* 294.

[45]    Picard *et al. Liability* 383. See also Osode 1993 *AALR* 294.

[46]    Osode 1993 *AALR* 294–295. Picard *et al. Liability* 384.

any of the two above-mentioned categories. They are members of hospitals' staff who are not subject to the hospital administration's control in performing their duties. These professionals consist of surgeons, doctors, interns, radiologists, pharmacists, anaesthetists and nurses whose conduct is also frequently called into question.[47]

Consequently, the majority of doctors working in Canada whose acts are in dispute, do not have contracts of service with hospitals,[48] and would traditionally not be employees of the hospital.

Regarding the doctor in the first category, the patient retains the power to employ, pay and dismiss the doctor. The medical professional is then considered an independent contractor and is directly liable to the patient for negligent actions.[49] With regard to the doctor who is employed as house staff by the hospital, vicarious liability of the institution can follow easily. The relationship between the hospital and the doctor is usually prescribed by means of a written contract and institutional attempts at control of such staff are evident from manuals and directives issued by the hospital.[50] In this case it is the hospital that holds the power to employ, pay and dismiss. Cases which involve professionals such as anaesthetists, deserve careful consideration. In some cases hospitals will be found vicariously liable, and in others not.[51] Direct hospital liability can also ensue in these cases.

As is evident from Australian and Canadian law — as derived from the English common law case of *Cassidy* — this power to employ, pay and dismiss forms the foundation to a particular legal ground of hospital liability, and lack thereof excludes it altogether. Denying the patient this power and forfeiting the power to the hospital, could establish hospital liability vicariously,[52] (or under the non-delegable duty).[53] When the patient is

---

[47]  *Ibid.*

[48]  Osode 1993 *AALR* 295.

[49]  In *Petite* v. *MacLeod and St Mary's Hospital* [1955] 1 DLR 147 (NSSC), the Supreme Court held that a hospital is liable for the negligence of employed doctors and nurses, but it is not liable for the negligence of doctors who are engaged and paid by the patient, even when they make use of the facilities, operating room and nurses of the hospital. Sharpe *Canada* 112. Picard *et al. Liability* 383, 385–386. Rozovsky *Law* 18–19.

[50]  Picard *et al. Liability* 384.

[51]  *Ibid:* These doctors do not fit into any of the two above-mentioned categories: In such cases the facts must be carefully analyzed as suggested in *Cassidy* v. *Ministry of Health* [1951] 1 ALL ER 574 (CA).

[52]  Picard *et al. Liability* 383–384, 386. Osode 1993 *AALR* 294–295. Rozovsky *Law* 18–19.

[53]  As is the case in Australian law.

afforded this power, it excludes hospital liability vicariously[54] (or under the non-delegable duty),[55] but could cause the independent contractor to be directly liable to the patient.[56]

In *Martel* v. *Hôtel-Dieu St-Vallier* [57] the court found that the anaesthetist performed his duties under his contract of employment with the hospital. His remuneration also included a portion of the service charges of the hospital. The hospital provided anaesthesia services and he was not selected by the patient. The anaesthetist was found to be an employee of the hospital and the hospital was consequently held vicariously liable. In *Beausoleil* v. *La Communauté des Soeurs de la Charité*[58] the Quebec Court of Appeal found the hospital vicariously liable under similar circumstances.

In **Vancouver General Hospital v. Fraser** [59] the following occurred: The respondent's husband was in a motor vehicle accident, as a result of which he was admitted to the appellant hospital's emergency ward, at night. In the emergency ward of the hospital, the interns on duty examined the patient. X-rays were taken, although these films were not submitted to the radiologist on call. Unfortunately, the interns who had no required skills or competency to read the films, proceeded to do so, and advised the family physician that they had found nothing abnormal. The interns failed to detect the injury. The patient was therefore discharged from hospital with a dislocated fracture of the neck. After a radiologist had examined the X-ray films, the patient's own physician had him re-admitted to the hospital the following day. The patient died a few days later as a result of the injury. The Supreme Court of Canada held the hospital liable for the negligence of its interns, and held that the hospital undertook to treat the patient.

---

[54] Picard *et al. Liability* 383–384, 386. Osode 1993 *AALR* 294–295.

[55] As is the case in Australian law.

[56] Picard *et al. Liability* 384.

[57] (1969) 14 DLR (3d) 445 (SCC). See also Picard *et al. Liability* 384–385.

[58] (1964) 53 DLR (2d) 65 [1965] QB 37 (Que CA) at 43: 'It is established that Dr Forest was employed by the hospital as chief anaesthetist and despite the efforts made to show that the salary paid him was for services rendered in a special and restricted field I am satisfied that he was held out to plaintiff as the hospital's anaesthetist, that he acted in this capacity and that plaintiff accepted him because of this. In this case the patient contracted with the hospital for all necessary services; of these, one was the giving of the anaesthetic. On this premise and since for the purposes of this action I see no essential difference between the position of Dr Forest and that of any other employee, the hospital must answer for his fault.' See Picard *et al. Liability* 285.

[59] (1952) 2 SCR 36. See also Osode 1993 *AALR* 298 and Sharpe *Canada* 112. Sneiderman *et al. Canadian* 131. Jones *Negligence* 394 and footnote 11.

In *Aynsley et al.* v. *Toronto General Hospital et al.* [60] Elizabeth Aynsley, the plaintiff, suffered from an atrial septum defect for which she underwent corrective surgery at the hospital. During the course of preliminaries to open-heart surgery to be performed, air escaped from the manometer to the transducer, which entered her venous system. The patient suffered from cardiac arrest. Consequently the plaintiff suffered serious permanent injuries to her brain, as a result of which her mental age was permanently reduced to that of a seven-year-old child which necessitated lifelong care commensurate with that age.

In this case, two anaesthetists were involved in the procedure that caused the injury or disablement. The first senior anaesthetist had been privately employed by the patient and had many years of experience. The second anaesthetist was a post-graduate student in anaesthesiology, a senior resident and hospital employee who was assigned by the hospital to assist the private anaesthetist.[61]

The trial judge had found that the negligence of both the anaesthetists — the private physician to the extent of 60 per cent and the resident to the extent of 40 per cent — had caused the plaintiff's damages. He found the hospital vicariously liable for the resident's negligence in terms of the master-servant relationship.[62] He found that Dr Porteous, the resident, was expected to use his training and abilities independently from Dr Matthews. Dr Porteous was also expected to use professional skill in the manner in which the manometer was pumped. This he had failed to do and as a permanent employee of the hospital, the hospital was vicariously liable for his negligence.[63] With these findings of the trial judge, Aylesworth JA concurred.

**The Ontario Court of Appeal:** Aylesworth JA first of all rejected the distinction created in Hillyer in terms of which a hospital is held liable only for the negligent acts committed by employees which are of an administrative nature and not for acts involving professional skills.[64]

The Supreme Court case of *Sisters of St Joseph of the Diocese of London in Ontario* v. *Fleming* [65] was referred to, in which it was confirmed that the

---

[60]  (1970) 7 DLR (3rd) 193: See also Osode 1993 *AALR* 298. Sharpe *Canada* 114–115: [1968] 1 OR 425; affd [1969] 2 OR 829; affd [1972] SCR 435 (sub nom. *Toronto General Hospital Trustees* v. *Matthews*). Picard *et al. Liability* 365.

[61]  *Aynsley* 194–195.

[62]  *Aynsley* 194, 210.

[63]  *Aynsley* 210. Aylesworth JA concurred.

[64]  *Aynsley* 201–203.

[65]  [1938] SCR 172, [1938] 2 DLR 417.

*Hillyer* decision was not binding then, and therefore not now. The principle enunciated there, to determine the situation was considered to be 'the test of the relation of master and servant or of principal and agent to the particular work in which the nurse was engaged at the moment when the act of negligence occurred'.[66] After careful consideration of the famous trilogy of cases[67] in the English law, the judge concluded on the judgments of Denning LJ[68] that the latter was of the opinion that hospital authorities were liable for the negligence of a doctor on the permanent staff of a hospital irrespective of the fact whether the doctor is employed under a contract of service or under a contract for services. It was to depend 'solely on the question of who employs him'.[69] The judge also reiterated that Denning LJ thought hospital authorities were responsible for the whole of their staff, not only for nurses and doctors, but also for the anaesthetists and surgeons whether permanent or temporary, resident or visiting, whole-time or part-time. This was stated on 'the ground that even if they are not servants of the hospital, they are its agents to give treatment'.[70]

Thus relying greatly on English authorities, Aylesworth JA formulated a principle for hospital liability. The hospital's liability for the negligent acts or omissions of employees regarding patients 'depends primarily upon the particular facts of the case, that is to say, the services which the hospital undertakes to provide and the relationship of the physician and surgeon to the hospital'.[71] On the facts Dr Porteous, the resident, was found to be a highly skilled, trained anaesthetist. He was a full-time member of the hospital staff, paid by the hospital, and assigned by the hospital to assist in certain procedures. He was not controlled in his work — either in the manner or execution of his duties — by the other anaesthetist, Dr Matthews.[72] The Court of Appeal thus found that the resident's negligence 'was a failure by the hospital staff itself to discharge efficiently its undertaking to the patient.'[73] The hospital's vicarious liability was confirmed.[74]

---

[66] *Aynsley* 203.

[67] Ie *Gold* v. *Essex County Council* [1942] 2 ALL ER 237; *Cassidy* v. *Ministry of Health* [1951] 1 ALL ER 574; *Roe* v. *Ministry of Health* [1954] 2 ALL ER 131.

[68] In the cases *supra.*

[69] *Aynsley* 206.

[70] *Aynsley* 208.

[71] *Aynsley* 208.

[72] *Aynsley* 208.

[73] *Aynsley* 208.

[74] *Aynsley* 208.

Most interesting, though, are the remarks made by Aylesworth JA after he confirmed the hospital's liability. He stated that Dr Porteous was 'I think, under a contract of service with the hospital but, in my view, the legal result would be the same if his had been a contract for services'.[75] Apparently this court had also implicitly abandoned the distinction between the 'contract of service' and 'contract for services', in order to establish hospital liability. The court determined that the hospital would be liable in cases of both contract arrangements. Although the resident was under a contract of service with the hospital, the court had stated that hospital liability would still ensue even if the contract had been for services. This can be considered as great progress in the development of Canadian hospital liability law.

This had been the first time that hospital liability had been extended to 'contracts for services' in Canada.[76] It is in accordance with the British view that hospitals should be liable for the negligent acts of all staff, whether they are permanent or temporary, resident or visiting, full or part-time, predicating that they are agents of the hospital in providing treatment.[77]

The fact that Aylesworth JA had stated that the hospital would be liable even if the doctor had been employed under a contract for services, could also suggest that the hospital was under a non-delegable duty. The negligence could have been that of an independent contractor for which the non-delegable duty makes provision and is applied. The contractual relationship between the hospital and the patient can well create a non-delegable duty.[78]

In Canada, hospital liability is determined independently in every case by consideration of the unique set of facts; by the determination of who employed the medical professional or physician; and by the relationship of the hospital with the physician which renders the physician an agent of the hospital or only a member privately engaged by a patient who is a privileged user of hospital facilities. If the hospital employed the physician, the hospital will be liable; whereas if the patient engaged the medical professional, the latter will bear responsibility for his own negligence. If the physician is an employee of the hospital or an agent providing medical care, assigned by the hospital to assist, the hospital will be vicariously liable. If the patient privately engages a physician who enjoys privileges at the hospital, the physician will be liable in cases of negligence.

---

[75] *Aynsley* 209. See *supra* Aylesworth JA's quote from Denning LJ who formulated this conclusion.

[76] Sharpe *Canada* 114.

[77] *Ibid.* See *supra* Chapter 5. *Aynsley supra* 203–208.

[78] Jones *Negligence* 407 footnote 82.

Canadian courts have also found hospitals not to be vicariously liable for anaesthetists who allegedly acted negligently. In both *Aynsley* v. *Toronto General Hospital* [79] and *Crits* v. *Sylvester*,[80] the patients employed certain doctors, and no liability ensued for the hospitals. In *Gorback* v. *Ting* [81] the patient engaged the doctor on a direct contractual fee-for-service basis, whilst the hospital provided no compensation for services rendered. The hospital was once again not found vicariously liable.

In *Tiesmaki* v. *Wilson* [82] the principles set out in *Aynsley* v. *Toronto General Hospital* [83] on vicarious liability and the master-servant relationships and responsibilities, were confirmed. The court indicated that vicarious hospital liability would only be established on evidence of negligence of those servants involved. In *Serre* v. *de Tilly*,[84] hospital liability was denied for the behaviour of the patient's own physician in the quality of care he had provided. He was in no way acting as an employee or agent of the hospital. It was furthermore advocated that a hospital should not interfere with or depart from the instructions of a patient's physician, if it is not clear or obvious that the physician is negligent or incompetent. Where the patient engages, pays and has the power to dismiss the physician, no hospital liability will usually ensue.[85]

In **MacDonald v. York County Hospital Corp.**,[86] the following facts were presented: David MacDonald suffered a fracture dislocation of his left ankle in a motorcycle accident. He was admitted to the emergency department of the York County Hospital. Dr Vail, a well-qualified general surgeon applied a thin plaster cast which was too tight. Gangrene unfortunately set in as a result of vascular insufficiency. Three successive amputations were required. Action was brought against the hospital and two doctors. The trial judge found Dr Vail had acted negligently and held the hospital liable for the negligence of its nursing staff. The nurses' negligence was found to exist in their failure to alert Dr Vail or any other physician to the dramatically

---

[79]　[1972] SCR 435: Only concerning the one privately employed anaesthetist.

[80]　[1956] SCR 991.

[81]　[1974] 5 WWR 606 (Man QB).

[82]　[1974] 4 WWR 19; affd [1975] 6 WWR 639 (Alta CA).Sharpe *Canada* 116.

[83]　[1972] SCR 435, see *supra.*

[84]　(1975) 8 OR (2d) 490. See also Sharpe *Canada* 116.

[85]　See also Picard *et al. Liability* 383–384.

[86]　[1972] 3 OR 469, 28 DLR (3d) 521 aff in part 1 OR (2d) 653, 41 DLR (3d) 321, affd [1976] 2 SCR 825 (sub nom Vail v MacDonald) 66 DLR (3d) 530 8 NR 155. Sneiderman *Canadian* 1–17. Sharpe *Law* 117.

worsening condition of the patient's foot over the 19-hour period he spent in hospital. Both Dr Vail and the hospital appealed. Dr Vail's appeal was dismissed. The hospital's appeal was however granted, since it was found that the negligence of the nurses did not cause or contribute to the plaintiff's injury. The court found that even if Dr Vail had been called, he would have done nothing for his patient. Dr Vail appealed to the Supreme Court who dismissed the appeal. It was concluded that there was sufficient evidence of negligence.

This case serves to illustrate that a hospital can be found vicariously liable for the negligent behaviour of its staff, for failing to alert attending physicians to certain serious conditions. It was also confirmed that physicians are not responsible for the actions of hospital staff to execute instructions on the treatment and care of patients.[87] Surgeons may delegate procedures without any duty to supervise qualified staff in performance of such instructions. Surgeons are however responsible, as part of a general duty to patients, to identify potential dangerous situations and to take remedial action where necessary or indicated.[88]

In **Kolesar v. Jeffries**,[89] later the *Joseph Brant Memorial Hospital et al.* v. *Koziol et al.* [90] case, the following transpired: The deceased was involved in a motorcar accident which was due solely to the negligence of the other driver. As a result, he underwent a spinal fusion operation. After the operation, while still unconscious, the patient was placed in a Stryker frame. He was strapped onto a narrow bed in order to remain in a fixed position to allow healing to proceed. He was transferred to the surgical ward of the hospital. He was found dead the next morning at 5 o'clock.

Action for wrongful death was brought *inter alia* against the hospital and five of its nurses. The trial judge gave judgment for the plaintiffs. He had the benefit of having the evidence and cross-examination before him upon which he could reasonably base his conclusion.[91] He heard the evidence, judged it to be credible and accepted it as a basis for his conclusion according to Spence J of the Supreme Court.[92] The trial judge's assessment of the evidence was thus accepted. Haines J found that the deceased had died

---

[87]  See also Sharpe *Canada* 117.

[88]  *Ibid.*

[89]  68 DLR (3d) 198, 12 OR (2d) 142; 59 DLR (3d) 367, 9 OR (2d) 41.

[90]  (1977) 77 DLR (3d) 161 (SCC); affd (1976) 12 OR (2d) 142 (CA);varying (1974) 9 OR (2d) 41 (HC).

[91]  *Kolesar* 169.

[92]  *Kolesar* 169.

due to aspiration resulting from regurgitation of gastric juices which was caused by a failure of the nurses to give him proper care and attention between the time of his removal in an unconscious state from the operating-room encased in a Stryker frame and the time of his death, seventeen hours later.[93] The hospital was therefore found (vicariously) liable for the negligence of the nurses who caused the patient's death.

The hospital and five nurses appealed to the Ontario Court of Appeal. This court allowed the appeal of four nurses on the ground that the evidence did not support the conclusion as to the cause of death. The court dismissed the appeal of the hospital and the fifth nurse. It was justified on the ground that the mystery of his death resulted from negligence of the nurse in failing to record the deceased's vital signs during the night.[94]

The hospital and fifth nurse appealed to the Supreme Court of Canada. The appeal was dismissed. The Supreme Court found that negligence by Nurse Malette had been established, for which negligence the hospital was held responsible in law, and that that negligence had resulted in the late William Kolesar's regurgitation. The court found that the cause of death was regurgitation which would not have occurred if adequate nursing had been provided. The negligent nursing had been brought about by the nurse's conduct in allowing the patient to sleep soundly all night, although he was observed as being very pale and quiet. This conduct which had been described as being 'absolutely contra the course of treatment advised by medical witnesses and ... two nursing experts', constituted the nurse's negligent conduct and established the hospital's liability.[95]

This case had provided proof of how simple hospital liability can be formulated and established by the negligence of a servant who had acted negligently within the scope of her employment, which negligent behaviour caused the death (injury) of a patient.

In *Ferguson v. Hamilton Civic Hospitals et al*,[96] vicarious hospital liability could not be established. Krever J delivered an in-depth discussion of the *res ipsa loquitur* rule. Thereafter he found that neither of the doctors who were residents in radiology and surgery, had been negligent.[97] Consequently the question for vicarious liability of the hospitals could not arise for decision. Since the submission of counsel with respect to the defendant

---

[93]   *Kolesar* 163.

[94]   *Kolesar* 166–168.

[95]   *Kolesar* 168.

[96]   (1983) 144 DLR (3d) 214.

[97]   *Ferguson* 253.

hospitals' liability was limited to the basis of vicarious liability,[98] hospital liability could not be established. However, had the issue arisen for determination, he stated that he would have found that the two residents 'were indeed employees of the defendant hospitals whose boards of governors had the right to engage and discharge residents[99] (and direct the manner in which residents were to provide services to patients[100])'. This finding would have been made despite the fact that the residents were paid by the McMaster University, to which the hospital was affiliated.[101]

It should be considered whether hospital liability might have ensued if the basis of the action had been direct hospital liability or the non-delegable duty, or breach of contract. In case of direct hospital liability, the negligence of the hospital itself is at stake and an improper system or organizational failure could render the hospital liable without pinpointing negligence on any individual. The outcome of this case is particularly sad if one considers that the plaintiff suffered from quadriplegia after having had surgery, for almost ten years before the trial, and thereafter received no compensation.[102]

**Conclusion on doctors**

In conclusion, Canadian courts have preferred to determine the obligations and ultimately the possible liability of hospitals by the careful consideration of the circumstances'[103] or facts of each case. Certain factors have been found to be common to Canadian, and some Australian and English law cases which can be identified in the founding of hospital liability for a doctor's negligence. Concerning the patient, the latter is in lack of control.[104] The patient will usually not engage or choose the doctor. The hospital will usually provide the doctor or the public expectation might be that such a doctor or service will be provided by the hospital. According to Canadian law the doctor could be an integral part of the organization rather than being an accessory to it. Remuneration received from the hospital is often regarded as an indicative factor,[105] which could lead to vicarious hospital liability.

---

[98] *Ferguson* 253.

[99] *Ferguson* 253.

[100] *Ferguson* 253. This part is selected by the author and is not recommended, since it invokes or implies some form of control by the hospital, which is undesirable.

[101] *Ferguson* 253–254. See also Osode 1993 *AALR* 298.

[102] See also *Ferguson* 258–259.

[103] Picard *et al. Liability* 385.

[104] *Op. cit.* 386–387. Rozovsky *Law* 18–19.

[105] *Ibid.*

## (3) Nurses

Canadian courts have held hospitals vicariously liable for the negligent actions of nurses committed within the scope of the nurse's employment.[106] This was not always the case.[107] The modern Canadian hospital has many employee nurses, although the nurse is a professional with skills, knowledge and judgment[108] of her own. The nurse forms an indispensable part of a health care team. Whenever she does not comply with the standard of the reasonable nurse or does not comply with the duty to follow doctor's orders or other duties, she will be negligent and vicarious liability could follow for the hospital.[109]

The underlying principle upon which hospital liability is established here, entails that it is an implied term of the contract between the hospital and the patient that the hospital not only undertakes to employ competent nurses, but also to nurse or treat the patient.[110] This principle can also found an alternative legal ground, namely the direct liability upon which hospital liability is founded.[111]

The general principle is upheld that a nurse should competently carry out the doctor's orders and that the doctor is entitled to rely on her for doing so.[112] Concern for the hospital's liability is however prevalent where the nurse believes that the doctor's orders are inappropriate or wrong.[113] A balance of interests indicate that the doctor controls medical treatment, but that the nurse is in close contact with the patient and has exceptional skills and experience.[114] A professional can however be found to act negligently on doctor's orders only if the order should have been recognized as being

---

[106] *Kolesar* v. *Jeffries* (1974) 59 DLR (3d) 367 at 376; affirmed 2 CCLT 170 (SCC). *Petite* v. *MacLeod supra. Sisters of St Joseph of the Diocese of London* v. *Fleming supra. Hôpital Générale* v. *Perron* [1979] 3 ACWS 410 (Que Ca). Rozovsky *Law* 22–23. Picard *et al. Liability* 392 and footnote 195.

[107] Picard *et al. Liability* 392: This is evident from cases decided in the first half of the century.

[108] Picard *et al. Liability* 393. *Foote* v. *Royal Columbian Hospital* July 5 1982, No 811062 (BCSC); affirmed (1983), 19 ACWS (2d) 304 (CA). See also Rozovsky *Law* 22.

[109] Rozovsky *Law* 22. Picard *et al. Liability* 393.

[110] Rozovsky *Law* 22. Picard *et al. Liability* 392.

[111] *Ibid.* See *supra.*

[112] Rozovsky *Law* 23. Picard *et al. Liability* 393.

[113] Picard *et al. Liability* 393.

[114] *Ibid.*

'manifestly wrong' by a reasonable professional.[115] No Canadian cases exist on this point.[116] It is however advocated that a mechanism should be devised by which concern for doubtful doctor's orders could be solved, in order to prevent vicarious hospital liability for nurses following negligent orders.[117]

A health care provider or hospital will not be vicariously liable for the negligence of a **private or special nurse** employed and paid by the patient.[118] When the nurse is engaged by the patient, she is not an employee of the hospital acting within the scope of her employment.[119] Hospital liability for the negligent private nurse is however possible (i) when the hospital selects nurses from and maintains lists of them or recommends a nurse while the hospital knows or ought to have known that the nurse was not qualified or competent or (ii) when the hospital knew or ought to have known of negligent acts of the nurse towards patient(s) but did not prevent it.[120] Negligence could be constructed in terms of a breach of duty owed to the patient by the hospital, rendering the hospital liable.[121]

Concerning interns and medical, nursing and technical **students**, hospital liability can ensue for their negligent behaviour causing injury to patients.[122] First, the hospital chooses, pays, supervises and controls the student employee. A typical employer-employee relationship exists for which an employer liability follows.[123] Second, (direct)[124] hospital liability can also ensue for breach of the hospital's responsibility (duty) to provide qualified and competent staff or for failing to train, instruct or supervise them.[125] In *Farrel* v. *Regina* [126] and *Harkies* v. *Lord Dufferin Hospital* [127] the hospitals

---

[115] *Ibid:* This was the principle formulated in a House of Lords decision in *Junor* v. *McNicol*, *The Times* March 25, 1959 (HL). Rozovsky *Law* 23.

[116] Picard *et al. Liability* 393.

[117] *Op. cit.* 394.

[118] Rozovsky *Law* 24. *Tiesmaki* v. *Wilson* [1974] 4 WWR 19; affirmed [1975] 6 WWR 639 (Alta CA). Picard *et al. Liability* 394.

[119] Rozovsky *Law* 24.

[120] *Ibid.* Picard *et al. Liability* 394.

[121] *Ibid.*

[122] Rozovsky *Law* 25. Picard *et al. Liability* 394.

[123] Rozovsky *Law* 25.

[124] My interpretation.

[125] Rozovsky *Law* 25. Picard *et al. Liability* 394.

[126] [1949] 1 WWR 429 (Sask KB). See also Picard *et al. Liability* 394.

[127] [1931] 2 DLR 440 (Ont HC). See also Picard *et al. Liability* 394.

were held vicariously liable for the negligence of nurses who injured infants in their care.

Incidents which involve the negligence of nurses for which a hospital will be held liable, are rife. Cases involve patients burning from hot water bottles, steam inhalators and X-ray machines.[128] Negligent behaviour of nurses in the recovery room also led to hospital liability.[129] Administration of wrong drug(s)[130] or the administration of an injection in the wrong location,[131] has caused liability. The failure to observe patients who injure themselves or to report signs of circulatory impairment[132] have been reported not to be generally successful. In *Joseph Brant Memorial Hospital* v. *Koziol*,[133] gross negligence of the nurses which followed back surgery, resulted in the patient's death and the hospital was held vicariously liable.

In *Sisters of St Joseph of Diocese of Sault Ste Marie* v. *Villeneuve*[134] the Supreme Court of Canada clearly indicated that vicarious hospital liability could have been established for the conduct of two nurses. In the light of the fact that no such relevant or satisfactory evidence was presented — concerning the alleged negligence of the nurses regarding their conduct in

---

[128]   Osode 1993 *AALR 298.* Picard *et al. Liability* 395 and footnote 220. *Eek* v. *Bd of High River Mun Hospital* [1926] 1 WWR 36 (Alta SC). *Davis* v. *Colchester* [1933] 4 DLR 68 (NSSC). *Craig* v. *Soeurs de Charité de la Providence* [1940] 2 WWR 80; affirmed [1940] 3 WWR 336 (Sask CA). *Sinclair* v. *Victoria Hospital* [1943] 1 WWR 30 (Man CA). *Shaw* v. *Swift Current Union Hospital Bd* [1950] 1 WWR 736 (Sask CA). *Sisters of St Joseph of the Diocese of London* v. *Fleming supra. Nyberg* v. *Provost supra. Abel* v. *Cooke supra. Lavere* v. *Smith's Falls Public Hospital supra.*

[129]   Vicarious hospital liability was imposed due to the negligent behaviour of nurses who failed to take care of patients who either were totally disabled or who died as a result of such neglect. Picard *et al. Liability* 395 and footnote 221. *Laidlow* v. *Lions Gate Hospital* (1969) 70 WWR 727 (BCSC). *Krujelis* v. *Esdale* [1972] 2 WWR 495 (BCSC). See also *Bernier* v. *Sisters of Service* [1948] 1 WWR 113 (Alta SC).

[130]   Picard *et al. Liability* 395 and footnote 223. *Barker* v. *Lockhart* [1940] 3 DLR 427 (NBCA). *Bugden* v. *Harbour View Hospital* [1947] 2 DLR 338 (NSSC). *Walker* v. *Sydney City Hospital* (1983) 19 ACWS (2d) 57 (NSSC). *Misericordia Hospital* v. *Bustillo* [1983] Alta D 2632–01 (Alta CA).

[131]   Picard *et al. Liability* 395 and footnote 224. *Laughlin* v. *Royal Columbian Hospital* [1971] DRS 694 (BCCA). *Huber* v. *Burnaby General Hospital* [1973] DRS 653 (BSCS). *Cavan* v. *Wilcox* (1974) 2 NR 618, 50 DLR (3d) 687; reversing 44 DLR (3d) 42 SCC. *Fiege* v. *Cornwall General Hospital* (1980) 4 L Med Q 124 (Ont SC).

[132]   Picard *et al. Liability* 395 and footnote 226. *Vail* v. *MacDonald* (1976) 66 DLR (3d) 530 (SCC).

[133]   (1977) 2 CCLT 170 (SCC). Picard *et al. Liability* 395–396.

[134]   (1975) 1 SCR 285. See also *Sisters of St Joseph of Diocese of London in Ontario* v. *Fleming* (1938) SCR 172. See also Osode 1993 *AALR* 298–299. Sharpe *Canada* 111: The court had also evolved away from the *Hillyer* doctrine in Canada, by this judgment.

the operating room — such liability became impossible. In *Fiege* v. *Cornwall General Hospital et al.* [135] the defendant-nurse was an employee of the defendant-hospital. The nurse had, whilst in employment, improperly injected the plaintiff. The court found that the instructions which she had been given were not improper, but that her manner of injecting the patient was contrary to accepted medical practice. The hospital was held vicariously liable for her acts, since she had acted negligently in her capacity as an employee of the hospital. In *Meyer* v. *Gordon* [136] the hospital was held 75 per cent liable as a result of negligent nursing, which caused brain damage to a baby whose birth was unattended.

As regards the theory or rule of the borrowed servant — in terms of which the doctor is held responsible for the negligence of the nurse — no cases have been reported in Canadian law where the hospital was relieved of liability on such a basis.[137]

The Canadian law with respect to nurses indicates that the relationship between the hospital and nurse is paramount. Nurses are usually selected, employed and paid by hospitals as members of the permanent staff. The Canadian courts establish vicarious hospital liability with ease, for the negligent behaviour of staff which results in death or injury to patients.[138]

## (4) Other employees

The health care provider, health institution or hospital will be vicariously liable for all its employees who commit wrongs within the scope of their employment.[139] Employee staff members may include cleaners, kitchen staff,[140] pharmacists,[141] physiotherapists,[142] X-ray[143] and laboratory techni-

---

[135] (1980) 30 OR (2d) 691 (HC). See also Sharpe *Canada* 111.

[136] (1981) 17 CCLT 1 (BCSC). Two nurses testified that the patient was not theirs while the third nurse — whose patient she might have been — went on lunch.

[137] Rozovsky *Law* 23. Picard *et al. Liability* 392. Sharpe *Canada* 115.

[138] Osode 1993 *AALR* 298.

[139] Rozovsky *Law* 26. Picard *et al. Liability* 396.

[140] Rozovsky *Law* 26.

[141] Picard *et al. Liability* 396. *Misericordia Hospital* v. *Bustillo supra.*

[142] Picard *et al. Liability* 396. *McKay* v. *Royal Inland Hospital* (1964) 48 DLR (2d) 665 (BCSC).

[143] Picard *et al. Liability* 396. *Murphy* v. *General Hospital* (1980) 25 Nfld & PEIR 355 (Nfld TD). *Pepin* v. *Hôpital du Haut Richelieu* (1983) 24 CCLT 259 (Que CA). *Abel* v. *Cooke supra.*

cians,[144] audiologists,[145] ward aides,[146] orderlies[147] and many more.[148]

This expanded hospital liability will also possibly be inclusive of a liability for paramedical assistants such as nursing assistants as well as volunteers and auxiliaries.[149]

(5)    Conclusion on employees

Canadian jurisprudence has kept pace with the English law by establishing vicarious liability for full-time employees of the hospital, who exercise professional skills, by discarding the infamous control test, relegating it to the background and by rejecting the distinction adopted in the *Hillyer* case.[150]

*7.3.1.1.1.1 Relevant tests*

(a)    The control test

(b)    The organization test

(a)  The control test

Control was at first deemed to be the most obvious justification for the master's accountability for the wrongs committed by the employee. But the control test has experienced universal criticism primarily due to its inefficiency with regard to professional people.[151] The employer of professional people not only has no competency to control such professionals, but will experience severe resistance when trying to do so.[152] The inappropriateness of the control test has specifically been displayed in its application to hospital liability.[153]

(b)  The organization test

The organization test basically enquires whether the perpetrator or medical officer involved, functioned as an integral part of the defendant organiza-

---

[144]  Picard *et al. Liability* 397. *Neufville* v. *Sobers* (1983) 18 ACWS (2d) 407 (Ont HC).

[145]  Picard *et al. Liability* 397. *Bartlett* v. *Children's Hospital Corp.* (1983) 40 Nfld & PEIR 88 (Nfld TD), revised (1985), 55 Nfld & PEIR 350 (Nfld CA).

[146]  Picard *et al. Liability* 397. *Wyndham* v. *Toronto General Hospital* [1938] OWN 55 (Ont HC).

[147]  Rozovsky *Law* 26. *Brennan* v. *Director of Mental Health* unreported Feb 18, 1977 No 83414 (Alta SC).

[148]  Rozovsky *Law* 26.

[149]  Rozovsky *Law* 26–29. Picard *et al. Liability* 397.

[150]  Osode 1993 *AALR* 299.

[151]  See also Picard 1981 *MGLJ* 1017 and Osode 1993 *AALR* 301–303.

[152]  Picard 1981 *MGLJ* 1017.

[153]  Especially in the *Cassidy* case where it was rejected without condition. Picard 1981 *MGLJ* 1017. See 4.3.1.

tion.[154] The organization test has systematically gained recognition and ground as a test or criteria to determine the employer-employee relationship. The test had its origin in English common law, from which both Australian and Canadian law have derived their 'entitlement' to this criteria. Authors in the Canadian[155] and Australian[156] law refer to the common law sources. The organization test has also been preferred to the control test in both English[157] and Canadian law. Most Canadian authors commend the functionality of the organization test.[158] The hospital is also no longer regarded only as an institutional facility and equipment provider for the use of surgeons, but is regarded and held responsible as an institutional provider of treatment and care to patients. This perspective, coupled with the effectiveness of the organization test, has resulted in an increased tendency to find hospitals vicariously liable.[159]

Canadian courts have also implemented the organization test. The Supreme Court of Canada accepted and applied the test in *Co-operative Insurance Association* v. *Kearney*.[160] The Supreme Court of Ontario also applied the test in *Kennedy* v. *CNA Assurance*,[161] in which case Linden J found a dentist to be the employee of another. Picard has emphasized that the evidence of each case must be examined and generalization of relationships concerning hospitals should be avoided, of which the latter case was a good

---

[154] Picard 1981 *MGLJ* 1017. Osode 1993 *AALR* 301. Picard *et al. Liability* 382. Chapman *Medicine* 64. See also Rozovsky *Law* 17.

[155] *Ibid.*

[156] See the discussion on the organization test in Chapter 6 *supra.*

[157] See the discussion on the development of the organization test in the English common law in Chapter 6. See also Bettle 1987 *NLJ* 573.

[158] Picard 1981 *MGLJ* 1017. Picard *et al. Liability* 382. Osode 1993 *AALR* 301. Chapman *Medicine* 532 states: 'The real source of the distinction between vicarious hospital liability and independent contractor liability, at least in the English cases, now seems to turn on whether the physician, rather than being provided by the hospital as an integral part of its overall organization of health care delivery, was engaged directly by the patient.' See also the comment of professor Magnet in Picard 1981 *MGLJ* 1018 and that of Fanjoy in Osode 1993 *AALR* 302 where Fanjoy is quoted as saying that in hospital context 'the test would be whether the servant is subordinate to the managerial powers of the employer's organization'. Such a test was mandated by changes in the industrial organization of the modern hospital.

[159] Osode 1993 *AALR* 301 footnote 32. Bettle 1987 *NLJ* 573.

[160] (1965) SCR 106. The employee was an insurance agent. See also Picard 1981 *MGLJ* 1018.

[161] (1978) 20 OR (2d) 674 (HC). See also Picard 1981 *MGLJ* 1018.

example.[162] Canadian academics considered the two cases as 'good law'.[163] Osode further submitted that if Canadian courts were to apply the organization test willingly and objectively to the modern hospital (which he suggested should be done), 'the consistent result will be hospital vicarious liability for the negligence of private, privilege-holding physicians in situations such as that in *Yepremian's* case. This would go a long way towards improving the present state of the doctrine of vicarious liability as a potent legal weapon in the armoury of the Canadian patient who has suffered injury as a result of medical malpractice occurring within the precincts of the hospital.'[164]

The second (7.3.1.1.2) and third (7.3.1.1.3) requirements of vicarious liability deserve no independent discussion in Canadian law.

### 7.3.1.2 Other instances of vicarious liability

#### 7.3.1.2.1 The private practitioner

A doctor-employer could be vicariously liable if his employee — a nurse or office staff member — behaves negligently towards a patient.[165]

#### 7.3.1.2.2 Partnerships

All the partners in a partnership will be jointly and severally liable for the negligent actions of each other, done in the course of the partnership as well as for the negligent actions of their servants.[166] The liability is unlimited. Once judgment is received, it can be enforced against partnership assets even — if necessary — to the point of exhaustion. One can then proceed against the personal assets of any partner or partners.[167] In the case of *Dowey* v. *Rothwell*,[168] Dr M who was a member of the defendant partnership, had treated Mrs Dowey for grand mal epileptic seizures, for years. On a particular day, anticipating such a seizure, she went to the clinic. After describing the symptoms, the attending nurse left her alone on the examining table for one minute. During this time, she fell off the table while suffering a seizure, and sustained a severely comminuted fracture of the arm. The court

---

[162]  Picard 1981 *MGLJ* 1018.

[163]  *Ibid.*

[164]  Osode 1993 *AALR* 302.

[165]  Sneiderman *et al. Canadian* 111.

[166]  *Ibid.*

[167]  *Ibid.*

[168]  [1974] 5 WWR 311, 49 DLR (3d) 82 (Alta TD).

held the partnership as a whole vicariously liable for the negligence of the nurse, in leaving the patient unattended under those circumstances. The nurse was not sued.

### 7.3.1.3 Conclusion on vicarious liability in Canadian law

As will be conclusively argued in Chapter 10, the problematic distinction between independent contractors and employees which inhibits vicarious hospital liability and needlessly limits a justified mode of compensation for ill-fated patients, is with all respect actually an unnecessary prerequisite.

Support for this argument has also been found in the writings of professor Chapman, a Canadian author. He argues that in Canadian law, no formal or systematic outlay of the grounds for vicarious hospital liability has been formulated. It has not expressly been dictated when and why a hospital will be vicariously liable for the negligent behaviour of personnel or medical professionals. It is, however, indicated that on the ratio of Denning LJ's 'power of dismissal' both independent contractors and employees in a master-servant relationship, could introduce hospital liability. Chapman then suggests that 'the analysis to follow argues for an expansion of vicarious hospital liability, but in a way that does not depend on the problematic distinction between independent contractors and employees'.[169]

### 7.3.2 The Doctrine of Ostensible or Apparent Agency

American courts have successfully implemented the doctrine of ostensible or apparent agency in order to hold hospitals (vicariously[170]) liable for the malpractice of independent contractors, especially in cases which involve emergency department medical professionals or physicians, radiologists, pathologists and anaesthesiologists.[171] Hospital liability has been expanded by this doctrine by American courts in an enviable manner.[172] Canadian authors have found justification for the implementation of this doctrine, but Canadian courts have not been as well-disposed towards such imposition.[173]

---

[169] Chapman *Medicine* 65.

[170] Osode defines this hospital liability as a form of vicarious liability. Osode 1993 *AALR* 303–307.

[171] Louisell and Williams *Medical Malpractice* § 15.04 15–22. Anesthesia is the US variant of anaesthesia.

[172] Osode 1993 *AALR* 303–304.

[173] *Op. cit.* 303.

The doctrine will be discussed in detail in Chapter 8, but the following information will suffice for this discussion. In order to determine whether an ostensible agency exists, courts will consider the following factors:[174]

(1)   Whether the patient in emergency had a pre-existing relationship with the treating physician;

(2)   Whether the physician was an independent contractor;

(3)   Whether the patient at the time of his admission to the hospital looked primarily to the hospital for treatment; and

(4)   Whether the patient reasonably relied on the hospital's representation that the treating physician was acting on behalf of the hospital.

Osode also presents four indicia to indicate when an ostensible agency will be acknowledged in American law:[175]

(i)    Where the patient did not select the physician (the hospital supplied the physician);

(ii)   Where the patient at the time of admission looked up to the hospital for cure;

(iii)  Where there was nothing to indicate to him/her the precise legal status of those who attended to him/her *vis-à-vis* the hospital;

(iv)   It is immaterial whether the physician is an employee or an independent contractor.

---

[174] *Op. cit.* 304.

[175] *Op. cit.* 304–305. *Adamski* v. *Takoma General Hospital* 20 Wash App 98, 579 P 2d 970 (1978). *Seneris* v. *Haas* 45 Cal 2d 811, 291 P 2d 915 (1955). *Arthur* v. *St Peter's Hospital* 169 NJ Super 575, 405 A 2d 443 (1979). Compare Louisell and Williams *Medical Malpractice* § 15.04 15–20 to 15–21. The factors presented by Osode can combinedly be summarized as follows:

(i)    Whether the patient looked primarily to the hospital for treatment upon admission;

(ii)   Whether the hospital represented that the physician was acting on behalf of the hospital;

(iii)  Whether the patient reasonably relied on such representation;

(iv)   Whether the physician was indeed an independent contractor;

(v)    Whether the patient admitted to an emergency centre had a pre-existing relationship with the treating physician;

(vi)   Whether anything/nothing indicated the precise legal status of those who attended the patient concerning the hospital;

(vii)  Whether the physician was an employee or an independent contractor is immaterial;

(viii) Whether the patient himself selected the physician or whether the hospital provided the physician.

Canadian courts have not yet accepted or implemented the doctrine of ostensible agency.[176] In the case of *Yepremian* v. *Scarborough General Hospital*,[177] the facts presented a young man who was hyperventilating and semi-comatose when admitted to the emergency department and later to the intensive care unit. The patient was therefore in no condition to select a physician or to inquire about the legal status of the medical professionals who attended him. Although the doctrine was not proposed or argued by counsel, the circumstances could quite successfully have been related to the most important indicia mentioned above,[178] which could have led to the ostensible agency doctrine being invoked.

In *Hopital Notre-Dame de L'Esperance* v. *Laurent*,[179] the facts were the following: The patient fell and twisted her hip. At the emergency room of the hospital, the surgeon who attended her took no X-rays, and only diagnosed a simple contusion. The surgeon prescribed medicine which prescription was later renewed. Dame Laurent was not admitted to the hospital. The patient eventually, after 3 months of pain, consulted a second doctor who diagnosed the fracture from which she had been suffering since the accident. As a result, the surgical treatment was long and complicated and the resulting permanent disability was increased. The surgeon was a member of the hospital medical staff by which he obtained the privilege to practise there. He was not employed by the hospital. His attendance in the emergency department was voluntary, and was not a condition to his association with the hospital.

The Supreme Court of Canada delivered judgment by word of Pigeon J. The judge found that no master and servant relationship existed between Dr Théoret and the hospital with respect to the professional services rendered by him in the emergency room.[180] He was not considered an employee of the hospital and therefore the hospital was exonerated from all liability.[181] The physician had acted on his own account and Dame Laurent received medical treatment under a contract with Dr Théoret, and not under a contract with the hospital.[182] The appeal of the appellant was allowed.

---

[176] Osode 1993 *AALR* 305–306.

[177] (1980) 110 DLR (3d) 513 (Ont CA).

[178] Osode 1993 *AALR* 305; i.e. the indicia discussed at 304–305.

[179] 3 CCLT 109; [1974] CA 543; reversed in [1978] 1 SCR 605.

[180] *Hopital Notre-Dame* 611.

[181] *Hopital Notre-Dame* 606, 609, 612.

[182] *Hopital Notre-Dame* 613.

Professor Magnet has criticized the judgment of the Supreme Court in no subtle way. He submitted that the relationship of the doctor with the hospital, irrespective of him being an employee or an independent contractor, is absolutely irrelevant in limiting the hospital's liability. The hospital had undertaken to supply medical services by the doctor who is then its agent, and therefore the hospital should in no way escape liability. The patient is in need and seeks help from the hospital.[183]

It would be advisable to expand Canadian hospital liability by introducing the doctrine of ostensible agency, and Canadian courts can only benefit from importing this tested legal doctrine from the United States.[184]

### 7.3.3  Direct (or) Corporate Hospital Liability[185]

The hospital as an institutional health care provider, is in law regarded as a person (although an artificial one) with a separate legal personality, which has responsibilities to a patient both directly as a corporate legal entity and indirectly through the acts of its personnel.[186] Hospital and other health corporations are subjected to two sets of general law, which are the law governing institutional providers of health services and the law that governs corporations in the jurisdiction in which they operate. Principles of company law sometimes also applies.[187]

A patient usually takes action against a hospital as a result of various other wrongful acts committed against him/her. The hospital can be sued for negligence, breach of contract, assault and battery, false imprisonment and defamation or loss of property.[188] The hospital can raise any of the following defences: approved practice, error of judgment, contributory negligence or consent.[189]

However, where the focus is on the conduct of the institutional health care provider or hospital itself, corporate negligence[190] and ultimately

---

[183]  Professor Magnet at 141 was quoted extensively by Osode 1993 *AALR* 306.

[184]  See also Osode 1993 *AALR* 306–307.

[185]  The discussion under 4.3.2 serves as general introduction to this section.

[186]  Rozovsky *Law* 8, 65. Picard *et al. Liability* 363. This describes the legal position of the hospital in terms of direct or corporate hospital liability. Sharpe *Canada* 123.

[187]  Rozovsky *Law* 7.

[188]  Rozovsky *Law* 16. Picard *et al. Liability* 364.

[189]  Picard *et al. Liability* 364.

[190]  This is also referred to as direct, institutional or independent negligence, or corporate negligence.

corporate, institutional or direct hospital liability is applicable. The principles of negligence law are then applied to the hospitals, as they are to persons or institutions.[191] The negligent conduct of the hospital must be established. In order to succeed with a suit against a hospital, the plaintiff must prove,[192] on a balance of probabilities, first, that the hospital owed him/her a duty of care; second, that this duty was breached; third, that the plaintiff thereby suffered injury and/or loss; fourth, that the hospital's breach of duty was the cause-in-fact as well as the proximate cause of his/her injury.

The most critical constituent element of the negligence action against hospitals, is considered to be the duty of care. Hospital liability and the extent thereof, is formulated with dependence on the extensive construction of the duty.[193] The hospital has, however, all the available defences such as the expiry of any statutory limitation periods, or the contributory negligence of the plaintiff.[194] Together with the evolution of the modern hospital, Canadian courts have not been as liberal in extending hospital liability by means of the concept of the duty of care as has been the case in the United States and the United Kingdom.[195]

In the process of establishing and demarcating duties, every case must be assessed independently and unique obligations imposed with reference to the unique relationships and facts of every incident. Generalizations or uniform findings are inappropriate.[196] Duties are formulated in consideration of various sources, such as statutes which govern hospitals. In Canada, relevant statutes are derived from the Provincial Hospital Acts, Health Insurance Acts and regulations. Hospital bylaws and the regulations of professional bodies should also be scrutinized. Public expectations are referred to by courts, but it is kept in mind that reasonable expectancies change. Duties are also enforced by undertakings or contracts.[197] New duties are created and enforced by means of value-judgments, interests and relationships. New law

---

[191] Osode 1993 *AALR* 307. Chapman *Medicine* 59. Picard 1981 *MGLJ* 1003. Also refer to Kennedy and Grubb *Medical Law* 397.

[192] *Ibid.* Rozovsky *Law* 59.

[193] *Ibid.*

[194] Chapman *Medicine* 527. See also Picard 1981 *MGLJ* 1004.

[195] Osode 1993 *AALR* 307–308. Southwick and Slee *Law of Hospital* 541–542, 554–582. See Chapter 5 on the English law. Sharpe *Canada* 124.

[196] Picard 1981 *MGLJ* 1004–1006.

[197] *Ibid.* Osode 1993 *AALR* 308–309.

is made when institutions evolve, relationships change and new evidence comes to light.[198]

### 7.3.3.1 The hospital's direct duties

Direct duties are owed by hospitals to patients.[199] Direct duties are founded fundamentally on the principle that the hospital must at all times provide an effective system or structure, good organization and proper treatment. The hospital itself has a direct duty to fulfil and upon non-compliance is itself at fault or to blame. The hospital itself, must maintain good systems and order, whereas under the non-delegable duty the hospital must ensure that other medical professionals do their work properly. The direct duty therefore focuses on formal systems and structures whereas the non-delegable duty concentrates on the malpractice of medical professionals, where the latter is at fault. Corporate liability is about organizational failure, while the non-delegable duty entails a stricter duty to ensure that reasonable care was taken. Corporate direct liability involves the duty to provide reasonable health care whereas the non-delegable duty involves the duty to ensure that reasonable care is/was provided. Corporate direct liability therefore focuses on the provision of formal structures or systems, and organizational frameworks.

The most basic direct duties owed by hospitals to patients which had been supported by precedents, had already been stated in 4.3.2.[200] Those duties and other duties which evolved from them will now be discussed shortly, with special application to Canadian law.

### 7.3.3.2 Categories

**Category 1: Duty to select competent and qualified employees/staff[201]**
Historically this was the first duty[202] a hospital was held to owe a patient. The scope of this direct, personal or corporate duty was at first limited to the

---

[198]  Picard 1981 *MGLJ* 1006.

[199]  See the discussion under 4.3.2, 8.3.3, 8.3.4 and 10.

[200]  Those direct duties were — according to Picard 1981 *MGLJ* 1007–1008 and Picard *et al. Liability* 367–380: The duty to: (1) select competent and qualified employees (2) to instruct and supervise them (3) to provide proper facilities and equipment (4) to establish systems and procedures necessary to the safe operation of the hospital.

[201]  Picard 1981 *MGLJ* 1007; Picard *et al. Liability* 367. Osode 1993 *AALR* 309–312. Rozovsky *Law* 65–66. Sharpe *Canada* 119, 123–124.

[202]  This was stated by Kennedy LJ in the *Hillyer* case. The English Court of Appeal confirmed the principle beyond doubt in the famous trilogy of cases. Osode 1993 *AALR* 309.

hospital's ascertainment that its professionals were qualified and competent.[203] The scope of the direct duty was expanded to include — the duty to instruct and supervise personnel, then — the duty to provide the systems and organization of the hospital to co-ordinate the activities for the patient to receive reasonable care, then — the duty to provide and maintain proper facilities and equipment. Other duties developed later which required procedures to protect patients from themselves and others, and procedures to protect all from infection.[204] This duty undeniably forms part of Canadian law.[205] In Canada, boards of governors are vested with the power to appoint doctors by virtue of s 33 of the Public Hospitals Act.[206] But in awe of the fact that hospital liability is eminent upon the appointment of an incompetent doctor, Boards rely heavily on the recommendations of the Medical Advisory Committee.[207] Courts have also greatly assisted hospital governing boards in preserving their medical staff appointing powers, by holding that the grant of hospital privileges is a privilege and not a right inherent in medical practitioners.[208] In discharging this duty, the hospital should adhere to the standard of the 'reasonable hospital' in compliance with all applicable statutory provisions, regulations and hospital bylaws.[209] Where a hospital had no actual knowledge of a physician's incompetence — according to evidence — but sufficient facts were available in order to make an inquiry, the hospital can be charged with 'constructive knowledge' on the ground that a 'reasonable hospital' with knowledge of the facts would have conducted further investigations which would have led to the discovery of the physician's incompetence'.[210]

---

Rozovsky *Law* 65. Picard 1981 *MGLJ* 1007. Picard *et al. Liability* 367. Sharpe *Canada* 123.

[203] Picard 1981 *MGLJ* 1007. Picard *et al. Liability* 367. Osode 1993 *AALR* 309. This duty was invented in order to ensure that patients receive quality care, diagnosis and treatment, according to Osode.

[204] Picard 1981 *MGLJ* 1007.

[205] *Yepremian* v. *Scarborough General Hospital* (1980) 110 DLR (3d) 513. Picard 1981 *MGLJ* 1007–1008. Osode 1993 *AALR* 309.

[206] C410 RSO (1980). See *supra*.

[207] Osode 1993 *AALR* 309–310.

[208] *Op. cit.* 310. *Re MacDonald and North York General Hospital* (1976) 59 DLR (3d) 647. *Re Streedhar and Outlook Union Hospital Board* (1944) 4 DLR 192.

[209] Osode 1993 *AALR* 310.

[210] Osode 1993 *AALR* 310. *Johnson* v. *Misericordia Community Hospital* (1981) 99 Wis 2d 708, 301 NW 2d 156.

**Category 2: Duty to provide instruction and supervision**
The hospital is under a duty to instruct and supervise its personnel. This responsibility necessitates job descriptions, training programs, testing and screening procedures, evaluations and systems for supervision.[211] Related to this duty is the non-delegable duty to ensure that each person is working within his competence, which flows from this duty,[212] in Canadian law.

The provision of the Ontario Public Hospitals Act, which permits censorship of attending physicians by either the chief of medical staff or the latter together with the departmental head, concerning particular patients' treatment, supports this duty.[213]

In *Murphy* v. *St Catherine's General Hospital* [214] the hospital was held liable for permitting an intern to negligently administer an intravenous injection. The hospital had not complied with the duty to provide instruction, direction and supervision to its staff regarding use of such a unit, and was therefore negligent. Similarly, in *Bartlett* v. *Children's Hospital Corp.*[215] the hospital was held liable for failure to provide a properly organized and supervised training programme.

**Category 3: Duties on the provision of adequate systems and organizational procedures in the provision of health care**[216]

(i)      *Duties concerning emergency centres*
In American cases, patients rely on the doctrine of ostensible agency or apparent agency in cases involving emergency departments with possible resultant (vicarious) hospital liability.[217] Canadian courts have not accommodated the doctrine yet.

In Canadian law, no absolute duty to provide emergency care has been formulated. Whether or not the duty exists to provide emergency care, will depend on the following factors:[218]

---

[211]  Picard *et al. Liability* 369. Osode 1993 *AALR* 314. This responsibility is applicable also to student professionals and employees-in-training.

[212]  Picard *et al. Liability* 369. Osode 1993 *AALR* 314. Rozovsky *Law* 66.

[213]  RSO (1980) ss 31 (1)–(7). See also Osode 1993 *AALR* 314.

[214]  (1964) 41 DLR (2d) 697 (Ont HC). See Picard *et al. Liability* 369.

[215]  (1983) 40 Nfld & PEIR 88 (Nfld TD), revised (1985), 55 Nfld & PEIR 350 (Nfld CA). See Picard *et al. Liability* 369.

[216]  Chapman *Medicine* 59. Rozovsky *Law* 66. Picard *et al. Liability* 369–378. Picard 1981 *MGLJ* 1007. *Yepremian* v. *Scarborough General Hospital* (1980) 110 DLR (3d) 513 at 558 (Ont CA) Blair JA.

[217]  Refer to the discussion on the doctrine of ostensible agency *supra*, and *infra*.

[218]  Picard *et al. Liability* 370–371.

- public expectations that medical care can be obtained at any emergency centre
- government funding of hospitals
- the hospital's undertaking to provide care
- whether the required standard of care has been met. If so, the hospital (and/or doctor) will not be liable
- whether its negligence has caused the patient's injury. If not so, the hospital (and/or doctor) will not be liable.

Once such a duty is constructed, the hospital must adhere to a standard of reasonable care, provide proper systems, competent personnel and adequate facilities and equipment, in the operation of an emergency centre or department.[219] It must also be kept in mind that emergency centres nowadays not only function as emergency facilities, but also serve as consultation centres for less serious conditions.[220]

In a 1973 case,[221] it was held that a patient received harmful treatment in an emergency unit. However, the negligent conduct of the hospital in using incorrect procedures, was held not to constitute a *novus actus interveniens* and the hospital was not held liable. In 1977, an action against a hospital was barred by a limitation period. In this Canadian case,[222] a hospital report indicated that the observation of patients and monitoring of systems were ineffective. However, in *Osburn* v. *Mohindra* (1980), a hospital was found to be directly liable.[223] The direct liability of the hospital was due to the malfunction of a system concerning X-rays. The system was inadequate for not assuring that the X-ray report of a radiologist be sent to the doctor in the emergency department who attended a patient, which resulted in the misdiagnosis of a fracture not being detected for some time.

(ii)  *Duties concerning the recovery room*

The recovery room is a higher risk area than the emergency room.[224] The hospital is thus required to establish proper systems and organizational procedures to monitor and observe patients in a post-anaesthetic state

---

[219]  *Op. cit.* 371.

[220]  *Ibid.*

[221]  *Thompson* v. *Toorenburg* (1973) 50 DLR (3d) 717 (BCCA), affirmed 1973, 50 DLR (3d) 717n (SCC). See Picard *et al. Liability* 372–373.

[222]  *Mumford* v. *Children's Hospital of Winnipeg* [1977] 1 WWR 666 (Man CA). See Picard *et al. Liability* 372.

[223]  *Osburn* v. *Mohindra* (1980) 29 NBR (2d) 340 (QB). See Picard *et al. Liability* 371.

[224]  Picard *et al. Liability* 373–374.

constantly and effectively. Sufficient staff must be provided to control facilities and patients. It could be suggested that hospitals should establish efficient systems to run the recovery room. Lack of compliance with this duty to organize, could lead to direct hospital liability.

In Canadian law, however, two cases where proper recovery room systems were established but negligent nurses failed to comply, by not adequately monitoring patients, rendered the hospitals vicariously liable.[225]

With all respect, it could be recommended that a breakdown of systems or organization which even manifests in the insufficient monitoring of patients, could also be classified as direct hospital liability due to the non-compliance with a direct duty to provide such systems.

### (iii)  *Duties on drugs*

Every hospital has a duty to construct an effective system for the safe and proper handling of drugs.[226] The hospital's liability 'has usually been vicarious rather than direct'[227] in drug related problems, as in the case of the recovery room. It should be considered to review the hospital's system for handling drugs, when injury is caused to patients through human negligence when obtaining or administering drugs.[228] Direct liability could be the proper solution for non-compliance with this duty.

### (iv)  *Duties on infection control*

The hospital has a distinct duty to protect patients, staff and visitors from infection.[229] The hospital is also under a duty not to discharge a patient whom it knows or ought to know, is infectious.[230] Responsibilities, concerning the

---

[225] *Op. cit.* 373–374. *Laidlow* v. *Lions Gate Hospital* (1969) 70 WWR 727 (BCSC). *Krujelis* v. *Esdale* [1972] 2 WWR 495 (BCSC). See also *Meyer* v. *Gordon* (1981) 17 CCLT 1 (BCSC).

[226] Picard *et al. Liability* 374.

[227] *Ibid. Misericordia Hospital* v. *Bustillo* [1983] Alta D 2632–01 (Alta CA).

[228] Picard *et al. Liability* 374.

[229] Rozovsky *Law* 66. Sharpe *Canada* 123. Osode 1993 *AALR* 313. Picard *et al. Liability* 374–375: *McDaniel* v. *Vancouver General Hospital* [1934] 4 DLR 593 (PC). According to Picard ( the *Science Digest* 27 (April 1982)), more deaths have been caused by infection than by any other iatrogenic illness. See also *Peters* v. *University Hospital Bd.* (1983) 1 Admin. LR 221, 147 DLR (3d) 385, 23 Sask. R. 123 [1983] 5 WWR 193 (CA), from which it is clear that hospital liability is expanding.

[230] *Hajgato* v. *London Health Association* (1982) 36 OR (2d) 669 at 682 (Ont HC), affirmed (1983) 44 OR (2d) 264 (CA). Picard *et al. Liability* 375. Osode 1993 *AALR* 313.

control of infection by the implementation of aseptic, quarantine and other necessary procedures, are basic duties which evolve from this duty.[231]

In *Vancouver General Hospital* v. *McDaniel and Another* [232] the plaintiff entered a hospital for infectious diseases, to be treated for diphtheria. She did, however, contract smallpox. The plaintiff claimed negligence in the system of infection control of the hospital. The alleged negligence existed in the juxtaposition of smallpox patients to the plaintiff, and the latter's and other smallpox patients' attendance by the same nurses. Lord Aldness remarked that the case against the appellant was one of direct responsibility and not vicarious liability. The negligence was claimed to exist not in the execution of duties by any employee of the hospital, but in 'the technique adopted by the appellants'.[233] The direct negligence of the hospital was therefore established by an inadequate procedure to safeguard patients from cross-infection.[234] This constituted a primary or direct liability for the hospital.

### (v) Duties on patient surveillance

The modern hospital owes a corporate duty to protect its patients from injury or death whilst on its premises.[235] It also involves the duty to establish sufficient procedures in terms of surveillance and safeguards in this respect. Patients must be protected from injuring themselves and/or others.[236]

### - Patient suicide, window leaping and other harm

Health institutions have a direct duty to take all reasonable steps to prevent suicide or injury, where such risks present themselves and are reasonably foreseeable.[237]

In 1973, the Supreme Court of Canada[238] found a hospital liable, where a psychiatric patient with suicidal tendencies fell to his death from a hospital

---

[231] *Voller* v. *Portsmouth Corporation* (1974) 203 LTJ 264 (KB). See also *Savoie* v. *Bouchard* (1982) 23 CCLT 83; (NBQB), varied (1983), 26 CCLT 173 (CA). No 8/83/CA (NBCA). Picard *et al. Liability* 374–375.

[232] (1934) 152 LT 56.

[233] *Vancouver* 57: 'The complaint is that the technique was adopted by the appellants, not that it failed in its execution. In other words, the case made against the appellant is one, not of vicarious, but of direct responsibility.'

[234] See also Jones *Negligence* 401.

[235] Osode 1993 *AALR* 312. Chapman *Medicine* 59.

[236] Picard *et al. Liability* 375–378.

[237] Rozovsky *Law* 67. Picard *et al. Liability* 375–378.

[238] *Villemure* v. *Turcot* (1973) SCR 716. See Picard *et al. Liability* 376. Osode 1993 AALR 313.

window. He had been transferred from a psychiatric ward to a semi-private room, and had been known to be a 'patient to be watched'. The liability had apparently been both direct and vicarious.[239] The health institution therefore has a duty to establish procedures in preventing suicide or injury, where such risks are foreseeable.[240]

In the first five cases,[241] the hospitals were exonerated on the ground that the patient's self-inflicted injuries were not a foreseeable risk.

In 1978, the Supreme Court dealt with an interesting legal question in *Lawson* v. *Wellesley Memorial Hospital*.[242] The court held that the action against the hospital could not be barred by a statute which purported to exempt the hospital for a tort of a patient. It was found that the section could not protect the hospital against its own direct negligence and the case was to proceed to trial.[243] From the court's reasoning it could be argued that a hospital will be directly liable for breach of an independent duty to protect a patient from injuring another (patient) or himself, by failing to provide sufficient surveillance and safeguards. The hospital could be directly liable for its own direct negligence in failing to provide adequate organization and supervision of patients.

In 1980,[244] the Court of Appeal introduced an 'open door policy' as an appropriate standard of care and a subjective test with regard to the patient. In this case the hospital was found neither vicariously nor directly liable where a patient injured herself trying to escape.

---

[239] According to Picard *et al. Liability* 376. The judgment of the dissenting member of the Court of Appeal, was adopted by the majority of the Supreme Court who wrote no judgment.

[240] Picard *et al. Liability* 375.

[241] (i) *Brandeis* v. *Weldon* (1916) 27 DLR 235 (BCCA);

(ii) *Flynn* v. *Hamilton* [1950] OWN 224 (CA);

(iii)*Stadel* v. *Albertson* [1954] 2 DLR 328 (Sask CA);

(iv)*University Hospital Bd* v. *Lepine* [1966] SCR 561;

(v) *Child* v. *Vancouver General Hospital* [1970] SCR 477.

Cases (iv) and (v) were presented in the Supreme Court. In case (v) direct hospital liability was denied, because it was held that the hospital had established procedures and treatment for the patient's care which met the expected standard of care.

[242] (1978) 1 SCR 893; see also Osode 1993 *AALR* 312–313 and Picard *et al. Liability* 378.

[243] Picard *et al. Liability* 378 footnote 107: The case was no doubt settled out of court, since it was not reported to have gone to trial.

[244] *Worth* v. *Royal Jubilee Hospital* (1980) 4 L Med Q 59 (BCCA). Picard *et al. Liability* 377. See also *H (M)* v. *Bederman* (1995) 27 CCLT (2d) 152 which dealt with the hospital's duty to protect patients from other patients. See also Picard *et al. Liability* 378.

## Category 4: Duties on equipment, facilities and premises

A hospital has a direct duty — breach of which will render the hospital directly liable — to provide and maintain adequate and proper equipment, facilities and premises which is inclusive of the grounds and buildings.[245] The hospital does not need to have the most modern or best equipment and facilities,[246] but can also not ignore those in common use.[247] In *Vuchar* v. *Trustees of Toronto General Hospital*,[248] a hospital was held directly liable for failing to provide suitable medical facilities or equipment. In *Dagenais* v. *Children's Hospital of Eastern Ontario*,[249] the hospital was held liable for injuries a person sustained on the premises of the hospital, after falling as a result of a gap in the asphalt at the edge of a ramp. The corporate responsibility of hospitals includes the liability for the maintenance and safety of its premises.[250]

## Category 5: Statutory duties and breach thereof

As in English law,[251] breach of statutory duty could lead to hospital liability in Canadian law. According to Picard, breach of statutory duty does not automatically / necessarily induce a civil remedy for damages nor constitute negligence, except where expressly so conferred or indicated. The court could, where appropriate, consider the statutory standard 'as an indication of what was reasonable practice in the circumstances'.[252]

### 7.3.3.3 Conclusion on direct or corporate hospital liability

The direct or corporate liability of a hospital entails that the hospital, as an independent corporate entity, can accrue a corporate responsibility in law for its own corporate negligence, as a result of which the corporate entity will

---

[245] *Vuchar* v. *Trustees of Toronto General Hospital* [1937] 1 DLR 298 (Ont CA). See also Jones *Negligence* 401 and footnote 46. Chapman *Medicine* 59 and footnote 11. Osode 1993 *AALR* 314. Picard *et al. Liability* 379–380. Sharpe *Canada* 123.

[246] *Thomas* v. *Port Colbourne Hospital* (1982) 12 ACWS (2d) 535 (Ont HC). Picard *et al. Liability* 379 and footnote 112. Osode 1993 *AALR* 314. Hospitals have the responsibility to monitor, check and repair such equipment in use in the hospital. See Picard *et al. Liability* 380.

[247] *Meyer* v. *Gordon* (1981) 17 CCLT 1 at 37 (BCSC). Picard *et al. Liability* 379.

[248] [1937] 1 DLR 298 (Ont CA).

[249] (1980) 1 ACWS (2d) 432 (Ont HC). See also Sharpe *Canada* 123.

[250] Sharpe *Canada* 123. Picard *et al. Liability* 380.

[251] *Supra* 5.4.2.

[252] Picard *et al. Liability* 380–381. Her statement is founded on *Saskatchewan Wheat Pool* v. *R* [1983] 1 SCR.

directly owe its patients a direct duty (duties), which operates independently of its vicarious responsibility for professional medical officers, and operates independently of its non-delegable duties to patients in terms of the negligence of both employees and independent contractors for which it can be held liable. Direct duties, breach of which establish direct hospital liability, are therefore not to be characterized as non-delegable duties.[253]

The direct corporate liability of Canadian hospitals is recommended by Canadian academics, or at least recognized[254] as a valid legal ground to found hospital liability. Corporate negligence has, however, been developed far more in the United States than in Canada.[255]

The implications of allocating the responsibility and ultimately the liability to an institution like the hospital, are manifold: Compensation is ensured from a financially viable and heavily insured corporate entity.[256] The hospital as main corporate entity is at best the most obvious and appropriate legal representative to ascertain the truth in cases of medical malpractice. They can initiate settlements or seek indemnification from negligent employees.[257] The hospital can also by means of its comprehensive powers rectify organizational failures and bad systems by regulating, controlling and setting standards for all involved.[258]

### 7.3.4  Breach of Contract

In Canadian law, the hospital's liability can also be founded on another independent legal ground, namely breach of contract. An injured patient can claim recompense under this doctrine, when treated negligently in a modern hospital.[259] This legal category is, however, the most undeveloped one upon which to proceed,[260] for '... courts have been most reluctant to subject the hospital-patient relationship to a thorough, conclusive contractual analy-

---

[253]  See Picard *et al. Liability* 364 who, unfortunately, does so.

[254]  Sharpe *Canada* 119, 123–124. Chapman *Medicine* 58–62. Picard *et al. Liability* 367–381. Osode 1993 *AALR* 307–314.

[255]  *Supra.* See also Sharpe *Canada* 124. See Chapter 8.

[256]  Sharpe *Canada* 119.

[257]  *Ibid.*

[258]  *Ibid.*

[259]  Osode 1993 *AALR* 315–317. Picard *et al. Liability* 365–366.

[260]  *Ibid.*

sis'.[261] It is also true that 'recent trends indicate an emerging change'.[262] Osode suggests developing this legal ground.[263]

When relying on this doctrine, the following applies: If the patient relies upon the existence of a contract (express or implied) between himself/herself and the hospital, it is accepted that the contract comes into existence upon the patient's entry into the hospital or upon the completion of hospital forms.[264] When breach of contract is alleged against the hospital, the court must then seek to construct a contract and determine its terms. Sources on which the court relies when determining a contract are the following: Written contracts, express terms (if any), relevant legislation, regulations, hospital by-laws, public expectations as well as the conduct of the parties themselves.[265] Terms which are easily implied are, for example, to provide competent staff, adequate equipment and facilities and efficient organization.[266] The duty to provide medical care is not easily inferred, although it should be implied in all emergency cases.[267]

In *Osborn* v. *Mohindra*,[268] Stratton J held a hospital liable on account of breach of contract, firstly, by failing to have an organized 'system of work' by means of which the radiologist's report must reach the attending doctor and, secondly, for failing to provide non-negligent medical treatment. The terms of the contract were determined by considering 'all the circumstances of the entrance of the patient into the hospital, of what is sought by him and the nature of what is done to and for him.'[269] In *Yepremian* v. *Scarborough General Hospital* [270] Blair JA, who dissented, founded the hospital's responsibility to provide medical care on a contract implied from all the circumstances.[271]

---

[261] Picard *et al. Liability* 366. Osode 1993 *AALR* 315 and footnote 89. Osode remarks that the reasons for this judicial attitude were alluded to by Blair JA in *Yepremian* v. *Scarborough et al.* at 566.

[262] Osode 1993 *AALR* 315.

[263] *Ibid.*

[264] *Ibid.*

[265] *Ibid.* Picard *et al. Liability* 365. *Lavere* v. *Smith's Falls Public Hospital* (1915), 26 DLR 346 (Ont CA).

[266] Picard *et al. Liability* 365. Osode 1993 *AALR* 315.

[267] *Ibid.*

[268] (1980) 29 NBR (2d) 340 (QB).

[269] *Osborn* at 353–354. Picard *et al. Liability* 366. Osode 1993 *AALR* 315–316.

[270] (1980) 110 DLR (3d) 513 at 565 (Ont CA).

[271] Yepremian *supra* per Blair JA at 567–568: '... the hospital held itself out as offering emergency medical service to persons in Tony's condition. It became contractually bound

Some duties which are derived from the hospital's contractual liability, have been typified as being non-delegable.[272] The writer would, with respect, prefer to classify duties that relate to organizational failures or improper systems, which become relevant to contractual liability — as direct duties and not as non-delegable duties.[273]

It has also been suggested that due to the obvious inequality of the two parties to these contracts, courts should not be hesitant to negate contractual terms which seem to be harmful or *contra bonos mores*, and should diligently stipulate the responsibilities and duties of institutional health providers.[274]

This legal ground is, however, problematic when considering the position of unconscious persons, persons who are not capable of forming consent, persons incapable of volition and those who do not have the full legal capacity to act. The afore-mentioned persons cannot give their consent to the formation of a contract, and consequently no contract is established — either explicitly or implicitly — as a result of the lack of consensus.

### 7.3.5  The Non-Delegable Duty[275]

In Canadian hospital liability law, there is no clear distinction between direct duties and non-delegable duties. It is submitted, however, that these duties can be distinguished and the non-delegable duty as an independent legal ground which can establish hospital liability will, therefore, be discussed.[276] This legal ground is discussed shortly in relevance to the Canadian hospital liability law.

In *Pickard* v. *Smith*,[277] a 1861 case, a duty was for the first time held to be a non-delegable duty. The trial judge stated that the employer will be answerable where:

> ... the act which occasions the injury is one which the contractor was employed to do;

and also where:

---

to provide such service in a non-negligent manner when its offer was accepted by the admission of Tony, and his complete submission to its care.' *Infra* 7.3.6.

[272] Picard *et al. Liability* 366. Osode 1993 *AALR* 316.

[273] See 4.3.2, 4.3.3, 4.4, 8.3.3, 8.3.4 and 10.

[274] Picard *et al. Liability* 366. Osode 1993 *AALR* 317.

[275] You are referred to the discussion on non-delegable duties under 4.3.3.

[276] See 4.3.2, 4.3.3, 4.4, 7.3.3, 8.3.3, 8.3.4 and 10.

[277] (1861) 10 CBNS 470, 142 ER 535 (CP). Picard 1981 *MGLJ* 1008.

... the contractor is entrusted with the performance of a duty incumbent upon his employer, and neglects its fulfilment, whereby an injury is occasioned.[278]

The non-delegable duty of care concept was also introduced where statutory duties were involved.[279] In *Dalton* v. *Angus*,[280] the concept came to life. Lord Blackburn stated:

> ... a person causing something to be done, the doing of which casts on him a duty, cannot escape from the responsibility attaching on him of seeing that duty performed by delegating it to a contractor. He may bargain with the contractor that he shall perform the duty and stipulate for an indemnity from him if it is not performed, but he cannot thereby relieve himself from liability to those injured by the failure to perform it.[281]

Canadian academics have, however, when discussing the direct (hospital) liability, and its duties, referred to the relevant (direct) duties as non-delegable duties:

(i)    Picard has, in terms of the direct hospital liability, discussed the expansion of the hospital's function as well as its responsibility to patients, and stated:

> These **responsibilities** may be characterized as **non-delegable duties** owed to the patient and a failure to discharge them properly may result in an action against the hospital for breach of contract or negligence.[282]

Even in the discussion of the direct duties, the latter were classified as being non-delegable duties.[283]

Concerning the duty to provide competent medical care, Osode formulated as follows:

> This is because this duty being a direct, personal or institutional duty is non-delegable.[284]

---

[278]  *Pickard* v. *Smith supra* at 539. Picard 1981 *MGLJ* 1009.

[279]  Picard 1981 *MGLJ* 1009.

[280]  (1881) 6 App. Cas. 740 (HL). Picard 1981 *MGLJ* 1009.

[281]  *Dalton* v. *Angus supra* at 829.

[282]  Picard *et al. Liability* 364. My accentuation.

[283]  *Op. cit.* 303.

[284]  Osode 1993 *AALR* 310. At 308 Osode interpreted as follows: '... it is important to note that wherever the courts find that a **direct duty is** owed, a necessary corollary is the finding that the duty is **non-delegable**. It is a rule of significant antiquity that **a person who owes a duty of care cannot**, in the event of injury occurring as a result of its breach, successfully contend that he **had delegated** the doing of the thing in question to another and it is inconsequential that the person to whom delegation is alleged to have been made is an employee or independent contractor. A duty of care is found to exist wherever there

**Comment on (i)**

When direct (hospital) liability is discussed with reference to specific duties, and the whole approach is founded on a fault-based direct corporate liability which necessitates corporate hospital-employer negligence for breach of the hospital's own personal duty (in other words when all the requirements of direct liability are complied with), then the relevant duties ought not be referred to as non-delegable duties. In such context, the duties are only direct, corporate or institutional duties, breach of which found direct hospital liability. A direct duty can not simultaneously be a non-delegable duty, since they represent two different fault systems. The non-delegable duty induces strict liability, whereas breach of the direct duty induces a fault-based liability.

(ii)    It has also been stated that: 'The quality of the duties owed by a hospital has led to their sometimes being referred to as '**non-delegable**'. This has the significant effect of making the **employer** of an independent contractor **strictly liable** for any negligence of the contractor in carrying out the duty of care which was the employer's, but which he had contracted or delegated to the independent contractor. This is an exception to the general rule that an employer is not liable for the negligence of an independent contractor employed by him.' (my accentuation).[285]

**Comment on (ii)**

When, however, the concept and content of a specific given duty is taken, and it is exalted or promoted to the status of a non-delegable duty, with full recognition of and full adherence to all the non-delegable duty's requirements and characteristics (for example the strict employer liability which is not fault-based liability; and the strict duty to ensure that care is taken), then the non-delegable duty becomes an independent legal ground *sui generis* which founds hospital liability.

This non-delegable duty is not a direct duty which founds fault-based direct (hospital) liability, but an independent legal ground of hospital liability. In the case of the non-delegable duty, the performance of the duty (to ensure that reasonable care is provided) is delegated, but the responsibility for that duty of care is not delegated.

---

is a relationship between the parties such that each is required to avoid acts or omissions which could be foreseen as likely to injure the other.' (my accentuation).

[285]    Picard 1981 *MGLJ* 1007.

The non-delegable duty has been said to provide justification for liability for the acts of independent contractors, but it has also been criticized to have no rational foundation for its implementation.[286]

A test has been proposed to distinguish between delegable and non-delegable duties: It is 'whether there is imposed on the person by the nature of the acts he is getting done a duty to those people whom as a reasonable man he ought to foresee as being affected by the performance of those acts'.[287] After finding various reasons[288] worthy of acknowledging the non-delegable duty, and considering an outstanding quote of Atiyah,[289] Picard concludes that the non-delegable duty should only be validated independently in every case, 'after a thorough examination of the hospital-patient relationship involved'.[290]

### 7.3.5.1 Non-delegable duties[291]

The following duty/duties can be presented as non-delegable duties, breach of which can found hospital liability:

---

[286] Picard 1981 *MGLJ* 1009. Atiyah *Vicarious* 332.

[287] Picard 1981 *MGLJ* 1009–1010.

[288] Factors are: The employer benefits from the contractor's work; he chooses the contractor; he sets up the relationship on his own terms; the employer can make arrangements to cope with a risk; the employer can be indemnified for liabilities imposed by the contractor.

[289] 'In many circumstances there is little doubt that the man in the street would find it hard to grasp the law's fine distinctions between a servant and an independent contractor, and would not wish to enquire too closely into the precise relationships existing in one organization. This is particularly true where the liability is of a contractual or semi-contractual nature, as e.g. in the case of hospitals. A person injured through the negligence of someone in a hospital tends to think of the hospital as a unit which ought to be responsible for the consequences, and he is unlikely to be impressed by arguments that the negligent party was, say, a visiting consultant who ought to be treated as an independent contractor.' Atiyah *Vicarious* 335.

[290] Picard 1981 *MGLJ* 1011.

[291] There are of course manifold non-delegable duties, but for the purpose of this discussion the two duties will suffice. These duties are therefore not a comprehensive compilation of all possible non-delegable duties.
  **The duty to ensure that staff remain competent**: This duty is more problematic but one could endeavour to transform it into a non-delegable duty. Hospitals are under a non-delegable duty to constantly review and monitor competency and qualifications of medical professionals. If a doctor acted negligently without skill, knowledge or judgment, a hospital would be liable if it knew or ought to have known about such incompetency and still granted him privileges. The hospital is under a non-delegable duty to ensure that staff remain instructed, trained, supervised and monitored in order for them to treat patients competently.

## (i)     Duty to provide reasonably competent medical treatment and care/ services[292]

The modern hospital owes a patient this duty. This duty is a non-delegable duty,[293] which renders the fact that the physician was either an independent contractor with hospital privileges or a proper employee, immaterial. Even the fact that the hospital exercised due care and good judgment in selecting medical professionals — who act negligently — will not exonerate the hospital from liability.[294] This duty is representative of an over-riding duty which institutional health care providers adhere to contemporarily, all over the world.[295] A prerequisite for the implementation of this duty, is that the patient sought competent medical care from the hospital alone.[296]

### 7.3.6  *Yepremian v. Scarborough General Hospital*[297] (1980):

Tony Yepremian, the plaintiff, who was 19 years old, had felt unwell and suffered from the following symptoms: he vomited, and had increased frequency of urination and drinking. His family took him to see Dr Gold-bach, a physician who filled in some week-ends as a doctor's replacement for the family doctor who was away. Dr Goldbach had obtained his degree in medicine a year earlier. He diagnosed tonsillitis, prescribed an antibiotic and found it unnecessary to refer the plaintiff to hospital. The plaintiff started to hyperventilate later that night at home. He was taken to the emergency department of the defendant hospital. At that time he was semi-comatose and in a wheelchair. Dr Chin, a general practitioner with hospital privileges was on duty. This doctor did not order a urinalysis and made no diagnosis. He noted the hyperventilation on the emergency record and prescribed medicine which deepened Tony's comatose condition. After two telephone calls to the home of Dr Rosen, the internist on call, the latter directed the plaintiff to be admitted to the intensive care unit of the hospital. Only at that stage some

---

[292]  See 4.3.3.

[293]  Osode 1993 *AALR* 310.

[294]  *Ibid.*

[295]  *Ibid.*

[296]  *Op. cit.* 310–311.

[297]  (1980) 110 DLR (3d) 513; (1980) 13 CCLT 105 (Ont Ca). (1981) 120 DLR (3d) 341: The action was settled before the appeal to the Supreme Court was heard. Kennedy and Grubb *Medical Law* 410–411. Giesen *International* 25, 62. Jones *Negligence* 407, 408–409. Lewis *Negligence* 183. Chapman *Medicine* 60–62. Picard *et al. Liability* 386–391. Picard 1981 *MGLJ* 1012–1016. Sneiderman *et al. Canadian* 104–106, 110–11. Sharpe *Canada* 120–123. Osode 1993 *AALR* 299–301.

tests were done. A neurologist examined him with negative results. Eleven hours after being admitted, a nurse detected a 'fruity' odour on the patient's breath and correctly diagnosed diabetes. Only then, did Dr Rosen instruct that insulin be administered. The dosage of sodium bicarbonate he prescribed was excessive. Potassium was also not administered soon enough and sufficiently. Tony remained semi-conscious and suffered a cardiac arrest almost 12 hours later. He suffered permanent brain damage. Action for damages was brought by the plaintiff against the hospital and Dr Goldbach. Neither Dr Rosen nor Dr Chin was sued.[298] Both gave evidence at the trial as witnesses called by counsel for the hospital.

Mr Justice RE Holland tried the action without a jury, and gave the following judgment: Both Dr Goldbach and Dr Chin were found negligent in the treatment of the patient. They did not provide the correct diagnosis or treatment. However, they were both 'insulated from liability', because their liability did not effectively cause the cardiac arrest which injured the patient. It was furthermore not foreseeable that an internist and specialist in endocrinology would treat the patient negligently.[299]

Dr Rosen, the internist, had been negligent in failing to correctly diagnose diabetes, and in the treatment and care of his patient. Potassium should have been administered sooner and in sufficient quantity by him. His negligence in treatment caused the cardiac arrest. Tony would have recovered without harm, if he had been properly treated after the diagnosis of diabetes had been made.[300]

The trial judge concluded that both Dr Chin and Dr Goldbach, although negligent, would not have been liable if sued. The hospital could therefore not be liable for their negligence.[301] This was accepted by Arnup JA of the Appeal Court.[302] The hospital was not found vicariously liable for the laboratory staff or nursing staff of the ICU, since there was no negligence on their part.[303] The hospital was only found responsible in law for the negligence of Dr Rosen.[304]

The undisputed facts were that, neither Dr Rosen nor Dr Chin were employees of the hospital. They did not receive any remuneration from the

---

[298] *Yepremian* (1980) 520.

[299] *Yepremian* (1980) 520–521.

[300] *Yepremian* (1980) 521.

[301] *Yepremian* (1980) 523.

[302] *Yepremian* (1980) 523.

[303] *Yepremian* (1980) 521.

[304] *Yepremian* (1980) 521.

hospital. They had only the right to practise there and were privileged in making use of hospital facilities. Responsibilities to attend the emergency department were also assigned to them as well as attending staff meetings. They billed patients or their funds, and paid nothing to the hospital. They were both thus regarded as independent contractors.[305] To such distinctions in appointments the trial judge remarked:

> In a large city such as Toronto with a population of over two million people, and with many doctors loath to make house calls, people go to the local hospital for care. Such people anticipate a high standard of care. They anticipate the best of equipment, laboratory services, nursing services and above all, they anticipate competent skilled medical attention and treatment. These people do not, I think, differentiate between a teaching and non-teaching hospital and I do not think that such people would understand that liability might be imposed on a hospital for the negligence of an intern or resident but not for the negligence of a newly-qualified general practitioner in a non-teaching hospital who takes his turn in the emergency department in order to obtain certain admitting privileges.[306]

The trial judge examined the relevant provisions of the Public Hospitals Act[307] especially section 41 of that act which, he argued, clearly reflected 'the intention that hospitals be directly responsible to their patients for the quality of care provided in the hospitals'.[308] He also found that 'the legislature recognizes the institutional responsibility for care as opposed simply to a responsibility for providing staff'.[309]

In view of the trial court's finding, Arnup JA stated that neither the Public Hospitals Act nor Regulation 729 — expressly imposed any statutory responsibility on a public hospital for the negligence of a specialist on its medial staff when treating a patient in the hospital or — expressly imposed upon a public hospital the obligation to provide competent medical care to patients admitted to the hospital. The judge, however, admitted that 'both are premised, in my view, on the existence of an obligation **to see** that such care is provided. Neither furnishes any real assistance ... in answering the crucial question: how does a hospital satisfy that obligation?'[310]

---

[305] *Yepremian* (1980) 525, 527.

[306] *Yepremian* (1980) 527, as quoted from p. 522 OR, p. 172 DLR.

[307] RSO 1970 c 378 s 41 as am RSO 1980 c 410 s 31.

[308] (1978) 88 DLR (3d) 161 at 175 (Ont HC). *Yepremian* (1980) 528–530. Chapman *Medicine* 528. Picard *et al. Liability* 387.

[309] (1978) 88 DLR (3d) 161 at 175 (Ont HC).

[310] *Yepremian* (1980) 530. (my accentuation) The 'obligation **to see**' implicates with respect the non-delegable duty which endeavours to **ensure** that care is provided. His formulation implies such a duty.

The trial judge then reviewed at length the relevant decided cases in England, Canada and one American decision.[311] He formulated the following principles on hospital liability in conclusion:

> Except in exceptional circumstances:
>
> 1. A hospital is not responsible for negligence of a doctor not employed by the hospital when the doctor was personally retained by the patient;
>
> 2. A hospital is liable for the negligence of a doctor employed by the hospital;
>
> 3. Where a doctor is not an employee of the hospital and is not personally retained by the patient, all of the circumstances must be considered in order to decide whether or not the hospital is under a non-delegable duty of care which imposes liability on the hospital.
>
> The present case falls into the third category.[312]

The trial judge had consequently founded the hospital's liability on breach of the non-delegable duty which constitutes an independent duty of its own to provide non-negligent medical care to patients, by ensuring that its staff use reasonable skill and competence in treating patients.[313] In other words, the hospital delegates performance, but responsibility for performance is non-delegable. The hospital was held liable under the non-delegable duty for the negligent performance of the independent contractor specialist who was assigned to provide reasonable care and treatment in the emergency department of that hospital, which he did not.[314] The trial judge gave judgment for the plaintiff against the hospital for the amount of $390,262.11, but dismissed action against Dr Goldbach.

The hospital appealed and the plaintiff cross-appealed to the Court of Appeal.

The Ontario Court of Appeal reversed the trial decision. The majority of the court which consisted of Arnup JA, Morden JA and MacKinnon ACJO, held that the plaintiff's appeal should be dismissed, and Blair and Holden JJA, dissenting, held that the hospital's appeal should be dismissed, and the cross-appeal against the hospital allowed with costs.[315]

The majority of the Court of Appeal held that in Canada a hospital does not undertake a non-delegable duty to a patient.[316]

---

[311] *Yepremian* (1980) 530. The American case was *Darling* v. *Charleston Community Hospital* (1965) 211 NE (2d) 253 (Ill CA).

[312] *Yepremian* (1980) 530–531. Picard *et al. Liability* 387–388. Sharpe *Canada* 120.

[313] See *Yepremian* (1980) 531–532.

[314] See also Sharpe *Canada* 120.

[315] *Yepremian* (1980) 517, 548, 553, 554, 580.

[316] *Yepremian* (1980) 517–554. Jones *Negligence* 407.

Arnup JA seemed to be critical of non-delegable duties, because it seemed to him to be a case of saying:

> In all the circumstances, the hospital **ought** to be liable.[317]

But Jones remarks to this: 'This, however, is the very point, and it is as true of the principle of vicarious liability, and indeed most tort duties'.[318]

The learned judge furthermore limited the hospital's duty dramatically. He suggested that:

> There being no finding that Dr Rosen was unqualified or incompetent, nor that there was anything other than careful consideration and good judgment on the part of the hospital before appointing him tot the staff, the hospital fully discharged its obligation to provide competent internal medicine services to Tony Yepremian following his admission to the hospital.[319]

He thereby limited the hospital's duty to the careful selection of competent and qualified staff. This was to come about by the hospital's

- picking its medical staff with great care;
- checking out the credentials of every applicant;
- causing existing staff to make a recommendation in every case;
- making no appointment for longer than one year at a time; and
- reviewing the performance of staff at regular intervals.

After considering the relevant case law, especially the English case law, he pondered on his caution to apply the English cases. He quoted Professor Allen Linden who considered whether English authorities should be adopted in Canada, in the light of 'different attitudes and practices in Canada', and again suggested that the reception of 'the English rule' might not be justified.[320] In England a non-delegable duty had been imposed on the Minister of Health by section 3 of the National Health Service Act, 1946 to provide 'medical, nursing or other services required at or for the purposes of hospitals' and 'the services of specialists'. The judge found that no similar duty had been imposed by the Public Hospitals Act, upon the Ontario

---

[317] *Yepremian* (1980) 532: Arnup JA also stated: 'I agree with the trial judge … that the Yepremians had every right to expect that a large public hospital like Scarborough General would provide whatever was required to treat seriously ill or injured people, but I do not think it follows that the public is entitled to add the further expectation: 'and if any doctor on the medical staff makes a negligent mistake, the hospital will pay for it'.'

[318] Jones *Negligence* 409.

[319] *Yepremian* (1980) 532.

[320] *Yepremian* (1980) 545. See also Lewis *Negligence* 12, 183.

hospitals, with respect to the services of specialists or other medical practitioners.[321]

Arnup JA concluded:

> The Government exercises a substantial degree of control over public hospitals, through Regulations and especially through the hospitals' finances. If liability is to be imposed upon hospitals for the negligence of its medical staff, including specialists, not employed by the hospitals, whether directly or by imposing a statutory duty to provide such services, it should be the function of the Legislature, as a policy question, to decide whether and under what conditions such liability is to attach.[322]

He accordingly allowed the hospital's appeal and dismissed the action against it, but without costs.[323]

MacKinnon ACJO did not want to part with the old ways of acknowledging the independence of the medical profession and of evading hospital liability except in the cases of vicarious hospital liability. He preferred not to reverse the long-standing experience and law which would have resulted in entering into a 'matter of policy'. He stated that such a change would require legislative intervention and not judicial legislation.[324]

Blair JA, dissented in part. He confirmed the judgment of the trial judge RE Holland J, in finding that the hospital was liable for the negligent treatment of a patient by a doctor who was a member of its medical staff (and thus an independent contractor), but not a salaried employee.[325] This hospital liability was founded on the legal ground of the non-delegable duty of the hospital to provide non-negligent medical care. The judge stated that his decision did 'not involve a quest for new jurisprudence but rather the more prosaic task of analysing established principles and applying them to the facts.'[326] He proceeded to do just that.

**Vicarious liability**: Blair JA decided that the hospital would have been vicariously liable for the negligence of Dr Rosen if he had been a paid employee.[327] In other words the vicarious liability of the hospital was

---

[321] *Yepremian* (1980) 545.

[322] *Yepremian* (1980) 545.

[323] *Yepremian* (1980) 545.

[324] *Yepremian* (1980) 553–545.

[325] *Yepremian* (1980) 545, 556. Sharpe *Canada* 122: 'It should be noted that two judges in dissent favoured expanding the responsibility of hospitals for the negligence of physicians and surgeons who are not employees of the hospitals'. Holden and Blair JJA (dissenting in part).

[326] *Yepremian* (1980) 558.

[327] *Yepremian* (1980) 558, 580.

inapplicable *in casu*, in the light of the fact that he presupposed the test to be the payment of a salary.

He also formulated the often-quoted passage:

> The oft-told tale of how the courts in a period of less than 50 years eliminated the anomaly which exempted hospitals from the ordinary rules of liability for negligence of doctors, nurses and other professionals acting within the scope of their employment need not be repeated.[328]

Since the retreat from the *Hillyer*[329] case, Courts have been trying to find alternative legal grounds to found hospital liability. There is a tendency to try and 'sweep all such cases under the rubric of vicarious liability'.[330] The judge did however advocate that in appropriate cases, alternative grounds for hospital liability, such as implied contract and the non-delegable duty have to be applied. He suggested that these alternative grounds for liability be applied in the present case.[331]

**Direct liability of hospitals**: Blair JA discussed the direct liability of hospitals. It is considered well established that a hospital is liable to a patient directly for failure to provide a 'safe system', or adequate or properly maintained equipment; or for failure to select competent and qualified doctors; or for failure to protect patients from injuring themselves or others; or for failure to provide sufficient staff.'[332]

He concluded:

> Whatever the relationship between the Hospital and its medical staff, the Hospital itself remains responsible for the proper operation of the Hospital system and the related functions of record-keeping and the effective transmission of information within the institution. However the system operates, the Hospital, in the final analysis, is responsible for it and must accept liability in the event of its failure.[333]

This, with respect, is the acceptable, formal description of direct hospital liability which, with respect, does not encompass the non-delegable duty.

Of great importance is his following distinction:

---

[328] *Yepremian* (1980) 558.

[329] *Hillyer* v. *Governors of St Bartholomew's Hospital* [1909] 2 KB 820 (CA).

[330] *Yepremian* (1980) 558.

[331] *Yepremian* (1980) 558.

[332] *Yepremian* (1980) 558–559. He quoted relevant Canadian case law.

[333] *Yepremian* (1980) 559–560.

> In some cases, the line is blurred between injury caused by the failure of the hospital to provide proper equipment or organization and injury caused by the negligence of employees: none the less, the principle of direct liability is well established by the authorities.[334]

It is submitted, with respect, that herein lies part of the distinction between direct hospital liability and the non-delegable duty. When the focus is on the formal organizational failures or improper provision of systems of the institution, by the institution itself, it constitutes direct hospital or institutional liability. Whereas, if the focus is on the delegation of performances to staff, and such performance of independent contractors *or* employees is negligent, the hospital's undelegable independent duty or responsibility to ensure that reasonable care or treatment is provided, is breached. It is once again the institution's responsibility, but the focus is on the negligence of the performers.

**The novelty of the issue:** All parties to the case conceded that the issue presented to the Court was novel. There was no authority binding on the Court which established that the hospital should be liable or not liable in those circumstances.[335]

Courts have acknowledge that whether a duty of care exists or not in such a novel situation, involves a policy decision.[336] When the court finds itself in a novel situation and makes a policy decision whether it decides to expand liability or refuses to do so, the decision will be open to legislative review. But, this fact does not, according to Blair JA, 'relieve the Court of its obligation to reach a decision on the case presented to it.'[337] The duty of the court's decision could not be avoided by classifying the review of the Hospital's duty as being a 'legislative and not a judicial responsibility'.[338]

---

[334] *Yepremian* (1980) 559.

[335] *Yepremian* (1980) 560. The judge further stated at 560: 'On countless occasions, common law Courts have asserted that the novelty of an issue is not a defence. If the Courts had followed the policy of rejecting cases because they had never occurred before, it is obvious that the common law would have atrophied and would not have expanded, as it has done over the many centuries, to meet new problems as society developed and changed. The past half-century has been marked by the expansion of the law of tort and, especially, responsibility for negligence. No citation of authority is necessary to show that, **in order to meet new situations in a rapidly-changing society, Courts have greatly expanded the concept of the duty owed to others by persons and institutions.'** (My accentuation).

[336] *Yepremian* (1980) 562.

[337] *Yepremian* (1980) 563.

[338] *Yepremian* (1980) 563.

**No duty of care from statute**: Blair JA confirmed Arnup JA's finding that no duty to provide non-negligent medical treatment arose from Canadian statute.[339] Nonetheless, he stated that the fact that liability in the United Kingdom is now founded on a clear statutory basis, in no way detracts from the value of the English case law in their discussions of alternate bases for liability.[340]

**Contractual duty of care**: Blair JA found that the contractual hospital liability for the negligent treatment in hospitals remains difficult by implying terms in contracts for hospital care and because of the 'unequal bargaining positions of hospitals and patients'.[341] He proposed the modern law of negligence as a more responsive and flexible instrument, than contract, for determining hospital liability.[342]

**Duty of care in tort**: Blair JA declared that the basis for liability in contract and tort is coextensive in this case, and the use of the word 'undertaking' by Holland J, in describing the hospital's obligation, also covers both situations.[343] He added that in terms of the common law, the non-delegable duty of care also avails liability for the negligence of independent contractors who are not employees. In addition, he stated that a 'non-delegable duty gives rise to direct and not vicarious liability',[344] after relying on a lengthy quote from 'Salmond on the Law of Torts'.[345]

It is submitted that the non-delegable duty is neither a form of direct liability nor a form of vicarious liability. It is a legal ground *sui generis*, and a unique and independent legal ground which establishes hospital liability.

Blair JA formulated two questions in order to determine whether the hospital was under a duty to provide non-negligent medical treatment:

> The first is whether a hospital could have undertaken such a duty. The second is whether it did.

In his view, both questions were to be answered in the affirmative.[346]

---

[339] *Yepremian* (1980) 564.

[340] *Yepremian* (1980) 565.

[341] *Yepremian* (1980) 566.

[342] *Yepremian* (1980) 566.

[343] *Yepremian* (1980) 568.

[344] *Yepremian* (1980) 568.

[345] 17th ed. (1977) 486 in *Yepremian* (1980) 568.

[346] *Yepremian* (1980) 568. At 576 he indicated that 'The expansion of direct liability of hospitals for negligent medical treatment by doctors who are not employees is also evident in the United States'. It must, however, be kept in mind that American law also differentiates

The judge considered it of paramount importance, in the circumstances of this case, to determine the relationship between the hospital and the patient in order to ascertain the extent of the hospital's duty. The relationship between the hospital and the doctor could be more important in other cases.[347]

Blair JA stated:

> The recognition of a direct duty of hospitals to provide non-negligent medical treatment reflects the reality of the relationship between hospitals and the public in contemporary society. This direct duty arises from profound changes in social structures and public attitudes relating to medical services and the concomitant changes in the function of hospitals in providing them. It is obvious that as a result of these changes the role of hospitals in the delivery of medical services has expanded. The public increasingly relies on hospitals to provide medical treatment and, in particular, on emergency services. Hospitals to a growing extent hold out to the public that they provide such treatment and such services.[348]

He concluded that in this case, the hospital's obligation to the patient could not be limited to the mere provision of qualified doctors. 'The Hospital assumed and would be expected to assume complete responsibility for Tony's treatment.'[349]

Blair JA found the hospital liable on account of the breach of its non-delegable duty to provide non-negligent medical treatment by an independent contractor. The hospital's appeal was dismissed.[350] Houlden JA, who also dissented in part, concurred with Blair JA.[351]

Leave to appeal the Ontario Court of Appeal decision in *Yepremian* to the Supreme Court of Canada, was subsequently granted.[352] The action was however settled by an astronomic amount, before the appeal to the Supreme Court could be heard.[353] This was probably done to avoid the risk of an adverse judgment at the Supreme Court level, which could have established an overriding non-delegable duty for all Canadian hospitals to provide non-negligent medical care to patients, or other similar non-delegable duties.

---

between the non-delegable duty and direct hospital liability, as separate legal grounds. See *infra* chapter 8.

[347] *Yepremian* (1980) 578.

[348] *Yepremian* (1980) 579. Giesen *International* 62.

[349] *Yepremian* (1980) 579.

[350] *Yepremian* (1980) 579–580.

[351] *Yepremian* (1980) 580–582.

[352] (1981) 120 DLR (3d) 341.

[353] See also Chapman *Medicine* 62. Picard *et al. Liability* 390. Sharpe *Canada* 122. Osode 1993 *AALR* 312: Nearly 2 million, see *infra* footnote 358.

## Comment on *Yepremian*

(i)     The non-delegable duty as legal ground to found hospital liability:
        In the Canadian case law, courts were first afforded the opportunity to
        apply the comprehensive non-delegable duty to provide non-negligent
        medical care to hospitals, in the case of *Yepremian*.[354] The court was
        supposed to discern the hospital for not only being an institutional
        provider of proper equipment, facilities and medical professionals,[355]
        but for being a comprehensive and extensive provider of medical care.
        The trial judge proclaimed such a duty to exist in this case founded on
        relevant statute.[356] The trial judge together with the dissent of two of
        the Appeal Court Judges also founded the duty on the legitimate pub-
        lic expectations of what a hospital undertakes to a patient in such a
        case.[357] This finding was based on a thorough analysis of the law by
        each one of them.[358] The Ontario Court of Appeal's majority of three
        Judges, however, disclaimed the existence of such a duty. They found
        that the hospital did not owe the patient such a duty and therefore
        overruled the trial Judge and two appeal Judges[359] who had dissented.
        The majority found that hospitals were not compelled by any statutory
        provision, regulation or contract to provide competent medical care
        via specialists and that there was indeed no precedent to establish such
        a principle.[360] The reigning Canadian academic poll[361] indicates that it
        is thought that the Supreme Court of Canada would have set aside the
        majority opinion, if it had adjudicated the matter. After leave to appeal
        to the Supreme Court had been granted, the hospital did, however, of-
        fer the patient a settlement. It is argued that the settlement was offered
        in fear of the fact that the Supreme Court of Canada would have up-
        held the minority judgments.[362] Consequently, it is also argued that

---

[354]   *Yepremian* v. *Scarborough General Hospital.* Osode 1993 *AALR* 311–312.

[355]   *Ibid.*

[356]   Public Hospitals Act.

[357]   *Yepremian* (1980) at 554–580 per Blair JA.

[358]   *Yepremian*; Osode 1993 *AALR* 312.

[359]   *Ibid.* The two appeal Judges had adopted the reasoning of the trial Judge.

[360]   *Yepremian* at 545.

[361]   Picard *et al. Liability* 389–391. Chapman *Medicine* 62. Osode 1993 *AALR* 312. Sharpe
        *Canada* 122.

[362]   *Ibid.* The settlement was for $1,839,095.28.

Canadian hospitals owe a duty to provide competent medical care in emergency and other cases similar to that of the case of *Yepremian*.[363]

(ii)    Vicarious hospital liability:

In the *Yepremian* case, the trial judge did not establish his finding of hospital liability on vicarious liability. In fact the complete Ontario Court of Appeal and in total al six judges who heard this case, decided that vicarious liability was inapplicable. With special reference to the English trilogy of cases, this finding is not altogether clear. In these cases the test for the application of vicarious hospital liability was not stated to exist in the distinction between employees and independent contractors. This test together with the control test was discarded. The test accepted in those cases was, whether the hospital or the patient had chosen and employed the doctor and whether that party had the power to dismiss the medical professional. In short the determinant factor was: the right to employ and dismiss. The party who accommodated this description, could be vicariously liable for another. The prominent factor to distinguish a party for whom a hospital would be liable or not, did not rely on whether the professional received a salary or not as suggested by Blair JA. Blair JA stated at 556, 558, 574 and 580 that the hospital would have been vicariously liable for the negligence of Dr Rosen if he had been a paid employee.

If one discards the employee and independent contractor distinction, and realize hospitals have the same power to employ and dismiss over independent contractors who have been granted hospital privileges, as they do over employees, then 'it would not be an incorrect application of the principles of vicarious liability if Canadian hospitals are held liable for the negligence of such private physicians. Indeed such an application would be a progressive development.'[364]

If the organization test[365] had been applied Dr Rosen would also have been considered part and parcel of the organization, in which case the hospital would have been held vicariously liable for him. Applying the organization test could bring about vicarious hospital liability for both hospital employees and privilege-holding physicians.[366]

---

[363]  Osode 1993 *AALR* 312.

[364]  Osode 1993 *AALR* 300–301.

[365]  Picard 1981 *MGLJ* 1018–1019. Osode 1993 *AALR* 301. *Yepremian* (1980) 575.

[366]  *Ibid.*

Furthermore, under vicarious liability both the employer and 'employee' are jointly liable, and the hospital has the right to be indemnified by the negligent doctor.[367]

(iii)    The direct liability of the hospital:

It is also, with respect, contended that the hospital's liability could have been argued on the basis of direct liability. This argument could have sought to establish that there was a serious organizational failure concerning the hospital's emergency services or a lack of a proper emergency system, which incorporated a duty to provide emergency services or a proper emergency system, of which the hospital was in breach. The lack of the system was portrayed by inefficient and insufficient manpower in the emergency centre; the negligent non-appearance of Dr Rosen (on call) after the first telephone call and negligent treatment after the second telephone call.

(iv)    The ostensible agency doctrine:

If this doctrine had been argued, applied and accepted, hospital liability could easily have been established. This doctrine has already been discussed *supra*. Unfortunately it has not yet been imported by Canadian courts.

(v)    Foreign application:

In the United States, the doctrine of ostensible agency makes ample provision for cases like this. It can also be said to be encompassing of the non-delegable duty to provide comprehensive competent medical care, in relevant situations,[368] such as these.

The (non-delegable) duty of hospitals to provide competent medical services,[369] has been part of the law of the United Kingdom for more than half a century.[370] Those courts[371] have unanimously held that the 'minister' is subject to this non-delegable duty in terms of the cu-

---

[367]    Picard 1981 *MGLJ* 1019.

[368]    See chapter 8 *infra*. Osode 1993 *AALR* 311.

[369]    In addition to many other duties.

[370]    Osode 1993 *AALR* 311.

[371]    *Ibid. Roe* v. *Minister of Health* per Denning LJ at 81–82. See also *Yepremian* at 574 per Blair JA. In *Razzel* v. *Snowball* [1954] 3 ALL ER 429 at 432, Downing LJ stated that the minister: 'Does not discharge his duty by appointing competent doctors and nurses and competent specialists. He has not merely to provide the staff. He has to provide their services; and, in as much as their services consist of treating the sick, it is his duty to treat the sick by means of their services.'

mulative effect of section 1(1) and section 3(1) of the National Health Service Act.

## After Yepremian

No major developments have occurred concerning the legal liability of hospitals in Canada, since the *Yepremian* case. In fact, as Picard[372] remarks, courts have adhered to the policy limitations expressed in that case. The Prichard Report, has recommended: no legislative intervention concerning the expansion of the doctrines of liability for health care institutions, but expanded hospital liability in areas of quality assurance and risk management, and (of course) appropriate development of relevant legal doctrines by the judiciary.[373]

### 7.4 CONTRIBUTION AND JOINT LIABILITY

The hospital is usually sued in preference to the employee, because of its financial viability. The hospital's liability is then discharged by the liability insurer.[374] The insurance company can, however, in terms of the 'subrogated right of action' sue the employee and recover whatever damage it had incurred as a result of the employee's breach of duty to its employer.[375] Employees should therefore be explicitly specified as an insured party in the employer's liability policy, or seek individual protection under a personal liability insurance scheme of through membership in the CMPA.[376]

Joint liability of a hospital and a doctor was also raised as a possibility in *Considine* v. *Camp Hill Hospital*.[377] It brings about the responsibility of both the health institution or hospital and the wrongdoing employee for the wrong(s) committed. Consequently they will be jointly and severally liable, meaning that both can be held responsible or either one can be held responsible.[378] When only one party i.e. the employer or employee is sued, either can have the other party added as a co-defendant.[379]

---

[372] Picard *et al. Liability* 391.

[373] *Ibid.*

[374] Sharpe *Canada* 109. Sneiderman *et al. Canadian* 112. See also Sharpe and Sawyer *Doctors* 73.

[375] *Ibid.* Rozovsky *Law* 17.

[376] Sneiderman *et al. Canadian* 112. Rozovsky *Law* 17.

[377] (1982) 133 DLR (3d) 11 NSSC. See also *Lloyd* v. *Milner* (1981) 15 Man R (2d) 87.

[378] Rozovsky *Law* 17. See also Sharpe and Sawyer *Doctors* 73.

[379] *Ibid.*

## 7.5 Conclusion

The Canadian health care liability system has been developed and expanded with regard to institutional responsibilities and the legal foundation of such liabilities, as well as in the determination of legal relationships[380] amongst institutional health care providers (hospitals), medical professionals or other staff, and patients. Canadian health care providers or hospitals have achieved professional sophistication, which requires of them the provision of (complete[381]) health care which is inclusive of all other necessary organizational arrangements, which in turn affects the courts' verdicts concerning hospital liability.[382]

It is, however, contended that Canadian hospital liability should be expanded even more.[383] The Canadian medical malpractice law and hospital liability law in particular has been criticized as being inefficient, dysfunctional and unsatisfactory and the courts have been described as being 'overly restrictive and conservative'.[384]

The legal establishment which is inclusive of the courts, lawyers and the legislature should direct a proper investigation into the availability of all legal grounds which found hospital liability and should develop their discretion as to when and how to apply them appropriately and independently.

The legal grounds which have been identified in discussing the Canadian hospital liability law, which can found hospital liability, are: Vicarious hospital liability; direct or corporate hospital liability; contractual hospital liability, the ostensible agency doctrine and the non-delegable duty.

Canadian Courts have primarily set out and stuck with vicarious hospital liability, and direct hospital liability to a certain extent,[385] forsaking all other grounds of hospital liability and leaving them undetected and undeveloped. Courts should implement other relevant legal grounds and formulate judicial

---

[380] Picard *et al. Liability* 397.

[381] See the judgment of Blair JA in *Yepremian* at 579. It is, however, not yet completely accepted and confirmed in Canadian hospital liability law.

[382] Picard *et al. Liability* 397.

[383] See also Chapman *Medicine* 55–102. Osode 1993 *AALR* 317–320. See also Picard et al. *Liability* 397.

[384] Osode 1993 *AALR* 317, 320.

[385] Canadian Courts have relied on direct hospital liability although confusing direct duties with non-delegable duties. There is no clear correct formulation or distinction yet between the two legal grounds of direct hospital liability and non-delegable duty which found hospital liability.

policies for novel situations. They should not evade judicial opportunities by enhancing the legislature's responsibilities, when they can themselves solve situations by creating new law within their boundaries. This recommendation is of course restricted by the courts' responsibility to create new (applications of) law by means of common or known principles, but not to necessarily create new principles of law.[386]

Chapman has, quite clearly formulated an opinion on the necessary expansion of hospital liability. He argues as follows:

> Except in cases of gross physician negligence, where a hospital indemnity action against the physician should be allowed, strict hospital liability for physician malpractice targets the defendant who is best able to take action to avoid the recurrence of the malpractice, and does so without encouraging overly cautious, and costly, defensive medicine.[387]

Other consequences of expanded hospital liability involve the shift of the burden of liability from the doctor or individual to the hospital or institution. This would preclude the doctor from practising defensive medicine and reduce the resulting costs involved.[388]

Whilst arguing for an expansion of hospital liability, an expansion of institutional liability can also be considered.[389] By targeting the institution which obviously suggests the hospital corporation, other levels of institutional liability are introduced which could be presented as possible appropriate institutional defendants. Other institutional possibilities include departments or sections within the hospital (e.g. the anaesthesiology department, the emergency room, etc) or other sub-groups of individual hospital staff members (e.g. hospital physicians in partnership).[390] The only problem with such a development is that no hospital by-laws or legal foundation yet exist, to provide such institutional possible defendants with the necessary legal authority to enforce themselves and protect themselves from liability.[391] Chapman suggests that:

> Perhaps the better view is to continue to focus the incentives of a harm-based liability rule on the whole hospital and hope that the effect of such liability will be that senior administrators will become more informed (either directly or by constant consultation with departmental chiefs) than they currently are

---

[386] The maxim *ius dicere, non facere* comes to mind.

[387] Chapman *Medicine* 100. He therefore suggests a standard of strict liability rather than negligence.

[388] *Op. cit.* 57.

[389] *Op. cit.* 65.

[390] *Op. cit.* 65–66, 71–72.

[391] *Op. cit.* 72–73.

about the systematic medical misadventures that do occur and how best to avoid them.[392]

Final arguments in favour of an expanded hospital liability, are that threats of litigation force hospitals to inspect their systems for organizational failures, probable medical misadventures or possible negligent behaviour of medical professionals. The hospitals are in control, they have the necessary legal authority and are in the best position to rectify bad situations, misdemeanours or procedural failures. This increases the quality of health care, consequently reduces the frequency of medical accidents, and cuts health care costs. Most importantly, patients are compensated where they had suffered a legal wrong with consequential injury.[393]

---

[392] *Op. cit.* 74. At 66 he says that 'the goal of a health care liability system is to provide incentives to reduce the frequency of incidents giving rise to medical misadventure'.

[393] See also Chapman *Medicine* 68–71, 100–102 and also Osode 1993 *AALR* 317–320.

# Chapter 8

# The Law in the USA

## 8.1. HEALTH CARE IN THE USA
## LAND AREA: 16,300,000 SQ. KM.[1]

### 8.1.1 Health Financing[2]

Health financing is provided by:

(i)     Private health insurance for the general population

(ii)    National insurance schemes which offer:
-       Medicare for the population aged over 65 years,
-       Medicaid for the needy regardless of age.

### 8.1.2 Health Care System[3]

Primary health care is provided by:

(i)     Specialists and general practitioners (mainly).

(ii)    Government Public Health Agencies which run community health, maternal and child health, school health and preventive health services.

Institutional care is provided by:

(i)     Mostly private hospitals providing short-term acute curative services. There is a free movement of generalists and specialists between hospitals and doctors' clinics.

---

[1]   Affordable Health Care Singapore 1993: Appendix B Subject 1.

[2]   *Op cit*: Appendix B Subject 9.

[3]   *Op cit*: Appendix B Subject 10.

(ii)    The government which runs the Veterans' Hospitals and hospitals for Eskimos and Indians.

(iii)   Nursing Homes (of which 75% are private).

### 8.1.3  The Health Care Industry

The following discussions will give a brief overview of the American health care industry, introducing important concepts and terminology without which it is impossible to form an adequate perspective on this complex issue. Where the hospital industry as well as hospitals' or other health care providers'[4] liability are scrutinized, the exposition of appropriate or important participants in the health-care field, is mandatory.

**Government financing** of health care was first introduced at the beginning of the twentieth century.[5] Government involvement, being branded as 'socialized medicine', was at first greeted with great suspicion by many wary organizations.[6] By the end of the 1930s, health care reforms of the CCMC were adopted.[7] These reforms involved 'the reorganisation and integration of medical services, the extension of private and public prepayment mechanisms (and) the collective planning of health care resources'.[8] These issues dominated American health policy debates for the next forty years.[9] Contemporarily the complex public policy of government-financed health and health insurance[10] has been adopted universally in a substantial manner.

In stark contrast with the history of the hospital, when people (from previous centuries) seeking health tried to stay out of the hospital, health care planning is now requested at governmental level to get ill people into hospital. Government has therefore increased its expenditure on health care in order to facilitate access to those who could not afford it otherwise.[11] Government expenditure can be stated as follows: Federal government spent

---

[4]   Other health-care providers also include Health Maintenance Organizations (HMOs).

[5]   Annas *et al. American Health Law* 13.

[6]   *Op. cit.* 13–17. The AMA especially objected to the CCMC's (Committee on the Costs of Medical Care) health care reforms.

[7]   Annas *et al. American Health Law* 17.

[8]   *Ibid.*

[9]   *Ibid.*

[10]  *Op. cit.* 13: Nationalized health insurance had been invented by the Germans.

[11]  Furrow *et al. Health Law* 666.

$12 billion on health care, the state and local governments $7 billion in 1967.[12] Federal government spent $196 billion, the state and local governments $73 billion in 1990.[13] In 1988 federal health care expenditures consumed 12% of the federal budget.[14] In 1991 government paid 41% of all personal health care and 54% of all hospital care.[15]

### 8.1.4 National Health Care Spending

The increased demand for health care has also led to the increase of the total amount society spends on health care and costs experienced by other payers.[16] National health care spending has increased steadily since the turn of the century.

National health care spending data was collected for the first time in 1929.[17] Physician services then consumed 28 per cent of all expenditures for health care, and hospitals only 19 per cent.[18] Hospital expenditure increased steadily and consumed 40 per cent of all national health costs by 1979.[19]

National expenditures on health care averaged $12.7 billion in 1950 and $41.9 billion in 1965.[20] In 1981, the total national health care expenditures amounted to $286 billion.[21] The United States spent $335 billion on national health care, in 1983. This amount equalled 10.8 per cent of the gross national product.[22] In 1990, national expenditures averaged $647 billion.[23] In 1991, the total national health care expenditures averaged $750 billion, of which

---

[12]  *Op. cit.* 661.

[13]  *Ibid.*

[14]  *Ibid.*

[15]  *Ibid.*

[16]  *Op. cit.* 666.

[17]  Annas *et al. American Health Law* 12.

[18]  *Ibid.*

[19]  Christoffel *Health* 105: *Id est* 85 billion dollars went towards hospital care. Annas *et al. American Health Law* 13: In the light of the fact that patient charges were insufficient to finance hospital care, unemployment increased and catastrophic medical bills emerged, major structural changes in health care financing seemed imminent. The hospital industry introduced major financial reforms, such as some sort of prepayment or insurance financing for hospital care.

[20]  Furrow *et al. Health Law* 661.

[21]  Silver *Health Costs and Payments* 1993 Grolier Electronic Publishing Inc.

[22]  Carlucci 1986 *Case & Comment* 34.

[23]  Furrow *et al. Health Law* 661.

physicians received 20% and hospitals 40%. 'The remainder was spent on private- and government-funded research, on construction and equipment purchases, public-health services, and other health-related expenditures. Private insurance covered about 50% of individual medical costs; federal and state governments spent close to $120 billion for reimbursement of Medicare and Medicaid costs.'[24] The Americans spent about $3900 per person on health care, totalling $942.5 billion in 1993. It has been predicted that if the current rate of growth continues, health care expenditures will consume almost a third of GNP (gross national product) by the year 2030.[25] Comprehensive reform of the health care delivery system has therefore become imperative.[26]

## 8.1.5  Health Care Costs

The unrealistic escalation of health costs has been attributed to certain factors: The inefficient consumption of health care costs has been caused by excess use of services by beneficiaries and excess expenditures by providers due to 'the 'free' nature of government care, and the cost-based form of reimbursement relied on until recently ...'.[27] The federal tax subsidy for employee health insurance has not only resulted in high insurance expenditures but has also escalated health costs.[28] Medical malpractice litigation which leads to the practise of defensive medicine has also been stated as a contributing factor.[29] Finally licensing laws have kept the cost of professional services exceptionally high.[30]

Furrow, Johnson, Jost and Schwartz[31] have most aptly selected and discussed approaches that can be considered as problem solving scenarios in the health care cost debate. The following approaches[32] were submitted: Competition, regulation, health (care) planning and rate review. Private

---

[24]  Silver *Health Costs and Payments* 1993 Grolier Electronic Publishing Inc.

[25]  Frankel 1994 *YLJ* 1297.

[26]  *Op. cit.* 1297, 1330–1331.

[27]  Furrow *et al. Health Law* 666.

[28]  *Ibid.*

[29]  *Ibid.*

[30]  *Ibid.*

[31]  *Op. cit.* 667. See also Christoffel *Health* 141.

[32]  All approaches and solutions herein stated are found in Furrow *et al. Health Law* 667. Compare Christoffel *Health* 141.

approaches namely utilization review, health maintenance organizations and preferred provider organizations were also proposed.

Other solutions comprise of governmental attempts to control costs of government health care programs by means of a Medicare prospective payment for hospitals and relative value payment schedules for doctors, Medicare and Medicaid fraud and abuse laws, and Peer Review Organizations. The latter solution involves national health insurance.

Only a brief overview of some of these solutions will be given, selecting them in accordance with their highest relevance to the subject matter.

### 8.1.5.1 Health care planning

Health care planning primarily involved state and national governmental efforts to 'mandate and regulate health planning'[33] in an attempt to curb health care costs. In the observance of governmental health goals, it concentrated foremost on the health needs of the community and therefore placed the hospital as individual institution (and its service area needs) first.[34]

Federal health planning was attempted through local health planning,[35] local planning funds,[36] federal funding of states,[37] and mandates provided by federal laws[38] which included the Hill-Burton Act of 1946,[39] the Comprehensive Health Planning and Public Health Service Amendments of 1966,[40] the Social Security Amendments of 1972,[41] the National Health Planning and Resources Development Act of 1974,[42] and the Social Security Amendments of 1983.[43]

---

[33]   Miller *Hospital Law* 95 (1986). Christoffel *Health* 141–145.

[34]   Miller *Hospital Law* 95 (1986).

[35]   Furrow *et al. Health Law* 684.

[36]   Miller *Hospital Law* 95 (1986).

[37]   Furrow *et al. Health Law* 684.

[38]   Miller *Hospital Law* 95 (1986).

[39]   Furrow *et al. Health Law* 684. Annas *et al. American Health Law* 25. Koeze *Healthcare* 411–414. Miller *Hospital Law* 95 (1986).

[40]   Miller *Hospital Law* 95 (1986).

[41]   *Ibid.*

[42]   *Op. cit.* 97–98. Furrow *et al. Health Law* 684. Christoffel *Health* 143.

[43]   Miller *Hospital Law* 95 (1986).

## 8.1.5.2  Antitrust

Antitrust is an approach to cost control which rejects planning and regulation in order to preserve a private competitive 'free market' system.[44] Federal state antitrust laws achieve this by prohibiting and eliminating anti-competitive practices and encouraging competition.[45] The primary federal laws such as the Sherman Anti-Trust Act, the Clayton Act, the Federal Trade Commission Act, and the Robinson-Patman Act forbid conspiracies to restrain trade, monopolization or attempts to monopolize, some exclusive dealing arrangements, acquisitions and mergers that have an anti-competitive effect, unfair or deceptive practices affecting competition and discriminatory pricing that lessens competition.[46]

Antitrust laws were also victoriously introduced to the health care field[47] and became applicable to the hospital industry and indeed all health care providers. Supreme court verdicts have confirmed this ruling exempting only certain state-compelled activities from antitrust liability.[48]

### 8.1.5.3  Health Maintenance Organization

A Health Maintenance Organization (HMO) 'is an entity that provides comprehensive health care services to an enrolled membership for a fixed, per capita, fee'.[49] HMOs are both providers and insurers of medical care.[50] There are usually four categories of HMOs based on their relationship with medical care providers.[51] Both federal and state law govern HMOs.[52] This

---

[44] Christoffel *Health* 145. Miller *Hospital Law* 83.

[45] *Ibid.*

[46] Miller *Hospital Law* 83–90. Christoffel *Health* 145–147. Furrow *et al. Health Law* 785–789.

[47] Furrow *et al. Health Law* 785–789. Miller *Hospital Law* 83–92. Christoffel *Health* 145–148. Hall and Ellman *Health Care* 186–215. Annas *et al. American Health Law* 796–797. Colton *Healthcare* 165–256.

[48] *Ibid.*

[49] Furrow *et al. Health Law* 716. Colton *Healthcare* 241–243.

[50] *Ibid.*

[51] *Ibid.* Furrow *et al. Health Law* 716 states: 'staff model HMOs directly employ physicians to provide medical care; group model HMOs contract with an independent, multi spe-cialty corporation or partnership of physicians to delivery care; network HMOs contract with a number of groups of physicians who also may serve patients not belonging to the HMO; and individual practice association (IPA) HMOs contract with an IPA, which in turn contracts with individual physicians to provide care in their offices'.

[52] Furrow *et al. Health Law* 716.

alternative health care delivery system is an employer-sponsored health plan enrolled by employees.[53] In 1981, 4% of employees were enrolled in HMOs and PPOs (Preferred Provider Organizations) compared to a 17% employee enrolment in HMOs and 16% in PPOs in 1989.[54] Employers in the private sector thus invest heavily in competitive strategies as a cure for their health cost problems.[55]

Health Maintenance Organizations (HMOs) and Independent Practice Associations (IPAs) have become a major party in the health care delivery system because they negotiate lower health care costs which the government and employers desperately seek.[56] HMOs and IPAs face the same vicarious and corporate liability as hospitals, since their services are provided by physicians who are either salaried or act as independent contractors.[57]

### 8.1.5.4 Preferred Provider organizations

Preferred Provider Organizations (PPOs) are organized systems of health care providers that agree to provide services on a negotiated basis to subscribers.[58] PPO subscribers may chose non-preferred providers — and are not limited to plan providers, (as in an HMO) — in which case they face financial disincentives such as deductibles or larger co-payments.[59] PPOs usually pay providers not on a capitation but on a fee-for-service basis.[60] PPOs usually face utilization review and quality assurance requirements. PPOs may be sponsored by physician groups, commercial insurers, hospitals, Blue-Cross/Blue Shield plans, investors, union trusts, or others.[61] PPOs have grown very rapidly and are heavily concentrated in certain states.[62]

---

[53] *Op. cit.* 715.

[54] *Op. cit.* 716.

[55] *Op. cit.* 716–717: Studies found that HMOs admit patients to hospitals 40% less often than do fee for service plans and use 40% less hospital days.

[56] Furrow *et al. Health Law* 273.

[57] *Ibid.* See *Boyd* v. *Albert Einstein Medical Center* 377 Pa. Super. 609, 547 A 2d 1229 (1988). The Superior Court of Pennsylvania discussed these issues.

[58] Furrow *et al. Health Law* 723. Colton *Healthcare* 241–243.

[59] Furrow *et al. Health Law* 723–724.

[60] *Op. cit.* 724.

[61] *Ibid.*

[62] *Ibid.*

## 8.1.5.5 Medicare

Medicare, which is a two-part programme of health insurance for the aged, was established by the 1965 Amendments to the Social Security Act.[63] All people who are 65 or older, or do comply with other relevant requirements, qualify for federal assistance with uniform benefits across the country.[64] Qualification rests without regard to financial need.[65] Medicare has assured broad and equitable access to qualitative health care for the elderly.[66]

## 8.1.5.6 Medicaid

Medicaid, authorized by Title XIX of the Social Security Act, is a federal law that provides medical care for those who cannot afford it.[67] Medical assistance is rendered to families with dependent children, the aged, blind, disabled and those who need rehabilitation and other services.[68] States pass their own laws to participate in funding, but all states have joined in the light of the fact that federal government grants more than fifty per cent of the financial support for Medicaid.[69] State implementation of this program therefore varies tremendously.[70]

Medicare and Medicaid fraud and abuse laws were promulgated to combat crime and — most importantly — to cut health care costs and the excessive provision and utilization of medical services.[71] The policing of cost-containment has also resulted in two programmes:

> First, the Medicare and Medicaid fraud and abuse laws attempt to police provider conduct to control costs, protect quality and encourage professional fidelity to patient interests. Second, the Medicare Utilization and Quality

---

[63]   It was established by Title XVIII of that Act. Miller *Hospital Law* 53–55. Annas *et al. American Health Law* 30. Peters *et al. Medical Practice* 27.

[64]   Miller *Hospital Law* 53. Furrow *et al. Health Law* 567–568. Nelson *Hospital Liability Law* 43. Annas *et al. American Health Law* 29–32. Christoffel *Health* 162–163. There are some regional variations.

[65]   Miller *Hospital Law* 53. Christoffel *Health* 162.

[66]   Furrow *et al. Health Law* 568.

[67]   Miller *Hospital Law* 57–59. Christoffel *Health* 164. Furrow *et al. Health Law* 568–570.

[68]   Annas *et al. American Health Law* 30–31. Miller *Hospital Law* 57. Christoffel *Health* 164–165. Furrow *et al. Health Law* 568–569.

[69]   Furrow *et al. Health Law* 570. Miller *Hospital Law* 58. Christoffel *Health* 164.

[70]   Christoffel *Health* 163–164. Miller *Hospital Law* 58–59.

[71]   Furrow *et al. Health Law* 748, 749–767. Miller *Hospital Law* 59–60.

Control Peer Review Organisation (PRO) program ... attempts to police the utilization and quality of Medicare financed care.[72]

Finally, lawyers have been more than encouraged to master the intricacies of Medicare and Medicaid reimbursement and relevant laws and to unravel forbidden schemes by earning the so-called 'pot of gold' by specializing in this field.[73]

### 8.1.5.7 Private insurance

The unique American private insurance market for health care or health service financing steadily emerged from the 1930s.[74] The AHA (American Hospital Association) along with state and local hospital groups initiated 'service-benefit' plans with exemption from tax benefits, to set up contracts between hospitals (providers) and subscribers.[75] The AHA sponsored the national Blue Cross Association (BCA), which was followed by the Blue Shield and Blue Cross plans.[76] Commercial insurance companies also emerged.[77] *In toto* this created private, employment-based insurance-type financing schemes and other schemes that separated the delivery of medical services from their financing.[78] This had left the elderly and the poor unattended,[79] which was later rectified.

### 8.1.5.8 National Health Insurance

National Health Insurance is accomplished by government involvement in health which assures universal access to medical care.[80] The United Kingdom and Sweden ensures direct government provision of health care; Canada furnishes government financing of privately provided health care and Germany has procured mandatory employer provision of health insurance.[81] The implementation of such a program in the United States of American has received some interest and was investigated by the Pepper

---

[72] Furrow *et al. Health Law* 748.

[73] *Op. cit.* 748–749.

[74] Annas *et al. American Health Law* 17, 21. Furrow *et al. Health Law* 534–535.

[75] Annas *et al. American Health Law* 18.

[76] *Op. cit.* 18–21. Furrow *et al. Health Law* 534–535.

[77] Annas *et al. American Health Law* 19. Furrow *et al. Health Law* 535.

[78] Annas *et al. American Health Law* 21. This issue became critical in the 1970s and 1980s.

[79] *Op. cit.* 22.

[80] Furrow *et al. Health Law* 602.

[81] *Op. cit.* 602.

Commission who failed to come up with a consensus proposal for health insurance.[82] Their proposal was accompanied by a price tag of $ 86.2 billion.[83] Recently other proposals have seen the light.[84]

### 8.1.5.9  Licensure and accreditation

Introduction: Governmental regulation and private accreditation of hospitals and other health care providers or facilities take place in virtually every state[85] of the United States. Multiple regulation which results from governmental involvement at every level and numerous agencies' prescriptions, create conflicting mandates for all health care facilities which is illustrated (for example) in the tension between health planning laws which seek co-operation and antitrust laws which seek competition.[86]

The regulating mechanisms that exist of standard-making organizations, can be divided into governmental agencies which grant licenses to hospitals and other health care facilities and private accrediting agencies or organizations which grant accreditation to hospitals and other health care providers. Governmental regulation is thus effected by licensure and the hospital industry makes use of a private authority which grants accreditation.[87] Licensure mainly differs from accreditation therein that it is a function of government and mandatory for hospitals.[88]

Providers of health care which are affected and restricted by these formidable regulating structures in a bid for quality assurance, are hospitals, nursing homes, freestanding emergency centers ('FECs'), ambulatory surgery clinics and other similar facilities.[89] Hospitals are, however, by far the most extensively regulated facilities of all.[90]

Agencies that are either regulatory or accrediting may focus on the institution as a whole. Other agencies focus on individual services such as a pharmacy or elevators and some agencies may direct either the entire

---

[82]  *Op. cit.* 783.

[83]  *Ibid.*

[84]  *Ibid.*

[85]  Hall *et* Ellman *Health Care* 134. Miller *Hospital Law* 38.

[86]  Miller *Hospital Law* 38.

[87]  Christoffel *Health* 121. Miller *Hospital Law* 38–39. Hall *et* Ellman *Health Care* 134–135.

[88]  Miller *Hospital Law* 38.

[89]  Hall *et* Ellman *Health Care* 134: The above-mentioned facilities are regulated by states through licensure statutes and regulations. States are now commencing to cover FECs and ambulatory surgery clinics by facilities licensing laws.

[90]  Miller *Hospital Law* 38.

hospital *or* its individual facilities depending on the special circumstances of a given situation.[91] The latter may be illustrated in the case of a certificate-of-need agency which must provide permission for a new hospital (*in toto*) or any new service(s) at a hospital.[92]

### 8.1.5.9.1 Licensure

Licensing statutes and regulations are promulgated by each state.[93] The state legislature establishes by law an administrative agency authority, which imposes standards that hospitals must meet, which grants licenses upon compliance and enforces continual performance.[94] In default of a license, a hospital cannot operate and when failing to comply with prescribed standards, loss of license or penalization follows.[95]

Major legal issues that are encountered in regulating hospitals through institutional licensure are: the authority for licensure, the scope of regulations, and the penalties for violations.[96] The statutory authority which is granted to the Department of Health of a state — in order to regulate hospitals — is protected and enforced by the Supreme Court, and the police power provides the state government with the necessary executive powers.[97]

Hospital licensing regulations regulate the organization of the hospital, requiring an organized governing body, an administrator and an organized medical staff.[98] The provision of certain basic services, an adequate nursing personnel and standards for facilities, equipment, personnel, safety, sanitation, infection control etc., building codes and fire safety codes are also addressed.[99] Courts have assessed the validity of prescribed standards on the merits of each case giving preference to more objective standards but have even 'upheld enforcement of subjective standards if fairly applied'.[100]

---

[91] *Op. cit.* 38–39.

[92] *Ibid.* The most recent form of health care facility regulation is certificate of need laws: Hall *et* Ellman *Health Care* 134.

[93] Miller *Hospital Law* 39.

[94] *Op. cit.* 39–40.

[95] *Ibid.*

[96] *Op. cit.* 39–42.

[97] *Op. cit.* 39: In 1980 the Pennsylvania Supreme Court confirmed the statutory authority of the department even though it interfered with and replaced the traditional authority of the hospital management: *Hospital Ass'n of Pa.* v. *MacLeod*, 487 Pa 516, 410 A 2d 731 (1980).

[98] Miller *Hospital Law* 40.

[99] *Ibid.*

[100] *Ibid.*

Administrative agencies have also been empowered to grant a waiver or variance as exceptions to specific rules or standards.[101] Waivers are however only granted when certain requirements are met.[102]

Non-compliance by hospitals to licensing laws or violation thereof leads to sanctions, which result in either revocation or suspension of hospital licenses, criminal penalties or fines, after being notified of specific violations and being granted an opportunity to be heard on the issue(s).[103] Hospitals can seek a judicial review in the case of an adverse decision by an agency in which case the court may overrule the agency's decision.[104]

### 8.1.5.9.2 Accreditation

The private hospital industry has established privately funded hospital standards-making organizations,[105] which regulate quality hospital care for American health care providers. These private authorities or organizations[106] grant private accreditation on substantial compliance with the standards promulgated,[107] and also provide a foundation for licensing and eligibility for federal funds.[108]

The most important and leading health care provider accreditation agency (private authority), is the Joint Commission on Accreditation of Health Care Organizations (JCAHO), (formerly Joint Commission on Accreditation of Hospitals (Standards) (JCAH)).[109] This body grants accreditation to hospitals and other health care facilities.[110] The JCAHO consists of representatives

---

[101] *Op. cit.* 40–41.

[102] *Ibid.* There must be '(1) … a substantial need for relief from the rule; (2) the public purpose will be better served by the exception; and (3) the exception will not create a hazard to the health and well-being of patients or others that is excessive in light of the public purpose being served.'

[103] Miller *Hospital Law* 41–42.

[104] *Ibid.*

[105] Dornette *Hospital Liability* 302. Miller *Hospital Law* 38.

[106] The American Osteopathic Association (AOA), Liaison Committee on Medical Education and the National Fire Protection Association (NFPA) are other accrediting bodies with accreditation programs: Christoffel *Health* 121. Dornette *Hospital Liability* 302. Miller *Hospital Law* 38–39.

[107] Dornette *Hospital Liability* 302. Miller *Hospital Law* 38. Christoffel *Health* 121. Hall *et* Ellman *Health Care* 135.

[108] Dornette *Hospital Liability* 302. Miller *Hospital Law* 38.

[109] Miller *Hospital Law* 38. Furrow *et al. Health Law* 100. Christoffel *Health* 121. Hall *et* Ellman *Health Care* 135. Rutchik 1994 *VLR* 556–558.

[110] Hall *et* Ellman *Health Care* 135. Dornette *Hospital Liability* 302. Miller *Hospital Law* 38–39.

from the American Dental Association, the American College of Physicians, the American College of Surgeons, the American Medical Association (AMA) and the American Hospital Association (AHA).[111] The JCAH was founded in 1952, being the successor to the American College of Surgeons Hospital Standardization Program, which was established in 1919.[112] The JCAH was organized by the American Medical Association, the American College of Physicians, the American Hospital Association, the American College of Surgeons and the Canadian Hospital Association.[113]

The Accreditation Manual for Hospitals (AMH), comprises of an exposition of the minimum national standards that hospitals must follow to receive accreditation, and is published annually.[114] JCAHO standards relate basically to patient care and the safety of hospital buildings.[115] These standards dictate to a large extent the contents of a hospital's bylaws and its internal organizational structure.[116] JCAHO accreditation is vitally important to a hospital's economic viability, since the status of the hospital can only benefit from a voluntary accreditation because of fierce competition in the market-place.[117]

Several states delegate their licensing function to the JCAHO,[118] whereby the accreditation of the organization serves as a basis for partial or full licensure, without further state inspection.[119] Medicare and Medicaid participation is approved in a similar way. All JCAHO-accredited hospitals are automatically deemed acceptable by the Federal Medicare and Medicaid

---

[111] Miller *Hospital Law* 38. Christoffel *Health* 121. Furrow *et al. Health Law* 100. Dornette *Hospital Liability* 303 footnote 1.

[112] Furrow *et al. Health Law* 100. Christoffel *Health* 121. See Jost The Joint Commission on Accreditation of Hospitals: Private Regulation of Health Care and the Public Interest 24 BCL Rev 835 (1983), on the history of the JCAHO: Louisell *et* Williams *Medical Malpractice* § 15.02 15–9.

[113] *Johnson* v. *Misericordia Community Hospital* 99 Wis 2d 708, 301 NW 2d 156 (1981). Louisell and Williams *Medical Malpractice* §15.02 15–9. See also Rutchik 1994 *VLR* 556.

[114] The Accreditation Manual for Hospitals (AMH) is the primary source of minimum national standards: Louisell and Williams *Medical Malpractice* § 15.02 15–10. Rutchik 1994 *VLR* 556. Miller *Hospital Law* 38.

[115] Dornette *Hospital Liability* 302. Louisell and Williams *Medical Malpractice* §15.02 15–10.

[116] Louisell and Williams *Medical Malpractice* § 15.02 15–10.

[117] Rutchik 1994 *VLR* 556.

[118] This is done by incorporating its standards by reference: Hall *et* Ellman *Health Care* 135.

[119] Miller *Hospital Law* 38.

programs.[120] As a result of the far-reaching results flowing from JCAHO approval, most hospitals therefore seek JCAHO accreditation.[121]

The abdication of regulatory oversight by the public sector to the private industry has been heralded as a most controversial issue.[122] The fusing of private accreditation with public regulation regarding quality-control, ('deeming'), has, however, been upheld as constitutional.[123]

The JCAHO has accumulated unknown power, and this has resulted in the fact that hospitals do not risk jeopardizing its accreditation status in view of its potential business, liability and other consequences.[124] The detailed organizational, procedural[125] and other standards for the structure and operation of a hospital as imposed by the JCAHO, are therefore increasingly enjoying consideration.

The promulgated standards have the following important effect: Explicitly formulated standards establish specific duties of care[126] to be complied with by providers of health care. This in turn determines and expands directly the liability of hospitals and other providers of health care. Hospital liability[127] is therefore affected dramatically by the JCAHO and its regulatory powers. In the light of the far-reaching consequences the standards-making organizations and their promulgated standards have on the expanding liability of hospitals and other providers of health care, special precaution must be taken with the precise formulation and interpretation of standards.

Standards must be reasonably accessible and knowledgeable to relevant parties, reasonably achievable by hospitals and reasonably enforceable by pre-trial agreeing parties or by courts.[128] By sophisticating voluntary standard-making procedures and giving them due consideration before

---

[120] Hall *et* Ellman *Health Care* 135. Miller *Hospital Law* 38. Christoffel *Health* 122. Dornette *Hospital Liability* 305–306. Both internship and residency programs are also contingent upon JCAHO approval.

[121] Miller *Hospital Law* 38. Rutchik 1994 *VLR* 556.

[122] Furrow *et al. Health Law* 101. Hall *et* Ellman *Health Care* 135.

[123] Furrow *et al. Health Law* 101. Hall *et* Ellman *Health Care* 135. *Cospito* v. *Heckler* 742 F 2d 72 (3d *Circa* 1984).

[124] Hall *et* Ellman *Health Care* 135.

[125] *Ibid.*

[126] Dornette *Hospital Liability* 302.

[127] *Ibid.*

[128] *Op. cit.* 322.

necessitating their enforcement — for example in arranging proper education scenario's in hospitals — many a negligent tragedy may be averted.[129]

### 8.1.5.10  Conclusion

The American health care industry and its health care delivery system symbolizes a most complicated enigma consisting of political strategies, governmental laws and interventions, professional medical rationalized structures and 'free market' competition principles which strive for equality. It is also a mix of private and public payments, and is enormously costly.[130] A veritable objective perspective of the whole system, and ultimately the provision of valuable and redeeming solutions, are to say the least, extremely difficult.

## 8.2  THE HOSPITAL IN THE USA

### 8.2.1  The Hospital

The hospital industry and therefore the hospital in the USA, was once preceded by the infirmaries of public almshouses, which were public institutions.[131] Later, independent state or local institutions called 'hospitals' served the sick, the poor and the homeless.[132] The first American general hospital was established in 1751 by the Philadelphia Quakers, who built it for the sick.[133] The hospitals were also public institutions but were later supplemented by private, 'voluntary' hospitals, financed by bequest or donation, in the late eighteenth and early nineteenth centuries. The voluntary hospitals provided care for patients with some prospect of recovery. The public almshouse still attended to the incurable, to those with infectious diseases, the homeless, elderly and the destitute.[134]

The late 1800s, was a period which enhanced the hospital's image by introducing modern medicine, sophisticated surgical techniques, and the physician's attendance. The nineteenth century introduced antisepsis,

---

[129] In this regard compare Dornette *Hospital Liability* 324.

[130] Silver *Health-Care Systems* 1993 Grolier Electronic Publishing Inc.

[131] Annas *et al. American Health Law* 10. *Supra* 3.4.1.

[132] *Ibid.*

[133] Berkman *Hospital* 1993 Grolier Electronic Publishing Inc.

[134] Annas *et al. American Health Law* 10.

anaesthesia and X-ray diagnosis. The hospital of the late nineteenth-century, trained physicians, accommodated physicians in positions at the hospital and gave them the opportunity to expand their skills and financial status by treating private patients. The nursing profession developed simultaneously.[135]

The nineteenth-century hospitals only provided institutionalized care for the poor and desperate who were sometimes forced to go there and even apply for sponsorship for admission. These hospitals were characterized by abysmal hygienic conditions, were completely overcrowded and had little or primitive medical knowledge. Patients who were financially secure, were still treated at home or in the physician's office.[136]

The twentieth century brought the patient to the hospital and the physician's office, and traditional healing at home gave way to modern medicine.[137]

In 1900 only a small number of patients were paying hospitals.[138] During the 1920s about one half of hospital patients paid for their services which made up over two-thirds of all hospital income in the USA.[139]

The hospital's major transformation from shed for the poor to modern scientific-orientated institution was airborne in the 1930s.[140] The hospital became known for its medical healing technology, techniques and skills, supported and effected by a bureaucratic organizational personnel structure consisting of many capable medical professionals.[141]

Hospitals are nowadays operated by the federal government through the 'Veterans Administration, the Department of Defence, and the armed services as well as administering Public Health Service and Indian Health Service facilities, prison hospitals and special institutions run by the Alcohol, Drug Abuse and Mental Health Administration'.[142] One or more hospitals which provide care of the mentally ill, the retarded and those who

---

[135]  *Op. cit.* 10 –11. Berkman *Hospital* 1993 Grolier Electronic Publishing Inc.

[136]  Annas *et al. American Health Law* 10. Berkman *Hospital* 1993 Grolier Electronic Publishing Inc.

[137]  Annas *et al. American Health Law* 10.

[138]  *Op. cit.* 13.

[139]  *Ibid.*

[140]  Annas *et al. American Health Law* 12.

[141]  Physicians especially became dependent on hospitals for their livelihood (practising hospital-based medicine) — even remaining independent contractors — owing unknown loyalty to organized medicine and its discipline. See Annas *et al. American Health Law* 12 in this regard. See also Berkman *Hospital* 1993 Grolier Electronic Publishing Inc.

[142]  Berkman *Types of Hospitals* 1993 Grolier Electronic Publishing Inc.

suffer from tuberculosis, are operated by every state.[143] Hospitals have become modern institutional providers of health care and remain the centre of the American health-care system.[144]

### 8.2.2 The American Hospital Industry

The growth in the number of hospitals in the United States can be indicated as follows:

| Year | Hospitals | Beds |
|------|-----------|------|
| 1873[145] | 178 | |
| 1900[146] | 4,000 + | 35,500 |
| 1909[147] | 4,359 | |
| 1930[148] | 7,000 | 922, 000 |
| 1988[149] | 7,500 + | |
| 1991[150] | { 5,400 community hospitals | 900,000 |
| | {   500 long-term hospitals | 2,000,000 |
| | {20,000 nursing homes | 2,000,000 |

**Public hospitals[151]**
Public hospitals can be created by the acts of state, county or municipal authorities. Those governmental units control the public hospitals both economically and managerially. For example — unlike private hospitals — the members of the public hospital's governing body are often appointed by elected officials or elected by the public.

---

[143] *Ibid.*

[144] Koeze *Healthcare* 410.

[145] Christoffel *Health* 105. Annas *et al. American Health Law* 11. Berkman *Hospital* Grolier Electronic Publishing Inc.

[146] *Ibid.*

[147] *Ibid.*

[148] *Ibid.*

[149] Southwick and Slee *Hospital Law* 134: The United States had approximately 7,000–7,500 or more hospitals in the mid-1980s (1988) of which more than 1,200 were investor-owned, profit-making organizations. According to Berkman *Types of Hospitals* 1993 Grolier Electronic Publishing Inc., there were over 7,500 hospitals in the US in the mid-1980s.

[150] Silver *The US System* 1993 Grolier Electronic Publishing Inc.

[151] Smith *Hospital* § 1.01 [2] 1–3.

**Private hospitals**[152]

Privately owned hospitals can be categorized into three groups: (i) voluntary; (ii) investor-owned; and (iii) multi-unit hospital systems.

### 8.2.3  Hospital Organization

Most hospitals' organization includes a governing body or governing board, an administrator, and an organized medical staff,[153] regardless of the type of hospital. The governing board has the ultimate responsibility and legal authority (i) to establish policies and goals, (ii) to appoint the administrator, medical staff members and award individual clinical privileges and compensation, (iii) to review and evaluate the professional performance of lay administrators and medical staff.[154] The board delegates responsibility and authority to the administrator to manage everyday hospital business within the policies established by the board.[155] The medical staff are organized and have a delegated responsibility and authority to provide quality medical services in the hospital, subject to the board's ultimate responsibility.[156]

### 8.2.4  The Legal Basis

A hospital which is also an institutional provider of health care, is an independent legal entity.[157] The legal basis[158] of the hospital establishes the health facility and determines the type and nature of the hospital. American hospitals can be divided into various, but basically five types of organiza-tions.[159] On the ground of their legal basis, we distinguish between for-profit corporations, non-profit corporations, governmental institutions, as well as

---

[152] *Ibid.*

[153] Miller *Hospital Law* 14, 20. Pozgar *Health* 198–199. Berkman *Hospital Organization* 1993 Grolier Electronic Publishing Inc. Southwick and Slee *Law of Hospital* 114–120. Peters *et al. Medical Practice* 131–134.

[154] Southwick and Slee *Law of Hospital* 114–115. Miller *Hospital Law* 14, 20, 22. Pozgar *Health* 198–200.

[155] Miller *Hospital Law* 14.

[156] *Ibid.*

[157] Miller *Hospital Law* 14. Peters *et al. Medical Practice* 129.

[158] *Ibid.* 'Most hospitals are organized as corporations.'

[159] *Ibid.* Southwick and Slee *Law of Hospital* 106. Pozgar *Health* 198–199.

sole proprietorships and partnerships.[160] Hospitals may thus be classified as one of these five business organizations.[161] These health care facilities derive their specific powers, restricted duties, governance structure and therefore their discerning characteristics from their legal basis.[162]

## 8.3 HOSPITAL LIABILITY

### 8.3.1 Charitable Immunity in the USA

A law of medical malpractice was already established in every American state by the 1850s or later, and was based mainly on English precedents.[163] Most American hospitals enjoyed both charitable and sovereign immunity from liability for medical malpractice from 1861 until the 1950s.[164] The doctrine of charitable immunity (once again) relieved charitable institutions such as charitable hospitals from liability.[165] The doctrine was based on the assumption that donations and endowments which were kept in trust for charitable purposes, could not be diverted to the purpose of paying damages in cases of wrongful injury to patients by servants.[166] The American courts had adopted this English common law doctrine during the nineteenth century.[167]

In the United States, the doctrine of charitable immunity was first applied to a hospital in 1876, in the case of *McDonald* v. *Massachusetts General*

---

[160] Miller *Hospital Law* 14–15. Pozgar *Health* 198–199. Berkman *Types of Hospitals* 1993 Grolier Electronic Publishing Inc. Annas *et al. American Health Law* 11.

[161] Southwick and Slee *Law of Hospital* 103.

[162] Miller *Hospital Law* 14–15. See also Pozgar *Health* 199.

[163] Chapman *Physicians* 103.

[164] Louisell and Williams *Medical Malpractice* §15.01 15–2, §17.01 17–3.

[165] Granville *et al. Legal Medicine* 111. Roach *et al. Law* 205–207. Kelly and Jones *Healthcare* 329–332. Furrow *et al. Health Law* 222–224. Southwick *Hospital Liability* 235–237. Annas *et al. American Health Law* 437–439. Smith *Hospital* §2.01 2–2, §2.06 [1] 2–22. Richards and Rathbun *Risk* 75. Morris and Moritz *Law* 387. Southwick and Slee *Law of Hospital* 539–542. Pegalis and Wachsman *Law* 223. Mobilia 1985 *SCLR* 601. Moore and Kramer *Medical Malpractice* 103. Spero 1979 *TRIAL* 22. Oerlikoff and Vanagunas *Hospitals* 7, 9. Werthmann *Malpractice* 1–6. McWilliams and Russell 1996 *SCLR* 432, 434–438.

[166] *Ibid.*

[167] *Ibid.*

*Hospital.*[168] The court had relied upon an 1861 case of *Holliday* v. *St Leonard's*[169] which set an English precedent in holding that the hospital as charitable corporation, was immune from liability as long as it had exercised due care in selecting its employees. Unfortunately the court had failed to note that the Queen's Bench had rejected the *Holliday* case in 1871.[170] In 1885, the *McDonald* case was confirmed in *Perry* v. *House of Refuge*[171] in which charitable immunity was applied. However, a Rhode Island[172] court rejected this doctrine in 1879 and questioned the viability of the *Holliday* case.

'Historically, many jurisdictions applied some variant of the rule that private charitable hospitals were entitled to immunity from the tortious conduct of their doctors and nurses.'[173] The majority of jurisdictions have, however, on a state by state basis, revoked the doctrine of charitable immunity for hospitals over the last few decades.[174] Since the landmark decision of *President & Directors of Georgetown College* v. *Hughes*,[175] the majority of courts have not only abrogated the traditional doctrine of charitable immunity, but imposed tort liability on charitable hospitals as they do on other private institutions.[176] More than thirty jurisdictions have as a result rejected this doctrine, and the remainder have retained 'immunity to the extent of statutory ceilings on recoverable damages, or only up to available coverage, or as to charity care'.[177] The doctrine is now clearly discarded by the majority of courts, because the rationale or reasons for the

---

[168]    120 Mass 432, 21 Am Rep 529 (1876): A Massachusetts Supreme Court decision which has since been overruled by statute. Louisell and Williams *Medical Malpractice* § 17.02 17–5. Smith *Hospital* § 2.06 [1] 2–22. Granville *et al. Legal Medicine* 111. Kelly and Jones *Healthcare* 329. Annas *et al. American Health Law* 438–439.

[169]    142 Eng Rep 769 (1861). Louisell and Williams *Medical Malpractice* § 17.02 17–5.

[170]    *Foreman* v. *Mayor of Canterbury* LR 6 QB 214 (1871). Louisell and Williams *Medical Malpractice* § 17.02 17–5.

[171]    63 Md 20 52 Am Rep 495 (1885). A Maryland decision.

[172]    *Glavin* v. *Rhode Island Hospital* 12 RI 411 34 Am Rep 675 (1879). Louisell and Williams *Medical Malpractice* §17.02 17–6.

[173]    Louisell and Williams *Medical Malpractice* § 17.02 17–4. Smith *Hospital* § 2.06 [4] 2–23.

[174]    Smith *Hospital* § 2.06 [4] 2–23. Southwick *Hospital Liability* 235. Kelly and Jones *Healthcare* 331.

[175]    130 F 2d 810 (DC Cir 1942). Annas *et al. American Health Law* 444. Louisell and Williams *Medical Malpractice* § 17.02 17–9. Kelly and Jones *Healthcare* 330. Furrow *et al. Health Law* 224.

[176]    Louisell and Williams *Medical Malpractice* § 17.02 17–9.

[177]    Furrow *et al. Health Law* 224. Annas *et al. American Health Law* 444.

implementation of this doctrine no longer prevails in a modern society.[178] For example, profit and non-profit health-care enterprises, their medical professionals and other medical staff are sufficiently covered by insurance.[179] The national trend has therefore been toward the revocation of immunities both charitable and governmental.[180] Consequently, due to the decline of immunity, 'hospital liability has been one of the most dramatically changing areas of personal injury law'.[181] The dramatic expansion of hospital liability law,[182] has involved the development of various legal grounds, theories and/or doctrines which establish hospital liability for injuries to patients due to medical malpractice. The expansion of hospital liability thus acknowledges the hospital industry as the most dynamic health care provider industry, consisting of institutional health care providers of which the hospital is the most important health care facility, delivering vital health care and medical services. The hospital industry therefore has become the most important sector of the health care industry.

## 8.4 LEGAL GROUNDS OF HOSPITAL LIABILITY IN THE USA

### 8.4.1 Indirect or Vicarious Hospital Liability

#### 8.4.1.1 *Respondeat superior*

Vicarious liability founded on the legal doctrine of *respondeat superior* (let the master respond (or answer)) implies that the master or employer is liable to a third party for the wrong or tort of a servant or employee committed within the scope of employment.[183] This doctrine had already existed in

---

[178] Southwick *Hospital Liability* 235–236. Smith *Hospital* § 2.06 [4] 2–23, 2–25.

[179] *Ibid.* There are also other reasons not relevant to this discussion.

[180] Smith *Hospital* § 2.07 2–26. According to Louisell and Williams *Medical Malpractice* § 17.02 17–9: 'The current position on charitable immunity is summarized in section 895E of the Restatement (Second) of Torts, which provides that 'one engaged in a charitable, educational, religious or benevolent enterprise or activity is not for that reason immune from tort liability '. '

[181] Southwick *Hospital Liability* 236. The components of medical legal liability are found within the basic precepts of tort law: Hoffman *et al. Legal Medicine* 35.

[182] McWilliams and Russell 1996 *SCLR* 432–433.

[183] Southwick *Hospital Liability* 237, 238–250. Smith *Hospital* § 3.02 [1] 3–4, § 3.02 [3] 3–5 to 3–7. Kelly and Jones *Healthcare* 336–355. Louisell and Williams *Medical Malpractice* § 15.03 15–15 to 15–19, § 16.01 16–2. *McCafferty and Meyer* Liability 321–323. Annas

common law where the master had been held liable for the damage proximately caused by the wrongful conduct of his servant(s), and has been accepted and ultimately applied in American law inclusive of the American medical malpractice and American hospital liability law.[184]

The Restatement (Second) of Agency,[185] explicitly relates liability under *respondeat superior* as follows:

> A master is subject to liability for the torts of his servants committed while acting in the scope of their employment.

Vicarious liability for medical malpractice does not only include hospital liability but also[186] (i) the liability of a physician for an employee's torts; (ii) the liability of a physician for torts in a group practice; (iii) the liability of a corporation's individual shareholders for torts of a shareholder or employee of a corporation; (iv) the liability of a physician for the torts of other physicians all attending the same patient; (v) the liability of an attending staff physician at a hospital for the torts of another physician or employee of the hospital; (vi) the liability of an employment agency for the torts of an employee which it had provided on a temporary basis; (vii) the liability of an HMO or PPO for the torts of a physician under contract to provide services to subscribers of a medical plan; (viii) a hospital's medical staff's liability for malpractice committed in the hospital.

Concerning the health and medical care provider industry, the hospital can be held vicariously liable under the doctrine of *respondeat superior* by the American courts, for the negligent acts committed by its employees within the scope of their employment.[187]

---

*et al. American Health Law* 444–447. Furrow *et al. Health Law* 224–226. Southwick and Slee *Law of Hospital* 540–554. Pozgar *Health* 206–207. Miller *Hospital Law* 192–194.Pegalis and Wachsman *Law* 256–303. Werthmann *Malpractice* 8, 9–13. Oerlikoff and Vanagunas *Hospitals* 3. Reuter 1994 *JLM* 495. McWilliams and Russell 1996 *SCLR* 438–445. Mobilia 1985 *SCLR* 597–604. Cunningham 1975 *WLR* 385–397. Spero 1979 *TRIAL* 22–27. Moore and Kramer *Medical Malpractice* 103–112.

[184] *Ibid.* (With special reference to Smith *Hospital* § 3.02 [1] 3–4.)

[185] Restatement (Second) of Agency § 250. Louisell and Williams *Medical Malpractice* § 16.01 16–2, § 228 (1958). Smith *Hospital* § 3.02 [1] 3–4: § 250. McCafferty and Meyer *Liability* 321: §219 (1) (1958).

[186] Louisell and Williams *Medical Malpractice* § 16.01 16–2 to 16–3: (i) to (viii).

[187] *Supra* footnote 183. Smith *Hospital* § 3.01 3–2. McWilliams and Russell 1996 *SCLR* 438.

### *8.4.1.2 Background*

In 1914, the New York Court of Appeals considered the application of the doctrine of *respondeat superior* to hospitals in **Schloendorff v. Society of New York Hospital**.[188] Two surgeons had performed unauthorized surgery in a non-profit charitable hospital. Following the operation, gangrene developed in the plaintiff's left arm, resulting in several fingers being amputated. Action was brought by the plaintiff against the hospital and physicians. The Court of Appeals eventually confirmed the trial court's decision, in favour of the hospital. Judge Cardozo established the hospital's exemption from liability for the negligence of its physicians and nurses on two grounds. Firstly, the doctrine of charitable immunity which exempts the hospital from liability was approved. It was held that once the benefit or services of a charitable institution was accepted, such a person impliedly waived any rights of action for malpractice and for the negligence of the servants administering such charity. The implied waiver rationale was, however, found to be inapplicable because the unauthorized surgery was an intentional tort (battery) and not a negligent action.[189] Secondly, the court founded the hospital's immunity to liability on the application of the doctrine of *respondeat superior*. The true ground for the hospital's exemption from liability was held to be 'that the relation between a hospital and its physician is not that of master-servant'.[190] The physicians were supposedly independent contractors pursuing independent callings. The determination of the status of the relationship was held to be dependent upon the hospital's right to control the medical acts of the physicians. The hospital was held to lack the necessary element of control without which vicarious hospital liability could not be established. The court consequently held that the doctrine of *respondeat superior* did not impose hospital liability for the negligence of physicians whilst exercising professional judgment and expertise, where hospitals failed to be able to exercise control over such expertise to practice medicine.[191] It was, however, found that hospital liability could be incurred for the administration or ministerial acts of its employees.[192] Control was

---

[188] 211 NY 125 105 NE 92 (1914). Smith *Hospital* § 3.02 [1] 3–4 to 3–5. Louisell and Williams *Medical Malpractice* § 15.03 15–16 to 15–17. McCafferty and Meyer *Liability* 318–319. Granville *et al. Legal Medicine* 111. Mobilia 1985 *SCLR* 597–598. Cunningham 1975 *WLR* 389–390. Werthmann *Malpractice* 9 and footnote 3.

[189] *Schloendorff* 93.

[190] *Schloendorff* 94.

[191] *Schloendorff* 94.

[192] *Ibid.*

thus acknowledged as an essential element to determine the master-servant relationship.

As a consequence of this judgment, injured patients had no recourse against institutional or corporate hospital entities for injuries received as a result of negligent hospital treatment, for decades. More than forty years later, the hospital's immunity to liability based on *respondeat superior* was fortunately overruled.

In 1957, the New York Court of Appeals addressed the doctrine of charitable immunity and the distinction between professional and ministerial tasks in ***Bing* v. *Thunig*.**[193] The plaintiff had sustained severe burns to her body during surgery. The Court of Appeals in no uncertain terms stated their clear disapproval of, and indeed rejected, the charitable immunity doctrine. It was held that hospitals were to be liable and should bear their responsibilities as do all other employers. Hospitals were no longer to be excluded from liability by their exemption from the universal rule of *respondeat superior*. Hospital immunity from liability was no longer required to ensure economic existence, since liability insurance was available which protected the hospital as a business enterprise. The court also rejected the classification of physicians and nurses as independent contractors rather than employees for lack of control over their skills, as well as the 'highly elusive' distinction between medical and administrative acts.

The court stated:

> The doctrine of *respondeat superior* is grounded on firm principles of law and justice. Liability is the rule, immunity the exception. ... Present-day hospitals, as their manner or operation plainly demonstrates, do far more than furnish facilities for treatment. ... Certainly, the person who avails himself of 'hospital facilities' expects that the hospital will attempt to cure him, not that its nurses or other employees will act on their own responsibility. Hospitals should, in short, shoulder the responsibilities borne by everyone else. There is no reason to continue their exemption from the universal rule of *respondeat superior*. The test should be, for these institutions, whether charitable or profit-making, as it is for every other employer, was the person who committed the negligent injury-producing act one of its employees, and if he was, was he acting within the scope of his employment?[194]

---

[193] 2 NY 3d 656, 143 NE 2d 3, 163 NYS 2d 3 (NY 1957). Louisell and Williams *Medical Malpractice* § 15.03 15–16 to 15–17. Smith *Hospital* § 3.02 [2] 3–5 to 3–6. Werthmann *Malpractice* 9–10. Furrow *et al. Health Law* 222–223. Granville *et al. Legal Medicine* 111–112. Kelly and Jones *Healthcare* 330–331, 337–338. Southwick *Hospital Liability* 242–243. Southwick and Slee *Law of Hospital* 547. Mobilia 1985 *SCLR* 598–599. Cunningham 1975 *WLR* 390–392. Annas *et al. American Health Law* 444. Morris and Moritz *Law* 389–390. McWilliams and Russell 1996 *SCLR* 435.

[194] 2 NY 2d 666–667. 143 NE 2d at 8. 163 NYS 2d at 11–12 (NY 1957).

The doctrine of charitable immunity has subsequently been phased out. Courts are no longer exempting hospitals from liability and allow for full recovery for wrongful conduct which causes injury to patients. Except for the remnants of charitable immunity which is upheld through statute by a few states, 'the doctrine has been all but abolished'.[195] Various reasons[196] have been presented for the rejection of the doctrine of charitable immunity by most courts: The compensation of patients injured by medical malpractice has become an important public policy. Institutional and other health care providers have obtained liability insurance from insurance companies which provide compensation. Immunity from liability could adversely affect medical competence and the quality of care and diligence of medical personnel. Charitable hospital patients should also be compensated for injuries, as are patients of other hospitals.

### 8.4.1.3 Traditional elements of vicarious liability

Traditional elements[197] which impute liability under the *respondeat superior* doctrine are:

8.4.1.3.1    Master-servant relationship (employer-employee);

8.4.1.3.2    Wrongful act committed by the employee

8.4.1.3.3    Within the scope of his employment.

8.4.1.3.1    Employer-employee relationship

Hospitals have become vicariously liable under the *respondeat superior* theory for the malpractice and negligence of their employed physicians and nurses, which occur in the course of their employment.[198] Moore and Kramer have enumerated 43 cases in which hospitals have been held liable for the acts or omissions of employed physicians, nurses or other staff employees. The cases cited were instances 'in which liability was imposed or in which a factual issue as to the hospital's liability existed, for jury determination'.[199]

---

[195] Granville *et al. Legal Medicine* 112. See *supra* the discussion on Charitable Immunity.

[196] Granville *et al. Legal Medicine* 111–112. Annas *et al. American Health Law* 444–445. Southwick and Slee *Law of Hospital* 539.

[197] Pozgar *Health* 206–207. Southwick *Hospital Liability* 238. Louisell and Williams *Medical Malpractice* § 15.03 15–15 to 15–16. Southwick and Slee *Law of Hospital* 542. McCafferty and Meyer *Liability* 321–323. Reuter 1994 *JLM* 496. McWilliams and Russel 1996 *SCLR* 438–439.

[198] Moore and Kramer *Medical Malpractice* 103. Kelly and Jones *Healthcare* 337–348. Southwick *Hospital Liability* 237. Southwick and Slee *Law of Hospital* 542.

[199] Moore and Kramer *Medical Malpractice* 104–106.

(1)　　Physician-employees

In order to determine whether an employer-employee relationship exists for purposes of imposing vicarious hospital liability in terms of *respondeat superior*, courts scrutinize various factors. They review the

(i)　　the financial arrangement[200]

(ii)　　the physical (facility) setup[201] and

(iii)　　the patient choice[202]

*The financial arrangement*

The justification for the imposition of vicarious hospital liability in terms of the doctrine of *respondeat superior*, is amongst others contained in the payment of a salary or wage to the physician-employee.[203] American courts have paid attention to factors such as whether a salary arrangement existed between the hospital and the physician, in order to determine whether the

---

[200]　Kelly and Jones *Healthcare* 343:

The financial arrangement:

- whether the physician receives a salary form the hospital;
- whether the patient receives only one bill for the services of both the hospital and the physician;
- the extent to which the doctor's fees are included in the facility's combined bill; and
- in the case of an HMO, whether the member physician is on a lump-sum, 'capitation' system of compensation or the more traditional 'fee-for-services' system.

[201]　Kelly and Jones *Healthcare* 344:

The Physical Setup:

- whether the doctor is prohibited from having his or her own private office located outside of the facility;
- whether the physician has an office inside the facility;
- whether the hospital provides the equipment, staff, room, or radiology services used in the physician's practice;
- the explicit terms of the contract regarding facilities and services between the facility and its physicians;
- whether the physician is a 'resident' physician technically considered to be employed by the university that also operates the hospital; and
- whether a 'resident' physician on rotation at a non-university hospital is still within the control of the university hospital.

[202]　Kelly and Jones *Healthcare* 345:

Patient Choice:

- whether the patient has any choice in selecting the physician or whether the hospital arbitrarily assigns; and
- whether there is a pre-existing patient-physician relationship outside the facility's treatment plan.

[203]　Southwick and Slee *Law of Hospital* 546–547. Southwick *Hospital Liability* 242–243.

employer-employee relationship exists.[204] It has been held that where a hospital paid the physician a salary, the latter would be the employee of the hospital.[205] Even the payment of a part-time salary is considered adequate to render a physician an employee of the institution.[206] In *Niles* v. *City of San Rafael* [207] the hospital was held liable for a part-time salaried part-time employee, who was also a director of a hospital pediatrics department who happened to be in the emergency room of the hospital at the time of the incident. In *James* v. *Holder* [208] the hospital was held vicariously liable for a private practising physician who was also a part-time employee.

A list of other factors which are also taken into account in order to determine whether an agent is a servant or an independent contractor, is found in the Restatement (Second) of Agency §220 (1957).[209]

## Following physician's orders
The general principle that applies is that non-physician staff members are generally considered 'not responsible for the diagnosis and treatment of patients'.[210] Thus there is no staff negligence and consequently no health care

---

[204] McCafferty and Meyer *Liability* 323.

[205] In *Mayers* v. *Litow* 154 Cal App 2d 413, 316 P 2d 351 (1957), the physician did at no time receive any payment from the hospital, and was therefore considered an independent contractor of the hospital. McCafferty and Meyer *Liability* 323.

[206] Southwick and Slee *Law of Hospital* 546. Southwick *Hospital Liability* 242.

[207] 42 Cal App 3d 260, 116 Cal Rptr 801 (1974).

[208] 34 AD 2d 632, 309 NYS 2d 385 (1970). See also *Newton County* v. *Nicholson* 132 Ga App 164, 207 SE 2d 659 (1974).

[209] 1. The factors are:

  (a) the extent of control which, by the agreement, the master may exercise over the details of the work;

  (b) whether or not the one employed is engaged in a distinct occupation or business;

  (c) the kind of occupation, with reference to whether, in the locality, the work is usually done under the direction of the employer or by a specialist without supervision;

  (d) the skill required in the particular occupation;

  (e) whether the employer or the workman supplies the instrumentalities, tools, and the place of work for the person doing the work;

  (f) the length of time for which the person is employed;

  (g) the method of payment, whether by time or by the job;

  (h) whether or not the work is a part of the regular business of the employer;

  (i) whether or not the parties believe they are creating the relation of master and servant; and

  (j) whether the principal is or is not in business.

In *Stewart* v. *Midani* 525 F Supp 843 (ND Ga 1981) a similar list of factors relevant to the hospital context was discussed. McWilliams and Russell 1996 *SCLR* 439–440.

[210] Kelly and Jones *Healthcare* 340.

facility (hospital) liability, for failure to question physician's orders where the handling of the case was not so obviously negligent that the staff member was obliged to intervene and order a different treatment.[211] The employing healthcare facility and their nurses have been exonerated for following physicians orders. But some cases imply that the institution will be liable when its staff fails to question the doctor's order.[212] The duty to disagree, disobey or interfere with a doctor's orders is, however, only imposed — with consequential hospital liability for nurses and other staff — in the most egregious circumstances. Nurses may disobey doctor's instructions which are patently wrong, but no duty to disobey exists where a mere disagreement in medical opinion arises.[213] The standard applied to discern whether the nurse breached such a duty, is 'established by expert testimony of similar providers in similar communities under similar circumstances'.[214]

## (2) Independent contractor physicians

The traditional prerequisite for the employment of vicarious hospital liability under the doctrine of *respondeat superior*, is that the acts or omissions of those for whom the hospital is held liable, must be that of employees and not independent contractors.[215] In *Cooper* v. *Curry* [216] and *Heins* v. *Synkonis* [217] the hospital's liability was rejected pursuant to the fact that the malpractice transpired by a physician who was identified as an independent contractor.

There are, however, exceptions to the rule that the employer is not liable to a third party for the negligent acts of the independent contractor. The employer is liable for the torts of the independent contractor where the employer is under a non-delegable duty to the third party, for which he delegates performance but not responsibility to the independent contractor.[218] Another exception to the general rule of non-liability, is where the independent contractor performs work which is inherently dangerous. This essentially means that 'the activity is dangerous to others even if all reasonable care is

---

[211] *Op. cit.* 340–341.

[212] *Op. cit.* 340.

[213] *Op. cit.* 341.

[214] *Ibid.*

[215] *Supra* footnote 197. McWilliams and Russell 1996 *SCLR* 439.

[216] 589 P 2d 201 (NM App 1978). The finding that the hospital was not vicariously liable for the negligence of an independent contractor was affirmed on appeal. See also *Fiorentino* v. *Wenger* 19 NY 2d 407, 227 NE 2d 296, 280 NYS 2d 373 (1967).

[217] 58 Mich App 119, 227 NW 2d 247 (1975).

[218] See also Southwick and Slee *Law of Hospital* 543 and Southwick *Hospital Liability* 239.

exercised'.[219] This occurs when blasting with dynamite, during use of fireworks, crop dusting and excavations near a public highway.[220]

Hospital liability has also been extended to the degree that hospitals have even been held vicariously liable for the malpractice of certain independent contractors.[221]In certain instances the element of control procures hospital liability for the independent contractor who is assigned to the patient by the hospital.[222] Hospitals have been held liable for the malpractice of independent contractor physicians whom they furnish to patients, only if such contractors were at no time privately hired by the patient.[223] Consequently, hospital liability has, under certain circumstances, been imposed for the malpractice of an emergency room physician,[224] orthopaedic surgeon,[225] anaesthesiologist,[226] radiologist[227] or pathologist[228] who were independent contractors.

Hospitals do, however, try to evade hospital liability for independent contractors by creating and formulating contracts for services with physicians. The contracts produce or encourage agency-based defences and yield physicians as true independent contractors.[229] The well-drafted contracts

---

[219] Southwick and Slee *Law of Hospital* 544. Southwick *Hospital Liability* 239.

[220] *Ibid.*

[221] Moore and Kramer *Medical Malpractice* 103. Southwick and Slee *Law of Hospital* 545. McWilliams and Russell 1996 *SCLR* 443.

[222] Moore and Kramer *Medical Malpractice* 107. McWilliams and Russell 1996 *SCLR* 443.

[223] Moore and Kramer *Medical Malpractice* 107.

[224] *Mduba* v. *Benedictine Hospital* 52 AD 2d 450, 384 NYS 2d 527 (3d Dep't 1976). *Mangen* v. *White Plains Hospital Medical Center* 136 AD 2d 608, 523 NYS 2d 587 (2d Dep't 1988). *Martell* v. *St Charles Hospital* 137 Misc 2d 980, 523 NYS 2d 342 (Sup Ct 1987). See also *Heinsohn* v. *Putnam Community Hospital* 65 AD 2d 767, 409 NYS 2d 785 (2d Dep't 1978). Moore and Kramer *Medical Malpractice* 107.

[225] *Rivera* v. *Bronx-Lebanon Hospital Center* 70 AD 2d 794, 417 NYS 2d 79 (1st Dep't 1979). See also *Calvaruso* v. *Our Lady of Peace Roman Catholic Church* 36 AD 2d 755, 319 NYS 2d 727 (2d Dep't 1971). Moore and Kramer *Medical Malpractice* 107.

[226] *Mertsaris* v. *73rd Corp.* 105 AD 2d 67, 482 NYS 2d 792 (2d Dep't 1984). *Robinson* v. *Jewish Hospital* 136 Misc 2d 880, 519 NYS 2d 459 (Sup Ct 1987). See also *Felice* v. *St Agnes* Hospital 65 AD 2d 389, 396, 411 NYS 2d 901 (2d Dep't 1978). Moore and Kramer *Medical Malpractice* 107.

[227] *Facklam* v. *Rosner* 145 AD 2d 955, 536 NYS 2d 326 (4th Dep't 1988). *Pamperin* v. *Trinity Memorial Hospital* 423 NW 2d 848 (Wis 1988). Moore and Kramer *Medical Malpractice* 107.

[228] *Sharsmith* v. *Hill* 764 P 2d 667 (Wyo 1988). Moore and Kramer *Medical Malpractice* 107.

[229] McWilliams and Russell 1996 *SCLR* 444–445.

explicitly describe the relationship as that of principal and independent contractor, stipulate that the physician does not receive a salary and that the hospital has no right of control over the physician as professional health care provider.[230] But '... characterizations in employment agreements are far from conclusive in the tort context. Some courts have denounced the independent contractor designations as self-serving 'secret arrangements' between physician and hospital not binding upon patients or the courts'.[231] Some courts have — when assessing hospital liability — discarded the bargained-for relationship between the hospital and physician and the policies which traditionally found principal liability for the negligence of agents.[232] Courts have preferred to attach more weight to the patients' reasonable expectations and public perceptions.[233] 'In so deciding, these courts ignore or overlook the traditional distinction between servant and independent contractor, which is oriented toward allocating to the employer that burden directly flowing from an employer/employee relationship.'[234]

The vicarious hospital liability which is established for the malpractice of an independent contractor (physician) when the hospital exerts some control over such a physician, is obviously similar and indeed overlaps with the apparent or ostensible agency doctrine. The latter doctrine will be discussed in this chapter, as an independent legal ground which also founds hospital liability.

---

[230]  *Op. cit.* 444.

[231]  In *Smith* v. *St Francis Hospital* 676 P 2d 279 (Okla Ct App 1983) the court stated at 282: '[T]he hospital must be held accountable for the negligence, if any, of its authorized emergency room physician regardless of whether or not he is an independent contractor by secret limitations contained in a private contract between the hospital and doctor or by virtue of some other business relationship unknown to the patient and contrary to the hospital's conduct and representations.' *Fulton* 1993 WL 19674 at 5: '... it is unfair to allow 'secret limitations' on liability, ... premised on a doctor/hospital contract to bind the unknowing patient.' (Citing *Arthur* 405 A 2d at 447. *Mduba* 384 NYS 2d at 529 (same). *Kashishian* 481 NW 2d at 282 (same).) *Hardy* 471 So 2d at 371: 'the details of any undisclosed agreement between the hospital and the person acting on its behalf' was regarded as ineffectual. Classen 1987 *ALR* 471: 'Though widely utilized, most courts now view (independent contractor clauses) as thinly veiled attempts by hospitals to shirk their responsibility to the patient.' See also *Drexel* v. *Union Prescription Ctrs.* 582 F 2d 781, 796 (3d Cir 1978). See also McWilliams and Russell 1996 *SCLR* 444.

[232]  McWilliams and Russell 1996 *SCLR* 445.

[233]  *Ibid.*

[234]  *Ibid.*

Other medical personnel

### (3)  Nurses

The medical personnel for which a hospital can be held vicariously liable, includes nurses.[235] In order to establish vicarious hospital liability, the court will determine whether the nurse was a servant or employee of the hospital acting within the scope of her employment, at the time of the wrongful conduct.

*Respondeat superior* is invoked to impose vicarious hospital liability for the negligent acts of employees. Cases in which nurses have acted negligently are the following: Patients have either been burned or mistreated by nurses;[236] Surgical swabs or instruments have been left inside the patient and the nurse has improperly counted instruments;[237] A nurse has negligently failed to take action where a patient was in distress.[238]

### (4)  Special duty nurses

It has been contended that hospitals are not vicariously liable under the doctrine of *respondeat superior* for special duty nurses.[239] This is supposedly due to the fact that a special duty nurse is usually hired directly by the patient, the hospital cannot exercise authority over the nurse nor supervise the care given by him/her, and cannot be considered that nurse's employer.[240]

### (5)  Residents

The hospital, medical school or the attending physician should be held vicariously liable for the house staff negligence.[241] Liability is determined for the negligent acts of hospital employees and is established in non-hospital employment settings, by the application of agency principles, and should also be applied to determine liability for house staff negligence.[242] Hospital liability will generally be founded upon these rules for the negligent acts of employees, unless the hospital had no control over the acting professional.[243]

---

[235]  McCafferty and Meyer *Liability* 328. Southwick and Slee *Law of Hospital* 547. Southwick *Hospital Liability* 242. Kramer and Kramer *Medical Malpractice* 55.

[236]  *Bing* v. *Thunig* 2NY 2d 656, 143 NE 2d 3, 163 NYS 2d 3 (1957)

[237]  *Ramone* v. *Mani* 535 SW 2d 654 (Tex Civ App 1975).

[238]  *Goff* v. *Doctors General Hospital* 166 Cal 2d 314, 333 P 2d 29 (1958).

[239]  McCafferty and Meyer *Liability* 329.

[240]  *Ibid.*

[241]  Reuter 1994 *JLM* 531.

[242]  *Ibid.*

[243]  *Ibid.*

(6)    Non-medical personnel

Both medical and non-medical personnel employed by the hospital, place the hospital in the *respondeat superior* relationship[244] leading to vicarious hospital liability. In *Hipp* v. *Hospital Authority*[245] the hospital's liability was under scrutiny after an orderly of the hospital — who had a criminal record as a 'peeping Tom' — had molested a nine year old patient. The Georgia Court of Appeals found that the hospital's liability for negligent selection of an employee was a jury question.

*8.4.1.3.1.1 Relevant tests:*

(a)    The control test

(b)    Rejection of the right of control test

(c)    The Brown test

(d)    Other factors

(a)    The control test

Traditionally, the basic rationale for imposing vicarious liability on the employer for the wrongs of the employee, was founded on the fact that the employer could control or had the right, power or authority to control the time, means and methods of the employees' acts or work.[246] Therefore, traditionally, the hospital was not held vicariously liable for the wrongful acts of medical personnel or professionals who were independent contractors.[247] The doctrine of *respondeat superior* did not apply, because in terms of the independent contractor relationship, the principal had no right of control over the manner and method of the agent's work.[248]

Although the employer/principal employs, hires or appoints the independent contractor, and 'retains the right of control and power of approval

---

[244] McCafferty and Meyer *Liability* 331.

[245] 104 Ga App 174, 121 SE 2d 273 (1961).

[246] Southwick and Slee *Law of Hospital* 542. Southwick *Hospital Liability* 238. Pozgar *Health* 206. Miller *Hospital Law* 193. Cunningham 1975 *WLR* 387–388. Louisell and Williams *Medical Malpractice* §15.03 15–18. Miller *Hospital Law* 193. Kelly and Jones *Healthcare* 345–346: Courts also look at the JCAHO's standards, hospital by-laws and quality assurance mechanisms as indicia of control. McWilliams and Russell 1996 *SCLR* 439–440.

[247] *Ibid.* Louisell and Williams *Medical Malpractice* §15.03 15–16.

[248] Southwick and Slee *Law of Hospital* 542–544. Southwick *Hospital Liability* 238–239. Pozgar *Health* 207.

over the final result of the work',[249] the independent contractor would be held responsible for his own acts in terms of this doctrine.[250]

In this context American hospital liability law[251] acknowledged the element of control (in a disguised form) to found vicarious liability. Many American courts and authors still acknowledge the right of control test, unlike some Canadian and other authors who outright reject any form of control.

In *Hodges* v. *Doctors Hospital* [252] the court stated that it was extremely difficult to determine whether an employer-employee or employer-independent contractor relationship existed. The test was 'whether the employer, under the contract either oral or written, assumes the right to control the time, manner and method of executing the work, as distinguished from the right merely to require certain definite results in conformity to the contract '.[253] In the light of the fact that the physician was required to serve in the emergency room to retain his staff privileges, and received a fixed fee for his services, he was considered to be an employee for which the hospital was held vicariously liable under the *respondeat superior* doctrine.

In *Beck* v. *Lovell*,[254] the court refused to impose vicarious liability on the hospital, based upon the hospital's absence of control over the individual physician's surgery. In *Mduba* v. *Benedictine Hospital* [255] it was found that the doctor's salary was guaranteed by the hospital, and that the hospital controlled his activities. Consequently, the court held the doctor to be an employee. In *Beeck* v. *Tucson General Hospital* [256] the court found the hospital to be the employer of a non-salaried radiologist. The finding was based on the hospital's right to control medical staff members' professional

---

[249] Southwick and Slee *Law of Hospital* 543. Southwick *Hospital Liability* 238–239.

[250] Pozgar *Health* 207.

[251] *Ibid.* Southwick and Slee *Law of Hospital* 543. Southwick *Hospital Liability* 238–239. Furrow *et al. Health Law* 226. Werthmann *Malpractice* 9. Miller *Hospital Law* 193: The Restatement (Second) of Agency §220 (1958) describes control as an essential element of an agency or master-servant relationship as follows: 'Agency is the fiduciary relation which results from the manifestation of consent by one person to another that the other shall act on his behalf and subject to his control, and consent by the other so to act.' See also Smith *Hospital* §3.02 [2] 3–5.

[252] 141 Ga App 649, 234 SE 2d 116 (1977).

[253] 234 SW 2d at 177. McCafferty and Meyer *Liability* 322.

[254] 361 So 2d 245 (La Ct App 1978). McCafferty and Meyer *Liability* 323.

[255] 52 AD 2d 450, 384 NYS 2d 527 (3d Dept 1976). In *Kober* v. *Stewart* 148 Mont 117, 417 P 2d 476 (1966) it was found that the contract established the method by which the hospital hired the doctor as supervisor. See also Furrow *et al. Health Law* 226.

[256] 18 Ariz App 165, 500 P 2d 1153 (1972). Miller *Hospital Law* 193.

performance, the stipulations of the contract, the hospital's role as billing agent and the patient's lack of choice in selecting a radiologist. The court even discarded a statement in the hospital admission form which the patient had signed, acknowledging that the radiologist was not an employee but an independent contractor. 'The first judicial approach was simply to test whether the doctor was an employee or subject to the control of the hospital, applying a number of standard criteria for evaluating the existence of a master-servant relationship. If the contract gave the hospital substantial control over the doctor's choice of patients or if the hospital furnished equipment, then an employee relationship might be found. The case law reflects divergent applications of the 'control' test, because of the breadth of the factors involved.'[257]

(b)    Rejection of the right of control test
The right of control test is/was the traditional test for determining the existence of a master-servant relationship.[258] The traditional right of control test has, however, been found unworkable in the hospital setting, when applying the ***respondeat superior*** doctrine to the hospital-physician relationship.[259] 'Central to the control test is the master's right of physical control over the details of the servant's work.'[260] The hospital's directors or administrators do not control the professional medical judgment of or medical treatment rendered by physicians, even if the physicians are salaried.[261] They are not only unqualified to do so, but it would constitute a violation of most state medical practices, acts/statutes to attempt to exercise such control.[262] Following the failure of the right of control test in these circumstances, courts created other tests for liability in the medical context.

---

[257]  Furrow *et al. Health Law* 226.

[258]  Louisell and Williams *Medical Malpractice* §15.03 15–18. Cunningham 1975 *WLR* 392. Mobilia 1985 *SCLR* 602.

[259]  Cunningham 1975 *WLR* 392.

[260]  *Ibid.*

[261]  *Ibid.* Mobilia 1985 *SCLR* 602.

[262]  *Ibid.* Werthmann *Malpractice* at 9 made the following remarks whilst discussing the special category of the employer-employee relationship and the hospital's consequential vicarious liability: 'Due to the high degree of skill exercised by physicians in their work, the question necessarily arises whether the hospital does indeed have the right to control the manner in which the physician works. If the hospital has no right of control, the physician is an independent contractor and the hospital will not be held vicariously liable for his or her torts.'

(c)    The Brown test

In *Brown* v. *La Société Française de Bien Faisance Mutuelle*,[263] the California Supreme Court suggested a two-pronged test for the application of *respondeat superior* to the hospital setting. The **Brown** test consisted of two elements: (i) Did the patient seek treatment primarily from the hospital, or look to the physician for treatment: (relationship between the hospital and patient). Malpractice plaintiffs choose their tortfeasors. (ii) Did the hospital pay the negligent physician a salary: (relationship between the hospital and the physician).

If the patient sought treatment primarily from the hospital and the physician is a salaried employee of the hospital, hospital liability is clearly established. 'The courts which apply the doctrine of *respondeat superior* to the hospital — physician relationship have *sub silentio* substituted this two-pronged **Brown** test for the unworkable right of control test.'[264] Where staff members were clearly not salaried employees, courts have held hospitals liable for their tortious conduct under the ostensible agency theory.[265] But many courts have used the Brown test to hold hospitals liable for the negligence of their interns and resident physicians.[266] However, where the physician is neither employed nor paid by the hospital, vicarious hospital liability will not follow.[267]

(d)    Other factors

Courts also rely on other factors in establishing a master-servant relationship.[268]

---

[263]  138 Cal 475, 71 P 516 (1903). Cunningham 1975 *WLR* 393–396. Mobilia 1985 *SCLR* 602–603. Louisell and Williams *Medical Malpractice* §15.03 15–18.

[264]  Cunningham 1975 *WLR* 393.

[265]  *Howard* v. *Park* 37 Mich App 496, 195 NW 2d 39 (1972). The medical center was held liable under the ostensible agency doctrine, although the physician was actually an independent contractor. Cunningham 1975 *WLR* 394, 396. Mobilia 1985 *SCLR* 603.

[266]  Louisell and Williams *Medical Malpractice* §15.03 15–18.

[267]  *Op. cit.* §15.04 15–19.

[268]  Louisell and Williams *Medical Malpractice* §15.03 15–18 to 15–19: The other factors include:

(1)    Hospital control over billing.
(2)    Setting of fees by the hospital.
(3)    Provision of clerical and medical support by the hospital at no cost.
(4)    Provision of facility and equipment by the hospital at no cost.
(5)    Exclusivity of contract between hospital and physician.
(6)    Receipt of a percentage of gross fees by the physician.
(7)    Lack of other employment by the physician.

### 8.4.1.3.2 The 'wrongful act'

The **'wrongful act'** requirement needs no discussion in this chapter.

### 8.4.1.3.3 Within the scope of employment.

This requirement presents fewer problems to the courts. The courts have seldom refused to impute liability as a result of a person acting outside the scope of his/her employment.[269] In *Haven* v. *Randolph* [270] the court did decline hospital liability for the physician's act on the ground that the latter acted not as an employee or an agent of the hospital, but completely independent of the hospital. The court confirmed that:

> The doctrine of *respondeat superior* does not apply to a physician who acts upon his own initiative, and in the exercise of his own judgment and skill, without direction or control of an employer.[271]

### 8.4.1.3.4 Comment on employer-employee requirement

Concerning the legal ground of vicarious hospital liability which is based on *respondeat superior*, it has been suggested that the traditional employer-employee requirement, should be eliminated. The inquiry should no longer be 'whether the physician was a servant, but whether the tort occurred within the scope of the hospital enterprise'.[272] The scope of the enterprise is defined as 'any service, medical or otherwise, the hospital purports to provide the patient.'[273] Included in the scope of the enterprise would be

-      specialist services the hospital provides, such as anaesthesiologists, radiologists and pathologists for whose malpractice the hospital will be held liable.

---

(8)      Long term contract between the hospital and the physician for provision of a service which is an inherent function of the hospital.

(9)      Lack of patient control over physician selection.

(10)      Hospital control over working hours and scheduling of vacations.

(11)      Contractual requirement that physicians comply with hospital rules and regulations.

(12)      Standardized procedure whereby hospital contracts physician on call.

[269]      McCafferty and Meyer *Liability* 322. See also Cunningham 1975 *WLR* 396–397.

[270]      342 F Supp 538 (DDC 1972). McCafferty and Meyer *Liability* 322.

[271]      *Haven* v. *Randolph* at 542: The Court quoted from *Smith* v. *Duke University* 219 NC 628, 634 14 SE 2d 643, 647 (1941).

[272]      Cunningham 1975 *WLR* 417–418.

[273]      *Op. cit.* 418.

- acts of non-salaried physicians who do rotating service pursuant to active staff membership. This is a service rendered by the hospital.[274]

The malpractice of a private attending physician would, however, not fall within the scope of the enterprise. The private physician-patient relationship is therefore respected and the autonomy of the private physician is maintained.[275]

This is in trend with modern hospital liability law developments and discards the superficial quest for an employee identification which is irrelevant to the injured patient. The enterprise tort liability expands vicarious hospital liability but ensures indemnification from a 'deep pocket' which is covered by malpractice insurance.

### 8.4.1.4 No-fault or strict liability

In application of the doctrine of *respondeat superior* to the institutional health care provider or hospital, it must be clear that the employer is not negligent, neither had the enterprise committed a personal or direct wrong to the third party.[276] The employer self has no fault, but the blame or fault of the employee is imputed to the employer for which he is vicariously liable. Consequently, vicarious liability is a non-fault liability[277] or strict liability.[278]

### 8.4.1.5 Exceptions

**Private attending physicians and nurses**
As in Australian and Canadian hospital liability law, courts have created an exemption from vicarious liability for hospitals under the doctrine of **respondeat superior**: there will be no hospital liability 'for the malpractice of a patient's independently retained private attending physician or private nurse unless the hospital had reason to know that the malpractice would take place. The reason is that the status of the private attending physician and private nurse as independent contractors is insufficient to impute their negligent treatment, acts or omissions to the hospital, which in such instances 'serves the function only of a specialized facility, not a direct

---

[274] *Ibid.*

[275] *Op. cit.* 418–419.

[276] Southwick and Slee *Law of Hospital* 542. Southwick *Hospital Liability* 237–238.

[277] *Ibid.*

[278] McWilliams and Russell 1996 *SCLR* 438. They state: '*Respondeat superior* is agency-based strict liability.'

service healing institution …'.'[279] The law protects a hospital from liability if it follows the direct and explicit orders of the private physician, unless the staff knows that the doctor's orders are 'so clearly contra-indicated by normal practice that ordinary prudence requires inquiry into [their] correctness'.[280] The hospital will also be liable if the employed physicians or nurses do not carry out the orders of the private attending physician.[281]

### 8.4.1.6 Expansion

Southwick[282] has formulated several reasons for the courts' tendency to expand the applicability of ***respondeat superior***:

- The hospital or employer rather than the patient himself, increasingly selects or provides the doctor.

- The emergency room is used more frequently.

- The institutional health care provider or hospital has increased the number and frequency of salaried arrangements for physicians, providing increased institutionalized and specialized medical care.

- Contracts with hospital-based specialists have also increased in number and frequency.

### 8.4.1.7 Intentional acts

The hospital or healthcare facility can be liable for the intentional acts of an employee or agent, if they act within the scope of their employment.[283] This can be determined by the fact that the employee did not act in furtherance of his/her own interest, but with an intent to benefit the employer. The facility or hospital will only be liable if the employee acted outside the scope of his/her employment, if the intentional act of the employee was foreseeable to

---

[279] Moore and Kramer *Medical Malpractice* 104.

[280] *Toth* v. *Community Hospital* 22 NY 2d 255 at 265, 239 NE 2d 368, 292 NYS 2d 440 (1968). *Killeen* v. *Reinhardt* 71 AD 2d 851, 853, 419 NYS 2d 175 (2d Dep't 1979). See also *Christopher* v. *St Vincent's Hospital & Medical Center* 121 AD 2d 303 306, 504 NYS 2d 102 (1st Dep't 1986). Moore and Kramer *Medical Malpractice* 104, 116.

[281] *Toth* v. *Community Hospital supra. Beardsley* v. *Wyoming County Community Hospital* 79 AD 2d 1110, 435 NYS 2d 862 (4th Dep't 1981). *Bamert* v. *Central General Hospital* 77 AD 2d 559, 430 NYS 2d 336 (2d Dep't 1980), affd 53 NY 2d 656, 421 NE 2d 119, 438 NYS 2d 999 (1981). See also *Collins* v. *New York Hospital* 49 NY 2d 965, 406 NE 2d 743, 428 NYS 2d 885 (1980). Moore and Kramer *Medical Malpractice* 104, 116.

[282] Southwick and Slee *Law of Hospital* 546. Southwick *Hospital Liability* 241–242.

[283] Kelly and Jones *Healtcare* 341–342.

the facility or that the facility knew or should have known of propensities of the employee which could endanger patients or put them at risk.[284]

### 8.4.1.8 The decline of the 'Captain-of-the-Ship' and 'Borrowed-Servant' doctrines[285]

The 'captain of the ship' and 'borrowed servant' doctrines are theories of *respondeat superior* liability.[286] They were formulated and applied when hospitals were exempted from liability under the doctrine of charitable immunity, in order to create some other kind of 'deep pocket' who would be liable for the negligent acts of nurses and other non-physician employees.[287]

The 'captain of the ship' doctrine developed the concept that the chief surgeon was the captain of the ship during surgery and could consequently be held liable vicariously for the negligence of any person serving as a member of the surgical team.[288] The 'borrowed servant doctrine' is a similar concept but rules that one who is normally an employee of the hospital, providing a hospital function, may be temporarily borrowed by a private physician, making him a servant or employee of the physician, and thereby rendering the physician vicariously liable for the negligence of the hospital employee. The latter doctrine has a wider range of application.[289]

The two traditional doctrines thus operated to hold private physicians, rather than the institutional health care provider or hospital, vicariously liable for the negligent acts of (non-physician) employees.[290] The application

---

[284] *Op. cit.* 342.

[285] Southwick and Slee *Law of Hospital* 551–554. Southwick *Hospital Liability* 248–250. Kelly and Jones *Healthcare* 336–337. Price 1989 *JLM* 323–356. Richards and Rathbun *Risk* 75–77. Annas *et al. American Health Law* 445–446. Louisell and Williams *Medical Malpractice* §16.06 16–18 to 16–23. Werthmann *Malpractice* 15–18. Furrow *et al. Health Law* 224–225. See also Reuter 1994 *JLM* 495–507. Restatement (Second) of Agency §227 (1958) defines the borrowed-servant rule as follows: 'A servant directed or permitted by his master to perform services for another may become the servant of such other in performing the services. He may become the other's servant as to some acts and not as to others.'

[286] Kelly and Jones *Healthcare* 336.

[287] *Ibid.* Price 1989 *JLM* 325, 332, 355.

[288] Southwick and Slee *Law of Hospital* 551–552. Southwick *Hospital Liability* 248–249. Price 1989 *JLM* 330–339, 326–328.

[289] *Ibid.*

[290] Kelly and Jones *Healthcare* 336.

of the doctrines were based on the theory that the staff members were under the 'actual control' or 'right to control' of the 'borrowing' physician.[291]

After the abolishment of the doctrine of charitable immunity by courts towards hospitals and the dispersion of responsibilities in the hospital and theatre, followed by the increasing sophistication and specialization of medical practice, most jurisdictions have altered the allocation of legal liability in and around the operating room.[292]

Southwick suggests that courts had in recent years restricted applicability of the two doctrines, thereby expanding hospital liability even further.[293] After citing from various cases[294] in which the doctrines had been abandoned and hospital liability established, he concluded that there had been an increased imposition of vicarious liability upon the hospital for more than two decades. 'When medical care is provided by a highly specialized, sophisticated team of professional individuals all working within an institutional setting, it is frequently difficult to determine who is exercising direct control over whom at any given time. When such difficulty in determination arises, it is only natural and logical that ultimate liability be placed upon the corporate institution and not upon the private physician.'[295] Thus, according to Southwick, hospitals are most likely awarded vicariously liability for the negligence of employees.

According to Price, the majority of jurisdictions have appropriately rejected the 'captain of the ship' doctrine, because the hospital can most easily absorb and spread liability costs and is in the best position to prevent future harm to patients.[296] It is also a fallacy to say that the modern operating surgeon has the right to control other assisting hospital personnel by the mere presence of the surgeon in the operating room.[297] He finds that the operating surgeon should only be held vicariously liable for the negligence of assisting hospital personnel where the surgeon has the right to control the manner of such personnel's performance.[298] Concerning the 'borrowed

---

[291]  *Ibid.* Price 1989 *JLM* 326, 334–335, 339. Southwick and Slee *Law of Hospital* 552. Southwick *Hospital Liability* 248.

[292]  Price 1989 *JLM* 323–324, 355.

[293]  Southwick and Slee *Law of Hospital* 551, 554. Southwick *Hospital Liability* 248, 250.

[294]  *Tonsic* v. *Wagner* 458 Pa. 246, 329 A 2d 497 (1974). *Sprager* v. *Worley Hospital* 547 SW 2d 582 (Tex 1977). *May* v. *Brown* 261 Or 28, 492 P 2d 776 (1972).

[295]  Southwick and Slee *Law of Hospital* 554. Southwick *Hospital Liability* 250.

[296]  Price 1989 *JLM* 324, 355.

[297]  *Op. cit.* 355.

[298]  *Op. cit.* 324.

servant' doctrine, he suggests that it should still be applied in employer-employee situations, but only where 'the surgeon has the right to control the details as to the manner of the employee's performance.'[299] *In toto* he concludes that occasions in which the surgeon will be liable will be fewer under the circumstances he advises i.e. when the surgeon 'has a genuine opportunity to control and possibly prevent the negligence of those providing assistance'.[300] Courts will be more likely to find hospitals and not the operating surgeons, vicariously liable for the negligence of employees.[301]

Annas' and Miller's reasoning, however, surpasses the finding that the trend is towards hospital liability only. Annas finds that the 'modern trend is to recognize that **both** the hospital and the physician may be supervising the employee, and hence both may be liable for the employee's negligence'.[302] In *Truhitte* v. *French Hospital* [303] the court rejected the reasoning that a hospital be exempted from liability by the two doctrines, and in *Brickner* v. *Normandy Osteopathic Hospital Inc.*,[304] the Missouri Supreme Court held that an employee could be under the control of two masters, and that the hospital could only successfully evade liability when it showed that it had 'relinquished all control and authority ... to the special employer.'[305]

In conclusion, it is most clear that the doctrines of 'borrowed servant' and 'captain of the ship' are declining if not already sunk. Hospitals are increasingly being held liable (vicariously also) and in some instances which could traditionally have qualified for the application of the above-mentioned doctrines, vicarious liability for both the hospital and the operating or private physician could be a possibility. All taken into account, the reasonableness of the two doctrines just seem to 'become less clear with the evolution of the modern hospital and the concomitant development of high technology medicine'.[306]

---

[299] *Op. cit.* 355–356.

[300] Price 1989 *JLM* 356.

[301] *Op. cit.* 323.

[302] Annas *et al. American Health Law* 445. Miller *Hospital Law* 193 calls it the dual servant doctrine, under which both the physician and the hospital are vicariously liable under **respondeat superior** for the acts of the employee.

[303] 128 Cal App 3d 332, 180 Cal Rptr 152 (1982).

[304] 746 SW 2d 108 (MO 1988).

[305] *Brickner* at 114.

[306] Richards and Rathbun *Risk* 76. See also their discussion. See also Price 1989 *JLM* 323.

## 8.4.2  Hospital Liability in Terms of the Doctrines of Apparent (or Ostensible) Agency[307] and Agency by Estoppel[308]

The general rule of non-liability for the negligent acts of independent contractors has been evaded by the formulation of various legal grounds and doctrines such as the doctrine of 'apparent or ostensible agency'[309] and the later doctrine of 'agency by estoppel'.[310] Courts have applied agency and estoppel theories in order to hold the hospital liable for the malpractice of independent contractors.[311]

Many authors refer to the doctrine of apparent (or ostensible) agency as apparent authority. It has, however, been suggested that they differ both in respect of context and application.[312] Furthermore apparent authority[313] 'has no application in tort', whereas apparent agency 'can be effective in either contract or tort'.[314] Agency by estoppel on the other hand is thought to be

---

[307] Louisell and Williams *Medical Malpractice* §15.04 15–19 to 15–24. Smith *Hospital* §3.03 [3] 3–21 to 3–22. Southwick and Slee *Law of Hospital* 547–551. Southwick *Hospital Liability* 243–247. Moore and Kramer *Medical Malpractice* 107–112. Kelly and Jones *Healthcare* 348–355. Furrow *et al. Health Law* 226–235. Miller *Hospital Law* 194. Werthmann *Malpractice* 8–13. McCafferty and Meyer *Liability* 324–326. Annas *et al. American Health Law* 447. Owens 1990 *WLR* 1129–1154. Ferraro and Camarra 1988 *IBJ* 364–370. Zaslow 1978 *PBAQ* 466–470. Janulis and Hornstein 1985 *NLR* 696–702. Pegalis and Wachsman *Law* 225–232. Cunningham 1975 *WLR* 398–403. Ferraro and Camarra 1998 *IBJ* 364–370. Brown 1988 *DCJ* 164–165. Reuter 1994 *JLM* 510–511. Morgan 1995 *JLM* 397–403. McWilliams and Russell 1996 *SCLR* 432–474.

[308] *Ibid.* With special reference to: Kelly and Jones *Healthcare* 348–355. Janulis and Hornstein 1985 *NLR* 696–702. Morgan 1995 *JLM* 398–403. Ferraro and Camarra 1988 *IBJ* 364–370.

[309] Louisell and Williams *Medical Malpractice* §15.04 15–19: It was also referred to as estoppel to deny agency. See also Kelly and Jones *Healthcare* 348. McWilliams and Russell 1996 *SCLR* 445–452.

[310] Kelly and Jones *Healthcare* 348–349. McWilliams and Russell 1996 *SCLR* 445–452. Morgan 1995 *JLM* 398–403.

[311] See *supra* footnote 307. Kelly and Jones *Healthcare* 348. McWilliams and Russell 1996 *SCLR* 434. Morgan 1995 *JLM* 401.

[312] McWilliams and Russell 1996 *SCLR* 445 footnote 75.

[313] Restatement (Second) of Agency §8 (1957) defines apparent authority as: 'the power to affect the legal relations of another person by transactions with third persons, professedly as agent for the other, arising from and in accordance with the other's manifestations to such third persons.' The agent can bind the principal in contract by means of apparent authority. McWilliams and Russell 1996 *SCLR* 445–446 footnote 75.

[314] McWilliams and Russell 1995 *SCLR* 446 footnote 75. Also: 'Apparent agency, by contrast, estops an assertion of nonagency, in effect supplying the missing agency, and defines the scope of the agency.'

based on the same principles as apparent agency and is traditionally limited in application to contracts, as is apparent authority.[315] Some courts are of the opinion that there is no meaningful differentiation between apparent agency and agency by estoppel.[316]

The relevant doctrines are summarized as follows:

Restatement (Second) of Torts §429 (1966) provides:

> One who employs an independent contractor to perform services for another which are accepted in the reasonable belief that the services are being rendered by the employer or by his servants, is subject to liability for physical harm caused by the negligence of the contractor in supplying such services, to the same extent as though the employer were supplying them himself or by his servants.

Restatement (Second) of Agency §267 (1958) provides:

> One who represents that another is his servant or other agent and thereby causes a third person justifiably to rely upon the care or skill of such apparent agent is subject to liability to the third person for harm caused by the lack of care or skill of the one appearing to be a servant or other agent as if he were such.

Comment a to Restatement (Second) of Agency §267 (1958) states:

> The mere fact that acts are done by one whom the injured party believes to be the defendant's servant is not sufficient to cause the apparent master to be liable. There must be such reliance upon the manifestation as exposes the plaintiff to the negligent conduct.

It must be noted that there exists no consensus amongst American authors on which doctrine(s) the respective Restatement paragraphs 429 and 267 are founded. Some authors state that apparent agency is based on §267[317] and

---

[315] McWilliams and Russell 1996 *SCLR* 446 footnote 76.

[316] *Ibid.* The Restatement (Second) of Agency §8B (1957) does, however, treat them separately defining apparent agency in terms of injury and agency by estoppel in terms of liability.

[317] McWilliams and Russell 1996 *SCLR* 445, 446. Owens 1990 *WLR* 1153. Reuter 1994 *JLM* 510. According to the McWilliams and Russell at 450, the traditional requisites of apparent agency (in terms of §267) are:

(1) The defendant must either have represented the contractor to be his servant
   - with reason to believe that the representation would be relied upon
   - or to have remained silent unreasonably
   - or not in good faith.

(2) The plaintiff must thereby have been induced to rely upon the care or skill of the apparent servant with resulting harm.

(3) The harm must be within the scope of the agency represented.

others found apparent agency on §429;[318] some found apparent authority on §429[319] whilst others base agency by estoppel on §267.[320] Some authors found 'apparent or ostensible agency' on both §267 and §429,[321] whilst other authors do not even refer to the relevant paragraphs.[322] Most courts also differ on their interpretation and foundation of paragraphs 267 and 429.[323]

### 8.4.2.1 Apparent agency

The majority of authors only discuss the apparent ostensible agency doctrine. Only this doctrine was initially applied by courts. The doctrine basically purports that the hospital will be liable for the independent contractor physician's negligence when the patient proceeds directly to the hospital and seeks treatment primarily from the hospital,[324] relies on the hospital for such treatment and reasonably believes the physician is the servant of the hospital-employer, though he is not. 'The doctrine provides that a plaintiff seeking medical help, and ultimately, redress for malpractice, should not be

---

[318] Kelly and Jones *Healthcare* 349. Southwick and Slee *Law of Hospital* 551 footnote 35. Southwick *Hospital Liability* 247.

[319] Morgan 1995 *JLM* 397. But Werthmann *Malpractice* 12 implicates that apparent authority is founded on §267.

[320] Morgan 1995 *JLM* 398. Kelly and Jones *Healthcare* 349–350.

[321] Louisell and Williams *Medical Malpractice* §15.04 15–19 to 15–21. Louisell and Williams *Medical Malpractice* §15.04 15–20 state that three elements must be proved under §267 in order to establish hospital liability under the doctrine of ostensible agency:

(1) a justifiable belief by the patient that the physician is the hospital's agent;
(2) which arises from a representation by the hospital; and
(3) causes the injury.

They further find at 15–21 that the approach of Comment a to Restatement (Second) of Agency §267 (1958) is consistent with the Restatement (Second) of Torts §429 (1966).

[322] Smith *Hospital* §3.03 [3] 3–21 to 3–22. Moore and Kramer *Medical Malpractice* 109–112. Miller *Hospital Law* 194. But Ferraro and Camarra 1988 *IBJ* 366 states: Apparent agency, also referred to as apparent authority or agency by estoppel, arises when a principal, through words or conduct, creates a reasonable impression that the agent has authority to perform a certain act, and where the third party in actual reliance on that impression changes position or forbears a change of position to his or her detriment.
At 368 they distinguish between apparent agency and agency by estoppel.

[323] *Jackson* v. *Power* see *infra*: Apparent agency is grounded in §429. *Arthur* v. *St Peters Hospital* see *infra*: relied on §429. *Mehlman* v. *Powell* see *infra*: relied on §267. *Pamperin* v. *Trinity Memorial Hospital* see *infra*: relied on §267.

[324] See *supra* footnote 1. See also Cunningham 1975 *WLR* 398.

bound by secret limitations contained in private contracts.'[325] Under this doctrine, the hospital is therefore estopped from denying liability for the attending physician's negligent acts where the patient had a rational basis upon which he based his belief that the physician was a hospital employee.[326] In order to establish liability, the relevant facts must be analysed carefully 'to determine whether a sufficient indicia of an agency relationship existed to allow the patient to rationally assume that his/her care was being administered and supervised by the hospital.'[327] The rule of ostensible agency is thus applied in order 'to bring the hospital into the suit as an additional, potentially vicariously liable, defendant'.[328] In jurisdictions where apparent agency is applied, liability is strongly considered on impressions, public expectations and perceptions of hospital operations (subjective issues) rather than on actual proof of justifiable reliance (an objective issue), or actual legal arrangements between the hospital and the physician.[329]

The ostensible or apparent agency doctrine had been used most frequently to hold hospitals liable for the wrongful acts of physicians with hospital-based practices, for example radiologists, pathologists, anaesthesiologists, clinical laboratory and emergency room physicians.[330] When the patient is treated in the hospital emergency room which is run either by employees of an independent contractor service group or by hospital employees, hospital liability is often predicated upon this doctrine.[331]

By comparison, *respondeat superior* and apparent agency are similar in that both bring about imputed liability for the physical torts of another. They differ fundamentally as regards their basic doctrine and application in that *respondeat superior* proceeds from a servant-type agency and is based upon

---

[325] Moore and Kramer *Medical Malpractice* 111: '… A plaintiff has the right to expect not only that the person initially relied upon for special services will hire skilful employees, but also that, if the employee is guilty of any malpractice, the person upon whom plaintiff relied in the first instance will be answerable in damages.' *Mduba* v. *Benedictine Hospital* 384 NYS 2d at 529.

[326] Smith *Hospital* §3.03 [3] 3–21 to 3–22. See also Ferraro and Camarra 1988 *IBJ* 366.

[327] Smith *Hospital* §3.03 [3] 3–22.

[328] Reuter 1994 *JLM* 511.

[329] Kelly and Jones *Healthcare* 353. Brown 1988 *DCJ* 164.

[330] Louisell and Williams *Medical Malpractice* §15.04 15–22. Southwick and Slee *Law of Hospital* 547. Southwick *Hospital Liability* 243. Werthmann *Malpractice* 10. Reuter 1994 *JLM* 511. Williams and Russell 1996 *SCLR* 437. Brown 1988 *DCJ* 164–165. Ferraro and Camarra 1988 *IBJ* 367–368.

[331] Smith *Hospital* §3.03 [3] 3–22. Louisell and Williams *Medical Malpractice* §15.04 15–22.

a master/servant relationship whereas apparent agency is estoppel-based and not agency-based.[332]

### 8.4.2.2 Agency by estoppel

The doctrine of apparent agency has been developed and expanded in order to establish hospital liability for independent contractor malpractice. It had become a popular rationale in many jurisdictions,[333] although some jurisdictions still refuse to apply it.[334] The doctrine of apparent agency may, however, despite its earlier popularity — be giving way to the doctrine of 'agency by estoppel' which embodies a somewhat higher standard of proof which 'requires more facility conduct to justify the patient's asserted reliance'.[335] The doctrines of apparent agency and estoppel to deny agency are not theoretically identical, although apparent agency is steeped in principles of estoppel.[336] 'In practice, however, commentators and courts often use these terms as if they were interchangeable, causing confusion and possible misapplication of the law.'[337]

Agency by estoppel is the emerging legal ground which founds health care facility liability for independent contractors.[338] The doctrine of agency by estoppel is most often described in terms of Restatement (Second) of Agency §267.[339] The important distinction between apparent agency and estoppel to deny agency, is that under apparent agency the ostensible principal is 'holding out' the ostensible agent in such a way, that the reasonable plaintiff would conclude that an agency relationship existed.[340] Agency by estoppel, however, requires (good faith) actual reliance on the representations or identity of the principal by the plaintiff which causes or induces the latter to act to his detriment or forbear before the hospital can be

---

[332] McWilliams and Russell 1996 *SCLR* 446–447.

[333] *Op. cit.* 445, 447, 450–451. Smith *Hospital* §3.03 [3] 3–21 to 3–22.

[334] Kelly and Jones *Healthcare* 348.

[335] *Op. cit.* 348–349. Morgan 1995 *JLM* 398.

[336] *Stewart* v. *Midani* 525 F Supp 843, 850 (ND Ga 1981). Janulis and Hornstein 1985 *NLR* 696.

[337] Janulis and Hornstein 1985 *NLR* 696. Morgan 1995 *JLM* 401. Ferraro and Camarra 1988 *IBJ* 366.

[338] Kelly and Jones *Healthcare* 353.

[339] *Op. cit.* 350, 353. Morgan 1995 *JLM* 398. Janulis and Hornstein 1985 *NLR* 697 footnote 52.

[340] Restatement (Second) of Agency §8 (1958). Janulis and Hornstein 1985 *NLR* 696–697. Ferraro and Camarra 1988 *IBJ* 366.

estopped from denying agency.[341] This higher standard of proof is more strict for under apparent agency no showing of justifiable reliance is necessary.[342] Thus, in order to warrant a conclusion of apparent agency, there need be no causal relationship between the principal's conduct and the plaintiff's reliance.[343] However, the essence of agency by estoppel is the causal relationship between the principal's conduct and the plaintiff's reliance, and such a change of position by the plaintiff.[344]

Under the doctrine of agency by estoppel, the plaintiffs must plead and prove that if they had prior knowledge that the purported agents were not the hospital's employees, they would have refused treatment by them or would have taken a different course of action.[345] Only when the plaintiff meets the higher requirement of proof of agency by estoppel — which is proof of inducing acts and actual reliance — is the hospital estopped from denying agency.[346]

### 8.4.2.3 Relevant case law

1901:   *Hannon* v. *Siegel-Cooper Co* 167 NY 244, 60 NE 597 (1901)

1942:   *Stanhope* v. *Los Angeles College of Chiropractics* 54 Cal 2d 141, 128 P 2d 705 (Cal App 1942) (California)

1955:   *Seneris* v. *Haas* 45 Cal 2d 811, 291 P 2d 915 (1955) (California)

1963:   *Lundberg* v. *Bayview Hospital* 175 Ohio St 133, 191 NE 2d 821 (1963) (Ohio)

1966:   *Kober* v. *Stewart* 148 Mont. 117, 417 P 2d 476 (1966) (Montana)

1970:   *Vanaman* v. *Milford Memorial Hospital* 262 A 2d 263 (Super Ct 1970), 272 A 2d 718 (1970) (Delaware)

1972:   *Beeck* v. *Tucson General Hospital* 18 Ariz. App 165, 500 P 2d 1153 (1972) (Arizona)

1972:   *Howard* v. *Park* 37 Mich App 496, 195 NW 2d 39 (1972) (Michigan)

1973:   *Schagrin* v. *Wilmington Medical Center Inc.* 304 A 2d 61 (Del Super Ct 1973) (Delaware)

---

[341] Kelly and Jones *Healthcare* 350, 353. Morgan 1995 *JLM* 398. Janulis and Hornstein 1985 *NLR* 697.

[342] In terms of §429, for apparent agency. Morgan 1995 *JLM* 398. Kelly and Jones *Healthcare* 350, 353. Janulis and Hornstein 1985 *NLR* 697.

[343] Janulis and Hornstein 1985 *NLR* 697. Morgan 1995 *JLM* 398.

[344] *Ibid.* Ferraro and Camarra 1988 *IBJ* 368.

[345] Kelly and Jones *Healthcare* 353–354.

[346] *Op. cit.* 354.

1976:    *Mduba* v. *Benedictine Hospital* 52 AD 2d 450, 384 NYS 2d 527 (3d Dep't 1976) (New York)

1977:    *Mehlman* v. *Powell* 281 Md 269, 378 A 2d 1121 (1977) (Maryland)

1977:    *Overstreet* v. *Doctors Hospital* 142 Ga App 895, 237 SE 2d 213 (1977)

1978:    *Adamski* v. *Tacoma General Hospital* 20 Wash App 98, 579 P 2d 970 (1978) (Washington)

1978:    *Felice* v. *St Agnes Hospital* 65 AD 2d 388, 411 NYS 2d 901 (1978)(New York)

1979:    *Grewe* v. *Mt Clemens General Hospital* 404 Mich 240, 273 NW 2d 429 (1979) (Michigan)

1979:    *Arthur* v. *St Peters Hospital* 169 NJ Super 575, 405 A 2d 443 (1979)

1979:    *Rivera* v. *Bronx-Lebanon Hospital Center* 70 AD 2d 794, 417 NYS 2d 79 (1979) (New York)

1980:    *Capan* v. *Divine Providence Hospital* 410 A 2d 1282 (Pa Super Ct 1979), 287 Pa Super 364, 430 A 2d 647 (1980) (Pennsylvania)

1980:    *Gasbarra* v. *St James Hospital* 85 Ill App 3d 32, 406 NE 2d 544 (Ill App 1980) (Illinois)

1980:    *Hannola* v. *City of Lakewood* 68 Ohio App 2d 61, 426 NE 2d 1187 (1980) (Ohio)

1980:    *Anderson* v. *Wagner* 79 Ill 2d 295, 301–302, 402 NE 2d 560, 568–569 (1980) (Illinois)

1981:    *Stewart* v. *Midani* 525 F Supp 843 (ND Ga 1981)

1981:    *Edmonds* v. *Chamberlain Memorial Hospital* 629 SW 2d 28 (Tenn Ct App 1981)(Tennessee)

1981:    *Themins* v. *Emanuel Lutheran Charity Board* 637 P 2d 155 (Or App 1981)

1982:    *Irving* v. *Doctors Hospital of Lake Worth* 415 So 2d 55 (Fla App 1982) (Florida)

1982:    *Walker* v. *United States* 549 F Supp 973 (WD Okla 1982) (Oklahoma)

1983:    *Smith* v. *St Francis Hospital* 676 P 2d 279 (Okla Ct App 1983) (Oklahoma)

1984:    *Barun* v. *Rycyna* 473 NYS 2d 627 (App Div 1984) (New York)

1985:    *Bernier* v. *Burris* 113 Ill 2d 219, 497 NE 2d 763 (1985) (Illinois)

1985:    *Paintsville Hospital Co* v. *Rose* 683 SW 2d 255 (Ky 1985) (Kentucky)

1985:    *Porter* v. *Sisters of St Mary* 756 F 2d 669 (8th Cir 1985) (Missouri law)

1985:    *Hardy* v. *Brantley* 471 So 2d 358 (Mississippi)

1986:    *Sztorc* v. *Northwest Hospital* 146 Ill App 3d 275, 496 NE 2d 1200 (1st Dist. 1986) (Illinois)

1986:    *Greene* v. *Rogers* 147 Ill App 3d 1009, 498 NE 2d 867 (3d Dist 1986) (Illinois)

1986:    *Mega* v. *Holy Cross Hospital* 111 Ill 2d 416, 428, 490 NE 2d 665, 670 (1986) (Illinois)

1986:    *Hill* v. *St Clare's Hospital* 67 NY 2d 72, 490 NE 2d 823, 499 NYS 2d 904 (1986) (New York)

1986:    *Smith* v. *Baptist Memorial Hospital System* 720 SW 2d 618 (Tex App 1986) (Texas)

1987:    *Griffin* v. *Matthews* 522 NE 2d 1100, 36 Ohio App 3d 228 (1987)

1987:    *Richmond County Hospital Authority* v. *Brown* 361 SE 2d 164 (Ga 1987) (Georgia)

1987:    *Jackson* v. *Power* 743 P 2d 1376 (Alaska 1987)

1988:  *Pamperin* v. *Trinity Memorial Hospital* 144 Wis 2d 188, 423 NW 2d 848 (1988) (Wisconsin)

1990:  *Siggers* v. *Barlow* 906 F 2d 241 (6th Cir 1990)

1990:  *Malone* v. *State Department of Health and Human Services, Office of Hospitals* 569 So 2d 1098, 1099 (La App 1990)

1993:  *Shuler* v. *Tuomey Regional Medical Center* 313 SC 225, 437 SE 2d 128 (Ct App 1993)

1994:  *Strickland* v. *Madden* 448 SE 2d 581 (Ct App 1994)

### 8.4.2.4 Discussion

#### 1. 1901: *Hannon* v. *Siegel-Cooper Co.*[347]
The court of appeals first recognized the doctrine of apparent or ostensible agency as a predicate for vicarious malpractice liability, in this case.[348] The department store which had advertised itself as providing a practice of dentistry in one of its departments, was held liable for the malpractice of Dr Cooney. The department had in fact been leased to a person who employed the doctor to render dental services.

#### 2. 1942: *Stanhope* v. *Los Angeles College of Chiropractics*[349]
The California Court of Appeals found that in view of the fact that the college did not inform the plaintiff that the X-ray laboratory was an independent contractor and not an integral part of the college, the college could not evade liability. Ostensible agency was defined as one in which 'the principal intentionally, or by want of ordinary care, causes a third person to believe another to be his agent who is really not employed by him'.[350]

#### 3. 1970: *Vanaman* v. *Milford Memorial Hospital*[351]
The Delaware court decided that the hospital's liability could be established for the doctor's negligence, if the hospital had represented the doctor as it's employee upon which representation the patient relied justifiably. The jury had to decide whether the doctor had acted whilst providing emergency care and thus performed a hospital function, or if he had treated the patient in a private capacity in which case the hospital would not have been liable.

---

[347]  167 NY 244, 60 NE 597 (1901)(New York).

[348]  Moore and Kramer *Medical Malpractice* 109–111.

[349]  54 Cal 2d 141, 128 P 2d 705 (Cal App 1942)(California). Cunningham 1975 *WLR* 398 footnote 73. Spero 1979 *TRIAL* 24.

[350]  *Ibid.* This passage was quoted in *Seneris* v. *Haas* 45 Cal 2d 811, 291 P 2d 915 at 927 (1955).

[351]  262 A 2d 263 (Super Ct 1970), 272 A 2d 718 (1970)(Delaware). Southwick and Slee *Law of Hospital* 548. Southwick *Hospital Liability* 244. Cunningham 1975 *WLR* 402–403.

## 4. 1972: *Beeck* v. *Tucson General Hospital*[352]

An Arizona court established an employment relationship between a hospital and radiologist group based on several relevant facts.[353] The court concluded that the radiologist was an employee, and held the hospital liable. The decision was maintained without resorting to the doctrines of apparent agency or agency by estoppel.

## 5. 1976: *Mduba* v. *Benedictine Hospital*[354]

The hospital was held liable *in casu*, for the negligence of a physician providing services in the emergency room. The court found that even if no employer-employee relationship existed and the physician had been an independent contractor, hospital liability would still have ensued in terms of apparent agency. The court held:

> Patients entering the hospital through the emergency room, could properly assume that the treating doctors and staff of the hospital were acting on behalf of the hospital. Such patients are not bound by secret limitations as are contained in a private contract between the hospital and the doctor.[355]

It was found that the defendant hospital had held itself out to the public as an institution furnishing doctors, staff and facilities for emergency treatment. It was therefore under a duty to perform those services and was liable for the negligent performance of those services by the doctors and staff it hired and furnished to the decedent.[356] The 'right of control' that the hospital exercised

---

[352]  18 Ariz. App 165, 500 P 2d 1153 (1972) (Arizona). Southwick and Slee *Law of Hospital* 549. Southwick *Hospital Liability* 245. Furrow *et al. Health Law* 232–235. Werthmann *Malpractice* 10.

[353]  *Ibid.* The relevant facts were:

- An exclusive agreement for radiological services was made, which would be effective for five years.
- A given percentage of the department's gross revenue was paid to the doctors.
- The hospital provided employed technicians and all the 'facilities and instrumentalities'.
- The hospital had control over the vacation periods and working hours of physicians, the billing and employment of the technicians.
- The hospital could control the services and professional standards of performance of radiologists for the department, via a peer review evaluation process, overseeing boards and supervisors.
- The hospital chose the physicians and the patient's choice was eliminated.

[354]  52 AD 2d 450, 384 NYS 2d 527 (3d Dep't 1976) (New York). Moore and Kramer *Medical Malpractice* 107–109. Werthmann *Malpractice* 11. Janulis and Hornstein 1985 *NLR* 695–696.

[355]  *Mduba* 384 NYS 2d at 529.

[356]  *Mduba* 52 AD 2d at 453–454.

over the functioning of the emergency room was also considered a decisive factor in establishing hospital liability by the Appellate Division.[357]

### 6. 1977: *Mehlman v. Powell*[358]

The Maryland Court of Appeals held *in casu* that the Holy Cross Hospital indeed represented to the decedent that the staff of the hospital's emergency room were its employees, thereby causing the decedent to rely on the emergency room staff's care or skill, and that the hospital was consequently vicariously liable to the decedent as if the emergency room staff were its employees.[359] The court considered the emergency room, staffed by a group of independent contractors — which was an unknown fact to the decedent — as an integral part of the institution. Although the court found that no employer-employee relationship existed between the hospital and emergency room doctors, the hospital's liability for the emergency doctor was founded on the Restatement (Second) of Agency §267 (1958).[360]

### 7. 1979: *Grewe v. Mt Clemens General Hospital*[361]

The Supreme Court of Michigan established hospital liability on the doctrine of agency by estoppel. The patient had gone to the hospital with the expectation that the hospital would provide him with care and treatment and had not personally selected the independent contractor physicians. The hospital was therefore estopped to deny that no employment relationship existed for which they could be held responsible.

### 8. 1979: *Arthur v. St Peters Hospital*[362]

The plaintiff attended the emergency room after injuring his wrist. No fracture was found after diagnosis and X-rays were taken, whereupon the plaintiff was sent home. Eventually an outside physician diagnosed a fracture of the wrist. The plaintiff sued the hospital and physicians. The court held the hospital liable for the independent contractor physician's conduct, since the patient could reasonably have believed the physician was an employee and the hospital had not done anything to dispel the belief.

---

[357] Janulis and Hornstein 1985 *NLR* 696. Moore and Kramer *Medical Malpractice* 109.

[358] 281 Md 269, 378 A 2d 1121 (1977)(Maryland). Janulis and Hornstein 1985 *NLR* 698–700. Zaslow 1978 *PBAQ* 468–469. Pozgar *Health* 207. Spero 1979 *TRIAL* 24. McCafferty and Meyer *Liability* 324–325.

[359] *Mehlman* 281 Md at 275, 378 A 2d at 1124.

[360] *Mehlman* 281 Md at 273, 378 A 2d at 1123, applying the doctrine of apparent agency.

[361] 404 Mich 240, 273 NW 2d 429 (1979)(Michigan). Southwick and Slee *Law of Hospital* 549–550. Southwick *Hospital Liability* 245–246. McCafferty and Meyer *Liability* 324.

[362] 169 NJ Super 575, 405 A 2d 443 (1979). Janulis and Hornstein 1985 *NLR* 697–698.

In this case, most remarkable, is the fact that the court did not distinguish clearly between apparent agency and agency by estoppel. The court did seem to rely on apparent agency, since it referred to 'holding out' but at the same time used language which suggested an estoppel theory.[363] Furthermore cases relevant to both doctrines were cited, 'with no perceivable distinction drawn among them'.[364] In any case, this court relied on Restatement (Second) of Torts §429 (1965).

### 9. 1980: *Capan* v. *Divine Providence Hospital*[365]

In this case the intermediate appellate court adopted the doctrine of apparent or ostensible agency and found that the hospital could be liable for the physician's alleged negligence even if the latter had been an independent contractor. It was held:

> Similarly, it would be unfair to allow the 'secret limitations' on liability contained in a doctor's contract with the hospital to bind the unknowing patient.[366]

### 10. 1980: *Gasbarra* v. *St James Hospital*[367]

An Illinois appellate court decided that a hospital could indeed be held liable under the doctrine of equitable estoppel (agency by estoppel) for the torts of the independent contractor physician who provides emergency room treatment. The court did, however, find that the doctrine did not apply *in casu* and that the hospital could consequently not be held vicariously liable, because the requirements of the doctrine were not met. It was found that agency by estoppel 'must be proved by clear and unequivocal evidence and that there must be reliance in good faith upon conduct of another which leads a person to change position for the worse'.[368]

---

[363]  *Ibid.*

[364]  Janulis and Hornstein 1985 *NLR* 698.

[365]  287 Pa Super 364, 430 A 2d 647 (1980)(Pennsylvania). See also Southwick and Slee *Law of Hospital* 550–551. Southwick *Hospital Liability* 246–247.

[366]  *Capan* 430 A 2d at 649.

[367]  85, Ill App 3d 32, 406 NE 2d 544 (1st Dist 1980)(Illinois). Ferraro and Camarra 1988 *IBJ* 364–370. Werthmann *Malpractice* 12.

[368]  Ferraro and Camarra 1988 *IBJ* 365. Gasbarra 85 Ill App 3d at 45, 406 NE 2d at 555: 'She brought decedent to the hospital for medical care which she received, albeit allegedly improper. She does not contend, and it does not appear, that she would have taken any other action had she been informed that the emergency room doctors were not employees of the hospital, and we find nothing in the record from which a conclusion could be made. We find that the record discloses no change of position by the plaintiff for the worse, and, accordingly, we hold that the doctrine of equitable estoppel is not applicable.'

## 11. 1980: *Hannola* v. *City of Lakewood*[369]

The Ohio court established hospital liability for a physician member of an independent foundation which operated an emergency room — regardless of the contractual arrangements — by application of agency by estoppel. The court provided the following reasons for its finding:[370]

- The hospital was holding itself out to the public as being a provider of emergency care.
- The hospital governing body exercised control over the appointments of physicians employed by the foundation.
- The hospital could revoke privileges of individual emergency room doctors for justifiable cause and monitored the quality of care provided.

> Thus a hospital or other corporate institution cannot contractually insulate itself from liability to a patient by providing in its agreement with the independent specialists that the hospital shall not be liable for their negligence. In fact, with increasing frequency the courts are inclined in these circumstances to find the hospital liable under principles of vicarious liability.[371]

## 12. 1981: *Themins* v. *Emanuel Lutheran Charity Board*[372]

In this case, the plaintiff was treated negligently by an orthopaedic resident who was on rotation from the University of Oregon Health Sciences Center and whose employer was the Health Sciences Center. The resident treated the plaintiff at the Emanuel Hospital, and appeared to the plaintiff to be an employee of the hospital. According to the plaintiff's testimony, he would not have admitted the resident to treat him if he had known otherwise. The court applied the doctrine of ostensible agency in terms of which they found the resident to be an ostensible agent of the Emanuel Hospital for which the hospital became vicariously liable.

## 13. 1982: *Irving* v. *Doctors Hospital of Lake Worth*[373]

The Florida Appellate Court did apply the doctrine of apparent authority but in addition the court introduced another ground to ensure hospital liability. The court confirmed that the hospital could be held liable for the independent contractor emergency-room physician since there was an implied

---

[369] 68 Ohio App 2d 61, 426 NE 2d 1187 (1980)(Ohio). Southwick and Slee *law of Hospital* 548–549. Southwick *Hospital Liability* 244–245.

[370] *Ibid.*

[371] Southwick and Slee *Law of Hospital* 549. Southwick *Hospital Liability* 245.

[372] 637 P 2d 155 (Or App 1981). Reuter 1994 *JLM* 511–512.

[373] 415 So 2d 55 (Fla App 1982)(Florida). Werthmann *Malpractice* 12.

contract between the hospital and the emergency-room patient, in terms of which the hospital could not evade responsibility by their delegation to the independent contractor. This would — it is submitted — constitute nothing other than the non-delegable duty as legal ground to establish hospital liability.

### 14. 1985: *Paintsville Hospital Co* v. *Rose* [374]

The 16-year-old patient was taken to the emergency room, after being found in an unconscious state. The private physician on call failed to diagnose a skull fracture with subdural haematoma, which resulted in the patient's death. The Appellate Court reversed the trial court's decision on the issue of ostensible agency which the Supreme Court affirmed. The Kentucky Supreme Court, by relying on §267 of the Restatement (Second) of Agency, found that the hospital's emergency room operation 'where the public comes expecting medical care to be provided through normal operating procedures within the hospital, falls within the limits for application of the principles of ostensible agency and apparent authority'.[375]

### 15. 1986: *Hill* v. *St Clare's Hospital* [376]

The Court of Appeals discussed the apparent or ostensible agency doctrine as well as the control theory.

### 16. 1987: *Griffin* v. *Matthews* [377]

The patient who suffered from chest and arm pains was taken to the Middletown Hospital Association emergency room. After several tests were performed and a diagnosis was made, the patient was discharged and sent home, but died less than an hour later after being taken back to hospital. The emergency room was provided with physicians by a company under contract with the hospital. On appeal, the court rejected all arguments related to reliance, as it would have produced inequitable results. The court pointed out that unconscious patients cannot establish reliance since they have no choice, whereas the conscious person chooses the hospital where he wants to be treated and thus establishes reliance on the hospital and emergency room. Conclusively the court maintained that a full-service hospital should be held

---

[374] 683 SW 2d 255 (Ky 1985)(Kentucky). Morgan 1995 *JLM* 401. Kelly and Jones *Healthcare* 350–351.

[375] *Paintsville* 683 SW 2d at 258. The majority seemed to blend the doctrines of ostensible agency and apparent authority which was criticized by Vance J who delivered the dissenting opinion.

[376] 67 NY 2d 72, 490 NE 2d 823, 499 NYS 2d 904 (1986)(New York). Moore and Kramer *Medical Malpractice* 111.

[377] 522 NE 2d 1100, 36 Ohio App 3d 228 (1987). Morgan 1995 *JLM* 399.

accountable for emergency room malpractice regardless of the patient's induced or actual reliance, in the light of the nature of emergency medical care.[378] The legal ground on which the court chose to found the hospital's liability, was in the end the non-delegable duty. The court stated:

> [W]here the full-service hospital assumes a non-delegable duty such as the operation of an emergency room facility, the hospital cannot contractually insulate itself from liability for acts of medical malpractice committed in its emergency room by entering into a contract with a third party whereby the third party is to operate the emergency room. In such a situation, the party asserting the agency need not prove induced reliance on his or her part in order to establish the agency relationship.[379]

### 17. 1987: *Richmond County Hospital Authority* v. *Brown*[380]

The Georgia Supreme Court held the hospital liable in terms of the doctrine[381] of apparent or ostensible authority for the malpractice or negligent acts of hospital emergency room physicians who were independent contractors and not hospital employees. The Supreme Court cited section 267 of the Restatement (Second) of Agency in noting the relevant doctrine. It was found that if the hospital had represented to the plaintiff that the emergency room physicians were its employees and if the plaintiff had justifiably relied on the skill of the physicians suffering consequential injury due to their negligence, the hospital's liability could ensue for such negligence.

### 18. 1987: *Jackson* v. *Power*[382]

The plaintiff fell from a cliff, was airlifted to the hospital and admitted to the emergency room. Due to an insufficient examination by the emergency room physician on duty at the time, the young boy lost both his kidneys. The plaintiff alleged negligence in diagnosis, care and treatment when filing suit.

---

[378] Morgan 1995 *JLM* 399.

[379] *Griffin* 522 NE 2d at 1104.

[380] 361 SE 2d 164 (Ga 1987)(Georgia). Louisell and Williams *Medical Malpractice* §15.04 15–22 to 15–23. Morgan 1995 *JLM* 400–401.

[381] Louisell and Williams Medical Malpractice §15.04 15–22 denote the doctrine as 'apparent or ostensible authority'. Morgan 1995 *JLM* 400–401 points out that the plaintiff relied on apparent authority, but that the Supreme Court noted the doctrine of 'agency by estoppel' and cited §267 of the Restatement (Second) of Agency, as founding such finding. The court did in fact refer to the doctrine as the doctrine of 'apparent or ostensible authority' and not agency by estoppel.

[382] 743 P 2d 1376 (Alaska 1987). Furrow *et al. Health Law* 226–230. Kelly and Jones *Healthcare* 349–350. Annas *et al. American Health Law* 448–453. Louisell and Williams *Medical Malpractice* §15.05 15–24 to 15–25. McWilliams and Russell 1996 *SCLR* 454–455. Smith *Hospital* §15.05 15–24 to 15–25.

Three legal grounds were proposed for the founding of hospital liability: (1) enterprise liability (2) apparent authority and (3) non-delegable duty.

There was consensus on the fact that the physician Dr Power was not an employee of Fairbanks Memorial Hospital (FMH), but an independent contractor employed by respondent Emergency Room Inc. (ERI) and that both ERI and FMH were separate legal entities.

The Supreme Court of Alaska came to some remarkable conclusions:

(1)   The court found that vicarious liability is not equivalent to enterprise liability in Alaska. The plaintiff's argument that the negligent act occurred during an activity performed for the benefit or in the interest of the enterprise and therefore rendered the enterprise liable, was rejected.[383]

(2)   The court took cognizance of the fact that courts have held hospitals vicariously liable under doctrines known as 'ostensible or apparent agency' or 'agency by estoppel'.[384] It was clearly articulated that the two doctrines differed and were not theoretically identical.[385] The court stipulated that 'apparent or ostensible agency' is predicated on §429 of the Restatement (Second) of Torts (1966) and that 'agency by estoppel' is based on §267 of the Restatement (Second) of Agency (1958).[386] The court defined the requirements for both apparent agency[387] and agency by estoppel.[388] Although the court specified these doctrines, it refrained from applying either, since the court found no reason to adopt a special rule in this jurisdiction.[389] On the facts of the

---

[383]   Furrow *et al. Health Law* 228. Annas *et al. American Health Law* 448–449.

[384]   *Jackson* 743 P 2d at 1380.

[385]   Furrow *et al. Health Law* 228. Kelly and Jones *Healthcare* 349.

[386]   *Jackson* 743 P 2d at 1380.

[387]   Ostensible agency requires two elements:

    (1) whether the patient looks to the institution, rather than the individual physician for care and
    (2) whether the hospital 'holds out' the physician as its employee.

    See also Furrow *et al. Health Law* 228. Kelly and Jones *Healthcare* 350.

[388]   Agency by estoppel requires actual reliance upon the representations of the principal by the injured person. See also Furrow *et al. Health Law* 229. Kelly and Jones *Healthcare* 350.

[389]   Jackson 743 P 2d at 1380–1382. Kelly and Jones *Healthcare* 349. Furrow *et al. Health Law* 229. On the facts the court also found that it was advertised on a sign that the physicians working in the emergency room were from ERI, and that Jackson was not unconscious when he arrived at the hospital. See also Annas *et al. American Health Law* 449.

case, the court determined that there was a jury question as to apparent authority.[390]

(3)    The Supreme Court did find that the hospital had a duty to provide emergency services which duty was non-delegable, due to 'public policy' considerations.[391] The hospital was thus held liable in terms of the legal ground of a non-delegable duty to provide non-negligent medical care in the emergency room by means of the independent contractor physicians, whether the latter were deemed to be agents of the hospital or not.

## 19. 1988: *Pamperin* v. *Trinity Memorial Hospital*[392]

In this case the Wisconsin Supreme Court adopted the principle of 'apparent authority', and applied it for the first time in a medical malpractice action. Other jurisdictions had — according to the court — applied 'apparent or ostensible authority' in order to hold hospitals liable for the negligence of independent contractor physicians, and this court decided to join them.[393] The court held that '... when a hospital holds itself out to the public as providing complete medical care, a hospital can be held liable under the doctrine of apparent authority for the negligent acts of the physicians retained by the hospital to provide emergency room care ... '.[394] The court also explicitly endorsed §267 of the Restatement (Second) of Agency (1957).[395]

It has been suggested that the *Pamperin* decision is justified because, as hospitals have evolved, the extension of hospital liability has come to match 'the extension of the hospital's role and the expectations of its increasingly affluent patients'.[396] The formidable financial burden placed on hospitals should also be processed by hospital administrators by co-ordinating insurance coverage with affiliates, eliminating needless litigation and easing the burden of injured victims of malpractice.[397] 'By accepting the court's ruling as not only binding, but logical, and accepting responsibility for the

---

[390]  Smith *Hospital* §15.05 15–25.

[391]  Jackson 743 P 2d at 1376. Kelly and Jones *Healthcare* 355. Furrow *et al. Health Law* 226.

[392]  144 Wis 2d 188, 423 NW 2d 848 (1988)(Wisconsin). Morgan 1995 *JLM* 401–403. Owens 1990 *WLR* 1129–1154. McWilliams and Russell 1996 *SCLR* 442.

[393]  *Pamperin* 144 Wis 2d at 203–207, 423 NW 2d at 854–855.

[394]  *Pamperin* 144 Wis 2d at 193–194, 423 NW 2d at 849–850.

[395]  *Pamperin* 144 Wis 2d at 206, 423 NW 2d at 855.

[396]  Owens 1990 *WLR* 1153. Brown 1988 *DCJ* 165.

[397]  Owens 1990*WLR* 1153–1154.

treatment rendered by the hospital, administrators can contribute greatly to a lessening of distrust between the health care community and its patients.'[398]

## 20. 1993: *Shuler* v. *Tuomey Regional Medical Center* [399]

The South Carolina Court of Appeals conceded to the possible expansion of hospital liability for independent contractor physicians, by accepting the theory of apparent agency to found such hospital liability. The court proposed a multiple test in order to establish apparent agency for the plaintiff.

> To establish an apparent agency ... [the plaintiff] must prove:
>
> (1)    that the purported principal consciously or impliedly represented another to be his agent;
>
> (2)    that there was a reliance upon the representation; and
>
> (3)    that there was a change of position to the relying party's detriment.'[400]

This was the first time that the doctrine of apparent agency had been applied in a hospital context in South Carolina.[401] The *Shuler* case was followed in *Strickland* v. *Madden*,[402] in which the Shuler test was cited. *In casu* the court applied the theory 'in terms consistent with section 267'.[403]

### 8.4.2.5 Conclusion

The doctrines of ostensible or apparent agency and agency by estoppel are independent legal grounds which can be implemented to establish hospital liability for independent contractor malpractice. It is, however, a great pity that a more uniform or general approach could not be formulated or recommended by the law of the USA, in order to create legal certainty or from which other legal systems could be instructed by legal comparison. Since these doctrines have their undeniable merits, it is submitted, that technicalities such as the founding of the relevant doctrines on definite statutory clauses be revised and prerequisites be included so as to create proper foundations for hospital liability which courts can apply justly, fairly and equally under all circumstances to the advantage of all plaintiffs.

---

[398]  *Op. cit.* 1154.

[399]  313 SC 225, 437 SE 2d 128 (Ct App 1993).

[400]  *Shuler* 313 SC at 227, 437 SE 2d at 129.

[401]  The application of the doctrine was, however, not successful due to the lack of relevant evidence. McWilliams and Russell 1996 *SCLR* 433, 471–472.

[402]  448 SE 2d 581, 585 (Ct App 1994). McWilliams and Russell 1996 *SCLR* 433, 471–472.

[403]  McWilliams and Russell 1996 *SCLR* 472.

There is a 'generalized confusion of terminology'[404] concerning these doctrines and their namesakes among all jurisdictions, which needs clarification. It is also recommended that the application of the doctrine of apparent agency which is based on a public policy rationale, rather be based on a well grounded legal approach.[405]

The evolution of the doctrines of apparent agency, agency by estoppel and other possible relevant theories is once again proof of the systematic expansion of hospital liability for the negligent acts of independent contractor physicians and independent contractor groups or companies consisting of medical professionals which are accommodated on the hospital premises.

### 8.4.3 Hospital Liability in Terms of the Non-Delegable Duty

The non-delegable duty has been improvised as a rationale or independent legal ground to establish hospital liability for the malpractice or negligent acts of independent contractors.[406] The concept of the non-delegable duty had already been established in 1811:

> A person causing something to be done, the doing of which casts upon him a duty, cannot escape from the responsibility attaching to him of seeing that duty performed, by delegating it to a contractor. He may bargain with the contractor that he shall perform the duty, and stipulate for an indemnity from him if it is not performed, but he cannot thereby relieve himself from liability to those injured by the failure to perform it.[407]

---

[404] Ferraro and Camarra 1988 *IBJ* 370.

[405] *Op. cit.* 370, 364–370: Such as was taken by Illinois courts defining 'a conservative *prima facie* case of 'agency by estoppel' which strikes a balance between the rights of the health care consumer and provider.' Such an approach 'is consistent with the public policy of this state, as announced by the legislature and supreme court, in recognizing the legitimate governmental interest in mitigating the costs and burdens of a perceived malpractice crisis in the interest of providing affordable health care.'

[406] See also Louisell and Williams *Medical Malpractice* §15.05 15–24 to 15–26, §16.08 16–39. Smith *Hospital* §3.03 [2] 3–10 to 3–11. Southwick and Slee *Law of Hospital* 543–544. Southwick *Hospital Liability* 239. Annas *et al. American Health Law* 447–453. McWilliams and Russell 1996 *SCLR* 452–462. Furrow *et al. Health Law* 226–230, 266–269. According to Louisell and Williams *Medical Malpractice* §15.05 15–24 the non-delegable duty rationale is based on the Restatement (Second) of Agency §214 (1958) and according to McWilliams and Russell 1996 *SCLR* 457–462, it is based on Restatement (Second) of Torts §429 (1965).

[407] *Ft Lowell-NSS Ltd Partnership* 800 P 2d at 966–967. McWilliams and Russell 1996 *SCLR* 452–453.

As has already been discussed, the non-delegable duty is only non-delegable concerning the responsibility or liability of the delegator, but is delegable in the sense that only performance of the duty is delegable to the independent contractor or other delegatee.[408] The delegator therefore retains responsibility or liability to third parties, without any fault on the delegator's part, but for the negligence of the delegatee.[409] Liability is therefore not evaded by delegation of (the performance of) the duty to an independent contractor.[410] The non-delegable duty is therefore an exception both to the rule of non-liability for the torts of independent contractors and to the fault-based tort system which requires that the liability should be based on fault.[411] Non-delegable duty comprises employer liability without (employer) fault.[412]

The non-delegable duty has been classified as being a form of direct liability in the Australian hospital liability law,[413] whereas in the American hospital liability law, the non-delegable duty has frequently been referred to as vicarious liability.[414] McWilliams and Russell state:

> Similarly clear is that nondelegable duty does not describe direct liability in the sense of breach by or fault of the delegator; it is a species of vicarious liability, liability for the fault of another based not on the delegator's fault but on policy considerations.[415]

However, under the discussion of direct corporate liability, McWilliams and Russell refer to the courts' questionable usage of direct corporate liability

---

[408] *Supra* at 4.2.3, 4.3.3, 5.5, 6.3.3. See also McWilliams and Russell 1996 *SCLR* 452–453.

[409] *Ibid.*

[410] *Ibid.*

[411] *Ibid.* Southwick and Slee *Law of Hospital* 543. Southwick *Hospital Liability* 239. Louisell and Williams *Medical Malpractice* §15.05 15–24.

[412] *Supra* at 4.2.3, 4.3.3, 5.5. McWilliams and Russell 1996 *SCLR* 453.

[413] *Supra* at 6.3.3 and 6.5.

[414] Louisell and Williams *Medical Malpractice* §15.05 15–24, §16.01 16–2. Southwick and Slee *Law of Hospital* 543. Southwick *Hospital Liability* 239. McWilliams and Russell 1996 *SCLR* 452–453, 454, 468.

[415] McWilliams and Russell 1996 *SCLR* 453, and at 452: 'The doctrine of nondelegable duty has traditionally been used to describe a form of vicarious liability, ... .' And at 454: 'Although a number of courts have used the term 'nondelegable duty' to refer to certain duties owed directly by hospitals to patients, in most such cases the term is being used not in the traditional sense; rather, the hospital is found liable for its own negligence in breaching a duty owed directly to the patient, not for the negligence of an attempted delegee.'

duties as 'nondelegable duties',[416] yet do not seem to substantially differentiate between these duties, themselves.

It is submitted, that the non-delegable duty is first and foremost an independent legal ground *sui generis* which founds hospital liability. Preferably, it should not be classified as a form of direct or indirect (vicarious) liability.[417] American courts have, however, introduced the non-delegable duty formulation when referring to direct corporate duties breach of which induces direct corporate hospital liability. It is then, however, not used in the full traditional sense of referring to a separate legal ground which initiates strict liability, but rather implies that an employer will not escape liability for his *own* negligence, if performance of health care is delegated. The employer has a personal direct duty to fulfil to his patients, breach of which induces direct fault-based liability.[418]

Non-delegable duties[419] are created by contract, franchise or charter, statute or common law.[420] It has been concluded that duties are perceived to be non-delegable at common law, where the responsibility to the community is so important, that the employer should not be allowed to transfer it to another.[421] Apart from this criterion no other common justification has been formulated.[422] Non-delegable duties which are established by common law have also been described as 'reflections of particularly significant public policy, as perceived by courts'.[423]

The non-delegable duty was discussed and employed in *Jackson* v. *Power*.[424] On appeal, the Alaska Supreme Court explored the grounds,

---

[416] McWilliams and Russell 1996 *SCLR* 452, 454, 468, 469–471. See *infra*.

[417] See the Comparative Diagram at 4.4, and see the Conclusion at 10.

[418] See also McWilliams and Russel 1996 *SCLR* 468–471.

[419] According to Southwick and Slee *Law of Hospital* 543 and Southwick *Hospital Liability* 239, such a duty exists where an enterprise owes duties to the public or community. 'For example, the duty of a public or common carrier to exercise reasonable care in the transport of passengers is non-delegable, likewise the duty of a city to repair streets or other public facilities is nondelegable … a landowner to refrain from obstructing an adjoining public way.'

[420] Southwick and Slee *Law of Hospital* 543. Southwick *Hospital Liability* 239. McWilliams and Russell 1996 *SCLR* 453–454, who indicate that the common law category includes the identification of inherently dangerous activities.

[421] McWilliams and Russell 1996 *SCLR* 454.

[422] *Ibid.*

[423] *Ibid.*

[424] 743 P 2d 1376 (Alaska 1987). For a detailed discussion of the facts and outlay of this case refer to Apparent Agency: Relevant Case Law, in this chapter. Furrow *et al. Health Law* 226–230. Kelly and Jones *Healthcare* 349–350. Annas *et al. American Health Law* 448–453. Louisell and Williams *Medical Malpractice* §15.05 15–24 to 15–25. McWilliams and

criterions or justification by means of which the non-delegable duty is established and imposed in given circumstances. In terms of the state regulations, the JCAH's standards and the hospital's own bylaws, the court determined that the hospital (FMH) indeed had a duty to provide emergency room services and that part of the duty was to provide physician care in its emergency room.

Furthermore, in the light of the 'importance to the community of a hospital's duty to provide emergency room physicians...'[425] and the operation of the hospital as 'one of the most regulated activities in this state',[426] the court found that the hospital bears final accountability for the provision of physicians in the emergency room. The court concluded 'that a general acute care hospital's duty to provide physicians for emergency room care is non-delegable. Thus, a hospital ... may not shield itself from liability by claiming that it is not responsible for the results of negligently performed health care when the law imposes a duty on the hospital to provide that health care'[427]

Unfortunately, after founding the non-delegable duty and establishing the hospital's liability the court proceeded to find the hospital **vicariously** liable for damages proximately caused by the physician's negligence or malpractice. The fortunate finding was that the hospital's liability should not depend upon the technical employment status of the emergency room physician who had treated the patient. In other words, hospital liability should follow for emergency room physicians irrespective of the fact whether such a physician was an employee or an independent contractor. This case once again established hospital liability for the negligence of an independent contractor.[428]

The *Jackson* case has not been widely followed.[429] In *Albain* v. *Flower Hospital*[430] the Ohio Supreme Court went so far as to characterize the 'extensions of nondelegable duty to hospitals employing independent contractors as 'misdirected attempts to circumvent the necessity of proving

---

53. Louisell and Williams *Medical Malpractice* §15.05 15–24 to 15–25. McWilliams and Russell 1996 *SCLR* 454–455. Smith *Hospital* §15.05 15–24 to 15–25.

[425] Jackson 1384. McWilliams and Russell 1996 *SCLR* at 455 conclude that the characterization of the *'duty as nondelegable, ... is based on a determination of public policy, ... .'*

[426] *Jackson* 1384.

[427] *Jackson* 1385.

[428] See the comment of Annas *et al. American Health Law* at 451, on this aspect. The independent contractor aspect did, however, refrain the court from applying the apparent authority theory.

[429] McWilliams and Russell 1996 *SCLR* 455.

[430] 553 NE 2d 1038 (Ohio 1990).

agency by estoppel [that] confuse the proper scope of a hospital's duty in selecting competent physicians.'[431]'[432]

### 8.4.3.1 The inherent function test

Pursuant to the concept of the non-delegable duty, the hospital is considered liable for the independent contractor's malpractice when the services which are provided are part of the inherent function of the hospital.[433] In *Beeck* v. *Tucson General Hospital*,[434] the plaintiff had contracted pneumonia after the insertion of a needle into her spine during a lumbar myelogram, which occurred due to a collision by the X-ray machine screen with the needle. After careful consideration of all relevant facts, an employer-employee relationship was identified as existing between the radiologist Dr Rente and the hospital, as a result of which *respondeat superior* applied. The court also employed the inherent function test as a result of which it found that the radiology service was an inherent function of the hospital without which the hospital could not properly operate or achieve its responsibility, or properly achieve its purpose.[435] The court found the hospital liable for the acts of radiologists who operated and provided the radiology services of the hospital, by employing this theory. '*Beeck* stands for the proposition that when certain inherent functions are essential to the purposes of the hospital and those functions are performed by independent contractor physicians, the hospital may not delegate responsibility for injuries sustained from the negligent performance of those duties.'[436]

The inherent function test investigates those functions of the hospital which are essential to its operation of which two are its radiology and emergency services.[437] This test overlaps substantially with the non-delegable duty rule in agency law.[438]

---

[431]  *Albain* 1047.

[432]  McWilliams and Russell 1996 *SCLR* 456.

[433]  Louisell and Williams *Medical Malpractice* §16.08 16–39, §15.05 15–25. Werthmann *Malpractice* 10. Furrow *et al. Health Law* 232–235.

[434]  18 Ariz App 165, 500 P 2d 1153 (1972)(Arizona). See a discussion of this case under Apparent Agency-Relevant Case Law.

[435]  See also Werthmann *Malpractice* 10, and Furrow *et al. Health Law* 233.

[436]  Louisell and Williams *Medical Malpractice* §16.08 16–39.

[437]  Furrow *et al. Health Law* 233.

[438]  *Ibid.*

### 8.4.4 Direct or Corporate Hospital Liability

#### 8.4.4.1 *The hospital as corporate institution*

Hospitals and other institutional health care providers or health care facilities, mostly operate as corporations.[439] A corporate health care facility is a legal person with 'recognized rights, duties, powers and responsibilities'.[440] In *Trustees of Dartmouth College* v. *Woodward*[441] the corporation was defined as being 'an artificial being, invisible, intangible, and existing only in contemplation of law'.[442] A corporation is therefore a fictitious person created by law, existing separately and distinct from those who create it, own it or serve it.[443] Natural persons are however designated to form a governing body and are generally known as the board of directors or board of trustees.[444] These individuals exercise corporate powers and may be held liable for their corporate decision-making.[445] Institutions that are not incorporated, are not fictitious persons and powers and responsibilities are held by one or more natural persons.[446]

Most hospitals have become sophisticated comprehensive health care institutions, which are comprehensive health care providers arranging total health care, furnished with modern equipment and necessary facilities.[447] Most of these hospitals function as corporations, and courts have described them as corporate institutions that provide and monitor all aspects of health care.[448] Private hospitals are often owned by large corporations which subject these hospitals or corporate entities to corporate structures or hierarchies.[449] These corporate legal entities or hospitals are designed as businesses, are managed to obtain optimal profits and are traded on the Stock Exchange.[450] Statistics have revealed that 'community hospitals throughout the USA

---

[439] Southwick and Slee *Law of Hospital* 103. Peters *et al. Medical Practice* 129.

[440] Pozgar *Health* 199.

[441] 17 US (4 Wheat) 518 (1819) at 636.

[442] *Ibid*: As held by Chief Justice John Marshall of the United States Supreme Court.

[443] Southwick and Slee *Law of Hospital* 106. Pozgar *Health* 199.

[444] Pozgar *Health* 199, 200.

[445] *Ibid*.

[446] *Op. cit.* 145.

[447] See also Rutchik 1994 *VLR* 538 and Peters 1988 *TRIAL* 82.

[448] Rutchik 1994 *VLR* 538. Peters 1988 *TRIAL* 82. Peters *et al. Medical Practice* 129–130.

[449] Rutchik 1994 *VLR* 538–539.

[450] *Ibid*. Peters *et al. Medical Practice* 129.

realized an annual net total revenue of more than \$235 billion'.[451] Corporate hospital liability has been justified by courts on the basis of public reliance on this sophisticated, profit-generating hospital industry, which provides comprehensive, competent, high-quality medical care.[452]

### 8.4.4.2 Hospital liability

Direct or corporate (hospital) liability qualifies as an independent legal ground which establishes hospital liability, and has evolved over more than thirty years in American law.[453] Direct hospital liability or institutional responsibility or corporate liability[454] implies the direct liability of the hospital or institutional health care provider, which centres on the hospital's own liability for its own acts[455] or omissions.

The concept of corporate liability is predicated on the rule of agency[456] (Restatement [Second] of Agency §2.13) in terms of which a principal is held liable for his own negligence for placing an agent in a position to do harm.

> A person conducting an activity through servants or other agents is subject to liability for harm resulting from his conduct if he is negligent or reckless:
> (b)    in the employment of improper persons or instrumentalities in work involving risk of harm to others;
> (c)    in the supervision of the activity ... .

---

[451]  Rutchik 1994 *VLR* 539. The statistics relied on 1991 data.

[452]  Mason and McCall-Smith 1987 *Encyclopaedia* 582. Rutchik 1994 *VLR* 539. Peters 1988 *TRIAL* 82.

[453]  Annas *et al. American Health Law* 455. Fiscina *Legal Medicine* 424. Rutchik 1994 *VLR* 540.

[454]  Annas *et al. American Health Law* 453–470. Mason and McCall-Smith 1987 Encyclopaedia at 582. Fiscina *Legal Medicine* 420–426. Fiesta *Nurses* 24–27. Furrow *et al. Health Law* 235–241. Christoffel *Health* 117–121. Kelly and Jones *Healthcare* 355–368. Kramer and Kramer *Medical Malpractice* 50–53. Louisell and Williams *Medical Malpractice* §15.06 15–26 to 15–41. McCafferty and Meyer *Liability* 319–321. Miller *Hospital Law* 194–195, 206–225. Oerlikoff and Vanagunas *Hospitals* 4–6. Pozgar *Health* 207–228. Roach *et al. Law* 208–211. Smith *Hospital* §3.03 [1] 3–8 to 3–9; §3.03 [3] 3–18 to 3–20. Southwick *Hospital Liability* 251–263, 279–280. Southwick and Slee *Law of Hospital* 554–565, 580–581. Werthmann *Malpractice* 19–25. Brown 1988 *DCJ* 165–167. Cunningham 1975 *WLR* 411–416. Janulis and Hornstein 1985 *NLR* 702–708. McWilliams and Russell 1996 *SCLR* 462–471. Morgan 1995 *JLM* 403–406. Peters 1988 *TRIAL* 82–90. Reuter 1994 *JLM* 512–513. Rutchik 1994 *VLR* 540–548. Spero 1979 *TRIAL* 24–27. Trial and Claybrook 1985 *BLR* 323–330, 363.

[455]  Annas *et al. American Health Law* 453.

[456]  Werthmann *Malpractice* 19.

Corporate or direct hospital liability especially creates a hospital liability zone for the malpractice of professional independent contractors.[457] Hospital liability in terms of this legal ground can also ensue for the acts performed by the hospital board, board of directors, senior administrative and medical officials, and any employee or other medical staff member who fulfils an institutional duty or function of the hospital in an organizational role.[458]

Corporate or direct liability is consequently established by breach of the hospital's independent direct duty of care which it owes the patients.[459] Corporate negligence is established by the breach of the duty of care through one of the corporation's agents,[460] employees, members or independent contractors.

### 8.4.4.3  The concept of duty

Direct or corporate hospital liability embodies a concept of duty.[461] Upon investigation of the formation of this independent legal ground, an extensive structure of direct legal duties[462] which are ascribed to the hospital, is uncovered. A uniform description which summarizes the constellation of comprehensive duties runs as follows: The hospital as institution, and other institutional health care providers owe a direct and independent duty of care to its patients,[463] to refrain from any act or omission which could in any way

---

[457]  See footnote 454. McWilliams and Russell 1996 *SCLR* 463: Direct hospital liability follows regardless of the fact of whether the patient was treated by a hospital employee, an independent contractor staff physician of the hospital or the patient's personal physician. Morgan 1995 *JLM* 403. Rutchik 1994 *VLR* 536.

[458]  Annas *et al. American Health Law* 453. Pozgar *Health* 212–214.

[459]  Werthmann *Malpractice* 19. Pozgar *Health* 207–208. McCafferty and Meyer *Liability* 319. Roach *et al. Law* 210. Rutchik 1994 *VLR* 540. Fiesta *Nurses* 51–84: Breach of Duty.

[460]  *Ibid.*

[461]  *Johnson* v. *Misericordia* 99 Wis 2d 708, 301 NW 2d 156 (1981). See also Fiscina *Legal Medicine* 424.

[462]  Janulis and Hornstein 1985 *NLR* 703. Louisell and Williams *Medical Malpractice* §15.06 15–26 to 15–41: They discuss six duties which found corporate hospital liability. Peters 1988 *TRIAL* 82–90 discussed 'Eleven Theories of Direct Liability' or eleven direct duties which found hospital corporate liability and induces corporate negligence. Cunningham 1975 *WLR* 412–416 discussed at least four duties. Pozgar *Health* 207–228, discusses twelve relevant corporative duties. Kramer and Kramer *Medical Malpractice* 50–54 listed fifteen hospital duties. Miller *Hospital Law* 194–195.

[463]  Janulis and Hornstein 1985 *NLR* 702–703. Oerlikoff and Vanagunas *Hospitals* 4. Werthmann *Malpractice* 19. McCafferty and Meyer *Liability* 319. Pozgar *Health* 207–208. Mason and McCall-Smith 1987 Encyclopaedia at 582. Trial and Claybrook 1985 *BLR* 323, 330, 363. Fiesta *Nurses* 25–26, 51–84.

cause (foreseeable) harm or create an unreasonable risk of danger.[464] Identification of duties has been so extensive, that courts and writers have succeeded in categorizing the direct hospital duties. These categories, which are not finite nor yet inclusive of all possible direct duties, comprise of many direct hospital duties which the hospital should fulfil.[465] The duties which a hospital owes a patient, are expanded and altered by case law at any time, can overlap in certain areas, and are indeed very broad.[466] The comprehensive concept of direct duty evolved in order to monitor the quality of medical care by controlling the standards of that care by organizational methods, supervising, overseeing and reviewing procedures and other possible means.[467]

The hospital's direct duties which are owed to patients, stem from the common law duty of care owed to patients by the hospital.[468] It is also a moral duty and is contemporarily also founded by relevant legislation.[469] The direct duties which a corporation owes the general public and its patients, usually arise from statutes, regulations, principles of law which the courts develop and internal operating rules of the institution.[470]

---

[464] *Johnson* v. *Misericordia* 99 Wis 2d 708, 301 NW 2d 156 (1981). Fiscina *Legal Medicine* 424. The concept of duty induces corporate negligence of which foreseeability is a fundamental element.

[465] See a detailed discussion of all relevant categories *infra*. Klages 1988 *IBJ* 40–41 states: 'Although the more recent trend in both legislation and case law has been to limit the hospital's duty and the damages for which it can be liable, there still remains the potential of liability for new and expanded breaches of duty. Suits ... have yet to reach their full potential as sources of malpractice claims. One of the results of the expansion of professional healing negligence claims has been an enormous rise in the malpractice insurance premiums for both physicians and hospitals.'

[466] Oerlikoff and Vanagunas *Hospitals* 6.

[467] Fiscina *Legal Medicine* 425. Annas *et al. American Health Law* 455.

[468] *Johnson* v. *Misericordia* 99 Wis 2d 708, 301 NW 2d 156 (1981). Fiscina *Legal Medicine* 424.

[469] *Ibid.*

[470] Pozgar *Health* 207–208.

## *8.4.4.4 The hospital's direct duties*

### 8.4.4.4.1 **Categories**[471]

---

[471] The categories formulated in *Thompson* v. *Nason Hospital* 527 Pa 330, 591 A 2d 703 (Pa 1991) at 707 will be discussed first and foremost, and all relevant hospital duties as formulated by courts and writers will be categorized accordingly. Morgan 1995 *JLM* 403–404 reiterated the classification of the *Thompson* case *supra*, as did Rutchik 1994 *VLR* 540–548. Reuter 1994 *JLM* 512–513 also confirmed the *Thompson* classification, as did McWilliams and Russell 1996 *SCLR* 463.

Southwick *Hospital Liability* 251–278 and Southwick and Slee *Law of Hospital* 554–578 highlighted the following duties: (1) Duty of reasonable care in the maintenance and use of equipment. (2) Duty of reasonable care in selecting and retaining of employees and medical staff. (3) Duties concerning the 'Violation of rules and failure to adopt rules as corporate negligence'.

Kelly and Jones *Healthcare* 355–377 discuss several categories of duties which relate to: (1) Negligent selection and retention (of staff). (2) Selection of equipment, supplies and devices. (3) Design, maintenance and security of the physical plant. (4) Innovative (non-standard) therapies. (5) Liability of Trustees or Directors.

Louisell and Williams *Medical Malpractice* §15.06 15–27 to 15–41, categorized hospital liability as follows:

(1) Liability for negligent selection of professional staff.
(2) Liability for negligent monitoring or supervision of staff physicians.
(3) Liability for acts of emergency room physicians.
(4) Liability for refusal to treat in emergency room or Improper transfer of patient to another facility.
(5) Liability for negligent supervision of surgical and anaesthesia services.
(6) Hospital liability for malpractice in staff physician's office.

Oerlikoff and Vanagunas *Hospitals* 5–6 expounded five areas of obligations a hospital owes a patient: (1) The duty of the hospital to exercise reasonable care in providing proper medical equipment, supplies, medication, and food for its patients. (2) The duty of the hospital to exercise reasonable care in providing safe physical premises for its patients. (3) The duty of the hospital to adopt internal policies and procedures reasonably estimated to protect the safety and the interests of its patients. (4) The duty of the hospital to exercise reasonable care in the selection and retention of hospital employees and in the granting of staff privileges. (5) The duty of the hospital to exercise reasonable care to guarantee that adequate patient care is being administered.

Brown 1988 *DCJ* 165 who only discusses three traditional areas of direct corporate hospital liability:

(1) Physical condition of buildings and grounds.
(2) Selection and maintenance of equipment.
(3) Selection and evaluation of hospital staff, to which he added the hospital duty to supervise medical care.

Trail and Claybrook 1985 *BLR* 323–330 identifies three traditional areas of direct corporate hospital liability: 1) Maintenance and use of equipment. 2) The availability of services to those who seek to use them. 3) Selection and retention of hospital employees.

In *Thompson* v. *Nason Hospital*,[472] the Pennsylvania Supreme Court adopted the doctrine of corporate negligence (which relates to institutions) and proceeded to note that the hospital's duties had been classified into four primary categories by other jurisdictions.[473] The classifications had been founded on case law that had evolved over the last twenty-five years.[474] Corporate liability could ensue for breach of any of the hospital duties under these categories.[475]

The categories formulated in *Thompson*[476] are:

(1) A duty to use reasonable care in the maintenance of safe and adequate facilities and equipment.

(2) A duty to select and retain only competent physicians.

(3) A duty to oversee all persons who practice medicine within its walls, as to patient care.

(4) A duty to formulate, adopt and enforce adequate rules and policies to ensure quality care for the patients.

## Category 1: A duty to use reasonable care in the maintenance of safe and adequate facilities and equipment[477]

Hospitals have a direct duty to patients (and others) to reasonably maintain facilities and equipment. Of all the direct corporate liabilities, this duty is the least controversial of all. It is established by traditional tort doctrine which

---

They also discuss the expansion and recent developments concerning direct corporate liability, which include for example the duty to maintain reasonable rules and standards.

According to Rutchik 1994 *VLR* 540 footnote 28, Perdue in 'Direct Corporate Liability of Hospital: A Modern Day Legal Concept of Liability for Injury Occurring in the Modern Day Hospital' 24 *S Tex LJ* (1983) 773 note 2, there are six categories of corporate liability: (1) Negligence in relation to premises, equipment or facilities. (2) Negligence in selection or retention of physicians. (3) Negligence in supervision of physicians. (4) Failure to formulate medical rules or policies. (5) Negligence in formulating medical rules or policies. (6) Negligence in enforcing medical rules or policies.

See also Klages 1988 *IBJ* 34–41.

[472] 527 Pa 330, 591 A 2d 703 (Pa 1991) at 707.

[473] *Ibid.* See also Morgan 1995 *JLM* 403.

[474] *Thompson* 591 A 2d 703 (1991) at 707. Rutchik 1994 *VLR* 540. Seminal cases were cited in the *Thompson* case.

[475] *Ibid.*

[476] *Thompson* 591 A 2d 703 (Pa 1991) at 707.

[477] Most courts and writers acknowledge this duty: McWilliams and Russell 1996 *SCLR* 463. Morgan 1995 *JLM* 403. Rutchik 1994 *VLR* 540. Trail and Claybrook 1985 *BLR* 323. Cunningham 1975 *WLR* 412. Brown 1988 *DCJ* 165. Peters 1988 *TRIAL* 85. Southwick *Hospital Liability* 252–254. Southwick and Slee *Law of Hospital* 555–557. Kelly and Jones *Healthcare* 364–368. Miller *Hospital Law* 206–209. Oerlikoff and Vanagunas *Hospitals* 5. Pozgar *Health* 221. Klages 1988 *IBJ* 36. Christoffel *Health* 117.

requires commercial entities to reasonably maintain all the equipment and facilities offered to the public.[478]

This category is also inclusive of the following duties:

(1)     The hospital's duty to exercise reasonable care in providing proper medical supplies, medication and food for its patients.[479]

(2)     The hospital's duty to exercise reasonable care in providing safe physical premises and environment for its patients and employees.[480]

(3)     The hospital's duty to use reasonable care in the maintenance of buildings and grounds for the protection of the hospital's invitees.[481]

(4)     The duty of the hospital to safeguard patient valuables.[482]

(5)     The hospital has a duty to effectively control infection.[483]

(6)     The hospital must provide reasonably adequate diagnostic equipment and safe hardware for the care and treatment of its patients.[484]

(7)     The hospital must establish an effective system for the handling of drugs.[485]

## Category 2: A duty to select and retain only competent physicians[486]

Hospitals should verify and scrutinize physicians' competence, qualifications and medical credibility or background with an acceptable level of care,

---

[478]   Rutchik 1994 *VLR* 540.

[479]   Oerlikoff and Vanagunas *Hospitals* 5.

[480]   *Ibid.* Pozgar *Health* 223–227. Christoffel *Health* 117.

[481]   Cunningham 1975 *WLR* 412. Brown 1988 *DCJ* 165. Kelly and Jones *Healthcare* 367–368. Kramer and Kramer *Medical Malpractice* 54.

[482]   Pozgar *Health* 227–228.

[483]   *Op. cit.* 163. Klages 1988 *IBJ* 36–37. Miller *Hospital Law* 221–223.

[484]   Klages 1988 *IBJ* 36.

[485]   *Op. cit.* 37. Brushwood *Law* 214–217.

[486]   Most courts and writers acknowledge this duty: McWilliams and Russell 1996 *SCLR* 463, 464–465. Morgan 1995 *JLM* 403. Rutchik 1994 *VLR* 541–546. Trail and Claybrook 1985 *BLR* 330–334. Cunningham 1975 *WLR* 412, 415–416. Fiscina *Legal Medicine* 420–426. Peters 1988 *TRIAL* 82–84. Miller *Hospital Law* 209. Southwick *Hospital Liability* 257–258, 263–278. Southwick and Slee *Law of Hospital* 559–560, 565–578. Kelly and Jones *Healthcare* 355–364. Louisell and Williams *Medical Malpractice* §15.06 15–27 to 15–30. Oerlikoff and Vanagunas *Hospitals* 6. Klages 1988 *IBJ* 38. Brown 1988 *DCJ* 165. Hirsh 1988 *Med Law* 128. Christoffel *Health* 117–119. See the discussions that involve this duty *infra*.

before inviting them to join hospital staffs and granting them privileges.[487] When assessing applications and in consideration of their appointments, hospitals are responsible for any relevant information that they knew or should have known.[488] Whenever original employment applications are screened negligently or inadequately, institutions are held liable for the malpractice of staff physicians even where such negligent acts occurred several years after they were hired.[489]

The plaintiff must prove negligence on the part of the hospital in the course of selection or supervision. If the hospital's negligence is not active, 'but constitutes a failure to act, foreseeability of the harm that resulted, is required.'[490]

## Category 3: A duty to oversee all persons who practice medicine within its walls as to patient care[491]

The Restatement (Second) of Agency §213 (1958) provides:

> A person conducting an activity through servants or other agents is subject to liability for harm resulting from his conduct if he is negligent or reckless: ...
> (c) in the supervision of the activity ... .

This duty could be the most controversial component of the corporate liability doctrine.[492] 'Two factors complicate courts' determinations of liability for breach of the duty to properly supervise: physicians are independent contractors and negligent supervision may be difficult to ascertain.'[493]

The duty to *supervise* health care provided by medical professionals, (or all persons who practice medicine within the hospitals walls), has been

---

[487] See also Rutchik 1994 *VLR* 541, and McWilliams and Russell 1996 *SCLR* 467.

[488] *Ibid. Thompson* 591 A 2d at 707. See *infra*.

[489] *Johnson* v. *Misericordia Community Hospital* 301 NW 2d 156 (Wis 1981) at 169–171. Rutchik 1994 *VLR* 541.

[490] McWilliams and Russell 1996 *SCLR* 467. *Corleto* v. *Shore Memorial Hospital* 350 A 2d 534 (NJ Super Ct Law Div 1975) at 538.

[491] Most courts and writers acknowledge this duty: McWilliams and Russel 1996 *SCLR* 463, 465. Morgan 1995 *JLM* 403. Rutchik 1994 *VLR* 546–548. Reuter 1994 *JLM* 512–513, 517–526. Cunningham 1975 *WLR* 412. Fiscina *Legal Medicine* 420–426. Miller *Hospital Law* 209. Southwick *Hospital Liability* 263–278. Southwick and Slee *Law of Hospital* 565–578. Kelly and Jones *Healthcare* 355–364. Louisell and Williams *Medical Malpractice* §15.06 15–30 to 15–32. Brown 1988 *DCJ* 165. Trail and Claybrook 1985 *BLR* 323–330. Hirsh 1988 *Med Law* 128. Christoffel *Health 117.*

[492] Rutchik 1994 *VLR* 546.

[493] *Ibid.* Reuter 1994 *JLM* 517–526 also discusses the duty to supervise.

enunciated by some courts or truncated by others.[494] Courts who have limited this sphere of the expansion of corporate hospital liability, represent judicial recognition (of the facts) (i) that the physician-patient relationship is of a personal nature which necessitates physician discretion, (ii) for which it is impractical to continually 'stand over a physician and personally supervise the quality of medical care rendered.'[495] and (iii) for which the hospital is not well-equipped to actively and concurrently supervise patient care.[496]

Therefore, it has been suggested that the correct procedure to be enunciated in the formulation of such a duty, is the duty to *oversee* — rather than supervise — the quality of physician performance and other relevant medical performances, which represents a different perspective. Overseeing or review of medical staff clinical performance signifies a retrospective process.[497] Hospitals delegate their review function to medical staff committees, such as quality assurance, risk management and credentials, who use historical data base describing the physician's training, prior experience and performance to project future performance.[498] Whereas the process of supervision requires current data to concurrently determine present performance to provide appropriate contemporaneous intervention.[499]

This category is inclusive of many duties:

(i)     *The duty to exercise reasonable care in the provision of patient care* is also inclusive of the following duties:

    (1)     The hospital's duty to exercise reasonable care to guarantee that adequate and satisfactory patient care is being administered.[500]

    (2)     The duty of employees to follow physicians' instructions concerning medical care. Failure to comply with this duty has resulted in direct hospital liability.[501]

---

[494]   Fiscina *Legal Medicine* 424.

[495]   *Op. cit.* 425.

[496]   *Op. cit.* 424–425 for the three judicial expositions. Reuter 1994 *JLM* 518 states that the duty to supervise, by university faculty or attending staff — in the medical house staff context — arises in various ways depending on the type of teaching hospital. Likewise, the attending physician or medical school faculty member who accepts the responsibility for supervising residents, must do so in a reasonable manner.

[497]   Fiscina *Legal Medicine* 425. *Thompson supra* (at 707) and category 3 *supra*.

[498]   Fiscina *Legal Medicine* 425.

[499]   *Ibid.*

[500]   Pozgar *Health* 216, 222–223. Oerlikoff and Vanagunas *Hospitals* 6.

[501]   *Albain* v. *Flower Hospital* 553 NE 2d 1038 at 1050 (Ohio 1990). McWilliams and Russell 1996 *SCLR* 463. Kramer and Kramer *Medical Malpractice* 54. Bruchmwood *Law* 221.

(3)  The duty to keep the attending physician informed of a patient's condition to permit appropriate diagnosis and treatment.[502] Failure to adhere to this duty has also resulted in direct hospital liability.[503]

(4)  The hospital is under a duty not to use non-standard or experimental treatment that can cause injuries or death to patients.[504]

(5)  The hospital may not prematurely discharge a patient or improperly move the patient from one hospital to another.[505]

(6)  The hospital has a duty to properly supervise a patient who is in the delivery room and becomes mentally deranged or had shown signs of mental instability.[506]

(7)  The hospital must not give the patient mismatched blood or improper medication.[507]

(8)  The patient must not be burned with a hot-water bottle, heat-lamp or other devices.[508]

(9)  Nurses must be competent to administer injections appropriately.[509]

(10)  Procedures for the insertion of needles for intravenous fluids must be handled properly.[510]

(11)  A sufficient number of trained nurses must be provided to recognize deterioration in a patient's condition or gangrene in a patient's leg. They must require consultation with, or examination, by hospital staff members as required by the hospital's own rules.[511]

---

[502]  *Albain* at 1051. *Lambert* v. *Sister of Mercy Health Corp.* 369 NW 2d 417 (Iowa 1985) at 420 was cited: Additionally, 'it must be ... shown that such breach was the proximate cause of the patient's injury before the hospital will be held vicariously liable therefore.' McWilliams and Russell 1996 *SCLR* 463. Kramer and Kramer *Medical Malpractice* 53.

[503]  See also McWilliams and Russell 1996 *SCLR* 463.

[504]  Kelly and Jones *Healthcare* 368–371.

[505]  Kramer and Kramer *Medical Malpractice* 51. Peters 1988 *TRIAL* 89–90. The hospital is also responsible for the quality care at the other facility.

[506]  Kramer and Kramer *Medical Malpractice* 51.

[507]  *Op. cit.* 53. Klages 1988 *IBJ* 36–37.

[508]  Kramer and Kramer *Medical Malpractice* 53.

[509]  *Ibid.* Brushwood *Law* 219–220.

[510]  Kramer and Kramer *Medical Malpractice* 53.

[511]  *Darling* v. *Charleston Community Memorial Hospital* 50 Ill App 2d 253, 200 NE 2d 149 (1964), affd, 33 Ill 2 d 326, 211 NE 2d 253 (1965), cert. denied, 383 US 946 (1966). Kramer and Kramer *Medical Malpractice* 53–54.

(12)   Adequate personnel assistance is required to help the elderly patient to the bathroom.[512]

(13)   A hospital may not give a patient illegal treatment with the knowledge of the hospital administration.[513]

(14)   Hospitals must respond promptly to patients' calls for help.[514]

(15)   The hospital has a duty to provide adequate staff.[515]

(ii)   *The duty to exercise reasonable care in the provision of specialized patient care.* Hospital liability can ensue in the following circumstances:

(1)   The hospital has a duty to provide adequate emergency room care by means of emergency room physicians,[516] when providing such services.

(2)   Liability will ensue for refusal to admit or treat patients in the emergency room or for the improper transfer of a patient to another facility.[517]

(3)   Liability will ensue for the negligent supervision of surgical and anaesthesia services.[518]

(4)   Hospitals have a duty to employ qualified, trained and supervised non-physician staff, for example nurses, and X-ray and laboratory technicians.[519]

(5)   Hospitals can encounter liability with regard to pharmacists, physical therapists, pathology and radiology.[520]

(iii)   *Hospitals have a duty to inform the patient or his survivors of a known deviation from the standard of care that caused injury or death.*[521]

---

[512]   Kramer and Kramer *Medical Malpractice* 54.

[513]   *Ibid.*

[514]   Peters 1988 *TRIAL 88.*

[515]   Pozgar *Health* 218–221. Fiesta *Nurses* 51–84.

[516]   Louisell and Williams *Medical Malpractice* §15.07 15–32 to 15–33. Miller *Hospital Law* 223–224.

[517]   Louisell and Williams *Medical Malpractice* §15.07 15–33 to 15–40. Kramer and Kramer *Medical Malpractice* 50.

[518]   Louisell and Williams *Medical Malpractice* §15.07 15–40 to 15–41.

[519]   Peters 1988 *TRIAL* 88.

[520]   Miller *Hospital Law* 216–221.

[521]   Peters 1988 *TRIAL* 88–89.

(iv) *The hospital has a duty to compile and maintain proper medical records.*

When this does not transpire — to the detriment of the patient — separate action will lie against the hospital for this impropriety, in a subsequent action.[522]

## Category 4: A duty to formulate, adopt and enforce adequate rules and policies to ensure quality care for the patients[523]

Courts can find a hospital *per se* negligent, when such a hospital declines to establish rules or necessary procedures for its physicians or other health-care practitioners.[524] A lack of substantive rules, policies or procedures or related problems should induce direct liability. Usually, the corporate liability controversies involve the degree and manner in which the hospitals had applied the rules and regulations which they had established.[525]

This category is also inclusive of the following duties:

(1) The hospital's duty to adopt internal policies and procedures reasonably estimated to protect the safety and the interests of its patients.[526]

(2) The hospital's governing board's duty to implement an operating certification committee to supervise physician practice within the hospital. Failure of this duty might establish direct hospital liability, constituting a negligent breach of a direct duty to patients.[527]

(3) The hospital should carry out the mandates of the JCAHO, and must abide by its own bylaws and rules,[528] statutes and regulations.[529]

(4) Hospitals have a duty to arrange or make proper contracts with subcontractors and vendors.[530]

(5) Hospitals must have adequate institutional policies.[531]

---

[522] Kramer and Kramer *Medical Malpractice* 54.

[523] Most corporate liability litigation does not address this duty: Rutchik 1994 *VLR* 541. Most writers acknowledge this duty: McWilliams and Russell 1996 *SCLR* 463. Morgan 1995 *JLM* 403. Rutchik 1994 *VLR* 540–541. Peters 1988 *TRIAL* 85. Christoffel *Health* 117.

[524] Rutchik 1994 *VLR* 541.

[525] *Ibid.*

[526] Oerlikoff and Vanagunas *Hospitals* 6.

[527] McWilliams and Russell 1996 *SCLR* 464.

[528] Peters 1988 *TRIAL* 85–86.

[529] Pozgar *Health* 215–216.

[530] Peters 1988 *TRIAL* 86–87.

[531] *Op. cit.* 87.

(6)    Hospitals must employ a competent hospital administrator.[532]

(7)    Hospitals are under a duty to avoid self-dealing and conflict-of-interest situations concerning board members.[533]

(8)    The hospital has a duty to provide adequate insurance.[534]

(9)    The hospital has a duty to require competitive bidding.[535]

### 8.4.4.5  Standards to determine corporate liability

Courts establish corporate or direct hospital liability when determining potential hospital negligence by means of objective standards.[536] Courts detect these standards in guidelines promulgated by the Joint Commission on Accreditation of Healthcare Organizations (JCAHO), in state statutes and state regulations.[537] As hospitals have evolved into modern corporations, so have these standards which define the scope and extent of potential liability for hospitals.

Most courts throughout the country nowadays assess all types of medical malpractice by using a national standard of care.[538] The national JCAHO standards[539] are based on the knowledge and practices of the ordinary hospital, regardless of the hospital's location and allow courts to apply the corporate liability doctrine in a responsible and practical manner.[540] Arguments against implementation of national standards concentrate on urban and rural as well as wealthy and poor discrepancies.

A national corporate liability standard is also recommended.[541] It has been advised that courts should apply a uniform set of corporate liability standards and select these standards consistently.[542] Corporate liability duties should be assessed by courts and hospitals by means of a national standards frame-

---

[532]  *Op. cit.* 87–88. Pozgar *Health* 213–214.

[533]  Pozgar *Health* 216–218.

[534]  *Op. cit.* 161.

[535]  *Op. cit.* 162.

[536]  Rutchik 1994 *VLR* 555.

[537]  *Ibid.*

[538]  *Op. cit.* 566.

[539]  *Id est* the national standard as codified in the JCAHO guidelines.

[540]  *Op. cit.* 566–567.

[541]  *Op. cit.* 567.

[542]  *Op. cit.* 555, 566.

work.[543] When establishing hospital duties concerning physician selection and supervision, the JCAHO guidelines are considered appropriate for courts to rely on. 'The guidelines are updated annually, are representative of industry changes, and are subscribed to on a national basis. They also are written by and for the hospital industry, and hospitals subscribe to them on a voluntary basis.'[544]

### 8.4.4.5.1 The JCAHO guidelines

The JCAHO guidelines necessitate a hospital organizational structure which consists of people creating policy, ensuring quality care and establishing internal management and planning.[545] A hospital governing body is required which adopts bylaws concerning its legal accountability and responsibility to patients, and develops rules and bylaws for physician staff selection and supervision.[546] A hospital is also required to have an organized medical staff who are responsible for the quality of professional services and who report to the governing body.[547]

Medical staff

(1)     The American hospital has come under a (non-delegable[548]) duty to take all necessary and reasonable steps to ensure that physicians who are granted medical staff memberships or privileges are competent and properly qualified and to ensure that this competency be continually examined or reviewed and revoked if necessary.[549]

---

[543]   *Op. cit.* 567. Proper JCAHO national standards should be considered.

[544]   Rutchik 1994 *VLR* 566.

[545]   Rutchik 1994 *VLR* 556.

[546]   JCAHO's Accreditation Manual for Hospitals GB 1 at 113, GB 1.13 at 115 (1994). Rutchik 1994 *VLR* 556.

[547]   JCAH's Accreditation Manual for Hospitals/ 88 MS.1 at 115 (1988). Rutchik 1994 *VLR* 556.

[548]   Although this duty is a direct corporate duty breach of which establishes direct corporate hospital liability, Smith *Hospital* §3.03 [2] 3–10 and McWilliams and Russell 1996 *SCLR* 468–471 have indicated that courts define this duty as a non-delegable duty. A detailed discussion on this subject follows *infra*. In actual fact these duties remain and are nothing other than direct corporate (liability) duties.

[549]   Smith *Hospital* §3.03 [2] 3–10. Richards and Rathbun *Risk* 78–82: The latter authors have formulated the duty in 'non-delegable duty' terminology. They state that the duty entails that the hospital should **ensure** that physicians are competent and should **ensure** that they are supervised which could imply a non-delegable duty connotation. Trail and Claybrook 1985 *BLR* 330–335: They also specify procedures in this regard.

The ultimate responsibility for the competency of medical staff has been allotted to the governing body by the JCAH.[550] Courts have consequently applied a legal duty commensurate with this responsibility.[551] Hospital liability is incurred and negligence is ruled:

(i)     where the physician's competence is determined by insufficient criteria

(ii)    if the hospital or hospital board knew that the physician was incompetent

(iii)   if the hospital or hospital board should have known that the physician was incompetent.[552]

In such cases the court would find that the hospital did not act in good faith or with reasonable care in granting the physician privileges.[553] When board members had personal knowledge of negligent behaviour but still failed to act, both personal and corporate liability could ensue.[554]

As a matter of law, it has been ruled that the medical staff execute an assumed duty of supervising the competency of staff physicians, whereby they act for and on behalf of the hospital.[555] Therefore, if the medical staff do not take any action against a physician or recommend revocation of privileges to the governing body, the medical staff and the hospital are deemed negligent and hospital liability ensues.[556]

(2)     The hospital also has a duty to oversee all persons who practice medicine within its walls as to patient care. From the previous discussion it can be concluded that the hospital governing body does there-

---

[550] Smith *Hospital* §3.03 [2] 3–10

[551] *Ibid.*

[552] Smith *Hospital* §3.03 [2] 3–10. Richards and Rathbun *Risk* 79.

[553] *Joiner* v. *Mitchell County Hospital* 125 Ga App 1, 186 SE 2d 307 at 308. See also *Penn Tanker Co* v. *United States* 310 F Supp 613 (SD Tex 1970)(Texas). Smith *Hospital* §3.03 [2] 3–10.

[554] Richards and Rathbun *Risk* 79.

[555] *Purcell* v. *Zimbelman* 18 Ariz App 75, 500 P 2d 335, 341 (1972). In this case the hospital negligently failed to revoke a private attending physician's staff privileges. The defendant doctor had negligently performed an abdominal surgical operation. It was contended that the hospital (against whom action was also brought) knew or had reason to know that the defendant-doctor lacked the skill to perform the procedure in accordance with appropriate medical standards. The court found that the Department of Surgery's negligence was imputable to the hospital as a matter of law. Smith *Hospital* §3.03 [2] 3–10.

[556] See *Foley* v. *Bishop Clarkson Memorial Hospital* 185 Neb 89, 173 NW 2d 881 (1970) in this regard. Smith *Hospital* §3.03 [2] 3–10.

fore not have an ultimate authority to dismiss physicians or hospital staff. The governing body can only do this when other staff physicians initiate ousting and only after consultation with the medical staff.[557] 'Thus the JCAHO guidelines and the corresponding exposure to corporate liability for the failure to supervise their staff physicians adequately limit hospital administrator's freedom. The governing body has the ultimate legal responsibility for its staff physicians, but it must defer to physician autonomy to satisfy the JCAHO guidelines, which are virtually necessary to run a successful and profitable hospital.'[558]

The JCAHO guidelines only stipulate broad organizational requirements with which the hospitals should comply and do not exactly specify the manner in which a hospital should select or supervise its patients. This transpires out of respect for hospital autonomy and their geographical and cultural diversity throughout the country. However, if more specified standards were introduced, a more uniform and consistent application of standards by courts would avail, by which modern hospitals could protect themselves from future liability.[559]

In conclusion, the JCAHO guidelines have been recommended as the ideal uniform national set of standards which could provide a specific framework for the proper application of the corporate liability doctrine, which should be applied consistently by courts and with which hospitals — upon full compliance — should be safeguarded from corporate hospital liability.[560]

It has been suggested that the JCAHO guidelines should be more specific, which in turn would create legal certainty and accountability.[561] Courts should, however, retain the privilege to formulate independent, clear and uniform or consistent decisions regardless of the Guidelines' specificity.[562] Proper judicial application can only strengthen if not save the doctrine of corporate hospital liability,[563] in due time.

At the moment, hospitals face a dilemma: If they do not terminate a staff physician after receiving complaints, they are exposed to corpo-

---

[557] Rutchik 1994 *VLR* 556–557. Trail and Claybrook 1985 *BLR* 334–335.

[558] Rutchik 1994 *VLR* 556–557.

[559] *Op. cit.* 557–558.

[560] *Op. cit.* 567–569.

[561] *Op. cit.* 569.

[562] *Op. cit.* 570.

[563] *Op. cit.* 571.

rate hospital liability for negligent physician supervision. However, upon termination of the physician, the hospital faces a potential anti-trust action from the physician. Hospital decisions should therefore be executed on greater information based on certain legal guidelines which would not only benefit hospitals, but the patients who suffer most.[564]

### 8.4.4.5.2 The National Practitioner Data Bank

A National Practitioner Data Bank (Data Bank) has been established by the United States Department of Health and Human Services by means of promulgated regulations.[565] The Data Bank documents all events of malpractice and physician incompetence on a national level, which reduces the overall risk of malpractice.[566] When a payment is made in settlement of a malpractice claim, the entity making the payment must report the circum-stances of such payment to the Data Bank.[567] State licensing boards must also report any disciplinary actions and adverse clinical actions taken against a health-care provider.[568]

The Data Bank regulations require a hospital — upon consideration of physician staff — to check for prior malpractice events and adverse licensing proceedings.[569] The hospital is presumed to have constructive knowledge of any information available at the Data Bank.[570] If a hospital properly checks the Data Bank, it may rely on the obtained information without future liability.[571] This creates a defence *per se* to negligent selection liability, if a plaintiff would later claim that the hospital did not check the Data Bank in selection of physician staff.[572] Hospitals may, however, still be held liable for negligent selection based on criteria and information not available at the Data Bank, if courts were to enforce a Data Bank requirement.[573] A hospital could be held liable for negligent selection on the grounds of a physician's

---

[564]  *Ibid.*

[565]  National Practitioner Data Bank for Adverse Information on Physicians and Other Health Care Practitioners 45 CFR 60.7 (1992). Rutchik 1994 *VLR* 558.

[566]  *Ibid.*

[567]  *Ibid.*

[568]  45 CFR §60.8 & §60.9 (1992). Rutchik 1994 *VLR* 558.

[569]  45 CFR §60.10 (a)(1)(1992). Rutchik 1994 *VLR* 558.

[570]  45 CFR §60.10 (b)(1992). Rutchik 1994 *VLR* 558.

[571]  45 CFR §60.10 (c)(1992). Rutchik 1994 *VLR* 558.

[572]  Rutchik 1994 *VLR* 558 and footnote 197.

[573]  *Op. cit.* 559. See also 45 CFR §60.10 (a)(1992).

poor references or questionable educational background. In other words, only if the negligence pertains to information included in the Data Bank i.e. a physician's prior malpractice or adverse licensure events, would Data Bank information constitute a valid defence for a hospital.[574] 'Therefore, the guidelines still need further comprehensive and well-defined selection criteria.'[575]

### 8.4.4.6 *Direct or corporate liability duties: non-delegable or not*

The American courts have in recent hospital cases termed the direct or corporate duties — breach of which is established by corporate negligence — non-delegable duties.[576] It has been applied where hospitals were held liable if their negligence had been proven, and where it was shown that their negligence had had a causal relationship to the plaintiff's injury.[577]

In terms of the non-delegable duty, an employer is held liable because of the independent contractor's negligence even though the employer had exercised reasonable care.[578] In case of the non-delegable duty, the employer has no personal fault or blame. The exercise of reasonable care is not enough. The employer has to ensure that reasonable care was/is taken, thus suggesting a stricter duty and a higher standard to which to conform. This is no ordinary duty, but a stricter duty, implying strict liability.[579]

It is, however, clear that the direct or corporate duty breach of which establishes direct liability, does indeed require personal fault or blame from the employer in order to succeed. The direct duty, followed by direct liability thus requires the employer's corporate negligence to be proven in hospital cases. This emphasizes the main difference between the non-delegable duty and the direct (corporate) duty. The direct or corporate hospital liability necessitates proof of negligence of the employer and thus is still a fault-based liability whereas the non-delegable duty necessitates no employer-negligence and initiates strict liability.[580]

---

[574] Rutchik 1994 *VLR* 559.

[575] *Ibid.*

[576] See also McWilliams and Russell 1996 *SCLR* 468–471 and Smith *Hospital* §3.03 [2] 3–10 to 3–11.

[577] McWilliams and Russell 1996 *SCLR* 468. See *infra.*

[578] See *supra* 4.3.3 and 4.3.3.3 and 4.4. See also McWilliams and Russell 1996 *SCLR* 468 footnote 212 citing 'Keeton *et al.* (*supra* note 3 §71) at 511.'

[579] *Ibid.*

[580] See *supra* 4.3.3 and 4.3.3.3. and 4.4.

In *Johnson* v. *Misericordia Community Hospital*,[581] the Wisconsin Supreme Court stated the nature and extent of the duty to 'exercise reasonable care in the selection of its medical staff ... . This is not to say that hospitals are *insurers* of the competence of their medical staff, for a hospital will not be negligent if it exercises the noted standard of care in selecting its staff.'[582] The court thus indicated that duties concerning the selection of staff were direct and not non-delegable.

In 1989, in *Mason* v. *Labig*,[583] the Ohio court of Appeals observed in an unpublished opinion that the full service hospital should be held accountable for emergency room malpractice because sound public policy considerations require it.[584] The court also confirmed the finding at the Alaska Supreme Court in *Jackson* v. *Power* wherein it was held that 'a general acute care hospital's duty to provide physicians for emergency room care was non-delegable.'[585] The court did, however, proceed to discuss hospital liability in terms of the breach for which it was sought, and found that the hospital had deviated from acceptable standards in not ensuring that an appropriate consultant was available to the emergency room. The basis of the latter finding was the hospital-employer's own negligence for non-compliance with an ordinary direct duty. Thus 'the hospital had itself been negligent in performing a duty that it owed directly. This is direct liability, not vicarious liability for the tort of another regardless of the delegator's fault.'[586]

This was indeed direct liability which is fault based, and not vicarious liability which is strict liability, nor the non-delegable duty which is also strict liability, and requires no fault or blame from the hospital-employer.

In *Douglas* v. *Freeman* [587] (1990), the Washington Court of Appeals stated:

> Under the doctrine of corporate negligence, a hospital owes a nondelegable duty directly to the patient to 'exercise reasonable care to ensure that only competent physicians are selected as members of the hospital staff'.[588]

[581]   99 Wis 2d 708, 301 NW 2d 156 (1981).

[582]   *Johnson* 301 NW 2d 156 (1981) at 174–175.

[583]   1989 WL 72234 (Ohio Ct App June 29, 1989). McWilliams and Russel 1996 *SCLR* 470.

[584]   *Mason* at 12: '[s]ound public policy considerations require that the full service hospital be held accountable for emergency room malpractice.'

[585]   *Mason* at 12 (citing *Jackson* v. *Power* 743 P 2d 1376 (Alaska 1987)).

[586]   McWilliams and Russel 1996 *SCLR* 470.

[587]   787 P 2d 76 (Wash Ct App 1990). McWilliams and Russell 1996 *SCLR* 468–469.

[588]   *Douglas* at 79 (quoting *Alexander* v. *Gonser* 711 P 2d 347, 351 (Wash Ct App 1986) and citing *Pedroza* v. *Bryant* 677 P 2d 166 (Wash 1984)).

The court did, however, absolve the clinic from liability after ample evidence of the clinic's negligence in permitting an unlicensed dentist to perform extractions was provided, because of a lack of adequate connection between the clinic's negligence and the patient's injury.[589]

Once again the foundation of the court's findings was direct hospital liability, based on the probable breach of a direct duty to provide competent physicians or dentists — owed to patients — which necessitated proof of the clinic's negligence and an adequate causal connection of the negligence to the patient's injury. The usage of the term 'non-delegable duty' and its incorporation into the findings was highly unnecessary and had no valuable effect on the outcome of the proceedings.

In *Thompson* v. *Nason Hospital*[590] (1991), four categories of 'non-delegable' duties were defined for breach of which the hospital could be found liable 'independently of the negligence of its employees or ostensible agents.'[591] However, the court applied further requirements, in that the plaintiffs had to prove that the hospital itself had breached a duty as well as that the hospital knew or should have known of the negligent acts.[592] In *Edwards* v. *Brandywine Hospital*[593] (1995), the Pennsylvania Superior Court concluded on *Thompson* that 'a hospital's corporate negligence will be measured against what a reasonable hospital under similar circumstances should have done … . *Thompson* does not propound a theory of strict liability … . Though broadly defined, *Thompson* liability is still fault based.'[594]

In *Engel* v. *Minissale*[595] (1995), the United States District Court for the Eastern District of Pennsylvania, granted summary judgment for the hospital. *In casu* the court referred to the *Thompson* case in proposing that in a corporate negligence action 'a plaintiff must 'show that the hospital had actual or constructive knowledge of the defect or procedures which created the harm and that the hospital's negligence must have been a substantial

---

[589] *Douglas* at 81.

[590] 527 Pa 330, 591 A 2d 703 (Pa 1991).

[591] *Thompson* 591 A 2d 703 (1991) at 707.

[592] *Thompson* 591 A 2d 703 (1991) at 708.

[593] 652 A 2d 1382 (Pa Super Ct 1995).

[594] *Edwards* at 1387.

[595] No. CIV. A. 90–4400, 1995 WL 478506 (E.D. Pa Aug 10, 1995). McWilliams and Russell 1996 *SCLR* 470.

factor in bringing about the harm'.'[596] What is as remarkable, is that the court did not define the duties categorized by *Thompson*, as non-delegable.[597]

### 8.4.4.6.1 Conclusion on direct duties: non-delegable or not

The courts have not applied the non-delegable duty in the traditional sense, of it being an independent legal ground which implies strict employer liability and establishes hospital liability. Ultimately, it could have been used to imply 'that hospitals cannot, by delegating patient care to independent contractors, escape liability for their **own** negligence in performing directly owed duties'.[598]

In each of the above-mentioned cases the courts established hospital direct (corporate) liability due to the hospital's own corporate negligence which took effect as a result of breach of the hospital's own direct duty it owed patients. Breach of the hospital's direct duty, resulting in the hospital's own independent negligence, which proximately caused the plaintiff's injuries, signalled a successful finding of hospital liability every time.

The relevant hospital duties were only direct corporate duties, for breach of which direct corporate liability ensues. There were no non-delegable duties in the relevant direct liability discussions, nor was there any need to describe the relevant hospital duties as non-delegable. The courts would have reached the same conclusions and the same outcome, without describing the duties as non-delegable. In other words, in terms of direct corporate liability as legal ground, which is established by breach of (direct) hospital duties, hospital liability follows reasonably when such hospital duties are classified as only direct (corporate) hospital duties. The principles on which such a hospital liability is founded is fault-based, whereas the non-delegable duty implies strict employer liability. There is thus no need to label the direct corporate hospital duties as non-delegable duties, since the whole judicial approach substantiates a finding of fault-based hospital liability in these cases. The liability induced by the non-delegable duty (strict liability) and direct (corporate) liability (fault-based liability) cannot be equated.

It is furthermore scientifically incorrect to mix concepts or terminology which are peculiar to a specific legal ground, when not discussing that particular legal ground, in order to establish hospital liability. Specific

---

[596] *Engel* at 2.

[597] *Engel* at 1.

[598] McWilliams and Russell 1996 *SCLR* 470. At 470–471 they indicate: 'That the term 'nondelegable' is used at all, however, reflects the trend of public reliance on the hospital itself as the care provider and therefore as the responsible party, driving perceived public policy toward enhanced hospital responsibility for the fate of patients.'

concepts or terminology akin to a specific legal ground, should be kept apart. Courts and commentators should apply concepts cautiously, in a disciplined manner, to ensure a clear and concise approach to hospital liability. Courts and commentators should therefore, with respect, refrain from calling direct corporate duties, non-delegable duties when applying the doctrine of direct corporate liability.

### 8.4.4.7 Justification

The imposition of corporate hospital liability has been justified on several grounds:

(1)  It has been stated that the modern hospital has evolved into a comprehensive health care provider which initiates an expanded role and necessitates increased liability.[599]

(2)  Corporate liability induces greater caution in the selection and monitoring of medical staff, by the threat of possible hospital or institutional liability.[600]

(3)  The financial responsibility which corporate liability anticipates, forces the hospital to ensure that a high quality of health care will be provided by quality staff physicians. It does not negate physician negligence completely, but supplies the necessary incentives to reach such goals.[601]

(4)  In terms of the deeper-pocket theory, the corporate liability doctrine provides a financially viable source of compensation for the injured claimant, which is a very important practical solution to such a serious circumstance.[602]

(5)  It has also been suggested that a hospital itself is in the best position to monitor the provision of medical care effectively. This does not, however, imply automatic liability for hospitals.[603]

---

[599]  Rutchik 1994 *VLR* 539, 548. See Mason and McCall-Smith 1987 *Encyclopaedia* at 582. Peters 1988 *TRIAL* 82.

[600]  Rutchik 1994 *VLR* 548.

[601]  *Op. cit.* 549.

[602]  *Op. cit.* 1994 *VLR* 549.

[603]  *Ibid. Pedroza* v. *Bryant* 101 Wash 2d 266, 677 P 2d 166 (1984) at 169–170.

## Criticisms

(1)    Corporate liability, when viewed negatively could cause bad publicity which is a great incentive for a hospital to carefully select and supervise competent physicians. The free market system could address this problem in a more positive way and encourage competition which could have the same effect.[604]

(2)    Some critics have gone so far as to say that corporate liability is focused more on establishing a deep pocket compensator than finding an appropriate tortfeasor. In view of the traditional concept of fault-based liability, some have equated corporate liability with a 'quasi-strict liability system in which hospitals serve as the ultimate insurers.'[605]

### 8.4.4.8 Other relevant case law

1.  1939:  *Stuart Circle Hospital Corp.* v. *Curry* 3 SE 2d 153 (Va 1939)

2.  1965:  *Darling* v. *Charleston Community Memorial Hospital* 33 Ill 2d 326, 211 NE 2d 253 (Ill 1965) certiorari denied 383 US 946. 86 S Ct 1204, 16 L Ed 2d 209 (1966)

3.  1972:  *Purcell and Tucson General Hospital* v. *Zimbelman* 18 Ariz App 75, 500 P 2d 335 (1972)

4.  1974:  *Gonzales* v. *Nork* No 228566 (Cal. Super Ct Sacramento County (filed Nov 19, 1973) (1974)

5.  1975:  *Corleto* v. *Shore Memorial Hospital* 350 A 2d 534 (1975)

6.  1976:  *Tucson Medical Center* v. *Misevch* 545 P 2d 958 (1976)

7.  1980:  *Bost* v. *Riley* 44 NC App 638, 262 SE 2d 391 (1980)

8.  1981:  *Johnson* v. *Misericordia* 99 Wis 2d 708, 301 NW 2d 156 (1981)

9.  1982:  *Elam* v. *College Park Hospital* 4 Civ No 24479 (Cal Ct App filed May 27, 1982, modification filed, June 25, 1982). 132 Cal App 3d 332, 183 Cal Rptr 156 (1982)

1.  In **Stuart Circle Hospital Corp. v. Curry**[606] a 1939 case, the doctrine of corporate liability for hospitals was most aptly preceded by the court's insight that could have initiated such a development. The court stated:

---

[604]  Rutchik 1994 *VLR* 549–550.

[605]  *Op. cit.* 550. In *Thompson* v. *Nason Hospital* 591 A 2d at 709 Flaherty J (dissenting) intimated that corporate liability was nothing more than an irresponsible search for a deep-pocket compensator, and that **respondeat superior** was sufficient to protect claimants.

[606]  3 SE 2d 153 (Va 1939) at 157. Reuter 1994 *JLM* 513.

The particular nature of a corporation prevents it as such from practising medicine, but there is no ban against the performance of duties by its qualified agents, servants and employees, that they are qualified to perform, and that they are held out by the hospital as being able to perform … . The interne [sic] is not an independent contractor so far as the patient is concerned. His contract is with the hospital. His service is part of the numerous duties prescribed by the hospital, and he is selected, employed, directed, supervised, and paid by the hospital.[607]

### 2. *Darling v. Charleston Community Memorial Hospital*[608] (1965).

Hospital liability was significantly expanded by the formal introduction of corporate hospital liability as a legal ground in *Darling*. This decision established the basis for this theory of hospital liability.[609] The concept of the duty of care with which the hospital should comply, was expanded dramatically. The hospital's independent liability and its independent duty/duties were formulated in no uncertain terms.

Dorrence Darling II, (the plaintiff), was eighteen years old when he played in a college football game and broke his leg. He was taken to the emergency room at Charleston Community Memorial Hospital, a small facility accredited by the Joint Commission on Accreditation of Hospitals and licensed by the state of Illinois. The doctor on emergency call, Dr Alexander — who was inexperienced in orthopaedic work of this nature — applied traction and placed the leg in a plaster cast. In the following days, the plaintiff experienced great pain, his toes were swollen and dark in colour,

---

[607] *Stuart* 157 and 158. See also *Comess* v. *Norfolk General Hospital* 52 SE 2d 125 (1949) which is also illustrative of corporate negligence. A visitor to a hospital incurred injuries when tripping over a chain across a path which led to the front entrance, and was permitted to recover for injuries sustained. The court found the hospital negligent in not placing a sign or giving notice that the entrance was no longer in use. The court found that the hospital had a duty to give notice to the public, and failure to comply with this duty led to its liability.

[608] 50 Ill App 2d 253, 200 NE 2d 149 (1964), aff'd 33 Ill 2d 326, 211 NE 2d 253 (1965), certiorari denied 383 US 946, 86 S Ct 1204, 16 LEd 2d 209 (1966). Annas *et al. American Health Law* 457–462. Christoffel *Health* 119. Dornette *Hospital Liability* 317–319. Esquire *Liability* 80–83. Furrow *et al. Health Law* 241, 248–251. Giesen *International* 63. Fiscina *Legal Medicine* 421. Jones *Negligence* 124–125. Kelly and Jones *Healthcare* 356–360. Louisell and Williams *Medical Malpractice* §15.06 15–26. McCafferty and Meyer *Liability* 319–321. Oerlikoff and Vanagunas *Hospitals* 4–5. Pegalis and Wachsman *Law* 232–234. Pozgar *Health* 208–210. Roach *et al. Law* 208–210. Smith *Hospital* §3.03 [1] 3–8 to 3–9. Southwick *Hospital Liability* 263–265. Southwick and Slee *Law of Hospital* 561, 565–567. Werthmann *Malpractice* 21. Brown 1988 *DCJ* 165. Cunningham 1975 *WLR* 411–414. Janulis and Hornstein 1985 *NLR* 702–705. McWilliams and Russell 1996 *SCLR* 464. Mobilia 1985 *SCLR* 603–605. Reuter 1994 *JLM* 512. Rutchik 1994 *VLR* 546–548. Spero 1979 *trial* 25–27. Trail and Claybrook 1985 *BLR* 326, 328–329.

[609] McCafferty and Meyer *Liability* 320.

and eventually became cold and insensitive. At one stage, when the cast was removed, a foul odour — the worst a witness had smelled since World War II — was detected from the leg. Eventually, the plaintiff was transferred to Barnes Hospital in St Louis, where Dr Fred Reynolds ultimately had to amputate the leg eight inches below the knee, due to a gangrenous condition which had become life-threatening.[610]

In a subsequent lawsuit, Dr Alexander paid $40,000 in settlement. A verdict was returned by the jury against the hospital for $150,000, which amount was reduced by the $40,000 the doctor had paid. Judgment against the hospital was affirmed by the intermediate Appellate Court.[611]

The Illinois Supreme Court[612] decision was significant in several respects:

(i)     The doctrine of charitable immunity was hereby abolished in Illinois.[613]

(ii)     The court found that the hospital's observance of local custom did not sufficiently or conclusively establish that the hospital had exercised due care. Custom was only deemed **relevant** in determining the standard of care.[614] The court therefore departed from the traditional 'locality rule'.[615]

(iii)     The court held that the (national) standards of the Joint Commission on the Accreditation of Hospitals (now the Joint Commission on Accreditation of Healthcare Organizations), the state licensing regulations and the hospital's bylaws (policies, rules and regulations), could be introduced as evidence of the duty or standard of care the hospital owed its patients, in order to determine negligence.[616] They did not, however, conclusively determine the standard of care but performed almost the same function as did evidence of custom. The standards, regulations and bylaws 'demonstrate that the medical profession and other responsible authorities

---

[610]  *Darling* 33 Ill 2d 326, 211 NE 2d at 255–256.

[611]  *Darling* 50 Ill App 2d 253, 200 NE 2d 149. 33 Ill 2d 326, 211 NE 2d 253.

[612]  *Darling* 33 Ill 2d 326, 211 NE 2d 253 (1965). The Illinois Supreme Court decision was delivered by Schaefer J.

[613]  *Darling* 33 Ill 2d 326, 211 NE 2d at 260. According to Roach *et al. Law* 208, this was consistent with a nation-wide trend to abrogate that doctrine.

[614]  *Darling* 33 Ill 2d 326, 211 NE 2d at 257.

[615]  Cunningham 1975 *WLR* 413. Dornette *Hospital Liability* 317–319, 322.

[616]  *Darling* 33 Ill 2d 326, 211 NE 2d at 257.

regard it as both desirable and feasible that a hospital assume certain responsibilities for the care of the patient.'[617]

(iv)     The Supreme Court did not analyse all the issues submitted to the jury; they only discussed two issues: 'Two of them were that the defendant had negligently: '5. Failed to have a sufficient number of trained nurses for bedside care of all patients at all times capable of recognizing the progressive gangrenous condition of the plaintiff's right leg, and of bringing the same to the attention of the hospital administration and to the medical staff so that adequate consultation could have been secured and such conditions rectified: *** 7. Failed to require consultation with or examination by members of the hospital surgical staff skilled in such treatment; or to review the treatment rendered to the plaintiff and to require consultants, to be called in as needed.' ... We believe that the jury verdict is supportable on **either** of these grounds.'[618]

The Supreme Court concluded on the evidence before the jury, that the nurses did not test for circulation (in the leg) as frequently as necessary; that skilled nurses would have recognized the dangerous condition and ultimately should have informed the attending physician or the hospital authorities to take appropriate action. The hospital failed to review Dr Alexander's work or require consultation. Failure to do so, constituted negligence.[619]

The Supreme Court found that the hospital owed the patient an independent duty of medical care and treatment which included the following duties:

(i)     the duty of nurses to adhere to proper procedures by supervising patients adequately and regularly,[620]

(ii)    the duty that nurses should inform medical staff, the attending physician or the hospital administration of (dangerous) conditions,[621]

(iii)   the duty to obtain the necessary consultation, especially where complications had developed,[622]

(iv)    the duty to review the (independent contractor) physician's work.[623]

---

[617] *Darling* 33 Ill 2d 236, 211 NE 2d at 257.

[618] *Darling* 33 Ill 2d 326, 211 NE 2d at 258. (my accentuation).

[619] *Darling* 33 Ill 2d 326, 211 NE 2d at 258.

[620] *Darling* 33 Ill 2d 326, 211 NE 2d at 258.

[621] *Darling* 33 Ill 2d 326, 211 NE 2d at 258.

[622] *Darling* 33 Ill 2d 326, 211 NE 2d at 258.

[623] *Darling* 33 Ill 2d 326, 211 NE 2d at 258.

## Comment on Darling

It is submitted, with respect, that the *Darling* Supreme Court decision was founded entirely on the direct corporate liability of the hospital. The court only pronounced systemic or organizational failures and explicitly formulated direct duties with which the hospital should have complied. Furthermore, the court's statement that the jury verdict was supportable on 'either ... grounds', does not implicate, with respect, that both the grounds that were discussed, could not have been founded on the same legal ground. It should not be interpreted as proposing two different or alternative legal grounds. Even if not so, the terminology of both grounds and content would only allow for direct liability. The hospital's failure to supply a sufficient number of trained nurses, the failure to comply with a procedural requirement to recognize gangrenous conditions and the failure to inform the authority of such conditions could — with respect — be classified as organizational failures or improper system(s). Failure to require consultation or review the physician's work, were also organizational failures which imply direct corporate liability. Vicarious liability based on *respondeat superior* was not mentioned once, and should — in the light of the foregoing — not be regarded as an appropriate legal ground *in casu*. To suggest that the first ground was founded on vicarious hospital liability, based on the doctrine of *respondeat superior*, can only be allowed in so far as the nurses were employees of the hospital for which the hospital would have been liable in the correctly formulated or expounded circumstances and/or statements. The direct duties which were indeed formulated by the Supreme Court, however, indicate the intention to provide a legal ground that is founded on the direct corporate liability for the hospital in these circumstances in this case.

Direct corporate liability was imposed on the hospital for its own negligence in the failure of its employee nurses to adequately monitor or supervise or examine the plaintiff, and/or inform the hospital and/or obtain consultation and/or review the physician's work.[624]

## Post Darling

Courts have, however, not been consistent in their application of this expanded theory of corporate negligence. Some courts have followed this exposition of direct corporate liability, or have even expanded the finding, whilst others have limited the scope of the duty to supervise physicians who are only employees and not independent contractors or treating physicians.[625]

---

[624] Pegalis and Wachsman *Law* 234.

[625] Smith *Hospital* §3.03 [3] 3–18 to 3–20. Roach *et al. Law* 209–210. Oerlikoff and Vanagunas *Hospitals* 5. Rutchik 1994 *VLR* 547–548, 559–561.

3. *Purcell and Tucson General Hospital v. Zimbelman* [626] (1972). In this case, a physician named Purcell had performed surgery on the plaintiff, Zimbelman in the defendant hospital. Due to the alleged malpractice, the plaintiff suffered from catastrophic consequences. At the time of the alleged negligent surgery, the doctor had been sued for malpractice on at least four prior occasions, concerning his surgical performances, which the hospital knew.

The court held that medical malpractice suits constitute notice of incompetence. It was also held that the hospital had a duty to supervise the competence of the staff doctors. Since the department of surgery fulfilled the duty to supervise doctors on behalf of the hospital, and since the department of surgery knew of the doctor's questionable competence, the department and consequently the hospital was negligent in allowing the doctor to treat patients. The hospital was thus held liable for not terminating the doctor's privileges.

4. *Gonzales v. Nork* [627] (1974). In this case, Dr Nork, a private physician member of the medical staff had performed unnecessary and negligent spinal surgery on a twenty-seven- year-old man, which resulted in constant pain in his back and legs. Only three years after this operation, did the hospital become aware of the problems surrounding the surgeon. The surgeon's malpractice insurance had been cancelled. The surgeon had also been sued for malpractice earlier, which the hospital had failed to investigate. During the trial, the surgeon admitted to having performed at least twenty-six other unnecessary operations. A scheme of fraud was uncovered.

The court held that the hospital's corporate liability was founded on its duty to protect patients from malpractice by members of its medical staff. If the hospital knew, had reason to know or should have known that negligent acts were likely to occur, the hospital or the hospital governing board was corporately responsible for the (negligent) conduct of its medical staff.

The court also reiterated that compliance with the 'JCAHO standards alone was insufficient to insulate the hospital from corporate liability for negligent selection. ... Because courts have treated compliance with JCAHO standards inconsistently, hospitals must hope that the particular court in which they appear does not ignore these accepted standards and impose

---

[626] 18 Ariz App 75, 500 P 2d 335 (1972). Spero 1979 *TRIAL* 24–25. Werthmann *Malpractice* 21.

[627] No 228566 (Cal Super Ct Sacramento County (filed Nov 19, 1973) 1974). Janulis and Hornstein 1985 *NLR* 706. Rutchik 1994 *VLR* 562. Mobilia 1985 *SCLR* 608–609. Fiscina *Legal Medicine* 422–423. Pegalis and Wachsman *Law* 237–238.

corporate liability despite the hospital's actual compliance with industry guidelines.'[628] The hospital was thus held liable despite good faith compliance with industry standards.[629]

The court found that the hospital did not have an effective system or mechanism to supervise quality medical care, to detect fraudulent physicians, uncover substandard operations or handle relevant information or knowledge of incompetence. A duty was constructed in terms of which a hospital has to have a proper system by means of which important data or information on risk creating activities could be compiled or acquired.[630]

### 5. *Corleto v. Shore Memorial Hospital* [631] (1975)

Joyce Corleto had died following abdominal surgery. A wrongful death action was filed. The defendant doctor (an independent contractor), the hospital, the administrator, the board of directors and medical staff were all sued. The court held the hospital liable for allowing a doctor who they knew or should have known to be incompetent, to perform a surgical procedure and for failing to remove such a known incompetent physician from the case and to allow him surgical privileges. The hospital was held to have a duty to patients to protect them from malpractice. The hospital was held responsible for the care of its patients. This liability was explicitly formulated as (being a corporate direct liability and) nót being a **vicarious liability**.

### 6. *Tucson Medical Center v. Misevch* [632] (1976)

The plaintiff's wife underwent surgery during which anaesthesia was administered negligently. As a result, she suffered cardiac arrest and died. It was alleged that the anaesthesiologist was under the influence of alcohol at the time of the procedure, and that the hospital was consequently negligent in retaining him on its medical staff.

The court stated that actual or constructive knowledge, is an essential factor in determining whether the hospital had exercised reasonable care under the circumstances. In terms of the hospital's responsibilities for the care of its patients, the hospital would be negligent if not complying with the duty to supervise the physician staff members, to supervise their competence or when failing to recommend action by the hospital's governing body prior

---

[628] Rutchik 1994 *VLR* 562–563.

[629] Janulis and Hornstein 1985 *NLR* 706. Mobilia 1985 *SCLR* 609.

[630] See also Janulis and Hornstein 1985 *NLR* 706 and Fiscina *Legal Medicine* 423.

[631] 350 A 2d 534 (1975). Spero 1979 *TRIAL* 25. Fiscina *Legal Medicine* 421. Annas *et al.* *American Health Law* 464–467.

[632] 545 P 2d 958 (1976). Fiscina *Legal Medicine* 422.

to injury. The court explored the concept of corporate liability and indicated that the hospital and its governing body could be liable for negligent supervision of medical staff members which result in injuries to patients. The hospital was under a duty to ensure that medical staff were competent.

## 7. *Bost v. Riley* [633] (1980)

In this case the patient suffered from a ruptured spleen after he had been in an accident. After being admitted to hospital, Dr Riley, the attending surgeon performed a splenectomy after which the patient was placed in the intensive care unit. The surgeon subsequently went on vacation, leaving the patient in the care of his associates who discovered a volvulus of the intestine twelve days later. They resected the gangrenous bowel, but the patient died of complications of the surgery five months later.[634]

The North Carolina Court of Appeals found that the doctrine of corporate liability had not been expressly adopted or rejected by courts in North Carolina, but that it had been implicitly accepted and applied in a number of decisions.[635] After exploring numerous cases which formulated direct hospital duties in the state of North Carolina, the judge proceeded to find that 'we acknowledge that a breach of any such duty may correctly be termed corporate negligence, and that our State recognizes this as a basis for liability apart and distinct from *respondeat superior*'.[636]

The court therefore expressly adopted the concept of corporate negligence pertaining to the duty to supervise medical treatment, violation of which could render the hospital corporately liable. The court interpreted the hospital's duty to supervise most liberally,[637] in construing that the hospital had a duty (to make reasonable effort[638]) to monitor and oversee the physicians (non-employees[639]) prescribing and rendering treatment and medical care at the facility.[640]

---

[633] 44 NC App 638, 262 SE 2d 391 (1980). Fiscina *Legal Medicine* 425. Kelly and Jones *Healthcare* 360. Brown 1988 *DCJ* 165.

[634] *Bost* 44 NC App 638, 262 SE 2d at 392.

[635] *Bost* 44 NC App 638, 262 SE 2d at 396.

[636] *Bost* 44 NC App 638, 262 SE 2d at 396.

[637] Brown 1988 *DCJ* 166. Brown describes this duty as being an 'unqualified duty'.

[638] *Bost* 44 NC App 638, 262 SE 2d at 396.

[639] Wells J stated at *Bost* 395 that physicians treating Lee (in this case) were not acting as employees, agents, or servants of Catawba, and therefore the principle of *respondeat superior* was inapplicable to this case.

[640] *Bost* 44 NC App 638, 262 SE 2d at 396. Kelly and Jones *Healthcare* 360 state that 'subsequent case law in North Carolina has not supported a duty to monitor treatment'.

The court also found that the surgeons had failed to keep accurate progress notes on the patient's condition, which induced breach of the hospital's duty to the patient to enforce its own internal rules on keeping such notes.[641] No evidence was, however, produced to show that this omission had contributed to Lee's death.[642] On account of other relevant circumstances, a new trial was ordered.[643]

## 8. *Johnson v. Misericordia Community Hospital* [644] (1981)

Dr Solinsky had negligently performed an operation on the plaintiff, as a result of which the plaintiff's right thigh was permanently paralysed. The plaintiff had settled a malpractice claim against the surgeon (and his insurance carrier) prior to the trial, and therefore proceeded only against the hospital. The plaintiff's malpractice suit against the hospital, was founded on the hospital's duty of care which it owes its patients to use reasonable care in the appointment of staff and the granting of staff (surgical) privileges.[645]

The Supreme Court of Wisconsin eventually reviewed the case.

It had been alleged that the hospital was negligent by:

(a)     its careless and imprudent selection of the surgeon to its staff;

(b)     allowing the surgeon to perform surgical procedures when it knew or should have known that he was not qualified to perform such procedures;

(c)     failing to investigate the surgeon's abilities when they knew or should have known that he was not capable.[646]

The surgeon's negligence had been established at trial, by undisputed expert testimony.[647] It also came to light that the surgeon was appointed before his application was investigated.[648] In fact, the surgeon himself endorsed the

---

[641]   *Bost* 44 NC App 638, 262 SE 2d at 397.

[642]   *Bost* 44 NC App 638, 262 SE 2d at 397.

[643]   *Bost* 44 NC App 638, 262 SE 2d at 397.

[644]   99 Wis 2d 708, 301 NW 2d 156 (1981). Annas *et al. American Health Law* 455–457. Fiscina *Legal Medicine* 423–425. Janulis and Hornstein 1985 *NLR* 706–707. Trail and Claybrook 1985 *BLR* 329–330. Werthmann *Malpractice* 22–23. Rutchik 1994 *VLR* 565. McCafferty and Meyer *Liability* 320–321.

[645]   *Johnson* 99 Wis 2d 708, 301 NW 2d at 158. The plaintiff's malpractice claim against the hospital was not based on **respondeat superior**. The hospital was also not accredited by the Joint Commission on the Accreditation of Hospitals.

[646]   *Johnson* 99 Wis 2d 708, 301 NW 2d at 258.

[647]   *Johnson* 99 Wis 2d 708, 301 NW 2d at 158.

[648]   *Johnson* 99 Wis 2d 708, 301 NW 2d at 160.

approval of his application, because soon after his 'appointment', he assumed the duties as chief of the medical staff organization.[649]

The Supreme Court of Wisconsin, dealt with the following two leading issues:

1. Whether the hospital owed a duty to its patients to use due care in the selection of its medical staff and the granting of specialized surgical (orthopaedic) privileges;

2. What the standard of care was that the hospital had to exercise to discharge the duty to its patients, and whether Misericordia indeed had failed to exercise that standard of care.[650]

The Supreme Court explored that applicability of the legal ground of corporate liability in other states and adopted the theory of corporate negligence, applying it to the circumstances.[651]

Coffey J recognized that hospitals owe a duty of ordinary care in selecting and maintaining only qualified members on their medical staff, to ensure quality care, diagnosis and treatment of their patients.[652] It was confirmed and concluded that a 'hospital is under a duty to exercise reasonable care to permit only competent medical doctors the privilege of using their facilities.[653] The court also found that the standard of 'ordinary care under the circumstances' applies to hospitals.[654] It 'meant that degree of care, skill and judgment usually exercised under like or similar circumstances by the average hospital'.[655]

The court found that under the doctrine of constructive knowledge, Misericordia could readily have obtained the following information concerning Salinsky's application, that: (i) Salinsky's orthopaedic privileges had been revoked at Doctors Hospital two months before he had applied for orthopaedic privileges at Misericordia; (ii) St Anthony's Hospital had denied him staff privileges in 1971; (iii) he was never on the staff of New Berlin Memorial Hospital or Northwest General Hospital; and (iv) Mt. Sinai Hospital had granted him privileges to perform simple orthopedic procedures, later reduced his rank, and ultimately revoked all his privileges for

---

[649] *Johnson* 99 Wis 2d 708, 301 NW 2d at 159.

[650] *Johnson* 99 Wis 2d 708, 301 NW 2d at 163.

[651] *Johnson* 99 Wis 2d 708, 301 NW 2d at 163–171.

[652] *Johnson* 99 Wis 2d 708, 301 NW 2d at 170–171.

[653] *Johnson* 99 Wis 2d 708, 301 NW 2d at 171.

[654] *Johnson* 99 Wis 2d 708, 301 NW 2d at 171.

[655] *Johnson* 99 Wis 2d 708, 301 NW 2d at 172.

failure to use their clinical departments, (v) Misericordia had access to Court files which indicated that ten malpractice suits had been filed against Salinsky, seven of which had been filed prior to his application.[656]

The court had to establish whether a hospital with knowledge of such facts, would, in the exercise of ordinary care, have granted Salinsky orthopaedic surgical privileges. It was eventually decided that a hospital exercising ordinary care would not have appointed Salinsky to its medical staff.[657]

The court summarized:

(i)     A hospital owes a duty to its patients to exercise reasonable care in the selection of its medical staff and in granting specialized privileges.[658]

(ii)    The court explicitly stated that the hospital's governing body had the final appointing authority, although there was some delegation of responsibility 'to investigate and evaluate the professional competence of applicants for clinical privileges'.[659]

(iii)   The hospital should:
-   ensure that the application is completed and verify the applicant's statements, especially regarding his medical education, training and experience;
-   'solicit information from the applicant's peers, including those not referenced in his application, who are knowledgeable about his education, training, experience, health, competence and ethical character;
-   determine if the applicant is currently licensed to practice in this state and if his licensure or registration has been or is currently being challenged; and
-   inquire whether the applicant has been involved in any adverse malpractice action and whether he has experienced a loss of medical organization membership or medical privileges or membership at any other hospital. The investigating committee must also evaluate the information gained through its inquiries and make a reasonable judgment as to the approval or denial of each application for staff privileges. The hospital will be charged with gaining and evaluating the knowledge that would

---

[656]   *Johnson* 99 Wis 2d 708, 301 NW 2d at 161, 162, 173.

[657]   *Johnson* 99 Wis 2d 708, 301 NW 2d at 174.

[658]   *Johnson* 99 Wis 2d 708, 301 NW 2d at 174.

[659]   *Johnson* 99 Wis 2d 708, 301 NW 2d at 174.

have been acquired had it exercised ordinary care in investigating its medical staff applicants and the hospital's failure to exercise that degree of care, skill and judgment that is exercised by the average hospital in approving an applicant's request for privileges is negligence.'[660]

The decision of the Court of Appeals was affirmed.[661] The hospital was held directly liable in terms of its corporate negligence.

### 9. *Elam v. College Park Hospital* [662] (1982)

In this case the patient brought a malpractice action against the physician due to negligent podiatric surgery and against the hospital where the independent contractor physician performed the surgery. In this instance, several malpractice suits had already been filed against Dr Schur, the licensed podiatrist, in 1974 and 1976. The court held that the hospital could be liable under the doctrine of corporate liability for the negligent conduct of independent physicians who were not employees nor agents of the hospital.

The court constructed an extensive duty. It was found that the hospital had a duty to ensure the competence of its staff physicians who performed surgery on hospital patients through careful selection and review, as well as a duty of 'continuing evaluation' to 'monitor, review and oversee trends in the quality of treatment given by a staff physician over time (both within and outside of its facility) in determining whether or not it is appropriate to renew or continue to extend privileges.'[663] It was added that the hospital would be accountable for the negligent screening of the medical staff's competency in order to ensure the quality or adequacy of medical care which is rendered to patients at health care facilities.[664] Failure by the hospital to ensure competent medical staff through careful selection, review and supervision, created an unreasonable risk of harm to its patients.[665]

---

[660] *Johnson* 99 Wis 2d 708, 301 NW 2d at 174–175.

[661] *Johnson* 99 Wis 2d 708, 301 NW 2d at 175.

[662] 4 Civ No 24479 (Cal Ct App filed May 27, 1982, modification filed June 25, 1982). 132 Cal App 3d 332, 183 Cal Rptr 156 (1982). Annas *et al. American Health Law* 462–464. McCafferty and Meyer *Liability* 320. Fiscina *Legal Medicine* 425–426. Pozgar *Health* 210. Janulis and Hornstein 1985 *NLR* 707. Rutchik 1994 *VLR* 565. Kelly and Jones *Healthcare* 360–361. Southwick and Slee *Law of Hospital* 575–578.

[663] Kelly and Jones *Healthcare* 361.

[664] Fiscina *Legal Medicine* 426.

[665] *Ibid.* Annas *et al. American Health Law* 463.

### *8.4.4.9  Conclusion on direct or corporate liability*[666]

Direct or corporate liability is perhaps the most potent legal ground in contemporary hospital liability law. It acknowledges the sovereign independent or corporate responsibility of a legal entity which embraces a legal liability for the negligent acts of independent contractors, employees, agents and even unidentifiable individuals. In American hospital liability law, this legal ground has been expounded most scientifically, except for the equation of direct duties with non-delegable duties in the corporate liability context. The relevant case law is vast but centres on the courts' identification of relevant direct or corporate duties, violation of which results in corporate negligence and ultimately in direct or corporate hospital liability.

It has been suggested that the doctrines of *respondeat superior* and corporate negligence have become one.[667] It is submitted, with all respect, that this perception is only formed due to an inability by some courts and others to approach hospital liability in a scientifically correct manner and by keeping concepts and terminology which is akin to specific legal grounds apart. Once distinct structures of legal grounds are formulated and set out in statutes or relevant laws, a more dogmatic approach which reflects clear reasoning and argumentation, will reign. American hospital liability law has produced remarkable independent legal grounds which should be guarded, but should be developed independently without confusing them, which could stifle its potential.

### 8.4.5  Strict Liability

Although the theory of negligence has developed dramatically and still prevails, a finding of liability without fault has been assessed by many as providing a more equitable basis for assessing damages than by requiring a determination of fault.[668] The growing social policy, which evolved during the past century, seeks to impose liability on the party who can best bear the loss. Those who create an unusual risk of harm to others, are subjected to liability arising from such activities.[669]

---

[666] See also Smith *Hospital* §3.04 3–23 to 3–26.

[667] Southwick *Hospital Liability* 279–280. Southwick and Slee *Law of Hospital* 578–580.

[668] Hoffman *et al. Legal Medicine* 37.

[669] *Ibid.* For example companies (e.g. blasting), zoos, private persons (e.g. those who keep animals) and heavy construction companies who operate dangerous equipment.

American courts have not directly applied the substance of legal doctrine of strict liability in any action by a patient-plaintiff against a physician-defendant.[670] The health-care provider has, however, been held strictly liable in a handful of cases.[671]

## 8.5 JOINT AND SEVERAL LIABILITY

The doctrine of joint and several liability provides a legal mechanism to the plaintiff, whereby multiple tortfeasors can be held liable, individually, for the full factual loss or entire judgment awarded by a court. The doctrine entails that each defendant who had caused damage, is jointly and severally liable for the total assessed damages.[672] In other words, the total can be collected by the plaintiff from either of them or from each of them in any combination.[673] The loss can be adjusted between the defendants through actions for contribution.[674] However, where causal apportionment between tortfeasors is not feasible upon the factual basis of the situation, the tortfeasors should be held jointly and severally liable for the entire damage.[675] The law of joint and several liability thus implies that each tortfeasor can become liable to pay for more harm than he actually caused.[676] Thus, where it is practically impossible to apportion various incidents/parts of a cluster of theoretically separable injuries, the cluster is treated as a single indivisible injury.[677]

However, in more recent times there has been a tendency to advocate that each defendant in medical negligence multi-defendant actions, only be responsible in payment for their own percentage of fault ascribed to them.[678] Various state legislatures have made defendants severally, rather than jointly

---

[670] Hoffman *et al. Legal Medicine* 38. Pharmaceutical and medical appliance industries have, however, been affected. See also McCafferty and Meyer *Liability* 362–363 and Mobilia 1985 *SCLR* 626–629.

[671] *Thomas* v. *St Joseph Hospital* 618 SW 2d 791 (Texas 1980). *Province Hospital* v. *Truly* 611 SW 2d 127 (Texas 1980). Brown 1988 *DCJ* 166.

[672] Markesinis and Deakin *Tort Law* 233: An American Perspective by Professor D W Robertson. Pozgar *Health* 666.

[673] Markesinis and Deakin *Tort Law* 233.

[674] *Ibid.*

[675] *Op. cit.* 234.

[676] *Ibid.*

[677] *Op. cit.* 234–235.

[678] Pozgar *Health* 666.

and severally liable. Consequently, defendants have become responsible only for a percentage of the damages.[679]

The health care industry has experienced tremendous problems as a result of the increasing number of malpractice claims, excessive jury awards, consequential medical malpractice insurance non-availability and the increase in malpractice insurance rates.[680] The medical malpractice insurance industry has to make provision for the potential liability of all health care providers i.e. hospitals, institutions/organizations, agencies, clinics and individual professional health care providers.[681] A crisis could well be expected in the future in this industry in the US, although the short-term outlook is good.[682] Medical professional liability insurance has become more available by the formation of medical malpractice insurance associations. They not only provide medical malpractice insurance for physicians, but also for institutions. Most physician-owed liability insurance companies, are non-profit enterprises, more accessible, offer better prices, and are mostly linked to medical societies.[683]

Professional health care providers such as physicians and nurses have acquired professional liability insurance, protecting themselves against any exposure to a potential legal loss.[684] Hospitals in the US have required staff to carry such personal professional liability insurance. Under policies which grant a 'maximum coverage of 1 million for each claim and 3 million for aggregate claims (the total amount payable to all injured parties), the insured is protected on each individual claim up to 1 million and up to 3 million in a policy period'.[685] The insurance company pays the injured party only the

---

[679] *Ibid*: Wyomi Statute § 1.1.109 (1986) provides that: 'each defendant to a lawsuit is only liable for that proportion of the total dollar amount of damages according to the percentage of the amount of fault attributed to him or her'. Minnesota Statute § 604.02 (1988) provides that: 'A defendant whose fault is 15 per cent or less may be jointly liable for a percentage of the whole award not greater than four times his or her percentage of fault.' See every individual state's own statutory provision for joint and/or several liability. Compare Louisell and Williams *Medical Malpractice* § 16.05, 16–16 to 16–17 (1996), for relevant case law.

[680] Pozgar *Health* 540–541.

[681] *Op. cit.* 550–551, 543.

[682] *Op. cit.* 541.

[683] Op. cit. 551. Furrow *et al. Health* (1995) 339.

[684] Pozgar *Health* 543. See also Furrow *et al. Health* (1995) 33.

[685] Pozgar *Health* 547.

expressly stated maximum limit of the insurance policy. Any exceeding damages must be personally paid by the insured professional.[686]

Several states have also imposed statutory limitations on medical malpractice recoveries. The total dollar amount of damages awarded in medical malpractice actions has been restricted.[687] Statutory limitations have been found to be constitutional by the courts in several instances.[688] Such statutory restrictions have, however, not deterred the public from filing malpractice claims.[689]

## 8.6 CONCLUSION

The health service industry has evolved the hospital into the most important and comprehensive provider of health care. Public policy and patient expectation of protection has demanded a financially viable defendant which can provide quality medical care and competent medical staff, enforced by adequate policies, rules and regulations. The hospital liability law in the USA has expanded considerably, sometimes bordering on strict liability.[690] The hospital liability law does, however, differ from state to state — being founded on a common law system.[691] It is submitted that greater uniformity concerning this law, would be to the advantage of all, and should be sought by all.

Vicarious liability has been expanded. The independent contractor defence no longer precludes a successful litigation based on *respondeat superior*. The doctrines of 'apparent agency' and 'agency by estoppel' have also expanded possible hospital liability, as has the decay of the doctrines of

---

[686] *Ibid.*

[687] Pozgar *Health* 666–667.

[688] *Ibid.* In *Jones* v. *State Board of Medicine* 555 P 2d 399 (Idaho 1976), The Supreme Court of Idaho held that the state's statutory limitation on malpractice recoveries (150,000) could be held constitutional. Pozgar *Health* 667: 'The court held that there was no inherent right to an unlimited amount of damages and that the state had a legitimate interest in controlling excessive medical costs caused by large malpractice recoveries, and thus the statute could be held constitutional'. In California, in *Fein* v. *Permanente Medical Group* (695 P 2d 665 (Cal 1985)), the Supreme Court came to the same conclusion, namely that the statutory limit concerning non-economic damage for pain and suffering in medical malpractice cases, was not unconstitutional. Compare similar restrictive statutes of Maryland, Kansas, Virginia, Indiana, Michigan and Ohio.

[689] Pozgar *Health* 667.

[690] McWilliams and Russell 1996 *SCLR* 473.

[691] *Ibid.*

'borrowed servant' and 'captain of the ship'. Direct corporate liability has experienced tremendous progress and the potential of this legal ground is vast. The legal ground of the non-delegable duty has, however, been confused with direct or corporate liability, but ought to be acknowledged and respected as an independent legal ground.

It is submitted that the American hospital liability law presents the most remarkable variation of legal grounds and doctrinal devices in order to impose hospital liability. These legal grounds should at all cost be respected as sovereign and independent legal grounds. A national legal commission could be introduced in the USA and elsewhere, in order to codify the legal grounds, and distinguish their distinct requirements, concepts and terminology, to save the legal grounds from extinguishing each other by mere confusion.[692]

---

[692] The appropriate body to research the South African hospital liability law would be the South African Law Commission.

# Chapter 9

# The South African Law

### 9.1 HEALTH CARE IN SOUTH AFRICA
### LAND AREA: 1,221,042 SQ. KM.[1]

South Africa was introduced to a new political dispensation in 1994. As a result, the South African health care industry has experienced radical changes. South African health care and health care services are now influenced by socialist ideals.[2]

### 9.1.1 The New National Health System

A 'single, comprehensive, equitable and integrated National Health System is planned and co-ordinated at the central government level.'[3] The system mainly comprises of the following:

- An intersectoral National Development Committee will be instituted which comprises of the relevant government Ministers. 'It will be responsible for intersectoral liaison with other ministries.'[4]
- A National Health Authority (NHA) is created which consists of the Minister of Health, the Secretary for Health, Heads of National Divisions and representatives from Provincial Health Authorities and District Health Authorities. This body will be responsible for the development and provision of all health care in South Africa.[5]

---

[1]  Wêreldfokus Vol. 14 1978, 2779.

[2]  Health Care *Financial Mail* November 22, 1996, 22.

[3]  A National Health Plan for South Africa May 1994, 68.

[4]  *Ibid.*

[5]  *Op. cit. 68–70.* National Health *Financial Mail* November 29, 1996, 44. Functions of the National Health Authority:

-     A National Health Advisory Body.[6]
-     Support Services.[7]
-     Administration and Finance.[8]
-     Planning and Human Resources.[9]

---

-     Formulation of national policy; including macro economic analyses in respect of inter- and intra-sectoral activities.
-     Determination of national priorities, plans and strategies and ensuring their implementation.
-     Determination of national norms, guidelines and standards of care.
-     Overall co-ordination of both public and private health care.
-     Co-ordination of organizations providing national services.
-     International liaison and co-ordination of international and donor support, including policies and guidelines for that support.
-     Planning, co-ordinating, supporting, supervising and evaluating all services in the provinces and districts, including establishing national norms, policies and guidelines for the building or expansion of public and private hospitals and clinics.
-     Promotion of health, and support for health education.
-     Support for the preventive interventions and programmes of provinces and districts.
-     Planning and controlling the national referral system.
-     Co-ordination of emergency services and disaster relief in collaboration with the PHAs, DHAs and other parties as necessary.

[6]   A National Health Plan for South Africa May 1994, 68. This body advises the NHA. It has:

-     representation from the 'statutory bodies, the national associations of health professionals, NGO's involved in health, trade unions and national community standards.'

[7]   A National Health Plan for South Africa May 1994, 70:

-     Procurement, storage and distribution of pharmaceuticals and of medical and laboratory supplies and equipment.
-     Providing backup services for highly specialized equipment.
-     Quality control of laboratory services and equipment.
-     Administering certain national programmes, such as vaccine production, virological services and medicine control.

[8]   A National Health Plan for South Africa May 1994, 70:

-     Establishing norms, standards and guidelines for all health resources (funds, human resources, facilities and equipment).
-     Negotiating with the Department of Finance for funds to provide the necessary health services and for training.
-     Development of financial allocation mechanisms, and monitoring and evaluation of the effectiveness and cost-efficiency of the health system.
-     Provision of the infrastructure and services needed to underpin the health facilities of the nation.
-     Preparing and tabling health and health related legislation for the National Assembly.

[9]   A National Health Plan for South Africa May 1994, 70:

-     National human resources planning and development.

'One of the greatest challenges facing the health care industry is finding new and innovative ways of bringing the whole population into the health care arena.'[10] Free primary health care (PHC) has been offered to pregnant women and children under six since May 1994.[11] In April 1996, free PHC was introduced for all.[12] This brought about the expansion of immunization, nutrition and disease prevention programmes. Substantial salary increases for doctors and nurses followed, as well as an infrastructural programme and an essential drug list.[13]

There has, consequently, been a reallocation of resources to PHC. This has 'resulted in 700 new PHC posts in under-served provinces and 60 new clinics'.[14] In order to finance the PHC programme, academic hospitals have experienced severe budget cuts as a result of which they are on the verge of collapse.[15] The Western Cape health minister Mr Ebrahim Rasool has remarked that the 'implementation of these cuts, especially in the short time frame proposed, is likely to prove destructive to the current and future standards of health services, training and research'.[16] The Financial Mail has reported that the new health reform policy is 'contributing to a reduction in the quality and availability of health care in parts of SA.'[17]

---

- Planning and coordination of national health and health-related research and research institutions.
- Coordination of academic health institutions.
- Establish and coordinate a national health information system.
- Provision of special technical advice and expertise to the provinces and districts.

[10] Gardner *Sunday Times* Business Times August 18, 1996, 8. Reported by Smith.

[11] Health Care *Financial Mail* November 22, 1996, 22.

[12] *Ibid.* 'The decision to extend free PHC was made before the effects of free PHC for pregnant women and children under six had been evaluated.'

[13] Health Care *Financial Mail* November 22, 1996, 22.

[14] *Ibid.*

[15] *Ibid.* Three world-renowned academic institutions, Groote Schuur, Red Cross Children's Hospital and Tygerberg in the Western Cape have to reduce staffing levels by 1600 posts before March 1997, and must close 500 hospital beds. The Western Cape lost R35 million from academic hospitals to other parts of the service according to Parker 1997 *Longevity* 57.

[16] Parker 1997 *Longevity* 57.

[17] Health Care *Financial Mail* November 22, 1996, 24.

## 9.1.2 New Legislation

The (draft) National Health Bill is due to be tabled in parliament in September 2000.[18] It grants excessive powers to the Health Minister and the central health authority to regulate the private sector.[19] The national health authority is given the power to award authorization or 'certificates of need' to enable the 'rational and equitable distribution of health services, technology, establishments and human resources by the use of objectively verifiable criteria.'[20] Whenever it will be decided to authorize the creation, enlargement or modification of a health facility (for example a hospital), the national health authority must consider criteria such as its 'compliance with government plans, relationships between existing and proposed establishments, demographic and geographic features, the availability of personnel and alternative establishments in the vicinity and funding conditions.'[21] The private sector is, however, not represented on the proposed National Health Advisory Council, which guides the National Health Authority in policy formulation.[22] A federal concept is also proposed by the Bill, whereby every

---

[18]   This was confirmed by the Department of Health on 9 February 2000. See also National Health *Financial Mail* November 29, 1996, 44. Health Care *Financial Mail* November 22, 1996, 24. The *'White Paper for the Transformation of the Health System in South Africa'*, was discussed in parliament in 1997. See Government Gazette No 17910 Notice No 667, 16 April 1997.

(( http: // www.health.gov.za/ ))

A *patient Bill of Rights* had also been agreed to and signed by 95% of South Africa's private hospitals in 1999. It enables patients of private hospitals to demand quality health care and professional services. The bill avails the patient of competent staff, a clean, safe and hygienic hospital, nutritious food and facilities in good working order. Most importantly an objective body — Discovery Health, a medical insurer — was nominated as medical industry watchdog to enforce protection of the rights of clients: Seeger *Sunday Times Business Times* April 11, 1999, 12.

Other new legislation:
Academic Health Centres Act No 86 of 1993, as amended by Act No 47 of 1997.
Medical Schemes Act No 131 of 1998.
Sterilisation Act No 44 of 1998.
Medical, Dental and Supplementary Health Service Professions Amendment Act No 1 of 1998.
South African Medicines and Medical Devices Regulatory Authority Act No 132 of 1998.
Prevention and Treatment of Drug Dependency Amendment Act, Act No 20 of 1992, as amended by Acts No 106 of 1996 and No 14 of 1999.

[19]   National Health *Financial Mail* November 29, 1996, 44.

[20]   *Ibid.*

[21]   *Ibid.*

[22]   *Ibid.* A National Health Plan for South Africa May 1994, 68–70.

provincial health authority addresses policy as well as the delivery of services within national guidelines.[23] The NHA's extensive powers could, however, limit the decentralization of decision-making.[24]

### 9.1.3 Health Financing

South Africa is described as a unitary state in terms of the Constitution. Provinces have only been awarded limited autonomous taxing and expenditure powers, which is in accordance with the unitary structure. The principle of decentralization of revenue collection and expenditure remains desirable, in terms of the principle of diffusion of power. However, the 'control of aggregate spending by the first and second tier levels of government is firmly in the hands of one authority only.'[25]

The public health sector is mainly funded by general tax revenue.[26] According to a report on National Health by the ANC, government expenditure on health fluctuated between 2.8 and 3.4% of GDP (11–12% of total government spending with a recent trend to decrease the latter portion), in recent years.[27] It was reported that South Africa spent 5.4% of GNP on health care in 1990.[28] The government allocated 11.2% of the budget to health care in 1985 and 11.7% at the 1990/1991 financial year.[29] In 1994, ± R21.6 billion was spent on health services in South Africa which is between 6–6.5% of GNP.[30] According to the Financial Mail, total public health expenditure was expected to average R16.8 billion in 1995–1996 and R19.98 bn in 2000–2001 which forecasts an annual average real increase of 3.4%.[31] 'It relies on foreign aid to reduce the State's requirement to a more feasible 0.6% real annual increase.'[32] If the health care costing principles flounder, 'the State could well face a financial crisis that would require the taxpayer to bail it out.'[33] It has, however, already been recommended that a compulsory

---

[23] National Health *Financial Mail* November 29, 1996, 44.

[24] *Ibid.*

[25] Provincial Revenue *Financial Mail* August 9, 1996, 28.

[26] A National Health Plan for South Africa May 1994, 76.

[27] *Ibid.*

[28] Greenblo *Finance Week* 14–20, 1996.

[29] A National Health Plan for South Africa May 1994, 32.

[30] *Ibid.*

[31] Health Care *Financial Mail* November 22, 1996, 24.

[32] *Ibid.*

[33] *Ibid.*

National Health Insurance (NHI) system be examined,[34] to make provision for relevant expenditures. Contributions to this system will be income-related and will be determined centrally.[35] It is most probable that this system will be constructed, in order to make provision for between 10-million and 12-million South Africans who are not insured through medical aids, because they cannot afford monthly premiums.[36]

## 9.2  THE HOSPITAL IN SOUTH AFRICA

The first hospital in South Africa, was built in 1883 at the small gold town of Barberton.[37] More than a century later in 1988, there were 693 hospitals and 158,567 hospital beds (public and private) and 2,218 health care clinics in the public sector in South Africa.[38] The Health Systems Trust and the World Bank compiled a report on health expenditure in 1995 in which it was stated that Gauteng had six hospital beds per 1,000, whilst KwaZulu/Natal had only 3.8 and Mpumalanga 2.1.[39]

South Africa had also reached the stage where hospitals had been transformed into sophisticated facilities where the sick could be treated.

## 9.3  LEGAL GROUNDS OF HOSPITAL LIABILITY IN SOUTH AFRICA

### 9.3.1  Indirect or Vicarious Hospital Liability[40]

South African law also acknowledges the principle of vicarious liability as founded on the doctrine of *respondeat superior*, even as a legal ground which establishes hospital liability.[41] In South African law, the principle of

---

[34]  A National Health Plan for South Africa May 1994, 77–78.

[35]  *Ibid.*

[36]  Hoffman *Business Day* August 1996, 20.

[37]  TPA Report 1988 — Hospital Services Branch 36.

[38]  A National Health Plan for South Africa May 1994, 31.

[39]  Parker 1997 *Longevity* 57.

[40]  The general discussion on Indirect or Vicarious Hospital Liability 4.3.1, serves as an introductory passage to this discussion.

[41]  Claassen and Verschoor *Negligence* 95–107. Van der Merwe and Olivier *Onregmatige Daad* 508–522. Gordon Turner and Price *Medical Jurisprudence* 127, 177–183, 187. Lipshitz *Responsa Meridiana* 117–125. Van Dokkum 1996 *De Rebus* 253–255. The Law of South Africa Vol. 17 153. Baxter *Administrative Law* 624–632. Wiechers *Adminis-*

vicarious liability purports that where an employee committed a wrong within the scope of his employment, against a third, such a third person can institute an action for compensation against the employer.[42] This principle was adopted by modern Roman-Dutch law from English law, with the traditional condition that the employer would not be liable for the negligent acts of an independent contractor.[43]

The law concerning the master's liability for the servant's acts, is also the result of a long historical development.[44] In Roman Law, the praetor applied the principle of the masters' legal responsibility for the wrongful acts of servants to specific cases on the ground of public policy.[45] Subsequently this principle was applied by the method of extensive interpretation to analogous cases, by bringing other masters and servants also within this ambit of responsibility.[46] Eventually, the principle was applied to all cases of master

---

*tratiefreg* 346, 347, 349, 366, 385. Strauss *Doctor* 299–304. Strauss and Strydom *Reg* 280–285. See also Simons *Malpractice* 266–273. Neethling *et al. Delict* 372–379, *Deliktereg* 362–369.

[42] Van der Merwe and Olivier *Onregmatige Daad* 508.

[43] Gordon Turner and Price *Medical Jurisprudence* 177. Neethling *et al. Delict* 373. See also *Masuku* v. *Mdlalose* 1998 (1) SA 1 (A) 13–14.

[44] *Feldman (Pty) Ltd* v. *Mall* 1945 AD 733 at 737. *Barkett* v. *SA National Trust and Assurance Co Ltd* 1951 (2) SA 353 (A) 362 B–C.

[45] *Ibid.*

[46] *Ibid.* In *Feldman* 737–738 Watermeyer CJ expounded as follows: In Dig 14.3.5, Ulpian dealt with the praetor's edict relating *institores*, who are factors or commercial agents. He extended the meaning of *institor*, to cover any one appointed to do any business e.g. the manager of a block of flats or a muleteer. He mentioned that *Labeo* thinks that an action resembling the Institorian action, as well as the *actio furti* and the *actio iniuriarum* should be given against an undertaker if he had employed a slave to embalm a corpse which corpse the slave robs. 'These exceptional Roman Law cases were instances of true vicarious liability, not dependent upon any fault of the master, and the master could not escape liability by proving absence of fault.' Several passages in the *corpus iuris* dealt with the justification of this principle. Inst. 4–5–3 indicated that the master was guilty of *culpa* (aliquatenus culpae reus est) for having made use of an incompetent servant. In Dig 4–9–7 Ulpian did not found the principle on the master's *culpa* but made him responsible because it is reasonable that he should be responsible for the acts of those he employed. Translated:

The exercitor is bound to answer for the behaviour of all his seamen, whether they be slaves or free, and it is quite reasonable that he should be answerable for their behaviour as he employed them at his own risk.

In Roman-Dutch law some writers, e.g. Voet 9–4–10 generalized the specific Roman Law cases into a general rule that all masters are responsible for the wrongs done by their servants: '*in officio aut ministerio cui ... domino fuerunt praepositi*'. Justification was founded by some writers on *culpa in eligendo*, whilst Voet maintained that 'the master is

and servant, in Roman-Dutch law.[47]

### 9.3.1.1 Strict liability

Vicarious liability has been classified in 4.3.1.7 as being a term of strict liability. It had also been classified as not being delictual by nature since the employer has no personal fault or blame.[48] However, Van der Walt describes vicarious liability as a strict or faultless delictual liability.[49] He argues that not only wrongful acts which are performed **with fault**, procure delictual liability.[50] Such a limitation would be contrary to our own positive law and in conflict with developments concerning the unlawful act (delict or tort) in the modern Continental legal systems since the middle of the previous century.

Van der Walt[51] then proceeds to illustrate several cases of faultless delictual liability in the positive law which includes (vicarious) liability of the master for the unlawful acts of the servant, indirect liability of certain employers for the accidents of their employees which occur within the scope of their employment, liability for damages resulting from aeroplanes,[52] and liability for damages resulting from the provision of electricity.[53] This he classifies as examples of **faultless delictual liability**.

It could therefore be concluded that in South African law, vicarious liability — at least — could be regarded as a form of faultless delictual liability.

---

responsible because the assignment of the work to an incompetent or untrustworthy servant was his act' (according to Watermeyer CJ).

[47]  *Feldman* 737–738. *Barkett* 362 B–C.

[48]  *Supra* 4.3.1.7. Van der Merwe and Olivier *Onregmatige Daad* 508. Claassen and Verschoor *Negligence* 95.

[49]  Van der Walt 1964 *THRHR* 212 at 213: 'skuldlose deliktuele aanspreeklikheid'.

[50]  *Ibid.* (my accentuation).

[51]  Van der Walt 1964 *THRHR* 213.

[52]  Aviation Act No 74 of 1962 section 11.

[53]  Electricity Act No 40 of 1958 section 50 (repealed). Now Electricity Act No 41 of 1987.

### 9.3.1.2 Traditional requirements of vicarious liability[54]

The three traditional requirements of vicarious liability are also acknowledged in South African law. They are:

9.3.1.2.1 Employer-employee relationship

9.3.1.2.2 An actionable wrong committed

9.3.1.2.3 In execution of duties.

9.3.1.2.1 Employer-employee relationship

This requirement is acknowledged and upheld in South African law.[55] It is a general rule of the South African law that the employer is not responsible for the negligent wrongful performances of an independent contractor employed by him.[56] This is also a general rule of the English law. However, English courts[57] (and Canadian, Australian and American courts) have recognized a number of exceptions to this rule for a very long time.

In *Gibbins v. Williams, Muller, Wright & Mostert Inc and Another*,[58] the court had found a university vicariously liable for the negligent behaviour of members of the university residence's house-committee. In order to determine whether the culprit(s) were indeed employees of the university four *indicia* were highlighted:[59]

(a)    the employer's right to employ the employee

(b)    the payment of wages or other compensation

(c)    the employer's right to control the method of work

(d)    the employer's right to dismiss the employee.

---

[54]    *Supra* 4.3.1.8. Claassen and Verschoor *Negligence* 96–98. Van der Merwe and Olivier *Onregmatige Daad* 509–519. Gordon Turner and Price *Medical Jurisprudence* 177–183, 187. Neethling *et al. Delict* 372–378, *Deliktereg* 362–368. Lipschitz *Responsa Meridiana* 117. Van Dokkum 1996 *De Rebus* 253–255. The Law of South Africa Vol. 17 153. Baxter *Administrative Law* 624–632. Wiechers *Administratiefreg* 346, 347, 349, 366, 385. Strauss and Strydom *Reg* 280–285. Strauss *Doctor* 299–304.

[55]    *Ibid. Supra* 4.3.1.8.1.

[56]    *Langley Fox Building Partnership (Pty) Ltd v. De Valence* 1991 (1) SA 1 (A), 8. *Colonial Mutual Life Assurance Society Ltd v. MacDonald* 1931 AD 412 at 428, 431–432. *Dukes v. Marthinusen* 1937 AD 12 at 17.

[57]    *Langley Fox Building Partnership (Pty) Ltd v. De Valence supra*, at 8: English courts have known these exceptions for well over a century.

[58]    1987 (2) SA 82 (T). See *infra* footnote 178 on *Dowling v. Diocesan College and Others.*

[59]    *Gibbins* 90.

*In casu* all four *indicia* had been present which established the employer-employee relationship. Since all necessary traditional requirements were met, the university was held liable vicariously. The court, per Eloff AJP, did however add that non-compliance with one of the four above-mentioned *indicia* will not negate such liability.

In terms of South African law, vicarious liability will be established even where:

- a contract of service was negotiated for a short period of time. A long period of time is not necessary to comply with this requirement.[60]

- the servant receives no remuneration, salary or wages for services rendered.[61]

- the servant is not bound contractually to render his services. The existence of a contract of service is not a prerequisite to establish vicarious liability. *De facto* provision of services is sufficient to found vicarious liability.[62]

- the servant disregarded the express instructions of the master.[63]

According to *Minister van Polisie en 'n Ander* v. *Gamble en 'n Ander*,[64] the Minister of Law and Order can now be held accountable for the performances (peccadilloes) of a policeman even if the policeman had exercised an independent discretion or a discretion of his own. Even so, in *Minister of Police* v. *Rabie*[65] liability followed where the policeman was not on duty. Consequently, by analogy, it could be argued that the Minister of Health is at risk whenever a member of the hospital staff (under his command), is negligent in the performance of any duties whether they be professional and not subject to dictation from others, or not.[66]

It has, however, already been suggested that the employer-employee distinction should be discarded in the hospital liability setting.[67] In English

---

[60]   Van der Merwe and Olivier *Onregmatige Daad* 514. *Infra* footnote 76.

[61]   *Ibid. Rodriques and Others* v. *Alves and Others* 1978 (4) SA 834 (A) at 814 E. *Gibbins supra* at 90.

[62]   Van der Merwe and Olivier *Onregmatige Daad* 514.

[63]   *Barkett* v. *SA National Trust & Assurance C Ltd* 1951 (2) SA 353 (AD) 362. *Feldman (Pty) Ltd* v. *Mall* 1945 AD 733.

[64]   1979 (4) SA 759 (A).

[65]   1986 (1) SA 117 (A).

[66]   *Mtetwa* v. *Minister of Health* 1989 (3) SA 600 (D), at 606 B–D. See also Van Dokkum 1996 *De Rebus* 255.

[67]   *Supra* 4.3.1.9 and 4.3.1.9.1.

law,[68] Canadian law,[69] and American law,[70] there have also been recom-mendations for the negation of this requirement. In South African law, such implied calls have been few and far between, but will be dealt with briefly *infra*.

### 9.3.1.2.1.1 Relevant tests

(a)  The control test

(b)  The organization test

(a)  The control test

The inadequacy of the control test has also already been expounded.[71] The control test was traditionally implemented in order to establish the existence of the employer-employee relationship. South African law mainly acknowl-edges the validity of this test in one form or another — 'the right to control' or as one of various indicia by which to ascertain the compliance of the employer-employee relationship.

The consideration of control, that is not factual control but the capacity (power) or right to control,[72] has been deemed to be the most important factor in determining whether a perpetrator is an employee or an independent contractor.[73] Control is, however, not the sole determining factor.[74] In South

---

[68]  *Supra* 4.3.1.9.1 and 5.3.1.

[69]  *Supra* 4.3.1.9.1 and 7.3.1.3.

[70]  *Supra* 4.3.1.9.1 and 8.4.1.3.4.

[71]  *Supra* 4.3.1.9.2, 5.3.1, 5.4.1, 5.5.1, 7.3.1.1.1.1, 8.3.1, 10.3.2.1.

[72]  Verschoor and Claassen *Negligence* 96. Neethling *et al. Delict* 374, *Deliktereg* 364. Van der Merwe and Olivier *Onregmatige Daad* 511. *Rodriques* v. *Alves* 1978 (4) SA 834 (A) 842. *Mhlongo and Another NO* v. *Minister of Police* 1978 (2) SA 551 (AD) at 567–568B. *Smit* v. *Workmen's Compensation Commissioner* 1979 (1) SA 51 (AD) 62. *Rofdo (Pty) Ltd t/a Castle Crane Hire* v. *B & E Quarries (Pty) Ltd* 1999 (3) SA 941 (SEC) per Zietsman JP at 948 G–I, 949 B–F.

[73]  *Colonial Mutual Life Assurance Society Ltd* v. *MacDonald* 1931 AD 412, 432–435, 444–445. *Lichaba* v. *Shield Versekeringsmaatskappy Bpk* 1977 (4) SA 623 (O) 635. *Gibbins* v. *Williams, Mulder, Wright en Mostert Ingelyf* 1987 (2) SA 82 (T) 90. *FPS Ltd* v. *Trident Construction (Pty) Ltd* 1989 (3) SA 537 (A) 542–543. Neethling *et al. Delict* 374–375.

[74]  Lipshitz 1981 Responsa Meridiana 124–125. Van der Merwe en Olivier Onregmatige Daad 511. Neethling et al. Delict 375, Deliktereg 365. Argent v. Minister of Social Security and Another 1968 1 WLR 1749. Ongevallekommissaris v. Onderlinge Verseker-ingsgenootskap AVBOB 1976 (4) SA 446 (A) 456–457. Mtetwa v. Minister of Health 1989 (3) SA 600 (D) 605 G–J, F–G: 'Control is merely one of the indicia to determine whether or not a person is a servant or an independent worker.' In Smit v. Workmen's Compensation Commissioner 1979 (1) SA 51 (A) 62D–G Joubert JA stated: 'Notwith-standing its importance the fact remains that the presence of such a right of supervision and control is not the sole indicium but merely one of the indicia albeit an important one,

African law, the relationship is judged in the light of all the circumstances of the specific case.[75]

All employers, inclusive of the state, are in the same position. The only way the state could escape liability is by showing that the particular official was not *pro hac vice* (in the particular case), an employee of the state at the time the delict was committed.[76] This occurs when the state did not have the power to control him at that stage.[77]

(b)  The organization test

The organization test was introduced in the English common law.[78] This test has, however, not experienced a particularly warm reception in South African law, as was the case in Australian law.

Kahn-Freund[79] had postulated the organization test as a better alternative to the control test. It was suggested that since the employer is not in control of the (modern) enterprise due to modern social conditions, the organization test would be the more suitable test in terms of which it should be asked: 'Was the employee part of the employer's organization in the sense that his work was an integral part of the master's business?' The employee's work would be integrated, but the independent contractor's work would not be integrated into, but only accessory to the employer's business.

In *Ready Mixed Concrete (South East) Ltd* v. *Minister of Pensions and National Insurance* [80] McKenna J stated that the organization test was vague,

---

and that there may also be other important indicia to be considered depending upon the provisions of the contract in question as a whole.' See also *Sasverbijl Beleggings en Verdiskonterings Maatskappy Bpk* v. *Van Rhynsdorp Town Council and Another* 1979 (2) SA 771 (W) 776.

[75]  *Supra* 4.3.1.8.1. Claassen and Verschoor *Negligence* 97. Lipshitz 1981 *Responsa Meridiana* 119. Neethling *et al. Delict* 375, *Deliktereg* 365. *R* v. *AMCA Services* 1959 (4) SA 207 (A) 211 per Schreiner JA. *Midway Two Engineering & Construction Services* v. *Transnet Bpk* 1998 (3) SA 17 (SCA) per Nienaber JA at 22 D–23 J, where the learned judge stated that the control test is outdated and that a multi-faceted test consisting of all relevant factors relating to reasonableness and policy, should be applied in order to determine the nature of a relationship. In the end the temporary employer was found vicariously liable for the temporary employee who performed services — according to the court's test — within the scope of the temporary employer's employment. (At 28 F–J).

[76]  Neethling *et al. Delict* 375–376, *Deliktereg* 365.

[77]  *Ibid.*

[78]  *Supra* 4.3.1.8.1 and footnote 113, and 6.3.1.1.1.1(b).

[79]  Kahn-Freund 1951 *MLR* 504–509. Millner 1958 *Journal of Forensic Medicine* 102–103: Millner quotes from Kahn-Freund and concludes that the control test has to be supplemented in a suitable case by the organization test.

[80]  [1968] 1 ALL ER 433 (QB) 445 G.

since the meaning of being part and parcel of an organization was nowhere defined, and this was necessary to distinguish between a servant and an independent contractor. The judge could therefore not conclude that the person who is a servant of an enterprise, necessarily forms an integral part of such an enterprise. It was to this case that Joubert JA had referred in *Smit* v. *Workmen's Compensation Commissioner*[81] when he discarded the organization test whilst stating:

> In my view the organisation test is juristically speaking of such a vague and nebulous nature that more often than not no useful assistance can be derived from it in distinguishing between an employee (*locator operarum*) and an independent contractor (*conductor operis*) in our common law.[82]

Lipshitz, however concludes:

> Notwithstanding the reservations which have been expressed about the organisation test in the above two cases, it is my opinion that doctors and nurses do indeed form part of the organisation of a hospital when they are performing professional duties, and the same is also true of a policeman who performs a negligent act in the course of his duties.[83]

Van Dokkum also suggests that control has given way to the organization test which is more in accord with 'modern economic and social realities, of whether he was part of his employer's organisation'. He finds that the hospital is no longer precluded from liability by pleading that there was no detailed supervision of the performances of professional staff, just as long as 'they are part of the hospital organisation and not employed by the patient himself'.[84]

### 9.3.1.2.2  An actionable wrong

This requirement was dealt with in 4.3.1.8.3 and needs no additional discussion here.

### 9.3.1.2.3  In execution of duties

This requirement was sufficiently discussed in 4.3.1.8.2. It should, however, be highlighted that an exceptional test was introduced in *Minister of Police*

---

[81]  1979 1 SA 51 (AD).

[82]  *Smit* 63 G.

[83]  Lipshitz 1981 *Responsa Meridiana* 123. See also Burchell and Schaffer 1977 *Businessman's Law* 110: 'It is possible on this criterion to hold that a nurse is clearly part of the organization of the hospital even when she is performing professional duties.'

[84]  Van Dokkum 1996 *De Rebus* 255.

v. *Rabie*,[85] by which it could be determined whether a person acted within the scope of his employment. The test was subjective on the one hand and objective on the other. The employer will therefore not be vicariously liable only if the employee, 'viewed subjectively, has not only exclusively promoted his own interests, but, viewed objectively, has also completely disengaged himself from the duties of his contract of employment.'[86]

When a wrongful act is committed by means of a forbidden act, and the forbidden act is connected with the work generally authorized by the employer and thus falls within the extent thereof, the employer will also be liable vicariously.[87]

Furthermore, compliance with the requirement whether the employee had acted within the scope of his employment had been judged — in decided cases — on the basis of the creation of a risk by the employer.[88]

However, in *Minister of Law and Order* v. *Ngobo*,[89] two police constables who had been off-duty, fatally wounded a son who was supporting his

---

[85]   1986 (1) SA 117 (A) 134, at 774: 'It seems clear that an act done by a servant solely for his own interests and purposes, although occasioned by his employment, may fall outside the course or scope of his employment, and that in deciding whether an act by the servant does so fall, some reference is to be made to the servant's intention …'[124] The test is in this regard subjective. On the other hand, if there is nevertheless a sufficiently close link between the servant's acts for his own interests and purposes and the business of his master, the master may yet be liable.[125] This is an objective test. And it may be useful to add that '… a master … is liable even for acts which he has not authorized provided that they are so connected with acts which he has authorised that they may rightly be regarded as modes — although improper modes — of doing them ….'

The latter case was followed in *Smit* v. *Minister van Polisie* 1997 (4) SA 893 (T) per De Villiers J at 905 E–G, 909 E, 908 A and *Viljoen* v. *Smith* 1997 (1) SA 309 (A) 315–316, 318 and *Ess Kay Electronics Pte Ltd and Another* v. *First National Bank of Southern Africa Ltd* 1998 (4) SA 1102 (W) per Baruchowitz J at 1108 F–J. See also *Witham* v. *Minister of Home Affairs* 1989 (1) SA 116 (ZH) 126. Neethling *et al. Delict* 376, *Deliktereg* 366. *Canadian Pacific Railway Co* v. *Lockhart* 1942 AC 591: 'On the other hand, if the unauthorised and wrongful act of the servant is not so connected with the authorised act as to be a mode of doing it but is an independent act, the master is not responsible.'

[86]   Neethling *et al. Delict* 376–377, *Deliktereg* 366. *Compare Greater Johannesburg Transitional Metropolitan Council* v. *ABSA Bank Ltd T/A Volkskas Bank* 1997 (2) SA 591 (W) per Goldstein J at 600 where the bank was held vicariously liable for damage caused by the theft of an employee performing the exact functions for which she had been employed, but in an improper fashion.

[87]   *Ibid.* See also their explanation of risk-creation by the employer. *Maxalanga* v. *Mpela and Another* 1998 (3) SA 987 (T).

[88]   Neethling *et al. Delict* 378, *Deliktereg* 367–368. These decisions have been critized by other authors. *Minister of Police* v. *Rabie* 1986 1 SA 117(A) 134. *Feldman (Pty) Ltd* v. *Mall* 1945 AD 733 741.

[89]   1992 (4) SA 822 (A). They shot the man with their service revolvers.

mother. The vicarious liability of the Minister for the policemen who were off-duty, was expounded by means of ascertaining whether they had acted within the scope of their employment. The standard test for vicarious liability, which comprises of the subjective and objective tests, was accepted. The 'creation of risk principle' was rejected. The claim failed.

### 9.3.1.3 Comment on the master-servant relationship and the control test

#### 9.3.1.3.1 In general

(a)   Gordon, Turner and Price have observed that the master and servant relationship is not precluded by the fact that the servant is employed to perform work which is of a highly skilled or technical kind, which the employer might be incapable of doing himself.[90] They quote from Goodhart where the latter states that:

> The aviation company which employs an aviator to fly an aeroplane on a difficult course is liable for his negligence ... . Similarly, a steamship company is liable for the negligence of the certified ship-masters who are navigating its ships. In such cases the employers are liable even though they cannot tell their servants how to perform the tasks they have employed them to do, and would, in fact, make themselves criminally liable if they attempted to do so.[91]
>
> It is suggested that this proposition is of great significance in considering the liability of hospitals and others for the acts of practitioners employed by them, and that some cases have been wrongly decided in the past because it has been overlooked.[92]

On the contrary Goodhart remarks that:

> It might with equal force be said that the directors of an aviation company do not undertake in any way themselves to fly their aeroplanes ... but that the aviators were therefore doing their own work as skilled pilots and not as servants of the aviation company'.[93]

(b)   In *Lee* v. *Lee's Air Farming Ltd* [94] an air company of which the 'servant' was the 'managing director', was found vicariously liable

---

[90]   Gordon, Turner and Price *Medical Jurisprudence* 177.

[91]   *Op. cit.* 177–178.

[92]   *Op. cit.* 178.

[93]   *Op. cit.* 183 footnote 278. On the contrary Goodhart remarks that: 'It might with equal force be said that the directors of an aviation company do not undertake in any way themselves to fly their aeroplanes... but that the aviators were therefore doing their own work as skilled pilots and not as servants of the aviation company.'

[94]   1961 AC 12.

despite a complete lack of control. Lee was the sole director of the company, owned all the shares in the company and was employed as chief pilot. Regardless of the fact that Lee controlled the company rather than the company controlling him, the Privy Council found a contract of service to exist between Lee and the Company. Consequently, since a normal contract of service was identified, the master-servant relationship or contract was held to exist in spite of 'the absence of any real control'.[95]

In other words, the element of control or absence thereof cannot preclude a finding of (vicarious) liability, nor the existence of a master-servant relationship (although the latter finding could be unnecessary, with respect).

(c)    In *Colonial Mutual Life Assurance Society Ltd* v. *MacDonald*,[96] De Villiers CJ stated as follows:

> Although the opportunity of supervising and controlling which a master is able to exercise over a servant may vary greatly with the circumstances, it cannot be said to be altogether unreasonable to hold him liable for the torts of his servant. But because even **in the case of master and servant** efficient supervision and **control is** in some cases difficult **if not entirely absent,** ... .[97]

By this statement it is, with respect, acknowledged that control is not a prerequisite for the existence of a master-servant relationship.

(d)    Baxter has come to the ultimate conclusion. First of all he admitted that the control test was 'beginning to lose its dominance in the realm of private vicarious liability and even in so far as the liability of public authorities was concerned.'[98] He proceeded to find that the 'master/servant framework with its attendant control test, even in its more flexible modern form, is incapable of dealing with delicts committed by officials who exercise a personal statutory power.'[99] He stated that control by a superior could constitute interference with the exercise of

---

[95]    Lipshitz 1981 *Responsa Meridiana* 122. Lipshitz is one of the few South African authors that recognized the inadequacy of the control test (at 119).

[96]    1931 AD 412.

[97]    Colonial 433. The above-mentioned passage proceeds: '... that is no reason for extending the liability of the principal to include the torts of a man over whose actions he has no say whatever.' See also Gordon, Turner and Price *Medical Jurisprudence* 177.

[98]    Baxter *Administrative Law* 628.

[99]    *Op. cit.* 631.

discretionary powers by others.[100] He added that the concept of the employer-employee relationship has to keep abreast with the organizational realities of modern institutions.[101] In some instances no employer/employee situation existed.[102] He concludes:

> Since the official will be acting judicially and will therefore be exercising an independent discretion, the state will not be vicariously liable for his acts. There is no control and therefore no master/servant relationship. This seems unsatisfactory: while one might understand the need for immunity on the part of the decision-maker, there seems little reason why the state should not be liable for any delict he commits. ... This reveals one more deficiency in the model of vicarious liability as it operates in public law.[103]

It is submitted, with respect, that Baxter should have gone one step further: He should have found that the vicarious liability model is most valuable in establishing liability according to the principle of finding the most financially viable party with its appropriate funds to compensate the injured. But he should have recognized the inadequacies and limitations of the master/servant framework and the control test and have adapted or abandoned them, as is the contemporary international trend concerning the hospital setting. By analogy, the same conclusion can be drawn regarding the ineffectiveness of the master/servant requirement and the control test concerning the hospital liability law.

It must be noted that Wiechers has also acknowledged the inadequacy of the control test.[104]

### 9.3.1.3.1.1 Conclusion

The control test obviously fails where high skills are displayed or discretionary tasks rest not with the employer, and the typical master-servant subordination vanishes except for apparent contractual specifications or other minutiae, which succeeds in establishing such a relationship. Actually, with respect, the pilot who carries a heavy responsibility by exercising skills and discretion based on expertise as well as the shipmaster, are in effect

---

[100] *Ibid.*

[101] *Ibid.*

[102] *Op. cit.* 631–632.

[103] *Op. cit.* 634.

[104] Wiechers *Administatiefreg* 364: 'Hoe dit ook al sy, die kontroletoets is nog meer onvanpas by die staatlike diensverhouding as wat dit ooit by die private diensverhouding kon gewees het.' Compare Markesinis and Deakin *Tort Law* 535.

'independent contractors' by reason of their expertise. They are only employees in so far as their contracts make provision for their employment and in the determination of career prospects. The airline or ship company nevertheless have to take responsibility and can be held vicariously liable for the negligence of these 'servants'. Medical professionals, doctors or specialists who are highly skilled and trained and perform independently from the corporation or hospital by means of their discretion and expertise, could consequently also cause such institutions to be held vicariously liable for their negligent performances.

### 9.3.1.3.2 The owner and/or driver of a motor vehicle:

(a)  In *Braamfontein Food Centre* v. *Blake*,[105] Goldstone J concluded that the master-servant relationship was not a necessary requirement to establish the owner of a motor vehicle's vicarious liability.[106] The learned judge remarked:

> The vicarious liability of a master for the negligent driving of his servant rests upon the relationship between the master and the servant. Power to **control** the manner of driving of the servant **is not a requirement of such liability**. The right of control is relevant in the determination of the relationship of master and servant. If such a relationship is established then the master will be liable if a delict is committed by the servant acting in the course and scope of his employment. Where the **relationship of master and servant is absent (as in the present case)** liability for the negligent driving of a motor vehicle will arise where the vehicle is being driven on behalf of the owner or other person sought to be held liable, i.e. for the owner's or such other person's purposes, and the owner or such other person has the power to control the manner of driving the vehicle.[107]

(b)  In *Paton* v. *Caledonian Insurance Co*[108] the plaintiff was driven in her motor vehicle by a friend to whom she had given her consent for the common purpose of a holiday trip. They were in an accident with another motorcar whilst underway, which other car was ensured by the defendant in terms of Act 29 of 1942. The court found that both drivers were equally negligent. The plaintiff had become liable in terms of vicarious liability for the friend's negligence and was therefore only entitled to recover half her damages from the defendant.

---

[105]  1982 (3) SA 248 (T).

[106]  Van der Merwe and Olivier *Onregmatige Daad* 528.

[107]  *Braamfontein* 250 H–251 B.( My accentuation ).He thereby also disqualified control as a requirement to vicarious liability at first, but 'reinstated' control in the last sentence.

[108]  1962 (2) SA 691 (D).

Henning J found that vicarious liability could be established in three separate incidents: A person could be held vicariously liable as a master or as a principal or merely as the owner (of a car) who retained control of the car.[109]

In other words, the traditional master-servant requirement was not deemed necessary to found vicarious liability and the absence of such a relationship could not preclude such a finding.

The judge also found:

> It appears to me that the owner of a potentially dangerous thing, such as a motor vehicle, who retains control of it, although he allows another to handle it, is vicariously responsible to others for the harm caused to them by such handling. The liability is based on the retention of control and not on any negligent act or omission of the owner, and it seems to me that it is not essential that a person who handles the article should be either the servant or agent of the owner.'[110] 'The owner not only has the right to control the driver, but he is also under a duty to do so.[111]

It is rather unfortunate, with respect, that the judge had to persist with the control test. After abandoning the master-servant requirement, he might as well have discarded control which is traditionally only implemented to establish the relationship which he has just dismissed.

An alternative basis to vicarious liability — most appropriately — could have been the direct liability of the owner. By suggesting that the owner of a potentially dangerous thing was under a duty to control the manner in which such a thing was handled, could by concept and formulation easily have established direct liability.[112] At 697B the judge mentioned 'another basis upon which the plaintiff's liability is, in my opinion, established,' but never identifies or expounds this alternative legal ground or basis.

(c)    In *Feldman (Pty) Ltd* v. *Mall*,[113]the employer was held liable for the negligent or improper performance of the master's work by the so-called servant, which caused damage. The servant had negligently driven the master's van during which time he had collided with and

---

[109] *Paton* 697: '... the plaintiff is, in law, vicariously answerable for... negligence whether she was in the position of a master or principal or merely of an owner who retained control of the car.'

[110] *Paton* 695H–695A.

[111] *Paton* 696B–C.

[112] Van der Merwe and Olivier *Onregmatige Daad* 527.

[113] 1945 AD 733.

killed the father of two minor children. It was held that disobedience of or acting contrary to the master's instructions could still render the master liable. Watermeyer CJ accentuated that in such a case, non-compliance with direct orders or the disregard of control still founds vicarious liability.

In terms of this decision, employer or vicarious liability was established without complying with the control test. It was found that there was no submission to control. Control was ineffective, due to breach of contract between the employer and employee.[114]

- It could be argued that control was traditionally regarded as the indicium by which to establish the employer-employee relationship. Since there was no control, traditionally there could then be no employer-employee relationship. But vicarious liability ensued regardless of the fact that control was lacking by which the employer-employee relationship should be established.

- It could also be argued that the vicarious liability was established in spite of the fact that control was lacking, and that the existence of the employer-employee relationship also did not depend on the element of control.

Despite the lack of control, vicarious liability **or** both vicarious liability and the employer-employee relationship were established. The court referred to the master-servant relationship, so the latter approach would seem the more reasonable one.

### 9.3.1.3.1 Conclusion

It is apparent that in South African law either the master-servant requirement or the control test is sometimes deleted in the vicarious liability context. The non-adherence to these prerequisites indicates that either or both could be discarded in the formation of a modern vicarious liability law.

---

[114] Van der Merwe and Olivier *Onregmatige Daad* 517. See *Venter* v. *Boputhatswana Transport Holdings (Edms) Bpk* 1997 (3) SA 374 (HCA) per Olivier JA, where the owner of a vehicle was held vicariously liable for the negligent driver who was considered to have acted within the scope of his employment, in consideration of all the relevant factors.

### 9.3.1.4 Justification

In South African law, no absolute ground of justification has yet been found or formulated to justify the imposition of vicarious liability.[115] In *Feldman (Pty) Ltd v. Mall*,[116] Greenberg JA stated:

> But law is not always logical; on the very question underlying this liability, *viz.* the reason why a master should ever be liable for acts of the servant which are committed in disregard of his express instructions, judges and commentators have found difficulty in finding a logically satisfying basis, and the way in which the rule has been applied is probably a compromise between conflicting considerations.[117]

Watermeyer CJ expounded the justification of the principle of vicarious liability in *Feldman* as follows:

> I have gone in to this question more fully than seems necessary, in the hope that the reasons which have been advanced for the imposition of vicarious liability upon a master may give some indication of the limits of a master's legal responsibility, and the reasons are to some extent helpful. It appears from them that a master who does his work by the hand of a servant creates a risk of harm to others if the servant should prove to be negligent or inefficient or untrustworthy; that, because he has created this risk for his own ends he is under a duty to ensure that no one is injured by the servant's improper conduct or negligence in carrying on his work and that the mere giving by him of directions or orders to his servant is not a sufficient performance of that duty. It follows that if the servant's acts in doing his master's work or his activities incidental to or connected with it are carried out in a negligent or improper manner so as to cause harm to a third party the master is responsible for that harm.[118]

In *Barkett v. SA National Trust and Assurance Co Ltd*,[119] Centlivres CJ proclaimed that:

> Whatever the real reason may be for holding a master responsible for the harm done by a servant in the execution of his work it is clear that in modern South African Law it is not because the master himself has been at fault: whether he was at fault or not is irrelevant: all that has to be proved is that the harm was done by the servant in the execution of his master's work.

---

[115] See *supra* 4.3.1.10. *Midway Two Engineering & Construction Services v. Transnet Bpk* 1998 (3) SA 17 (SCA) per Nienaber JA at 22 A–D.

[116] 1945 AD 733.

[117] *Feldman* 779. See also Van der Merwe and Olivier *Onregmatige Daad* 509.

[118] *Feldman* 741.

[119] 1951 (2) SA 353 (A) at 360 H. Compare *Mkize v. Martens* 1914 AD 382 at 394. See also Van Der Merwe and Olivier *Onregmatige Daad* 509.

South African academics have founded justification for the principle of vicarious liability either on a variety of specific theories,[120] on the 'risk liability theory',[121] on the necessity of cost distribution in the light of increasing industrialization and increased industrial accidents (without a clearly identifiable tortfeasor),[122] or on public policy which necessitates a deep pocket to recompense the injured 'man of straw'.[123] However, Van der Merwe and Olivier have concluded that despite all such attempts, a satisfactory juridical basis has yet to be found.[124]

### 9.3.1.5 The 'Borrowed-Servant' and 'Captain-of-the-Ship' doctrines[125]

Both the above-mentioned doctrines are declining in the USA. Initially, they had been introduced to afford patients a 'deep pocket' when hospitals were precluded from liability under the doctrine of charitable immunity.[126]

These doctrines have not been adopted in South African law. In *Hartl* v. *Pretoria Hospital Committee*[127] the court had briefly applied the 'captain of the ship' doctrine. Wessels J held that:

> But if the nurse is engaged in an operation under the supervision of the med-
> ical officer who is actually in charge of the operation, then as long as she is
> under the charge of the medical officer who is conducting the operation she
> can in no way be said to be acting as the employee of the Hospital Committee.
> ... the nurse who assists the doctor in an operation is entirely under his control
> ... and the Hospital Committee is not liable for her acts.[128]

---

[120] Claassen and Verschoor *Negligence* 95–96. Lipschitz 1981 *Responsa Meridiana* 117. Neethling *et al. Delict* 373, *Deliktereg* 363.

[121] Scott 1979 *CILSA* 44, 49.

[122] Van Dokkum 1996 *De Rebus* 253.

[123] Strauss *Doctor* 302.

[124] Van der Merwe and Olivier *Onregmatige Daad* 509. Claassen and Verschoor *Negligence* 96.

[125] *Supra* 8.4.1.8. Claassen and Verschoor *Negligence* 110–113. Gordon Turner and Price *Medical Jurisprudence* 183. Strauss *Doctor* 302. Strauss and Strydom *Reg* 283: They criticized the 'captain of the ship' doctrine as well as the 'borrowed servant' doctrine.

[126] *Supra* 8.4.1.8. Distinguish between the separate meanings of the two doctrines.

[127] 1915 TPD 336.

[128] *Hartl* 341. This would, with respect, constitute implementation of the captain of the ship doctrine and not the borrowed servant doctrine as is suggested by Strauss and Strydom *Reg* 283 footnote 112.

However, in *Van Wyk* v. *Lewis*,[129] the Appellate Division denied any application of the afore-mentioned doctrines. Innes CJ held:

> But assuming (without determining) that she was negligent in her check, it does not follow that the surgeon is liable for the consequences. ... She was not the servant of the respondent; ... .[130]

Kotzé JA held:

> Her duty in counting and checking the swabs is quite independent of the operating surgeon.[131]

Wessels JA found:

> They are subordinate to the surgeons but they are in no way their servants. The surgeon is not responsible for what the nurse does in the sense that a master is responsible for the acts of his servant. The surgeon does not insure that he will be responsible for every misfeasance of the nurse. To make him so would make his position intolerable.[132]

The court thus found that the nurse remains the servant of the hospital at all times.[133]

Hitherto, any application or these doctrines have been non-existent in South African law.

### *9.3.1.6 Res Ipsa Loquitur*[134]

The maxim *res ipsa loquitur* means, the matter speaks for itself. The South African judicial literature has offered no objection(s) in principle that precludes the reasonable application of this maxim. Innes CJ stated in *Van Wyk* v. *Lewis* that:

> ... It is really a question of inference. No doubt it is sometimes said that in cases where the maxim applies the happening of the occurrence is in itself *prima facie* evidence of negligence. If by that is meant that the burden of

---

[129] 1924 AD 438. If any doctrine was to be applied here, it would have been the captain of the ship doctrine.

[130] *Van Wyk* 450.

[131] *Van Wyk* 454.

[132] *Van Wyk* 459. It would be interesting to know if Wessels JA, and Wessels J who gave the decision in *Hartl supra*, was the same judge.

[133] Gordon Turner and Price *Medical Jurisprudence* 183.

[134] *Supra* 4.3.3.3.3. Gordon Turner and Price *Medical Jurisprudence* 113–117, 139, 183. Van der Merwe and Olivier *Onregmatige Daad* 144. Neethling *et al. Delict* 149–150, *Delikte-reg* 146. Van Dokkum 1996 *De Rebus* 253.

proof is automatically shifted from the plaintiff to the defendant then I doubt the accuracy of the statement ... .[135]

*Res ipsa loquitur* has also been branded as being no doctrine 'but a convenient label to describe a result.' '**The maxim *res ipsa loquitur***, where applicable, gives rise to an inference rather than to a presumption.'[136]

It is submitted that this maxim is a useful and necessary tool of logic, which should be applied not only with caution, but also as an instrument to facilitate findings in hospital liability cases.[137]

### 9.3.2 Hospital Liability in Terms of the Doctrines of Apparent Agency and Agency by Estoppel[138]

The doctrines of apparent agency and agency by estoppel are the most correct contemporary phraseological expositions, (or doctrines) implemented by courts in the USA to hold hospitals liable where medical professionals are held out to be employees of hospitals whilst they are not.

These doctrines are most appropriately and conveniently implemented in the USA, especially when dealing with emergency medical services or the notorious emergency room, in order to render the hospital liable.[139] In Canadian law, academics have in no uncertain terms, recommended the use or adoption of especially the doctrine of apparent agency.[140]

Considering the position in South African law, these doctrines have not yet been adopted. It is, however, submitted that if a private hospital[141] would

---

[135] *Van Wyk* v. *Lewis* 1924 AD 438, at 445.

[136] *Arthur* v. *Bezuidenhout and Mieny* 1962 (2) SA 566 (A) per Ogilvie Thompson JA at 574. **Criticism** to the *res ipsa loquitur* maxim is found in *Van Wyk* v. *Lewis supra* at 464 per Wessels JA: 'Hence it seems to me that the maxim *res ipsa loquitur* has no application to cases of this kind.'

See also *Pringle* v. *Administrator Tvl* 1990 (2) SA 379 (W): Van Dokkum 1996 *De Rebus* 253. See also Simons *Malpractice* 270–271. *Res ipsa loquitur* was applied with both great caution and success in *MacLeod* v. *Rens* 1997 (3) SA 1039 (EC) per Erasmus J at 1046 C–H, and 1052 E.

[137] *Supra* 4.3.3.3.3.

[138] *Supra* 7.3.2 and 8.4.2. See also Claassen and Verschoor *Negligence* 103–104 who discuss the doctrine of 'apparent authority'.

[139] *Supra* 8.4.2.

[140] *Supra* 7.3.2.

[141] Strauss *Doctor* 303 negates the private hospital's potential liability for the provision of emergency services. This viewpoint is, with respect, not in line with contemporary hospital liability law. See also Claassen en Verschoor *Negligence* 103–104. See *Buls and Another* v. *Tsatsarolakis* 1976 (2) SA (T) 891 on the emergency services provided by a

undertake to provide emergency services by means of an independent contractor(s) or an independent contractor company on a contractual basis, the following liability options would be available:

(i)    Hospital liability could be established by means of the doctrines of apparent agency or agency by estoppel. The traditional doctrine of apparent authority is also still relevant in certain circumstances.[142]

(ii)   Direct hospital liability could also be founded on the breach of the hospital's duty to exercise reasonable care in the provision of specialized patient care: If the hospital chose to or provided or held itself out as entertaining or providing a specific speciality or specialized field of services or **specialized system**, e.g. emergency services or an emergency system, the hospital could be under a duty to take reasonable care in the provision of such services. Failure to provide proper emergency services or a proper emergency system, or relevant organizational failures could amount to breach of such a direct duty. This would consequently render the hospital directly liable due to breach of it's own direct duty founded on corporate negligence. It should be kept in mind that direct institutional (corporate) liability relates favourably to improper systems and organizational failures.[143]

(iii)  Hospital liability for poor emergency services that involve the negligent performance(s) of even independent contractors, can also be founded on the non-delegable duty. If the court can find that the hospital had indeed (a) delegated the performance of emergency services to independent contractor(s) or an independent contractor company, (b) but in the light of the *boni mores*, the public policy, relevant hospital regulations or other relevant factors, such a duty's responsibility cannot be considered delegable, hospital liability can ensue.[144]

### 9.3.3  The Non-Delegable Duty

The non-delegable duty has been acknowledged as an independent legal ground which founds hospital liability in English law, Australian law and the

---

public hospital. *Soobramoney* v. *Minister of Health, KwaZulu-Natal* 1998 (1) SA 765 (CC). *Infra* 9.3.5.1. Category 3 (iv) (2).

[142]  *Supra* 7.3.2 and 8.4.2. Claassen and Verschoor *Negligence* 103–104.

[143]  *Supra* 8.4.4.4.1 (Category 3) and 9.3.2 (Category 3).

[144]  *Supra* 7.3.2, 8.4.2 and 8.4.2.4. *Jackson* v. *Power* 743 P 2d 1376 (Alaska 1987).

law of the USA.[145] There have been recommendations[146] for such an adoption in the South African law, but implementation of the non-delegable duty as a proper independent legal ground, is either undetected or non-existent. There have been references to non-delegable duties in the South African case law, but not in the sense of acknowledging it as an independent legal ground on which to found (employer) or hospital liability.

The main characteristics of the non-delegable duty is that performance of the duty is delegated, but responsibility for it is undelegable. The non-delegable duty as an independent legal ground perpetuates a strict or faultless liability i.e. (employer) liability without blame, for even independent contractors.[147]

### 9.3.3.1 English law

In the **English law**,[148] it had been concluded that a non-delegable duty could be construed:

(i)  In terms of a **statute** or statutory clause. An examination of the construction of the statute is necessary to determine if it implied a non-delegable duty. The duty to use 'due diligence' could be such a duty.[149]

(ii)  A non-delegable duty could be raised contractually in terms of an express term in the **contract**, which would hardly occur.[150]

(iii)  If a hospital holds itself out or has a **reputation** in the 'market place' for rendering particular services, such a non-delegable duty could be inferred.[151]

### 9.3.3.2 Australian law

In **Australian law**,[152] the non-delegable duty was established, which induced a higher standard of responsibility due to modern and exceptional risks

---

[145]  *Supra* 4.3.3, 5.5, 6.3.3, 8.4.3.

[146]  Millner 1958 *Journal of Forensic Medicine* 103, 104. Burchell and Schaffer 1977 *Businessman's Law* 110.

[147]  *Supra* 4.3.3, 5.5, 6.3.3, 8.4.3. Millner 1958 *Journal of Forensic Medicine* 103.

[148]  *Supra* 5.5.2, 5.5.3, 5.5.4.

[149]  *Supra* 5.5.2.

[150]  *Supra* 5.5.3.

[151]  *Supra* 5.5.3.

[152]  *Supra* 6.3.3.

which induce special relationships in need of special protection. In Australian law,[153] the existence of the non-delegable duty in the hospital setting relies on the consideration of

(i)     the relationships amongst the hospital, the doctor and the patient and

(ii)    the obligations which the hospital had assumed.

In *Burnie Port Authority* v. *General Jones Pty Ltd* [154] the court had identified certain categories of cases which would give rise to the non-delegable duty to ensure that reasonable care is taken. Characteristics of such a situation was found to exist in a special relationship which generates a special responsibility for vulnerable people. The categories of cases related to:

-       owners (adjoining) of land in relation to work threatening walls;
-       master and servant in relation to a safe system of work;
-       hospital and patient;
-       school authority and principal;
-       occupier and invitee.

### 9.3.3.3 USA law

In the **USA**, the non-delegable duty is created by contract, franchise or charter, statute or common law.[155] At common law, duties are deemed to be non-delegable where the responsibility to the community is so important that the employer should not be allowed to transfer it to another.[156] The common law category therefore includes the identification of inherently dangerous activities.[157] The non-delegable duties which arise from common law are also acknowledged by courts to be reflections of significant public policy.[158]

### 9.3.3.4 South African law

In South African law, it is submitted, the non-delegable duty can also be construed to exist in terms of categories, could be founded on various

---

[153] *Ibid.*

[154] (1994) 120 ALR 42, 43, 61–69, 70–97.

[155] *Supra* 8.4.3. Southwick *Hospital Liability* 239. Southwick and Slee *Law of Hospital* 543. McWilliams and Russell 1996 *SCLR* 453–454.

[156] McWilliams and Russell 1996 *SCLR* 454.

[157] *Ibid.*

[158] *Ibid.*

grounds or by means of various *indicia*. The non-delegable duty could therefore exist as an independent legal ground on which employer liability and even hospital liability, is founded in South African law.

### 9.3.3.4.1 Categories

By virtue of a legal comparative perspective the following categories could be considered relevant in establishing the existence of a non-delegable duty:

**Category 1: Non-delegable duties founded on statutes**
In South African law, there are multiple statutory duties which concern health care, health and the treatment of persons or patients.[159] Great care must be taken to stay within the parameters of the powers granted or the limits drawn by these statutes.[160]

Statutory duties or clauses can also establish non-delegable duties in South African law. It will be necessary to investigate the relevant statutory duty/duties with great circumspection, before reaching such a conclusion.[161]

It must first be established whether the relevant statutory duty was indeed a non-delegable duty: In order to determine whether a breach of a statutory duty has taken place, the content and scope of the duty must be ascertained. **The exact nature of the duty is a question of interpretation. The duty can impose either an absolute standard of conduct, i.e. strict compliance**, or a standard requiring reasonable care in the exercise of the duty.[162]

It must be kept in mind that the non-delegable duty induces strict employer liability. Therefore a non-delegable duty will require strict compliance.[163]

Furthermore, when exercising a statutory power in discharging a duty of the defendant the following must be kept in mind: Where, however, a reasonable person in the position of the defendant would, in view of the circumstances of the case and in particular the dangerous nature of the work involved, have taken additional precautions, **the employment of an independent contractor is in itself not sufficient to discharge the duty**.[164]

---

[159] Gordon Turner and Price *Medical Jurisprudence* 167–168. This pertains to relevant acts or statutes of the past and their present substitutes.

[160] *Ibid.*

[161] See Van der Walt *Delict* 37–39, 46–47, 83–84 on statutory duties in the South African law. See also Van der Walt and Midgley *Delict* 37–38, 84–86.

[162] (My accentuation) Van der Walt *Delict* 39.

[163] *Supra* 4.3.3, 4.4, 5.5, 6.3.3, 8.4.3, 9.3.1.1.

[164] (My accentuation) Van der Walt *Delict* 47. Van der Walt and Midgley *Delict* 102.

One of the advantages of the application of the non-delegable duty is that it founds hospital liability for the negligent performance of even the independent contractor.[165] Furthermore the quote is indicative of a non-delegable duty, performance of which is indeed delegated but responsibility thereof, undelegable.[166]

Breach of the (non-delegable) statutory duty is accomplished by proving '(a) the particular statute was intended to give him a civil remedy; (b) he was a person for whose benefit and protection the duty was imposed; (c) the kind of harm and the manner of occurrence fell within the protective range of the duty; (d) the defendant's conduct breached the duty; and (e) the breach was causally connected to the harm.'[167]

### Conclusion on statutory duties
It is submitted that the South African law can reasonably apply the above-mentioned *indicia* to establish a possible non-delegable duty in terms of a statute, which could qualify as an independent ground on which to found hospital liability. If the statutes are formulated to the effect that it could be construed as placing a non-delegable duty on the Minister and/or delegates[168] (or on corporations or private health institutions), hospital liability can ensue in terms of the non-delegable duty.

### Category 2: The non-delegable duty in terms of situations which are inherently or *per se* dangerous
Millner had proposed another *indicium* by which to construe the non-delegable duty in the hospital setting. He stated that the South African law had indeed recognized exceptional cases where the employer is held liable for the independent contractor's negligence which caused harm. Such an exceptional case is, for example, where the employer had employed the contractor to do work which is '*per se* dangerous'.[169] In such a case the employer 'has not merely a duty to take care but a duty to provide that care is taken — per Langton J in the *Pass of Ballater*, 1942 P. 112 at 117. (See *Dukes* v. *Marthinusen*, 1937 A.D. 12).'[170] Millner suggested that the rule

---

[165] *Supra* 4.3.3, 4.4, 5.5, 6.3.3, 8.4.3. Millner 1958 *Journal of Forensic Medicine* 104. Burchell and Schaffer 1977 *Businessman's Law* 110.

[166] Millner 1958 *Journal of Forensic Medicine* 104.

[167] Van der Walt *Delict* 37–39. Neethling *et al. Delict* 72–73, *Deliktereg* 69–71.

[168] As has been the case in the English law *supra* 5.5, **5.5.2**, 5.5.3, 5.5.4. See *ABSA Insurance Brokers (Pty) Ltd* v. *Luttig and Another NNO* 1997 (4) SA 229 (SCA). If an agreement is prohibited by statute the agreement would be a nullity.

[169] Millner 1958 *Journal of Forensic Medicine* 104.

[170] *Ibid.*

which Denning LJ was contending for in *Roe's* case, coincided with this rule. Therefore, Millner argued that the work which the hospital provides through its servants is *'per se* dangerous' in as much 'as the health and life of the patients are at stake and that consequently it cannot, by means of delegation, relieve itself of responsibility for the manner in which its agents carry out that work.'[171] He did, however, suggest that such a novel idea might provoke judicial resistance.[172]

**Category 3: Non-delegable duties in terms of other *indicia***
Van der Walt presents a considerable number of *indicia* and relevant case law from which the non-delegable duty to ensure that reasonable care is taken, could be inferred:

(i)     The doctrine of previous conduct;[173]

(ii)    Control of a potentially dangerous thing;[174]

(iii)   Certain offices or positions;[175]

(iv)    Special relationship.[176]

The 'special relationship' could be said to exist between the hospital and patient, as well as the school and the pupil. The latter relationship could also be protected by the 'office or position' *indicium* of the principal in a school setting or the school authority, towards the pupils. In Australian law a school (authority) had been held responsible in terms of the non-delegable duty for the injury a pupil had sustained at the school.[177]

**Category 4: The non-delegable duty by virtue of the common law**

**Category 5: The non-delegable duty as a result of advertising, reputation or public policy and expectation**

---

[171]  *Ibid.*

[172]  *Ibid.*

[173]  Van der Walt *Delict* 31–32. Van der Walt and Midgley *Delict* 71.

[174]  Van der Walt *Delict* 32–33, 78–79. As discussed under category 2. Van der Walt and Midgley *Delict* 71–72.

[175]  Van der Walt *Delict* 33. This can also entail strict liability as does the non-delegable duty. Van der Walt and Midgley *Delict* 72.

[176]  Van der Walt *Delict* 33. This category is also acknowledged in Australian law as giving rise to the non-delegable duty. See also Van der Walt *Delict* 21–31. See also Neethling *et al. Delict* 57–71, *Deliktereg* 49–66. Van der Walt and Midgley *Delict* 72–73, 55–57.

[177]  *Supra* 6.3.3. In *Dowling* v. *Diocesan College and Others* 1999 (3) SA 847 (C), the school was held vicariously liable for a claim for damages arising out of unlawful assaults by duly appointed prefects. The traditional requirements of vicarious liability were upheld.

### 9.3.4 Hospital Liability in Terms of Breach of Contract

It is submitted, with respect, that the application of 'breach of contract' as an independent and sovereign ground to found hospital liability, should at least be considered.[178] It has only been taken cognizance of — in that capacity — in Canadian law.[179] It is therefore not favoured generally nor applied with ease, due to the inequality of the parties to such a contract.

This suggestion has been forwarded in view of the fact that breach of contract has been addressed in both the cases of *St Augustine's* and *Mtetwa*. In *St Augustine's* the 'breach of contract' approach and the court's subsequent findings, were more indicative of such acknowledgement of breach of contract as an independent legal ground which founds hospital liability, without having once referred to it in that way. However, in *Mtetwa* breach of contract was presented by plaintiff as a separate legal ground or cause of action on which to found hospital liability, but the ground was still based on suggestions of vicarious elements. The court, however, dealt with this problematic 'contract ground' by discussing whether it was a 'contract for services' or a 'contract of services', thus establishing it as a traditional requirement in order to found the employer-employee requirement in terms of vicarious liability. It should be kept in mind that the traditional differentiation between the 'contract for services' and 'contract of services' has long been discarded in English case law.[180] It should therefore not be clung to by South African courts as they have done so with the principles of the *Hillyer* and *Lower Umfolosi* cases.

Breach of contract should therefore either be regarded or acknowledged as an independent legal ground which founds hospital liability, but should no longer be dealt with in terms of the traditional distinction of 'contract for services' and 'contract of services'.

In ***Administrator, Natal* v. *Edouard***[181] (1990), the respondent had instituted an action for damages on behalf of his wife, who had contracted with

---

[178] Millner 1958 *Journal of Forensic Medicine* 96, 103–104, and Burchell and Schaffer 1977 *Businessman's Law* 110, had already acknowledged that hospital liability could ensue as a result of breach of contract.

[179] *Supra* 7.3.4.

[180] *Supra* chapter 5.

[181] 1990 (3) SA 581 (A). See also Van Dokkum 1996 *De Rebus* 252. *Silver* v. *Premier, Gauteng Provincial Government* 1998 (4) SA 569 (W); per Cloete J at 574 J–575 B: The plaintiff's claim was 'founded in contract and, in the alternative, in delict. ... The loss sustained by the plaintiff is said to have been caused by the breach of an implied term of an agreement that the hospital through its staff and employees would exercise due care, skill and diligence in providing nursing care. Precisely the same facts are relied upon as

the provincial hospital to have a tubal ligation (sterilization) performed during the course of a caesarean section for the birth of their third child. The sterilization was, however, not performed and they sued for both patrimonial loss and intangible loss, after the birth of the fourth child.

Hospital liability was established on account of breach of contract in failing to perform the operation they had agreed upon. Liability was allocated to the appellant who was cited in his capacity as head of the Natal Provincial Administration.[182]

### (i) Breach of contract

The court clearly stated that in principle, 'the precise nature of the breach of contract or neglect giving rise to'[183] (the birth of the unwanted child) is immaterial. Thus it was irrelevant whether the breach of contract consisted of 'a complete failure to carry out the agreed procedure, or of an ineffective surgical intervention.'[184]

Having found that the claim was indeed based on a breach of contract, Van Heerden JA stated that:

> ... it was common cause that the respondent suffered damages (i.e. child-raising expenses) as a result of the breach, that such damages were a direct and natural consequence thereof, and that the loss was contemplated by the parties as a likely consequence of failure to perform the agreed sterilization operation, more particularly because, to the knowledge of the Administration, the respondent and Andrae could not afford to support any more children. **The claim therefore satisfies all the requirements of our law for the recovery of damages flowing from breach of contract.**[185]

No policy considerations were forwarded that were successful in negating the validity of the claim.[186]

### (ii) Extension of liability

The court did, however, reward only patrimonial loss suffered in terms of breach of contract. The court held that courts had in 'later years consistently

---

constituting a breach of the implied term of the duty of care owed to the plaintiff.' The latter 'duty of care' (formulation) referred to, could also have founded another alternative/ sovereign legal ground for hospital liability, namely direct liability. *Mukheiber* v. *Raath and Another* 1999 (3) SA 1065 (SCA). This was a case with similar facts to the case of *Administrator, Natal* v. *Edouard* 1990 (3) SA 581 (A) but the former claim was founded in delict.

182  *Adm Natal* 584E.

183  *Adm Natal* 585H–I.

184  *Adm Natal* 588H–I.

185  *Adm Natal* 588D–F. (my accentuation).

186  *Adm Natal* 589–593.

indicated that only patrimonial loss may be recovered in contract and delict.'[187] It was submitted that damages for pain and suffering (which was actionable in delict), should also be recoverable for breach of contract.[188] The court persisted that it only had power to modify or alter the common law, in exceptional cases necessitating compelling reasons to do so.[189] For want of such compelling reasons, Van Heerden JA decided:

(1)     *Ex delicto* such damages may only be claimed if the tortfeasor acted intentionally or negligently. By contrast, fault is not a requirement for a claim for damages based upon a breach of contract. The proposed extension of liability would therefore result in the anomalous situation that damages may be recovered *ex contractu* under circumstances where no action *ex delicto* would lie.[190]

## Comment on Adm. *Natal* v. *Edouard*

### (a) *Extension of liability*

It should be kept in mind that not all cases of delictual liability are fault-based. Vicarious liability is a faultless or strict employer liability and so is liability based on the non-delegable duty. Van der Walt had described such liability as a strict or faultless delictual liability.[191] The fact that there is no fault, in no way affects the delictual nature of the action and in no way precludes parties from claiming and receiving damage awards. The same should apply to the legal ground of breach of contract. The absence of fault should in no way deter a necessary award of damages for non-patrimonial or intangible loss, based upon a breach of contract.

### (b) *Breach of contract*

In this case, hospital liability was definitely established upon breach of contract, which was acknowledged as the independent ground on which the defendant's claim was based.[192] This decision could have far-reaching consequences in that South African courts can now formally implement breach of contract as a ground to found hospital liability. This was, with respect, an exceptionally well-expounded hospital liability case. A definite scientific methodical approach ensured identification of the relevant legal ground and compliance with all its requirements.

---

[187]   *Adm Natal* 596A–B.

[188]   *Adm Natal* 597A.

[189]   *Adm Natal* 596D.

[190]   *Adm Natal* 597E–F.

[191]   *Supra* 9.3.3.1. Van Der Walt 1964 *THRHR* 212 at 213.

[192]   *Adm Natal* 588D.

## 9.3.5 Direct or Corporate Hospital Liability[193]

Direct or corporate or institutional liability is an independent legal ground which founds hospital liability. Direct liability arises form the defendant's (hospital's) own blameworthy conduct,[194] or own negligence[195] which constitutes corporate negligence, by his own delict.[196] This liability is therefore a fault-based liability. It is based on the employer's breach of his own personal duty which establishes his own negligence and independent direct liability.

Vicarious liability, by comparison, is a strict liability. Liability in terms of the non-delegable duty as legal ground which also founds hospital liability, is also strict liability. In terms of these two distinct legal grounds, the **employer** is held legally responsible and ultimately liable for the negligent wrongful behaviour of other person(s), without having performed negligently in any way. In case of vicarious liability, the employer is traditionally held liable for the negligent wrongful acts of the employee, whereas the non-delegable duty founds employer-liability for even independent contractors. Direct liability — which is fault-based liability — can therefore never be founded on breach of the non-delegable duty, which implies strict liability.

Unfortunately, South African hospital liability law has not yet fully expounded the legal ground of direct (or corporate) hospital liability. There is no thorough discussion of this subject in South African law.[197]

---

[193] Compare *supra* 4.3.2, 5.4, 6.3.2, 7.3.3, 8.4.4.

[194] Gordon Turner and Price *Medical Jurisprudence* 125.

[195] *Rhodes Fruit Farms Ltd* v. *Cape Town City Council* 1968 (3) SA 514 (C) at 519 Van Wyk held: 'It is the duty of the employer to take such precautions as a reasonable person would take in the circumstances.' He thus indicated that the employer's liability was founded on his own negligence. *Frank* v. *Van Rooy* 1927 OPD 231 at 236: '... it is negligence on the part of the employer ... it is only reasonable that he should be personally liable.' *Dukes* v. *Marthinusen* 1937 AD 12 at 20 and 29: '... duty of the employer ... and her failure to do so was negligence and she is liable ... for ... that negligence.' Van der Merwe and Olivier *Onregmatige Daad* 522. Strauss *Doctor* 304.

[196] Van der Merwe and Olivier *Onregmatige Daad* 521. Neethling *et al. Delict* 374 footnote 115, *Deliktereg* 364 footnote 110 where he quotes from Van der Merwe and Olivier.

[197] Gordon Turner and Price *Medical Jurisprudence* 125–127: They present a discussion of one hospital duty: the duty to provide qualified and competent medical personnel, and two relevant cases in South African law.

Claassen and Verschoor *Negligence* 104–108 discuss three direct hospital duties with reference to foreign case law, as well as direct corporate liability in the USA with reference to five direct hospital duties.

Van der Merwe and Olivier *Onregmatige Daad* 520–522, 527 discuss direct liability in general. Neethling *et al. Delict* 374 and footnote 115, *Deliktereg* 363–364 and footnote

Direct (hospital) liability should be constructed and formulated in South African law as has been done in other legal systems, e.g. English law, Canadian law and the law in the USA .[198] This legal ground is founded on the concept of duty. Categorization of relevant direct duties is helpful in order to achieve a systematic and helpful arrangement which is not finite yet comprehensive enough to assist in modern legal circumstances. The four categories which were presented in *Thompson* v. *Nason Hospital*,[199] were founded on the evolvement of direct (corporate) liability law over twenty-five years and should at least be considered as an adequate model for South African law.

### 9.3.5.1 Categories

**Category 1: A duty to use reasonable care in the maintenance of safe and adequate facilities and equipment**
Category 1 is also inclusive of the following duties:

(1)    The hospital must exercise reasonable care to maintain safe physical premises, buildings, grounds and environment for patients, medical staff and guests.[200]

---

110 refers to a liability, without identifying it as direct liability, which in actual fact is direct liability. Strauss *Doctor* 304–305 identifies 'Direct hospital liability' with reference to Giesen, but presents no exposition of this matter. He does, however, refer to 'breach of contract' in this brief discussion, which should be regarded as another independent legal ground which founds hospital liability. Van Dokkum 1996 *De Rebus* 252 only mentions the 'corporate defect affecting the institution as a whole.'

[198]    Compare *supra* 4.3.2, 5.4, 6.3.2, 7.3.3, 8.4.4.

[199]    527 Pa 330, 591 A 2d 703 (Pa 1991) at 707. The four categories are discussed *infra* — as formulated in *Thompson supra* 8.4.4.4 and 8.4.4.4.1.

[200]    *Dukes* v. *Marthinusen* 1937 AD 12 at 20 and 29: The defendant ordered the independent contractor to demolish a building next to a highway. A passer-by was injured. It was held that: 'In such circumstances it was the duty of the employer to see that such precautions were taken, and her failure to do so was negligence and she is liable in this case for the consequences of that negligence.'
Crawhill v. Minister of Transport and Another 1963 (3) SA 614 (T) at 617: 'But if work has to be done on premises to which the public have access, and that work can reasonably be expected to cause damage unless proper precautions are taken, the duty of the occupier to see that those precautions are taken and that the premises are safe persists, whether he does the work himself or through his own servants or delegates it to an independent contractor.'
In *Rhodes Fruit Farms Ltd and Others* v. *Cape Town City Council* 1968 (3) SA 514 (C) Van Wyk J found at 519 D: '... I come to the conclusion that it lays down no more than that if work entrusted to an independent contractor is of such a character that, if the contractor does the work and no more, danger will ensue, then liability for damages

(2) The hospital must exercise reasonable care in providing safe, proper and sufficient equipment, stocks, medication and food. The use of defective equipment which causes injury or death, leads to direct hospital liability.[201]

---

remains with the employer on the failure of his contractor to take precautions in addition to doing the work. It is the duty of the employer to take such precautions as a reasonable person would take in the circumstances.'

See also *Langley Fox Building Partnership (Pty) Ltd* v. *De Valence* 1991 (1) SA 1 (A) in which the above-mentioned case law was discussed.

In *Frank* v. *Van Rooy* 1927 OPD 231 a businessman had holes dug into the pavement in front of his business. He did not take the necessary precautions, as a result of which a passer-by fell into a hole and was injured. The judge found that: 'In these and similar cases the underlying idea is that in such circumstances it is negligence on the part of an employer not to take care to see that adequate precautions are adopted by the contractors for the protection of the public, and that for such failure it is only reasonable that he should be personally liable.'

In *Minister of Post and Telegraphs* v. *JCI Co Ltd* 1918 TPD 253 at 258 it was held that the municipality has a 'continuous duty' to supervise contractors who have to repair the streets and failure to do so amounts to liability for their own wrongful act.

Van der Walt *Delict* 31–32. At 32–33 he states: 'The occupier of premises has a duty to take care that persons whose presence might be reasonably foreseeable are not injured by dangerous conditions existing on the premises.' See also his exposition at 33 par 23(d) and at 34 footnote 47. *Burton* v. *The Real Estate Corp* 1903 TH 430. *Skinner* v. *Johannesburg Turf Club* 1907 TS 852. *Cape Town Municipality* v. *Paine* 1923 AD 207. *Cecil* v. *Champions Ltd* 1933 OPD 27. *Sangster* v. *Durban Corp* 1934 NPD 347. *Small* v. *Goldreich Buildings Ltd and Reid and Knuckey (Pty) Ltd* 1943 WLD 101. *Spencer* v. *Barclays Bank* 1947(3) SA 230 T. *King* v. *Arlington Court (Muizenberg) (Pty) Ltd* 1952 (2) SA 23 (C). *Alberts* v. *Engelbrecht* 1961 (2) SA 644 T. Van der Walt and Midgley *Delict* 72: 'The occupier of premises has a legal duty to ensure that persons whose presence might reasonably be foreseeable are not injured by dangerous conditions existing on the premises.' This could also initiate a non-delegable duty.

*Supra* 8.4.4.4.1 (Category 1). Gordon Turner and Price *Medical Jurisprudence* 151–152. Van der Merwe and Olivier *Onregmatige Daad* 521–522. Claassen and Verschoor *Negligence* 105. Neethling *et al. Delict* 46–57, *Delikwereg* 44–55. Burchell and Schaffer 1977 *Businessman's Law* 110(2). Van Dokkum 1996 *Stellenbosch Law Review* 255.

See also *Pretoria City Council* v. *De Jager* 1997 (2) SA 46 (A). *Faiga* v. *Body Corporate of Dumbarton Oaks and Another* 1997 (2) SA 651 (W). *Kritzinger* v. *Steyn en Andere* 1997 (3) SA 686 (C). *Cape Town Municipality* v. *Bakkerud* 1997 (4) SA 356 (C). *Graham* v. *Cape Metropolitan Council* 1999 (3) SA 356 (C).

[201] This is a most common duty to other legal systems. Compare *supra* 4.3.2, 5.4, 6.3.2, 7.3.3, 8.4.4.4.1. Claassen and Verschoor *Negligence* 105 and footnote 96.

Van der Walt *Delict* 31, 32 par 23(b), 33, 34 footnote 46. *Cambridge Municipality* v. *Millard* 1916 CPD 724. *Conrad* v. *Cambridge Municipality* 1921 EDL 4. *Colman* v. *Dunbar* 1933 AD 141, 157. *Silva's Fishing Corp (Pty) Ltd* v. *Maweza* 1957 (2) SA 256 (A); See the judgment of Steyn JA. *Regal* v. *African Superslate (Pty) Ltd* 1963 (1) SA 102 (A); See the judgment of Steyn CJ. *Ministry of Forestry* v. *Quathlamba (Pty) Ltd* 1973( 3) SA 69 (A). At 32 par 23(b) he states: 'Where a person is in control of a potentially

It is submitted that if a hospital has a duty to provide safe premises, the hospital would even more so owe a duty (duties) to patients to provide proper equipment since equipment directly affects patients' lives and their well-being. The provision of defective equipment, and failure to repair it, would also constitute non-compliance with this duty.

(3)    The hospital must exercise reasonable care in providing a safe and proper system regarding the provision and handling of medication, drugs, prescriptions and doctors' orders for necessary medicines and injections.[202]

(4)    The hospital has a duty to provide a proper system to effectively control infection and contagious diseases.[203]

---

dangerous thing, movable or immovable, he is under a duty to take care to prevent the risk materializing. Whether a particular thing is potentially dangerous depends on the circumstances of the case.' It is submitted, with respect, that this would also be applicable to the equipment of hospitals. Van der Walt and Midgley *Delict* 70–73.

See also Van Dokkum 1996 *De Rebus* 253, on the availability of equipment. *S v. Kramer and Another* 1987 (1) SA 887 (W).

[202]    This duty is common to most other legal systems. *Supra* 4.3.2, 5.4, 6.3.2, 7.3.3, 8.4.4.4.1. Gordon Turner and Price *Medical Jurisprudence* 130–134, 133: 'As far as the hospital authorities were concerned the learned judge considered that the **whole system** (my accentuation) in operation in regard to the preparation and use of dangerous drugs was 'utterly defective and dangerous'.' See also 136–139, on the insertion of a needle.

[203]    *Supra* 4.3.2, 5.4, 6.3 .2, 7.3.3, 8.4.4.4.1. Claassen and Verschoor *Negligence* 105. Gordon Turner and Price *Medical Jurisprudence* 134–136.

## Category 2: A duty to select and retain only competent physicians[204]

This category is also inclusive of the following duties:

(1)    The hospital has a duty to employ only qualified and competent medical personnel or medical professionals.

(2)    The hospital has a duty to grant privileges only to qualified and competent medical professionals.[205]

(3)    The hospital has a duty to take reasonable care in ascertaining the qualifications and/or competence of such medical personnel or professionals and should take all reasonable steps and/or precautions in establishing relevant facts or information which come to light, or

---

[204]    *Supra 7.3.3.2. Lower Umfolozi District War Memorial Hospital* v. *Lowe* 1937 NPD 31 as discussed in 9.6.

Gordon Turner and Price *Medical Jurisprudence* 183 footnote 279 suggest: '... if he is culpable in his selection or employment of such a person, he will be *directly* (not vicariously) liable for the harmful consequences of such culpability.

Van der Walt *Delict* 70: 'Lack of skill or knowledge is not *per se* negligence, but it is negligent to engage voluntarily in any potentially dangerous activity unless one has the skill and knowledge usually associated with the proper discharge of the duties connected with such an activity. This principle is expressed in the well-known maxim of Roman law: *imperitia culpae adnumeratur.* A person who engages in a profession, trade, calling or any other activity which demands special knowledge and skill must not only exercise reasonable care but measure up to the standard of competence of a reasonable man professing such knowledge and skill. Skill can be regarded as a special competence which is the result of aptitude developed by special training and experience.' In South African law the medical practitioner is expected to conform to 'the standard of reasonably competent and experienced practitioners of the time.' See Van der Walt *Delict* 71 for an exposition of relevant factors which are taken into account in order to establish the medical practitioner's negligence. Van der Walt and Midgley *Delict* 141.

In *Lymberg* v. *Jefferies* 1925 AD 236, the radiologist Mr Ensor, was unqualified but had a long practical experience. He nevertheless severely burnt the plaintiff. The action was, however, instituted against Dr Jefferies who had sent the plaintiff to Mr Ensor. The court found that he was in charge of the radiology department at Pretoria Hospital. It is submitted that the action should have been instituted against the hospital (1) on the ground of direct liability for having selected an unqualified radiologist, or, (2) on the ground of vicarious liability for the negligence of the hospital's employee.

In *Byrne* v. *East London Hospital Board* 1926 EDL 128, the radiologist was qualified but his experience was non-existent. *Infra* 9.3.2 gives a detailed discussion of this case.

Van der Merwe and Olivier *Onregmatige Daad* 521. Gordon Turner and Price *Medical Jurisprudence* 125–127. Claassen and Verschoor *Negligence* 105–106. Strauss *Doctor* 304 where he quotes from Giesen. Neethling *et al. Delict* 374 footnote 115, *Deliktereg* 364 where they quote from Van der Merwe and Olivier *Onregmatige Daad* 521–522. Burchell and Schaffer 1977 *Businessman's Law* 110.

[205]    Compare 4.3.2, 5.4, 6.3.2, 7.3.3, 8.4.4.4.1 and 9.3.2.

should be known. Proper steps should also be taken when dealing with known facts or facts that should be known.[206]

### Category 3: A duty to oversee all persons who practice medicine within its walls as to patient care

This category is also inclusive of the following duties:

(i)     *The hospital has a duty to exercise reasonable care by overseeing*[207] *(traditionally supervising*[208]*) patient care.*

The hospital has to persist in ascertaining continually whether all personnel are still competent by providing training and courses, and by following up all necessary information which may indicate the contrary. Hospitals are held liable on account of that which they had known or should have known which affects the competency of personnel/staff and ultimately affects the quality of patient care which is rendered.

(1)     The hospital, therefore, is under a duty to ensure that no patient suffers as a result of the performances of beginners, medical students or interns who could be incompetent. The hospital also has a duty to train and teach them.[209] Van der Walt suggests that no allowance can be made for the inexperienced doctor's lack of proficiency and experience, and the doctor cannot rely thereon.[210]

---

[206] *Ibid.*

[207] To oversee medical personnel or professionals is the correct modern or contemporary term. *Supra* 8.4.4.4.1.

[208] The South African case law discussed under category 2, is also relevant here. Van der Merwe and Olivier *Onregmatige Daad* 521. Claassen and Verschoor *Negligence* 106. *Durr* v. *ABSA Bank Ltd and Another* 1997 (3) SA 448 (SCA) per Schutz JA. Although the institution's liability was accepted as being vicarious, the judgement — in terms of the alternative ground mentioned at 464 E–G — could easily had founded direct liability on the basis of its own terminology and exposition.

[209] Gordon Turner and Price *Medical Jurisprudence* 127.Van der Walt *Delict* 71–72.

[210] Van der Walt *Delict* 71–72. *S* v. *Mkwetshana* 1965 ( 2) SA 493 (N). In *African Flying Services (Pty) Ltd* v. *Gildenhuys* 1941 AD 230, the flying instructor had entrusted his aeroplane to a pupil, which aeroplane the pupil crashed. It was found that with regard to the instructor who had voluntarily exposed his proprietary interests to risks, the objective standard of care required in respect of his property, was lowered concerning the pupil. '[T]he standard of care required was that degree of care and skill which could reasonably have been expected of such a pupil.' However, if a third party had suffered damage, the pupil's negligence would have been determined by the standard of care and skill expected of a reasonably proficient and experienced pilot. See also *Phillips* v. *William Whiteley Ltd*

(ii)    *The hospital has a duty to exercise reasonable care in the provision of patient care.*[211]

    (1)    The hospital may under certain circumstances not refuse to admit a patient, and should not move the patient.[212]

    (2)    Prompt and suitable treatment should be provided after a patient is admitted to a hospital.[213]

    (3)    A hospital could be liable for discharging a patient too soon.[214]

    (4)    Patients should be prevented from falling out of bed — especially children and the elderly.[215]

    (5)    The hospital must provide adequate staff.[216]

(iii)   *The hospital should provide proper and safe systems to safeguard all persons — including patients — from patients who have a tendency to commit suicide, or behave abnormally, are violent or do window-leaping, or are criminals.*[217]

(iv)    *The hospital has a duty to exercise reasonable care in the provision of specialized patient care.*[218]

---

[1938] 1 ALL ER 566. *The Insurance Commissioner* v. *Joyce* (1948–1949) 77 CLR 39 46.

[211]  *Supra* 8.4.4.4.1 (Category 3).

[212]  *Ibid.* Claassen and Verschoor *Negligence* 107. Gordon Turner and Price *Medical Jurisprudence* 121–122.

[213]  *Supra* 8.4.4.4.1. Claassen and Verschoor *Negligence* 107. Gordon Turner and Price *Medical Jurisprudence* 122–124.

[214]  *Supra* 8.4.4.4.1. Claassen and Verschoor *Negligence* 107–108.

[215]  *Supra* 4.3.2, 5.4, 6.3.2, 7.3.3, 8.4.4.4.1.

[216]  *Ibid.*

[217]  *Ibid.*

[218]  *Supra* 8.4.4.4.1 (Category 3). *S* v. *Mkwetshana* 1965 (2) SA 493 (N) it was held that if a general practitioner undertook work which necessitates a specialist skill which the practitioner did not have, the practitioner would be considered being negligent. Van der Walt *Delict* 72. Van der Walt and Midgley *Delict* 139–141. Van Dokkum 1996 *De Rebus* 253. A higher standard of care is also required where the medical practitioner holds himself out as having a form of specialist qualifications or expertise. In *Buls and Another* v. *Tsatsarolakis* 1976 (2) SA 891 (T), it was held that the average general practitioner could not be judged by the standard required of a specialist orthopaedic surgeon. The casualty officer was thus not negligent. Gordon Turner and Price *Medical Jurisprudence* 113 on the Specialist, 119–120 on Radiography, 144–150 on Anaesthesia, 162–167 on Emergency.

(1)     The hospital must provide reasonably competent specialists and ensure that they are qualified and competent enough to provide such specialized services or expertise. Hospital privileges may only be granted to such competent and qualified medical professionals and privileges should be restricted or refused when there is evidence which indicates the contrary.[219]

(2)     The hospital has a duty to provide reasonable emergency care when providing such services.[220]

(3)     Hospitals have a duty to employ only qualified, trained and competent non-physician staff such as nurses, X-ray and laboratory technicians and other staff.[221]

(v)     *The hospital has a duty to compile and maintain proper medical records.*[222]

## Category 4: A duty to formulate, adopt and enforce adequate rules and policies to ensure quality care for patients[223]

### 9.3.5.2 Relevant case law

1. 1895:   *Newman* v. *East London Town Council* 1895 12 SC 61

2. 1937:   *Dukes* v. *Marthinusen* 1937 AD 12

3. 1963:   *Crawhall* v. *Minister of Transport and Another* 1963 (3) SA 614 (T)

4. 1991:   *Langley Fox Building Partnership (Pty) Ltd* v. *De Valence* 1991 (1) SA 1 (A)

1.   In ***Newman*** v. ***East London Town Council*** [224] (1895), the Town Council had contracted with an independent contractor to reconstruct a road. The independent contractor was guilty of several acts of negligence. The Town Council had precluded itself from any possible liability as a result of the

---

[219]   *Ibid. Durr* v. *ABSA Bank Ltd and Another* 1997 (3) SA 448 (SCA). *Infra* 9.3.5.1, Category 3 (i).

[220]   *Ibid.* S 27(3) of the Constitution of the Republic of South Africa Act 108 of 1996 provides: 'No one may be refused emergency medical treatment' and s 11 stipulates 'Everyone has the right to life'. *Soobramoney* v. *Minister of Health, KwaZulu-Natal* 1998 (1) SA 765 (CC).

[221]   *Ibid.*

[222]   *Supra* 8.4.4.4.1. (Category 3). This duty also prevails in South African hospitals.

[223]   *Supra* 8.4.4.4.1. (Category 4).

[224]   1895 12 SC 61; at 68: 'Voet in 9.2.3 says a man cannot escape liability by passing a duty incumbent on him to another person.' Cf *Rhodes Fruit Farms Ltd and Others* v. *Cape Town City Council* 1968 (3) SA 514 (C) at 519, and D–F.

contractor's work, by means of an exemption clause in their contract with the contractor. The question arose whether the Town Council was liable for the acts of the independent contractor.

De Villiers CJ found:

> But assuming that the negligent acts of the contractor were not the acts of the defendants, the obvious question arises, Why did they not adopt some precautions against such negligent acts? I can well understand the doctrine that a person who employs an independent contractor upon works which, in the ordinary course, would entail no danger to the public, is not liable for incidental injuries caused by the contractor's negligence. But where, as in the present case, the work is to be performed upon and near a public road, and it may reasonably be anticipated that, without due precautions, the safety of the public using the road will occasionally be endangered by the carelessness of the workmen, **it is surely an act of negligence to order the work without the precautions.**[225]

To this the judge added:

> After authorising the reconstruction of the road without taking any precautions to avert dangers which might reasonably have been foreseen, and which they apparently did foresee, they cannot shelter themselves behind the terms of their contract.[226]

Buchanan J, held:

> ... when a municipality contract for the execution of a work which necessarily involves danger, it is their duty to contract that the work shall be done in such a manner and under such conditions as to protect the public against the dangers necessarily involved; and failure so to contract makes the municipality liable for damage caused by the absence of such precautions, even if the work be entrusted to a contractor under conditions which make him an independent contractor. ... the duties of fencing and lighting remain in the municipality, and they are liable for damages caused by the absence of these.[227]

Upington J, held:

> In my opinion, that was the **direct consequence** of the negligence of the defendants.[228]

The appeal was allowed by all three judges. In terms of the employer's breach of his own duty, which induced his own negligence, the Town Council was held directly liable for the (negligent) performance of the independent contractor in spite of an explicit contractual exemption clause.

---

[225] *Newman* 73. (my accentuation).

[226] *Newman* 73.

[227] *Newman* 79.

[228] *Newman* 82. (my accentuation).

This municipal liability was a fault-based liability and therefore a direct liability.

2. ***Dukes* v. *Marthinusen*** [229] (1937): In this case the court took note of the traditional principle that the employer would only be liable for the acts of the servant, and no more.[230] However, exceptions to the rule were formulated. '... it is **the existence of a duty** on the part of the employer of an independent contractor that determines his liability for injury resulting from the operation which he has authorised the contractor to do. ... the **employer is** made liable on the ordinary doctrine of **negligence**, and, on the supposition of an unperformed duty which results in injury to another, it is immaterial to consider whether the contractor is independent or a mere servant or agent.'[231] In case of direct liability, the status of the delegatee is irrelevant since the employer is held liable for what he himself had done or not done.

Stratford ACJ held that the employer's liability must result 'from the breach of a duty owed by the employer to the person injured as a consequence of such breach.'[232] In other words, it's the employer's own personal duty of which there must be breach.

Next, the honourable judge introduced the test concerning the employer's fault:

> Thus the test in this case narrows down to the question whether the demolition of these buildings abutting on the highway was a dangerous operation in the sense that public safety was imperilled by it unless precautions were taken to obviate that peril. If the answer is in the affirmative, the law casts upon the author of the operation the duty to take those precautions, and the breach of that duty is called *culpa* or negligence.[233]

The judge concluded that in such circumstances it was the duty of the employer to ensure that precautions were taken. The 'employer's' failure to do so was negligence for which consequences she was held liable.[234]

The appeal was dismissed.[235] The employer was held liable in terms of a fault-based direct liability for breach of her own duty which induced her own fault or negligence and resulted in the death of a passer-by.

---

[229] 1937 AD 12.

[230] *Dukes* 17.

[231] *Dukes* 18. (my accentuation).

[232] *Dukes* 20.

[233] *Dukes* 24.

[234] *Dukes* 29.

[235] *Dukes* 29.

The fact that the judge had referred to undelegable duties[236] in no way suggested that the decision was based on the non-delegable duty, since the latter represents strict or faultless liability.

3. In *Crawhall* v. *Minister of Transport and Another* [237] (1963), the plaintiff had fallen over a barricade which the independent contractor had erected whilst working on the floor of an airport. Plaintiff instituted an action for damages for personal injuries she had sustained, against the first defendant, the Minister of Transport who in law was deemed to be 'the lawful occupier of the **Jan Smuts air terminal** building at the material time, and an occupier of premises is under a duty to take reasonable care to see that persons who can be expected to be on those premises are not injured in consequence of the dangerous condition of those premises.'[238] Action was also instituted against the second defendant who had been the independent contractor employed by the first defendant.[239]

A legal duty was found to exist which was owed by the occupier to the public:[240]

> But if work has to be done on premises to which the public have access, and that work can reasonably be expected to cause damage unless proper precautions are taken, the duty of the occupier to see that those precautions are taken and that the premises are safe persists, whether he does the work himself or through his own servants or delegates it to an independent contractor.[241]

There was breach of duty by both the defendants. Both the defendants were held to be negligent.[242] Consequently both the defendants were held liable.[243] This constituted a fault-based liability.

It was submitted, with respect, that direct liability was the implied legal ground on which occupier — (employer) liability was founded.

4. *Langley Fox Building Partnership (Pty) Ltd* v. *De Valence* [244] (1991). A professional lady (a successful audiometrician in private practice) who was

---

[236] *Dukes* 21, 23.

[237] 1963 (3) SA 614 (T).

[238] *Crawhall* 617C–E.

[239] *Crawhall* 615F.

[240] *Crawhall* 617F–H.

[241] *Crawhall* 617G–H.

[242] *Crawhall* 616–617C, 618B–C.

[243] *Crawhall* 618C–D.

[244] 1991 (1) SA 1 (A). Knobel 1991 *THRHR* 661–666. Neethling *et al. Delict* 374 footnote 115, *Deliktereg* 364 footnote 110. Strauss *Doctor* 305. Cf. *Minister of Community*

the respondent in this case, injured herself whilst walking on the sidewalk. She had struck her forehead — on the left — against a wooden beam which was erected over the sidewalk at a building site. A subcontractor had been employed, who had erected the wooden beam on the busy city sidewalk. No warning signs had been placed near the beam, nor was the obstruction cordoned off. The respondent had suffered a serious injury as a result of which she claimed damages for loss of all future earning capacity. She claimed damages from the appellant as employer of the independent contractor.

The *crux* of this case centred on the question whether a legal duty had arisen, for breach of which the employer could be held liable where an independent contractor had performed negligently.

Goldstone AJA first of all highlighted the general rule of our law that an employer is not responsible for the negligent and unlawful performance of the independent contractor employed by him. He did acknowledge exceptions to the rule, which the English law had recognized.[245]

The judge then proceeded to quote from Percy[246] who discussed direct liability. He then quoted from Fleming[247] on the 'non-delegable duty' and finally from Salmond and Heuston[248] who had confused primary (direct) liability with what 'seems to be … talk of 'non-delegable duties'.'

After having found that the duty referred to in *Dukes* v. *Marthinusen*, was a non-delegable duty (as confirmed in *Crawhall* v. *Minister of Transport and Another)* the judge once again concluded that the duty and consequently the rule that was formulated, in effect established some 'kind of vicarious liability unknown in our law of delict.'[249]

It is submitted, with due respect, that some decisions which had been discussed, as well as the conclusions drawn from them, showed no clear distinction between the independent legal grounds which found hospital liability. It is also submitted, that in terms of the perspective presented *supra*, direct liability is not 'non-delegable duties' or founded thereon. Neither is the non-delegable duty some kind of vicarious liability. Direct liability, vicarious liability and hospital liability in terms of the non-delegable duty are all independent and separate legal grounds which found hospital liability.

---

*Development* v. *Koch* 1991 (3) SA 751 (A). *Randaree and Others NNO* v. *WH Dixon and Associates and Another* 1983 (2) SA 1 (A).

[245] *Langley Fox* 8 A–B.

[246] *Langley Fox* 8 B–D.

[247] *Langley Fox* 8 D–F.

[248] *Langley Fox* 8 F–H.

[249] *Langley Fox* 10 I–J.

In order to determine whether a legal duty existed, breach of which would render the employer liable to the respondent, the judgment was expounded as follows:

A.    Goldstone AJA concluded that 'whether or not the duty arises must depend on all the facts.'[250] He stated that 'the existence of a duty upon an employer of an independent contractor to take steps to prevent harm to members of the public will depend in each case upon the facts. It would be relevant to consider the nature of the danger; the context in which the danger may arise; the degree of expertise available to the employer and the independent contractor respectively; and the means available to the employer to avert the danger.'[251] It became apparent that a duty was likely to arise and employer liability to follow, where the work involved performances which were likely to create danger to the public.[252]

B.    The judge proceeded to formulate a test consisting of three questions in order to enquire whether a legal duty indeed existed:

(1)    Would a reasonable man have foreseen the risk of danger in consequence of the work he employed the contractor to perform? If so,

(2)    would a reasonable man have taken steps to guard against the danger? If so,

(3)    were such steps duly taken in the case in question?

Only where the answer to the first two questions is in the affirmative does a legal duty arise, the failure to comply with which can form the basis of liability.[253]

It is submitted, that the determination of wrongfulness — that is whether a legal duty had existed in terms of which the employer should have acted — should not be deliberated on grounds (tests) which could establish negligence or the element of fault but should be established by means of objective factors only.

Knobel suggests that the *boni mores* are applied in establishing wrongfulness in terms of an omission by the determination of the breach of a legal duty; 'Prior conduct' or control of a dangerous thing, knowledge of a dangerous situation and the objective possible execution of steps to prevent

---

[250]   *Langley Fox* 9 H–I.

[251]   *Langley Fox* 13 A–C.

[252]   *Langley Fox* 10 C–D.

[253]   *Langley Fox* 12 H–J.

damage, are also factors which should be considered when determining the existence of such a legal duty.[254] Van Der Walt also lists relevant objective factors: (a) prior positive conduct (b) control of a potentially dangerous thing — movable or immovable (c) persons who occupy certain offices or positions (d) a particular-relationship. These factors could be important 'in the determination of the existence of a duty owed by one party to the other.'[255]

Goldstone AJA resolved the questions with the following findings:

### (1) Question 1

'The appellant as a building contractor should reasonably have foreseen that danger.'[256] '... the appellant should have realised that the work was inherently dangerous.'[257]

This finding could rather entail that the **appellant** was **negligent**.

### (2) Question 2

The judge found that (the) 'duty rested upon the appellant.'[258] The 'appellant, as a substantial building contractor, should not simply have left it to the contractor to take adequate steps to protect such people from that danger.'[259] It had been established that the obstruction was inherently dangerous.[260] The duty was therefore owed to the public in general as well as to the respondent.[261] Therefore the judge found that the employer should have taken steps to guard against the danger, which he did not do.[262]

It is submitted that the duty was the **own personal duty** of the **employer** himself which he owed to the respondent. The employer did not comply with this duty. There was breach of the **employer's duty** by his own failure to take proper precaution.

---

[254] Knobel 1991 *THRHR* 665.

[255] Van Der Walt *Delict* 31–33. See also Van der Walt and Midgley *Delict* 71–73.

[256] *Langley Fox* 13 I–J.

[257] *Langley Fox* 13 I–J.

[258] *Langley Fox* 13 E–F, F–G.

[259] *Langley Fox* 13 C–D.

[260] *Langley Fox* 13 C.

[261] *Langley Fox* 13 E–F.

[262] *Langley Fox* 13 F–G.

### (3) Question 3

The judge found that in view of the fact that the only adequate precaution — i.e. to cordon off the obstruction — had not been taken, '... breach by the appellant of the duty resting upon it is manifest'.[263]

**Breach of the employer's own duty by his own negligent failure** to take proper precautions rendered him **liable**.

The employer was held liable to compensate the respondent for the damages sustained by her.[264] Milne JA and MT Steyn JA concurred in the judgment of Goldstone AJA.[265]

Botha JA, who presented the minority judgment, found that there was no legal duty on the employer to act positively, since the employer had no knowledge and was quite unaware of the existence of the dangerous situation.[266] He consequently found that no *prima facie* case of negligence had been established against the appellant.[267] Eksteen JA concurred.[268]

### Comment on Langley Fox

Firstly, it is submitted that there was indeed a legal duty to be found in this case, and it should have been found on objective grounds only. The existence of a dangerous situation which poses a threat to the public in general and which could be said to be *per se* dangerous, should under certain circumstances give rise to a legal duty to protect other parties from such an imminent danger.

Secondly, this case could pose as a clear example of direct liability.

- Direct liability is a certain example of employer liability for the (act or omission of the) independent contractor, which in this case it was.

- Furthermore, it was explicitly found that there existed a legal duty, which was owed by the employer to the respondent. This duty was owed by the employer himself, which is another feature of direct liability. There was also breach of the employer's own personal

---

[263] *Langley Fox* G–H.

[264] *Langley Fox* H.

[265] *Langley Fox* 16 D–E.

[266] *Langley Fox* 17–18, 20 F. Neethling *et al. Delict* 374 footnote 115, *Deliktereg* 364 footnote 110.

[267] *Langley Fox* 19 I.

[268] *Langley Fox* 20 H.

duty, also indicating direct liability. Breach of the employer's own personal duty induces his own personal fault or negligence for his own negligent omission or performance.

- The employer's own negligence was established thus indicating that this liability was a fault-based employer liability, what direct liability is. The negligence of the employer is inferred from the evidence, the court's tests, the court's findings and the court's enquiry into the respondents' possible contributory negligence. The latter enquiry would not have been lodged if there was no fault or negligence on the part of the employer or even the contractor. In any case it was a fault-based liability.

- The court's frequent referral to the non-delegable duty, in discussions of other case law, should not be seen as indicative of the fact that the decision in *Langley Fox* was founded on the non-delegable duty. Liability founded on the non-delegable duty is always a faultless or strict employer liability, whereas direct liability is a fault-based (employer) liability.

### 9.3.5.3 Conclusion on direct liability

In the above-mentioned cases, direct employer liability was established by virtue of the breach of the employer's own personal (legal) duty to prevent harm to others in an inherently dangerous situation, thus inducing the employer's own negligence or fault by which he caused harm to another for which he was held responsible in a claim of damages.

The legal ground of direct liability, which has been presented as an adequate independent cause of action by means of which to establish employer liability for the independent contractor, should be extended to the hospital setting. Direct hospital liability should also ensue for breach of the hospital's own personal duty which it owes patients or others, breach of which induces direct negligence in causing harm to patients or others, for which an order to pay damages could be awarded against such an institution.

The legal ground of direct liability should be extended as an appropriate cause of action to airlines, shipping companies, schools and even municipalities. This is an ideal legal ground on which to base an action which could be used against institutions, companies and even public or authoritative bodies or groups.

### 9.3.5.4 Requirements for direct liability

(i)     A (legal) duty must exist.

(ii)     The duty must be owed by the employer to another party.

(iii)    The duty must be the employer's own personal duty.

(iv)     There must be a breach of the employer's duty.

(v)      Breach of the employer's duty must result in the employer's own personal fault/blame or negligence. Direct liability is an (employer ...) fault-based liability.

(vi)     The breach of the duty and consequent negligence must cause or result in harm or damage or injury or death. Damages may include patrimonial and non-patrimonial loss.

(vii)    Independent contractors, employees or unidentifiable persons can be involved in the incident in terms of which the employer is held directly liable.

### 9.3.5.5  Exclusion of liability

Some private hospitals have attempted to exempt themselves from liability by having patients sign admission forms to the effect that the 'hospital will not be liable for any injury, loss or damage of whatever nature suffered by the patient arising out of any treatment or attention received or defect in the premises or instruments of the hospital, whether it is due to the negligence of the hospital or its staff or servants or not.'[269] Exemption clauses have been interpreted restrictively by South African courts.[270]

The latest trend in the South African environment is that other corporations such as health clubs or fitness corporations have also employed such terms or contracts for admission. Certain states in the USA have, however, found such exculpatory agreements or exemptions to be invalid.[271] Burchell and Schaffer did indicate — some twenty years ago — that the South African courts will not be at liberty to declare these clauses invalid.[272]

It is, however, unacceptable that big institutions, corporations or other groups with unrestricted financial resources and adequate insurance, can refrain from fulfilling their responsibilities by exempting themselves from liability in the easiest possible way. In terms of direct, institutional or

---

[269] Burchell and Schaffer 1977 *Businessman's Law* 109. Van Dokkum 1996 *Stell LR* 250–251.

[270] *Ibid*. See *Durban's Water Wonderland (Pty) Ltd* v. *Botha and Another* 1999 (1) SA 982 (SCA).

[271] Burchell and Schaffer 1997 *Businessman's Law* 109. Van Dokkum 1996 *Stell LR* 250–251.

[272] *Ibid*. Strauss *Doctor* 109. See also Claassen and Verschoor *Negligence* 102–103.

corporate liability which is established by breach of a comprehensive range of direct duties or responsibilities, liability could be enforced. It should be considered whether extensive exemption clauses are effectively *contra bonos mores*, against public policy and/or public interest and should be declared invalid by the courts. As has been suggested, the South African legislator could intervene,[273] as could the hospitals themselves.[274]

In *Newman* v. *East London Town Council* [275] (1895), the East London Town Council had been held liable, in spite of an exemption clause in a contract with an independent contractor. The clause provided that:

> ... the contractor is responsible for all damage to persons or property arising out of the contract; and in the event of accident to persons, cattle, horses, sheep, or stock of any sort, from insufficient protection, the protector shall indemnify the Council from all claims on account thereof.[276]

The court held the Council liable for injuries sustained and found that the Council **'cannot shelter themselves behind the terms of their contract.'**[277] It is a pity that the South African law had not progressed much in a century's time.

## 9.4 SOUTH AFRICAN CASE LAW

### Hospital liability

1. 1915: *Hartl* v. *Pretoria Hospital Committee* 1915 TPD 336
2. 1926: *Byrne* v. *East London Hospital Board* 1926 EDL 128
3. 1937: *Lower Umfolosi District War Memorial Hospital* v. *Lowe* 1937 NPD 31
4. 1957: *Esterhuizen* v. *Administrator Transvaal* 1957 (3) SA 710 (T)
5. 1963: *Dube* v. *Administrator Transvaal* 1963 (4) SA 260 (T)
6. 1975: *St Augustine Hospital (Pty) Ltd* v. *Le Breton* 1975 (2) SA 530 (D)
7. 1981: *Magware* v. *Minister of Health* 1981 (4) SA 472 (Z)
8. 1989: *Mtetwa* v. *Minister of Health* 1989 (3) SA 600 (D)

---

[273] Strauss *Doctor* 305. Claassen and Verschoor *Negligence* 103.

[274] See also Van Dokkum 1996 *Stell LR* 255.

[275] 1895 12 SC 61.

[276] *Newman* 72.

[277] *Newman* 73. (My accentuation). See also Upington J at 81.

**The *Hillyer* distraction**

South African courts also fell prey to the decision of *Hillyer* v. *Governors of St Bartholomew's Hospital*.[278] This decision established the doctrine of charitable immunity. It also founded the principle that hospitals would not be liable (vicariously) for the negligent performance by medical professionals or staff of professional duties, but only for the negligent performance or execution of administrative tasks by such staff. The medical professionals were not deemed to be employees of the hospital since they exercised an independent discretion over which the hospital was perceived to lack control. The implementation of these principles had far-reaching consequences for the South African hospital liability law.

It is clear from an international legal comparative perspective, that the legal systems of the United Kingdom, Australia, Canada and the USA, rid their hospital liability law from these untenable principles, at a very early stage. Therefore, it seems strange that South African law persisted so long to enforce such out-dated principles as enunciated in *Hillyer*.[279]

1.  In ***Hartl* v. *Pretoria Hospital Committee***[280] (1915) counsel for the plaintiff had relied, amongst others, on the *Hillyer* case.[281]
    Wessels J held that:

    -   the Pretoria hospital was a *quasi* public charitable institution.[282]

    -   neither the medical officers who were also members of the Medical Board, nor the resident medical officers, were considered servants or agents of the Hospital Committee.[283]

    -   Since the doctors were giving their services free and exercised an independent discretion, the Hospital Committee had no control over them, and precluded them from being employees.[284]

    -   The Hospital Committee was therefore not responsible for their professional acts.[285]

---

[278]  [1909] 2 KB 820 CA.

[279]  *Hillyer supra.*

[280]  1915 TPD 336. Claassen and Verschoor *Negligence* 98 footnote 33. Van der Merwe and Olivier *Onregmatige Daad* 512. Strauss *Doctor* 301.

[281]  *Hartl* 337.

[282]  *Hartl* 340.

[283]  *Hartl* 340.

[284]  *Hartl* 340–341.

[285]  *Hartl* 341.

It was held that:

> ... a doctor who is actually engaged in an operation is not, in the case of a *quasi*-public charitable institution, a servant of the Committee of that institution, but is an independent professional person, who is entitled to use his own discretion and who is quite outside the control of the hospital body.[286]

The court thus found that since the medical officers were exercising an independent discretion whilst performing professional tasks, the Hospital Committee had no control over them and therefore they were not employees of the Hospital Committee for which the Hospital Committee could be liable.

## 2. In *Byrne v. East London Hospital Board* [287] (1926):

In this case, the radiologist was qualified but lacked experience. The radiologist, Dr Hollis, had burnt both the doctor who operated (plaintiff), as well as the patient whom he had operated on and a nurse.[288] The operation was performed on the patient's hand, whilst the radiologist screened it under an X-ray plant which was operated by himself.[289]

At the time of his appointment (as radiologist) Dr Hollis discontinued an X-ray course after attending only two lectures on X-ray work. He had indicated on his application form that he was attending such a course but did not reveal discontinuance of the course to the defendants.[290] Dr Hollis did — in giving evidence — profess to be ignorant and inexperienced when employed and at the date of the operation.[291] He had only been assisted by the previous radiologist for two months.[292]

The question was whether the Hospital Board was negligent for employing an unskilled operator and for not making further enquiries into his radiological qualifications before appointing him.[293]

Graham JP relied on the *Hillyer* case and its application in the *Hartl* case. He found that the board was not negligent in the appointment of Dr Hollis. The 'board had every reason to suppose that they had procured in the person

---

[286] *Hartl* 342–343.

[287] 1926 EDL 128. See *supra* 9.3.2 (Category 3). Claassen and Verschoor *Negligence* 98 footnote 33. Strauss *Doctor* 301.

[288] *Byrne* 133.

[289] *Byrne* 131–133.

[290] *Byrne* 140.

[291] *Byrne* 138, 145.

[292] *Byrne* 140–141, 157.

[293] *Byrne* 134–135, 142.

of Dr Hollis the services of a competent and zealous radiologist.'[294] On account of the authorities he had referred to, he did not find the hospital liable.[295] This conclusion was drawn in spite of the fact that he had previously found that '... circumstances surrounding the operation ... tend to show either incompetency or negligence on his part'.[296]

Pittman J found that the board was negligent in failing to make 'adequate investigation into his radiological qualifications before placing him in control of its X-ray plant ...'.[297] Nevertheless, he found that Dr Hollis had sufficient knowledge and skill — at the time of the operation — to satisfy all reasonable requirements.[298] Whilst relying on the cases of *Hillyer* and *Hartl* he found that no proof had been given that Dr Hollis was inexpert at the time of the operation.[299]

**Comment on *Byrne***

The reliance on *Hillyer* and *Hartl* caused the disappointing outcome of this case. It is submitted, with respect, that it was clearly established that Dr Hollis had no proper training and was incompetent — according to his own evidence and other evidence. The hospital should have been found liable directly for non-compliance with the duties under category 2 and/or category 3.[300] The hospital was negligent for breach of:

(i)　　The duty to take reasonable care in selecting and appointing a qualified and competent medical officer who was also a radiologist rendering special services.[301]

(ii)　　The duty to take reasonable care in adequately investigating the radiological qualifications of the medical professional (or applicant) before placing him in control of its X-ray plant.[302]

(iii)　　The duty to take reasonable care in the provision of specialized services by (so-called) specialists, or specialized patient care.[303]

---

[294]　*Byrne* 147.

[295]　*Byrne* 147.

[296]　*Byrne* 146.

[297]　*Byrne* 151.

[298]　*Byrne* 158.

[299]　*Byrne* 158.

[300]　*Supra* 8.4.4.4.1 and 9.3.2: Compare their categories 2 and 3.

[301]　*Supra* 8.4.4.4.1 and 9.3.2: Compare their categories 2 and 3.

[302]　*Ibid. Byrne* 151.

[303]　*Supra* 8.4.4.4.1 and 9.3.2: Compare their categories 2 and 3.

3. *Lower Umfolosi District War Memorial Hospital* v. *Lowe* [304] (1937): *In casu*, the nurse had placed a warm water bottle in the bed of a patient who was recovering from the effects of an anaesthetic, after undergoing a liver operation. As a result his right leg was severely burnt, for which he claimed damages.[305]

On appeal, the decision was once again founded on the principles formulated in *Hillyer* [306] and cases kindred to it. Feetham JP held that the nurse was not an employee (servant) of the hospital since the latter could not control the (negligent) performance(s) of professional duties which was inclusive of the placing of a hot water bottle in the bed of a patient. Therefore the hospital could not be liable for the negligent performance of professional duties or delicts in the execution of professional tasks. The hospital could only be liable for the negligent execution of ministerial or administrative duties, in which case the nurses were considered servants of the hospital.[307]

The only duty that was repeatedly acknowledged being owed to patients by a hospital was: the duty of the hospital to select duly qualified nurses or medical staff, by using due care and skill.[308] This duty has been acknowledged and upheld by most legal systems and is the most common in terms of usage and historically, the first (direct) duty ever to be created in *Hillyer*.[309]

**Comment on Lower Umfolosi**

The hospital should have been held liable on one of the following grounds:

(i)    Vicarious hospital liability could have ensued by compliance to the traditional requirements of vicarious liability and by preclusion of the principles laid down in *Hillyer*, and other similar decisions.

(ii)   Direct hospital liability could have ensued for breach of the duty to properly train or supervise medical staff or for breach of the duty to provide a proper hot water bottle system.

---

[304]   1937 NPD 31. Claassen and Verschoor *Negligence* 98. Gordon Turner and Price *Medical Jurisprudence* 179. Van der Merwe and Olivier *Onregmatige Daad* 512 footnote 94. Van Dokkum 1996 *De Rebus* 255. Strauss *Doctor* 301. Cf. *Nock* v. *Minister of Internal Affairs* 1939 SR 286, 292–297. (*Strangeways-Lesmere* v. *Clayton* [1936] 2 KB 11.)

[305]   *Lower Umfolosi* 33–34.

[306]   *Lower Umfolosi* 35–42.

[307]   *Lower Umfolosi* 38. Hathorn J concurred.

[308]   *Lower Umfolosi* 35–39.

[309]   *Supra* 7.3.3.2.

## 4. *Esterhuizen v. Administrator Transvaal* [310] (1957).

The plaintiff, a child of fourteen years at the time of the incident, had suffered from Kaposi's disease since she was ten years old. She had twice received treatment — it is X-ray treatment by means of the Chaoul Unit — prior to the unfortunate incident at the Johannesburg General Hospital .[311] However, in 1949, Dr Cohen who took charge of the plaintiff decided that she required radical treatment. At this time, she received deep therapy treatment under the Maximar Unit.[312] Dr Cohen knew beforehand that she would suffer severe irradiation of the tissues, that she would suffer permanent harm to the epiphyses and skin and run the risk of possible amputation of the treated limbs.[313]

As a direct result of the X-ray treatment and the dosage applied to her — in an endeavour to 'cure' her of the disease — the plaintiff sustained the loss of both her legs (below the knees), the loss of the right hand (at the wrist), with the certain prospect that the whole of the left hand would also have to be amputated. The irony of the case was that a specialist pathologist, Dr Murray, had examined the amputated legs, and had found no evidence or trace of Kaposi's disease in these sections. The condition of the legs were due only to the radiation treatment and not to the so-called disease.[314]

The plaintiff claimed damages against the defendant in his capacity as Administrator of the Transvaal Province, thus representing the Provincial Administration under whose jurisdiction public hospitals in the Province were vested by the provisions of Ord. 19 of 1946, of which the Johannesburg General Hospital was one.[315] The plaintiff alleged that during October 1949, at the Johannesburg General Hospital, servants of the defendant were acting wrongfully and unlawfully and intentionally in the scope and course of their employment, whereby they (intentionally) assaulted her in that they subjected her to radium treatment which caused her serious injuries. In the alternative she introduced another cause of action whereby she alleged that these servants were unskilled or negligent in the application of the treatment and that defendant was therefore liable for the resultant injuries.[316] The

---

[310]   1957 (3) SA 710 (T). Claassen and Verschoor *Negligence* 99. Van der Merwe and Olivier *Onregmatige Daad* 512. Van Dokkum 1996 *De Rebus* 255. Simons *Malpractice* 267.

[311]   *Esterhuizen* 714–715.

[312]   *Esterhuizen 716–717.*

[313]   *Esterhuizen* 716.

[314]   *Esterhuizen* 717.

[315]   *Esterhuizen* 713.

[316]   *Esterhuizen* 713.

defendant relied on the defence of 'implied consent' to the treatment, concerning the cause of action based on assault and concerning the alternative cause of action, pleaded that his servants were neither unskilled nor negligent.[317]

The court dealt firstly with the main cause of action: Bekker J, proceeded to find that 'accordingly mere consent to undergo X-ray treatment, in the belief that it is harmless or being unaware of the risks it carries, cannot in my view amount to effective consent to undergo the risk or the consequent harm.'[318] It was therefore held that no consent to the treatment nor its catastrophic consequences could be construed.

The court also found that *dolus* had been proved which was necessary to establish assault, by subjecting the plaintiff to the particular treatment without her consent. It was remarked that the motive for the assault might be laudable but that it does not 'negative the fact that the intention to assault or the assault itself might nevertheless be wrongful.'[319]

Bekker J established the following principle:

> ... a therapist, not called upon to act in an emergency involving a matter of life or death, who decides to administer a dosage of such an order and to employ a particular technique for that purpose, which he knows beforehand will cause disfigurement, cosmetic changes and result in severe irradiation of the tissues to an extent that the possibility of necrosis and a risk of amputation of the limbs cannot be excluded, must explain the situation and resultant dangers to the patient — no matter how laudable his motives might be — and should he act without having done so and without having secured the patient's consent, he does so at his own peril.[320]

It was consequently held that the defendant was liable to the plaintiff for damage she had sustained as a result of the unlawful assault committed on her by his servants.[321]

The court then dealt with the alternative cause of action: In order to determine whether the doctor had acted negligently or unskilfully the negligence test as formulated in *Van Wyk* v. *Lewis*[322] per Wessels JA was adopted:

> ... the surgeon (must perform) the operation with such technical skill as the average medical practitioner in South Africa possesses and (must) apply that skill with reasonable care and judgment ...(he) is not expected to bring to bear

---

[317] *Esterhuizen* 713–714.

[318] *Esterhuizen* 719.

[319] *Esterhuizen* 722.

[320] *Esterhuizen* 721.

[321] *Esterhuizen* 721.

[322] 1924 AD 438 at 456.

on a case entrusted to him the highest possible professional skill but is bound to employ reasonable skill and care and is liable for the consequences if he does not.

The specialist test adopted from *R* v. *Van der Merwe* [323] per Roper J, ran as follows:

> ... not what a specialist would or would not do under the circumstances ... because a general practitioner is not expected to have the same degree of knowledge and skill and experience as a specialist has ... . The question is what is the common knowledge in the branch of the profession to which the accused belongs.

Bekker J found that the doctor had acted without ordinary diligence or reasonable care by employing a dosage and technique which resulted in the administration of excessive X-rays ('too high an order') which exceeded the limits of skin or tissue tolerance, causing necrosis and necessitating the amputation of limbs.[324]

The defendant was found liable to the plaintiff on both the main and the alternative cause of action. The amount of £10,000 was awarded in damages.[325]

### Comment on Esterhuizen

It is submitted that the plaintiff's first claim was basically founded on the principles of vicarious liability, constituting a delict by which hospital liability could have ensued without resorting to a superfluous or an unnecessary claim based on assault. The alternative cause of action could have been based on the legal ground of direct (or institutional) hospital liability which accommodates the duty of the hospital to select and retain only competent (skilled and qualified) medical personnel as well as the duty of the hospital to oversee (supervise) all persons who practice medicine within its walls as to patient care. The latter duty or category also includes duties of the hospital which relate to the provision of specialized patient care or specialist treatment(s).

The hospital's direct liability would have been founded on breach of the hospital's own duty (duties) as expounded above, which induces the hospital's own blame or fault by means of improper system of specialist services. The negligence of the medical officer or radiologist, is relevant

---

[323] WLD 20th May 1953 unreported. It should be kept in mind that nowadays, a stricter standard or higher standard of care is required where the medical practitioner professes to be a specialist. *Supra* 9.3.2 Category 3.

[324] *Esterhuizen* 725–726.

[325] *Esterhuizen* 726.

whether he be an employee or an independent contractor. This negligent performance of the radiologist of course has to result in injury or ultimately damages to the plaintiff which was the case *in casu*.

A third legal ground founded on the non-delegable duty could also have been implemented. The hospital is then held liable strictly (without any fault or blame of its own), for the negligence of the radiologist (who might be an employee or an independent contractor) in terms of the latter person's (negligent) delegated performance for which the hospital cannot delegate its responsibility.

Three alternative legal grounds could thus have been considered *in casu*, each of which founds hospital liability:

(i)    Vicarious hospital liability

(ii)   Direct hospital liability

(iii)  Hospital liability in terms of the non-delegable duty.

The *Esterhuizen* decision brought an end (at least in the Transvaal) to the application of the principles enunciated in *Hillyer*. Hospital liability was introduced in South Africa by holding the hospital authority liable. The same transpired in the next case:

5. In **Dube v. Administrator Transvaal** [326] (1963) the plaintiff had sustained a fracture to the left forearm below the elbow, after warding off an assault with a weapon. He attended the casualty section of a public hospital which, in terms of the Public Hospitals Ordinance 14 of 1958 (T), was controlled and managed by the Transvaal Provincial Administration.[327]

Plaster was applied to the arm after X-rays had been taken which revealed an uncomplicated fracture. The patient had returned to the casualty section several times, complaining of pain. The hand and arm had, however, become septic and gangrene set in which necessitated eventual amputation of the limb at about the middle of the left forearm.[328] Volkmann's ischemic contracture had been identified as the condition which had caused the patient's hand and fingers to be contracted, which is usually caused by plaster being applied too tightly and which ultimately caused the amputation.[329]

---

[326]  1963 (4) SA 260 (T).

[327]  *Dube* 261.

[328]  *Dube* 262.

[329]  *Dube* 262–263.

The court, per Trollip J found on the evidence, that the probable cause of the Volkmann was that the plaster had been applied too tightly,[330] but that arterial thrombosis or damage could not be ruled out as additional causes.[331]

In expounding the hospital's negligence, the court constructed the following duties: The hospital's acceptance of the plaintiff as a patient (paying or non-paying) caused its staff to owe him a 'duty to attend to and treat him with due and proper care and skill.'[332] The duty on the part of the people who plastered his arm and attended to him, 'was to exercise that degree of skill and care which the reasonable plasterman and general medical practitioner respectively would ordinarily have exercised in South Africa under similar circumstances (*Van Wyk* v. *Lewis* 1924 AD 438 at pp. 444, 456; *Esterhuizen* v. *Administrator of Transvaal* 1957 (3) SA 710 (T) at p. 723 C to E, 726 A to C).'[333] Breach of this duty would constitute negligence.

The servants of the hospital were found to be negligent in one or more of the following respects:

(1)    applying the plaster initially too tightly;

(2)    failing to diagnose the possible onset of a Volkmann on the 28th June and to take other measures to arrest the development of the Volkmann;

(3)    failing to give the plaintiff on the 28th June a clear and unambiguous instruction and warning to return immediately if the pain persisted and/or swelling developed in the hand and fingers.[334]

The hospital was found liable for the negligence of those servants who had treated and attended to the plaintiff.[335] It was also held that the plaintiff himself was not guilty of any contributory negligence.[336]

### Comment on Dube

This was a rather simple case of vicarious hospital liability in which all the traditional elements were not needlessly scrutinized, yet present.

However, in the light of the fact that the duties which were expounded carefully, could also qualify as direct duties of the hospital itself or could

---

[330]  *Dube* 265.

[331]  *Dube* 266.

[332]  *Dube* 266.

[333]  *Dube* 266–267.

[334]  *Dube* 267.

[335]  *Dube* 270.

[336]  *Dube* 270.

also be related to the organizational system(s) of the hospital, breach of such duties could also found direct hospital liability.

It must be pointed out that in *Darling* v. *Charleston Community Memorial Hospital* [337] precisely the same type of situation or facts had emerged. Except, this hospital had been a charitable corporation and the medical practitioner involved had been an independent contractor, but the nurses and other medical staff were considered to be servants of the hospital. The duties formulated in *Darling*[338] were almost identical or most similar to those duties formulated in *Dube*. Yet, in *Darling*, direct or corporate hospital liability was introduced which is founded on the breach of (a) direct duty/duties which induces direct or corporate negligence.

It is submitted that the fact that a hospital is a public hospital, should not deter a court from finding a public hospital **directly** liable. Direct or institutional or corporate liability works on the same principle of ascribing liability, breach of duty/duties and negligence to a body or institution or representative. What matters is the hospital's own fault or blame when considering this legal ground. If a health authority can be held liable in terms of the **hospital's servants'** negligence (or fault),[339] then it must surely follow that such a health authority can be held liable in terms of the **hospital's own** negligence or fault, on account of the hospital's direct liability. This direct liability of the public hospital will not be corporate, but direct. The health authority's responsibility will likewise exist, not in terms of vicarious hospital liability or corporate hospital liability but in terms of direct hospital liability. Whether the public hospital is vicariously or directly liable, the hospital is still liable, for which liability the hospital authority or other representative has to take full responsibility.

6. *St Augustine's Hospital (Pty) Ltd* v. *Le Breton* [340] (1975). A ninety-two year old lady suffering from a fractured arm fell out of bed at night. The sides of the cot had not been erected by nursing staff, in spite of an explicit written notice that it should be done at night. As a result of the fall, she sustained a fractured leg, which necessitated a longer stay in hospital. The hospital had insisted on full payment for the full period, whilst the plaintiff's son counter-claimed for damages resulting from the hospital staff's negligence.[341]

---

[337] 33 Ill 2d 326, 211 NE 2d 253.*Supra* 8.4.4.8.

[338] 33 Ill 2d 326, 211 NE 2d at 258. *Supra*.

[339] On account of vicarious hospital liability.

[340] 1975 (2) SA 530 (D).

[341] *St Augustine's* 531–533.

Fannin J, held that he was bound by the 1937 Natal case of *Lower Umfolosi District War Memorial Hospital* v. *Lowe*[342] by virtue of the precedent system.[343] The system precluded a single judge from overruling an earlier Full Bench decision delivered by two judges. The honourable judge most emphatically added that 'had I been free to do so, I would have been disposed to accept as more in accordance with our law the later English decisions, and to have applied the law as there applied and as applied in *Esterhuizen* ... and *Dube* ...'.[344]

The hospital could therefore not be found liable for the negligent performance of professional duties by the staff. The legal position in Natal therefore differed from the legal position in Transvaal.[345]

It should be added that the judge scrutinized the contract between the defendant and the plaintiff in order to establish the extent of the defendant's liability. It was, however, found that the contract could not be construed as casting upon the defendant any liability or burden considering the additional charges and disbursements in respect of hospitalization of the old lady's fractured leg.[346] It is submitted that the judge had gone to such great length in discerning the contractual clauses, in order to establish possible hospital liability, that it would, with respect, consume little effort in acknowledging **breach of contract** as an independent legal ground which founds hospital liability, in South African hospital liability law.[347]

This sad story did, however, have a happy ending. The appeal which had been noted was not proceeded with, in the light of the fact that this matter was settled.[348] Justice prevailed.

## 7. *Magware* v. *Minister of Health* [349] (1981)

In this Zimbabwean case, the hospital's liability was established without once identifying the type of liability. Liability was founded on a 'special relationship between defendant's employees, the casualty medical staff and the plaintiff, different from the relationship between the plaintiff and a

---

[342]  1937 NPD 31.

[343]  *St Augustine's* 537.

[344]  *St Augustine's* 538.

[345]  Claassen and Verschoor *Negligence* 99.

[346]  *St Augustine's* 531–532, 537–538.

[347]  This has been proposed in Canadian hospital liability law. *Mtetwa* v. *Minister of Health* 1989 (3) SA 600 (D).

[348]  *St Augustine's* 530, * the only footnote.

[349]  1981 (4) SA 472 (Z).

disinterested stranger',[350] and negligence was found to exist by breach of a legal duty. The court constructed a 'legal duty to act reasonably'[351] in the provision of care and treatment to the patient.

Of importance was the court's search for a basic test, to determine whether a legal duty existed in the particular circumstances of a case. The court found that 'all the facts of the case and the conceptions prevailing in the particular community at a given time'[352] were to be considered. The court referred to *Goldman* v. *Hargrave* (1967) 1 AC 645 where the existence of a legal duty was decided by factors such as '... knowledge of the hazard, ability to foresee the consequences of not checking or removing it, and the ability to abate it; ...'.[353]

These guidelines might be of use in constructing future hospital case law in South Africa, when the existence of a legal duty has to be determined.

## 8. *Mtetwa* v. *Minister of Health* [354] (1989)

The plaintiff had been treated negligently for tuberculosis at a public hospital. Public hospitals in the Province of Natal, at that time, were vested under the jurisdiction of the Minister of Health.[355] Plaintiff claimed damages and sought to hold the defendant liable on three separate alternative grounds or causes of action:

(i)    breach of contract with resultant liability

(ii)   vicarious liability for the alleged negligence of its employees

(iii)  vicarious liability for an alleged assault by the employees, for subjecting the plaintiff to harmful treatment.[356]

The defendant noted an exception against the claim which was based on the *Lower Umfolosi* [357] case.[358] In order to prevent the predicament which befell Fannin J in the *St Augustine's* [359] case, which compelled him to follow the view he did not prefer, the plaintiff — as respondent to the exception —

---

[350]  *Magware* 477.

[351]  *Magware* 477.

[352]  *Magware* 476.

[353]  *Magware* 476.

[354]  1989 (3) SA 600 (D).

[355]  *Mtetwa* 601.

[356]  *Mtetwa* 601.

[357]  *Supra.*

[358]  *Mtetwa* 601–602.

[359]  *Supra.*

initiated an application in terms of s 13(1)(b) of the Supreme Court Act 59 of 1959 to accomplish a hearing of the exception by a Full Court of the Natal Provincial Division.[360] The exception was dismissed since the test in question involved a factual analysis, which could not be dealt with by means of an exception.[361] However, it in no way deferred the court from making important findings and finally rejecting the findings of the *Lower Umfolosi* case.

The court found that the 'degree of supervision and control which is exercised by the person in authority over him is no longer regarded as the sole criterion to determine whether someone is a servant or something else. The deciding factor is the intention of the parties to the contract, which is to be gathered from a variety of facts and factors. Control is merely one of the *indicia* to determine whether or not a person is a servant or an independent worker.'[362]

Most importantly, Nienaber J emphasized that the more recent authorities by South African and English cases had overtaken the out-dated principles purported in *Lower Umfolosi*, by establishing hospital liability for the negligent professional acts of medical professionals.[363]

> Professor JC van der Walt suggests (1976 *THRHR* 399 at 405) that the later English cases have undermined the foundation on which the judgment in the *Lower Umfolosi* case was based. I agree. The *ratio decidendi* of that judgment, in my respectful view, is outmoded and no longer authoritative.[364]

## Comment on Mtetwa

The *Mtetwa* decision had not only established equality concerning the hospital liability law for the provinces of Transvaal and Natal, but has accomplished a uniform legal position for the whole of South Africa.[365]

## 9.5  CONCLUSION

The only independent legal ground to found hospital liability, which South African courts have knowingly expounded and applied, is vicarious liability. This legal ground was historically the first to be introduced and is generally applied mostly. There has, however, only been one other instance of hospital

---

[360]  *Mtetwa* 603–604.

[361]  *Mtetwa* 604–605.

[362]  *Mtetwa* 605.

[363]  *Mtetwa* 606.

[364]  *Mtetwa* 606.

[365]  See also Claassen and Verschoor *Negligence* 101. See also Strauss *Doctor* 302.

liability where the Administrator, Natal was held responsible for a public hospital's liability based on breach of contract.

The South African judicial system has been a solid system founded on solid principles. Concerning the development of hospital liability law, there is, with respect, need for further deliberations and considerations. South African hospital liability law is by legal comparison, still in infant shoes.

In the light of the fact that there has been a dramatic shift in emphasis in South African medical law, by which the South African patient is now protected, the development of South African hospital liability law is not impossible. South African courts have experienced a radical change in approach towards patients. The courts' protectionist attitude towards the 'paternalistic' medical profession has been displaced by an acknowledgement of patient 'autonomy' and the 'patient's fundamental right to self-determination'.[366] It has also been emphasized that the courts, and not the medical profession or group in the community, would determine the standard of reasonable care demanded of the medical profession.[367] Consequently the law will set the standards and make the decisions.[368]

It is submitted that the courts' protection of patients, which is enforced in terms of the medical profession, would ultimately affect hospitals and clinics. The latter will have to take responsibility for negligent performances, organizational failures, systemic defects and the provision of sub-standard health care. This will undoubtedly lead to the expansion of hospital liability in South African law.

---

[366] *Castell* v. *De Greeff* 1994 (4) SA 408 (C) at 420 J, 426 D–E. See also Van Dokkum 1996 *De Rebus* 252 and Dreyer 1995 *THRHR* 532–539.

[367] *Castell* 426 I–J.

[368] *Castell* 426 H–J.

# Chapter 10

# Conclusion

## 10.1 THE RIGHT TO HEALTH CARE

One of the most trying and controversial issues concerning the health care industry, has been assessed as the free market competition ideal versus the principle of equality. Both have valuable accents and both share elements which can either be implemented or need constant review.[1]

One of the most called for 'fundamental human right(s)'[2] has been acclaimed to comprise of the entitlement to unbiased medical care. The 'right to health care' has been acknowledged internationally and has been provided as freely as possible.[3]

The right to health care has captured international participation by various international organizations, such as the World Health Organization (WHO) on international level, and the Council of Europe on European level.[4] States have on national, regional and local levels[5] carried the responsibility of accommodating this right in most cost effective and suitable ways.

At this stage, the right to (access to) health care is incorporated as international treaty law. It is therefore binding on at least the European Union member states.[6]

---

[1]  Annas *et al. American Health Law* 40, states that 'a synthesis of the most effective and humane elements of both perspectives' is commended.

[2]  Annas *et al. American Health Law* 32–40. Christoffel *Health* 169–172.

[3]  It might appear, however, that unconditional entitlement without due or minimal responsibility could create an economic deficit and a national health crisis. In the extreme, an ideology based on responsibility, has always secured prosperity and ensured stability, whereas the sole egalitarian response — by contrast — has led to tremendous poverty and a lack of ambition.

[4]  Den Exter and Hermans *The Right to Health Care* 167 & 168.

[5]  *Op. cit.* 168. See the Diagram.

[6]  *Op. cit.* 3.

The universal challenge, however, remains of creating a balance between the right(s) of patients for health care and the discretionary cost control initiatives concerning health expenditure. The right to health care has not been[7] (and certainly never will be) qualified as an absolute right. Its implementation and consequential economic implications vary internationally, and are followed by all countries with great circumspection. However, what can be commended, is reasonable access to the best possible health care, for all.

## 10.2  THE HOSPITAL

Contemporarily, the health care industry is a billion dollar complex enterprise. The modern hospital has evolved into a comprehensive multi-faceted health-care facility or a sophisticated institutional health-care provider, which mostly offers quality health care and medical services by means of an industry comprising of medical professionals. Today's hospital should be effectively managed and financially sound, since it has become the primary litigation target by virtue of its vast economic resources, which is sustained by a remarkable framework of insurance benefits. Complex issues relating to hospitals and hospital liability law are universal and have extended beyond the hospital scenario and national dimensions. Both national and/or international intervention(s) by means of legal advisory group(s), organizations, the legislature(s) and courts, could procure viable solutions to this comprehensive and difficult matter.

## 10.3  HOSPITAL LIABILITY

### 10.3.1  Differentiation between Legal Grounds

**Some of the most eminent problems encountered in hospital liability case law, are the striking displays of confusion regarding the differentiation between distinct legal grounds and their distinct/separate requirements and the mixed usage of concepts and terminological phrases or**

---

[7]    *Op. cit.* 2. The economic long-term effects of unconditional gratifications to millions of people could be hazardous. Rather the 'right to have access to health care services' could be endorsed. See *Soobramoney* v. *Minister of Health, KwaZulu-Natal* 1998 (1) SA 765 (CC) per Chaskalson P (at 776–777) and Sachs J.

**idioms which are akin to and introduce independent legal grounds to found hospital liability.**

Courts are neither disciplined in their approach nor do they respect the sovereign independence of different legal grounds that found hospital liability. Concepts which relate to sovereign or independent legal forms of hospital liability are not kept apart, but are mixed confusingly, without reason, in order to arrive at the contemplated liability. Once realizing that certain key concepts and terminological phrases are the founding principles of or introduce certain independent legal grounds of hospital liability, the cautious formulation of sound hospital liability principles becomes indispensable. In other words, a **methodical scientific approach**

-    **by recognizing separate legal grounds and their separate requirements,**

-    **correct usage of concepts and terminology, and**

-    **non-confusing formulation of legal grounds,**

**will demystify hospital liability.**


### 10.3.2 Effective Hospital Liability System

In accomplishing an effective and unique national health care liability system and hospital liability system, the legislature should be involved in creating and formulating clearly defined legal or administrative procedures, relevant principles and legal grounds by which to establish hospital liability.[8] The function of the legislature, however, does not relieve the courts of their optimal responsibility and of their duty to create and enforce law within their general boundaries.[9] Both the courts and their professional colleagues from the legal fraternity should make a relentless effort to secure and stabilize hospital liability law.

By securing a clear and well-defined hospital liability system, courts will not be swayed by frivolous arguments, and security of justice will prevail. Hospital liability will be expanded in a responsible way and patients who are

---

[8]    For example: The legislator could provide necessary or useful guidelines which could be either effective in establishing hospital liability law, or could state/expound legal grounds or principles which have already been implemented or established in hospital liability law. Medical malpractice courts could be founded, and medical malpractice procedures could be established to save time, to be more cost effective and to benefit all witnesses concerned. See footnote 14 *infra.*

[9]    The power of courts to make, modify or change the law is in no way, disregarded.

wrongly injured will be compensated in a financially satisfactory manner. The quality of health care will be uplifted and ensured by enforcing valid legal principles or regulations. The level of health care services provided by hospitals and medical professionals will be standardized, but penalized by non-compliance. An effective hospital liability system will ultimately reduce the frequency of medical misadventures.

The regulation of hospital liability can be inclusive of:

- **Legal offices** and legal professionals specializing in medical malpractice cases and events;

- The creation of **independent medical malpractice boards and/or courts** that function independently and deal only with medical malpractice cases;

- The righteous yet **expedient hearings** of cases which would reduce costs and time spent on otherwise tiresome hearings years after the event;

- The creation of a **national medical insurance system** which would benefit all;

- The creation of a **national data bank** where the compulsory compilation of medical malpractice facts occurs. This would be inclusive of facts relating to medical malpractice cases and medical professionals who are involved in such cases;

- The creation of an **Official Monitoring Office(s) (OMO)**, which could be established in or outside hospitals, which is run by lawyers who monitor events in hospitals. This would entail the listing of: complaints, institution of actions against medical professionals and hospitals, wrongful deaths, outcome of medical malpractice actions, rehabilitative procedures and programs, the renewal of staff privileges, disciplinary proceedings and other relevant matters.

- A **statutory cap** on professional liability and hospital liability could be set. This entails that a maximum limit is set on liability. This has already transpired regarding the liability of auditing firms and auditors in Germany and New South Wales, Australia.[10] Statutory limitations on medical malpractice awards have been introduced in several States in the USA, and have been held to be constitutional.[11]

---

[10] Mockler 1996 *Financial Mail* August 9, 40. See also Chapman *Medicine* 56 and Kennedy and Grubb *Medical Law* 544; 528 and 538 for their proposed measures.

[11] See *supra* 8.5.

- **Proportionate liability** should at all times be taken into consideration.[12]

## 10.3.3 Legal Grounds and their Requirements

### *10.3.3.1 The employer-employee requirements in terms of vicarious liability* [13]

Modern hospital liability law acknowledges legal and social developments and also discards the employer-employee identification as a necessary requirement to establish vicarious hospital liability.[14] The legal ground of vicarious hospital liability should never be abolished completely.

---

[12] *Ibid.*

[13] Arguments in terms of this requirement are to be found in 4.3.1.9.1, 7.3.1.3, 8.4.1.3.4 and 9.3.1.2.

[14] *Ibid.* **The law in the Netherlands:** As a matter of interest, the development of the law of hospital liability, has given effect to the elimination of the traditional distinction between employees and independent contractors, in order to establish hospital liability. In terms of the WGBO ('Wet op de Geneeskundige behandelingsovereenkomst') section (artikel) 7: 462 of the 'Burgerlijk Wetboek', the central liability of the hospital (ziekenhuis) was established and came into effect from 1 April 1995.

Artikel 462

1. Indien ter uitvoering van een behandelingsovereenkomst verrichtingen plaatsvinden in een ziekenhuis dat bij die overeenkomst geen partij is, is het ziekenhuis voor een tekortkoming daarbij mede aansprakelijk, als ware het zelf bij de overeenkomst partij.

2. Onder ziekenhuis als bedoeld in lid 1 worden verstaan een voor de toepassing van de Ziekenfondswet of de Algemene Wet Bijzondere Ziektekosten als ziekenhuis, verpleeginrichting of zwakzinnigeninrichting erkende of aangewezen instelling of afdeling daarvan, een academisch ziekenhuis, een abortuskliniek in de zin van de Wet afbreking zwangerschap alsmede een tandheelkundige inrichting in de zin van de Wet tandheelkundige inrichtingen 1986.

This provision entails that the 'ziekenhuis' or hospital will be jointly liable in case of medical malpractice, regarding the performance of any wrongful acts in terms of an agreement for treatment, acts thus performed by employees or independent contractors, as if the hospital itself were a party to such agreement. The distinction between employees and independent contractors, in order to establish hospital liability, is thus eliminated.

'Dank zij deze bepaling wordt het verschil tussen een arts-in- en een arts-out-situatie bij aansprakelijkheid irrelevant. Ook de vroedvrouw of de huisarts, die de bevalling in het ziekenhuis voltooit, schept overigens zo'n aansprakelijkheid voor het ziekenhuis.' Hubben *et al. Arts, patiënt en ziekenhuis* 45.

The hospital is thus held liable, 'centrally' for all wrongful acts performed by professional health care providers. The ratio behind the legislation was twofold: first, the hospital is held responsible for quality health care in the complete provision of all health

Vicarious hospital liability should either

(i) be expanded to include an 'employer' liability for both independent contractors and employees — thus eliminating the problematic distinction (between independent contractors and employees)[15] which is irrelevant to injured patients, and is merely a contractual technicality of consequence to the employer, or

(ii) the traditional employer-employee requirement should be eliminated completely. The question should no longer be whether the perpetrator was an employee, but whether the wrongful act occurred within the scope of the hospital enterprise[16] — thus unifying the employer-employee requirement and the requirement that the wrongful act had to occur within the scope of his employment.

Needless to say, that in the hospital setting, the control test is even in more dire need of dismissal.[17] The dismissal or adaptation of these tests will ultimately lead to an increased hospital liability for independent contractors.

### 10.3.3.2 The non-delegable duty, vicarious liability and direct liability[18]

The non-delegable duty is neither direct nor indirect hospital liability. The non-delegable duty is a sovereign, independent legal ground which is *sui generis* and also founds hospital liability.

(i) The non-delegable duty is characterized by the lack of personal fault or blame of the employer, as is vicarious liability. Direct liability is known for the employer's personal fault.

(ii) The non-delegable duty as legal ground, entails liability for (mostly) the independent contractor's or other delegatee's or even unidentifiable perpetrator's negligence. Vicarious liability is traditionally related to the employee's negligence. Direct liability ensues as a result of the employer's own negligence.

---

care services to the patient and second, the reasonable reward of damages to a patient is thus guaranteed by means of an easier burden of proof for the helpless victim.

Direct and indirect hospital liability is acknowledged in the law of the Netherlands.

Verbogt *Hoofdstukken over gezondheidsrecht* 61–62; Hubben *et al. Arts, patiënt en ziekenhuis* 43–45, 74; Ledemaate *Verantwoordingsplicht en aansprakelijkheid in de gezondheidszorg* 52–54.

[15] *Supra* 7.3.1.3. Chapman *Medicine* 65.

[16] *Supra* 8.4.1.3.4. Cunningham 1975 *WLR* 417–418.

[17] *Supra* 4, 5, 6, 7, 8, 9, 10.

[18] Comparative diagram 4.4 and the discussion under 4.3.3.

(iii)   The non-delegable duty is related to employer responsibility/liability for another's negligence but the breach of the employer's own personal duty. Vicarious liability relates to the employee's breach of duty or negligence which is imputed to the employer. Direct liability relates to the employer's own negligence, and breach of own duty.

(iv)   Non-delegable duty entails employer liability as a result of a stricter duty to ensure reasonable performance. Vicarious liability entails employer liability founded on *respondeat superior*. Direct liability entails employer liability for organizational failure(s) or improper system(s).

(v)   The non-delegable duty centres on the employer's own personal duty of which performance can be delegated, but legal responsibility cannot be delegated . Vicarious liability is marked by the employee's duty, to whom performance is delegated but not the legal responsibility. Direct liability relates to the employer's direct own personal or corporate duty which necessitates personal performance of which breach entails liability for the employer.

(vi)   Non-delegable duty entails a duty to ensure that care is taken. Vicarious liability deals with the duty to take reasonable care. Direct liability implies the duty to provide or exercise (reasonable health-care).

(vii)   Hospital liability in terms of the non-delegable duty, is a faultless employer liability. Vicarious hospital liability is also a strict or faultless employer liability. Direct employer liability is a fault-based liability, which could also be a corporate liability.

## 10.4  LIABILITY OF AIRLINE(S)

Direct or corporate or institutional liability, is usually founded on the corporation's breach of it's own personal direct duty which it owes relevant persona, for example passengers, patients, other guests or the public. The institution or corporation or airline could be at fault for organizational failures or the implementation of improper systems. Improper systems most often initiate direct corporate liability.

Duties, breach of which reveal an improper or inefficient system, found direct or corporate liability. These duties which the airline could be held to owe passengers are vast in number, and relate to passenger and/or air safety. A relevant category could in this instance be distinguished as being the **'duty to provide a system which enhances passenger safety'**. This category would include the airline's or corporation's duty to provide and implement:

-   The use of seatbelts, oxygen masks and life vests;
-   Evacuation and emergency procedures should be provided;
-   The brace position should be demonstrated and made known to passengers;
-   Prohibitions on smoking (areas) should be displayed and/or explicitly made known to passengers;
-   A safe hand luggage system[19] must be provided;
-   Safety brochures should be provided in every seat pocket;
-   Pre-flight briefings are essential.

Such systems are imperative to ensure safe flying and ultimately a safe airline, and are undergirded by safety policies and relevant regulations.

Therefore, an airline is legally responsible to ensure that a comprehensive pre-flight safety briefing is given on the usage of seatbelts, oxygen masks and the donning of life vests as well as the brace position, emergency exits and escape slides and finally the correct stowage of hand luggage. Severe injuries can occur in turbulent conditions, mainly because of seatbelts not fastened or hand luggage that is incorrectly stowed or is overweight.

It is submitted that the airline could — according to international legal standards and principles, and according to acceptable international airline practice, perhaps be held liable. The airline could be held directly liable as corporation in terms of corporate negligence, for breach of such a safety duty or lack of a safe hand luggage system, where injury or death results from such an improper system.

It should be noted that a court would in all probability, when assessing any given situation, take cognizance of international standards and international practice and policies of other international airlines, when establishing appropriate standards to which an airline should comply. It would also be determined whether a specific airline did indeed have viable standards, and did indeed comply with acceptable standards. Non-existence and non-adherence to appropriate safety standards, and non-existence and non-adherence to a proper safety (e.g. use of seatbelts and stowage of hand

---

[19]   The provision of a safe hand-luggage system pertains to

   (1) hand luggage size, weight, number,

   (2) hand luggage X-raying, confiscation, etc.

   (3) hand luggage stowage in the aircraft, etc.

luggage) system, could imply corporate negligence which could in turn establish corporative or airline liability.

It would also be possible to found airline liability on the legal ground of the non-delegable duty. This type of liability could ensue by comparison to the Australian law, English law and the law of the USA, whereas the direct corporate liability is often founded in both English and American law. Vicarious liability, would of course be the most common ground by legal comparison, by which to establish a possible airline liability.

## 10.5 LIABILITY OF SHIPPING COMPANIES

The same principles and legal grounds which have been discussed under 10.4 which relate to airline liability, are also applicable to the liability of shipping companies.

Direct liability which is founded on breach of the shipping company's or the board of directors' own duty to other parties, which induces corporate negligence as a result of which harm, damage or injury ensues, is an ideal legal ground on which to found a shipping company's liability.

In 1987, a Townsend Thoresen passenger and freight ferry capsized as a result of which 187 passengers and crew lost their lives. The subsequent enquiry found:

> ... the Board of Directors did not appreciate their responsibility for the **safe management** of their ships ... and they must accept a heavy responsibility for their lamentable lack of direction.[20]

In terms of this finding and formulation, it could, with respect, be inferred that a direct corporate liability could be at stake as a result of an improper safety management system.

In proper circumstances, the non-delegable duty can also be construed, breach of which induces a faultless company liability which could also be relevant to establish the shipping company's possible liability. Vicarious liability could also ensue as a possible legal ground by which to found an employer liability in the shipping environment.

## 10.6 LIABILITY OF OTHER GROUPS

The liability of municipalities, outdoor leisure companies, health clubs, auditing firms and other groups, can likewise be established.

---

[20] My accentuation. Sharples 1996 *Focus on Commercial Aviation Safety* 12.

Direct or corporate or institutional liability can also ensue for these groups, as a result of an improper system or organizational failure. In 1993, the English Crown Court jailed the managing director of an outdoor leisure company for 'failing to devise, institute, enforce and maintain a **safer system** for the execution of an outdoor leisure activity.'[21] This could imply the company's direct liability.

Liability can also be established in terms of the non-delegable duty or vicarious liability in suitable circumstances. For the auditing firm, liability can also be founded on contract or breach thereof.[22]

## 10.7 CONCLUSION

A hospital liability system is recommended which is governed by relevant legislation, regulations, hospital by-laws or policies and relevant procedural directives. A hospital liability law is also recommended which is legally administered by means of valid principles, doctrines and distinct and independent legal grounds of which the latter display specific and distinct conceptual and other necessary requirements whereby differentiation between such legal grounds becomes possible, in order to obtain justice for all.

By these proposals, all patients — past, present and future — are wished a better future.

---

[21]  My accentuation. Sharples 1996 *Focus on Commercial Aviation Safety* 12.

[22]  Mockler 1996. *Financial Mail* August 9, 40.

# Summary

This thesis presents an international legal comparative perspective on hospital liability law. The legal systems that are expounded on this subject are: the English law, the Australian law, the Canadian law, the law of the USA and the South African law.

The health care systems of various countries are inspected. The hospital is researched in various contexts, and its historical development is researched. The health care system and hospital (setting) of the relevant legal systems are briefly discussed.

It is apparent that every legal system that is discussed has its own unique set of legal principles, legal doctrines and/or legal grounds which are implemented to establish hospital liability. No legal system acknowledges the same legal grounds nor follows the same approach towards hospital liability.

The **English hospital liability** law acknowledges the following legal grounds:

(i) Vicarious or indirect hospital liability;

(ii) Direct hospital liability;

(iii) Hospital liability in terms of the non-delegable duty.

The English law is still setting the pace for most other countries.

The **Canadian law** either acknowledges or implements the following legal grounds:

(i) Vicarious hospital liability;

(ii) Direct hospital liability;

(iii) Breach of contract;

(iv) The doctrine of ostensible agency is only recommended as a legal ground on which to found hospital liability, at this stage, but is not implemented by courts yet;

(v) The non-delegable duty: The existence of this duty had been discussed but has not yet been implemented as an independent legal ground on which to found hospital liability. The Ontario Court of Appeal in Canada has held in *Yepremian*, that a hospital in Canada does not undertake a non-delegable duty to a patient, whether he presents himself at the hospital or not. On the other hand, there is also a tendency in Canadian hospital liability law, to call the direct duties of the hospital — in terms of its direct or corporate liability — non-delegable duties.

The **Australian hospital liability law** has implemented:

(i)     Vicarious hospital liability;

(ii)    The non-delegable duty as an independent legal ground which founds hospital liability. However, the non-delegable duty has by such status as founding hospital liability, been referred to as direct liability. There is, however, no in-depth discussion of any case law founded on direct liability as an independent legal ground based on fault in the Australian law, *id est* in the sense of the employer or institution's direct fault-based liability founded on the breach of its direct duty which induces direct negligence resulting in harm or injury.

Most Australian decisions on hospital liability have been founded on the non-delegable duty. Australian courts have accepted that a hospital may undertake a non-delegable duty (of providing medical care) to its patients. The existence of the non-delegable duty has been accepted in various circumstances, although there is still a difference of opinion as to when the non-delegable duty exactly may arise.

**Hospital liability law in the USA** has by far, presented the most developed and widest variety of legal grounds on which to found hospital liability. They acknowledge and implement:

(i)     Vicarious hospital liability;

(ii)    The doctrines of apparent agency and agency by estoppel;

(iii)   The direct or corporate liability of a hospital;

(iv)    Hospital liability in terms of the non-delegable duty.

It is, however, unfortunate that some authors and some courts confuse the different independent legal grounds. Due to a lack of a scientific and a disciplined approach, concepts and requirements of distinct or specific legal grounds are not respected and kept apart, but confused.

The **South African hospital liability law** only implements two legal grounds:

(i)     Vicarious hospital liability; and

(ii)    Breach of contract.

Development of this area of the law is highly recommended.

# Opsomming

Hierdie tesis behels 'n regsvergelykende ondersoek op internasionale vlak, na hospitaal aanspreeklikheid. Die regstelsels wat indringend bestudeer word aangaande hierdie onderwerp, sluit in: die Engelse reg, die Australiese reg, die Kanadese reg, die reg van die VSA en die Suid-Afrikaanse reg.

Die gesondheidsorgstelsels van verskeie lande word ontleed. Die hospitaal word in verskeie kontekste ontleed en die hospitaal se historiese ontwikkeling is nagevors. Die gesondheidsorgstelsel en die hospitaal in die relevante regstelsels is kortliks bespreek.

Dit is duidelik dat elke regstelsel wat nagevors is, sy eie unieke stel regsbeginsels, leerstukke en/of regsgronde het wat geïmplementeer word om hospitaal regsaanspreeklikheid te vestig. Geen regstelsel erken dieselfde regsgronde of volg dieselfde benadering ten opsigte van hospitaal aanspreeklikheid nie.

Die **Engelse reg** aangaande hospitaal aanspreeklikheid erken die volgende regsgronde:

(i)     Middellike of indirekte hospitaal aanspreeklikheid;

(ii)    Direkte hospitaal aanspreeklikheid;

(iii)   Hospitaal aanspreeklikheid in terme van die nie-delegeerbare plig.

Die Engelse reg stel die pas vir ander lande.

Die **Kanadese reg** erken of implementeer die volgende regsgronde:

(i)     Middellike hospitaal aanspreeklikheid;

(ii)    Direkte hospitaal aanspreeklikheid;

(iii)   Kontrakbreuk;

(iv)    Die leerstuk van 'ostensible agency' word slegs aanbeveel as 'n regsgrond waarop hospitaal aanspreeklikheid gevestig word, in hierdie stadium. Die howe het dit nog nie geïmplementeer nie;

(v)     Die nie-delegeerbare plig: die bestaan van hierdie plig word bespreek, maar is nog nie geïmplementeer as 'n onafhanklike regsgrond waarop hospitaal aanspreeklikheid gevestig word nie. Die Ontario Appèlhof in Kanada het in *Yepremian* bevestig dat 'n hospitaal in Kanada nie 'n nie-delegeerbare plig aan 'n pasiënt onderneem nie; of die pasiënt homself by die hospitaal aanmeld of nie. Aan die ander kant, is daar ook 'n tendens in die Kanadese hospitaal aanspreeklikheidsreg, om die direkte pligte van die hospitaal — in terme van sy direkte of korporatiewe aanspreeklikheid — nie-delegeerbare pligte te noem.

Die **Australiese hospitaal aanspreeklikheidsreg** implementeer:

(i) Middellike hospitaal aanspreeklikheid; en

(ii) Die nie-delegeerbare plig as 'n onafhanklike regsgrond wat hospitaal aanspreeklikheid fundeer. Die nie-delegeerbare plig, is egter na verwys as 'n vorm van direkte aanspreeklikheid. Daar is ook geen indiepte bespreking van enige hofbeslissing wat gefundeer is op direkte aanspreeklikheid as 'n onafhanklike regsgrond — gebaseer op skuld — in dié Australiese reg nie, *id est* in die sin van die werkgewer of instituut se direkte skuld-gebaseerde aanspreeklikhed, wat gefundeer is op die breuk van die direkte plig, wat direkte nalatigheid veroorsaak met gevolglike skade of besering nie.

Die meeste Australiese hofbeslissings aangaande hospitaal aanspreeklikheid is gebaseer op die nie-delegeerbare plig. Australiese howe aanvaar dat 'n hospitaal 'n nie-delegeerbare plig jeens 'n pasiënt kan hê (om mediese sorg te verskaf). Die bestaan van so 'n plig was aanvaar vir verskeie omstandighede, behalwe dat daar meningsverskil bestaan aangaande die feit presies wanneer so 'n plig mag ontstaan.

Die reg aangaande **hospitaal aanspreeklikheid** in die **VSA**, het by verre die mees ontwikkelde en grootste verskeidenheid regsgronde wat hospitaal aanspreeklikheid fundeer. Hulle erken en implementeer:

(i) Middellike hospitaal aanspreeklikheid;

(ii) Die leerstukke van 'agency by estoppel' en 'apparent agency';

(iii) Die direkte of korporatiewe aanspreeklikheid van 'n hospitaal;

(iv) Hospitaal aanspreeklikheid in terme van die nie-delegeerbare plig.

Dit is egter jammer dat sommige skrywers en sommige howe die verskillende regsgronde verwar. As gevolg van 'n gebrek aan 'n wetenskaplike en 'n gedissiplineerde benadering, word konsepte en vereistes van verskillende of spesifieke regsgronde, nie gerespekteer of onderskei nie, maar verwar.

Die **Suid-Afrikaanse hopitaal aanspreeklikheidsreg** implementeer slegs twee regsgronde:

(i) Middellike hospitaal aanspreeklikheid; en

(ii) Kontrakbreuk.

Die ontwikkeling in hierdie area van die reg verdien aandag.

# Bibliography[*]

REFERENCE IN TEXT       REFERENCE IN FULL

BOOKS

Annas *Rights*

**Annas GJ** (An American Civil Liberties Union Handbook) *The Rights of Patients. The Basic ACLV Guide to Patient Rights* ed. Dorsen N 2nd edn. 1989 Southern Illinois University Press

Annas *et al. American Health Law*

**Annas GJ Law SA Rosenblatt RE Wing KR** *American Health Law* 1990 USA Law School Casebook Series

Atiyah *Vicarious*

**Atiyah PS** *Vicarious Liability in the Law of Torts* 1967 London Butterworths

Bates *et al. Hospital Liability*

**Bates PW** *et al.* 'Pleading A Medical Malpractice Claim' in *Hospital Liability and Medical Malpractice* A Seminar LAAMS Publications 1995

Baxter *Administrative Law*

**Baxter L** *Administrative Law* Reprint 1989 SA

Brazier *Law*

**Brazier M** *Medicine, Patients and the Law* 2nd edn. 1992 Penguin Books

---

[*] Where there is reference to two or more editions by the same author(s), references to page numbers in the text will be that of the latest edition except otherwise indicated. All editions referred to, have been consulted.

Brazier and Murphy *Street on Torts*

**Brazier M and Murphy J** *Street on Torts* 10th edn. 1999 London Butterworths

Bridgman and Roemer *Hospital*

**Bridgman RF and Roemer MI** *Hospital Legislation and Hospital Systems* 1973 Geneva World Health Organisation

Brushwood *Law*

**Brushwood DB** *Medical Malpractice Pharmacy Law* 1986 USA Shepards'/ McGraw-Hill

Cahill *et al. Hospital Liability*

**Cahill W** 'Emerging Trends in Hospital Liability' in *Hospital Liability and Medical Malpractice* A Seminar LAAMS Publications 1995

Carlin *Hospital*

**Carlin M** *et al.* 'Medieval English Hospitals' in *The Hospital in History* eds. Granshaw L and Porter R 1989 London Routledge

Carmi *Hospital Law*

**Carmi A** 'Hospital Law — New Trends' in *Hospital Law* eds. Carmi A and Schneider S 1988 Germany Springer-Verlag

Castiglioni *Medicine*

**Castiglioni A** *A History of Medicine* ed. Krumbhaar EB 1975 New York Jason Aronson Inc

Chapman *Medicine*

**Chapman B** 'Controlling the Costs of Medical Malpractice: An Argument for Strict Hospital Liability' in *Medicine and the Law* (International Library of Essays in Law and Legal Theory) ed. Dickens BM 1993 Great Britain Dartmouth

Chapman *Physicians*

**Chapman CB** *Physicians Law and Ethics* 1984 New York and London New York University Press

Christoffel *Health*

**Christoffel T** *Health and the Law* 1982 New York The Free Press

Claassen and Verschoor *Negligence*

**Claassen NJB and Verschoor T** *Medical Negligence in South Africa* 1992 Natal Digma Publications (Pty) Ltd

Clinton *et al. Health Care*

**Clinton M** *Management in The Australian Health Care Industry* eds. Clinton M and Schiewe D 1995 Australia Harper Educational (Australia) Pty Ltd

Cowdrey *Law*

**Cowdrey ML** *Basic Law for the Allied Health Professions* 1984 US (California) Wadsworth Health Sciences Division

Curran *Health*

**Curran WJ Hall MA Kaye DH** 'Perspectives in Health Law' in *Health Care Law, Forensic Science, and Public Policy* 4th edn. 1990 USA Law School Casebook Series

Davis and George *States*

**Davis D and George J** *States of Health: Health and Illness in Australia* 1989 Sydney Harper and Row Publishers

Den Exter and Hermans *The Right to Health Care*

**Den Exter A and Hermans H** *The Right to Health Care in Several European Countries* eds. Den Exter A and Hermans H 1999 The Hague Kluwer Law International

Dewdney *Health Policy*

**Dewdney** *et al.* 'Australia's Health System — A Brief Description' in *Perspectives on Health Policy: Australia, New Zealand, United States* eds. Raffel MW and Raffel NK 1987 Australia John Wiley and Sons

Dix *et al. Australia*

**Dix A Errington M Nicholson K Powe R** *Law for the Medical Profession in Australia* 2nd edn. 1996 Butterworth-Heinemann Australia

Dornette *Hospital Liability*

**Dornette WHL** *et al. Hospital Liability* eds. Bertolet MM and Goldsmith LS 4th edn. 1980 New York

Dugdale and Stanton *Negligence*

**Dugdale AM and Stanton KM** *Professional Negligence* eds. Evans DE and Parkinson JE 2nd edn. 1989 London and Edinburgh Butterworths; 3rd edn. 1998 London and Edinburgh Butterworths

Edelstein *Legacies*

**Edelstein L** 'The Hippocratic Oath; The Professional Ethics of the Greek Physician' in *Legacies in Ethics and Medicine* ed. Burns CR 1977 New York Science History Publications

Esquire *Liability*

**Esquire EH** *Nursing and Legal Liability* 1985 USA National Health Publishing

Field *Health*

**Field MG** 'Chapter 1: Theoretical Problems in Medical Sociology. The Comparative Evolution of Health Systems: Convergence, Diversity and Cross-Cutting Issues' in *Soziologie und Sozialpolitik Band 8 Health and Illness in America and Germany* eds. Lüschen G Cockerham WC Kunz G 1989 München Oldenbourg

Fiesta *Nurses*

**Fiesta J** *The Law and Liability. A Guide for Nurses* 2nd edn. 1988 USA Wiley Medical Publication

Finch *Law*

**Finch JD** *Health Services Law* 1981 London Sweet and Maxwell

Fleming *Torts*                     **Fleming JG** *The Law of Torts* 8th edn.
                                    1992 The Law Book Company
                                    Limited; 9th edn. 1998 NSW LBC
                                    Information Services

Furrow *et al. Health Law*          **Furrow BR Johnson SH Jost TS
                                    Schwartz RL** *Health Law Cases,
                                    Materials and Problems* American
                                    Casebook Series 2nd edn. 1991 USA
                                    West Publishing Company

Furrow *et al. Health* 1995         **Furrow BR Greaney TL Johnson SH
                                    Jost T Schwartz RL** *Health Law*
                                    1995 USA West Publishing
                                    Company

Gardner and McCoppin *Health*       **Gardner H and McCoppin B**
                                    Introduction in *The Politics of
                                    Health: the Australian experience*
                                    ed. Gardner H 1989 Churchill
                                    Livingstone

Giesen *International*               **Giesen D** *International Medical
                                    Malpractice Law: A comparative
                                    Law Study of Civil Liability Arising
                                    from Medical Care* 1988 Germany
                                    Martinus Nijhoff Publishers

Gordon, Turner and Price            **Gordon I Turner R Price TW**
*Medical Jurisprudence*             *Medical Jurisprudence* 3rd edn.
                                    1953 E & S Livingstone Ltd
                                    Edinburgh and London

Hall and Ellman *Health Care*       **Hall MA and Ellman IM** *Health Care
                                    Law and Ethics in a Nutshell* 1990
                                    USA West Publishing Company

Hoffman *et al. Legal Medicine*     **Hoffman AC Zimmerly JG Seifert JB
                                    (and other authors)** Chapter 7 (and
                                    other chapters) 'Torts' in *Legal
                                    Medicine. Legal Dynamics of
                                    Medical Encounters* American
                                    College of Legal Medicine 1988
                                    USA The CV Mosby Company

Granville *Legal Medicine*

**Hoffman AC Zimmerly JG Seifert JB (and other authors)** 'Immunity' in *Legal Medicine. Legal Dynamics of Medical Encounters* American College of Legal Medicine 1988 USA The CV Mosby Company

Fiscina *Legal Medicine*

**Hoffman AC Zimmerly JG Seifert JB (and other authors)** 'Corporate Liability' in *Legal Medicine. Legal Dynamics of Medical Encounters* American College of Legal Medicine 1988 USA The CV Mosby Company

Holdsworth 3 *History*

**Holdsworth Sir W** *A History of English Law* Volume III reprint 1966 London Methuen & Co Ltd Sweet and Maxwell

Hubben *et al. Arts, patiënt en ziekenhuis*

**Hubben JH, Gevers JKM, Kastelein WR, Teeuwissen JG, Joosten MEWH** *Arts, patiënt en ziekenhuis* 2nd edn. 1997 Deventer Gouda Quint

Hunter *Roman Law*

**Hunter WA** *Introduction to Roman Law* Revised by Lawson FH 9th edn. revised 1934 London Sweet and Maxwell Ltd

Jackson and Powell *Negligence*

**Jackson RM and Powell JL** *on Professional Negligence* The Common Law Library No 12 3rd edn. 1992 London Sweet and Maxwell

Jones *Negligence*

**Jones MA** *Medical Negligence* 1991 London Sweet and Maxwell; 1996 London Sweet and Maxwell

Kaser *Roman Private Law*

**Kaser M** *Roman Private Law* translated by Dannenbring R 3rd edn. 1965 SA Butterworth & Co

Kaser and Wubbe *Privaatrecht* | **Kaser M and Wubbe FBJ** *Romeins Privaatrecht* 2nd edn. 1977 NV Uitgeversmaatschappij

Kennedy *Medical Responsibility* | **Kennedy I** *Medical Responsibility in Western Europe. Research Study of the European Science Foundation* eds. Deutsch E and Schreiber HL 1985 Berlin Springer-Verlag

Kennedy and Grubb *Medical Law* | **Kennedy I and Grubb A** *Medical Law: Text with Materials* 2nd edn. 1995 reprinted London Butterworths

Kennedy and Grubb *et al. Principles* | **Kennedy I and Grubb A**. *Principles of Medical Law* eds. Kennedy I and Grubb A 1st edn. 1998 New York Oxford University Press and the 1999 Second Cumulative Supplement

Koeze *Healthcare* | **Koeze JS**. 'Access to Treatment' in *Healthcare Facilities Law Critical Issues for Hospitals, HMOs, and Extended Care Facilities* ed. Dellinger AM 1991 USA Little, Brown and Company

Calton *Healthcare* | **Calton DJ** 'Antitrust Law' in *Healthcare Facilities Law Critical Issues for Hospitals, HMOs, and Extended Care Facilities* ed. Dellinger AM 1991 USA Little, Brown and Company

Jost *Healthcare* | **Jost TS** 'Legal Characteristics of the Extended Care Facility' in *Healthcare Facilities Law Critical Issues for Hospitals, HMOs, and Extended Care Facilities* ed. Dellinger AM 1991 USA Little, Brown and Company

Kelly and Jones *Healthcare*     **Kelly K and Jones S** 'Tort Liability, Immunities, and Defenses' in *Healthcare Facilities Law Critical Issues for Hospitals, HMOs, and Extended Care Facilities* ed. Dellinger AM 1991 USA Little, Brown and Company

Kramer and Kramer *Medical Malpractice*     **Kramer C and Kramer D** *Medical Malpractice* 5th edn. 1983 New York Practising Law Institute

Lawson *Negligence*     **Lawson FH** *Negligence in the Civil Law* 1986 Oxford Claredon Press

Legemaate *Verantwoordingsplicht en aansprakelijkheid in de gezondheidzorg*     **Legemaate J** *Verantwoordingsplicht en aansprakelijkheid in de gezondheidzorg* 2nd edn. 1997 Deventer WEJ Tjeenk Willink

Lewis *Negligence*     **Lewis CJ** *Medical Negligence. A Plaintiff's Guide* 1988 London Frank Cass

Louisell and Williams *Medical Malpractice*     **Louisell DW and Williams H** 'Volume 1. Chapter XV Hospital Liability' in *Medical Malpractice* ed. Nelson LJ III 1990 USA Matthew Bender

MacFarlane *Health Law*     **MacFarlane P** *Health Law Commentary and Materials* 1993 Sydney The Federation Press

Markesinis and Deakin *Tort Law*     **Markesinis BS and Deakin SF** *Tort Law* 4th edn. 1999 London Oxford University Press

Martin *Law*     **Martin CRA** *Law Relating to Medical Practice* 1979 Great Britain Pitman Medical

McCafferty and Meyer *Liability*     **McCafferty MD and Meyer SM** *Hospital Liability in Medical Malpractice Bases of Liability* USA McGraw Hill Book Company

McConnell *Health Care*     **McConnell CR** *Managing the Health Care Professional* 1984 USA Aspen Systems Corporation

Miller *Hospital Law*     **Miller RD** *Problems in Hospital Law* 1986 edn. and 6th edn. 1990 USA Aspen Publishers

Moore and Kramer *Medical Malpractice*     **Moore TA and Kramer D** *Medical Malpractice: Discovery and Trial Basic Practice Skills Series* 6th edn. January 1990 New York Practising Law Institute

Morris and Moritz *Law*     **Morris RC and Moritz AR** *Doctor and Patient and the Law* 5th edn. 1971 Saint Louis CV Mosby Company

Munkman *Liability*     **Munkman J** *Employer's Liability* 11th edn. 1990 London Butterworths

Neethling *et al. Delict*     **Neethling J Potgieter JM Visser PJ** *Law of Delict* 1992 SA Butterworths; *Deliktereg* 3rd edn. 1996 SA Butterworths; *Law of Delict* 3rd edn. 1999 SA Butterworths

Nelson-Jones and Burton *Law*     **Nelson-Jones R Burton F** *Medical Negligence Case Law* 1990 London Fourmat Publishing; 2nd edn. 1995 London Butterworths

Oerlikoff and Vanagunas *Hospitals*     **Oerlikoff JE and Vanagunas AM** *Malpractice Prevention and Liability Control for Hospitals* 2nd edn. 1988 USA American Hospital Publishing Inc

Pegalis and Wachsman *Law* — **Pegalis SE and Wachsman HF** *American Law of Medical Malpractice* Vol. 1 Section 1:1-5:18 1980 New York The Lawyers Co-Operative Publishing Co

Peters *et al. Medical Practice* — **Peters JD Fineberg KS Kroll DA** *The Law of Medical Practice in Michigan* 1981 Michigan Health Administration Press

Picard *Liability* — **Picard EI** *Legal Liability of Doctors and Hospitals in Canada* 2nd edn. 1984 Canada Carswell Legal Publications

Picard *et al. Liability* — **Picard EI and Robertson GB** *Legal Liability of Doctors and Hospitals in Canada* 3rd edn. 1996 Canada Carswell Legal Publications

Pozgar *Health* — **Pozgar GD** *Legal Aspects of Health Care Administration* ed. Pozgar NS 5th edn. 1993 USA Aspen Publishers Inc; 6th edn. 1996 USA Aspen Publishers Inc

Richards and Rathbun *Risk* — **Richards EP III and Rathbun KC** *Medical Risk Management Preventive Legal Strategies for Health Care Providers* 1983 USA Aspen Publication

Roach *et al. Law* — **Roach WH Chernoff SN and Esley CL** *Medical Records and the Law* ed. Coyle J 1985 USA Aspen Systems Co

Roemer *World Perspective* — **Roemer MI** *Health Care Systems in World Perspective* 1976 Ann Arbor Health Administration Press

Roemer and Roemer *Health*

**Roemer MI and Roemer RJ** *Health Care Systems and Comparative Manpower Policies* 1981 USA Marcel Dekker Inc

Rozovsky *Law*

**Rozovsky LE** *Canadian Hospital Law* 2nd edn. Canada Canadian Hospital Association

Ryden and Mackay *Health*

**Ryden J and Mackay D** *Federalism and Health Services in The Politics of Health: The Australian Experience* ed. Gardner H 1989 Churchill Livingstone

Sax *Health*

**Sax S** *Organisation and delivery of health care in The Politics of Health: The Australian Experience* ed. Gardner H 1989 Churchill Livingstone

Scott *Middellike Aanspreeklikheid*

**Scott WE** *Middellike Aanspreeklikheid en die Risiko-Aanspreeklikheidsbeginsel* 1983 Butterworth Durban Pretoria

Scott *Negligence*

**Scott W** *The General Practitioner and the Law of Negligence* 2nd edn. 1995 London Cavendish Publishing Ltd

Scully *Health Care Facilities*

**Scully P.** 'The Legislative/Regulatory Setting for Risk Management' Chapter 2 in *Risk Management* Handbook for Health Care facilities eds. Harpster LM and Veach MS 1990 USA AHA American Hospital Publishing Inc

Sharpe *Canada*

**Sharpe G** *The Law and Medicine in Canada* 2nd edn. 1987 Canada Butterworths

Sharpe and Sawyer *Doctors* — **Sharpe G and Sawyer G** *Doctors and the Law* 1978 Toronto Butterworths

Smith *Hospital* — **Smith JW** *Hospital Liability* 1985 New York Law Journal Seminars-Press

Sneiderman *et al. Canadian* — **Sneiderman B Irvine JC Osborne PH** *Canadian Medical Law. An Introduction for Physicians and Other Health Care Professionals* 1989 Canada Carswell

Southwick *Hospital Liability* — **Southwick AF** 'Hospital Liability: Two Theories Have Been Merged' in *Hospital Liability Law and Practice* eds. Bertolet MM and Goldsmith LS 5th edn. 1987 New York Practising Law Institute

Southwick and Slee *Law of Hospital* — **Southwick AF and Slee DA** *The Law of Hospital and Health Care Administration* 1988 Michigan Health Administration Press

Speller *Hospitals* — **Speller SR** *Speller's Law Relating to Hospitals and Kindred Institutions* ed. Jacob J 6th edn. 1978 London HK Lewis & Co Ltd

Strauss *Doctor* — **Strauss SA** *Doctor Patient and the Law. A Selection of Practical Issues* 2nd revised ed. 1984 3rd revised edn. 1991 Pretoria JL van Schaik

Strauss and Strydom *Reg* — **Strauss SA and Strydom MJ** *Die Suid-Afrikaanse Geneeskundige Reg* 1967 Pretoria JL van Schaik Bpk Pretoria

Taylor *Malpractice* — **Taylor JL** 'Medical Negligence' in *Medical Malpractice* 1980 Bristol John Wright & Sons Ltd

Simons *Malpractice*

**Simons** 'Medical Malpractice in South Africa' in *Medical Malpractice* 1980 Bristol John Wright & Sons Ltd

Brown *Malpractice*

**Brown** 'Medical Malpractice in Canada' in *Medical Malpractice* 1980 Bristol John Wright & Sons Ltd

Trindade and Cane *Torts*

**Trindade F and Cane P** *The Law of Torts in Australia* 2nd edn. 1993 Oxford University Press; 3rd edn. 1999 Oxford University Press

Van der Merwe en Olivier *Onregmatige Daad*

**Van der Merwe NJ and Olivier PJJ** *Die Onregmatige Daad in die Suid-Afrikaanse Reg* 6th edn. 1989 Pretoria JP van der Walt en Seun (Edms) Bpk

Van der Walt *Delict*

**Van der Walt JC** Delict: *Principles and Cases* 1979 Durban Butterworths

Van der Walt and Midgley *Delict*

**Van der Walt JC and Midgley JR** *Delict: Principles and Cases* Vol. 1 & Vol. 2 1997 Durban Butterworths

Verbogt *Hoofdstukken over gezondheidsrecht*

**Verbogt S** *Hoofdstukken over gezond-heidsrecht* 7th edn. 1998 Deventer Gouda Quint

Van Zyl *Justice*

**Van Zyl DH** *Justice and Equity in Greek and Roman Legal Thought* 1991 Pretoria Academica

Wallace *Law*

**Wallace M** *Health Care and the Law. A Guide for Nurses* 2nd edn. 1995 Australia The Law Book Company Ltd

Werthmann *Malpractice*

**Werthmann B** *Medical Malpractice Law: How Medicine is Changing the Law* 1984 USA Lexington Books

Wiechers *Administratiefreg*

**Wiechers M** *Administratiefreg* 2nd edn. 1984 Pretoria Butterworths

JOURNALS

Bettle 1987 *NLJ*

**Bettle J** 'Suing Hospitals Direct: Whose Tort is it Anyhow?' 1987 *New LJ* 137 (pt 1) 573

Brown 1988 *DCJ*

**Brown HM** 'Hospital Liability Law: Cost Containment, Marketing and Consumer Expectation' April 1988 *Defense Counsel Journal* 159

Burchell and Schaffer 1977 *Businessman's Law*

**Burchell JM and Schaffer RP** 'Liability of Hospitals for Negligence' 1 February 1977 *Businessman's Law* 109

Burstein 1975 *LLR*

**Burstein CH** 'Medical Malpractice: A Move Towards Strict Liability' 1975 *Loyola Law Review* Vol 21 194

Carlucci 1986 *Case and Comment*

**Carlucci MA** 'Health Care Systems and Medical Malpractice' 1986 *Case & Comment* Vol 91 No 5 34

Carstens 1988 *De Rebus*

**Carstens PA** 'Prophylaxis Against Medical Negligence: A Practical Approach' May 1988 *De Rebus* 345

Classen 1987 *ALR*

**Classen HW** 'Hospital Liability for Independent Contractors: Where Do We Go From Here?' 1987 *Ark Law Review* Vol 40 469

Cunningham 1975 *WLR*

**Cunningham JD** 'Comment. The Hospital-Physician Relationship: Hospital Responsibility for Malpractice of Physicians' 1975 *Washington Law Review* Vol 50 385

Day 1996 *SLR*

**Day K** 'Medical Negligence — the Duty to Attend Emergencies and the Standard of Care: Lowns & Anor v Woods & Ors' September 1996 *The Sydney Law Review* Vol 18 No 3

Deutsch 1979 *IJML*

**Deutsch E** 'Medical Malpractice, Informed Consent and Human Experimentation in Western Europe' 1979 *International Journal of Medicine and Law* Vol 1 81

Dreyer 1995 *THRHR*

**Dreyer L** 'Redelike Dokter versus Redelike Pasiënt *Castell* v. *De Greeff* 1994 4 SA 408 (K)' 1995 (58) *THRHR* 532

Ferraro and Camarra 1988 *IBJ*

**Ferraro DA and Camarra JA** 'Hospital Liability: Apparent Agency or Agency by Estoppel' March 1988 *Illinois Bar Journal* Vol 76 No 7 364

Frankel 1994 *YLJ*

**Frank JJ** 'Medical Malpractice Law and Health Care Cost Containment: Lessons for Reformers from the Clash of Cultures' March 1994 *The Yale Law Journal* Vol 103 No 5 1297

Gorr 1988 *IBJ*

**Gorr KH** 'Strict Tort Liability/Negligence/Prescription Drugs' December 1988 *Illinois Bar Journal* 227

Hirsh 1988 *Med Law*

**Hirsh HL** 'Medical Law Hospital and Medical Staff Relations in the USA III. The Business of Practicing Medicine' September 1988 *Medicine and Law* Vol 77 No 1 121 (Springer-Verlag)

Janulis and Hornstein 1985
*NLR*

**Janulis DM and Hornstein AD**
'Damned If You Do, Damned If You Don't: Hospitals' Liability for Physicians' Malpractice' 1985 *Nebraska Law Review* Vol 64 No 4 689

Kahn-Freund 1951 *MLR*

**Kahn-Freund O** 'Servants and Independent Contractors' 1951 *Modern Law Review* 504-509

King 1987 *JAMA*

**King LS** 'Medicine 100 Years Ago: II. The Doctor and the Law' April 24 1987 *Journal of the American Medical Association* Vol 257 No 16 2204

Klages 1988 *IBJ*

**Klages GW** 'Medical Malpractice Liability from a Hospital's Perspective' September 1988 *Illinois Bar Journal* Vol 77 No1 34

Knobel 1991 *THRHR*

**Knobel JC** 'Deliktuele aanspreeklikheid vir skade aangerig deur 'n onafhanklike subkontrakteur *Langley Fox Building Partnership (Pty) Ltd* v. *De Valence* 1991 1 SA 1 (A)' 1991 *THRHR* 661

Lee 1979 *AALR*

**Lee RG** 'The Liability of Hospital Authorities for the Negligence of their Staff — A History' 1979 *Anglo-American Law Review* Vol 8 313

Lipshitz 1981 *Responsa Meridiana*

**Lipshitz IM** 'Control' as an Essential Element for Determining Whether a Vicarious Liability Exists or Not' 1981 *Responsa Meridiana* Vol 4 No 3 117

McWilliams and Russell 1996 *SCLR*

**McWilliams MC and Russell HE** 'Hospital Liability for Torts of Independent Contractor Physicians' 1996 *South Carolina Law Review* Vol 47 No 3 432

Millner 1958 *Journal of Forensic Medicine*

**Millner MA** 'Vicarious Liability for Medical Negligence' 1958 *Journal of Forensic Medicine* Vol 5 No 2 April-June 96

Mobilia 1985 *SCLR*

**Mobilia MA** 'Hospital Corporate Liability — Toward a Stricter Standard for Administrative Services' 1985 *South Carolina Law Review* Vol 36 597

Morgan 1995 *JLM*

**Morgan D** 'Emergency Room Follow-up Care and Malpractice Liability' 1995 *The Journal of Legal Medicine* Vol 16 No 3 373

Osode 1993 *AALR*

**Osode PO** 'The Modern Hospital and Responsibility for Negligence — Pointing Canadian Courts in the Right Direction' 1993 *Anglo-American Law Review* Vol 22 No 3 289

Owens 1990 *WLR*

**Owens SR** '*Pamperin* v. *Trinity Memorial Hospital* and the Evolution of Hospital Liability: Wisconsin Adopts Apparent Agency' 1990 *Wisconsin Law Review* 1129

Peters 1988 *TRIAL*

**Peters JD** 'Hospital Malpractice. Eleven Theories of Direct Liability' November 1988 *TRIAL* Vol 24 No 11 82

Picard 1981 *MGLJ*            **Picard E** 'The Liability of Hospitals in
                              Common Law Canada' 1981 (26)
                              *McGill Law Journal* 997

Price 1989 *JLM*             **Price SH** 'The Sinking of the 'Captain
                              of the Ship' Re-examining the
                              Vicarious Liability of an Operating
                              Surgeon for the Negligence of
                              Assisting Hospital Personnel' 1989
                              *The Journal of Legal Medicine* Vol
                              10 No 2 323

Reuter 1994 *JLM*            **Reuter SR** 'Professional Liability in
                              Postgraduate Medical Education:
                              Who is Liable for Resident
                              Negligence?' 1994 *The Journal of
                              Legal Medicine* Vol 15 No 4 485

Rutchik 1994 *VLR*           **Rutchik DH** 'The Emerging Trend of
                              Corporate Liability: Courts' Uneven
                              Treatment of Hospital Standards
                              Leaves Hospitals Uncertain and
                              Exposed' March 1994 *Vanderbilt
                              Law Review* Vol 47 No 2 535
                              Vanderbilt University School of Law

Scott 1979 *CILSA*           **Scott WE** 'The theory of risk liability
                              and its application to vicarious
                              liability' 1979 *Comparative and
                              International Law of South Africa* 44

Sharples 1996 *Focus on      **Sharples C** 'An Airlines view of
Commercial Aviation Safety*   Airline Safety Management (Part 1
                              of 2)' Autumn 1996 *Focus on
                              Commercial Aviation Safety* Issue 24
                              ISSN 1355-1523 12

Spero 1979 *TRIAL*           **Spero KE** 'Hospital Liability' 1979
                              *TRIAL* Vol 15 22

Trail and Claybrook 1985 *BLR*     **Trail WR and Claybrook S** 'Hospital Liability and the Staff Privileges Dilemma' 1985 *Baylor Law Review* Vol 37 No 2 316 Baylor University Law School

Van der Walt 1964 *THRHR*     **Van der Walt JC** 'Verborge Gebreke, Onskuldige Wanvoorstelling en Verrykingsaanspreeklikheid' 1964 *THRHR* 212

Van Dokkum 1996 *Stell LR*     **Van Dokkum N** 'Hospital Consent Forms' 1996 *Stellenbosch Law Review* Vol 7 No 2 249

Van Dokkum 1996 *De Rebus*     **Van Dokkum N** 'Medical Malpractice in South African Law' 1996 *De Rebus* April No 340 252

Whippy 1989 *ALJ*     **Whippy WP** 'A Hospital's Personal and Non-Delegable Duty to Care for its Patients — Novel Doctrine or Vicarious Liability Disguised?' 1989 *The Australian Law Journal* Vol 63 No 3 182

Zaslow 1978 *PBAQ*     **Zaslow J** 'Vicarious Liability of a Hospital for Tortious Acts of Its Independent Contractors Delivering Medical Care' 1978 *Pennsylvania Bar Association Quarterly* Vol 49 466

COMPUTER INFORMATION

Internet:     About Health Canada http://hpb 1. hwc.ca/links/healthcan/ abthc_e.htm 5/8/96 11:44 AM

Berkman (B):     *Hospital* 1993 Grolier Electronic Publishing Inc

Berkman:                          *Types of Hospitals* 1993 Grolier
                                  Electronic Publishing Inc

Silver (G.A.):                    *The US System* 1993 Grolier Electronic
                                  Publishing Inc

Silver:                           *Health Costs and Payments* 1993
                                  Grolier Electronic Publishing Inc

Silver:                           *Health-Care Systems in European
                                  Countries* 1993 Grolier Electronic
                                  Publishing Inc

Silver:                           *Health-Care Systems* 1993 Grolier
                                  Electronic Publishing Inc

HEALTH CARE DOCUMENTS

Affordable Health Care            A White Paper  Ministry of Health
Singapore 1993:                   Singapore 1993

A National Health Plan for        Prepared by the ANC South Africa May
South Africa May 1994:            1994

TPA Report 1988 — Hospital        TPA Report 1988 Hospital Services
Services Branch                   Branch 36–49

MAGAZINES AND NEWSPAPERS

Gardner *Sunday Times*            **Smith L** 'Bringing a holistic approach
Business Times August 18          to SA's health care industry'
1996. Reported by Smith           Northern Medical Society Corporate
                                  Survey *Sunday Times* Business
                                  Times August 18 1996, 8. An
                                  interview with Gardner J, MD of
                                  NMA Medical Fund Managers

Greenblo *Finance Week* 14–20     **Greenblo A** 'Unhealthy Conflict Better
1990                              primary care must become primary
                                  objective' *Finance Week* 14–20
                                  1996 9–13

Health Care Financial Mail November 22 1996

'Health Care Utopian Quest Flounders in Mire of Bad Planning' in Socialist Dream Clogs up Health Service. *Financial Mail* November 22 1996 22–24

Hoffman *Business Day* August 1996

**Hoffman H** 'Medical Schemes face crisis. Health Care provision and funding has become one of the most complex and dynamic issues facing corporate management. The Insurance Industry' *Business Day* August 1996 20

Mockler 1996 *Financial Mail* August 9

**Mockler K** 'The Deep Pocket Syndrome' 1996 *Financial Mail* August 9, 40

National Health *Financial Mail* November 29 1996

National Health 'Private Sector Faces Pain' in Nurturing the Wa-Benzi *Financial Mail* November 29 1996 44

Parker 1997 *Longevity*

**Parker H** 'How will the National Health Plan Affect You? The good, the bad and the sickly' 1997 *Longevity* January 54-58

Provincial Revenue *Financial Mail* August 9 1996

Provincial Revenue 'Formula Aims at Parity in Education and Health Care' *Financial Mail* August 9 1996 28

Seeger *Sunday Times* Business Times April 11 1999, 12

**Seeger D** 'You no longer have to be patient with bad hospitals' *Sunday Times* Business Times April 11 1999, 12

DICTIONARIES

Oxford

*Oxford Advanced Learner's Dictionary*
10th impression 1994 London,
Oxford University Press

*Oxford English Dictionary* Vol VII 2nd
edn. 1989 Oxford, Oxford
University Press

*The Concise Oxford Dictionary* Thumb
Index Edition 8th edn. 1990 Oxford,
Clarendon Press

*The Shorter Oxford English Dictionary
on Historical Principles* 1988 Vol 1
A Markworthy Oxford

Reader's Digest

*Reader's Digest Universal Dictionary*
1988 London, Reader's Digest
Association

ENCYCLOPAEDIA

Mason and McCall-Smith
1987 *Encyclopaedia*

**Mason JK and McCall-Smith RA**
*Butterworths Medico-Legal
Encyclopaedia* 1987 Butterworth
and Co

The Law of South Africa Vol
17

*The Law of South Africa* Vol 17 Durban
Butterworths

Wêreldfokus Vol 14 1978

Wêreldfokus: 'n Geïllustreerde
Ensiklopedie van Suid-Afrika en die
Wêreld Vol 14 1978 Uitg.
Ensiklopedie Africana Johannesburg

# Table of Cases

I ENGLAND

*Powell* v. *Streatham Manor Nursing Home* 1935 AC 243

*R* v. *Central Birmingham Health Authority, ex parte Collier* 6 January 1988 unreported CA

*R* v. *Central Birmingham Health Authority, ex parte Walker* (1987) 3 BMLR 32

*R* v. *North Derbyshire HA, ex parte Fisher* [1997] 8 Med LR 327

*R* v. *Secretary of State for Social Services, ex parte Hincks* 1979 123 SJ 436; (1980) 1 BMLR 93 (CA)

*Razzel* v. *Snowball* (1954) 1 WLR 1382; [1954] 3 ALL ER 439 CA

*Ready Mixed Concrete (South East) Ltd* v. *Minister of Pensions and National Insurance* [1968] 1 ALL ER 433 QB

*Re HIV Litigation* [1996] PNLR 290 (CA)

*Re HIV Haemophiliac Litigation* [1990] 140 NLJR 1349 (CA)

*Riverstone Meat Co Pty Ltd* v. *Lancashire Shipping Co Ltd* [1961] AC 807

*Robertson* v. *Nottingham HA* [1997] 8 Med LR 1

*Roe* v. *Minister of Health* [1954] 2 QB 66; [1954] 2 ALL ER 131

*Romford Ice and Cold Storage* v. *Lister* (1955) 3 WLR 631

*Salsbury* v. *Woodland* [1970] 1 QB 324

*Smith* v. *Cammell Laird & Co Ltd* [1940] AC 242

*Staveley Iron and Chemical Co Ltd* v. *Jones* [1956] AC 627

*Stevenson Jordan and Harrison Ltd* v. *MacDonald and Evans* 1952 1 TLR 101 (CA)

*Strangeways-Lesmere* v. *Clayton* [1936] 2 KB 11

*Tarry* v. *Ashton* (1876) 1 QBD 314

*The Pass of Ballater* [1942] P 112

*Yewens* v. *Noakes* (1880) 6 QBD 530

*Wardell* v. *Kent County Council* [1938] 3 ALL ER 473

*Wilsher* v. *Essex Area Heath Authority* [1987] 1 QB 730; [1986] 3 ALL ER 801 CA

*Woods* v. *Lowns* (1995) 36 NSWLR 344

*Zuijs* v. *Wirth Bros (Pty) Ltd* (1955) 93 CLR 561

## III Canada

*Abel* v. *Cooke* [1938] 1 WWR 49 (Alta CA)

*Aynsley et al. Toronto General Hospital et al.* (1970) 7 DLR (3rd) 193. [1968] 1 OR 425; affd [1969] OR 829 affd [1972] SCR 435

*Barker* v. *Lockhart* [1940] 3 DLR 427 (NBCA)

*Bartlett* v. *Childrens' Hospital Corp* (1983) 40 Nfld & PEIR 88 (Nfld TD), revised (1085) 44 Nfld & PEIR 350 (Nfld CA)

*Beausoleil* v. *La Communauté des Soeurs de la Charité* (1964) 53 DLR (2d) 65 [1965] QB 37 (Que CA)

*Bernier* v. *Sisters of Service*[1948] 1 WWR 113 (Alta SC)

*Brennan* v. *Director of Mental Health* unreported Feb 18, 1977 No 83414 (Alta SC)

*Bugden* v. *Harbour View Hospital* [1947] 2 DLR 338 (NSSC)

*Cavan* v. *Wilcox* (1974) 2 NR 618 50 DLR (3d) 687; reversing 44 DLR (3d) 42 SCC

*Considine* v. *Camp Hill Hospital* (1982) 133 DLR (3d) 11 NSSC

*Co-operative Insurance Association* v. *Kearney* (1965) SCR 106

*Craig* v. *Soeurs de Charité de la Providence* [1940] 2 WWR 80; affirmed [1940] 3 WWR 336 (Sask CA)

*Crits* v. *Sylvester* [1956] SCR 991

*Dagenais* v. *Children's Hospital of Eastern Ontario* (1980) 1 ACWS (2d) 432 (Ont HC)

*Dalton* v. *Angus* (1881) 6 App Cas 740 (HL)

*Davis* v. *Colchester* [1933] 4 DLR 68 (NSSC)

*Dowey* v. *Rothwell* [1974] 5 WWR 311, 49 DLR (3d) 82 (Alta TD)

*Eek* v. *Bd of High River Mun Hospital* [1926] 1 WWR 36 (Alta SC)

*Farrel* v. *Regina* [1949] 1 WWR 429 (Sask KB)

## IV THE USA

*Rofdo (Pty) Ltd T/A Castle Crane Hire* v. *B&E Quarries (Pty) Ltd* 1999 (3) SA 941 (SEC)

*S* v. *Kramer and Another* 1987 (1) SA 887 (W)

*S* v. *Mkwetshana* 1965 (2) SA 493 (N)

*Sangster* v. *Durban Corp* 1934 NPD 347

*Sasverbijl Beleggings en Verdiskonterings Maatskappy Bpk* v. *Van Rhynsdorp Town Council and Another* 1979 (2) SA 771 (W)

*Silva's Fishing Corp (Pty) Ltd* v. *Maweza* 1957 (2) SA 256 (A)

*Silver* v. *Premier, Gauteng Provincial Government* 1998 (4) SA 569 (W)

*Skinner* v. *Johannesburg Turf Club* 1907 TS 852

*Small* v. *Goldreich Buildings Ltd and Reid and Knuckey (Pty) Ltd* 1943 (W) 101

*Smit* v. *Minister van Polisie* 1997 (4) SA 893 (T)

*Smit* v. *Workmen's Compensation Commissioner* 1979 (1) SA 51 (A)

*Soobramoney* v. *Minister of Health, KwaZulu-Natal* 1998 (1) SA 765 (CC)

*Spencer* v. *Barclays Bank* 1947 (3) SA 230 T

*St Augustine Hospital (Pty) Ltd* v. *Le Breton* 1975 (2) SA 530 (D)

*Van Wyk* v. *Lewis* 1924 AD 438

*Venter* v. *Bophuthatswana Transport Holdings (Edms) Bpk* 1997 (3) SA 374 (HCA)

*Viljoen* v. *Smith* 1997 (1) SA 309 (A)

*Witham* v. *Minister of Home Affairs* 1989 (1) SA 116 (ZH)

# Subject Index